Refugee Entrepreneurship

This comprehensive volume explores the phenomenon of refugee entrepreneurship and advances the discussions and debates in the domain.

The growing number of refugees across the world creates a compelling need to study the social and economic activities of refugees in different contexts, and to share experiences and debate how to better support refugee populations. This book covers academic, practical, and policy issues in refugee entrepreneurship, seeking to present the current status of research in this evolving field. The topics include how to identify and differentiate refugee entrepreneurship; refugees' business practices; the personal, economic, and social values and impacts of refugee entrepreneurship; and the institutional support and role of ecosystems in facilitating refugee entrepreneurship. Future research directions are also outlined.

This book provides scholars with the theoretical foundations and evidence base to advance refugee entrepreneurship research. Support agencies will learn from the experiences of others about the delivery of tailored support and policymakers will recognise the need for empathy and consistency in developing host country strategies for refugees.

Nadeera Ranabahu is Senior Lecturer in the UC Business School at the University of Canterbury, New Zealand. Nadeera's main research interest is inclusive entrepreneurship. She has published papers on entrepreneurship among refugees, immigrants, low-income people, and women.

Huibert P. de Vries is Associate Professor in the UC Business School at the University of Canterbury, New Zealand. He has published papers on ethnic minority immigrant entrepreneurship, refugee entrepreneurship, and indigenous entrepreneurship among Māori and Pacific Peoples in New Zealand.

Robert T. Hamilton is Emeritus Professor in the UC Business School at the University of Canterbury, New Zealand, and Consulting Editor for *International Small Business Journal.* His recent publications have been on portfolio entrepreneurs and the nature and spread of high-growth firms in New Zealand.

Routledge Research Companions in Business and Economics

Contemporary Talent Management
A Research Companion
Edited by Ibraiz Tarique

Business with a Conscience
A Research Companion
Edited by Joan Marques

Entrepreneurial Finance, Innovation and Development
A Research Companion
Edited by Vi Dung Ngo, Duc Khuong Nguyen and Ngoc Thang Nguyen

Platform Labour and Global Logistics
A Research Companion
Edited by Immanuel Ness

Behavioural Economics and the Environment
A Research Companion
Edited by Alessandro Bucciol, Alessandro Tavoni and Marcella Veronesi

Responsible Marketing for Well-being and Society
A Research Companion
Edited by Michael Saren, Louise M. Hassan, Miriam McGowan, N. Craig Smith, Emma Surman and Rohit Varman

Islamic Green Finance
A Research Companion
Edited by Mohd Ma'Sum Billah, Rusni Hassan, Razali Haron, Romzie Rosman and Akhtarun Naba' Billah

Refugee Entrepreneurship
A Research Companion
Edited by Nadeera Ranabahu, Huibert P. de Vries, and Robert T. Hamilton

Refugee Entrepreneurship

A Research Companion

Edited by Nadeera Ranabahu, Huibert P. de Vries, and Robert T. Hamilton

Routledge
Taylor & Francis Group
LONDON AND NEW YORK

First published 2025
by Routledge
4 Park Square, Milton Park, Abingdon, Oxon OX14 4RN

and by Routledge
605 Third Avenue, New York, NY 10158

Routledge is an imprint of the Taylor & Francis Group, an informa business

British Library Cataloguing-in-Publication Data
A catalogue record for this book is available from the British Library

Library of Congress Cataloging-in-Publication Data
Names: Ranabahu, Nadeera, editor. | De Vries, Huibert P., editor. |
Hamilton, Robert T., editor.
Title: Refugee entrepreneurship: a research companion /
edited by Nadeera Ranabahu, Huibert P. de Vries, and Robert T. Hamilton.
Description: Abingdon, Oxon; New York, NY: Routledge, 2025. |
Series: Routledge research companions in business and economics |
Includes bibliographical references and index. |
Identifiers: LCCN 2024033048 (print) | LCCN 2024033049 (ebook) |
ISBN 9781032437125 (hardback) | ISBN 9781032437118 (paperback) |
ISBN 9781003368540 (ebook)
Subjects: LCSH: Immigrant business enterprises. |
Minority-owned business enterprises. | Entrepreneurship.
Classification: LCC HD2360 .R44 2025 (print) | LCC HD2360 (ebook) |
DDC 338.6/422–dc23/eng/20240801|
LC record available at https://lccn.loc.gov/2024033048
LC ebook record available at https://lccn.loc.gov/2024033049

ISBN: 9781032437125 (hbk)
ISBN: 9781032437118 (pbk)
ISBN: 9781003368540 (ebk)

DOI: 10.4324/9781003368540

Typeset in Galliard
by Newgen Publishing UK

Contents

Figures

Tables

About the editors

Nadeera Ranabahu is Senior Lecturer in the UC Business School at the University of Canterbury, New Zealand. Nadeera's main research interest is inclusive entrepreneurship. She also studies social entrepreneurship and social innovations and the intersection between microfinance and sustainability. She is passionate about reducing inequalities and promoting the social and economic inclusion of refugees, immigrants, low-income people and women. Her work has been published in the *Journal of International Migration*, *Small Business Economics*, and *Journal of Management & Organization*.

Huibert P. de Vries is Associate Professor in the UC Business School at the University of Canterbury, New Zealand. He has led research projects related to self-employment among immigrants and minority groups. He has published papers in the fields of ethnic minority immigrant entrepreneurship, refugee entrepreneurship and indigenous entrepreneurship among Māori and Pacific Peoples in New Zealand. Further, he has published on entrepreneurship education and entrepreneurial resilience.

Robert T. Hamilton is Emeritus Professor in the UC Business School at the University of Canterbury, New Zealand. His main areas of interest are small business management and entrepreneurship. He has led recent research projects on the nature and significance of high-growth firms in New Zealand. In addition to his role as a consulting editor of the *International Small Business Journal*, he reviews regularly for a range of international journals, including the *Journal of Business Research*, the *European Management Journal*, and the *International Journal of Entrepreneurial Behaviour & Research*.

Contributors

Solomon Akele Abebe is a final-year PhD candidate at the Sten K. Johnson Center for Entrepreneurship, Lund University School of Economics and Management, Sweden. Solomon's work ventures into the emerging research area of refugee entrepreneurship, providing a nuanced understanding of the phenomenon and unravelling its complexities through a weave of systematic, methodological, theoretical, and empirical analyses.

Yunizar Adiputera is Lecturer in the Department of International Relations at Universitas Gadjah Mada, and a researcher at the Institute of International Studies, Universitas Gadjah Mada. He completed his undergraduate degree and Master of Arts degree in International Relations from Universitas Gadjah Mada. Currently, he is also affiliated with the Department of Political Science at the University of Florida as a doctoral student. His research interests include topics around humanitarian issues in global politics, peace and conflict studies, and comparative politics. He has published research articles on the topic of refugees that address questions about state policy and the protection of refugee rights.

Fatih Aktas (PhD) born in Turhal, Türkiye in 1980, is Senior Researcher at the University of Applied Sciences Utrecht. His expertise lies in migration, post-migration integration, migrant entrepreneurship port and active lifestyle in post-migration period. He completed his bachelor's degree in public administration and master's degree in political science from Dumlupınar University and his PhD degree from Istanbul University in 2017, specialising in migration studies. With 15 years working in Türkiye's public sector, Aktas joined Utrecht University of Applied Science in 2023. He is fluent in Turkish, Dutch and English, and conversant in Arabic.

Cihan Aydiner is Assistant Professor and Program Director of Homeland Security at Embry-Riddle Aeronautical University Worldwide (ERAU-W). He has had prior academic and professional roles at Louisiana State University, Beyond the Horizon ISSG (a Belgium-based think tank), Hybridcore (an artificial intelligence [AI]-powered decision-making company), and Army. He has doctoral and master's degrees in Sociology from Louisiana State University and a master's degree in National and International Security Management from Army War College, Istanbul/Türkiye. He has many funded grant projects, publications, documentary films, and technical reports. Aydiner's current research focuses on the complex interdependencies among policy, homeland security, and international migration.

Ashenafi Biru is Senior Lecturer in Entrepreneurship and Innovation at the School of Management, RMIT University, Melbourne, Australia. His research interests lie at the intersection of entrepreneurship, business strategy, and institutional environments in mature and developing economies, with a particular emphasis on the strategic behaviours of entrepreneurs and exploring the dark side of entrepreneurship.

Rima M. Bizri is Associate Professor of Management at Canadian University Dubai. Her research interests are interdisciplinary, spanning the fields of entrepreneurship, HRM, and organisational behaviour and the dynamic relationships that connect them. Rima's research is published in Scopus-indexed journals like *Entrepreneurship and Regional Development, International Journal of Entrepreneurial Behavior & Research, Journal of Family Business Management, Journal of Management Development,* International Journal of Organizational Analysis and *Equality, Diversity and Inclusion.* She is currently working on a project that investigates the influence of high-performance work systems and their impact on employees' entrepreneurial orientation. Rima also offers consultations to nascent entrepreneurs on launching successful start-ups, and to professionals embarking on mid-life career shifts.

Abel Chikanda is Associate Professor in the School of Earth, Environment and Society at McMaster University in Hamilton, Ontario, Canada. His research interests include migration and development, immigrant and refugee integration, and food security in African cities.

Imon Chowdhooree (PhD) is serving as Assistant Director in the Postgraduate Programs in Disaster Management (PPDM) of the Department of Disaster Management at BRAC University, Dhaka, Bangladesh. Additionally, he is serving as Executive Director of the Cell for Adaptation, Resilience, Security, and Humanitarian Assistance (CARSHA) of the same department. His research interests include community resilience and vulnerability analysis, climate change adaptation practices, sustainable urban design and planning, humanitarian assistance and refugee crisis analysis. He earned his doctoral degree from Queensland University of Technology, Australia, and Master of Urban and Regional Planning degree from Bangladesh University of Engineering and Technology and University of Hawaii at Manoa, USA.

Lisa Jones Christensen is Associate Professor of Management at the Marriott School of Business at Brigham Young University. Her research focuses on female founders and innovation and entrepreneurship in extreme contexts. She publishes award-winning articles and cases focused on resilience, social value creation, and strategic innovation. She received her undergraduate degree from University of California Berkeley, an MBA and MA in International Development from Brigham Young University, and a PhD from University of North Carolina-Chapel Hill. Prior to academia, she worked in Silicon Valley, and co-founded a non-profit organisation which focuses on post-disaster humanitarian relief and invests in cross-cultural social entrepreneurship.

Jonathan Crush is Professor at the Balsillie School of International Affairs, Canada, and Honorary Professor at the University of the Western Cape, South Africa. He has published extensively on migration and food security issues in Africa. His most recent book is *Transforming Urban Food Systems in Secondary Cities in Africa* (Palgrave Macmillan, 2023) (co-edited with Liam Riley).

Alexandra David is a senior researcher on Migration, Innovation and Entrepreneurship at the Westphalian University. After her communication science studies at the University Duisburg-Essen (GER) and economic studies in Hagen (GER), she wrote her PhD in Sociology at the University of Twente (NL) while working at the IAT as a researcher and as a consultant in Bern (CH). She has advised the German Integration Commissioner of the Federal Government and the Ashoka Hello Europe on migrant and refugee entrepreneurship. She is a board member of Perspektive neuStart e.V., a German initiative helping minority groups in start-up activities.

Ziad El-Awad is Associate Professor of Business Administration specialising in entrepreneurship at Lund University's Sten K. Johnson Center for Entrepreneurship. His research focuses on organisational studies, new venture teams, entrepreneurial learning, entrepreneurial ecosystems, and circular entrepreneurship. Through advanced qualitative methods, Ziad delves into the human aspects of entrepreneurship, uncovering mechanisms, motivations, and challenges that impact innovation and success. His work contributes to an in-depth understanding of entrepreneurship and its various influences on the entrepreneurial landscape.

Muhammad Ferdaus is Director of the Human Security and Humanitarian Assistance Wing at the Cell for Adaption, Resilience, Security, and Humanitarian Assistance (CARSHA) at the Department of Disaster Management of BRAC University. He is an expert in youth leadership and rights-based responses to humanitarian crises. He is also Coordinator and Lecturer of the Postgraduate Programmes in Disaster Management (PPDM) in the same department. He earned his BA in Social Welfare from Islamic University, Kushtia, Bangladesh; an MA in Disaster Management from BRAC University, Dhaka; an MSc in International Development (Conflict, Security, and Development) from the University of Birmingham,

United Kingdom; and a professional certification in energy management from the Association of Energy Engineers, DC, USA.

Jörg Finsterwalder is Professor of Marketing in the UC Business School at the University of Canterbury (UC), New Zealand. His work has been published in international journals, such as *the European Journal of Marketing, Journal of Business Research, Journal of Public Policy & Marketing, Journal of Retailing and Consumer Services, Journal of Service Management, Journal of Services Marketing, Journal of Service Theory and Practice,* and *The Service Industries Journal.*

Burcin Hatipoglu holds a PhD in Human Resource Management from the University of New South Wales (UNSW). From 2006 to 2020, she worked as a full-time faculty at Bogazici University, Istanbul, where she taught courses on management, human resource management, and sustainability. In the last 15 years, Hatipoglu has been involved in several sustainable development projects and consulted regional development agencies and industry organisations for policy development. She has published various articles on employee participation, circular economy, education for sustainability, sustainable development, and refugee labour market integration. She is a visiting fellow at the School of Business, Canberra, and Industrial Relations Research Group (IRRG), UNSW.

Sibylle Heilbrunn's main area of scholarship, research and publication concerns entrepreneurship. Critical theory discourse accompanies her work and in most recent years, she has used intersectionality and social positioning as frameworks to uncover causes and consequences of advantaged and disadvantaged entrepreneurship. Her concern with antecedents and consequences of inequalities combines her agenda as Dean with teaching, exposing her students to global universalities while empowering and holding onto local particularities. She is part of the editorial board of several scientific journals, including the *Journal of Innovation and Entrepreneurship in Emerging Economies,* the *European Journal of International Management,* and the *International Journal of Entrepreneurship Behaviour & Research.* She has authored the award-winning *Dark Sides of the Startup Nation: Winners and Losers of Technological Innovation and Entrepreneurship in Israel* (2023) and has co-edited *Refugee Entrepreneurship: A Case-Based Topography* (2018).

Afreen Huq is Associate Professor in Entrepreneurship and Innovation in the School of Management, RMIT University, Melbourne, Australia. She is an entrepreneurship scholar and educator passionate about gender and entrepreneurship. Afreen takes a cross-disciplinary approach and examines how gender identity and sociocultural factors influence women's entrepreneurial behaviour and approach to growth. Afreen researches this phenomenon on women entrepreneurs in both developed countries and culturally restrictive societies. She also explores identity reconstruction, socialisation, and resilience of migrant and refugee women entrepreneurs.

Rosa Lisa Iannone has been an independent professional in higher education for the past 15 years, lecturing internationally in a variety of master's programmes and researching in a wide range of European collaborative projects. Her latest doctoral scholarship, undertaken at the University of Luxembourg, has focused on refugee entrepreneurship, identity formation and processes in social psychology. She has contributed to a number of academic journals as well as book chapters in *Cross-Cultural Lifelong Learning* (2010) and *Refugee Entrepreneurship: A Case-Based Topography* (2018). She holds a multidisciplinary BA in Global Governance from York University, Collège Glendon and an Erasmus Mundus Master's in Lifelong Learning: Policy and Management from the University of Aarhus, the University of Deusto and the Institute of Education, University of London. She is also a founding Board Member of Lëtz Art ASBL.

Fatima Junaid specialises in area of Organisational behaviour & HR, focusing on wellbeing and psychosocial risks. She has taught and worked as a consultant for more than a decade serving public and private sector entities. With a PhD in Management she works with migrant, refugee, and fisher communities; on exclusion and marginalisation; stress and wellbeing, and psychosocial risks. She is the New Zealand representative for the COPSOQ international network, member of American Psychological Association, and National Council of Women of New Zealand. Fatima runs a social media support group "Pakistani women in Academia" with 650+ women members which supports women's further education and research.

Tanya Jurado teaches and supervises doctoral students in entrepreneurship, business and society, and strategy. She has published on SME internationalisation and public policy support for SMEs, and current interests include Indigenous and refugee entrepreneurship. She also researches the participation and retention of women in IT professions. Tanya is actively involved in the wider SME international research community and serves as Editor-in-Chief of Small Enterprise Research, and as the Chair of the Small Enterprise Association of Australia and New Zealand.

Juha Kansikas is Senior Lecturer at Jyväskylä University School of Business and Economics, Jyväskylä, Finland. His research interests include entrepreneurship, family business, entrepreneurship education, and executive education. Kansikas has been lately invited to speak at the University of Lausanne in Switzerland and is a visiting researcher at the Copenhagen Business School (Denmark), and Telfer School of Management (University of Ottawa, Canada). He has published his research in the journals such as *Technological Forecasting and Social Change*, *Business History*, *Enterprise and Society*, *International Journal of Entrepreneurial Behavior and Research*, *Journal of Social Entrepreneurship*, and *Science and Public Policy*.

Nadeen Khoury is a former researcher at the Malmö Institute for Studies of Migration, Diversity, and Welfare at Malmö University. Her expertise lies in the fields of refugee integration, refugee women's empowerment, and social cohesion. Nadeen has contributed significantly to several EU-funded projects focusing on refugee integration. Through her research, Nadeen has shed light on key issues and contributed to the understanding of effective strategies for fostering integration and well-being among refugees and their host communities.

Antje Missbach is Professor of Sociology at Bielefeld University, Germany, specialising in global and transnational migration and mobility. She is the author of *Separatist Conflict in Indonesia: The Long-Distance Politics of the Acehnese Diaspora* (2012) and *Troubled Transit: Asylum Seekers Stuck in Indonesia* (2015) and co-author of *Indonesia: State and Society in Transition* (2019). Her latest book is *The Criminalisation of People Smuggling in Indonesia and Australia: Asylum Out of Reach* (2022).

Elke Murdock is Senior Researcher in the Department of Behavioural and Cognitive Sciences at the University of Luxembourg. Her research focuses on living with diversity – at the individual level: biculturalism, identity construal processes and at the societal level: understanding attitudes towards plurally composed societies, national identity and acculturation processes. She has contributed over 100 academic publications, and is the author of *Multiculturalism, Identity and Difference: Experiences of Culture Contact* (2016). Her academic training started in psychology at Saarland University, where her focus on cultural identity burgeoned. An Erasmus stipend took her to the University of Aberdeen and a Fulbright scholarship to Western Washington University where she earned a BA and an MSc degree. She also holds an MBA from the Edinburgh Business School and a PhD from the University of Luxembourg.

Arielle Badger Newman is Assistant Professor of Entrepreneurship at Syracuse University. Newman's research focuses on entrepreneurs outside the "mainstream", those who seek to legitimise themselves and their entrepreneurial endeavours despite institutions that were not made for them, or in fact, were made to exclude them. Her work focuses on the impact of their experiences on their overall entrepreneurial journey and well-being. Her work has been published in the *Journal of Business Venturing, Entrepreneurship Theory and Practice, Business and Society, Journal of International Business Policy,* and *Asia Pacific Journal of Management.*

Poh Yen Ng is Associate Professor of Entrepreneurship and Innovation at Aberdeen Business School, Robert Gordon University. She holds a PhD in Management from the University of Canterbury, New Zealand, and is currently a Senior Fellow of Advance HE in the United Kingdom. Her research spans many areas within the entrepreneurship and family business discipline, including the influence of socioemotional wealth in the family business, empowerment process and social network dynamics of women entrepreneurs, and environmental practices of small and medium-sized enterprises.

Section 1

The scope of refugee entrepreneurship

The following three chapters focus on providing the scope and boundaries for refugee entrepreneurship (RE) theory and practice. As alluded to in the introduction, there is no consensus as to whether RE merits a separate domain within entrepreneurship research. This is further complicated by the differing ways in which refugee entrepreneurs are defined, discussed, and classified in the literature. The chapters in this section discuss these domain and definition-related concerns.

In Chapter 2, David and Zaghow compare the similarities and differences between voluntary migrants and refugees who are forced to migrate and discuss whether RE needs to be recognised as a separate domain of research. The authors argue for finely grained taxonomies and categories to achieve conceptual and phenomenological clarity in RE.

In Chapter 3, Abebe et al. provide detailed guidelines on how to conceptualise RE. Grounded in refugee theories, these authors take into account the diversity of refugee entrepreneurs, contextual heterogeneity associated with RE, and temporality linked to refugees' legal status and life circumstances. This chapter provides an ontological foundation for RE research and delineates the boundary conditions for empirical studies.

In the final chapter (Chapter 4) of this section, Ranabahu et al. focus on the intention and behaviour gap among refugee entrepreneurs and provide a nomenclature for resettled refugees who have already started a business or intend to do so. This nomenclature provides a novel way to classify, describe, and provide business development services for resettled refugees who intend to start or have already started businesses.

DOI: 10.4324/9781003368540-2

1 Refugee entrepreneurship

Status of research and practice

Nadeera Ranabahu, Huibert P. de Vries, and Robert T. Hamilton

Introduction

In parallel with the increasing number of wars, conflicts, and religious and political persecutions, there is a growing academic and policy attention on the survival, (re)settlement, and integration of refugees and asylum seekers. Refugees differ from other migrant groups, such as temporary migrants, skilled migrants, or expatriates, because of the forced nature of their migration (Christensen et al., 2020; Connor, 2010; Duncan, 2022; Wauters & Lambrecht, 2006). They experience trauma, suffer from the stigmatised identity of being a stateless refugee, and live in precarious legal situations. They typically lack language proficiency in both transitional and host countries, struggle to transfer their education and professional experience into suitable work in host countries, and hence find many obstacles to finding employment (Christensen et al., 2020; Connor, 2010; Lee et al., 2020; Wauters & Lambrecht, 2006). Extant employment-related scholarship explains these challenges using metaphors such as 'refugee gap' (Connor, 2010; Ortensi & Ambrosetti, 2022), 'bamboo ceiling' (Huynh, 2022), 'sticky floor' (Morrar & Rios-Avila, 2021), and 'canvas ceiling' (Lee et al., 2020), pointing out that both skill and knowledge gaps and structural factors affect refugees' economic integration. Refugee entrepreneurship (RE) is considered an effective means to address some of these economic integration barriers.

Generally, RE is explained as entrepreneurial activities conducted by a person or a group of people forcibly displaced by their home country due to war, persecution, threats, or conflict (Abebe, 2023a; Duncan, 2022; Newman et al., 2023). It includes both formal and informal activities conducted during the flight from a home country, temporary stay in transition countries, and settlement in a host country (de Vries et al., 2021; Harima et al., 2021). RE also explains individual, business, and meso or macro level issues among asylum seekers, those under temporary protection visas, or those who have been recognised as refugees by the United Nations High Commissioner for Refugees (UNHCR). These perspectives and avenues through which RE can be explored have contributed to the growth, variability, and heterogeneity

DOI: 10.4324/9781003368540-1

of contemporary RE research and practice (Abebe, 2023a; Al-Dajani, 2022; Desai et al., 2021; Heilbrunn & Iannone, 2020; Newman et al., 2023).

Why this book?

There is a compelling and urgent need to share experiences, debate how to better support refugee populations, and develop support systems, practices, and policy initiatives. This book is a contribution towards meeting this need. With the adoption of the first-ever UN global agreement on a common approach to international migration,[1] there is a need for understanding and implementing sustainable livelihood activities and economic integration measures for refugees and displaced populations (Desai et al., 2021; UN, 2018). Along these lines, the 2030 Sustainable Development Goals (SDGs) make explicit references to populations at risk, such as refugees and displaced people. There are concerns related to these groups being 'left behind' due to adverse drivers or structural factors in achieving sustainable futures (UNHCR, 2019).

Academically, RE brings together multiple fields of literature, such as sociology, migration studies, political science, business, law, psychology, and history (Abebe, 2023a, 2023b; Heilbrunn & Iannone, 2020). Studying RE from these multiple perspectives has contributed to the growth of refugee studies and the variability in research themes (Heilbrunn & Iannone, 2020; Newman et al., 2023). Although such variability contributes to understanding the phenomenon, it has also led to a lack of conceptual and ontological clarity (Abebe, 2023a; Heilbrunn & Iannone, 2020). Further, ontological differences between immigrants and refugees have led to calls for considering RE as separate from immigrant entrepreneurship (Duncan, 2022; Gold, 1988). There are ongoing debates as to whether refugee entrepreneurship should also be considered a distinct domain of research from transnational, diaspora, or inclusive entrepreneurship (Bakker & McMullen, 2023; Gold, 1988). However, the lack of clarity regarding its relationship to similar domains and competing explanations of similarities and differences with other related domains hinders the RE field from moving forward.

From both policy and practice perspectives, the sheer number of refugees and internally displaced people in the world makes RE a promising avenue to enhance economic participation, income generation, and socioeconomic integration (Desai et al., 2021). The global interest levels in refugee integration vary with the flow of migrants and refugees (Desai et al., 2021). According to UNHCR (2023), there are more than 110 million forcibly displaced people around the world with 36.4 million refugees. Many of these refugees live in refugee camps or developing countries, such as the Islamic Republic of Iran, Türkiye, Pakistan, and Colombia (UNHCR, 2023). Around 2.5 million refugees are hosted by Germany with other EU countries, and countries such as the UK, Australia, and New Zealand. Yet, the refugee numbers are increasing on a daily basis with the current Ukraine-Russia war, the Israel-Palestine conflict within Gaza and the West Bank, the Rohingya crisis, and internal conflicts

in Sudan, and many more. This book shares experiences of multiple groups of refugees, in multiple geographies, and provides insights into refugee journeys, their resilience, business endeavours and challenges, and the institutional role in diverse contexts in enhancing RE.

Historical refugee migration trends and RE research and practice

The growth of RE research and practice has been attributed to refugee flows at different historical periods (Heilbrunn & Iannone, 2020). By considering countries of origin, countries of residence, and timeframes of forced migration, Heilbrunn and Iannone (2020) categorised RE publications under three main waves. The first wave of publications, which constitutes the early work on RE, focused on former Soviet Jewish and Vietnamese refugees who fled mainly to North America as a result of World War I and II, the Vietnam War, and the collapse of the Soviet Union (Gold, 1988, 1992; Heilbrunn & Iannone, 2020). In considering the example of Soviet Jewish and Vietnamese refugees, Gold (1988) identified that refugee networks are small, and even with financial and technical assistance from the US government, some opted to start small businesses to achieve independence and flexibility. The second wave of publications consists of studies on refugees from developing countries (e.g., Afghanistan, Iraq) who transitioned to developed countries. The studies of this second wave are prominent from mid-2010 onwards (Newman et al., 2023). Somewhat overlapping with the second wave, the current third wave consists of studies related to refugees from developing countries who start businesses in other developing countries, such as in refugee camps in Kenya (de la Chaux & Haugh, 2020; Luseno & Kolade, 2023). Although other researchers do not classify these forced migration trends as systematically as Heilbrunn and Iannone (2020) do, there appears to be a general consensus on the historical patterns, at least related to the first and second wave, in RE literature (see: Abebe, 2023a; Newman et al., 2023).

Key issues in RE research and practice

Despite early work during 1980, the RE literature has remained on the periphery of immigrant entrepreneurship research (Abebe, 2023b; Gold, 1988; Harima et al., 2021). Systematic reviews conducted by Abebe (2023a), Heilbrunn and Iannone (2020), and Newman et al. (2023) provide an overview of the key themes in RE since the 1980s. These reviews are comprehensive, as exemplified by Heilbrunn and Iannone (2020) having 68 sources (up to 2018), Abebe (2023a) having 105 articles for the period of 1980 to November 2020, while Newman et al. (2023) having 76 articles (up to end of June 2022). These demonstrate that RE research is concentrated into six main areas (Figure 1.1).

As Figure 1.1 demonstrates, similarities and differences between immigrant and refugee entrepreneurship are a prominent sub-theme in RE theory and

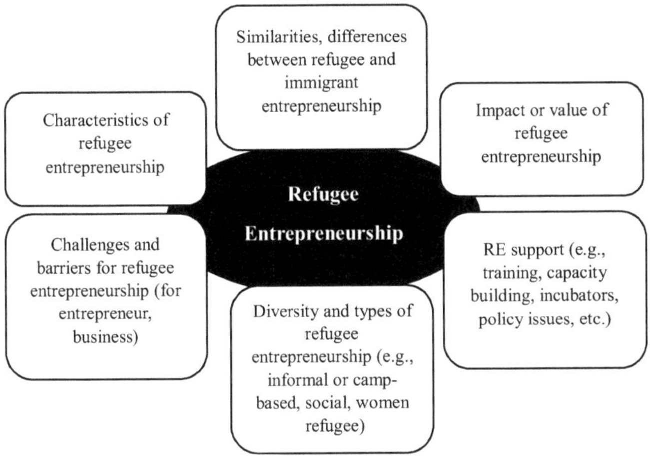

Figure 1.1 Key research areas in refugee entrepreneurship.

Source: Compiled by using Abebe (2023a), Heilbrunn & Iannone (2020), and Newman et al. (2023).

practice. This prominence stems from the early, first wave, publications such as Gold (1988, 1992) who compared Soviet Jews with Vietnamese refugees in the US. In later studies, Wauters and Lambrecht's (2006) 'six criteria' are also used in differentiating refugees from immigrants: (a) extent of social networks, (b) forced migration making it impossible for refugees to acquire funds, capital, or labour from home countries, (c) experience of trauma, (d) limited preparation for host destination settlement, (e) leaving all valuables and assets behind, and (f) potential unsuitability for host country labour markets. Further, the 2x2 framework of Christensen et al. (2020) takes into account the voluntary/involuntary nature of migration and relative permanency/non-permanency, which differentiates refugees, immigrants, sojourners, and exiles. These authors outline differences between human, physical, institutional, and social capital between these four groups.

A significant number of RE research and practice articles discuss the characteristics of refugee entrepreneurs or their enterprises. Freiling and Harima (2018) summarise these using cases from Heilbrunn et al. (2019) and illustrate refugees' push motivation, the age differences, and how they are affected by home country imprint, availability (or lack of) resources, and human capital. They also illustrate the types of industries and sectors in which refugees start businesses. Further, there are RE research and practice articles that explain refugees' resilience, adaptability, self-efficacy, and intentions (Klyver et al., 2022; Shepherd et al., 2020; Yeshi et al., 2022), how refugees take advantage of institutional voids, and how they dis-embed and re-embed

in home and host contexts for resource acquisition (de la Chaux & Haugh, 2020; Harima, 2022; Heilbrunn et al., 2019). Although most of the extant work is agent-centric which focuses on the cognition, action, or behaviour of refugees, Zalkat et al. (2023) present an entrepreneurship motivation measure by combining person-related factors and the perceptions of environment-related factors. Such work signals the integration of agent and context in RE research and practice.

RE literature also discusses the challenges and barriers of individual entrepreneurs or their businesses. These challenges, to name a few, include a lack of social capital, differing ethnic and cultural norms, lack of institutional and market understanding, lacking resources and entering into low-value-added business sectors (Bizri, 2017; Meister & Mauer, 2019; Ranabahu et al., 2021; Wauters & Lambrecht, 2006). These studies are closely linked with RE work that explains the characteristics of refugee entrepreneurs. Heilbrunn et al.'s (2019) case studies provide insights into both the challenges and how refugees navigate them while employing characteristics such as self-efficacy, motivation, resilience, and adaptability.

Of great interest to society are studies that demonstrate the value and impact of RE. These benefits are explained for multiple levels as for the individual refugee, the community level, and the national economic level (Bizri, 2017; Ranabahu et al., 2023; Tavakoli, 2020). For example, refugee entrepreneurs have been reported to create employment for either local or ethnic communities, advance the development of cultural or social values, and engage in civic activities (Ranabahu et al., 2023; Tavakoli, 2020; Weng & Lee, 2016). Further studies, such as Harb et al. (2019), report on the wider economic benefits of RE to host countries.

RE support and training initiatives are important for policy and practice. To this end, Harima and Freudenberg (2020) and Meister and Mauer (2019) examined incubator programmes. Furthermore, Richey et al. (2022) and Street et al. (2022) reported on the training, mentoring, and other support provided for refugees. These studies highlight the drawbacks of overemphasising the disadvantaged entrepreneurs' agency (Richey et al., 2022), and that there is a need for co-creative and supportive spaces for refugees to learn about the market and test their business ideas (Harima & Freudenberg, 2020; Meister & Mauer, 2019). Recent studies have also examined novel ways of providing finance to refugee entrepreneurs such as crowdsourcing or the use of peer-to-peer (P2P) platforms (Emanuel-Correia et al., 2022; Gama et al., 2023). These studies found that refugee entrepreneurs, through third parties such as microfinance institutions, offer positive signals to crowdfunders to invest in RE (Gama et al., 2023). This is also a way of funding refugee entrepreneurs in developing countries and reducing the refugee funding gap in RE (Emanuel-Correia et al., 2022; Gama et al., 2023).

Even within RE research and practice, there is diversity and a focus on different types of RE. The extant studies highlight sub-entrepreneurship (i.e.,

various self-employment forms that are undeclared to relevant authorities), informal entrepreneurship (de la Chaux & Haugh, 2020; Refai & McElwee, 2023), or illegal income-generation tasks (Missbach, 2015). Refugee women entrepreneurship research (e.g., Adeeko & Treanor, 2021; Al-Dajani, 2022; Al-Dajani et al., 2019; Huq & Venugopal, 2021; Ranabahu et al., 2021) is also gaining traction as they describe intersectional identity issues, specific challenges women refugees encounter, and how they navigate them. The focus of social entrepreneurship or digital entrepreneurship in RE, although only a few, explains how social enterprises shape self-efficacy and business intentions (Abou Chakra & Al Jardali, 2022) and how information technology shapes RE (Brown et al., 2022).

Key theories in shaping RE research and practice

RE has multidisciplinary roots and it has led to RE research and practice to adopt a mix of theories and concepts from sociology, psychology, business, and other fields (Abebe, 2023b; Heilbrunn & Iannone, 2020). Abebe (2023b) classifies these theories/concepts as culturally oriented, structurally oriented, agency-oriented, embedded agency-oriented, or combined perspectives. However, not all these theories are frequently used in RE literature. Some frequently used theories and concepts in RE research are outlined in Table 1.1.

Theories, such as cultural theory, ethnic enclave, disadvantaged, and mixed embeddedness outlined in Table 1.1, are frequently used in immigrant entrepreneurship studies. However, these theories have been extended or adapted in RE research to explain the phenomenon. For example, mixed embeddedness framing has been adapted and extended to RE by taking into account the transitional context or prolonged stays at refugee camps (de Vries et al., 2021; Harima et al., 2021) or embedding and de-embedding of practices of refugees (Harima, 2022).

More recent RE studies, albeit infrequently, have explored the RE phenomenon using other theories and concepts. Some of these include the opportunity production model (Jiang et al., 2021), Bourdieu's habitus concept (Refai et al., 2018), translocational positionality and intersectionality (Adeeko & Treanor, 2021), co-creation at incubator settings (Harima & Freudenberg, 2020), stakeholder theory and blended value creation (Ranabahu et al., 2023), acculturation and identity (Jones Christensen & Newman, 2024), Weber's iron cage of rationality (Refai & McElwee, 2023), and bricolage (Luseno & Kolade, 2023). There are also concepts such as defiance and resilience employed to explain the phenomenon of RE (Al-Dajani et al., 2019; Shepherd et al., 2020; Yeshi et al., 2022). These multiple theories/concepts provide rich insights into understanding and elaborating RE; hence, we consider theoretical/conceptual plurality as an advantage in understanding RE.

Table 1.1 Frequently used theories or concepts in refugee entrepreneurship

Theory or concept	*Explanation based on RE literature*
Cultural theory	Refugees from different ethnic backgrounds have cultural attributes which encourage and facilitate their participation in business activities (Gold, 1988).
Ethnic enclaves	Refugee groups who are concentrated into different spatial locations, through knowledge, resources sharing, organise themselves and form ethnic markets enhancing entrepreneurship (Andersson, 2020).
Disadvantage theory	Refugees are disadvantaged compared to other immigrants or host country individuals in the general labour market due to their poor English, lack of familiarity of the context, or limited education (Gold, 1988).
Mixed embeddedness	Refugees embed themselves in their social networks and the wider economic and political structure of the external environment of the home, transition, and host countries (Harima et al., 2021; Ram et al., 2022).
Social capital and social networks	Refugees use and employ their social relationships and networks to gain resources in business start-up and development (Bizri, 2017).
Institutions and institutional void	Formal and informal institutions shape RE as not having or weak institutional structures affect business start-up and development (Lehmann et al., 2022).
Entrepreneurial intention theories	Refugees' intentions or plans to set up a new business venture at some point in the future (Cifci & Cetin, 2023).

Methods and methodological plurality shaping RE research and practice

As the RE phenomena require in-depth explorations, many studies have employed qualitative, exploratory, inductive methods, such as data collected from interviews or case studies. Heilbrunn and Iannone (2020) found that around 58% (39 articles out of 68) in their systematic review used qualitative data. These studies have provided reliable and insightful findings of refugee journeys and their opportunities and challenges when starting and developing businesses. Although cross-sectional studies are prominent, longitudinal qualitative studies are emerging (e.g., Ram et al., 2022).

There are only very few studies which utilise surveys, quantitative techniques (e.g., Hartmann & Philipp, 2022; Klyver et al., 2022), or mixed methods (e.g., Abou Chakra & Al Jardali, 2022). We also see the emerging use of country-level, centrally administered statistical databases in RE research (e.g., Hartmann & Philipp, 2022). There are hardly any comparative quantitative studies or studies with panel data, but a few cross-country studies have

emerged in recent years (e.g., Zalkat et al., 2023). The lack of large-scale data sets or even quantitative studies is partly due to refugees being a hard-to-reach population where identification and contacting refugee entrepreneurs requires novel or non-traditional methods (Abebe, 2023b).

Contextual variability in RE research and practice

The RE phenomenon has been studied in different geographical regions and contexts. The main finding across these contexts seems to be the constrained nature of the institutions (Refai & McElwee, 2023). Such institutional context can be related to regulations, formal or informal norms or practices, and other resource-related constraints or institutional voids (de la Chaux & Haugh, 2020; Heilbrunn et al., 2019). These contextual constraints and how refugees or asylum seekers experience these vary between refugee groups or across countries (see examples such as Abou Chakra & Al Jardali, 2022; Adeeko & Treanor, 2021; de Vries et al., 2021; Wauters & Lambrecht, 2006; Zalkat et al., 2023). Although studies from North America, Europe, the UK, and Australia had dominated RE studies (Abebe, 2023a; Heilbrunn & Iannone, 2020), there are now studies in emerging markets or among south-to-south refugee movement (Luseno & Kolade, 2023; Shepherd et al., 2020). These studies have elaborated on refugee camps-based entrepreneurship (de la Chaux & Haugh, 2020).

Finally, RE literature has a broad industry focus. Beyond a few tourism and hospitality-focused studies which outline industry-specific personal, organisational, and environmental factors specific to the industry (e.g., Cifci & Cetin, 2023), existing studies focus more on low-entry barrier industries where resource requirements are low (e.g., retail shops, saloons, ethnic food) (Heilbrunn et al., 2019).

Format of the book

This book aims to address some of the conceptual and empirical gaps and debates in the RE domain. RE, although extant studies provide insights into the phenomenon, requires defining and extending its theoretical boundaries to find practical and policy solutions for refugee-related challenges. This book offers new insights into the phenomenon of RE, new conceptualisations and future directions to advance research in RE. Hence, this book is a useful tool to extend contemporary RE research, develop further scholarly clarity, improve practice and policy, and learn from shared experiences across different countries.

We also see RE as one initiative that can be used as a tool to address some, but not all, issues associated with the refugee crisis and refugees' economic and social integration. Specifically, beyond simply outlining challenges and barriers for RE, there is a need to learn from experiences across regions

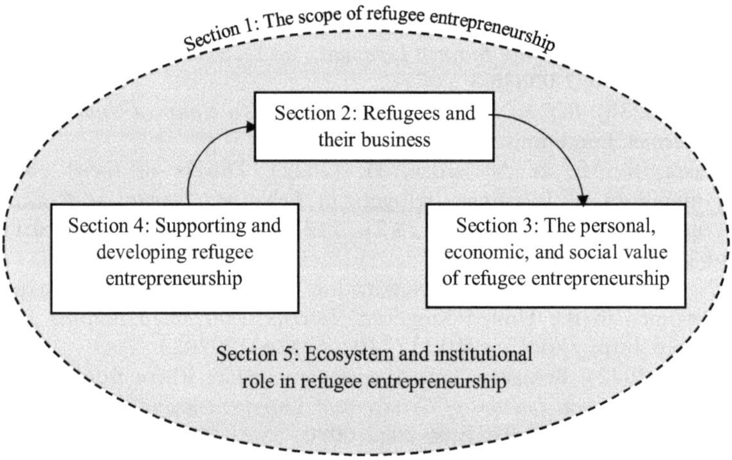

Figure 1.2 Book sections.

Source: Developed by editors.

and countries on what works and what does not. This includes debates on the types of activities public, private, and civil society organisations can conduct to enhance RE. Learnings from such discussions will be helpful to policymakers, refugee support organisations, or those agencies that develop local and regional incubators, as well as training and capacity development programmes.

The collection of chapters in this book is arranged into five sections. Section 1 addresses the current status of the RE domain and its definitional concerns. Section 2, refugees and their business, includes chapters which explain the RE phenomenon. Section 3 discusses the personal, economic, and social value and impact of RE. Section 4 examines the institutional support for and development of RE, while section 5 elaborates on the role of ecosystems and institutions in facilitating RE. See Figure 1.2 for an illustration of the interconnectedness between the sections.

Each section contains three to five chapters and contains a brief overview. The section overviews provide a brief overview about each chapter to allow the readers to identify chapters that meet their interests. The concluding chapter (Conclusion: Looking ahead) provides further areas of study and future research directions.

Note

1 This is known as Global Compact for Safe, Orderly and Regular Migration. It was built on the 2016 New York Declaration for Refugees and Migrants.

References

Abebe, S. A. (2023a). Refugee entrepreneurship: systematic and thematic analyses and a research agenda. *Small Business Economics*, *60*(1), 315–350. https://doi.org/10.1007/s11187-022-00636-3

Abebe, S. A. (2023b). *Refugee Entrepreneurship: Towards a Nuanced Understanding of the Phenomenon*. Lunds universitet, Media-Tryck.

Abou Chakra, S. M., & Al Jardali, H. (2022). Drivers of social entrepreneurial intentions of Palestinian refugees in Lebanon. *Journal of Research in Marketing and Entrepreneurship*, *24*(2), 242–269. https://doi.org/10.1108/JRME-02-2021-0014

Adeeko, N., & Treanor, L. (2021). Negotiating stigmatised identities: enterprising refugee women in the United Kingdom. *International Small Business Journal*, *40*(1), 23–46. https://doi.org/10.1177/0266242621997033

Al-Dajani, H. (2022). Refugee women's entrepreneurship: where from and where to next? *International Journal of Gender and Entrepreneurship*, *14*(4), 489–498. https://doi.org/10.1108/IJGE-06-2022-0090

Al-Dajani, H., Akbar, H., Carter, S., & Shaw, E. (2019). Defying contextual embeddedness: evidence from displaced women entrepreneurs in Jordan. *Entrepreneurship & Regional Development*, *31*(3–4), 198–212. https://doi.org/10.1080/08985626.2018.1551788

Andersson, H. (2020). Ethnic enclaves, self-employment, and the economic performance of refugees: evidence from a Swedish dispersal policy. *International Migration Review*, *55*(1), 58–83. https://doi.org/10.1177/0197918320912195

Bakker, R. M., & McMullen, J. S. (2023). Inclusive entrepreneurship: a call for a shared theoretical conversation about unconventional entrepreneurs. *Journal of Business Venturing*, *38*(1), 106268. https://doi.org/10.1016/j.jbusvent.2022.106268

Bizri, R. M. (2017). Refugee-entrepreneurship: a social capital perspective. *Entrepreneurship & Regional Development*, *29*(9–10), 847–868. https://doi.org/10.1080/08985626.2017.1364787

Brown, S., Saxena, D., & Wall, P. J. (2022). The role of information and communications technology in refugee entrepreneurship: a critical realist case study. *The Electronic Journal of Information Systems in Developing Countries*, *88*(1), e12195. https://doi.org/10.1002/isd2.12195

Christensen, L. J., Newman, A. B., Herrick, H., & Godfrey, P. (2020). Separate but not equal: toward a nomological net for migrants and migrant entrepreneurship. *Journal of International Business Policy*, *3*(1), 1–22. https://doi.org/10.1057/s42214-019-00041-w

Cifci, I., & Cetin, G. (2023). Identifying success factors of refugee entrepreneurs in the tourism and hospitality industry. International Journal of Contemporary Hospitality Management. https://doi.org/10.1108/IJCHM-11-2022-1439

Connor, P. (2010). Explaining the refugee gap: economic outcomes of refugees versus other immigrants. *Journal of Refugee Studies*, *23*(3), 377–397. https://heinonline.org/HOL/P?h=hein.journals/jrefst23&i=383

de la Chaux, M., & Haugh, H. (2020). When formal institutions impede entrepreneurship: how and why refugees establish new ventures in the Dadaab refugee camps. *Entrepreneurship & Regional Development*, *32*(9–10), 827–851. https://doi.org/10.1080/08985626.2020.1789752

de Vries, H. P., Ranabahu, N., & Basharati, Z. (2021). From taking flight to putting down roots: a narrative perspective of the entrepreneurial journey of a refugee. In T. M. Cooney (ed.), *The Palgrave Handbook of Minority Entrepreneurship* (pp. 365–389). Springer International Publishing. https://doi.org/10.1007/978-3-030-66603-3_17

Desai, S., Naudé, W., & Stel, N. (2021). Refugee entrepreneurship: context and directions for future research. *Small Business Economics*, *56*(3), 933–945. https://doi.org/10.1007/s11187-019-00310-1

Duncan, H. (2022). Commentary on immigrant and refugee entrepreneurship. *International Migration*, *60*(3), 261–263. https://doi.org/10.1111/imig.13010

Emanuel-Correia, R., Duarte, F., Gama, A. P. M., & Augusto, M. (2022). Does peer-to-peer crowdfunding boost refugee entrepreneurs? *Finance Research Letters*, *46*, 102264. https://doi.org/10.1016/j.frl.2021.102264

Finsterwalder, J. (2017). Refugee influx: repercussions and research agenda for service scholars. *Journal of Retailing and Consumer Services*, *37*, 177–181. https://doi.org/10.1016/j.jretconser.2016.11.001

Freiling, J., & Harima, A. (2018). Refugee entrepreneurship: learning from case evidence. In S. Heilbrunn, J. Freiling, & A. Harima (eds.), *Refugee Entrepreneurship: A Case-Based Topography* (pp. 255–277). https://doi.org/10.1007/978-3-319-92534-9_18

Gama, A. P. M., Correia, R. E., Augusto, M., & Duarte, F. (2023). Third-party signals in crowdfunded microfinance: which microfinance institutions boost crowdfunding among refugee entrepreneurs? *Small Business Economics*, *61*(2), 559–586. https://doi.org/10.1007/s11187-022-00708-4

Garnham, A. (2006). Refugees and the entrepreneurial process. *Labour, Employment and Work in New Zealand*. https://doi.org/10.26686/lew.v0i0.1375

Gold, S. J. (1988). Refugees and small business: the case of Soviet Jews and Vietnamese. *Ethnic & Racial Studies*, *11*(4), 411. https://doi.org/10.1080/01419870.1988.9993613

Gold, S. J. (1992). The employment potential of refugee entrepreneurship: Soviet Jews and Vietnamese in California. *Review of Policy Research*, *11*(2), 176–186. https://doi.org/10.1111/j.1541-1338.1992.tb00400.x

Harb, M., Kassem, A., & Najdi, W. (2019). Entrepreneurial refugees and the city: brief encounters in Beirut. *Journal of Refugee Studies*, *32*(1), 23–41. https://doi.org/10.1093/jrs/fey003

Harima, A. (2022). Theorizing disembedding and re-embedding: Resource mobilization in refugee entrepreneurship. *Entrepreneurship and Regional Development*, *34*(3–4), 269–293. https://doi.org/10.1080/08985626.2022.2047799

Harima, A., & Freudenberg, J. (2020). Co-creation of social entrepreneurial opportunities with refugees. *Journal of Social Entrepreneurship*, *11*(1), 40–64. https://doi.org/10.1080/19420676.2018.1561498

Harima, A., Periac, F., Murphy, T., & Picard, S. (2021). Entrepreneurial opportunities of Refugees in Germany, France, and Ireland: multiple embeddedness framework. *International Entrepreneurship and Management Journal*, *17*(2), 625–663. https://doi.org/10.1007/s11365-020-00707-5

Hartmann, C., & Philipp, R. (2022). Lost in space? Refugee entrepreneurship and cultural diversity in spatial contexts. *ZFW – Advances in Economic Geography*, *66*(3), 151–171. https://doi.org/10.1515/zfw-2021-0017

Heilbrunn, S., Harima, A., & Freiling, J. (eds.). (2019). *Refugee Entrepreneurship: A Case-based Topography*. Cham: Palgrave Macmillan. https://doi.org/10.1007/978-3-319-92534-9

Heilbrunn, S., & Iannone, R. L. (2020). From center to periphery and back again: a systematic literature review of refugee entrepreneurship. *Sustainability, 12*(18). https://doi.org/10.3390/su12187658

Huq, A., & Venugopal, V. (2021). DIY entrepreneurship? – Self-reliance for women refugees in Australia. *International Migration, 59*(1), 126–142. https://doi.org/10.1111/imig.12727

Huynh, J. A. (2022). Understanding internalized racial oppression and second-generation Vietnamese. *Asian American Journal of Psychology,13*(2), 129–140. https://doi.org/10.1037/aap0000211.supp

Jiang, Y. D., Straub, C., Klyver, K., & Mauer, R. (2021). Unfolding refugee entrepreneurs' opportunity-production process – patterns and embeddedness. *Journal of Business Venturing, 36*(5), 106138. https://doi.org/10.1016/j.jbusvent.2021.106138

Jones Christensen, L., & Newman, A. (2024). Who do I want to be now that I'm here? Refugee entrepreneurs, identity, and acculturation. *Business and Society, 63*(1), 242–275. https://doi.org/10.1177/00076503231158611

Klyver, K., Steffens, P., & Honig, B. (2022). Psychological factors explaining Ukrainian refugee entrepreneurs' venture idea novelty. *Journal of Business Venturing Insights, 18*, e00348. https://doi.org/10.1016/j.jbvi.2022.e00348

Lee, E. S., Szkudlarek, B., Nguyen, D. C., & Nardon, L. (2020). Unveiling the canvas ceiling: a multidisciplinary literature review of refugee employment and workforce integration. *International Journal of Management Reviews, 22*(2), 193–216. https://doi.org/10.1111/ijmr.12222

Lehmann, T., Albaba, H., & Kreiter-Sammet, S. (2022). Refugee entrepreneurship in Germany: an institutional voids perspective. In L.-P. Dana, N. Khachlou, A. Maâlaoui, & V. Ratten (eds.), *Disadvantaged Minorities in Business* (pp. 129–151). Springer.

Luseno, T., & Kolade, O. (2023). Displaced, excluded, and making do: a study of refugee entrepreneurship in Kenya. *Journal of Entrepreneurship in Emerging Economies, 15*(4), 808–834. https://doi.org/10.1108/JEEE-04-2021-0163

Meister, A. D., & Mauer, R. (2019). Understanding refugee entrepreneurship incubation – an embeddedness perspective. *International Journal of Entrepreneurial Behavior & Research, 25*(5), 1065–1092. https://doi.org/10.1108/IJEBR-02-2018-0108

Missbach, A. (2015). Making a "career" in people-smuggling in Indonesia: protracted transit, restricted mobility and the lack of legal work rights. *Sojourn: Journal of Social Issues in Southeast Asia, 30*(2), 423–454. www.jstor.org/stable/24779960

Morrar, R., & Rios-Avila, F. (2021). Discrimination against refugees in the Palestinian labor market. *International Journal of Manpower, 42*(6), 1002–1024. https://doi.org/10.1108/IJM-08-2019-0396

Newman A. B., & Jones Christensen, L. (2021). Doing it right, but getting it wrong: best practices for refugee focused incubators. *Journal of Developmental Entrepreneurship, 26*(3), 1–34. https://doi.org/10.1142/S1084946721500199

Newman, A., Macaulay, L., & Dunwoodie, K. (2023). Refugee entrepreneurship: a systematic review of prior research and agenda for future research. *International Migration Review*. https://doi.org/10.1177/01979183231182669

Ortensi, L. E., & Ambrosetti, E. (2022). Even worse than the undocumented? Assessing the refugees' integration in the labour market of Lombardy (Italy) in 2001–2014. *International Migration*, *60*(3), 20–37. https://doi.org/10.1111/imig.12884

Ram, M., Jones, T., Doldor, S., Villares-Varela, M., & Li, H. (2022). What happens to refugee-origin entrepreneurs? Combining mixed embeddedness and strategy perspectives in a longitudinal study. *Ethnic and Racial Studies*, *45*(16), 1–27. https://doi.org/10.1080/01419870.2021.1991970

Ranabahu, N., de Vries, H. P., & Basharati, Z. (2021). The economic integration of women refugee entrepreneurs in New Zealand. In M. McAdam & J. A. Cunningham (eds.), *Women and Global Entrepreneurship: Contextualising Everyday Experiences* (pp. 64–80). New York: Routledge.

Ranabahu, N., de Vries, H. P., & Basharati, Z. (2023). Refugee-owned small businesses: a typology for blended value creation. *International Migration*, *61*(4), 37–56. https://doi.org/10.1111/imig.13072

Refai, D., Haloub, R., & Lever, J. (2018). Contextualizing entrepreneurial identity among Syrian refugees in Jordan: the emergence of a destabilized habitus? *The International Journal of Entrepreneurship and Innovation*, *19*(4), 250–260. https://doi.org/10.1177/1465750317750322

Refai, D., & McElwee, G. (2023). Refugee subentrepreneurship: the emergence of a liquid cage. *Work, Employment and Society*, *37*(4), 1032–1051. https://doi.org/10.1177/09500170211062817

Richey, M., Brooks, J., & Ravishankar, M. N. (2022). Building self-determination of disadvantaged groups: insights from an entrepreneurship focused program for refugees. *International Journal of Entrepreneurial Behavior & Research*, *28*(7), 1828–1850. https://doi.org/10.1108/IJEBR-10-2021-0806

Shepherd, D. A., Saade, F. P., & Wincent, J. (2020). How to circumvent adversity? Refugee-entrepreneurs' resilience in the face of substantial and persistent adversity. *Journal of Business Venturing*, *35*(4), 105940. https://doi.org/10.1016/j.jbusvent.2019.06.001

Street, C. P., Ng, P. Y., & Al-Dajani, H. (2022). Refugee women business mentors: new evidence for women's empowerment. *Sustainability*, *14*(15), 9154. www.mdpi.com/2071-1050/14/15/9154

Tavakoli, J. (2020). Cultural entrepreneurship of Sahrawi refugees. *African Identities*, *18*(3), 279–294. https://doi.org/10.1080/14725843.2020.1777086

UN: United Nations (2018). Global compact for safe, orderly and regular migration. https://refugeesmigrants.un.org/sites/default/files/180713_agreed_outcome_global_compact_for_migration.pdf

UNHCR. (2019). UNHCR engagement with the Sustainable Development Goals – updated guidance note 2019. www.unhcr.org/media/unhcr-engagement-sustainable-development-goals-updated-guidance-note-2019

UNHCR. (2023). Refugee data finder. www.unhcr.org/refugee-statistics/

Wauters, B., & Lambrecht, J. (2006). Refugee entrepreneurship in Belgium: potential and practice. *The International Entrepreneurship and Management Journal*, *2*(4), 509–525. https://doi.org/10.1007/s11365-006-0008-x

Weng, S. S., & Lee, J. S. (2016). Why do immigrants and refugees give back to their communities and what can we learn from their civic engagement? *VOLUNTAS: International Journal of Voluntary and Nonprofit Organizations*, *27*(2), 509–524. https://doi.org/10.1007/s11266-015-9636-5

Yeshi, T., Harima, A., & Freiling, J. (2022). Resilience on an emotional rollercoaster: refugee entrepreneurship under adversity. *European Management Journal.* https://doi.org/10.1016/j.emj.2022.12.009

Zalkat, G., Barth, H., & Rashid, L. (2023). Refugee entrepreneurship motivations in Sweden and Germany: a comparative case study. *Small Business Economics.* https://doi.org/10.1007/s11187-023-00830-x

She works with multidisciplinary research projects, which gives her the opportunity to interact with entrepreneurs, immigrants, and different organisations to design and implement innovative programmes and tools that support entrepreneurship and socio-economic integration. She has worked on different European Union projects, and now she is the coordinator for the PLOUTOS project, which aims to improve immigrants' financial independence through financial services and entrepreneurship.

Judith Terstriep is an economist and Head of the Research Department "Innovation, Space & Culture" at Westphalian University Gelsenkirchen, Institute for Work and Technology, and lecturer for Social Innovation, Regional Innovation Systems and Migrant Entrepreneurship at the Ruhr-University Bochum. She has extensive experience in entrepreneurship and (social) innovation research. Her research work focuses on social innovation and its measurement, societal innovativeness, (social) innovation and entrepreneurial ecosystems, (regional) challenge-oriented innovation policies and impact measurement. She holds a doctoral degree from the TU Hamburg. Judith is chairwoman of the Federal Ministry for Economic Affairs and Climate Action's Programme Monitoring Committee "Go-cluster".

Nirosha Hewa Wellalage is Associate Professor at UniSA Business, University of South Australia, Adelaide, Australia. Her main research goal is to explore the ways marginalised firms, such as micro, small and medium-sized enterprises (SMEs), firms owned by females and ethnic minorities, and refugees finance their firms and find ways to be sustainable in the long run while contributing to the economic development. Her h-index is 24 and she has published 20 refereed articles in leading international journals, 16 of which (14 as lead author) are in journals ranked as A or A* by the Australian Business Deans Council.

Fatih Yilmaz, a dedicated research fellow and director of projects at Beyond the Horizon ISSG in Belgium, holds a Master of Arts in Interdisciplinary Studies from the University of Oklahoma and a Master of Science in European Politics and Policies from Catholic University of Leuven. His research interest lies in migrant and refugee integration. Proficient in English, Dutch, and Turkish, he passionately navigates the intersections of diverse cultures to foster inclusive communities. Beyond his professional pursuits, Fatih finds joy in his role as a spouse and a parent to two incredible children, inspiring him to create a more inclusive world for future generations.

Lukas R. Zaghow is a researcher at the Institute for Work and Technology (IAT) and pursues a PhD at Technical University of Berlin's (TU) Institute for Urban and Regional Planning (ISR). Building on experience in organisational and regional transformation scholarship, he entered the domain of entrepreneurial ecosystems research. He is concerned with spatialities under transformational pressures and entrepreneurial activity as drivers of change and competitiveness. He earned degrees in Management Science (MSc) and European Studies (MA) from Ruhr University Bochum (RUB), while attending universities in Lisbon, Oklahoma, Pisa, Osaka, and Istanbul on different scholarships.

Ghazal Zalkat holds a doctoral degree in innovation management and entrepreneurship from the Engineering and Innovation Department, School of Business, Innovation, and Sustainability at Halmstad University, Sweden.

2 What is refugee entrepreneurship?

Reflections for a growing field

Alexandra David and Lukas R. Zaghow

Introduction

According to the United Nations High Commissioner for Refugees (UNHCR), the number of displaced people around the world is increasing. However, the influx of refugees to Europe is not a new phenomenon. Since the 1990s, Western European countries have been popular destinations for international (forced) migration movements (United Nations: UN, 2015). Nevertheless, only in the years following the so-called 2015–2017 *European Union (EU) refugee crisis* did an increasing number of refugee entrepreneurship (RE) studies emerge globally that were rooted in the European research community (e.g., Abebe, 2023; Hartmann & Phillip, 2022; Harima, 2022a; Ranabahu et al., 2023; Stoewe, 2021; Heilbrunn & Iannone, 2020; David & Coenen, 2017). At the time, most refugees entered Europe as protection seekers from Iraq and Afghanistan or evading the conflict in Syria. With the Russian invasion of Ukraine in 2022, Ukrainian refugees are an additional group seeking shelter.

A prevalent opinion among scholars is that refugee entrepreneurs – as self-employed displaced individuals – are distinct from other (ethnic) minority entrepreneurs (Abebe, 2023), such as migrant entrepreneurs. This line of thought is based on arguments drawing from different levels of analysis, involving (1) refugee entrepreneurs' individual characteristics (micro level), such as, the modalities of their flight (cf. Kunz, 1973), their entrepreneurial process, and temporal aspects as to the receipt of refugee status and initiation of the founding process in relation to their flight, as well as (2) characteristics of their *organisation* (meso level), and (3) the conditions in the receiving country or *country of residence* (macro level; cf. Shepherd et al., 2020. To exemplify this, Hugo (2013) argues that the migration process (respective *choice-compulsive-spectrum*) introduces a perspective for differentiating or demarcating refugee and migrant entrepreneurs as analytical or ontological categories. Hartmann and Philipp (2022) emphasise refugee entrepreneurs' *entrepreneurial process* as a differentiator, while Bakker and McMullen (2023) enlist cultural diversity factors viewed through the lens of *inclusive entrepreneurship*. Yeshi et al. (2022) stress the receiving environment and its implied challenges for refugee

DOI: 10.4324/9781003368540-3

entrepreneurs, for example, for opportunity identification, resource acquisition, or structural barriers such as discrimination and segregation tendencies in market interactions and local ecosystems. Heilbrunn and Iannone (2020) provide a comprehensive review of RE research as a quickly emerging, eclectic field. Going beyond the quest of establishing order and dissecting the domain of RE itself (which we deem as necessary, e.g., Abebe in this volume), we seek to (re-)contextualise it in the overall migrant entrepreneurship domain and differentiate between other migrant groups in entrepreneurship such as economic migrants.

However, the terms refugee and migrant entrepreneurs are (still and often) employed interchangeably, and refugee entrepreneurs are widely referred to as migrant entrepreneurs (David et al., 2022). Evidently, the introduction of a clear ontological demarcation of sameness and difference in the field of inclusive entrepreneurship research poses challenges. What, if anything, distinguishes refugees from other minority group entrepreneurs(hip)? The challenge for scholars is striking a balance between emphasising those differences, that is, specific particularities and otherness of refugee entrepreneurs, while not neglecting the similarities to existing groups. We thereby seek to stress the entanglements between both the categories on one hand, while welcoming new rigour in attempting to make precise distinctions *within* the category of refugee entrepreneurs – doing justice to the striking heterogeneities within this ever-expanding group. We therefore question whether there is a basis for introducing RE as a distinct field of its own, asking:

> What is refugee entrepreneurship? Who are refugee entrepreneurs and in how far do existing taxonomies aid or obstruct a better understanding of this phenomenon? Do we need to revise and establish new categories or refine the existing categories and taxonomies to maintain conceptual clarity and order?

Against this backdrop, we subsequently discuss whether *refugee entrepreneurs* serve as a conducive overarching label for those categorised as 'refugees'. First, we set the terms of refugee and migrant entrepreneurs into a broader terminological context. Afterwards, we use a literature review providing a concise overview contrasting (relative) structural advantages and disadvantages of (1) migrant entrepreneurs compared to incumbent country of residence (CoR) entrepreneurs and (2) refugee entrepreneurs compared to (economic) migrant entrepreneurs. Building on a discussion of these findings, we deduce implications for framing RE in existing taxonomies and discuss labelling.

The emergence of refugee entrepreneurship

The refugee phenomenon is increasingly reflected in academic literature (cf. Heilbrunn & Iannone, 2020; Heilbrunn et al., 2019) and has grown in prominence since 2018 (Kleist, 2018). A scoping review with *Google Scholar* using the terms 'refugee entrepreneurship' (in English) before 2015–2017 points to only three reviewed articles, whereas the period 2015–2023 includes 62 reviewed articles. Of these, 58 were written between 2018 and 2023. In this vein, Abebe (2023, p. 315) finds an "increased scholarly mobilisation and drastic growth in the volume of salient scientific research". Within the same line, Heilbrunn and Iannone (2020, p. 2) state that "[...] refugee entrepreneurship studies have largely been positioned at the margins of entrepreneurship inquiry, up to 2018".

Nonetheless, it remains unclear whether the interest in RE is the result of the striking public discourse on refugee migration and integration or whether the starting point was truly rooted in observations of refugees displaying distinguishable entrepreneurial behaviours (Betts et al., 2017). Earlier, Sternberg and colleagues (2015) gave evidence "[...] that refugees are more likely to start a business than natives, based on GEM (Global Entrepreneurship Monitor) data". However, there is less evidence that they start businesses more often than economic migrants based on recent studies from Poland comparing Ukrainian refugees with Ukrainian economic migrants. Either way, the domain lacks a shared understanding and conceptualisation (Abebe, 2023). In particular, a demarcation of the phenomenon in (dis)similarity – likeness and difference – from other (marginalised) entrepreneur groups is missing.

But who is a *refugee*? Based on Article 1 of the Geneva Convention relating to the status of refugees of 1951, *refugee* refers to a person who has fled from war, violence, conflict, or persecution and who has crossed an international border to find safety in another country (UNHCR, 2019). In contrast to migrants who leave their country of origin (CoO) voluntarily, refugees are forced to leave. However, recognition as a refugee depends on the legal ramifications of each receiving country. This status is fluid and changes over time due to country regulations. Despite said definition, in the literature we find different groups and concepts subsumed under this label. The basic classification into the sub-category *refugee* is often provided by *nationality* (e.g., *Syrian*, Harb et al., 2014 *Afghan*, Jauhiainen & Eyvazlu, 2020), *ethnicity* (e.g., *Palestinians*, Shepherd et al., 2020), by belonging to a *specific migration context* (e.g., *flight from the Syrian civil war*, Alrawadieh et al., 2018; *the Russo-Ukrainian War*, Klyver et al., 2022), to the stage in which conflict was fled (*acute vs. anticipatory flight*, Kunz, 1973), or *in relation to a specific place* (*CoR or city*, e.g., *Berlin*, Embiricos, 2020; *Lebanon*, Alexandre et al., 2019). In summary, extant literature suggests that *refugee entrepreneurs* have a broad set of characteristics and act in a wide range of contexts.

Considering the wider *migrant entrepreneurship* research before 2015–2017, entrepreneurs with forced migration history are frequently subsumed under migrant entrepreneurs who share similar characteristics referring to their nationality, a common CoR, or even city of residence (e.g., *Iranian entrepreneurs in Scotland*, Haghighi & Lynch, 2012; *Somali entrepreneurs in Leicester*, Ram et al., 2008). Furthermore, refugee entrepreneurs are included in a wider group of migrants, such as *new migrants* in the UK (Jones et al., 2010) or in the Netherlands (Kloosterman et al., 2016). In studies where a country, city, neighbourhood, or a specific time is used as a point of origination or lines of demarcation for data collection, one can only assume that refugees were a part of the study population. As such, refugee entrepreneurs have been covered by migrant entrepreneurship scholarships in the past decades, but in a rather implicit, rather than explicit, manner. However, as the Old Greek origins of the word *catēgoria* highlight and group matter, as they reduce complexity and shape both quotidian and abstract thought, more sensitivity and precision are therefore required, both for research and policy generation purposes.

Thus, the central research questions are as follows: What added value does the concept/term *refugee entrepreneurship* offer compared to existing terms such as *migrant entrepreneurship*? Is the recent hike in the quantity and scope of literature referring to refugee entrepreneurs warranted? Is the heightened publications volume constructed on a firm ontological basis, an intuitively pleasing, and conceptually sound understanding of the phenomena? Are views of RE sufficiently finely grained understanding and distinctions between phenomena, resulting in likewise appropriate categories? What follows seeks to answer these fundamental questions.

Methodology

The systematic review of the literature was employed as it limits bias, with the overall aim of producing a scientific summary of extant evidence (cf. Petticrew, 2006) in RE scholarship.

The articles were identified using the electronic databases EBSCO, EconLit, Google Scholar, and the ISI Web of Knowledge. Consistent with prior approaches to identify relevant articles (Nielsen, 2010; Thorpe et al., 2005), some keywords on the subject were identified and constructed into search strings. For example, the main keywords were 'refugee', 'immigrant' and 'migrant', and 'entrepreneurship'. Consequently, literature research could be conducted employing refugee(s)* AND/OR (im)migrant AND entrepreneur* OR foreign* business AND creation. Consequently, these keywords were searched for in the titles and abstracts of each paper. When reading the abstract, particular care was devoted to filtering for only those studies on first-generation migrants (immigrants). Some articles did not explicitly mention the generation of migrants, but when the title and abstract mentioned 'immigrant(s)' or 'refugee(s)', they passed the first selection. The first selection comprised 70 articles. Following, the authors re-scrutinised each of these articles, re-reading the abstract and the introduction to make sure that they fit the established criteria. From these 70 articles, those published in journals without an impact factor and those that evolved around ethnic communities, minority entrepreneurs in general (including women and other groups), books, doctoral theses, conference proceedings, and other kinds of material were excluded (Jones et al., 2011). After scrutinising these papers, only 45 articles were finally selected for this systematic literature review. This proceeding allowed us to identify, review, and synthesise relevant literature both on (economic) migrants starting and leading businesses and on the group of refugee entrepreneurs in comparison to migrant entrepreneurs.

To gain a comprehensive understanding of the current state of knowledge, we have departed with a short overview of migrant entrepreneurship. We hereafter utilised comparative literature analysis, contrasting different literary bodies of migrant and RE to identify similarities, differences, and patterns in their business activities and present them clustered as (relative) structural dis- and advantages for better answering the posed question of whether the concept of RE contributes an added value when describing the underlying phenomenon in comparison to existing categories such as 'migrant entrepreneurship'.

Refugee and migrant entrepreneurs: Same, but different (- and how)?

Migrant entrepreneurship refers to a specific aspect of entrepreneurship that is often considered within the broader context of minority entrepreneurship or as part of inclusive entrepreneurship (David and Schäfer, 2022; OECD, 2021; Ram et al., 2017). While *minority entrepreneurship* (Ram et al., 2000) refers to the establishment, ownership, and operation of businesses by individuals who belong to marginalised or underrepresented groups within a particular society or economy. These groups can include racial and ethnic minorities, women, immigrants, LGBTQ+ individuals, and individuals with disabilities, among others. *Inclusive entrepreneurship* (Bakker & McMullen, 2023) refers to the entrepreneurial process as being embedded in societal circumstances striving for equal opportunities for all, in every aspect, and particularly in terms of economic participation. In this context, the term *inclusive* implies the normative ideal that entrepreneurship-related resources and *access* must not be restricted to specific groups of people, but ought to be readily available to all entrepreneurial hopefuls equally. Therefore, inclusive entrepreneurship is not about who can participate or how they participate, but rather about supporting entrepreneurs from diverse backgrounds (OECD, 2021) by fostering an inclusive environment. In this context, inclusive entrepreneurial ecosystems, (semi-) organised networks of actors operating as supportive infrastructure, are discussed (Wang et al., 2022 and Wang, 2023). Applying this contextual framework to migrant and RE, both groups can be subsumed under minority entrepreneurship and are part of *inclusive* entrepreneurship discourse.

Historically, the USA is the cradle of migrant entrepreneurship research (Aliaga-Isla & Rialp, 2013). In the USA, the impact of immigrant entrepreneurial activity on its economy is considered, a matter of course due to early mass migration between 1815 and 1914 (Wadhwani, 2016). It is therefore not surprising that the research field of *ethnic entrepreneurship* also originated in the USA as a subfield *of migrant entrepreneurship*. Studies were conducted as early as the 1960s and 1970s (Blalock, 1967; Bonacich, 1973;). Relevant

USA statistics revealed that the start-up rates of diverse ethnic groups differ from the overall population's start-up rates (Drinkwater, 2017). The focus on ethnic grouping as a determinant of entrepreneurial activity among migrants was also adopted in Europe, where the research field has grown in significance since the 1980s, primarily in the UK (Soni et al., 1987; McGoldrick & Reeve, 1989; Ram & Sparrow, 1993). Like in the USA, it was observed that certain ethnic groups were more likely to engage in self-employment, including those with Chinese, Pakistani, Bangladeshi, and Indian roots (Clark & Drinkwater, 1998). The riots in Brixton in 1981 and 1985, where the police and young people of colour clashed in the socioeconomically deprived London neighbourhood, proved to be another catalyst for addressing entrepreneurship as a pathway to social mobility for specific migrant groups and putting it on the political agenda (Scarman, 1986). This, in turn, prompted increased empirical research on *ethnic entrepreneurship* (Ram et al., 2017). Lastly, the low regulatory barriers to starting a business in the USA and the UK have contributed to the heightened presence of the topic of (migrant) entrepreneurship until today.

In contrast, the first prominent studies on the European continent emerged in the late 1990s through research conducted in the Netherlands (Kloosterman et al., 1999). Initially, this research focused on observing the phenomenon of first generation of migrants (Dheer, 2018) clustering as entrepreneurs in local markets and urban areas, as well as the concept of *mixed embeddedness*, which highlights the integration of this group in various settings as a contribution to opportunity structures.

Unlike in the UK, there were no comparable triggers that brought this topic to the forefront of the political agenda on the European mainland, but rather observations were made of the agglomeration of *migrant entrepreneurs* in metropolitan areas and their often different and unconventional ways of running businesses. However, the topic did receive occasional attention at the EU level, recognising it as an opportunity for the social and economic integration and mobility of disadvantaged groups, including first-generation migrants (Liikanen, 2003). Although the research strand of *ethnic entrepreneurship* continues to be pursued, primarily in the UK, more recent publications have increasingly referred to the term *immigrant entrepreneur* (Rath, 2000; Zhou, 2004). This shift in terminology suggests that the focus is generally set on first-generation immigrant entrepreneurs rather than on ethnicity. In parallel, since the turn of the millennium, there has been a related research branch known as *migrant entrepreneurship* (David et al., 2022; Ram et al., 2017), which implies that the term encompasses both descendants and first-generation immigrants as entrepreneurs.

Today, the striking variety of migrant entrepreneurship contexts has been addressed in scholars' publications. For instance, the rise of *transnational entrepreneurship* among migrants occurred at the latest since the early 2000s (Lundberg & Rehnfors, 2018; Portes et al., 2002). The *transnational* perspective replaces the understanding of migration as a one-time process (Harima, 2022a; Schmitz, 2013) in favour of a circular understanding (David,

2015). More often, ***migrant start-ups*** are also becoming the focus of academic interest (Terstriep et al., 2023). In addition, ***diaspora entrepreneurship*** as a characteristic of migrant entrepreneurship can also be seen as a manifestation of international entrepreneurship (Elo et al., 2018). In the context of a primarily political debate, ***female migrant entrepreneurs*** entered the academic agenda (e.g., Aman et al., 2024; Haandrikman & Webster, 2020), ensuring that the untapped resources and capabilities of migrant women entrepreneurs and female self-employed are identified and activated (OECD, 2021).

Finally, the spatial dimension of migrant entrepreneurs (David & Schäfer, 2022), originating from the mixed embeddedness concept of Kloosterman et al. (1999), often refers to the phenomenon of the embeddedness of migrant entrepreneurs into multi-scalar settings and two or more context at a time. This phenomenon is at times, also coined ***multifocal embeddedness*** (Solano et al., 2022), characterised by multiculturalism and diversity of social structures. Lastly, it is mainly ***refugee entrepreneurs*** who have been shaping the scientific agenda in the last 5–8 years. As enunciated earlier, however, a lack of common understandings and conceptual clarity hinder further advancements in this domain. Table 2.1 contrasts scholars' findings on (relative) structural advantages and disadvantages of (economic) migrant entrepreneur experiences when compared to incumbent, native CoR entrepreneurs. This is to serve as a basis for later juxtapositions of (economic) migrant and refugee entrepreneurs to carve out and uncover the lines of demarcation and similarity.

To date, refugee and migrant entrepreneurship literature share several continuities. For instance, publications are based on various disciplines, albeit with a focus on social sciences (Heilbrunn & Iannone, 2020). RE literature has borrowed theoretical vantage points from economic geography, urban sociology, or entrepreneurship research, such as the ***mixed embeddedness*** approach (Kloosterman et al., 1999; Wauters & Lambrecht, 2008) or ***social capital*** theory (Bizri, 2017). Like (im)migrant entrepreneurship (cf. Kerr & Kerr, 2017), initial attempts to explain RE point towards ***disadvantage mechanisms***, including language barriers, cultural alienation, legal status, adaptation to economic structures, institutional obstacles, segregation, and discrimination on the labour markets (Gold, 1992; Desai et al., 2021; Yeshi et al., 2022). While research focuses mainly on a certain country, city and legal context for refugees and entrepreneurship, the impact of this context on refugee entrepreneurs typically appears as a blurry background variable (Heilbrunn & Iannone, 2020). Furthermore, the focus is on refugees' economic ***participation*** through entrepreneurship, rather than on business performance (Stoewe, 2021).

In addition, scholars have elaborated on the ***specificity of refugee entrepreneurs' starting positions*** and resources (Hartmann & Philipp, 2022). They have referred to the abrupt, potentially severely traumatising, alienating, and detaching character of migration, which sets refugee-origin individuals and their entrepreneurial process apart from other migrants (Wauters & Lambrecht, 2008). The forced nature of migration and its personal and legal implications (e.g., lack of access to labour markets) can leave a lasting imprint on refugees' economic activity in the CoR (Desai et al., 2021). Further, literature points to the *(lack of) embeddedness* within local ecosystems (Harima, 2022b). Hartmann and Philipp (2022) find that refugee entrepreneurs can be 'Lost in Space' when entering local ecosystems, or struggle with power relations in specific locations (David & Schäfer, 2022).

Compared to other migrant groups, (structural) ***disadvantages and advantages*** of refugee entrepreneurs(hip) have been identified, albeit at a smaller scale. Advantages are described as reactions to initial barriers, including the capability of resilience even in the most adverse circumstances (Heilbrunn, 2019) and refugees´ resources such as transnational embeddedness (Sandberg et al., 2019), showing the ability to complement sole economic value by social and cultural value creation within CoRs (Ranabahu et al., 2023).

Akin to Table 2.1, Table 2.2 compares differences – represented as (relative) structural disadvantages and advantages – between *refugee entrepreneurs*

Table 2.1 Parameters on the (relative) structural advantages and disadvantages of economic migrant entrepreneurs versus CoR incumbent entrepreneurs

Structural advantage/ disadvantage	*Explanation of parameters*
Structural disadvantages of migrant entrepreneurs when compared with incumbent CoR national entrepreneurs	**Limited access to resources and capital:** Migrant entrepreneurs may have limited access to financial resources, such as loans, due to their lack of established credit history or collateral in the host country (cf. William & Krasnigi, 2018) **'Foreignness'** (cf. Gurău et al., 2020) and 'Othering' (cf. David & Terstriep, 2023; Rashid & Cepeda-García, 2021) **Discrimination:** Migrant entrepreneurs may face discrimination and bias in the form of reduced access to markets, contracts, and funding due to their ethnicity, race, or nationality (e.g., Teixeira et al., 2007) **Language and symbolic barriers:** Migrant entrepreneurs may face language barriers when trying to communicate with customers, suppliers, or government officials, which can make it difficult to establish and grow a business. (cf. Guerrero & Wanjiru, 2021) **Social capital and network constraints:** Migrant entrepreneurs may have limited social networks in the CoR, which affects perceptions and realities of opportunity structures, acquiring business partners, employees, or mentors (cf. Lassalle et al., 2020)

Table 2.1 (Continued)

Structural advantage/ disadvantage	*Explanation of parameters*
	Legal barriers: Migrant entrepreneurs may face legal barriers related to their immigration status, such as restrictions on working or starting a business (Solano et al., 2023) **Lack of knowledge and skills:** Migrant entrepreneurs may lack knowledge and skills related to business practices, regulations, and cultural norms in the host country, which can make it difficult to establish and grow a business (Ram et al., 2017)
Structural advantages of migrant entrepreneurs when compared with incumbent CoR national entrepreneurs	**International networks:** Migrant entrepreneurs may have access to international networks, including contacts in their country of origin and other countries, which can help them identify business opportunities and markets (Elo, 2014) **Multicultural skills:** Migrant entrepreneurs may possess multicultural skills, including language proficiency and knowledge of cultural norms, that can give them a competitive advantage in accessing diverse markets and building relationships with customers (Walsh & Cooney, 2022) **Cultural diversity:** Migrant entrepreneurs may bring cultural diversity to the business environment, which can lead to innovation, creativity, new perspectives, and co-ethnic networking (Zhang et al., 2023) **Niche markets:** Migrant entrepreneurs may be able to identify and capitalise on niche markets based on their knowledge of specific cultural or ethnic communities (Kloosterman et al., 1999) **Lower overhead costs:** Migrant entrepreneurs may have lower overhead costs due to their ability to leverage existing social and cultural networks to obtain resources such as business advice, office space, and labour (cf. David et al., 2023; Kloosterman et al., 1999) **Flexibility and adaptability:** Migrant entrepreneurs may have a higher degree of flexibility and adaptability due to their experience in navigating new and challenging environments, including cultural, legal, and regulatory differences (David et al., 2023) **'Elective affinity' or 'ethnic solidarity':** The sense of shared fate in ethnic groups and in immigrant communities across ethnicities (cf. Waldinger 1989)

Table 2.2 Parameters on the (relative) structural advantages and disadvantages of 'refugee' versus (economic) migrant entrepreneurs

Structural advantage/ disadvantage	*Explanation of parameters*
Structural disadvantages for refugee entrepreneurs versus (economic) migrant entrepreneurs	**Forced/disruptive separation from family and community life:** e.g., lost connections (social capital), struggle in strenuous mobility journeys, unplanned country of resettlement (Sossou et al. 2008; Yeshi et al. 2022)
	Forced resource scarcity: Lost assets (financial, physical capital) through the flight process (Gold, 1992; Shneikat & Ryan, 2018), limited finances before leaving CoO
	Psychological trauma also limiting cognitive capacity: e.g., war exposure, repeatedly threatened physical safety, violence, prolonged separation from family members, destruction of home and property, trauma as an explanation for struggles to move into and remain in (self-)employment (Gold, 1992; Yeshi et al., 2022)
	Exacerbated institutional barriers: Discrimination, segregation, lost identity and legitimacy (e.g., through deskilling), and power distances (Desai et al., 2021; Yeshi et al., 2022)
	Strict regulatory regimes and institutional voids: Especially shortly after arrival in the CoR, e.g., legal frameworks prohibiting asylum seekers from (formal) economic participation (Heilbrunn, 2019)
	Structural mismatch with labour markets in CoR: In forced migration contexts, the percentage of employees with culture/country-specific skills who would not leave their own country under normal circumstances is much higher than among economic migrants (Gold, 1992)
	Exacerbated blocked mobility: Limited transferability of professional degrees, especially when moving from less to more regulated CoRs (Gold & Kibria, 1993)
	Loss of (connection to) resource base in the CoO: Links to CoO cannot be activated (easily) (Wauters & Lambrecht, 2008)
	Smaller social capital and networks in CoR compared to other groups of immigrants (Gold, 1992; Wauters & Lambrecht, 2008)
Structural advantages (for entrepreneurship) produced by the refugee experience	**Resilience** (individual, relational, institutional; Heilbrunn, 2019; Shepherd et al., 2020; Shepherd et al., 2022) and **bricolage**, i.e., ability to employ limited resources to start a business (Heilbrunn, 2019; Kwong et al., 2018)
	Trauma and psychological impacts potentially beneficial for entrepreneurial thinking (e.g., 'venture ideal novelty', entrepreneurial rigour; [David & Terstriep, 2023; Wauters & Lambrecht, 2008])

Table 2.2 (Continued)

Structural advantage/ disadvantage	*Explanation of parameters*
	Blended value creation in ethnic/co-ethnic and local host communities: i.e., complementation of economic value by social and cultural outcomes (Ranabahu et al., 2023; Williams & Krasniqi, 2018) **Specific transnationality:** Social and economic embeddedness in the CoR and CoO, and diaspora networks around the world as resources (Halilovich & Efendić, 2019; Ram et al., 2022; Sandberg et al., 2019; Williams & Krasniqi, 2018)

and (economic) *migrant entrepreneurs.* Said analysis provides sufficient cause for demarcating between both concepts while highlighting their ontological affinity.

Discussion and conclusion

RE is a growing research field and in most studies it is presented within its own domain. Researchers have thus emphasised that the realities of refugees, due to their forced migration and their different treatment in the CoRs (compared to other migrants), differentiate them from other migrant-origin entrepreneurs. While there are calls for context sensitivity within the field (Abebe, 2023), little attention is given to the diversity within *RE* in contrast to the situation within migrant entrepreneurship (David et al., 2022).

In accordance with the previous works of Heilbrunn and Iannone (2020) and Abebe (2023), our literature review highlights the importance of recognising the heterogeneity of refugee entrepreneur experiences, even among individuals with similar demographic characteristics who engage in entrepreneurship in the same CoR. The presented heterogeneity of refugee-origin entrepreneurs underscores the need for a nuanced understanding of RE that goes beyond group assumptions of refugeeness and generalised related factors of disadvantage and advantage.

In this vein, we argue RE indeed shares similar characteristics with the *overarching* concepts of both migrant entrepreneurship for inclusive entrepreneurship. Hence, we argue for RE research to be *framed* within and explored from a vantage point informed by the tradition, extant theories, methodology, and overarching category systems in migration and migrant entrepreneurship scholarship. However, we provide backing for RE to be given special attention and to be carved out and explored as its distinct subfield. Our literature review explicitly emphasises how – both phenomenologically and ontologically – *refugee entrepreneurs* are a sufficiently distinct and sufficiently heterogeneous/stratified group/cohort/class and highlights how the refugee entrepreneur category itself must be deemed reductive and generalising. We thus call for more sensitivity and precision in research going forward. Thus, our contribution lies in the (1) emphasis on the lineages and precursors to RE scholarship (and the things we can learn from its antecedents), while simultaneously underscoring the need to establish (2) conceptual and ontological clarity to then solidify and substantiate and tailor research, exploring how one might make sense of the temporal, contextual, and motivational differences *among* refugee entrepreneurs. Thus, we find that while RE warrants specific scholarly attention, the domain lacks refinement and nuance in its current, rather unorderly and unharmonised use of terminology. This situation would be mitigated by framing the discourse of RE within the existing (migrant) entrepreneurship domain.

Based on migrant entrepreneurship categorisation (David et al., 2022), among others, micro, meso, and macro level considerations distinguish and differentiate refugee entrepreneurs both among each other *and* from other (economic) migrant entrepreneurs: (1) *individual/personal* characteristics such as age, gender, ethnic or religious affiliation, CoO, education level, histories or experience with entrepreneurship, the CoO context, temporality and acuteness of flight, trauma, individual motivation and entrepreneurial orientation, and recognition status as refugee by the time of starting a business (Ram et al., 2022); (2) *organisational* characteristics such as resource transferability or constraints, sectoral affiliation, path dependencies, transnational action radius, innovativeness, growth potential, and employment prospects; and (3) *institutional/contextual* factors such as the embeddedness in the local or regional entrepreneurial ecosystem in the CoR, the degree of institutionalised/formalised support received, and the larger CoR sociocultural and market context must be accounted for.

To better understand these distinctions and their consequences, we underscore the need to reframe the burgeoning domain of RE research. This involves placing greater emphasis on the uniqueness and diversity among phenomena attributed to this analytical category. We recommend that the future of RE studies should focus on achieving a balance between accentuating the group-specific particularities of refugees, analysing the consequences of these distinctive traits, and integrating emerging theoretical and conceptual findings into broader studies on entrepreneurship, including those related to migrant entrepreneurs.

References

Abebe, S.A. (2023). Refugee entrepreneurship: Systematic and thematic analyses and a research agenda. *Small Business Economics*, *60*, 315–350. https://doi.org/10.1007/s11187-022-00636-3

Alexandre, L., Salloum, C., & Alalam, A. (2019). An investigation of migrant entrepreneurs: The case of Syrian refugees in Lebanon. *International Journal of Entrepreneurial Behavior & Research*, *25*(5), 1147–1164. https://doi.org/10.1108/IJEBR-03-2018-0171

Aliaga-Isla, R., & Rialp, A. (2013). Systematic review of immigrant entrepreneurship literature – Previous findings and ways forward. *Entrepreneurship & Regional Development*, *25*(9–10), 819–844. https://doi.org/10.1080/08985626.2013.845694

Alrawadieh, Z., Karayilan, E., & Cetin, G. (2018). Understanding the challenges of refugee entrepreneurship in tourism and hospitality. *The Service Industries Journal*, *39*(9–10), 717–740. https://doi.org/10.1080/02642069.2018.1440550

Aman, R., Elo, M., Ahokangas, P., & Zhang, X. (2024). Empowering migrant women's entrepreneurship: stakeholder perspectives from the entrepreneurial ecosystem. *International Journal of Entrepreneurial Behavior & Research*, *30*(7), 1698–1724. https://doi.org/10.1108/IJEBR-04-2023-042

Bakker, R.M., & McMullen, J.S. (2023). Inclusive entrepreneurship: A call for a shared theoretical conversation about unconventional entrepreneurs. *Journal of Business Venturing*, *38*(1). https://doi.org/10.1016/j.jbusvent.2022.106268

Betts, A., Bloom, L., Kaplan, J.D., & Omata, N. (2017). *Refugee Economies: Forced Displacement and Development* (1st ed.). Oxford: Oxford University Press.

Bizri, R.M. (2017). Refugee-entrepreneurship: A social capital perspective. *Entrepreneurship & Regional Development*, *27*(1), 1–22. https://doi.org/10.1080/08985626.2017.1364787

Blalock, H.M. (1967). *Toward a Theory of Minority-Group Relations* (Vol. 325). New York: John Wiley & Sons.

Bonacich, E. (1973). A theory of middleman minorities. *American Sociological Review*, *38*(5), 583–594. www.jstor.org/stable/2094409

Clark, K., & Drinkwater, S. (1998). Ethnicity and self-employment in Britain. *Oxford Bulletin of Economics and Statistics*, *60*(3), 383–407. https://doi.org/10.1111/1468-0084.00105

David, A. (2015). *Scientia Est Potentia: Human Capital and the Role of Networks; Migration, Inclusion and New Qualification for A Sustainable Regional Economy.* [dissertation]. Twente: University of Twente.

David, A., & Coenen, F. (2017). Immigrant entrepreneurship – A chance for labour market integration of refugees? In A. David & I. Hamburg (Eds.), *Entrepreneurship and Entrepreneurial Skills in Europe* (pp. 77–101). Leverkusen: Barbara Budrich Publishers.

David, A., & Schäfer, S. (2022). Spatial perspectives on migrant entrepreneurship. *ZFW – Advances in Economic Geography*, *66*(3), 131–136. https://doi.org/10.1515/zfw-2022-0033

David, A., & Terstriep, J. (2023). *Transformational Hubs for Recognised Refugees – Policy Recommendations by the Enter to Transform Project.* Gelsenkirchen: Institute for Work and Technology, 6. Gelsenkirchen: Institut Arbeit und Technik. https://doi.org/10.53190

David, A., Terstriep, J., Stoewe, K., Ruthemeier, A., Elo, M., & Garcia Schmidt, A. (2022). Migrantisches Unternehmer: innentum in Deutschland. *Bertelsmann Stiftung*. https://doi.org/10.11586/2022002

David, A., Terstriep, J. & Zbierowski, P. (2023). Riding the wave – Resilient Polish migrant entrepreneurs navigating through Brexit and Covid-19 in the UK. In R. Sternberg, E. Amoros, M. Elo, & J. Levie (Eds.), *Research Handbook on Transnational*

Diaspora Entrepreneurship (pp. 220–245). Cheltenham: Edward Elgar Publishing. https://doi.org/10.4337/9781788118699.00021

de Lange, T., Berntsen, L., Hanoeman, R., & Haidar, O. (2020). Highly skilled entrepreneurial refugees: Legal and practical barriers and enablers to start up in the Netherlands. *International Migration*, 1–14. https://doi.org/10.1111/imig.12745

Desai, S., Naudé, W., & Stel, N. (2021). Refugee entrepreneurship: Context and directions for future research. *Small Business Economics*, *56*(3), 933–945. https://doi.org/10.1007/s11187-019-00310-1

Dheer, R.J.S. (2018). Entrepreneurship by immigrants: A review of existing literature and directions for future research. *International Entrepreneurship and Management Journal*, *14*(3), 555–614. https://doi.org/10.1007/s11365-018-0506-7

Drinkwater, S. (2017). Migrant entrepreneurship. In R. Blackburn, D.d. Clercq, & J. Heinonen (Eds.), *The Sage Handbook of Small Business and Entrepreneurship* (pp. 94–106). London: SAGE Publications.

Elo, M. (2014). Diaspora networks in international business and transnational entrepreneurship – A literature review. *ZenTra Working Paper in Transnational Studies*, 40. http://dx.doi.org/10.2139/ssrn.2518428

Elo, M., Sandberg, S., Servais, P., Basco, R., Cruz, A.D., Riddle, L., & Täube, F. (2018). Advancing the views on migrant and diaspora entrepreneurs in international entrepreneurship. *Journal of International Entrepreneurship*, *16*(2), 119–133. https://doi.org/10.1007/s10843-018-0231-x

Embiricos, A. (2020). From refugee to entrepreneur? Challenges to refugee self-reliance in Berlin, Germany. *Journal of Refugee Studies*, *33*(1), 245–267. https://doi.org/10.1093/jrs/fez073

Gold, S.J. (1992). The employment potential of refugee entrepreneurship: Soviet Jews and Vietnamese in California. *Review of Policy Research*, *11*(2), 176–186. https://doi.org/10.1111/j.1541-1338.1992.tb00400.x

Gold, S., & Kibria, N. (1993). Vietnamese refugees and blocked mobility. *Asian and Pacific Migration Journal*, *2*(1), 27–56. https://doi.org/10.1177/011719689300200102

Guerrero, M., & Wanjiru, R. (2021). Entrepreneurial migrants from/in emerging economies: Breaking taboos and stereotypes. *International Entrepreneurship and Management Journal*, *17*(2), 477–506. https://doi.org/10.1007/s11365-021-00754-6

Gurău, C., Dana, L.-P., & Light, I. (2020). Overcoming the liability of foreignness: A typology and model of immigrant entrepreneurs. *European Management Review*, *17*, 701–717. https://doi.org/10.1111/emre.12392

Haandrikman, K., & Webster, N.A. (2020). Migrant, woman and business owner: A heterogeneous group with diverse needs. *Kulturgeografisk Seminarium*, 1. Stockholm University.

Haghighi, A.M., & Lynch, P. (2012). Entrepreneurship and the social integration of new minorities: Iranian hospitality entrepreneurs in Scotland. *Tourism Review*, *67*(1), 4–10. https://doi.org/10.1108/16605371211216323

Halilovich, H., & Efendić, N. (2019). From refugees to trans-local entrepreneurs: Crossing the borders between formal institutions and informal practices in Bosnia and Herzegovina. *Journal of Refugee Studies*, *23*(4), 663–680. https://doi.org/10.1093/jrs/fey066

Harb, M., Kassem, A., & Najdi, W. (2019). Entrepreneurial refugees and the city: Brief encounters in Beirut. *Journal of Refugee Studies*, *32*(1), 23–41. https://doi.org/10.1093/jrs/fey003

Harb, C., & Saab, R. (2014). *Social Cohesion and CLI Assessment* – Save the Children report.

Harima, A. (2022a). Transnational migration entrepreneurship during a crisis: Immediate response to challenges and opportunities emerging through the COVID-19 pandemic. *Business and Society Review*, *127*(S1), 223–251. https://doi.org/10.1111/basr.12266

Harima, A. (2022b). Theorizing disembedding and re-embedding: Resource mobilization in refugee entrepreneurship. *Entrepreneurship & Regional Development*, *34*(3–4), 269–293. https://doi.org/10.1080/08985626.2022.2047799

Hartmann, C., & Philipp, R. (2022). Lost in space? Refugee entrepreneurship and cultural diversity in spatial contexts. *ZFW – Advances in Economic Geography*, *66*(3), 151–171. https://doi.org/10.1515/zfw-2021-0017

Heilbrunn, S. (2019). Against all odds: Refugees bricoleuring in the void. *International Journal of Entrepreneurial Behavior & Research*, *1*(3), 85–104. https://doi.org/10.1108/IJEBR-10-2017-0393

Heilbrunn, S., Freiling, J., & Harima, A. (2019). *Refugee Entrepreneurship: A Case-Based Topography*. London: Macmillan.

Heilbrunn S., & Iannone. Y. (2020). From center to periphery and back again: A systematic literature review of refugee entrepreneurship. *Sustainability*, *12*(18), 7658. https://doi.org/10.3390/su12187658

Hugo, G. (2013). The economic contribution of humanitarian settlers in Australia. *International Migration*, *52*, 31–52. https://doi.org/10.1111/imig.12092

Jauhiainen, J.S., & Eyvazlu, D. (2020). Entrepreneurialism through self-management in Afghan guest towns in Iran. *Urban Science*, *4*(4), 51. https://doi.org/10.3390/urbansci4040051

Jones, T., Ram, M., & Theodorakopoulos, N. (2010). Transnationalism as a force for ethnic minority enterprise? The case of Somalis in Leicester. *International Journal of Urban and Regional Research*, *34*(3), 565–585. https://doi.org/10.1111/j.1468-2427.2010.00913.x

Jones, N.A., Ross, H., Lynam, T., Perez, P., & A. Leitch, A. (2011). Mental models: An interdisciplinary synthesis of theory and methods. *Ecology and Society*, *16*(1), 46. www.jstor.org/stable/26268859

Kerr, S.P., & Kerr, W.R. (2017). Immigrant entrepreneurship. In J. Haltiwanger, E. Hurst, J. Miranda, & A. Schoar (Eds.), *Measuring Entrepreneurial Businesses: Current Knowledge and Challenges* (pp. 187–249). Chicago, IL: University of Chicago Press.

Kleist, J.O. (2018). *Flucht-und Flüchtlingsforschung in Deutschland: Akteure, Themen und Strukturen. State-of-research Papier 01.* Retrieved from: https://flucht-forschung-transfer.de/wp-content/uploads/2018/02/State-of-Research-01-J-Olaf-Kleist-web.pdf

Kloosterman, R.C., Rusinovic, K., & Yeboah, D. (2016). Super-diverse migrants – similar trajectories? Ghanaian entrepreneurship in the Netherlands seen from a mixed embeddedness perspective. *Journal of Ethnic and Migration Studies*, *42*(6), 913–932. https://doi.org/10.1080/1369183X.2015.1126091

Kloosterman, R., van der Leun, J., & Rath, J. (1999). Mixed embeddedness: (In)formal economic activities and immigrant businesses in the Netherlands. *International*

Journal of Urban and Regional Research, *23*(2), 253–267. https://doi.org/10.1111/1468-2427.00194
Klyver, K., Steffens, P., & Honig, B. (2022). Psychological factors explaining Ukrainian refugee entrepreneurs' venture idea novelty. *Journal of Business Venturing Insights*, 18. https://doi.org/10.1016/j.jbvi.2022.e00348
Kunz, E.F. (1973). The refugee in flight: Kinetic models and forms of displacement. *International Migration Review*, *7*(2), 125–146. www.jstor.org/stable/3002424
Kwong, C.C.Y., Cheung, C.W.M., Manzoor, H., & Rashid, M.U. (2018). Entrepreneurship through bricolage: A study of displaced entrepreneurs at times of war and conflict. *Entrepreneurship & Regional Development*, *7*, 1–21. https://doi.org/10.1080/08985626.2018.1541592
Lassalle, P., Johanson, M., Nicholson, J.D., & Ratajczak-Mrozek, M. (2020). Migrant entrepreneurship and markets: The dynamic role of embeddedness in networks in the creation of opportunities. *Industrial Marketing Management*, *91*, 523–536. https://doi.org/10.1016/j.indmarman.2020.04.009
Liikanen, E. (2003). EGovernment for Europe's Public Services of the Future. www.uoc.edu/inaugural03/esp/article/index.html
Lundberg, H., & Rehnfors, A. (2018). Transnational entrepreneurship: Opportunity identification and venture creation. *Journal of International Entrepreneurship*, *16*(2), 150–175. https://doi.org/10.1007/s10843-018-0228-5
McGoldrick C, Reeve D, 1989, *"Black business in Kirklees Huddersfield"*, Employment Development Unit, Kirklees Metropolitan Council, Huddersfield.
Nielsen, S. (2010). Top management team diversity: A review of theories and methodologies. *International Journal of Management Reviews*, (12), 301–316. https://doi.org/10.1111/j.1468-2370.2009.00263.x
OECD/European Commission (2021). *The Missing Entrepreneurs 2021: Policies for Inclusive Entrepreneurship and Self-employment*. Paris: OECD Publishing. https://doi.org/10.1787/71b7a9bb-en
Petticrew, M., & Roberts, H. (2006). *Systematic Reviews in the Social Sciences: A Practical Guide*. Blackwell Publishing. https://doi.org/10.1002/9780470754887
Portes, A., Haller, W., & Guarnizo, L. (2002). Transnational entrepreneurs: An alternative form of immigrant economic adaptation. *American Sociological Review*, *67*(2), 278–298. www.jstor.org/stable/3088896
Ram, M., Jones, T., Doldor, S., Villares-Varela, M., & Li, H. (2022). What happens to refugee-origin entrepreneurs? Combining mixed embeddedness and strategy perspectives in a longitudinal study. *Ethnic and Racial Studies*, *45*(16), 1–27. https://doi.org/10.1080/01419870.2021.1991970
Ram, M., Jones, T., & Villares-Varela, M. (2017). Migrant entrepreneurship: Reflections on research and practice. *International Small Business Journal*, *35*(1), 3–18. https://doi.org/10.1177/0266242616678051
Ram, M., Sanghera, B., Abbas, T., Barlow, G., & Jones, T. (2000). Ethnic minority business in comparative perspective: The case of the independent restaurant sector. *Journal of Ethnic and Migration Studies*, *26*(3), 495–510. https://doi.org/10.1080/713680492
Ram, M., & Sparrow, J. (1993). Minority firms, racism and economic development. *Local Economy*, *8*(2), 117–129. https://doi.org/10.1080/02690949308726181
Ram, M., Theodorakopoulos, N., & Jones, T. (2008). Forms of capital, mixed embeddedness and Somali enterprise. *Work, Employment and Society*, *22*(3), 427–446. https://doi.org/10.1177/0950017008093477

Ranabahu, N., de Vries, H.P., & Basharati, Z. (2023). Refugee-owned small businesses: A typology for blended value creation. *International Migration*, *61*(4), 37–56. https://doi.org/10.1111/imig.13072

Rashid, L., & Cepeda-García, S. (2021). Self-categorising and othering in migrant integration: The case of entrepreneurs in Berlin. *Sustainability*, *13*(4), 2145. https://doi.org/10.3390/su13042145

Rath, J. (Ed.) (2000). *Immigrant Businesses: The Economic, Political and Social Environment*. London: Macmillan.

Sandberg, S., Immonen, R., & Kok, S. (2019). Refugee entrepreneurship: Taking a social network view on immigrants with refugee backgrounds starting transnational businesses in Sweden. *International Journal of Entrepreneurship and Small Business*, *36*(1/2), 216–241. https://doi.org/10.1504/IJESB.2019.096967

Scarman, L.G. (1986). *The Scarman Report: The Brixton Disorders 10–12 April 1981: Report of an Inquiry:* Puffin.

Schmitz, A. (2013). *Transnational leben. Bildungserfolgreiche (Spät-)Aussiedler zwischen Deutschland und Russland*. Bielefeld: Transcript. ISBN 978-3-8376-2328-4.

Shepherd, D.A., Parida, V., & Wincent, J. (2022). Refugee entrepreneurs building and displaying resilience. In D. A. Shepherd, V. Parida, & J. Wincent (Eds.), *Entrepreneurial Responses to Chronic Adversity: The Bright, the Dark, and the in Between*. Palgrave Macmillan. https://doi.org/10.1007/978-3-031-04884-5_3.

Shepherd, D.A., Saade, F.P., & Wincent, J. (2020). How to circumvent adversity? Refugee-entrepreneurs' resilience in the face of substantial and persistent adversity. *Journal of Business Venturing*, *35*(4). https://doi.org/10.1016/j.jbusvent.2019.06.001

Shneikat, B., & Ryan, C. (2018). Syrian refugees and their re-entry to 'normality': The role of service industries. *The Service Industries Journal*, *38*(3–4), 201–227. https://doi.org/10.1080/02642069.2017.1387539

Solano, G., Ram, M., & Rath, J. (2023). Regulation of migrant entrepreneurship: The strained conjunction of laws, policies and practices. *International Migration*. https://doi.org/10.1111/imig.13128

Solano, G., Schutjens, V., & Rath, J. (2022). Multifocality and opportunity structure: towards a mixed embeddedness model for transnational migrant entrepreneurship. *CMS* 10, 3 https://doi.org/10.1186/s40878-021-00270-0.

Soni, S., Tricker, M., & Ward, R. (1987). *Ethnic Minority Business in Leicester*. Birmingham: Aston University.

Sossou, M.A., Craig, C.D., Ogren, H., & Schnak, M. (2008). A qualitative study of resilience factors of Bosnian refugee women resettled in the southern United States. *Journal of Ethnic & Cultural Diversity in Social Work*, *17*(4), 365–385. https://doi.org/10.1080/15313200802467908

Sternberg, R., von Bloh, J., & Brixy, U. (2015). Unternehmensgründung im weltweiten Vergleich. *Global Entrepreneurship Monitor*; Länderbericht Deutschland; Hannover: Institut für Arbeitsmarkt-und Berufsforschung.

Stoewe, K. (2021). *Entrepreneurship and Integration in the global city: The Cases of Refugee-Origin Entrepreneurship in Birmingham and Cologne* (PhD dissertation). Birmingham: University of Birmingham.

Teixeira, C., Lo, L., & Truelove, M. (2007). Immigrant entrepreneurship, institutional discrimination, and implications for public policy: A case study in Toronto. *Environment and Planning C: Government and Policy*, *25*(2), 176–193. https://doi.org/10.1068/c18r

Terstriep, J., David, A., Ruthemeier, A., & Elo, M. (2023). The role of embeddedness of migrant start-ups in local entrepreneurship ecosystems during the COVID-19 crisis. *Journal of Comparative International Management (JCIM)*. https://doi.org/10.55482/jcim.2023.33532

Thorpe, R., Holt, R., Macpherson, A., & Pittaway, L. (2005). Using knowledge within small and medium-sized firms: A systematic review of the evidence. *International Journal of Management Reviews*, *7*, 257–281. https://doi.org/10.1111/j.1468-2370.2005.00116.x

UNHCR (2019). Global Trends. Forced Displacements in 2019.

UN Human Development Report (2015). *Work for Human Development*. New York: United Nations Development Programme (UNDP).

Wadhwani, D. (2016). Entrepreneurship in historical context: Using history to develop theory and understand process. In F. Welter, & W.B. Gartner (Eds.), *A Research Agenda for Entrepreneurship and Context* (pp. 65–78). Cheltenham: Elgar Research Agendas. doi:10.4337/9781784716844.00010.

Waldinger, R. (1989). Structural opportunity or ethnic advantage? Immigrant business development in New York. *International Migration Review*, *23*(1), 48–72. www.jstor.org/stable/2546182

Walsh, L., & Cooney, T. (2022). Understanding the interplay between immigrant nascent entrepreneurship and cross-cultural adaptation. *Journal of Small Business and Enterprise Development*. https://doi.org/10.1108/JSBED-12-2021-0472

Wang, Q. (2023). Planning for an inclusive entrepreneurial ecosystem. *Journal of the American Planning Association*, *89*(3), 295–309. https://doi.org/10.1080/01944363.2022.2105740

Wang, H., Zhao, T., Cooper, S.Y. et al. (2023). Effective policy mixes in entrepreneurial ecosystems: a configurational analysis in China. *Small Bus Econ*, *60*, 1509–1542. https://doi.org/10.1007/s11187-022-00658-x

Wauters, B., & Lambrecht, J. (2008). Barriers to refugee entrepreneurship in Belgium: Towards an explanatory model. *Journal of Ethnic and Migration Studies*, *34*(6), 895–915. https://doi.org/10.1080/13691830802211190

Williams, N., & Krasniqi, B.A. (2018). Coming out of conflict: How migrant entrepreneurs utilise human and social capital. *Journal of International Entrepreneurship*, *16*(2), 301–323. https://doi.org/10.1007/s10843-017-0221-4

Yeshi, T., Harima, A., & Freiling, J. (2022). Resilience on an emotional rollercoaster: Refugee entrepreneurship under adversity. *European Management Journal*. https://doi.org/10.1016/j.emj.2022.12.009

Zhang, P., Wei, X., & Mao, G. (2023). Cultural diversity, social integration, and migrant entrepreneurship: Evidence from the China migrants dynamic survey. *Small Business Economics*. https://doi.org/10.1007/s11187-023-00791-1

Zhou, M. (2004). Revisiting ethnic entrepreneurship: Convergencies, controversies, and conceptual advancements. *International Migration Review*, *38*(3), 1040–1074. www.jstor.org/stable/27645425

3 Towards conceptualising refugee entrepreneur/ship

Solomon Akele Abebe, Nadeen Khoury, and Ziad El-Awad

Introduction

In recent years, refugee entrepreneurship (RE) has emerged as a distinct area of scholarship within the broader realm of migrant entrepreneurship (Heilbrunn & Iannone, 2020). RE research investigates the complex interplay between factors such as life disruption caused by war and violent conflicts, forced displacement, and entrepreneurial behaviour in unfamiliar locations, as well as the impact of individual characteristics like gender and social standing on these factors (Adeeko & Treanor, 2021). There have been calls for a more nuanced and detailed examination of RE, highlighting the need for a separate research stream devoted to this issue (Gold, 1992; Wauters & Lambrecht, 2008). This demand has grown increasingly compelling due to the global 'refugee crisis' in the mid-2010s, leading to a vigorous scholarly focus on the phenomenon and substantial growth in both the quantity and quality of RE research (Abebe, 2023).

While the RE literature is expected to continue expanding, as a field of study it still faces challenges as research remains inconsistent and fragmented, potentially impeding further progress. The primary reason for this is the lack of a unified understanding of RE, both as a phenomenon and as a scholarly area of investigation. The research area is currently characterised by a collection of loosely connected studies that focus on the intersection between forced cross-border migration and entrepreneurship (Adeeko & Treanor, 2021). Moreover, the diversity of entrepreneurial refugees, along with their varied flight and settlement patterns and circumstances, leads to complexities that cause scholars to work independently and provide their own accounts of the phenomenon (Harima et al., 2021).

As a result, existing studies vary in their explanation of RE, with some providing no definition at all, leading to conceptual ambiguities and inconsistencies. The lack of established boundaries for empirical work makes it difficult to conceptually distinguish RE from neighbouring disciplines, such as immigrant, diaspora, and transnational entrepreneurship (see Sandberg et al., 2019). Additionally, evaluating and comparing results across different studies is challenging. Overall, RE currently lacks an agreed-upon research scope that

DOI: 10.4324/9781003368540-4

unites scholars in a common and distinguishing intellectual project. While this situation is typical for emerging fields (Keupp & Gassmann, 2009), it hinders the accumulation of RE knowledge and raises concerns about its viability as a separate research stream.

In this chapter, we aim to conceptualise RE and define its research scope. We start by revisiting the fundamental relationship between refugeehood and entrepreneurship as the scope of RE research, acknowledging that ontologically it lies at the intersection of the two. Theoretical explanations of RE are based on the unique nature of refugees, connected to their flight, displacement, and settlement patterns. To understand the distinctions and diversity inherent in the phenomenon, we draw on refugee theories (George, 2010; Kunz, 1973, 1981), which offer insight into refugees' exclusive experiences and how such experiences shape their entrepreneurial motivations and opportunities. Additionally, we consider the contextual heterogeneity inherent in the phenomenon, stemming from diverse circumstances, and the temporality of the refugee experience, which is linked to refugees' specific legal standing and living conditions in their host locations.

By integrating these aspects, we propose a conceptualisation of RE that captures its specificity and considers the unique experiences and challenges faced by refugees in their host countries. Our contribution lies in establishing an ontological foundation for RE research, delineating the scope of inquiry, and creating an epistemological basis for scholars by providing boundary conditions for empirical studies. We believe these outcomes will support current scholarly efforts to establish RE as a viable research stream distinct from other disciplines investigating related phenomena and enhance its theoretical foundations. Our discussion also informs policies and programmes that support refugee entrepreneurs and researchers in the selection of appropriate samples for RE research.

Baseline definition: Recurring to the fundamental relationship between refugeehood and entrepreneurship

RE is a growing strand of migrant entrepreneurship that was insignificant a few decades ago but has now become central due to the current global refugee migration trends (Desai et al., 2021). This phenomenon occupies the intersection between 'refugeehood,' the state and experience of being a refugee, and entrepreneurship (Adeeko & Treanor, 2021; Wauters & Lambrecht, 2008). Although the 'politics of bounding' renders categorisation and labelling of 'immigrants' and 'refugees' problematic (Crawley & Skleparis, 2018), differentiating between them is essential due to their distinct causes and experiences of migration, nature of movement, legal circumstances, and structural positions, which all influence their entrepreneurial behaviour and outcomes differently.

In line with Desai et al. (2021), we argue that the category of 'refugee' is unambiguous and that clarifying its distinctions from other categories is crucial for conceptualising RE. Despite multiple ontological understandings of the term 'refugee' (Arar & FitzGerald, 2023), we adopt the classical realist approach based on the 1951 Convention, upheld by the United Nations High Commissioner for Refugees (UNHCR). This definition informs both academic and practical understanding of the term, describing refugees as individuals located outside their country of origin granted international protection due to well-founded reasons of persecution, conflicts, generalised violence, or other extreme circumstances threatening their ontological security (Whittaker, 2006).

Refugees differ from proactive migrants, such as professionals, expatriates, and guest workers, who are referred to as immigrants (Cortes, 2004). These distinctions arise from their forced departure, limited freedom to decide on their mobility, blocked access to their home country, and complex legal circumstances. International laws and conventions further differentiate refugees from internally displaced persons by defining refugees as those who have crossed an international border. Additionally, not all displaced people are refugees; many flee due to economic crises, environmental issues, or other factors not covered by the UNHCR definition (Richmond, 1993). Therefore, our discussion focuses on refugees as per the conventional definition.

Defining entrepreneurship has been challenging due to its multifaceted nature. Scholars use behavioural and cognitive approaches to understand the phenomenon (Landström, 2005). The behavioural approach sees entrepreneurship as the process of creating new ventures and entrepreneurs as those involved in the process (Gartner, 1985). In contrast, the cognitive approach views entrepreneurship as the nexus between opportunities and individuals pursuing them (Shane, 2007). In this study, we define entrepreneurship as the process of identifying and exploiting potential opportunities to establish and develop businesses, combining both approaches. This definition is crucial in the context of RE since it accounts for various forms of entrepreneurial endeavours and outcomes, including self-employment businesses, regardless of how the venture was established (either through founding or acquisition).

Therefore, RE can be defined as the process through which individuals forcibly displaced from their home countries due to persecution, war, and violent conflicts discover, recognise, and exploit opportunities to establish and grow their ventures in their new host country (Abebe, 2023; Wauters & Lambrecht, 2008). Refugee entrepreneurs are forced migrants who create and develop their businesses in the country where they have sought and obtained 'refugee status' as defined under international convention (Fuller-Love et al., 2006).

While these definitions provide a foundation for understanding RE, the nature of refugees' flight and movement, varied situational factors for their entrepreneurial activity, and legal circumstances after relocation further impact the phenomenon. Therefore, in the subsequent sections, we will elaborate on these issues to analyse the distinctions and diversity in the concept and arrive at a definition relevant for a nuanced understanding of the phenomenon by capturing its specificity.

Understanding the nature of refugee movements

As previously discussed, the theoretical explanation of RE is associated with reactive or forced migration, in contrast to proactive migration (Gold, 1988, 1992). To analytically understand its distinctions, it is necessary to examine the factors contributing to refugee movements. In this section, we explore widely used refugee theories, focusing on the Kinetic Model of Refugee Theory (Kunz, 1973, 1981), which offers insights into flight and settlement patterns as conforming to either 'anticipatory' or 'acute' refugee movement types. This model serves as the foundation for understanding how the nature of refugee movements influences their entrepreneurial behaviour.

Refugee entrepreneurs arriving in the host country through 'anticipatory' refugee movements have foreseen a crisis early on and planned their escape before it escalated. They have a clear knowledge of their destination and an orderly departure from their home country, often accompanied by their families (Kunz, 1973). In contrast, those with 'acute' refugee movements are forced to leave everything behind suddenly, reacting to intense and concentrated push situations. They experience shock from unforeseen events and endure perilous migration experiences before reaching a country willing to grant them asylum (Palalić et al., 2018).

Intermediate refugee entrepreneurs embody characteristics of both 'anticipatory' and 'acute' refugee movements (Richmond, 1993). For instance, many refugee entrepreneurs from Central America and the Caribbean, specifically from Guatemala, Honduras, and El Salvador, left their countries of origin in an 'anticipatory' manner to pursue 'the American Dream' but became 'acute' refugees in a third country of asylum, such as Mexico (Santamaria-Velasco et al., 2021).

Understanding RE requires distinguishing different types of refugee movements since the conditions for starting a business vary. 'Anticipatory' movements involve self-alienated refugees who flee their homes for personal reasons, often rooted in ideology (Palalić et al., 2018; Kunz, 1981). They may have similar entrepreneurial characteristics, conditions, and behaviours as immigrant entrepreneurs, as they have more time to plan their resettlement, resources, and information about re-entering entrepreneurship (Tömöry, 2008).

However, refugees in 'acute' movements face higher risks, such as destruction, dangerous journeys, and the loss of essential resources like finances and credentials, which are crucial for entrepreneurial activities (Harima, 2022). Additionally, refugees in 'acute' movements emerge from significant social and political events, are referred to as 'majority-identified' refugees by Kunz (1981), and arrive in the host country after experiencing violent conflicts, destruction, injury, and death, unlike 'anticipatory' refugees. Trauma and sudden displacement disrupt their cognitive anchors and abilities (e.g., imagination, knowledge, and motivation), which are vital for a successful entrepreneurial opportunity creation process (Jiang et al., 2021). While all types of refugees can experience barriers to entrepreneurship due to their disconnection from their home countries and legal circumstances, refugees in 'acute' movements face greater disadvantages during the business start-up phase. Therefore, focusing on refugees with 'acute' movements for empirical study helps capture the distinctive refugee entrepreneurial characteristics and behaviours and contributes to a nuanced understanding of RE.

Contextual heterogeneity of refugee entrepreneurship

The concept of contextual heterogeneity in RE refers to the diverse situational circumstances, conditions, and environments present in refugee host locations, which could significantly influence entrepreneurial behaviour and outcomes for refugees (cf. Welter, 2011). Contextual heterogeneity is multidimensional, and two interrelated dimensions must be considered for conceptualising RE.

One dimension to consider involves the differences or distances in cultural and institutional contexts between the refugees' country of origin and the host country. This can be made based on the classification of refugees as 'traditional' or 'new' (Harima et al., 2021; Paludan, 1974). 'Traditional' refugees typically possess cultural and ethnic similarities with the host society and originate from countries with comparable stages of development. Consequently, these refugees may adapt more easily to their new environment as they share cultural practices, beliefs, and values with the host community (Bizri, 2017). This cultural compatibility can facilitate the formation of social networks and mutual aid groups, assisting refugees in establishing themselves in their new country and pursuing entrepreneurial opportunities.

For instance, Syrian refugees who have resettled in neighbouring countries like Lebanon and Jordan share many cultural commonalities with their host societies (Harb et al., 2019). They speak the same language, share similar religious beliefs, and engage in similar social and cultural practices. This cultural alignment can ease network formation and resource access, enabling them to launch businesses (Bizri, 2017). Similarly, Somali refugees who have resettled in Kenya may also be considered traditional refugees, as they share numerous cultural similarities with the host communities (Campbell, 2007). These refugees rely on existing social networks and mutual aid groups to help them overcome the challenges of resettlement and entrepreneurship.

Conversely, 'new' refugees are ethnically, culturally, and racially distinct from the host societies and come from less-developed countries (Paludan, 1974). These refugees may encounter additional barriers to entrepreneurship compared to traditional refugees due to the lack of common cultural and linguistic traits with the host society. Therefore, new refugees may struggle to access the same networks and resources, making it more challenging for them to integrate into their new environment and pursue entrepreneurial opportunities (Lyon et al., 2007; Wauters & Lambrecht, 2008). For example, Syrian refugees in Sweden and Afghan refugees in the US face challenges in establishing themselves as entrepreneurs due to language and cultural barriers, as well as institutional disparities in regulations and legal systems (Strang & Ager, 2010). These challenges hinder their ability to start and grow a business, access necessary resources, and build support networks.

In essence, the differentiation between 'traditional' and 'new' refugees highlights the significance of accounting for the cultural and institutional contexts of both their home and host countries when investigating RE. Recognising these differences is imperative to understanding their influence on the entrepreneurial journey and outcomes of refugees.

Another dimension of RE is linked to the diverse experiences of refugee entrepreneurs in different locations around the world. Resource availability, societal attitudes towards refugees, and politico-regulatory circumstances are factors that greatly influence the feasibility and success of RE. For instance, in some host settings, refugees may have access to special federal grants (Miyares, 1998) as well as assistance in the form of microfinance initiatives and entrepreneurship education programmes provided by charitable organisations (Idris, 2019; Nayak et al., 2019). In contrast, in settings such as refugee camps or areas with institutional voids, these resources may be unavailable, forcing refugees to rely on their limited networks and resourcefulness to launch a business (Heilbrunn, 2019; Shepherd et al., 2020; Werker, 2007).

Societal attitudes towards refugees can also impact the success of RE. In some locations, refugees may confront xenophobia and social exclusion, which can hinder their ability to attract customers, access resources, and gain recognition for their businesses (Bhagat, 2020; Hawthorne, 2019; Tengh, 2018). In other areas, refugees may be welcomed and integrated into the host society, creating a favourable environment for establishing a business (Singh, 1994).

The politico-regulatory circumstances concerning refugees and entrepreneurship vary widely between countries. For example, some Western European countries, such as Germany, provide favourable conditions for refugees to start a business by establishing tailored entrepreneurial support structures like RE incubators (Harima et al., 2019; Meister & Mauer, 2019). In contrast, other countries, may foster hostile, repressive, and extremely precarious environments where refugees encounter significant barriers and complex requirements that obstruct their access to entrepreneurial resources (Barak-Bianco & Raijman, 2015).

Overall, refugees' entrepreneurial motivations, experiences, journeys, and outcomes depend on the institutional context of their host country. The contextual heterogeneity of RE contributes to differing accounts and understandings of it (Harima et al., 2021). Therefore, it is crucial to consider the specific situational circumstances, conditions, and contexts in which refugees start businesses when examining the phenomenon.

Temporality of the refugee experience

The final aspect of conceptualising RE requires understanding the legal circumstances related to the cessation of refugee status. Cessation pertains to the temporality or duration of refugee status, indicating when an individual is no longer considered a refugee (Masoumi, 2022; Nguyen, 2019). In practice, the cessation of refugeehood is influenced by factors such as developments in the country of origin, political views in the host country, and changes in the refugees' circumstances, where their status and protection are no longer necessary (Whittaker, 2006). As stated in the 1951 Convention, refugees should either integrate into a new country with a clear path to citizenship or be repatriated and reintegrated into their home country. However, many refugees face lifelong civic and social exclusion, and the options of citizenship or repatriation may be inaccessible (Nguyen, 2019).

We identify three scenarios associated with refugeehood temporality that impact our understanding of RE, emphasising the need to consider the temporal aspects of the refugee experience and select samples accordingly. In some cases, refugees find themselves in 'protracted refugee situations,' where they endure extended periods in exile without prospects for local integration or repatriation (Costello, 2017). For example, refugees living in camps for two or three decades may raise their children in these resource-poor camps, resulting in intergenerational refugeehood and socially isolated communities dependent on international aid and organisations like UNHCR (Nguyen, 2019; Werker, 2007). In such circumstances, refugees operate their businesses amidst 'substantial and persistent adversity.' These adversities are highlighted in the challenges faced by Palestinian refugee entrepreneurs in Lebanon (Shepherd et al., 2020) and Tibetan refugees (Nayak et al., 2019).

In contrast, 'new' refugees in advanced European countries such as the United Kingdom, Germany, and Sweden have provisional status with a specified duration. These refugees can obtain indefinite settlement and eventual citizenship after meeting economic self-sufficiency and integration requirements (Adeeko & Treanor, 2021; Harima, 2022). Afterward, they can choose to remain in their new home or relocate to another country, engaging in transnational business activities with access to resources in their home country and third countries. Lastly, when the situation that led to refugee status no longer exists, refugees may voluntarily return to their home countries and establish businesses after repatriation (Whittaker, 2006). These legal frameworks provide stability and long-term prospects for refugee entrepreneurs, enabling them to plan for the future and pursue better business opportunities.

The above discussion acknowledges the complexity of the refugee experience and the ongoing impact of trauma and feelings of otherness that may persist indefinitely (Silove et al., 2019). However, we argue that refugee entrepreneurs differ from other migrant entrepreneurs during the early resettlement stages, when liabilities stemming from their 'refugeehood' and 'foreignness' are most pronounced (Harima et al., 2021). As refugees progress in their resettlement process and advance their integration (e.g., acquire a new nationality and gain access to home country resources), they may not differ significantly from other entrepreneurs. Establishing themselves firmly in their host country fosters embeddedness, allowing refugees access to crucial entrepreneurial resources

(Kloosterman, 2010). Becoming a naturalised citizen of the host country can facilitate access to homeland resources and engagement in cross-border entrepreneurial activities (Halilovich & Efendic, 2021). To better understand and conceptualise RE, we must consider the temporal aspect of refugee status, the characteristics that define the acute refugee situation, and the factors that influence their transition from refugee entrepreneurs to other entrepreneurial categories.

Discussion and conclusion

The field of RE is an expanding research area within migrant entrepreneurship, amassing an emerging body of knowledge (Heilbrunn & Iannone, 2020). Yet the lack of coherent understanding and research scope among RE researchers hinders the development of a unified and distinctive intellectual project (Abebe, 2023). To address this, we undertook a scholarly exercise to conceptualise the phenomenon of RE. Our analysis emphasises that RE is an intriguing research area that merges theories of refugees and entrepreneurship to explore the complex interplay between experiences of conflict, forced displacement, and entrepreneurial behaviour in unfamiliar contexts. Moreover, it holds significant implications for understanding small business and entrepreneurship, particularly concerning the unique challenges and opportunities refugees face in various host country contexts (Desai et al., 2021). Nevertheless, the multitude of factors shaping refugee experiences in entrepreneurship make RE a complex phenomenon. These factors include refugees' heterogeneous backgrounds (e.g., gender, education, ethnicity, and social class) (Adeeko & Treanor, 2021), displacement and flight nature (Mawson & Kasem, 2019), host countries' sociocultural and institutional conditions, and legal circumstances.

To understand the phenomenon of RE, we need to consider the complexity of factors that shape the experiences of refugees in entrepreneurship (see Table 3.1 for an illustration). We contend that our conceptualisation of RE should consider the initial cause and mechanism of refugee movement, contextual heterogeneity, and the temporality of refugee experience.

We propose researchers to focus their empirical investigations on refugees with 'acute' movements as opposed to 'anticipatory' ones, who share similarities with voluntary immigrants. This suggestion stems from the hard-to-overcome barriers faced by refugees with acute movements, which can hinder their entrepreneurial pursuits. These barriers include losses of resources such as assets, finances, and credentials, which are vital for entrepreneurship but are often abandoned during conflicts and wars, resulting in a lack of the necessary resources to start or maintain a business.

Moreover, refugees with 'acute' movements experience traumatic events, which can negatively impact entrepreneurial behaviours like opportunity recognition and exploitation. Trauma can severely affect refugees' well-being, making it difficult to engage with entrepreneurial opportunities and overcome

Table 3.1 Factors that shape the study of refugee entrepreneurship

Factors	*Variance*	*Choice of sample*
Refugee movement	Refugee movements can be categorised as either 'acute,' resulting from traumatic events, or 'anticipatory,' where individuals have foreseen a crisis and planned their flight before it unfolds.	Focusing the investigation on acute refugee movements can provide more profound insights into the specific entrepreneurial challenges and opportunities faced by this group. By doing so, policies and programmes can be better designed to address their specific needs.
Contextual heterogeneity	The distance in the cultural and institutional context between refugees' country of origin and host influences RE (see 'new' versus 'traditional' refugees). Besides, the social, politico-regulatory, and institutional conditions for RE vary in different host countries.	Scholars must acknowledge the diversity of RE and contextualise this phenomenon by considering the specific situational circumstances and conditions that give rise to it.
Temporality of refugee experience	The cessation of refugeehood is determined by factors such as the latest developments in the country of origin, political views in the host country, and changes in the refugees' own circumstances. In order to comprehend the unique entrepreneurial tendencies displayed by refugees in advanced host country environments, considering the temporal aspect of their experiences is essential.	It is important to select samples that do not reflect the termination of their refugee status among the different categories of refugee entrepreneurs identified.

associated hurdles. Due to the sudden nature of displacement, 'acute' refugees face restrained cognitive function (Jiang et al., 2021), affecting their capacity to process information, make decisions, and take action. As the authors note, the cognitive impairments caused by trauma pose challenges in conceptualising, objectifying and enacting entrepreneurial ideas, which are the stages in the opportunity-production process for new ventures.

Therefore, researchers must select samples with 'acute' refugee experiences to capture the unique entrepreneurial characteristics and behaviours of refugees. This selection involves identifying refugees who have experienced traumatic events and significant resource losses and analysing how they navigate the challenges of entrepreneurship under such circumstances. By focusing on refugees with acute movements, scholars can better understand refugees' distinct entrepreneurial challenges and opportunities, which are relevant for developing policies and programmes catering to their specific needs.

Second, we argue that RE varies based on situational circumstances, conditions, and environments in host countries where refugees establish and operate their ventures. The cultural and institutional gap or distance between home and host countries significantly influences this aspect (Alexandre et al., 2019; Harima et al., 2021), as seen in Paludan's (1974) notion of 'new' versus 'traditional' refugees. The former refers to refugees who start and grow their businesses in culturally, ethnically, and racially distinct host contexts, originating from comparatively less-developed countries. Consequently, they face numerous obstacles related to language and culture, both crucial for understanding market opportunities, translating human capital, accessing local social networks, and navigating the institutional and societal environment (Embiricos, 2020; Lyon et al., 2007; Wauters & Lambrecht, 2008). It is vital to note that social networks are key platforms for forging local connections and serving as an information repertoire for recognising entrepreneurial opportunities (Sanders et al., 2002; Garcia, 2005). These networks allow refugees to build on local experience and adapt to the business culture (Drever & Hoffmeister, 2008).

On the other hand, Bizri's (2017) study of a Syrian refugee entrepreneur in Lebanon demonstrates that 'traditional' refugee entrepreneurs can benefit from shared language, heritage, values, and traditions, which ease access to resources and increase opportunities. However, the author contends that a similar study of Syrian entrepreneurs in Germany or Canada would yield contrasting results due to cultural and institutional differences. This emphasises the importance for RE researchers to consider the cultural and institutional contexts of both home and host countries and how these differences may impact the phenomenon.

Another critical aspect is the substantial variation in social, politico-regulatory, and institutional conditions in different host countries for refugees. Some environments are favourable for RE, offering supportive social attitudes, policies, legal frameworks, and infrastructure that bolster refugees' entrepreneurial participation and competence (De Jager, 2015; Meister & Mauer, 2019). In contrast, other contexts may be xenophobic (Bhagat, 2020), institutionally void (Heilbrunn, 2019; Heilbrunn & Rosenfeld, 2018), or resource poor (de la Chaux & Haugh, 2020), resulting in marginal and precarious conditions for refugee entrepreneurs.

As such, refugees' entrepreneurial motivations, experiences, and outcomes vary based on their host country's context (Harima et al., 2021). These diverse situational and institutional factors contribute to the heterogeneity of the RE phenomenon. Research in different and contrasting institutional contexts provides diverse accounts and understandings, making it challenging to generalise findings beyond a given study's empirical setting. Given this diversity, it is crucial for scholars to recognise RE's heterogeneity and contextualise the phenomenon by capturing the specific situational circumstances and conditions in which it unfolds.

Furthermore, we argue for the need to consider temporal aspects related to the cessation of refugeehood for a nuanced understanding of RE. We identify three relevant scenarios for RE. In protracted refugee situations, refugeehood becomes a way of life, and many refugees operate their businesses under 'substantial and persistent adversity' (Shepherd et al., 2020). Here, the legal designation and subjective experience of being a refugee are not temporary or short-lived (Nguyen, 2019), and scholars do not encounter sampling challenges that might affect a nuanced understanding of the phenomenon. However, in most advanced host countries, refugeehood is temporarily bounded, and a clear path toward naturalisation exists based on fulfilling certain institutional requirements (Adeeko & Treanor, 2021).

Refugees who become naturalised citizens can access their home country and third countries (Sandberg et al., 2019). This allows for critical global relationships and resource optimisation due to their embeddedness in different socioeconomic arenas (Halilovich & Efendic, 2021). Refugees may evolve into transnational and diaspora entrepreneurs, depending on their businesses' reach (Drori et al., 2009). If refugees repatriate to their home countries and start businesses, they become returnee entrepreneurs (Gruenhagen & Davidsson, 2020). Therefore, to capture the distinctive entrepreneurial behaviour of refugees from the various migrant entrepreneur categories identified above in advanced host country settings, we must consider the temporal aspect of the refugee experience and select samples that do not reflect the cessation of refugeehood.

This chapter highlights the complexity of conceptualising RE due to various factors, such as the diversity of entrepreneurial activities by refugees across different contexts, leading to the heterogeneity of the phenomenon (Harima et al., 2021). Nevertheless, the chapter highlights the importance of examining the intersection of 'acute' cross-border forced migration and entrepreneurship in the realm of RE.

Scholars can adopt a definition of RE as the process through which individuals forcibly displaced from their home countries due to persecution, war, or violent conflicts recognise and exploit opportunities to establish and grow their ventures in their host countries (Jiang et al., 2021; Wauters & Lambrecht, 2008). Refugee entrepreneurs can be defined as involuntary migrants who establish and grow businesses in the country where they have obtained refugee status as per international conventions (Fuller-Love et al., 2006). While these definitions lay the groundwork for understanding RE, researchers should also consider the context of migration, identifying acutely displaced refugees in the early stages of resettlement (before cessation of their refugeehood) for their empirical work while acknowledging the influence of context (Refai et al., 2018; Welter, 2011). Taking these factors into account captures the specificity of RE and enables a nuanced understanding of the phenomenon.

Practitioners should also acknowledge the complexity and diversity of RE and tailor support mechanisms to the specific characteristics, experiences, and needs of refugee entrepreneurs. Our discussion offers insights into the multifaceted nature of RE, which encompasses the various experiences and complexities faced by refugee entrepreneurs. We highlight the factors that contribute to the heterogeneity of RE, including the reason and mechanism for migration, institutional and cultural gaps between countries of origin and relocation, and legal circumstances and level of embeddedness in the host country. These factors can lead to diverse outcomes for refugees' entrepreneurial activities. Understanding the heterogeneity of RE allows practitioners to tailor their support based on individual refugee entrepreneurs' experiences and needs. Through customised support, practitioners can enhance refugee entrepreneurs' success, foster their economic self-sufficiency, and contribute to the socioeconomic development of their host countries.

References

Abebe, S.A. (2023). Refugee entrepreneurship: Systematic and thematic analyses and a research agenda. *Small Business Economics*, *60*(1), 315–350. https://doi.org/10.1007/s11187-022-00636-3

Adeeko, N., & Treanor, L. (2021). Negotiating stigmatised identities: Enterprising refugee women in the United Kingdom. *International Small Business Journal*, *40*(1), 23–46. https://doi.org/10.1177/02662426219970

Alexandre, L., Salloum, C., & Alalam, A. (2019). An investigation of migrant entrepreneurs: The case of Syrian refugees in Lebanon. *International Journal of Entrepreneurial Behavior & Research*, *25*(5), 1147–1164. https://doi.org/10.1108/IJEBR-03-2018-0171

Arar, R., & FitzGerald, D.S. (2023). *The Refugee System: A Sociological Approach*. Cambridge: Polity.

Barak-Bianco, A., & Raijman, R. (2015). Asylum seeker entrepreneurs in Israel. *Economic Sociology_The European Electronic Newsletter*, *16*(2), 4–13.

Bhagat, A. (2020). Governing refugees in raced markets: Displacement and disposability from Europe's frontier to the streets of Paris. *Review of International Political Economy*, 1–24. https://doi.org/10.1080/09692290.2020.1844781

Bizri, R.M. (2017). Refugee-entrepreneurship: A social capital perspective. *Entrepreneurship & Regional Development*, *29*(9–10), 847–868. https://doi.org/10.1080/08985626.2017.1364787

Campbell, E.H. (2007). Economic globalization from below: Transnational refugee trade networks in Nairobi. In M. Murray & G. Myers (Eds.), *Cities in Contemporary Africa* (pp. 125–148). New York: Palgrave Macmillan.

Cortes, K.E. (2004). Are refugees different from economic immigrants? Some empirical evidence on the heterogeneity of immigrant groups in the United States. *Review of Economics & Statistics*, *86*(2), 465–480. www.jstor.org/stable/3211641

Costello, C. (2017). On refugeehood and citizenship. In A. Shachar, R. Bauböck, I. Bloemraad, & M. Vink (Eds.), *The Oxford Handbook of Citizenship* (pp. 717–742). Oxford: Oxford University Press.

Crawley, H., & Skleparis, D. (2018). Refugees, migrants, neither, both: Categorical fetishism and the politics of bounding in Europe's 'migration crisis'. *Journal of Ethnic and Migration Studies*, *44*(1), 48–64. https://doi.org/10.1080/1369183X.2017.1348224

De Jager, J. (2015). The right of asylum seekers and refugees in South Africa to self-employment: A comment on Somali Association of South Africa V Limpopo Department of Economic Development, Environment and Tourism. *South African Journal on Human Rights*, *31*(2), 401–409. https://doi.org/10.1080/19962126.2015.11865253

de la Chaux, M., & Haugh, H. (2020). When formal institutions impede entrepreneurship: How and why refugees establish new ventures in the Dadaab refugee camps. *Entrepreneurship & Regional Development*, *32*(9–10), 827–851. https://doi.org/10.1080/08985626.2020.1789752

Desai, S., Naudé, W., & Stel, N. (2021). Refugee entrepreneurship: Context and directions for future research. *Small Business Economics*, *56*(1), 933–945. https://doi.org/10.1007/s11187-019-00310-1

Drever, I., & Hoffmeister, O. (2008). Immigrants and social networks in a job-scarce environment: The case of Germany. *International Migration Review*, *42*(2), 425–448. https://doi.org/10.1111/j.1747-7379.2008.00130

Drori, I., Honig, B., & Wright, M. (2009). Transnational entrepreneurship: An emergent field of study. *Entrepreneurship Theory and Practice*, *33*(5), 1001–1022. https://doi.org/10.1111/j.1540-6520.2009.00332.x

Embiricos, A. (2020). From refugee to entrepreneur? Challenges to refugee self-reliance in Berlin, Germany. *Journal of Refugee Studies*, *33*(1), 245–267. https://doi.org/10.1093/jrs/fez073

Fuller-Love, N., Lim, L., & Akehurst, G. (2006). Guest editorial: Female and ethnic minority entrepreneurship. *The International Entrepreneurship & Management Journal*, *2*(4), 429–439. https://doi.org/10.1007/s11365-006-0007-y

Garcia, C. (2005). Buscando Trabajo: Social networking among immigrants from Mexico to the United States. *Hispanic Journal of Behavioral Sciences*, *27*(1), 3–20. https://doi.org/10.1177/0739986304272353

Gartner, W.B. (1985). A conceptual framework for describing the phenomenon of new venture creation. *Academy of Management Review*, *10*(4), 696–706. www.jstor.org/stable/258039

George, M. (2010). A theoretical understanding of refugee trauma. *Clinical Social Work Journal*, *38*(4), 379–387. https://doi.org/10.1007/s10615-009-0252-y

Gold, S.J. (1988). Refugees and small business: The case of Soviet Jews and Vietnamese. *Ethnic and Racial Studies*, *11*(4), 411–438. https://doi.org/10.1080/01419870.1988.9993613

Gold, S.J. (1992). The employment potential of refugee entrepreneurship: Soviet Jews and Vietnamese in California. *Review of Policy Research*, *11*(2), 176–186. https://doi.org/10.1111/j.1541-1338.1992.tb00400.x

Gruenhagen, J.H., Davidsson, P., & Sawang, S. (2020). Returnee entrepreneurs: A systematic literature review, thematic analysis, and research agenda. *Foundations and Trends in Entrepreneurship*, *16*(4), 310–392. http://dx.doi.org/10.1561/0300000096

Halilovich, H., & Efendić, N. (2021). From refugees to trans-local entrepreneurs: Crossing the borders between formal institutions and informal practices in Bosnia and Herzegovina. *Journal of Refugee Studies*, *34*(1), 663–680. https://doi.org/10.1093/jrs/fey066

Harb, M., Kassem, A., & Najdi, W. (2019). Entrepreneurial refugees and the city: Brief encounters in Beirut. *Journal of Refugee Studies*, *32*(1), 23–41. https://doi.org/10.1093/jrs/fey003

Harima, A. (2022). Theorizing disembedding and re-embedding: Resource mobilization in refugee entrepreneurship. *Entrepreneurship & Regional Development*, *34*(3–4), 269–293. https://doi.org/10.1080/08985626.2022.2047799

Harima, A., Freudenberg, J., & Halberstadt, J. (2019). Functional domains of business incubators for refugee entrepreneurs. *Journal of Enterprising Communities: People and Places in the Global Economy*, *14*(5), 687–711. https://doi.org/10.1108/JEC-11-2018-0081

Harima, A., Periac, F., Murphy, T., & Picard, S. (2021). Entrepreneurial opportunities of refugees in Germany, France, and Ireland: Multiple embeddedness framework. *International Entrepreneurship and Management Journal*, *17*(2), 625–663. https://doi.org/10.1007/s11365-020-00707-5

Hawthorne, C. (2019). Making Italy: Afro-Italian entrepreneurs and the racial boundaries of citizenship. *Social & Cultural Geography*, *22*(5), 704–724. https://doi.org/10.1080/14649365.2019.1597151

Heilbrunn, S. (2019). Against all odds: Refugees bricoleuring in the void. *International Journal of Entrepreneurial Behavior & Research*, *25*(5), 1045–1064. https://doi.org/10.1108/IJEBR-10-2017-0393

Heilbrunn, S., & Iannone, R.L. (2020). From center to periphery and back again: A systematic literature review of refugee entrepreneurship. *Sustainability*, *12*(18), 1–37. https://doi.org/10.3390/su12187658

Heilbrunn, S., & Rosenfeld, A. (2018). The story of Jonny, an Eritrean entrepreneur in Tel Aviv, Israel. In S. Heilbrunn, J. Freiling, & Harima, A. (Eds.), *Refugee Entrepreneurship: A Case-Based Topography* (pp. 101–113). Cham: Palgrave Macmillan. https://doi.org/10.1007/978-3-319-92534-9_7

Idris, M. (2019). A microenterprise initiative among newly resettled refugees in a city of the US south: Challenges, successes, and lessons learned. *Annals of Anthropological Practice*, *43*(2), 39–52. https://doi.org/10.1111/napa.12129

Jiang, Y.D., Straub, C., Klyver, K., & Mauer, R. (2021). Unfolding refugee entrepreneurs' opportunity-production process: Patterns and embeddedness. *Journal of Business Venturing*, *36*(5), 106138. https://doi.org/10.1016/j.jbusvent.2021.106138

Keupp, M.M., & Gassmann, O. (2009). The past and the future of international entrepreneurship: A review and suggestions for developing the field. *Journal of Management*, *35*(3), 600–633. https://doi.org/10.1177/0149206308330558

Kloosterman, R.C. (2010). Matching opportunities with resources: A framework for analysing (migrant) entrepreneurship from a mixed embeddedness perspective. *Entrepreneurship and Regional Development*, *22*(1), 25–45. https://doi.org/10.1080/08985620903220488

Kunz, E.F. (1973). The refugee in flight: Kinetic models and forms of displacement. *International Migration Review*, *7*(2), 125–146. https://doi.org/10.2307/3002424

Kunz, E.F. (1981). Part II: The analytic framework: Exile and resettlement: Refugee theory. *International Migration Review*, *15*(1–2), 42–51. https://doi.org/10.2307/2545323

Landström, H. (2005). *Pioneers in Entrepreneurship and Small Business Research* (Vol. 8). Boston, MA: Springer Science + Business Media, Inc.

Lyon, F., Sepulveda, L., & Syrett, S. (2007). Enterprising refugees: Contributions and challenges in deprived urban areas. *Local Economy*, *22*(4), 362–375. https://doi.org/10.1080/02690940701736760

Masoumi, A. (2022). Fast refugee protection: Temporality and migration control. *Social & Legal Studies*, *31*(2), 197–215. https://doi.org/10.1177/09646639211015340

Mawson, S. & Kasem, L. (2019). Exploring the entrepreneurial intentions of Syrian refugees in the UK. *International Journal of Entrepreneurial Behaviour & Research*, *25*(5), 1128–1146. https://doi.org/10.1108/IJEBR-02-2018-0103

Meister, A.D., & Mauer, R. (2019). Understanding refugee entrepreneurship incubation: An embeddedness perspective. *International Journal of Entrepreneurial Behavior & Research*, *25*(5), 1065–1092. https://doi.org/10.1108/IJEBR-02-2018-0108

Miyares, I.M. (1998). "Little Odessa"—Brighton beach, Brooklyn: An examination of the former soviet refugee economy in New York city. *Urban Geography*, *19*(6), 518–530. https://doi.org/10.2747/0272-3638.19.6.518

Nayak, G., Salovaara, I.M., & Wade, J. (2019). Self-regulated learning in refugee entrepreneurship education: A university-based program for Tibetan entrepreneurs in India. *Diaspora, Indigenous, and Minority Education*, *13*(2), 81–96. https://doi.org/10.1080/15595692.2018.1557632

Nguyen, V. (2019). Refugeetude: When does a refugee stop being a refugee. *Social Text*, *37*(2), 109–131. https://doi.org/10.1215/01642472-7371003

Palalić, R., Dana, L.P., & Ramadani, V. (2018). Refugee entrepreneurship: A case study from the Sultanate of Oman. In S. Heilbrunn, J. Freiling, & H. Aki (Eds.), *Refugee Entrepreneurship: A Case-Based Topography* (pp. 207–219). Cham: Palgrave Macmillan. https://doi.org/10.1007/978-3-319-92534-9_14

Paludan, A. (1974). *The New Refugees in Europe*. Geneva, Switzerland: University Exchange Fund.

Paludan, A. (1981). Refugees in Europe. *International Migration Review*, *15*(1–2), 69–73. https://doi.org/10.1177/0197918381015001-209

Refai, D., Haloub, R., & Lever, J. (2018). Contextualizing entrepreneurial identity among Syrian refugees in Jordan: The emergence of a destabilized habitus? *The International Journal of Entrepreneurship and Innovation*, *19*(4), 250–260. https://doi.org/10.1177/1465750317750322

Richmond, A.H. (1993). Reactive migration: Sociological perspectives on refugee movements. *Journal of refugee Studies*, *6*(1), 7–24. https://doi.org/10.1093/jrs/6.1.7

Sandberg, S., Immonen, R., & Kok, S. (2019). Refugee entrepreneurship: Taking a social network view on immigrants with refugee backgrounds starting transnational businesses in Sweden. *International Journal of Entrepreneurship and Small Business*, *36*(1–2), 216–241. https://doi.org/10.1504/IJESB.2019.096967

Sanders, J., Nee, V., & Sernau, S. (2002). Asian Immigrants' reliance on social ties in a multiethnic labor market. *Social Forces*, *81*(1), 281–314. www.jstor.org/stable/3086535

Santamaria-Velasco, C.A., Benavides-Espinosa, M.D.M., & Simón-Moya, V. (2021). The refugee entrepreneurship process from/in emerging economies. *International Entrepreneurship and Management Journal*, *17*, 549–570. https://doi.org/10.1007/s11365-020-00712-8

Shane, S. (2007). *A General Theory of Entrepreneurship: The Individual-Opportunity Nexus*. Aldershot: Edward Elgar.

Shepherd, D.A., Saade, F.P., & Wincent, J. (2020). How to circumvent adversity? Refugee-entrepreneurs' resilience in the face of substantial and persistent adversity. *Journal of Business Venturing*, *35*(4). https://doi.org/10.1016/j.jbusvent.2019.06.001

Silove, D., Tay, A., & Rees, S. (2019). Psychotherapy for refugees and other populations exposed to conflict. In D. Silove, A. Tay, & S. Rees (Eds.), *Global Mental Health and Psychotherapy* (pp. 341–362). San Diego, CA: Academic Press.

Singh, S. (1994). Refugees as entrepreneurs: The case of the Indian bicycle industry. *The Journal of Entrepreneurship*, *3*(1), 81–96. https://doi.org/10.1177/097135579400300105

Strang, A., & Ager, A. (2010). Refugee integration: Emerging trends and remaining agendas. *Journal of Refugee Studies*, *23*(4), 589–607. https://doi.org/10.1093/jrs/feq046

Tengeh, R.K. (2018). From Cameroon to South Africa: From refugee to successful businessman. In S. Heilbrunn, J. Freiling, & Harima, A. (Eds.), *Refugee Entrepreneurship: A Case-Based Topography* (pp. 231–240). Cham: Palgrave Macmillan. https://doi.org/10.1007/978-3-319-92534-9_16

Tömöry, E. (2008). Immigrant entrepreneurship: How the '56-ers helped to build Canada's economy. *Hungarian Studies Review*, *35*(1–2), 125–142.

Wauters, B., & Lambrecht, J. (2008). Barriers to refugee entrepreneurship in Belgium: Towards an explanatory model. *Journal of Ethnic and Migration Studies*, *34*(6), 895–915. https://doi.org/10.1080/13691830802211190

Welter, F. (2011). Contextualizing entrepreneurship-Conceptual challenges and ways forward. *Entrepreneurship Theory and Practice*, *35*(1), 165–184. https://doi.org/10.1111/j.1540-6520.2010.00427.x

Werker, E. (2007). Refugee camp economies. *Journal of Refugee Studies*, *20*(3), 461–480. https://doi.org/10.1093/jrs/fem001

Whittaker, D.J. (2006). *Asylum Seekers and Refugees in the Contemporary World*. London: Routledge.

4 Dreamers, delayers, or doers

Entrepreneurial intentions and behaviours of former refugees in New Zealand

Nadeera Ranabahu, Ruth Helen Samujh, Sandya Rajapakshe, Nirosha Hewa Wellalage, and Huibert P. de Vries

Introduction

Former refugees' integration into a host country is a multifaceted two-way process that depends on their ability to adapt to the host country and the corresponding readiness of the host community to accept the new citizens (New Zealand Immigration, 2023; United Nations High Commissioner for Refugees [UNHCR], 2014). The extant literature depicts refugees as a "most vulnerable" minority group within society (Henkelmann et al., 2020). This vulnerability is exacerbated due to labour market challenges associated with employment, as former refugees often rely on welfare benefits or are confined to self-employment (de Vries et al., 2021). Yet, starting and developing a business is also difficult and refugees face numerous personal and structural barriers (Kazlou & Wennberg, 2023). This is despite bringing entrepreneurial skills, experience, knowledge, and capacity to their host communities. However, the entrepreneurial value and benefits that former refugees offer at economic and individual levels are not clearly understood or supported within host societies (Ranabahu et al., 2023). This points to the potential impasse that if former refugees do not have the confidence to enter into self-employment or do not have access to the local opportunity structures (Kloosterman, 2010), they will become an underutilised human resource (de Vries et al., 2023). Yet, there are few discussions on such matters, in particular former refugees' self-employment aspirations, entrepreneurial intentions, and what skill sets or assistance they believe are needed.

This chapter seeks to address this research gap and explores the underlying reasons, beliefs, attitudes, and aspirations related to former refugees' entrepreneurial intentions and actions. We posed the research question: What factors shape entrepreneurial intentions and behaviours among former refugees in New Zealand? A challenge to posing this question to New Zealand's former refugees appears to be in their diverse demographic differences in relation to age, race, religion, and culture, as well as various economic and social needs (Strategic Social Policy Group, 2008). To capture some of this diversity, our study employed focus groups and individual interviews with former refugees originating from Congo, Afghanistan, Pakistan, and Colombia. We focused on

DOI: 10.4324/9781003368540-5

ascertaining the participants' views on becoming employed and self-employed. Using the theory of planned behaviour (TPB) (Ajzen, 1985), this chapter reports on former refugees' entrepreneurial intentions and behaviours. Our findings, aligning with the TPB, reveal former refugees' attitudes towards entrepreneurship, subjective norms related to employment versus self-employment, and their perceived behavioural control or self-efficacy. These three themes also shape behaviours as to whether to consider self-employment as an option (dream), start a business sometime in the future (delay), or start a small business by engaging in start-up activity (do). We outline these themes in detail, develop a nomenclature based on former refugees' entrepreneurial intentions and behaviours (i.e., Dreamers, Delayers, and Doers), and conclude by discussing our contribution and implications.

Theory and literature review

In defining refugee entrepreneurship, we refer to the business start-up and development behaviour of displaced people, asylum seekers, and refugees. It infers actions that seek to sustain the refugees themselves and their families during their flight to a host country, including their stay in temporary but often long-term stays in transition countries, and during their resettlement in host countries (de Vries et al. 2021; Harima et al., 2021; Heilbrunn et al., 2019). These refugee entrepreneurs' lived experiences from flight to resettlement, unlike other immigrants such as skilled migrants or expatriates who opt to migrate, are far more challenging. Refugees are displaced due to nationality, religion, ethnicity, political or religious affiliations, or environmental turmoil (Moberg, 2009; Rankin, 2005). During displacement, they experience persecution, violence, and high levels of trauma (de Vries et al., 2021; Fazel et al., 2012; Shacknove, 1985) and typically have limited resources as they leave behind their livelihoods, material belongings, and social connections (Abebe, 2023). Furthermore, the course by which they arrive in a particular host country is extemporised and can involve prolonged periods of stay in transition countries or refugee camps (Abebe, 2023; de Vries et al., 2021). Such dire and deprived experiences can lead refugees to reject who they are and shape their identities (Gemignani, 2011), including their entrepreneurial intentions and behaviours.

Typically, a managed resettlement programme occurs in countries that voluntarily host refugees (de Vries et al., 2021), but such programmes are not available in developing countries (Mousa & Abdelgaffar, 2023). Furthermore, refugees are constrained by language comprehension, communication constraints, poor mental health, and social and regulatory incongruence. They can also face labour market discrimination, exacerbated by the incompatibility of their homeland qualifications, documentation, and credentials with host country requirements (Freiling & Harima, 2019; Hebbani & Khawaja, 2019; Refai et al., 2018; Shneikat & Alrawadieh, 2019; Wauters & Lambrecht, 2008). An outcome of such constraints is that refugees are pushed into entrepreneurial behaviours and actions to sustain themselves and their families (Freiling & Harima, 2019). Nevertheless, beyond survival, refugee entrepreneurs' business tasks allow them to participate in the host country's socio-economic, cultural, and political activities. Hence, entrepreneurship shapes former refugees' acculturation (Sidler et al., 2021) and their value creation in host communities (Ranabahu et al., 2023).

The literature, although not comprehensive, depicts cases of value generation by former refugee businesses in host countries at the individual, family, community, and country levels (Ranabahu et al., 2023; Tavakoli, 2020). At individual and family levels, refugees gain a great sense of achievement and empowerment by establishing their businesses, irrespective of where they are in their refuge-seeking journey (de Vries et al., 2021; Turner, 2020). They need to be engaged in valued work that drives their achievement orientation, self-esteem, integration, involvement, contribution, status, and self-worth (Cheung & Phillimore, 2014; Correa-Velez et al., 2010; Ruiz & Vargas-Silva, 2017). At the community level, refugee entrepreneurs employ people from similar ethnic backgrounds to create economic benefits for themselves and others and provide social spaces for former refugees to interact (Bizri, 2017). Further, at the host country level, refugee entrepreneurs provide visibility to culturally specific artisan products (Tavakoli, 2020; Ranabahu et al., 2023) and boost the host country's domestic economies (Wauters & Lambrecht, 2008).

Refugees' entrepreneurial behaviours, even though they are often pushed into starting a business, require some planning. That is, starting a business aligns with the basic premise of the TPB as it is a goal-directed activity with conscious self-regulatory processes (Ajzen, 1985; Krueger et al., 2000). Hence, we use the TPB as the theoretical lens in this study to explore former refugees' self-employment intentions.

Theory of planned behaviour (TPB) in entrepreneurship

Entrepreneurial intention is defined as "a self-acknowledged conviction by a person that they intend to set up a new business venture and consciously plan to do so at some point in the future" (Thompson, 2009, p. 676). Intention is considered the best predictor of behaviour in cases where phenomena are difficult to observe (Fayolle & Liñán, 2014; Krueger & Carsrud, 1993). Three core models are usually used in entrepreneurship research to discuss a person's intention to start a business (Fayolle & Liñán, 2014): Shapero and Sokol's (1982) entrepreneurial event model, Bird's (1988) rationality versus intuition model, and Ajzen's TPB (1985).

In this study, we use the TPB (Ajzen, 1985) to study the intentions and behaviours of former refugees who start businesses in New Zealand. According to Ajzen (2002), behavioural beliefs (i.e., views about the likely consequences of behaviour), normative beliefs (i.e., views about the normative expectations of other people), and control beliefs (i.e., views about the presence of factors that may further or hinder performance) form the foundation of TPB.

Based on these behavioural beliefs, TPB has three key dimensions: attitudes towards a behaviour, subjective norms, and perceived behavioural controls (Ajzen, 1985).

The first dimension, attitude towards the behaviour, is explained as "an individual's positive or negative evaluation of performing a behaviour" (Ajzen, 1985, p. 12). Behavioural beliefs form the foundation of this dimension (Ajzen, 2002). The second dimension denotes how individuals perform a behaviour if they assess an action positively or if they believe that their immediate social networks think they should perform it (Ajzen, 1985); this dimension, grounded on normative beliefs, is termed as subjective norms (Ajzen, 2022). The third dimension of perceived behavioural control refers to the ease or difficulty perceived by individuals in performing certain behaviours (Ajzen, 1985). This third dimension, grounded on control beliefs (Ajzen, 2002), captures situational factors and even the availability of critical resources. In combination, the three dimensions of attitudes towards a behaviour, subjective norms, and perceived behavioural controls form behavioural intentions, such as starting a business.

The degree and intensity of individuals' entrepreneurial intent vary from person to person and even for the "same person at different points in time depending on circumstances" (Thompson, 2009, p. 676). The TPB reasons that time and intervening events change people's behavioural control beliefs, modify attitudes, and shape subjective norms; hence, all lead to revised intentions (Ajzen, 2002). Yet, one of the main critiques against intention-based models, including TPB, is that they do not capture the time dimension; that is, a person with entrepreneurial intentions can take a relatively long or short time to commit to the venture (Fayolle & Liñán, 2014). The rationale for business promotion events, education, or training and capacity-building programmes (e.g., Ahmed et al., 2020; Souitaris et al., 2007), including entrepreneurship development programmes for refugees (Richey et al., 2022), is to shape intentions and enhance their business commitment. Hence, ascertainment of the intentions is critical and may need to be updated from time to time.

Refugees' entrepreneurial intentions and behaviour

The existing literature on refugee entrepreneurship discusses the personal, institutional, and contextual challenges of starting and operating businesses in host countries (e.g., Freiling & Harima, 2019; Harima & Freudenberg, 2019; Heilbrunn et al., 2019; Meister & Mauer, 2018; Refai et al., 2018; Shneikat & Alrawadieh, 2019; Valtonen, 2004; Wauters & Lambrecht, 2006, 2008). Furthermore, the refugee entrepreneurship literature discusses different types of ventures, the impact of refugee entrepreneurship, the value it creates, policy issues, and the institutional environment (Abebe, 2023; Heilbrunn & Iannone, 2020; Newman et al., 2023). A key finding in almost all of these studies is the need to address home and host country differences such as familiarity (or unfamiliarity) with formal and informal systems, availability (or unavailability) of resources, having (or not having) social networks, and access (or not having access) to information that shape the entrepreneurial behaviours of refugees (Heilbrunn et al., 2019; Wauters & Lambrecht, 2006, 2008).

The entrepreneurial intentions of refugees are also a prominent domain of research (Heilbrunn & Iannone, 2020; Newman et al., 2023) as self-employment provides a way of developing new identities (Adeeko & Treanor, 2022; Huq & Venugopal, 2021). The existing refugee entrepreneurship intention literature often highlights an intention-behavioural gap in business start-ups (e.g., Abou Chakra and Jardali, 2022; Mousa & Abdelgaffar, 2023). Among these studies, Cifci and Cetin (2023), Kachkar and Djafri (2022), Kassab et al. (2023), and Uder (2019) used TPB. In addition, the refugee entrepreneurial intention literature discusses the way self-efficacy and risk tolerance shape refugees' self-employment behaviours (Mawson & Kasem, 2019; Newman et al., 2023; Obschonka et al., 2018), the benefits of self-employment in generating emancipative value (Mousa & Abdelgaffar, 2023), and the role of social enterprises in influencing refugees' engagement in businesses (Abou Chakra & Jardali, 2022). Refugees are seen to prefer starting family businesses due to the high level of trust among family members, the ability to be cost-effective in relation to labour, and the opportunity to rely on family members' competence and expertise (Mousa & Abdelgaffar, 2023). In some host countries, governmental support exists for family businesses, as in the case of refugees who start businesses in Egypt (Mousa & Abdelgaffar, 2023).

Entrepreneurship development programmes for refugees aim to conduct activities that shape their intentions to start a business (Richey et al., 2022). On one hand, asylum-seeking journeys, hardships, and traumatic prior experiences damage refugees' autonomy and self-belief and shape their entrepreneurial intentions (Kassab et al., 2023; Mawson & Kasem, 2019; Santamaria-Velasco et al., 2021). Hence, they may not have self-efficacy or high alertness to opportunities (Baluku et al., 2023). On the other hand, refugees' ability to withstand hardships, manage uncertainty, and adjust to situations enhances their resilience (de Vries et al., 2021; Ranabahu et al. (2024). Similarly, refugees' psychological capital (i.e., the combination of psychological resources of confidence, hope, optimism, and resilience) boosts their entrepreneurial agency (Baluku et al., 2023). As a result, entrepreneurial programmes use the refugee journey as a starting point and conduct activities to enhance self-belief and confidence, ultimately affecting entrepreneurial intentions and behaviours (Richey et al., 2022). Such efforts can also shape refugees to move from a necessity-driven to an opportunity-driven mindset (Kassab et al., 2023).

Context: New Zealand

New Zealand is one of around 37 countries that work in partnership with the UNHCR. Individuals who are granted refugee status by the UNHCR become eligible for resettlement in New Zealand. The country has an annual refugee quota that determines the number of refugees it is willing to accept for resettlement. The quota is currently set at 1,500 refugees per year until 2024/2025, with a commitment to increasing it over time. The selection process considers various factors, such as vulnerability, family unity, and medical conditions (UNHCR, 2023). Refugees arriving through the quota programme are granted permanent residence by the government on arrival in New Zealand; hence, the term former refugees (New Zealand Immigration, 2023).

Resettlement agencies and non-governmental organisations (NGOs) in New Zealand play a crucial role in assisting former refugees with their settlement process. These organisations provide support in areas such as housing, employment, education, and cultural orientation. Nonetheless, finding secure employment in New Zealand is challenging for former refugees, especially for women, due to child-care responsibilities, limited English language proficiencies, and cultural obstacles (Labour and Immigration Research Centre, 2012; Ranabahu et al., 2021). According to recent findings, educational and training programmes that offer essential skills, such as the English language and driving, help former refugees interact with the community (de Vries et al., 2023). Currently, New Zealand provides skill training programmes and support services to former refugees through government organisations or by third-party providers (New Zealand Immigration, 2023).

Former refugees who engage in entrepreneurial behaviour strive to be seen as "Kiwis" and wish to participate wholeheartedly in society and the economy as soon as possible (Strategic Social Policy Group, 2008). They seek to undertake the same responsibilities and exercise the same rights as other New Zealanders while retaining a dual sense of belonging to their community and the host country (New Zealand Immigration, 2004). Supporting former refugees in New Zealand to become entrepreneurs and achieve economic self-sufficiency is an important way to help them integrate into their new society (de Vries et al., 2021). Collaboration among government agencies, NGOs, local businesses, and other former refugees creates a supportive ecosystem for refugee entrepreneurs. By empowering them with the skills, resources, and opportunities they need, New Zealand can harness the potential of refugee entrepreneurs to contribute to the country's economy and social fabric (de Vries et al., 2023). Inclusive policies such as the "Refugee Resettlement Strategy", introduced in 2012, promote diversity and inclusion in the business ecosystem and contribute to the support of refugee entrepreneurs (New Zealand Immigration, 2019, 2023). Further, organisations like the Auckland Regional Migrant Services offer mentorship programmes and training workshops to refugees interested in entrepreneurship (Ministry for Ethnic Communities, 2023). These programmes help former refugees build the necessary skills and knowledge. Business incubators and accelerators such as the Impact Hub and Creative HQ have programmes tailored to support former refugees as entrepreneurs. These programmes provide mentorship, resources, and access to networks. Further, the existing former refugee communities often play a crucial role in supporting entrepreneurial efforts through local organisations, cultural groups, and community centres that can provide assistance and networking opportunities.

Method

The data used in this chapter were drawn from a larger research project examining the employment and self-employment aspirations of former refugees in New Zealand. The Refugee Orientation Centre Trust (ROC), in Hamilton, New Zealand, coordinated and conducted the research (see de Vries et al., 2023 for the full report). The project collected data using focus groups and interviews with both youth and adult former refugees. The youth participants (18–25 years old) were drawn from attendees at holiday camps, while the adult participants were drawn from road code training classes; these activities were regularly conducted by ROC. In all, 111 former refugees originating from four countries, namely Congo, Afghanistan, Pakistan, and Colombia, participated in the project. In developing this chapter, we drew on the self-employment data.

The focus groups were used as the primary source of data. Interviewers and translators associated with ROC conducted nine focus group sessions. These sessions were conducted in a way that was sensitive to the ethnic and cultural norms and social issues that might arise when working with minority groups. This included conducting focus groups for the adult men separately from those for the adult women to facilitate free discussion.

The focus group participants were former refugees who had been displaced from their home countries, had lived in differing environments and country contexts, experienced multiple cultures and conflicting laws, and had proficiency in multiple languages. However, most of the participants were not confident in speaking English. Thus, focus groups were held separately for those originating from the Congo, Colombia, Afghanistan, and Pakistan. This division also aided in providing interpretation, translation, and later in analysis of the responses.

Following the focus group interviews, ROC conducted 23 interviews with adult former refugees (who were not part of the focus groups). The purpose of the interviews was to collect in-depth information on the matters raised by those who participated in the focus groups. Each of the interviews lasted between 30 and 60 minutes. A semi-structured interview guide was used, and the questions focused on ascertaining the participants' perspectives on becoming economically integrated into New Zealand society. The interviewers specifically asked for views on becoming employed and self-employed.

We analysed the data from the larger project by open coding, axial coding, and then forming analytical codes (Gioia et al., 2013). During this process, we identified multiple codes related to self-employment attitudes and aspirations.

We then searched the literature and used the TPB as the theoretical lens to make sense of our data; hence, our theoretical lens emerged abductively.

Findings

Our findings revealed that participants' attitudes towards entrepreneurship, subjective norms related to employment/self-employment, and perceived behavioural control or self-efficacy contributed to their business start-up intentions. These factors led to three key actions: dreaming to start a business, delaying their business start-up activities, or doing tasks by starting small. We explain these findings in detail in the following sections.

Entrepreneurial intentions

Attitudes towards self-employment

Our research exposed the degree to which former refugees held a favourable or unfavourable evaluation or appraisal of self-employment and how these attitudes shaped their entrepreneurship intentions. Our findings show that not all participants wanted to start or own a business. In our sample, one to three participants from focus groups 1, 2, 4, and 6 and interviewees 1, 4, 9, 11, 15, 18, and 20 mentioned that they would like to be self-employed. Interviewees 1, 15, and 20 wanted to start a business as a secondary source of income:

> *I'd have also a place where I can do my own business. Like a small [place]. I know a lot of people from back home, they want to have our own food, but they don't know where to go. If I get support, I can open a small shop, or open a small restaurant, so they can say, "oh, we can get our stuff from there".*
>
> (Interviewee 20)

Our participants, especially women, spoke of opening businesses in areas where they have skills such as cooking and sewing (Focus group 2). Their business ideas were "*retail business, like [a] shop*" (Focus group 2), "*cultural shop for our community*" (Interviewee 20), or owning a business for selling "*African dress*" (Focus group 6). The only exception was the participant from Focus group 1 who wanted to use his experience from the home country. In addition, the participants with a favourable attitude towards self-employment did not want to work for others ("*I don't want to work for people, I want people to work for me*": Focus group 4) and wanted to create employment in the community ("*It's another way to give other people the opportunity to find a job where I'm working*": Interviewee 20). Others were interested in entrepreneurship due to their hobbies, as media production (e.g., Interviewee 1).

The host country's context also shaped participants' attitudes towards self-employment. For example, one participant wanted to start a business because he perceived that the New Zealand business environment was good for self-employment:

> *We want, myself and my family our own business. Because I think New Zealand is a great country for having business. [...] We want to make a business of clothing or beautician.*
>
> (Interviewee 11)

Some participants had negative experiences when trying to find employment in New Zealand and considered self-employment as an alternative:

> *I went to Work and Income and told them I wanted a job. They sent me to a few places, but that experience was not useful. I just couldn't get a job. So now I want to start my own business, that's my goal.*
>
> (A participant in Focus group 2)

Hence, aspirations related to the types of businesses varied across participants.

Subjective norms

According to TPB, subjective norms refer to the perceived social pressure to perform or not perform a specific behaviour (Tornikoski & Maalaoui, 2019). Our participants talked broadly about employment and self-employment and how the norms within the ethnic community shaped their ideas of work. There seem to be two contrasting norms or views among former refugees: Having welfare is equal to earning a basic income versus welfare is not enough for good livelihood.

Those who held the view that having welfare is equal to earning a basic income talked about the unemployment benefit as "*free money*" (Focus group 6, interviewees 4, 11, and 14). Two participants (interviewees 4 and 9) spoke about the dilemma of choosing between full-time work and welfare support. One explained how the former refugees have to make a subjective choice.

> *If you find a job, and then you're gonna get the minimum wage, the rent is going to increase, everything is going to increase. [...] you get your wages, and then you have only a little bit of money left. So, you realise, okay, we have to work until 3 pm or 5 pm every day. Or maybe for nights or 20 hours a week. So, when you combine how much you gain from the government, then maybe you decide to stop the work and then stay in the government benefit.*
>
> (Interviewee 4)

Others talked about getting out of welfare, stating that it is insufficient for a comfortable life. They considered welfare provided only enough to cover the basic expenses (Focus group 5 and interviewees 3, 11, 15, 16, and 18). They expressed the desire to do something. One participant believed that owning a business was a way to move out of being a welfare recipient:

> *We can still do something. I also don't want to stay on government benefits. I believe that we should have our own business. [...] I also feel like we are, a*

> *burden to the government. So if we can do something, we must do something and we should have our own business.*
>
> (Interviewee 8)

Another former refugee expressed the need for changing attitudes in ethnic communities towards employment and self-employment.

> *[…] you may see some youth, people aged 18, 19, 20 and above, they are not maybe even going to class and they are not going to work. They say they are getting the benefit. I would say like, those people, they might need to open up their minds.*
>
> (Interviewee 12)

This participant mentioned that he would like to work in an area to help new arrivals change their attitudes towards working and self-employment:

> *[…] the new arrivals, to open up their minds; helping them to earn their licence; encouraging them in their English; to work hard. Just motivate new arrivals […]to share with them that it is possible in one year, in two years to adapt, even three years, even to open up a small business or to start work.*
>
> (Interviewee 12)

In summary, community norms of working (or not working) and self-employment contributed to their business intentions.

Perceived behavioural control/self-efficacy

The participants who wanted to start a business were at different levels of self-efficacy. Their level of perceived behavioural control heavily influenced their attitudes towards becoming self-employed. More specifically, context-related challenges contributed to whether they opened a business or not.

A main concern for most was the lack of available finance: *"no money to start a business"* (A participant in Focus group 6), *"We need money for this"* (Interview 16). They were also not able to access loans (a participant in Focus group 1). In addition, the participants identified a lack of knowledge, not having access to information, and a lack of understanding of laws and regulations about small business in New Zealand as hurdles to overcome:

> *We need to know more about this [small business start-up]. Because we don't know exactly how this works.*
>
> (Interviewee 16)

> *I think it's just that lack of knowledge of what you need to do. For example, how do you do your taxes, what are all the rules and regulations that you should follow? So, I think we should have programs like that, definitely.*
>
> (Interviewee 22)

Hence, the participants required information and knowledge about the New Zealand context. Some information they needed relates to business in general, and other information is specific to the industry in which they intend to operate a business (such as hospitality).

> *My profession is I'm a cook. We have different kinds of challenges like if we open our own business. [...] I love New Zealand but there are laws to be complied with. When we go to try to apply for the food license, the first thing we hear that is when we cook something and someone has an allergic reaction of any kind, and they eat, it is under the law in New Zealand that it's almost always the fault of the cook.*
>
> (Interviewee 8)

One participant suggested that information about small businesses needs to be provided with other career advice provided by support services.

> *I don't know how to start my own business. We need a little bit more information about this support from the organisations, volunteers. [...] But, we want career support as with any information we need to know about work, about business, about how we can grow it.*
>
> (Interviewee 16)

Therefore, contextual factors shaped former refugees' entrepreneurial self-efficacy.

Entrepreneurial behaviour

Our findings revealed that the attitudes, norms of self-employment, and self-efficacy led to three types of entrepreneurial actions among former refugees. Many thought that starting a business would be a good option but they were constrained by a lack of information and lack of support from NGOs or the government. They were "dreaming" about starting a business but had not taken any initiative to do so:

> *I have experience of 25 years in furniture polishing, house painting and polishing [...] for the last 25 years I did it in my own country. That's my dream to have my own business and I can do the job.*
>
> (A participant in Focus group 1)

Others who had intentions of owning a business had delayed their start-up activities until they were more familiar with the context: *"I want to own my business in the future. Not now"* (Interviewee 18). This was partly because participants wanted to learn the language and upskill themselves before starting a business:

> *I would just love to [start a business]. First, I need to improve my language because this is one of the biggest barriers that I'm feeling. Second, I would love*

> *to start some mechanic job, I mean, motor mechanic, that is. My dream job is to become a big businessman, but first I have to become a mechanic.*
>
> (A participant in Focus group 1)

Some already had plans to start their businesses in the future in an area where they were interested in:

> *In five year time, I have my own business, I have on production house. My dream is some FM radio channel here [...] because my son is also good in media. So we are doing making some documentaries and all those things.*
>
> (Interviewee 1)

A small number of participants explained that they had started very small and were now in the process of developing the business:

> *You can start with anything, you can start with small things, just start with things that you're good at. And then you can start doing business but that can be small. I started with knitting at home. So start with something that yeah, cooking and anything, just start with anything that you're good at, so like start with something small.*
>
> (A participant in Focus group 2)

These participants started with something they knew or were good at and were focused on translating that into a business.

Discussion

In this chapter, we explore the research question: What factors shape entrepreneurial intentions and behaviours among former refugees in New Zealand? We used the data collected from a project on the employment and self-employment aspirations of former refugees living in the city of Hamilton. Using the TPB, we analysed the self-employment data from the project. We found that the motivations and aspirations for self-employment, their ethnic norms of working or relying on welfare benefits, and contextual conditions shaped their intentions and actions. These led participants to either dream, delay, or take action in business start-up activities.

In synthesising our findings, we identified three categories of former refugees' according to their entrepreneurial intention-behaviour gap: *Dreamers, Delayers, and Doers.* As illustrated in the findings, some hoped to become self-employed but were not taking any actions to start a business due to unfamiliarity with the market, poor language skills, a lack of information, or limited finances. We termed this group *Dreamers*; that is, they aspired to own a business but had not taken any active steps as they were waiting for NGOs, the government, or others to provide "support". Their challenges for starting a business were personal, institutional, and context-related, as identified in this study and underscored in the wider refugee entrepreneurship literature (e.g., Freiling & Harima, 2019; Harima & Freudenberg, 2019; Heilbrunn et al., 2019; Meister & Mauer, 2018; Refai et al., 2018; Shneikat & Alrawadieh, 2019; Wauters & Lambrecht, 2006, 2008).

The second group of participants were *Delayers*. These participants aimed to start a business in a few years' time after becoming familiar with the market or learning the trade. Most of them wanted to own a business as a second source of income. Our findings, through the theoretical lens of TPB (Ajzen, 1985), emphasise that home country skills, personal interests, and the generally favourable self-employment environment shaped entrepreneurial intentions. A few were opportunity-driven entrepreneurs who wanted to be self-employed. Yet, there is a time delay in transforming their intentions to behaviours as they wanted to learn the language and sharpen their skills by first being employed.

The third group were *Doers*. They acted, started small, and learnt about business operations as they "went along" trading and developing their businesses. This group wanted to improve their economic circumstances in New Zealand or have a sense of purpose, but they were not destitute as they were eligible for unemployment benefits if they were not engaging in self-employment. Hence, the nature of necessity-driven motivations for self-employment is different in our sample from the findings reported in the extant literature (e.g., Heilbrunn et al., 2019). This could be because of the New Zealand's immigration policy, under which refugees arriving through the quota system are provided with government welfare benefits (Rafferty et al., 2020). However, this may not be the case for asylum seekers waiting for their claims of refuge to be assessed in New Zealand, as government support is not provided until their claims are accepted (Ferns et al., 2022). Nevertheless, we found that some former refugees were "resolved" to be entrepreneurs as they could not find employment. This desire is partly due to the stigma (Adeeko & Treanor, 2022) of being a welfare recipient or not wanting to be a "burden" to the system. Regardless of the motivation, they had taken steps to start small by relying on the skills they had.

The nomenclature of Dreamers, Delayers, and Doers, developed based on TPB (Ajzen, 1985), also shows the complex time-related variations in the entrepreneurial intentions and behaviours of former refugees. As Fayolle and Liñán (2014) explained, a person with entrepreneurial intentions can take a relatively long or short time to commit to a venture. In the case of former refugees, ethnic community norms and context-related complexities also contribute to the time it takes former refugees to start a business.

Our nomenclature provides a way of screening potential entrepreneurs and providing targeted support according to their intentions and the stage of development of their businesses. For example, identifying *Dreamers* will help organisations in supporting former refugees to develop their plans and goals, align their needs with available support, or strengthen/test their business ideas. Dreamers may also need assistance in identifying how they should prepare in order to fulfil their entrepreneurial dreams. Developing a business plan may help to identify the many aspects that need to be considered when bringing a business idea to fruition. *Delayers* may value specialised market-related assistance to own and operate a business in their specialised fields. The support they require is to reduce the "delay time" in starting a business. For example, a home-based business that aims to produce tourist items may need assistance in finding markets or online sales skills to reduce the delay time. *Doers* may need support in finding alliances and partnerships which will be helpful to grow their businesses. In addition, they may also require advice on formalising their existing businesses and expanding their marketing through alternate channels such as social media.

Contributions and implications

We contribute both theoretically and empirically to refugee entrepreneurship research and practice. Our main theoretical contribution to refugee entrepreneurship literature is developing the nomenclature for former refugees' self-employment intentions and behaviours: *Dreamers, Delayers, and Doers.* Our nomenclature, utilising TPB, provides a new perspective, beyond necessity and opportunity entrepreneurship, to identify various types of business start-up intentions, behaviours, and actions. It further shows novel ways in which TPB can be used in understanding refugees' entrepreneurial intentions beyond the existing work such as Cifci and Cetin (2023), Kachkar and Djafri (2022), Kassab et al. (2023), and Uder (2019).

This nomenclature also contributes empirically to practice and policy. As discussed earlier, the Dreamers, Delayers, and Doers nomenclature provides a foundation to develop targeted support, provides an avenue to review available entrepreneurship development programmes in organisations, such as ROC Trust in Hamilton, New Zealand, and to design programmes to address the challenges that have been identified for each group. Former refugees have considerable skills and experiences that are underutilised, but they lack essentials such as finance and knowledge of country-specific factors such as laws, regulations, and markets to achieve their aspirations. Our discussion identified the need for a range of specialised support according to the stage at which former refugees are on their entrepreneurial journey towards self-employment. Such support includes specialised education, financial support, and mentoring. In addition, fostering partnerships to provide former refugees with training, mentorship, and financial management can develop a supportive environment for them to contribute to the economy. Such an approach will help in refugee support organisations to make effective use of their limited resources in assisting former refugees to reach their potential and become economically self-sufficient. Thus, policymakers can use this nomenclature to strengthen their entrepreneurial support strategies in converting former refugees' business start-up intents into behaviours.

Conclusion

In conclusion, this chapter, using data collected from New Zealand, shows the complexities in relation to entrepreneurial intentions and the behaviour gap among former refugees. We introduce a new nomenclature (Dreamers, Delayers, and Doers) which can be used to categorise former refugees according to their business start-up inspirations. Our nomenclature takes into account attitudes, norms of self-employment, and behavioural controls. This nomenclature can be used in developing targeted programmes to reduce the intention-behaviour gap in self-employment among former refugees.

Acknowledgements

We would like to acknowledge the financial support of the Lottery Community Sector Research (LCSR-2020-147498) provided to Refugee Orientation Centre Trust (ROC Trust) to conduct this research.

References

Abebe, S.A. (2023). Refugee entrepreneurship: Systematic and thematic analyses and a research agenda. *Small Business Economics*, *60*(1), 315–350. https://doi.org/10.1007/s11187-022-00636-3

Abou Chakra, S.M., & Al Jardali, H. (2022). Drivers of social entrepreneurial intentions of Palestinian refugees in Lebanon. *Journal of Research in Marketing and Entrepreneurship*, *24* (2), 242–269. https://doi.org/10.1108/JRME-02-2021-0014

Adeeko, N., & Treanor, L. (2022). Negotiating stigmatised identities: Enterprising refugee women in the United Kingdom. *International Small Business Journal*, *40*(1), 23–46. https://doi.org/10.1177/0266242621997033

Ahmed, T., Chandran, V.G.R., Klobas, J.E., Liñán, F., & Kokkalis, P. (2020). Entrepreneurship education programmes: How learning, inspiration and resources affect intentions for new venture creation in a developing economy. *The International Journal of Management Education*, *18*(1), https://doi.org/10.1016/j.ijme.2019.100327

Ajzen, I. (1985). From intentions to actions: A theory of planned behavior. In Kuhl, J., Beckmann, J. (Eds.), *Action Control* (pp. 11–39). Springer, Berlin, Heidelberg: SSSP Springer Series in Social Psychology. https://doi.org/10.1007/978-3-642-69746-3_2

Ajzen, I. (2002). Perceived behavioral control, self-efficacy, locus of control, and the theory of planned behavior. *Journal of Applied Social Psychology*, *32*, 665–683. https://doi.org/10.1111/j.1559-1816.2002.tb00236.x

Baluku, M.M., Nansubuga, F., Nantamu, S., Musanje, K., Kawooya, K., Nansamba, J., & Ruto, G. (2023). Psychological capital, entrepreneurial efficacy, alertness and agency among refugees in Uganda: Perceived behavioural control as a moderator. *Journal of Entrepreneurship and Innovation in Emerging Economies*. https://doi.org/10.1177/23939575231194554

Bird, B. (1988). Implementing entrepreneurial ideas: The case for intention. *Academy of Management Review*, *13*(3), 442–453. https://doi.org/10.5465/amr.1988.4306970

Bizri, R.M. (2017). Refugee-entrepreneurship: A social capital perspective. *Entrepreneurship & Regional Development*, *29*(9–10), 847–868. https://doi.org/10.1080/08985626.2017.1364787

Cheung, S.Y., & Phillimore, J. (2014). Refugees, social capital, and labour market integration in the UK. *Sociology*, *48*(3), 518–536. https://doi.org/10.1177/0038038513491467

Cifci, I., & Cetin, G. (2023). Identifying success factors of refugee entrepreneurs in the tourism and hospitality industry. *International Journal of Contemporary Hospitality Management*. https://doi.org/10.1108/IJCHM-11-2022-1439

Correa-Velez, I., Gifford, S.M., & Barnett, A.G. (2010). Longing to belong: Social inclusion and wellbeing among youth with refugee backgrounds in the first three years in Melbourne, Australia. *Social Science & Medicine*, *71*(8), 1399–1408. https://doi:10.1016/j.socscimed.2010.07.018

de Vries, H.P., Rajapakshe, S., Ranabahu, N., Samujh, H., & Wellalage, N. (2023). *"We Want to Contribute": Former Refugee's Perspectives and Aspirations on Economic Integration*. Hamilton: Refugee Orientation Trust.

de Vries, H., Ranabahu, N., & Basharati, Z. (2021). From taking flight to putting down roots: A narrative perspective of the entrepreneurial journey of a refugee. In T. Cooney (Ed.), *Palgrave Handbook on Minority Entrepreneurship* (pp. 365–389). Cham: Palgrave Macmillan. http://dx.doi.org/10.1007/978-3-030-66603-3_17

Fayolle, A., & Liñán, F. (2014). The future of research on entrepreneurial intentions. *Journal of Business Research*, *67*(5), 663–666. https://doi.org/10.1016/j.jbusres.2013.11.024

Fazel, M., Reed, R.V., Panter-Brick, C., & Stein, A. (2012). Mental health of displaced and refugee children resettled in high-income countries: Risk and protective factors. *Lancet (London)*, *379*(9812), 266–282. https://doi.org/10.1016/S0140-6736(11)60051-2

Ferns, M., Stephens, M., Sama, B.N., Maurice, T., Perinpanayagam, U., Stocker, F., Malihi, Z., & Marlowe, J. (2022). *Safe Start. Fair Future: Refugee Equality*. Centre for Asia Pacific Refugee Studies and Asylum Seeker Support Trust, University of Auckland, Auckland, New Zealand . https://asst.org.nz/media/pages/file/7a/safe-start-fair-future-feb2022.pdf

Freiling, J., & Harima, A. (2019). Refugee entrepreneurship: Learning from case studies. In Heilbrunn, S., Freiling, J., & Harima, A. (Eds.), *Entrepreneurship – A Case-Based Topography* (pp. 255–278). Cham: Palgrave McMillan.

Gemignani, M. (2011). The past is past: The use of memories and self-healing narratives in refugees from the former Yugoslavia. *Journal of Refugee Studies*, *24*(1), 132–156. https://doi.org/10.1093/jrs/feq050

Gioia, D.A., Corley, K.G., & Hamilton, A.L. (2013). Seeking qualitative rigor in inductive research: Notes on the Gioia methodology. *Organizational Research Methods*, *16*(1), 15–31. https://doi.org/10.1177/1094428112452151

Harima, A., & Freudenberg, J. (2019). Co-creation of social entrepreneurial opportunities with refugees. *Journal of Social Entrepreneurship*, *11*(1), 1–25. https://doi.org/10.1080/19420676.2018.1561498

Harima, A., Periac, F., Murphy, T., & Picard, S. (2021). Entrepreneurial opportunities of refugees in Germany, France, and Ireland: Multiple embeddedness framework.

International Entrepreneurship Management Journal, *17*, 625–666. https://doi.org/10.1007/s11365-020-00707-5

Hebbani, A., & Khawaja, N.G. (2019). Employment aspirations of former refugees settled in Australia: A mixed methods study. *Journal of International Migration and Integration*, *20*(3), 907–924. https://doi.org/10.1007/s12134-018-0635-4

Heilbrunn, S., Freiling, J., & Harima, A. (2019). *Refugee Entrepreneurship – A Case-Based Topography*. Cham: Palgrave McMillan.

Heilbrunn, S., & Iannone, R.L. (2020). From center to periphery and back again: A systematic literature review of refugee entrepreneurship. *Sustainability*, *12*(18), 7658. https://doi.org/10.3390/su12187658

Henkelmann, J.-R., de Best, S., Deckers, C., Jensen, K., Shahab, M., Elzinga, B., & Molendijk, M. (2020). Anxiety, depression and post-traumatic stress disorder in refugees resettling in high-income countries: Systematic review and meta-analysis. *BJPsych Open*, *6*(4), e68. https://doi.org/10.1192/bjo.2020.54

Huq, A., & Venugopal, V. (2021). DIY entrepreneurship? – Self-reliance for women refugees in Australia. *International Migration*, *59*(1), 126–142. https://doi.org/10.1111/imig.12727

Kachkar, O., & Djafri, F. (2022). Exploring the intentional behaviour of refugees in participating in micro-enterprise support programmes (MESP): Is theory of planned behaviour (TPB) still relevant?. *Journal of Entrepreneurship in Emerging Economies*, *14*(4), 549–576. https://doi.org/10.1108/JEEE-05-2020-0150

Kassab, A., Omar, R., & Ghura, H. (2023). From intentions to actions: Exploring the entrepreneurial journey of Syrian refugees in Istanbul. In Alareeni, B., Hamdan, A. (Eds), *Explore Business, Technology Opportunities and Challenges after the Covid-19 Pandemic*. ICBT 2022. Lecture Notes in Networks and Systems, vol. 495. Cham: Springer. https://doi.org/10.1007/978-3-031-08954-1_9

Kazlou, A., & Wennberg, K. (2023). How kinship resources alleviate structural disadvantage: Self-employment duration among refugees and labor migrants. *Journal of Enterprising Communities: People and Places in the Global Economy*, *17*(1), 16–45. https://doi.org/10.1108/JEC-03-2020-0025

Kloosterman, R. (2010). Matching opportunities with resources: A framework for analysing immigrant entrepreneurship from a mixed embeddedness perspective. *Entrepreneurship & Regional Development*, *22*(2), 25–45. https://doi.org/10.1080/08985620903220488

Krueger, N.F., & Carsrud A.L. (1993). Entrepreneurial intentions: Applying the theory of planned behaviour. *Entrepreneurship & Regional Development*, *5*(4), 315–330. https://doi.org/10.1080/08985629300000020

Krueger, N.F., Reilly, M.D., & Carsrud, A.L. (2000). Competing models of entrepreneurial intentions. *Journal of Business Venturing*, *15*(5–6), 411–432. https://doi.org/10.1016/S0883-9026(98)00033-0

Labour and Immigration Research Centre. (2012). New land, new life: Long-term settlement of refugees in New Zealand. Wellington, New Zealand: Ministry of Business, Innovation and Employment. Retrieved from www.mbie.govt.nz/dmsdocument/2688-new-land-new-life-longterm-settlement-refugees-main-report-pdf

Mawson, S., & Kasem, L. (2019). Exploring the entrepreneurial intentions of Syrian refugees in the UK. *International Journal of Entrepreneurial Behavior & Research*, *25*(5), 1128–1146. https://doi.org/10.1108/IJEBR-02-2018-0103

Meister, A.D., & Mauer, R. (2018). Understanding refugee entrepreneurship incubation: An embeddedness perspective. *International Journal of Entrepreneurial*

Behavior & Research, *25*(5), 1065–1092. https://doi.org/10.1108/IJEBR-02-2018-0108
Ministry for Ethnic Communities. (2023). There is strength in diversity. Retrieved from www.ethniccommunities.govt.nz/
Moberg, K.K. (2009). Extending refugee definitions to cover environmentally displaced persons displaces necessary protection. *Iowa Law Review*, *94*(3), 1107–1136.
Mousa, M., & Abdelgaffar, H. (2023). Emancipation really matters: Why family firms might be a preferable choice for Syrian refugees in Egypt? An exploratory study. *International Migration*, 1–17. https://doi.org/10.1111/imig.13193
Newman, A., Macaulay, L., & Dunwoodie, K. (2023). Refugee Entrepreneurship: A Systematic review of prior research and agenda for future research. *International Migration Review*. https://doi.org/10.1177/01979183231182669
New Zealand Immigration. (2004). *Refugee Voices: A Journey towards Resettlement*. Wellington: Department of Labour.
New Zealand Immigration. (2019). Refugee Resettlement Strategy. Retrieved from www.immigration.govt.nz/about-us/what-we-do/our-strategies-and-projects/refugee-resettlement-strategy
New Zealand Immigration. (2023). New Zealand Refugee Quota Programme. Retrieved from www.immigration.govt.nz/about-us/what-we-do/our-strategies-and-projects/supporting-refugees-and-asylum-seekers/refugee-and-protection-unit/new-zealand-refugee-quota-programme
Obschonka, M., Hahn E., Bajwa N.U.H. (2018). Personal agency in newly arrived refugees: The role of personality, entrepreneurial cognitions and intentions, and career adaptability. *Journal of Vocational Behavior*, 105, 173–184. https://doi.org/10.1016/j.jvb.2018.01.003
Rafferty, R., Burgin, A., & Anderson, V. (2020). Do we really offer refuge? Using Galtung's concept of structural violence to interrogate refugee resettlement support in Aotearoa New Zealand. *Sites: A Journal of Social Anthropology and Cultural Studies*, *17*(1). https://doi.org/10.11157/sites-id455
Ranabahu, N., de Vries, H.P., & Basharati, Z. (2024). Refugee self-employment: How resettlement journeys shape entrepreneurial behavioural attributes. *International Journal of Entrepreneurship and Small Business*, *53*(1), 117–136. http://dx.doi.org/10.1504/IJESB.2024.10065262
Ranabahu, N., de Vries, H.P., & Basharati, Z. (2021). The economic integration of women refugee entrepreneurs in New Zealand. In M. McAdam & J. Cunningham (Eds.), *Women and Global Entrepreneurship: Contextualising Everyday Experiences* (pp. 64–80). New York: Routledge.
Ranabahu, N., de Vries, H.P, & Basharati, Z. (2023). *Refugee-owned small businesses: A typology for blended value creation. International Migration*, *61*(4), 37–56. http://dx.doi.org/10.1111/imig.13072
Rankin, M.B. (2005). Extending the limits or narrowing the scope? Deconstructing the Oau refugee definition thirty years on. *South African Journal on Human Rights*, *21*(3), 406–435. https://doi.org/10.1080/19962126.2005.11865141
Refai, D., Haloub, R., & Lever, J. (2018). Contextualizing entrepreneurial identity among Syrian refugees in Jordan: The emergence of a destabilized habitus? *The International Journal of Entrepreneurship and Innovation*, *19*(4), 250–260. https://doi.org/10.1177/1465750317750322
Richey, M., Brooks, J., & Ravishankar, M.N. (2022). Building self-determination of disadvantaged groups: Insights from an entrepreneurship focused program for

refugees. *International Journal of Entrepreneurial Behavior & Research, 28*(7), 1828–1850. https://doi.org/10.1108/IJEBR-10-2021-0806

Ruiz, I., & Vargas-Silva, C. (2017). Are refugees' labour market outcomes different from those of other migrants? Evidence from the United Kingdom in the 2005–2007 period. *Population, Space and Place, 23*(6), 1–15. https://doi.org/10.1002/psp.2049

Santamaria-Velasco, C.A., Benavides-Espinosa, M., & Simón-Moya, V. (2021). The refugee entrepreneurship process from/in emerging economies. *International Entrepreneurship and Management Journal, 17,* 549–570. https://doi.org/10.1007/s11365-020-00712-8

Shacknove, A. (1985) Who is a refugee. *Ethics, 95*(2), 274–284. www.https.jstor.org/stable/2380340

Shapero, A., & Sokol, L. (1982). The social dimensions of entrepreneurship. In C. Kent, D. Sexton, & K.H. Vesper (Eds.), *Encyclopaedia of Entrepreneurship* (pp. 72–90). Englewood Cliffs, NJ: Prentice-Hall.

Shneikat, B., & Alrawadieh, Z. (2019). Unraveling refugee entrepreneurship and its role in integration: Empirical evidence from the hospitality industry. *The Service Industries Journal,* 1–21. https://doi.org/10.1080/02642069.2019.1571046.

Sidler, P., Kassis., W., Makarova, E., & Janousch, C. (2021) Assessing attitudes towards mutual acculturation in multicultural schools: Conceptualisation and validation of a four-dimensional mutual acculturation attitudes scale. *International Journal of Intercultural Relations, 84,* 300–314. https://doi.org/10.1016/j.ijintrel.2021.08.009

Souitaris, V., Zerbinati, S., & Al-Laham, A. (2007). Do entrepreneurship programmes raise entrepreneurial intention of science and engineering students? The effect of learning, inspiration and resources. *Journal of Business Venturing, 22*(4), 566–591. https://doi.org/10.1016/j.jbusvent.2006.05.002

Strategic Social Policy Group. (2008). *Diverse Communities: Exploring the Migrant and Refugee Experience in New Zealand.* Wellington: Ministry of Social Development.

Tavakoli, J. (2020). Cultural entrepreneurship of Sahrawi refugees. *African Identities, 18*(3), 279–294. https://doi.org/10.1080/14725843.2020.1777086

Thompson, E.R. (2009). Individual entrepreneurial intent: Construct clarification and development of an internationally reliable metric. *Entrepreneurship Theory and Practice, 33*(3), 669–694. https://doi.org/10.1111/j.1540-6520.2009.00321.x

Tornikoski, E., & Maalaoui, A. (2019). Critical reflections – The theory of planned behaviour: An interview with Icek Ajzen with implications for entrepreneurship research. *International Small Business Journal, 37*(5), 536–550. https://doi.org/10.1177/0266242619829681

Turner, L. (2020). 'Refugees can be entrepreneurs too!' Humanitarianism, race, and the marketing of Syrian refugees. *Review of International Studies, 46*(1), 137–155. https://doi.org/10.1017/S0260210519000342

Uder, M.A. (2019). Now we are fighting to stand up again. Syrian refugees' perspectives on entrepreneurship in re-building their professional lives in the Netherlands [Master's thesis]. https://studenttheses.uu.nl/handle/20.500.12932/32941

UNHCR. (2014). The Integration of Refugees: A Discussion Paper. Retrieved from: www.unhcr.org/cy/wp-content/uploads/sites/41/2018/02/integration_discussion_paper_July_2014_EN.pdf

UNHCR. (2023). The UN Refugee Agency. New Zealand. Retrieved from www.unhcr.org/countries/new-zealand

Valtonen, K. (2004). From the margin to the mainstream: Conceptualizing refugee settlement processes. *Journal of Refugee Studies*, *17*(1), 70–95. https://doi.org/10.1093/jrs/17.1.70
Wauters, B., & Lambrecht, J. (2006). Refugee entrepreneurship in Belgium: Potential and practice. *The International Entrepreneurship and Management Journal*, *2*(4), 509–525. https://doi.org/10.1007/s11365-006-0008-x
Wauters, B., & Lambrecht, J. (2008). Barriers to refugee entrepreneurship in Belgium: Towards an explanatory model. *Journal of Ethnic and Migration Studies*, *34*(6), 895–915. https://doi.org/10.1080/13691830802211190

Section 2

Refugees and their businesses

This section, containing four chapters, illustrates the diversity of refugee entrepreneurs by elaborating on the contextual nuances and 'temporality' associated with refugees' legal status.

In Chapter 5, Huq and Biru explore the contextual and structural barriers faced by refugees in Australia. They bring to the forefront how neoliberal policies in respect to resilience and self-reliance expectations create unique hurdles for refugee entrepreneurs' economic survival and integration. Huq and Biru argue that the ability of refugees to successfully integrate into Australian society is also dependent on the willingness and ability of the host society to accommodate them.

Next, Adiputera et al. (Chapter 6) explain how refugees in Indonesia, a transition country which does not legally allow refugees to work and earn an income, manage to earn a living while waiting for resettlement. The authors provide accounts of how refugees engage in income-generation strategies that circumvent the prohibitions and subsequently illustrate how 'refugee' legal status shapes their entrepreneurial endeavours.

In Chapter 7, Aydiner and Rider study Turkish political exiles, following the 2016 attempted coup, who are now in the United States. The study outlines the adaptability and resilience of Turkish women exiles as they venture into entrepreneurship in an unfamiliar environment and with no past entrepreneurial experience.

The final chapter in this section (Chapter 8) focuses on how female refugees in Sweden use digital tools and social media in entrepreneurial activity. Zalkat takes an intersectionality perspective and presents the opportunities and challenges experienced by these female refugee entrepreneurs at the individual, business, and environmental levels. The chapter provides insights into how refugee entrepreneurs can digitise their businesses and policymakers can support them.

DOI: 10.4324/9781003368540-6

5 'Are we really safe here?'

The experience of refugee entrepreneurs in Australia

Afreen Huq and Ashenafi Biru

Introduction

Forced displacement because of war, human rights violations, and global warming is on the rise; 117 million people are currently displaced worldwide, more than at any time since the end of the Second World War (UNHCR, 2024). Nevertheless, the global architecture in place to support refugees is based on providing temporary humanitarian aid rather than long-term approaches that keep apace with sociopolitical development and address the broader crises that produce refugees (Betts et al., 2017). Complicating matters, neoliberal governance regimes abandon welfare support for refugees in the name of discouraging 'welfare dependency' (Collins, 2017; Cornwall & Rivas, 2015; de Angelis, 2003; Easton-Calabria & Omata, 2018; Hugo, 2014).

Despite the xenophobic stereotypes used against them, refugees, like migrants, typically provide a net economic benefit to their host society (Bizri, 2017). Refugee entrepreneurship reflects the desire of refugees to make good in, and give back to, countries that offer them a safe haven. They bring with them diverse cultural capital, knowledge, and experiences that can enrich their host societies. Yet this is conditional on the host society having the courage and willingness to support refugees to tackle the challenges they face, exercise their personal and social agency, and prosper. As displaced persons, refugees face unique barriers to their economic survival and integration, such as limited access to education and training, a lack of social networks, and hostile institutional and societal environments (Alrawadieh et al., 2019; Block & Koellinger, 2009; Wauters & Lambrecht, 2008).

These problems give rise to what is termed the 'refugee gap' (Bakker et al., 2017; Connor, 2010), whereby the problems all migrants face within a host society are magnified for the refugee cohort. According to Collins (2003), formal or informal discrimination can block labour market access and the social and economic mobility of refugees or confine them to unacceptable jobs in Australia. As a result of such problems and the long-term unemployment refugees frequently experience, many refugees become 'necessity entrepreneurs'. And the host society invariably holds up this 'necessity' or 'subsistence' entrepreneurship as evidence of the freedom and equality of

DOI: 10.4324/9781003368540-7

opportunity on offer, while citing 'welfare dependency' to rationalise the abandonment of adequate welfare and social supports for refugees (Cornwall & Rivas, 2015; Easton-Calabria & Omata, 2018; Turner, 2020). This has particularly deleterious consequences for women refugee entrepreneurs, who already suffer in other spheres as a result of the neoliberal and patriarchal co-option of democratic discourse (Bertocchi & Spagat, 2001; Huq & Venugopal, 2021; Huq et al., 2022).

This neoliberal recasting of necessity entrepreneurship as evidence of equality of opportunity disguises a profound lack of 'pull' factors that motivate refugees to embark on entrepreneurship. Lack of access to adequate support and justice and equality, which is needed to ensure their meaningful acculturation and integration into a new host society, is why refugees so often turn to entrepreneurship. This chapter examines the available research on entrepreneurship among refugees in Australia and internationally and explores the contextual and structural constraints on such entrepreneurship for male and female refugees in Australia. In the final analysis, we argue that the ability of refugees to successfully integrate is, in many crucial respects, a measure of the willingness and ability of the host society to accommodate them.

Refugee settlement and benefits to host society

Australia has had an immigration ministerial portfolio since 1945 and, since 1977, a formal Refugee and Humanitarian Program in place, after the fleeing of Indochinese refugees from the Vietnam War compelled the government of Malcolm Fraser to develop policy on the issue (Phillips, 2015). The 1951 United Nations *Convention Relating to the Status of Refugees* established refugee obligations for national governments to which the Australian Government responded with the introduction of the *Migration Act* in 1958. However, successive amendments by governments since have tended to undermine the relationship between the *Act* and the Convention and dilute the former's capacity to give effect to the latter (Refugee Council of Australia, 2017). While Australia has been viewed as a capable actor in resettling refugees, bringing in 870,000 displaced persons since 1945, Australia's commitment to international refugee conventions and the rights of refugees has been significantly diluted over time (Hugo et al., 2011; Hugo, 2014).

While neoliberal and conservative actors frame refugees as a net economic burden to Australia, research on the economic impacts of refugee resettlement is in fact too scarce to resolve this question one way or the other. Refugees have been found to have a negative overall economic impact during the first 12 years after arrival, yet researchers stress that refugee cohorts tend to represent younger age groups compared to the population mean (43% of offshore arrivals in 2006–2007 being under 14), and that they are more likely than the general population to be engaged in education and building a new identity for themselves (Sampson, 2016). Researchers further highlight the illogic of comparing refugees with the locally born population considering their radically divergent starting positions and life conditions and note that, as well as tending to make a greater contribution over the longer term, the second-generation children of refugees also have higher levels of labour market participation than the general population (Hugo, 2011; Sampson, 2016). Of the refugees interviewed in one study, a significant percentage were found to have backgrounds in professions like teaching, engineering, and information technology (Fleay et al., 2016).

Refugees are also found to bring benefits to struggling local communities. The resettlement of offshore refugees in rural communities in Australia in recent years has been used to address labour shortages and revitalise ailing local economies; the resettlement of 160 Karen refugees in Nhill, Victoria, in 2001 and of Afghan refugees in Young, New South Wales, being showcase examples (Hugo, 2011; Sampson, 2016).

The 'natural disadvantage' faced by refugees

Distinct from voluntary migrants who move internationally in pursuit of better opportunities, refugees are forced to flee their countries of origin due to life-threatening danger (Bizri, 2017, p. 848). Refugees face 'monumental' challenges when starting a business in their host country; after being warehoused in camps for anywhere between 5 and 25 years, they constitute 'the most unlikely' of entrepreneurs (Betts et al., 2017; Collins, 2017). Many lack formal education, capital, social capital, English-language skills, and knowledge of the local market, regulations, compliance requirements, and financial policies (Collins et al, 2017; Meister & Mauer, 2018, p. 1070). They rarely have a choice of destination and invariably arrive unskilled, with limited resources and no assurance of work, obstacles that are far more pronounced than those experienced by voluntary migrants (Alrawadieh et al., 2019; Cederberg & Villares-Varela, 2019).

Having no country of birth to return to provides refugees with added incentive to integrate and succeed in the host society (Bakker et al., 2017; Bizri, 2017). Nevertheless, many refugees lack family and social supports and become isolated within ghettoised communities (Legrain & Burridge, 2019). Insufficient command of the local language, poor treatment by the host society, and family objections to cultural adaptation create further barriers (Titzmann et al., 2011). Not knowing their destination country in advance, refugees are unable to prepare for their new life or bring with them resources, such as financial capital or evidence of qualifications. The 'blocked mobility' refugees face is compounded by a lack of assistance from the government, as such help is considered to foster a culture of dependency (Alaslani, 2019; Aliaga-Isla & Rialp, 2013).

Most refugees are condemned to poorly paid work due to their lack of language proficiency and the failure of host governments to recognise their prior education and training (International Labour Organization: ILO, 2020) and often experience workplace discrimination, 'pushing' them into necessity entrepreneurship (Betts et al., 2017; Chrysostome, 2010; Rametse et al., 2018). This is also the case in Australia where racialised assumptions about certain refugee groups as being 'innately entrepreneurial' and able to 'pull themselves up by their bootstraps' are often used to justify their official neglect (Collins & Low, 2010, p. 101). Njaramba et al. (2018) in their study of migrant and refugee entrepreneurs in North Queensland, Australia report that most are constrained by discrimination and a lack of support underpinned by the inaccurate assumption that they have access to adequate supports and education. The 'accent ceiling'—where employers view a job applicant's accent as reflecting an inability to communicate, rather than as an expression of diverse language skills and cultural knowledge (Collins & Low, 2010)—is a major obstacle to acculturation and social integration, and to the entrepreneurship through which such integration might be realised. In this regard, while facilitating a less-stressful process of acculturation, greater English-language proficiency can also mitigate issues associated with business start-up processes, like accessing capital, establishing contact with suppliers, and seeking feedback from customers and the market (Hauck et al., 2014; Immergluck, 2002).

Refugees arrive in the host country at a 'natural disadvantage' because of the traumatic effects of war, persecution, and the broader circumstances leading them to become a refugee (Boberg-Fazlic & Sharp, 2020). The experiences and fears that drive them to flee often produce trauma, which leads to psychological problems and hampers their resilience (Wauters & Lambrecht, 2008). The trauma of the flight experience itself, the lack of recognition of education and qualifications in the sanctuary country, and reception within the sanctuary country (including the length of time taken to process applications for asylum and visas) can compound the obstacles to recovery and integration (Meister & Mauer, 2018). Trauma can even intensify where conditions in the host country are bad enough; refugees report 'significantly lower levels' of physical health relative to voluntary migrants (Bakker et al., 2017; Connor, 2010; Meister & Mauer, 2018; Schweitzer et al., 2006; Silove et al., 2007; Stuart & Nowosad, 2020). This can then become the basis for what is known as 'cumulative disadvantage', arising from an initially unfavourable starting position that worsens with further obstacles or losses (Bakker et al., 2017; DiPrete & Eirich, 2006).

These challenges are worse still for women refugees, given the gendered structural inequalities present in host countries (Ahl & Marlow, 2017; Huq & Venugopal, 2021; Kelley et al., 2011; Pio, 2007). Similarly, the associated 'gendered geographies of power' create further barriers for refugee women in Australia, in addition to those produced by migrant enclaves and the web of hierarchical social relations based on factors like ethnicity and class (Huq & Venugopal, 2021).

Neoliberal ideology and refugee entrepreneurship

The economic choices available to refugees upon arriving in a host country have changed radically in recent decades. The rise of neoliberal ideology in the

1970s saw welfare nets dismantled in the name of deterring 'welfare dependency' (Harvey, 2007; Huq & Venugopal, 2021). While policymakers and refugee advocates agree that entrepreneurship can be a meaningful pathway to integration for refugees, the corrosive influence of neoliberalism means that these goals are articulated in terms of an ideology of self-reliance that serves to rationalise both the official abandonment of the socially vulnerable and supply-side austerity, which are known to exacerbate inequality (Bettache et al., 2020). Directed towards refugees, this extreme individualism alleges positive outcomes in promoting resilience. Evidence from Australia suggests, however, that refugee entrepreneurs develop resilience independently through the kinds of 'stopgap measures' that constitute necessity entrepreneurship—in short, by struggling against the conditions created by their abandonment (Huq & Venugopal, 2021). The pervasiveness of the abandonment and exclusion of refugee entrepreneurs in policy continues to remain almost two decades later since Collins (2003) undertook a review of Australian policy on migrant and refugee entrepreneurship at the turn of the century.

Under neoliberalism, the terms 'resilience' and 'self-reliance' are indicative of an 'almost evangelical approach to entrepreneurship articulated in emancipatory language but reflecting a hollowing out in fact of its emancipatory potential' (Easton-Calabria & Omata, 2018; Huq & Venugopal, 2021). Emancipatory ideals and concepts are co-opted in the name of transforming popular pressure to support refugees into institutional reform. The concept of self-reliance is 'reduced to buzzwords that garland policy discourses' that possess 'little or nothing of the clamour for equality' driving the popular movements from which they emerged (Cornwall & Rivas, 2015).

Self-reliance as a development ideal has been tied to various efforts to promote refugee self-sufficiency since before the start of the Second World War (Easton-Calabria & Omata, 2018; Omata, 2017). Long-term strategies for addressing the needs of refugees became necessary around this time as the standard duration of exile was prolonged, and the simple provision of humanitarian aid was therefore no longer sufficient. While these strategies were conceptualised in terms of 'helping refugees to help themselves', this self-reliance or self-sufficiency came to be conceived of as a collective endeavour for all refugee communities. In practical terms, this meant that groups of refugees fleeing war in Africa, for example, were provided with financial support and subsistence crops to produce, and their efforts were monitored to ascertain whether or not self-sufficiency was achieved (Easton-Calabria & Omata, 2018).

In discursive terms, this approach marked a conceptual shift from the 'evangelical approach to entrepreneurship' to active support and monitoring that puts faith in the 'entrepreneurial and hard-working spirit' of 'self-helped' individuals (Easton-Calabria & Omata, 2018). The core assumption driving this latter discourse is that success in self-reliance is a matter of cultivating the right personal qualities, and that if refugees fail to become self-sufficient, that is just cause for their stigmatisation (Easton-Calabria & Omata, 2018).

Consequently, refugee entrepreneurship became saddled with the need to overcome stigma *as well as* the need to meet refugees' day-to-day subsistence requirements (Adeeko & Treanor, 2022; Gao, 2021; Jaskulowski & Pawlak, 2022).

This neoliberal regime has predictably driven refugees into necessity entrepreneurship that lacks both the *de rigueur* supports provided to the locally born and the advantages arising from a native command of the local language and comparatively easy access to local markets. The neoliberal spin on necessity entrepreneurship also encourages economic activity that falls below the definitional threshold for a small-to-medium enterprise, although it is argued by proponents of neoliberalism that the nano-business economy is driving 'new forms of flexible working that allow workers to work when it suits them' and 'opening up new pools of workers who previously found it hard to work in a more formal environment' (Cottam, 2020). Despite these alleged benefits, the obstacles imposed on refugee entrepreneurs by neoliberal governments frustrate their ability to break out of 'ethnic enclaves' and into mainstream markets (Heilbrunn & Iannone, 2020).

While the neoliberal ideology of self-reliance emphasises individualism, the reality is that group solidarity is critical to the capacity of refugee entrepreneurs to survive.

Refugee entrepreneurship: Barriers and opportunities

Research on the refugee experience demonstrates that cultural blindness among the dominant ethnic group constrains the entrepreneurial opportunities available to refugees. Evidence in Australia demonstrates that the accent of refugees is perceived negatively by the 'gatekeepers' to employment or business support services (Collins & Low, 2010). This blindness needs to be overcome to allow refugees to adapt their existing knowledge, skills, and experience to the host country's market and establish a productive new identity (Hogan et al., 2022). In this, refugees must be freed from a reductionist identity politics that essentialises them as vulnerable subjects requiring the benevolent paternalism of institutions (Sampson, 2016).

For all of the reasons discussed in this chapter, the social integration of refugees is an 'extremely challenging process'. Knowledge of the ways to address these challenges, particularly from a vocational perspective, is limited and the identity politics based on a reductionist, paternalistic mindset remains the dominant paradigm (Morrice, 2011; Yakushko et al., 2008). Research tends also to focus on the experiences of skilled migrants rather than those of the forcibly displaced (Dunwoodie et al., 2020). Scholarship that seeks to fill this knowledge gap finds cumulative disadvantage to be the linchpin of many of the problems refugees face. Refugees fleeing conflict are more likely to be unemployed over the long term, more likely to experience job loss, and more likely to work informally (Ivlevs & Veliziotis, 2017). Such long-term harms are more pervasive among refugee women and younger refugees, the latter needing more education and training than older refugees to overcome their disadvantage (Newman et al., 2018).

The economic inclusion or exclusion of refugees can be decisive in their social integration. Refugees who experience institutional voids, societal rejection, and exploitation legitimation tend to feel, not without reason, that they are neither welcomed nor encouraged to participate in the economy (Morris, 2011). Therefore, economic support for refugees is critical to enable them to grow their business into a profitable venture in the mainstream market (Deloitte, 2019). However, this requires that refugees are visible, valued, and supported as individuals (Knappert et al., 2018). Another notable challenge is the undervaluing of refugees' social capital by the mainstream business community and business support service providers (Huq & Venugopal, 2021). As an issue that cannot be fixed by 'bootstrapping' measures, this undervaluing of refugee social capital requires 'proactive responses' on the part of governments (Eggenhofer-Rehart et al., 2018).

Where circumstances allow it, refugees can draw on their social capital to ease the transition into their new life (Deloitte, 2019). Building links with a mainstream society that values difference, cultural diversity, and the contributions of refugees, and encourages them to embrace their cultural identity, helps refugees to secure work or successfully run a business (Portes & Yiu, 2013). In contrast, being devalued and invisible in mainstream society reinforces the barriers refugees face, preventing them from overcoming their poverty, underemployment, downward occupational mobility, and economic marginalisation (Gericke et al., 2018). Refugees who 'frequently experience downward occupational mobility' need a model of career adaptability that embraces refugee-specific structural and personal barriers—particularly where they rely on social networks within marginalised enclaves that reinforce, rather than transcend, obstacles in terms of discrimination and the language barrier (Campion, 2018; Newman et al., 2018).

Vocational professionals working with refugees facing cumulative disadvantage require a 'significant realignment of practice' to acknowledge and address these issues (Vidhula & Huq, 2022). In particular, the subjectivity and voice of refugees must be recognised and supported. Yet the violent and traumatic experiences that make them refugees in the first place also often render them voiceless; the retelling of their stories to aid agencies and government departments tends to focus on themes of fear, hopelessness, helplessness, and trauma, reinforcing reductionist stereotypes of passive victims (Steel et al., 2022). Opportunities to voice personal career aspirations often fall by the wayside amid the struggle to survive (Stuart & Nowosad, 2020).

Women refugee entrepreneurs

Opportunities to voice career aspirations are particularly pressing for women refugee entrepreneurs, who need support to address gender-related barriers (Casimiro et al., 2007). Institutional voids, societal rejection, and discrimination that rationalises exploitation and exclusion are 'particularly disadvantageous for female refugees' and compound the problems they already experience because of gendered roles in the home and intersecting forms of hierarchical oppression in the host country (Knappert et al., 2018). Due to these intersecting oppressions, cumulative disadvantage is greater for women refugee entrepreneurs (Newman et al., 2018). Thus, women refugees not only need more tailored support in terms of education and training but also a platform through which to voice the impacts of their 'gendered experiences of oppressive and abusive relationships over a prolonged displacement period' (Abkhezr et al., 2018; Ivlevs & Veliziotis, 2017). In conceptualising refugee women entrepreneurs as active agents of their own destinies, rather than passive victims, the host society can lay a solid foundation for genuine resilience and agency.

Just as women in general tend to operate on the economic and social periphery, necessity entrepreneurship represents an avenue for pursuing economic security and independence for women refugees (Senthanar et al., 2021). As discussed earlier, however, women refugees face a unique set of cumulative disadvantages. For example, refugee women are expected to perform domestic care labour for no remuneration, as a second full-time job in addition to subsistence entrepreneurship (SBE Australia, 2022). These social and cultural expectations place additional stressors on their entrepreneurship, already encumbered by difficulties accessing start-up capital, a lack of education and training in financial skills, difficulties accessing affordable childcare, and fewer supports and networking opportunities (van Kooy, 2016).

Necessity entrepreneurship is the most common form of economic activity among refugee women, principally due to the immediate need to supplement and/or generate the household income (van Kooy, 2016). It often arises from the structural constraints that compel refugee women to sacrifice their own career prospects for those of their husbands, as entrepreneurship gives women the flexibility to balance income generation with domestic responsibilities in a country where they have no extended family support (Huq & Venugopal, 2021). Many refugee women see subsistence entrepreneurship as a temporary fix until their families can be settled and/or they can upgrade their professional qualifications (Senthanar et al., 2021). However, necessity entrepreneurship often becomes a permanent reality as the qualifications and knowledge refugee women bring with them become increasingly irrelevant over time (Huq & Venugopal, 2021). Having fled their country of origin, women refugees often arrive in their host country with only some members of their family, and often no husband, in which case they must defy their socialisation by assuming the role of breadwinner (Senthanar et al., 2021).

This can become a source of empowerment where refugee women develop forms of social entrepreneurship that enable them to network, skill share, and practise solidarity with other women in similar positions (Senthanar et al., 2021). Paradoxically enough, women refugees gain resilience as entrepreneurs as they learn to rely on their wits and their 'agency and underlying entrepreneurial cognitions and personality factors' to adapt to new social environments and often hostile neoliberal governments (Huq & Venugopal, 2021). While the funding models of neoliberal welfare have a narrow, reductionistic focus on service delivery based on individual case management, reflecting a 'diminishing architecture of supportive and holistic practice', women refugees must develop resilience by building what networks they can (Curry et al., 2018). They must rely on group solidarity and support to renegotiate their rights in an environment that reduces them to third-class citizens (Huq & Venugopal, 2021).

Networks of female migrant and refugee entrepreneurs are central to their resilience and success (van Kooy, 2016). This would appear to be at least partly due to the capacity of women refugees and migrants to insulate themselves from the harm done to their self-worth by the many barriers they face, and the discouragement that results (Baycan-Levent & Nijkamp, 2011; Collins & Low, 2010). These networks can also provide a forum for women to vent their outrage over injustice and build self-worth and resilience through a group solidarity that is defiant of the neoliberal paradigm. This reflects the finding in the scholarship that, rather than a product of individual case management, resilience depends on a broad variety of factors—individual, relational, communal, cultural, contextual, and cumulative (Huq & Venugopal, 2021; Sampson, 2016).

Conclusion and recommendations

In this chapter, we have argued that refugees are a unique group with experiences distinct from those of other migrant groups. In addition to their legal status, the distinction between economic migrants and refugees lies in their motivations. Economic migrants are primarily driven by the desire for better economic prospects, making intentional and proactive decisions to relocate in search of improved living conditions and opportunities. They aim to achieve their goals by leveraging market opportunities in the host country and often make calculated choices to enhance their lifestyle. On the other hand, refugees are classified as vulnerable groups who require support from humanitarian organisations to escape persecution, violence, or human rights abuses. Their movement is compelled by the urgent need for safety and protection rather than solely economic considerations (Hein, 1993; Schuster, 2016). These experiences shape their worldviews, challenge their capacity to exercise personal and social agency, and require supportive responses in equally unique and distinct ways. Like voluntary migrants, refugees experience obstacles to settlement and integration in specific ways, and the 'refugee gap' produces cumulative disadvantage for refugee entrepreneurs, which leads to their social and economic marginalisation. Essentialising refugees as helpless victims with no agency reflects a paternalistic mentality among western governments who abandon responsibility for welfare supports in the name of a ruggedly individualistic ideology of 'self-reliance'.

The approach of neoliberal governments has failed, demonstrating that the subjectivity and cultural identity of refugees must be acknowledged and addressed at the policy level in order for meaningful social and economic integration to occur. It is apparent that refugees develop resilience and self-reliance as entrepreneurs, and that they do so out of necessity, not opportunity; and not because of, but despite, the (inadequate) government and societal support provided to them. A democratic and compassionate approach would reflect the understanding that economies should serve people, and that to serve refugees, their experience must be acknowledged, to ensure that they can establish a new identity, and with it, a place in their adopted society.

Despite the difficulties they face in transitioning from countries of origin to host countries, refugees bring with them cultural and social capital that has great potential to enrich their host society. The reluctance of host countries, on ideological grounds, to provide refugees with long-term support can be seen as a squandered opportunity to reap the benefits of refugee settlement for all concerned. Indifference to refugee experiences of displacement and to refugee cultural identity prevents refugee entrepreneurs from recovering a sense of agency and asserting their individuality and identity in the host society.

We recommend that policymakers working towards sustainable outcomes for refugees seek to eliminate the constraints arising from the cultural blindness of the dominant ethnic group. We can hardly stress enough the value of the diverse cultural capital, knowledge, and experience refugees bring into the host country; and through recognition of refugees as capable and valuable members of society, refugee entrepreneurs can be supported to exercise their personal and social agency and become productive and fulfilled members of society. We also call for greater networking and coordination of programmes and interventions among support agencies, government initiatives, and not-for-profits to ensure that the host country entrepreneurial ecosystem is more accessible, effective, and responsive to the needs of refugee entrepreneurs. This is critical to enabling refugees to translate their existing knowledge, skills, and experience to suit the host country's market and to establish their new identity based on meaningful acculturation and integration into the host society.

References

Abkhezr, P., McMahon, M., Glasheen, K., & Campbell, M. (2018). Finding voice through narrative storytelling: An exploration of the career development of young African females with refugee backgrounds. *Journal of Vocational Behavior*, *105*, 17–30. https://doi.org/10.1016/j.jvb.2017.09.007

Adeeko, N., & Treanor, L. (2022). Negotiating stigmatised identities: Enterprising refugee women in the United Kingdom. *International Small Business Journal*, *40*(1), 23–46. https://doi.org/10.1177/0266242621997033

Ahl, H., & Marlow, S. (2017). Analysing entrepreneurial activity through a postfeminist perspective: A brave new world or the same old story? In P. Lewis, Y. Benschop, & R. Simpson (Eds.), *Postfeminism and Organization* (1st ed., pp. 141–159). New York: Routledge. https://doi.org/10.4324/9781315450933

Alaslani, M. A. (2019). *The Role of the Blocked Mobility Hypothesis in Explaining the Pathways to Entrepreneurship and the Entrepreneurial Aspirations of Muslim Migrants in Sydney, Australia*. (Doctoral dissertation). University of Technology Sydney.

Aliaga-Isla, R., & Rialp, A. (2013). Systematic review of immigrant entrepreneurship literature: Previous findings and ways forward. *Entrepreneurship & Regional Development*, *25*(9–10), 819–844. https://doi.org/10.1080/08985626.2013.845694

Alrawadieh, Z., Karayilan, E., & Cetin, G. (2019). Understanding the challenges of refugee entrepreneurship in tourism and hospitality. *The Service Industries Journal*, *39*(9–10), 717–740. https://doi.org/10.1080/02642069.2018.1440550

Bakker, L., Dagevos, J., & Engbersen, G. (2013). The importance of resources and security in socio-economic integration of refugees. *Journal of International Migration and Integration*, *15*(3), 431–448. https://doi.org/10.1007/s12134-013-0296-2

Bakker, L., Dagevos, J., & Engbersen, G. (2017). Explaining the refugee gap: A longitudinal study on labour market participation of refugees in the Netherlands. *Journal of Ethnic and Migration Studies*, *43*(11), 1775–1791. https://doi.org/10.1080/1369183X.2016.1251835

Baycan-Levent, T., & Nijkamp, P. (2009). Characteristics of migrant entrepreneurship in Europe. *Entrepreneurship and Regional Development*, *21*(4), 375–397. https://doi.org/10.1080/08985620903020060

Baycan-Levent, T., & Nijkamp, P. (2011). Migrant female entrepreneurship: Driving forces, motivation and performance. In. S. Desai, P. Nijkamp, & R. Stough (Eds.), *New Directions in Regional Economic Development: The Role of Entrepreneurship Theory and Methods, Practice and Policy*. Cheltenham: Edward Elgar Publishing. https://doi.org/10.4337/9780857933515.00017

Bertocchi, G., & Spagat, M. (2001). The politics of co-optation. *Journal of Comparative Economics*, *29*(4), 591–607. https://doi.org/10.1006/jcec.2001.1734

Bettache, K., Chiu, C. Y., & Beattie, P. (2020). The merciless mind in a dog-eat-dog society: Neoliberalism and the indifference to social inequality. *Current Opinion in Behavioural Sciences*, *34*, 217–222. https://doi.org/10.1016/j.cobeha.2020.06.002

Betts, A., Bloom, L., Kaplan, J. D., & Omata, N. (2017). *Refugee Economies: Forced Displacement and Development*. Oxford University Press.

Bizri, R. M. (2017). Refugee-entrepreneurship: A social capital perspective. *Entrepreneurship & Regional Development*, *29*(9–10), 847–868. https://doi.org/10.1080/08985626.2017.1364787

Block, J., & Koellinger, P. (2009). I can't get no satisfaction: Necessity entrepreneurship and procedural utility. *Kyklos*, *62*(2), 191–209. https://doi.org/10.1111/j.1467-6435.2009.00431.x

Boberg-Fazlic, N., & Sharp, P. R. (2020). *Is there a refugee gap? Evidence from over a century of Danish naturalizations*. EHES Working Paper. http://hdl.handle.net/10419/247124

Campion, E. D. (2018). The career adaptive refugee: Exploring the structural and personal barriers to refugee resettlement. *Journal of Vocational Behaviour*, *105*, 6–16. https://doi.org/10.1016/j.jvb.2017.10.008

Casimiro, S., Hancock, P., & Northcote, J. (2007). Isolation and insecurity: Resettlement issues among Muslim refugee women in Perth, Western Australia. *Australian Journal of Social Issues*, *42*(1), 55–69. https://doi.org/10.1002/j.1839-4655.2007.tb00039.x

Cederberg, M., & Villares-Varela, M. (2019). Ethnic entrepreneurship and the question of agency: The role of different forms of capital, and the relevance of social class. *Journal of Ethnic and Migration Studies*, *45*(1), 115–132. https://doi.org/10.1080/1369183X.2018.1459521

Chrysostome, E. (2010). The success factors of necessity immigrant entrepreneurs: In search of a model. *Thunderbird International Business Review*, *52*(2), 137–152. https://doi.org/10.1002/tie.20320

Collins, J. (2003). Cultural diversity and entrepreneurship: Policy responses to immigrant entrepreneurs in Australia. Entrepreneurship & Regional Development, *15*(2), 137–149. https://doi.org/10.1080/0898562032000075168

Collins, J. (2017). *From refugee to entrepreneur in Sydney in less than three years*. Final Evaluation Report on the SSI IGNITE, Small Business Start-ups Program. UTS Business School.

Collins, J., & Low, A. (2010). Asian female immigrant entrepreneurs in small and medium-sized businesses in Australia. *Entrepreneurship & Regional Development*, *22*(1), 97–111. https://doi.org/10.1080/08985620903220553

Collins, J., Watson, K., & Krivokapic- Skoko, B. (2017). *From Boats to Businesses: The Remarkable Journey of Hazara Refugee Entrepreneurs in Adelaide – Full Report*. Centre for Business and Social Innovation, UTS Business School.

Connor, P. (2010). Explaining the refugee gap: Economic outcomes of refugees versus other immigrants. *Journal of Refugee Studies*, *23*(3), 377–397. https://doi.org/10.1093/jrs/feq025

Cornwall, A., & Rivas, A. M. (2015). From 'gender equality' and 'women's empowerment' to global justice: Reclaiming a transformative agenda for gender and development. *Third World Quarterly*, *36*(2), 396–415. https://doi.org/10.1080/01436597.2015.1013341

Cottam, T. (2020). *Nanobusinesses: A new business category*. Omnisperience green paper. https://omnisperience.files.wordpress.com/2020/02/green-paper-new-business-category.pdf

Curry, O., Smedley, C., & Lenette, C. (2018). What is 'successful' resettlement? Refugee narratives from regional New South Wales in Australia. *Journal of Immigrant & Refugee Studies*, *16*(4), 430–448. https://doi.org/10.1080/15562948.2017.1358410

De Angelis, M. (2003). Neoliberal governance, reproduction and accumulation. *The Commoner*, *7*(Spring/Summer), 1–28. www.commoner.org.uk/07deangelis.pdf

Deloitte Access Economics (Firm). (2019). Economic and social impact of increasing Australia's humanitarian intake. http://hdl.voced.edu.au/10707/530968

DiPrete, T. A., & Eirich, G. M. (2006). Cumulative advantage as a mechanism for inequality: A review of theoretical and empirical developments. *Annual Review of Sociology*, *32*. 271–297. www.jstor.org/stable/29737740

Dunwoodie, K., Webb, S., Wilkinson, J., & Newman, A. (2020). Social capital and the career adaptability of refugees. *International Migration*, 1–20. https://doi.org/10.1111/imig.12787

Easton-Calabria, E., & Omata, N. (2018). Panacea for the refugee crisis? Rethinking the promotion of 'self-reliance' for refugees. *Third World Quarterly*, *39*(8), 1458–1474. https://doi.org/10.1080/01436597.2018.1458301

Eggenhofer-Rehart, P. M., Latzke, M., Pernkopf, K., Zellhofer, D., Mayrhofer, W., & Steyrer, J. (2018). Refugees' career capital welcome? Afghan and Syrian refugee job seekers in Austria. *Journal of Vocational Behavior*. http://dx.doi.org/10.1016/j.jvb.2018.01.004

Fleay, C., Lumbus, A., & Hartley, L. (2016). People seeking asylum in Australia and their access to employment: Just what do we know? *Cosmopolitan Civil Societies: An Interdisciplinary Journal*, *8*(2), 63–83. https://doi.org/10.5130/ccs.v8i2.4969

Gao, Q. (2021). Reconstituting the neoliberal subjectivity of migrants: Christian theo-ethics and migrant workers in Shenzhen, China. *Journal of Ethnic and Migration Studies*, *47*(12), 2725–2744. https://doi.org/10.1080/1369183X.2020.1739374

Gericke, D., Burmeister, A., Löwe, J., Deller, J., & Pundt, L. (2018). How do refugees use their social capital for successful labor market integration? An exploratory analysis in Germany. *Journal of Vocational Behavior*, *105*, 46–61. https://doi.org/10.1016/j.jvb.2017.12.002

Harvey, D. (2007). *A Brief History of Neoliberalism*. Oxford University Press.

Hauck, F. R., Lo, E., Maxwell, A., & Reynolds, P. P. (2014). Factors influencing the acculturation of Burmese, Bhutanese, and Iraqi refugees into American society: Cross-cultural comparisons. *Journal of Immigrant & Refugee Studies*, *12*(3), 331–352. https://doi.org/10.1080/15562948.2013.848007

Heilbrunn, S., & Iannone, R. L. (2020). From center to periphery and back again: A systematic literature review of refugee entrepreneurship. *Sustainability*, *12*(18), 7658. https://doi.org/10.3390/su12187658

Hein, J. (1993). Refugees, immigrants, and the state. *Annual Review of Sociology*, *19*(1), 43–59. www.jstor.org/stable/2083380

Hogan, O., Kortt, M. A., & Dollery, B. (2022). An empirical analysis of international migrant business ownership and employment in regional Australia. *Economic Papers: A Journal of Applied Economics and Policy*, *41*(1), 1–14. https://doi.org/10.1111/1759-3441.12315

Hugo, G. (2011). Future demographic change and its interactions with migration and climate change. *Global Environmental Change*, *21*, 21–33. https://doi.org/10.1016/j.gloenvcha.2011.09.008

Hugo, G. (2014). The economic contribution of humanitarian settlers in Australia. *International Migration*, *52*(2), 31–52. https://doi.org/10.1111/imig.12092

Hugo, G. J., Vas Dev, S., Wall, J., Young, M. E., Sharma, V., & Parker, K. (2011). *Economic, Social and Civic Contributions of First and Second Generation Humanitarian Entrants*. Australian Government, Department of Immigration and Citizenship.

Huq, A., Delaney, A., & Debney, B. (2022). Challenging the entrepreneurial discourse around women home-based workers' empowerment. *The Economic and Labour Relations Review*, *33*(2), 308–328. https://doi.org/10.1177/10353046211072539

Huq, A., & Venugopal, V. (2021). DIY entrepreneurship?: Self-reliance for women refugees in Australia. *International Migration*, *59*(1), 126–142. https://doi.org/10.1111/imig.12727

Immergluck, D. (2002). Redlining redux: Black neighborhoods, black-owned firms, and the regulatory cold shoulder. *Urban Affairs Review*, *38*(1), 22–41. https://doi.org/10.1177/107808702401097781

International Labour Organization (ILO). (2020). *How to Facilitate the Recognition of Skills of Migrant Workers*. Guide for Employment Services Providers.

Ivlevs, A., & Veliziotis, M. (2017). Beyond conflict: Long-term labour market integration of internally displaced persons in post-socialist countries. *Journal of Vocational Behavior*. http://dx.doi.org/10.1016/j.jvb.2017.12.003

Jaskulowski, K., & Pawlak, M. (2022). Middling migrants, neoliberalism and racism. *Journal of Ethnic and Migration Studies*, *48*(9), 2056–2072. https://doi.org/10.1080/1369183X.2020.1806046

Kelley, D. J., Brush, C. G., & Green, P. G. (2011). *Global Entrepreneurship Monitor: 2010 Women's Report*. Babson College.

Knappert, L., Kornau, A., & Figengül, M. (2018). Refugees' exclusion at work and the intersection with gender: Insights from the Turkish-Syrian border. *Journal of Vocational Behaviour*, *105*, 62–82. https://doi.org/10.1016/j.jvb.2017.11.002

Legrain, P., & Burridge, A. (2019). Seven steps to SUCCESS: Enabling refugee entrepreneurs to flourish. Centre for Policy Development and Open Political Economy Network. https://apo.org.au/node/229866

Meister, A. D., & Mauer, R. (2018). Understanding refugee entrepreneurship incubation: An embeddedness perspective. *International Journal of Entrepreneurial Behavior & Research*, *25*(5), 1065–1092. https://doi.org/10.1108/IJEBR-02-2018-0108

Morrice, L. (2011). *Being a Refugee: Learning and Identity – A Longitudinal Study of Refugees in the UK*. Trentham Books.

Newman, A., Bimrose, J., Nielsen, I., & Zacher, H. (2018). Vocational behavior of refugees: How do refugees seek employment, overcome work-related challenges, and navigate their careers?. *Journal of Vocational Behavior*, *105*, 1–5. https://doi.org/10.1016/j.jvb.2018.01.007

Njaramba, J., Chigeza, P., & Whitehouse, H. (2018). Barriers and challenges experienced by migrant African women entrepreneurs in North Queensland, Australia. *Entrepreneurship and Sustainability Issues*, *5*(4), 1054–1068. http://doi.org/10.9770/jesi.2018.5.3(25)

Omata, N. (2017). *The Myth of Self-Reliance: Economic Lives inside a Liberian Refugee Camp*. Berghahn Books.

Phillips, J. (2015). *Australia's Humanitarian Program: A Quick Guide to the Statistics since 1947*. Research Paper Series, 2014–2015, Canberra, Australia: Parliamentary Library. https://uploads.guim.co.uk/2016/08/18/QG-Humanitarian_(1).pdf

Pio, E. (2007). Ethnic entrepreneurship among Indian women in New Zealand: A bittersweet process. *Gender, Work & Organization*, *14*(5), 409–432. https://doi.org/10.1111/j.1468-0432.2007.00358.x

Portes, A., & Yiu, J. (2013). Entrepreneurship, transnationalism, and development. *Migration Studies*, *1*(1), 75–95. https://doi.org/10.1093/migration/mns036

Rametse, N., Moremong-Nganunu, T., Ding, M. J., & Arenius, P. (2018). Entrepreneurial motivations and capabilities of migrant entrepreneurs in Australia. *International Migration*, *56*(4), 217–234. https://doi.org/10.1111/imig.12452

Refugee Council of Australia. (2017). *State of the Nation: Refugees and People Seeking Asylum in Australia*. Surry Hills, NSW, Australia. https://www.refugeecouncil.org.au/wp-content/uploads/2018/12/State_Nation_2017_FINAL.pdf

Sampson, R. C. (2016). Caring, contributing, capacity building: Navigating contradictory narratives of refugee settlement in Australia. *Journal of Refugee Studies*, *29*(1), 98–116. https://doi.org/10.1093/jrs/fev010

SBE Australia. (2022). *Accelerating Women Founders: The Untapped Investment Opportunity*. Deloitte Access Economics.

Schuster, L. (2016). *Unmixing Migrants and Refugees* (pp. 297–303). In A. Triandafyllidou, & A. Triantaphyllidu (Eds.), *Routledge Handbook of Immigration and Refugee Studies*. London: Routledge.

Schweitzer, R., Melville, F., Steel, Z., & Lacherez, P. (2006). Trauma, post-migration living difficulties, and social support as predictors of psychological adjustment in resettled Sudanese refugees. *Australian & New Zealand Journal of Psychiatry*, *40*(2), 179–187. https://doi.org/10.1080/j.1440-1614.2006.0176

Senthanar, S., MacEachen, E., Premji, S., & Bigelow, P. (2021). Entrepreneurial experiences of Syrian refugee women in Canada: A feminist grounded qualitative study. *Small Business Economics*, *57*(2), 835–847. https://doi.org/10.1007/s11187-020-00385-1

Silove, D., Austin, P., & Steel, Z. (2007). No refuge from terror: The impact of detention on the mental health of trauma-affected refugees seeking asylum in Australia. *Transcultural Psychiatry*, *44*(3), 359–393. https://doi.org/10.1177/1363461507081637

Steel, Z., Silove, D., Phan, T., & Bauman, A. (2002). Long-term effect of psychological trauma on the mental health of Vietnamese refugees resettled in Australia: a population-based study. *The Lancet*, *360*(9339), 1056–1062. https://doi.org/10.1016/S0140-6736(02)11142-1

Stuart, J., & Nowosad, J. (2020). The influence of premigration trauma exposure and early postmigration stressors on changes in mental health over time among refugees in Australia. *Journal of Traumatic Stress*, *33*(6), 917–927. https://doi.org/10.1002/jts.22586

Titzmann, P. F., Silbereisen, R. K., Mesch, G. S., & Schmitt-Rodermund, E. (2011). Migration-specific hassles among adolescent immigrants from the former Soviet Union in Germany and Israel. *Journal of Cross-Cultural Psychology*, 42, 777–794. https://doi.org/10.1177/0022022110362756

Turner, L. (2020). '# Refugees can be entrepreneurs too!': Humanitarianism, race, and the marketing of Syrian refugees. *Review of International Studies*, *46*(1), 137–155. https://doi.org/10.1017/S0260210519000342

UNHCR, (2024). Global Trends Forced Displacement In 2023: https://www.unhcr.org/refugee-statistics

van Kooy, J. (2016). Refugee women as entrepreneurs in Australia. *Forced Migration Review*, (53), 71–73. www.bsl.org.au/knowledge

Venugopal, V., & Huq, A. (2022). Migrant trailing spouses: Career adaptability and occupational downshifting. *International Migration*, *60*(2), 143–159. https://doi.org/10.1111/imig.12864

Wauters, B., & Lambrecht, J. (2008). Barriers to refugee entrepreneurship in Belgium: Towards an explanatory model. *Journal of Ethnic and Migration Studies*, *34*(6), 895–915. https://doi.org/10.1080/13691830802211190

Yakushko, O., Backhaus, A., Watson, M., Ngaruiya, K., & Gonzalez, J. (2008). Career development concerns of recent immigrants and refugees. *Journal of Career Development*, *34*(4), 362–396. http://dx.doi.org/10.1177/0894845308316292

6 Making a living despite work prohibitions

Creativity, entrepreneurship and (self-) employment among refugees in Indonesia

Yunizar Adiputera, Mahardhika Sjamsoeoed Sadjad, and Antje Missbach

Introduction

Over the last decade, the increasing volume of literature on refugee entrepreneurship has mainly theorised refugee entrepreneurs as agents of economic action in the Global North or, less frequently, as subjects of development processes in the Global South (Heilbrunn & Iannone, 2020). Mostly consisting of single-site or country-specific explorative studies, research on refugee entrepreneurs highlights social-economic challenges and contributions in countries of residence (Lyon et al., 2007; Hugo, 2014), resilience in the face of precarity and uncertainty (Alkhaled, 2019; de la Chaux, 2019), and risks of refugees' further exploitation (Easton-Calabria & Omata, 2018; Ramsay, 2020).

Discussions on refugee entrepreneurship are inseparable from the asylum and migration regimes that govern the presence of refugees in different host societies. This is because many deterrence measures often involve restrictions on refugees' access to certain rights, including rights to livelihood (Carciotto, 2020). This chapter adds to this discussion through three case studies of refugee entrepreneurship during their protracted 'transit' in Indonesia. We demonstrate that refugees' navigation of grey areas and the United Nations High Commissioner for Refugees' (UNHCR) careful framing of entrepreneurship have allowed income generation to continue as a humanitarian compromise, despite government policies that aim to prohibit it.

Refugees in Indonesia

In mid-2022, there were close to 13,000 refugees spread across several urban centres in Indonesia (UNHCR, 2022b).[1] Most of them came from Afghanistan, Somalia, and Myanmar, and around 75% of them are men. About two-thirds of the refugees are accommodated in 84 community shelters, and they receive monthly cash-based assistance from the International Organisation for Migration (IOM Indonesia, 2021). Around 1,300 of the refugees who are designated as 'vulnerable' receive a monthly stipend from UNHCR (UNHCR,

DOI: 10.4324/9781003368540-8

2022b). The rest of them live autonomously with their own means; some can afford to rent a place to stay, while others are homeless. In terms of education level, a survey from Sandya Institute suggests that around 80% of refugees had education at high school level or below, with a majority educated either at elementary level or with no education at all (Locastro et al., 2019, p. 23).

Like most Southeast Asian countries, Indonesia is not a signatory to the 1951 Refugee Convention and its 1967 Protocol and in principle only offers temporary residence to refugees 'in transit' (Chen, 2021). Indonesia maintains that it is not under any obligation to go beyond being a transit country for refugees, nor is it prepared to formally allow for local integration, offering no legal pathway for refugees to become Indonesian citizens. However, the term 'transit' is perhaps misleading, given that most refugees spend over 8 years – some even over 13 years – in Indonesia before they can move somewhere else (Mohammadi & Askary, 2022). In 2014, Australia, which used to provide resettlement places for most refugees in Indonesia, announced that it would stop resettling refugees from Indonesia and at the same time began to turn back refugee boats, thus preventing unsanctioned journeys (Brown & Missbach, 2016). Conceptually, the term 'transit' is also inadequate to capture the lived experiences of refugees stuck in limbo for years without adequate protection of their rights (Missbach, 2015a; Sampson et al., 2016). With such extended stays, it is not tenable to maintain an emergency or crisis-based approach, which is typically characterised by relief-focused programmes and a suspension of rights, such as freedom of movement, right to education, and livelihood.

Refugees in Indonesia are generally prohibited from seeking employment or participating in any income-generating activities. The Presidential Regulation 125/2016 – the main legal reference for handling refugees in the country – contains no provisions at all on the right to work. As far as refugees' livelihoods are concerned, the regulation assumes that they will be facilitated by the relevant international organisations, which is neither appropriate nor realistic given the chronic funding shortages in these organisations (for further discussion, see Missbach et al., 2018; UNHCR, 2022c).

Since there is no specific provision for refugees in any specialised law and regulation, the government applies more general laws relating to the right to work, namely Law 13/2003 on Manpower (Labour Law) and Law 6/2011 on Immigration. These laws place restrictions on foreign nationals working in Indonesia, such as requiring a special work visa which refugees are in no position to obtain. Furthermore, an earlier regulation issued by the Director General of Immigration, No. IM.0352.GR.02.07 (2016), made explicit the active prohibition of refugees from working. From a legal standpoint, some argue that this regulation is problematic as it conflicts with its superseding legislation, Law 6/2011 on Immigration, which contains no provisions related to asylum seekers and refugees (Sianturi & Viartasiwi, 2021). Nevertheless, the regulation indicates that the government is very eager to deny work rights for refugees. Unemployment is a sensitive issue for the government which fears a backlash from the Indonesian people, who may see the presence of foreign workers as threatening their job security. Because its domestic labour market is very limited and has been further impacted by the Covid-19 pandemic, Indonesia supplies a large number of migrant workers to other countries.

Despite being legally prohibited from working, refugees *do* engage in various ways to sustain their lives while in Indonesia, as we will illustrate in more detail in this chapter. While there remains a segment of the refugee population in Indonesia whose daily sustenance is provided by IOM and UNHCR, most refugees must find some other way of making a livelihood (Locastro et al., 2019). Even those who receive monthly stipends find that the amount is not nearly enough to maintain an adequate standard of living in big cities like Jakarta, Medan, and Makassar. The recent Covid-19 pandemic and subsequent economic downturn, as well as high inflation rates, have caused the cost of living to increase, but the monthly stipends have remained at the same level for the last ten years.

To get around the prohibition, many refugees work in the informal sector, such as teaching foreign languages to Indonesians, Quran recitation, translation work, selling food and services, and even people smuggling and sex work (Missbach & Cameron, 2022; Missbach, 2015b). All these workarounds, however, have serious downsides. Although it offers flexibility and a degree of legal invisibility, (self-)employment in the informal sector also renders refugees vulnerable to exploitation and unfair work relations, not to mention arbitrary arrest (Palmer & Missbach, 2019). Often, these jobs are characterised by volatility and uncertainty as demand for them is often either unpredictable or temporary. Moreover, if self-employment and entrepreneurship require seed funding for equipment, tools, or goods, only privileged refugees will be able to access this. For these reasons, as well as anticipated social jealousy from the wider Indonesian population (Sadjad, 2022), self-driven entrepreneurship and employment are not actively encouraged.

Nevertheless, it is an open secret that refugees engage in these income-generating activities. After all, there is no way refugees can survive without getting money from somewhere. On several occasions, government officials have admitted that they know refugees have been working, with some even claiming to know where they work, but they tolerate these activities as long as they remain informal and do not compete in domains occupied by local labour. The ambiguity of the Indonesian state's position is not surprising. On the one hand, it prefers refugees to not work (nor to integrate permanently into Indonesian society at all), yet on the other hand, it lacks any will, ideas, or means for alternative solutions to address their seemingly permanent state of transit (Missbach & Adiputera, 2021). Consequently, the question of the right to work occupies an awkward place in the current policy discourse. It is increasingly difficult for the Indonesian government to ignore the fact that cash assistance is no longer sufficient nor sustainable to cover the basic needs of refugees.

Navigating grey areas

In this section, we offer three case studies on skill development, self-employment, and entrepreneurship, collected through online interviews in December 2022 and January 2023. Given that the three authors have been working in the realms of refugee protection in Indonesia for many years and maintain many personal contacts, it was possible to select three examples deemed typical. Most refugees interviewed for the purposes of this chapter wanted us to use their real names, which we advised against. As a compromise, we use their first name or nicknames. Our discussion in the subsequent sections is also grounded in interviews and observations during previous individual fieldwork by the authors in Indonesia and in our use of open access sources.

Case study 1: Hamideh

Hamideh is a 28-year-old Afghan woman, who spent most of her youth as a refugee in Iran. She arrived in Indonesia in mid-2016, accompanied by two younger siblings and her mother. Back in Iran she attended a refugee school, which offered her limited education. As a teenage girl she learned how to sew and developed a liking for this activity. She worked for four years in two different tailoring factories, sewing pants, dresses, and blouses that had been ordered by customers. She got paid per piece and '*it was good money for a teenager*'.

In Indonesia, where she applied for international protection under the UNHCR, she was informed that refugees are not allowed to work. Yet, at the same time she became aware that many fellow Afghans were using their skills to make some money. In fact, there were many refugee women who were making clothes on demand. Some had founded collectives and attracted interest from interested customers in Australia. Regular orders for higher prices than what could be charged in Indonesia helped those collectives to thrive, at least temporarily. When Hamideh was still new in Indonesia, she was very much interested in joining such a collective and reached out to the founder, but in vain.

Eventually she decided to try her own luck. An Indonesian friend gave her a sewing machine. Since she did not have money to buy a lot of fabrics, in the first years she relied solely on orders from customers. An American teacher, who had set up a refugee school in Jakarta, asked her to make some napkins and table runners. A friend then sold those items, and the profit was split between Hamideh and the school. The teacher helped her to receive more orders.

From the leftovers of the fabrics given to her, Hamideh started making pouches and bags. Markets and charity gatherings soon became the most frequented outlet for her sales. Many of her customers were expats and by selling her products to them in relatively safe places, she evaded the suspicion of local authorities. It takes Hamideh about one hour to sew a pouch that she can sell for Rp 80,000 (US$ 8).

An Indonesian friend recommended that she come up with a brand name. Because she liked bright colours, that friend suggested the brand name WarNa, which is Indonesian for colour. Hamideh accepted this suggestion, because, for her, that name also contains a political message, made more visible through a subtle change in spelling WarNa (no war) – a message that is very dear to her.

While there were times when her business went reasonably well, Hamideh has suffered setbacks. For example, a potential client asked her many details about her products, including measurements and sewing tricks. Later she found that that person had opened her own workshop, where she was producing pouches that very much resembled Hamideh's pouches. Although very disappointed by this experience, she decided not to confront that person and to keep silent, because *'as a refugee there is nothing I can do about cheating'*.

Although Hamideh is very much aware of Indonesian online shopping sites, such as Tokopedia, she has preferred not to sell her products through them, chiefly because she does not want her business activities to be known by people who 'cause her trouble' by reporting her to the Indonesian authorities.

Hamideh regrets that she didn't have a chance to attend any of the entrepreneurial training offered by the UNHCR in Jakarta. When the training programmes were offered, she did not know about them and only learned about them afterwards from friends who had managed to attend. Although she has plenty of experience in making clothes and accessories, she is interested in improving her skills and learning new techniques, especially pattern making. Moreover, she is interested in learning more about marketing and business administration. But, since she was not a minor when she arrived in Indonesia, she was excluded from educational and vocational training more often than not.

The Covid pandemic was also detrimental to her business, as she could no longer sell her products at the markets. Even after the pandemic had subsided and public life resumed, Hamideh found that people were no longer spending as they had before. Given that her sewing business was going very slowly, Hamideh considered finding something else to do, at least temporarily. She was offered an opportunity to teach Farsi at a school, which she found both appealing and frightening as she lacked previous experience.

Hamideh hopes that she will be able to utilise and improve her tailoring skills once she has been resettled to a third country. She has many ideas of what she would like to do but feels impeded by the uncertainty of waiting. For example, she has been considering paying for private tuition for dressmaking, which is not only very expensive but would also require time and energy – resources she cannot readily spare as her mother requires medical care.

Case study 2: Abdullah

Abdullah is a 34-year-old Hazara man, born in Iran, who came to Indonesia on his own in 2015. Although his family members were refugees in Iran, he managed to attend a public school for ten years. After graduation, he worked as a decorator whenever an opportunity occurred. His father worked as a shoemaker and baker. One of his brothers is a mason, while another is a businessman. His sister is an acupuncturist and is planning to follow her husband to Germany soon. Most of his fellow countrymen and friends he got to know after he came to Indonesia, rather than before.

For the first years, his family supported him financially, as he was not offered a monthly stipend by the UNHCR or IOM. In 2017, he opened a small grocery shop (*toko sembako*), where he sells products from Indonesia and some imported spices. Some of the capital for opening the shop and buying stock (approximately Rp 100 million or US$ 10,000) was his own money and some he borrowed, with flexible interest rates, from friends in Iran.

His first shop was in Kalibata, a suburb of Jakarta that is popular with refugees, but because of pressing competition from other shopkeepers and higher rents, he decided to move to Cisarua, a mountain village about 60 km from Jakarta. His relocation coincided with the departure of many other refugees from Jakarta for Cisarua during the Covid-19 pandemic, thus guaranteeing him more customers. His relocation was also triggered by an earlier arrest and a three-month stay in detention.

In late October 2018, several immigration officers wearing plain clothes came to his shop in Kalibata and started making random inquiries about prices. When he answered, they took this as evidence to arrest him for working illegally in Indonesia. They took him to their immigration office but did not confiscate his phone for the first three hours, so he was able to call several friends, ask them to take care of his shop and, most importantly, to find an Indonesian woman, who would come to the immigration office and testify that she was the rightful owner of the shop and that Abdullah was only helping her out. While in detention, this woman also took care of the business for him to avoid going broke (*rugi*). Although Abdullah reached out to the UNHCR for help, he was left to fend for himself, as the UNHCR did not want to be involved (*urus sendiri*). He had clearly breached Indonesian law, and he was surprised when he was let go after three months, without paying any bribes.

With his new shop in Cisarua, Abdullah is more careful. While he orders products and collects shipments, he has hired an Indonesian person to tend the shop. Not being seen in the shop protects him from raids conducted by immigration officers or the police every now and then. The lease for his shop (Rp 40 million a year or US$ 4,000) is in the name of another Indonesian friend, for whose service he has to provide 'mandatory friendship gifts' infrequently, usually payments around Rp 500,000 (US$ 50). While he is now taking greater precautions, he still faces threats from jealous neighbours and other refugees. For example, some people tried to report him to his landlord, revealing that the shop was in Abdullah's name and not in the name of his Indonesian friend, who had signed the lease, which could potentially cause the landlord trouble. Like any other Indonesian shop owner, he also must make monthly payments of Rp 50,000 (US$ 5) to the village head.

On an average day, Abdullah can make revenues of Rp 3–4 million (US$ 300–400) per day, which leaves him with a profit of 10–15% after deducting all related expenses. But additional pressure comes from fellow refugees, who shop without paying. Those relying on the meagre monthly stipends from the IOM or any other humanitarian organisation can often only pay at the end of the month, and some rely on Abdullah's charity.

Abdullah is interested in learning more about running a business. If the offer materialises, he may also participate in additional training. One of his friends who participated in a UNHCR training programme is now successfully running a small business selling homemade potato chips. Compared to Iran, where refugees face much greater restrictions when trying to open a business and getting licences, he much prefers Indonesia, where he sees many business opportunities. In fact, he has plans to expand his business in Indonesia, by, for example, opening a restaurant or coffee shop. Knowing how difficult it would be for him to be resettled in a third country, especially since the UNHCR has not even started his refugee status determination process, he is open to staying in Indonesia for good *'if only he could get proper papers'*.

Case study 3: Joshua

Joshua is a 28-year-old Afghan man from Iran. He attended a government school back in Iran, but only until grade 11 when he dropped out to help provide for his family. He mostly worked in construction, which was hard physical work but good money. Together with his brother he decided to come to Indonesia because life in Iran was very bad for refugees. He saw no future for himself there.

He arrived in Indonesia in 2013 and was determined to be a refugee by the UNHCR in 2015. Today they still mostly live off family remittances. He tried many times to find employment in Indonesia, but usually failed as prospective employers wanted to see a KITAS (a legal proof of residency), which as a refugee he does not have. Not being considered a legal resident made him feel very uncomfortable (*rasa nggak enak*).

He kept asking his friends about what to do about this problem and started searching the internet for ideas. Eventually he found that hairdressing (*pantas rambut*) might be a good niche for him. He set out in his neighbourhood to find somebody to train him. He was offered a trainee position for Rp 3 million (US$ 300) but could not afford to take that up as he didn't have the money at the time. Following the suggestion of an Indonesian friend, he asked the trainer whether he could get the training for free and then work in his salon and have parts of his salary deducted to repay the cost of his training. Unfortunately, this request was rejected, but later he met an Indonesian woman, whose father was also a foreigner, and she took him on as a trainee. Her salon was very far from Joshua's house, and he could only attend twice a week, but he was a quick learner. After six weeks, he had learned the basics, and she even gave him a proper certificate. The woman later offered him work in one of her salons (she then owned five and now owns ten) and to look after her house, but regretfully Joshua had to decline her offer. He needed to stay with his brother in Cisarua (a mountain village, where it is cooler than in the city), as his brother cannot stand the heat in the city.

So, instead, he started looking for jobs in salons near his rental house. Even though he could present a certificate, potential employers didn't want to hire him. They requested a minimum of one year's work experience. He did not want to lie to them, but wondered how he would ever get a foot into the job market. When he eventually got a job, he only stayed for about two months, as the employer imposed simply too many rules; even being just one minute late would result in a salary deduction.

At the time of the interview, he had resorted to cutting people's hair inside his rental home. While this has the advantage of avoiding any raids by the police or immigration officials, it means he has no walk-in customers. Most of his clients are people who have had an unfortunate encounter with another hairdresser and come to him to have it fixed. He charges Rp 30,000 (US$ 3) for a haircut and Rp 10,000 (US$ 1) for a shave or a combination of only Rp 35,000 (US$ 3.5). The number of customers is still low, and the money he earns is just a supplement to what he receives from his parents. He reinvests half of his earnings in new tools and cosmetics. So far, he does not advertise widely. He wanted to take before and after pictures of his customers to promote his business, but all of them are refugees who do not wish their photos to be circulated in public.

Joshua really likes his job and would like to learn more and get more training for colouring, straightening, and styling hair. He would especially like to extend his skill to dealing with women's hair. The training for this, however, would be substantially more expensive. He sometimes watches online tutorials for hair treatment, but, of course, this is not the same as learning by doing. Also, acquiring the new tools and cosmetics he would require a significant investment. One of his most meaningful job experiences so far was his participation in a hair-styling competition in Tasikmalaya. He was the only Afghan competitor among 19 Indonesians. Even though he did not win an award, several people came up to him and congratulated him for his work on the model.

When the UNHCR organised training for refugees, he was too late in applying, which he regrets as he would have loved to be part of this training. Not having anything to do makes him dizzy (*pusing*), almost drives him mad (*gila*). Just sitting around and wondering what the future will bring is stressful, particularly as he still depends on financial support from his family, even though it should be his turn now to support them. Against their advice and based on his own hope for a fast resettlement, he has refrained from finding an Indonesian spouse, who could have helped him with the legal side of the business. In the past, he also experimented with other business ideas, such as buying and selling chicken, but to be a serious salesperson, he would have been required to buy and sell huge quantities (100 kg), so he gave that up after only two months.

Joshua has managed to save up some money and he hopes he can open a salon in the city nearby. A six-month rental would cost him between Rp 6 and 8 million (US$ 600–800). He might have to borrow from friends or ask them to invest into his business. If he was to go ahead with the business, he would be serving Indonesian customers as well as refugees. An Indonesian acquaintance has offered to put his name on the lease. At the same time, Joshua remains hopeful that he will be resettled soon. Ideally, he would like to continue to work as a hairdresser in the future.

Work rights under another name?

Whenever the classic durable solutions (resettlement, repatriation, and local integration) are not forthcoming, the UNHCR will work towards 'comprehensive solutions' comprising temporary measures that give refugees access to opportunities that encourage self-reliance. While these measures are essentially humanitarian compromises rather than rights-based mechanisms, they are evidence of some small progress in improving the rights of refugees. Existing restrictions that prevent refugees from working in Indonesia have required UNHCR and its partner organisations to navigate between refugees' urgent need to earn a livelihood and local sensitivities around refugees working. One staff member of UNHCR Indonesia explained this by highlighting some institutional and social barriers that hinder the integration into local economies:

> *We would like refugees to be like normal people who have rights to obtain an income, even if a small one, perhaps not formal employment because that is still too sensitive, but a right to livelihood… We do a lot of activities that offer them [refugees] training skills according to their existing capacities. For example, with independent refugees, we offered training to make tempe [soy bean cake], soap, handicraft through partnering organisations, and they are able to sell what they make. The government does not reject these training programmes because we tell them that this is to help refugees avoid stress while living here and can become useful skills for them after resettlement. That is our line of advocacy.*
>
> (Interview with UNHCR staff, 10 June 2019)

During this interview, the UNHCR staff acknowledged that some refugees were able to generate an income with the support of UNHCR and partner organisations. To avoid possible scrutiny from Indonesian officials, income-generating activities were labelled as vocational training, and any money paid to refugees was as a lump sum to cover transportation costs.

UNHCR and IOM have been working with non-profit organisations, businesses, and universities to offer refugees various training opportunities, especially for young people who make up a significant percentage of the refugee population in Indonesia (UNHCR, 2022b; Masardi, 2021). In 2018, UNHCR worked with the International Labour Organization (ILO), an Indonesian university, and a local philanthropic organisation to offer entrepreneurship training for Hazara refugees. This training programme was described as linking 'refugees with local entrepreneurs to promote economic development in Indonesia and prepare refugees for the future' (UNHCR Indonesia Instagram, 18 December 2018). The programme was repeated in 2019 with refugees and Indonesians as participants, providing space for aspiring entrepreneurs to exhibit their collaborative entrepreneurial ideas. Most of these entrepreneurial projects displayed handicrafts and food products that could be produced at home. Somewhat surprisingly, the programmes emphasised social entrepreneurship and opportunities for refugees to expand their social network within Indonesia rather than in a future resettlement country. Entrepreneurship training programmes are a grey area within the practice of refugee reception, as entrepreneurship is arguably not employment, and the phrase 'training programme' frames activities as skills training and social networking opportunities rather than as income-generating options. They tend to encourage social integration with members of the Indonesian host society, while business-oriented projects for refugees are still considered taboo.

Although organisers cannot pay participants for their work or participation, they do offer reimbursements and transport allowances, which, in one way or another, allows for some money to be transferred to refugee participants. However, based on our observations, these workshops may potentially have exploitative features. For example, in a workshop offered to refugees in 2018 by a businessman whose family owns a chain of international hotels in Jakarta, the participants sewed small toiletry bags from recycled hotel linen that had been disposed of because it no longer met hotel standards. While the linen was donated to the refugees, the toiletry bags were supposedly bought back by the hotels. Upon closer inquiry, the workshop organisers were unwilling to reveal how much the hotels paid for the toiletry bags or even whether they had paid any money at all, besides the lump sum to cover transportation costs (Fieldwork notes, 18 September 2018). As well as the sewing course, designed with the aspiration of a self-sustaining business model, the businessman's foundation organised workshops where refugees learned to make soap to sell and connected refugees to a business that offered them computer programming courses. These training programmes and workshops tend to be rather small in scale and provide no immediate and living wages for refugees. While these training activities may help refugees fill time during long periods of waiting and learn new skills, it remains questionable whether the skills acquired through them will be actually useful and profitable.

In light of these adjustments and workarounds, there have been some positive signals from the Indonesian government regarding refugee rights in recent years, particularly regarding education, health, and livelihoods. This came after a sustained campaign by UNHCR and civil society organisations (Jesuit Refugee Service and SUAKA, among others) to advocate for the right to work, which began systematically in about 2017–2018. UNHCR commissioned an exploratory study on the right to work, published in 2018, and organised a series of workshops with government agencies on the topic (Adiputera & Prabandari, 2018). In 2018, a UNHCR official revealed that the campaign had broken new ground when the government started to openly allow refugees to receive formal remuneration for their work as translators for UNHCR.

Indonesia also supports the Global Compact on Refugees (GCR) adopted by the UN in 2018 and pledged during the 2019 Global Refugee Forum to 'design a refugee empowerment program', 'to support the implementation of the GCR', and develop 'relevant policies and budget in order to improve the lives of refugees in the country' (Hafid, 2019). Building upon the GCR calls for more comprehensive solutions to address refugees' needs during long-term displacement (United Nations, 2018). As part of the search for such solutions, there has been increased attention to refugee entrepreneurship. One of the key programmes of action stated in the Compact is the promotion of economic opportunities, decent work, job creation, and entrepreneurship programmes for host community members and refugees. Considering this new commitment to refugee empowerment, the Indonesian government has actually taken some positive steps towards recognition of the rights of refugees.

In 2019, the Ministry of Education and Culture issued a circular on the fulfilment of the rights to education, which provides a clear institutional policy for the inclusion of refugee children into the school system (UNHCR, 2022a). During the pandemic, the Health Ministry also issued a circular on the access to Covid-related health services for refugees. All these steps towards recognition, not only of the presence of refugees but also of their rights, may set the scene for eventually opening their access to livelihood. In fact, the policy discourse on work rights has been expanding in recent years as the government has perhaps become more open to such discussions. For example, in 2022, the Indonesian National Research and Innovation Agency (BRIN) conducted research and a series of workshops on the economic, social, and cultural rights of refugees in Indonesia, including the right to work (BRIN, 2023). In one of the workshops attended by representatives from the parliament, government ministries, and regional governments, discussions on the right to work took a noticeably positive tone as some of the government representatives indicated their support for arrangements that would allow refugees to work. Whether this reflects the official position of the government and whether there will be concrete follow-up in the form of a legislative change (as many civil society participants suggested) or under other policy frameworks, such as 'livelihoods' or 'productivity empowerment', remains to be seen.

Conclusion

In 2019, Indonesia made a public pledge to address the needs of refugees during their long-term displacement by promoting refugee entrepreneurship and supporting refugees' self-reliance and their socioeconomic integration into local economies. Exploring options for refugees to find employment and sustain a livelihood within the Indonesian context is, however, still perceived as a sensitive topic. As of 2023, refugees in Indonesia are still prohibited by law from participating in income-generating activities, despite the common understanding that they have for years been working within the informal sector. The government's ambivalence on this matter creates a legal grey area, which benefits neither the state nor the refugees. A series of positive signs from the government have been apparent in recent years regarding the recognition of refugee rights, most notably in access to education and health care. Nonetheless, it remains to be seen whether this recognition will soon extend to the right to work. While the numbers of refugees resettled from Indonesia have increased as the Covid-19 pandemic has eased, it seems highly unlikely that all refugees will be leaving Indonesia soon. Besides, more refugees keep coming to Indonesia, which makes the need for work rights more pressing. As our three case studies have shown, many refugees are not only keen to work but also to contribute to the Indonesian host society.

Note

1 The number has hovered around 11,000 and 14,000 for the last decade. It is considerably lower than in neighbouring countries such as Malaysia, Thailand, and Myanmar, whose refugee populations reach hundreds of thousands.

References

Adiputera, Y., & Prabandari, A. (2018). *Addressing Challenges and Identifying Opportunities for Refugee Access to Employment in Indonesia*. Yogyakarta: Institute of International Studies, Universitas Gadjah Mada.

Alkhaled, S. (2019). The resilience of a Syrian woman and her family through refugee entrepreneurship in Jordan. In S. Heilbrunn, J. Freiling, & A. Harima (Eds.), *Refugee Entrepreneurship – A Case-Based Topography* (pp. 241–253). Cham: Palgrave Macmillan. https://doi.org/10.1007/978-3-319-92534-9_17

BRIN. (2023, January 26). *BRIN Ulas pemenuhan hak-hak pengungsi luar negeri di Indonesia*. https://ipsh.brin.go.id/2023/01/26/brin-ulaspemenuhan-hak-hak-pengungsi-luar-negeri-di-indonesia/

Brown, T., & Missbach, A. (2016, March 22). The boats may have 'stopped', but more refugees are stuck in limbo in Indonesia. *The Conversation*. https://theconversation.com/the-boats-may-have-stopped-but-more-refugees-are-stuck-in-limboin-indonesia-56152

Carciotto, S. (2020). Making asylum seekers more vulnerable in South Africa: The negative effects of hostile asylum policies on livelihoods. *International Migration*, *59*(5), 3–18. https://doi.org/10.1111/imig.12788

Chen, E. (2021, December 21). Uneven refugee protections across Southeast Asia put migrants at risk. *CSIS Blogs: New Perspectives on Asia*. www.csis.org/blogs/new-perspectives-asia/uneven-refugee-protections-across-southeast-asia-put-migrants-risk.

de la Chaux, M. (2019). Entrepreneurship in extreme environments: Businesses in the Dadaab refugee camp in Kenya. In S. Heilbrunn, J. Freiling, & A. Harima (Eds.) *Refugee Entrepreneurship – A Case-Based Topography* (pp. 221–229). Cham: Palgrave Macmillan. https://doi.org/10.1007/978-3-319-92534-9_15

Easton-Calabria, E., & Omata, N. (2018). Panacea for the refugee crisis? Rethinking the promotion of 'self-reliance' for refugees. *Third World Quarterly*, *39*(8), 1458–1474. https://doi.org/10.1080/01436597.2018.1458301

Hafid, M. (2019). *Statement by Hon. Ms. Meutya Hafid, Chair of the Foreign Affairs and Defence Committee of the Indonesian House of Representatives for the First Global Refugee Forum 17-18 December 2019.* Genève, Switzerland. www.unhcr.org/5df9f35b4.pdf.

Heilbrunn, S., & Iannone, R. L. (2020). From center to periphery and back again: A systematic literature review of refugee entrepreneurship. *Sustainability*, *12*, 7658. https://doi.org/10.3390/su12187658

Hugo, G. (2014). The economic contribution of humanitarian settlers in Australia. *International Migration*, *52*(2), 31–52. https://doi.org/10.1111/imig.12092

IOM Indonesia. (2021). *IOM Indonesia – 2021 year in review*. https://indonesia.iom.int/sites/g/files/tmzbdl1491/files/documents/iom-indonesia-2021-year-in-review_final_1.pdf

Locastro, M., Alfath, D., & Hu, G. (2019). *Unlocking the Economic Potentials of Indonesia's Refugee Community: A Survey on Labour Characteristics.* Jakarta: Sandya Institute.

Lyon, F., Sepulveda, L., & Syrett, S. (2007). Enterprising refugees: Contributions and challenges in deprived urban areas. *Local Economy*, *22*(4), 362–375. https://doi.org/10.1080/02690940701736769

Masardi, R. (2021). *Independent Refugee Youth in Waiting: Social Navigations while in Transit in Indonesia* [Unpublished doctoral dissertation]. University of Amsterdam.

Missbach, A. (2015a). *Troubled Transit: Asylum Seekers Stuck in Indonesia.* Singapore: ISEAS-Yusof Ishak Institute.

Missbach, A. (2015b). Making a "career" in people-smuggling in Indonesia: Protracted transit, restricted mobility, and the lack of legal work rights. *Journal of Social Issues in Southeast Asia*, *30*(2), 423–454. www.jstor.org/stable/24779960

Missbach, A., & Adiputera, Y. (2021). The role of local governments in accommodating refugees in Indonesia: Investigating best-case and worst-case scenarios. *Asian Journal of Law and Society*, *8*(3), 490–506. https://doi.org/10.1017/als.2021.5

Missbach, A., Adiputera, Y., Prabandari, A., Cintika, G., Swastika, F. Y., & Darningtyas, R. (2018). *Stalemate: Refugees in Indonesia — Presidential Regulation No 125 of 2016* (Policy Paper No. 14). Centre for Indonesian Law, Islam and Society.

Missbach, A., & Cameron, T. (2022). Making do: How a Somali refugee woman experiences social mobility amidst precarity in transit in Indonesia. *TRaNS: Trans-Regional and -National Studies of Southeast Asia*, *10*(1), 85–101. https://doi.org/10.1017/trn.2021.9

Mohammadi, S., & Askary, S. (2022, January 11). *Refugees Live in Destitution in Indonesia: Years of Limbo and Suffering Lead Refugees to Protests for Many Weeks Now for Resettlement.* https://reliefweb.int/report/indonesia/refugees-live-destitution-indonesia-years-limbo-and-suffering-lead-refugees

Palmer, W., & Missbach, A. (2019). Enforcing labour rights of irregular migrants in Indonesia. *Third World Quarterly*, *40*(5), 908–925. https://doi.org/10.1080/01436597.2018.1522586

Ramsay, G. (2020). Humanitarian exploits: Ordinary displacement and the political economy of the global refugee regime. *Critique of Anthropology*, *40*(1), 3–27. https://doi.org/10.1177/0308275X19840417

Sadjad, M. S. (2022). Solidarity and social jealousy: Emotions and affect in Indonesian host societies' situated encounters with refugees. *Third World Quarterly*, *43*(3), 543–560. https://doi.org/10.1080/01436597.2021.1969228

Sampson, R. C., Gifford, S. M., & Taylor, S. (2016). The myth of transit: The making of a life by asylum seekers and refugees in Indonesia. *Journal of Ethnic and Migration Studies*, *42*(7), 1135–1152. https://doi.org/10.1080/1369183X.2015.1130611

Sianturi, M. H., & Viartasiwi, N. (2021). Advocating the temporary rights to work for refugees and asylum seekers in transit in Indonesia. *Indonesia Law Review*, *11*(3), 249–266. https://doi.org/10.15742/ilrev.v11n3.2

UNHCR. (2022a). *Indonesia Fact Sheet*. www.unhcr.org/id/wp-content/uploads/sites/42/2022/04/Indonesia-Fact-SheetFebruary-2022-FINAL.pdf

UNHCR. (2022b). *Sekilas data*. www.unhcr.org/id/figures-at-a-glance

UNHCR. (2022c, October 24). *UNHCR's Unprecedented US$700m Funding Gap Spells Catastrophe for Millions*. www.unhcr.org/news/press/2022/10/6356921e4/unhcrs-unprecedented-us700m-funding-gap-spells-catastrophe-millions.html

United Nations. (2018). *Global Compact on Refugees*. www.unhcr.org/5c658aed4.

7 Breaking barriers

Women refugee entrepreneurship and integration frameworks in the United States

Cihan Aydiner and Erin Rider

Introduction

In the United States (US), the federal government supports refugees and asylees through state contacts and independent business programmes nationwide. These services include employment preparation, business loans, and grants. For example, the Office of Refugee Resettlement (ORR) provides short-term financial assistance, job training, and funds to states for the employment of refugees. Accordingly, de Graauw and Bloemraad (2017) identify "the web of federal, voluntary sector, state and local partnerships [...] on getting refugees to economic self-sufficiency" (p. 109). However, awareness of these opportunities and readiness to apply for them is not an accessible and streamlined process for many women refugee entrepreneurs due to legal, financial, cultural, market-related, and gender-related challenges (see Brieger & Gielnik, 2021; Mehtap et al., 2019). Within the entrepreneurship context, women refugee entrepreneurs often face unique challenges that other business owners may not experience, such as language barriers, cultural differences, and less social capital (Mehtap et al., 2019; Nijhoff, 2021). Despite these obstacles, many refugees succeed in establishing successful businesses that contribute significantly to local economies around the world. Often their resilience is related to the necessity of and opportunity for entrepreneurship due, in the main, to barriers in the formal labour market (Desai et al., 2021; Zighan, 2021).

The aim of this research is to understand the economic integration of recently arrived Turkish women in the US. This research project provides an in-depth exploration of the challenging yet rewarding journey of economic independence experienced by Turkish asylum seeker/exiled individuals. In the US, "asylum is a protection grantable to foreign nationals already in the US or arriving at the border who meet the international law definition of a refugee" (American Immigration Council, 2022). We interchange the terminology of refugee with asylum seeker and exile due to the unique conditions of forced migration of participants. The participants entered the US legally through valid visas. Due to barriers in the formal economy, many turn to entrepreneurial endeavours to achieve economic stability. Of the six participants in our study, two were asylum seekers, three were granted asylum and permanent

DOI: 10.4324/9781003368540-9

residency, and one was an EB2 green card holder. However, we also identify that most participants had higher human capital in the form of education and professional work experience. We find that these exiled Turkish women were able to leverage their human capital, adaptability to the host country, and innovative spirit to create businesses with personal meaning and income generation. This provides insights into their multiple embeddedness to the US (Harima et al., 2021). The findings can aid in devising more inclusive policies to support refugee entrepreneurs during their transition into host societies, thus enabling their entrepreneurial spirit and motivation through the removal of bureaucratic barriers and increased access to social capital.

Literature review

Entrepreneurship has been described as both a necessity and an opportunity for refugees as they navigate both formal and informal labour markets (Desai et al., 2021; Zighan, 2021). A growing area of the literature is how entrepreneurship is linked to economic integration (Atasü-Topcuoğlu, 2019). Accordingly, van Kooy (2016) highlights that entrepreneurship is perceived as “positive, adventurous, and with the promise of rewards” while also raising doubts as to what it means for refugees (p. 71). As an economic strategy, refugee entrepreneurship has been demonstrated as not viable due to the nexus of barriers refugees face in comparison to native citizens (see Wauters & Lambrecht, 2008). Yet other research is emerging to identify government efforts to foster entrepreneurship among refugees to promote self-reliance and a greater likelihood of acceptance (Turner, 2020). In this literature review, using a framework of mixed embeddedness, we will explore the aspects of entrepreneurship as both a necessity and an opportunity, focusing particularly on how our female participants demonstrate agency.

Due to refugees’ experiences of a forced plight of migration and adjustment, with limited access to the formal economy in host countries, entrepreneurship has been mostly characterised as a necessity (Desai et al., 2021; Senthanar et al., 2021; Street et al., 2022; Zighan, 2021). However, this can be juxtaposed with the ability to pursue self-reliant forms of income activity to avoid or overcome formal market barriers (Hillmann & Toğral Koca, 2021; Mehtap et al., 2019; Sidhva et al., 2021; Turner, 2020). Using traditional push and pull language associated with migration, scholars have utilised the push factor to discuss refugee’s lack of access to formal labour and the pull factor to indicate the draw of entrepreneurship (Alexandre et al., 2019; Naicker & Nsengimana, 2020).

Refugee entrepreneurship has also been regularly framed by a mixed embeddedness theory addressing the agency of refugees to utilise their social networks and seek opportunities through the informal economy (Harima et al., 2021; Hedberg & Pettersson, 2012; Senthanar et al., 2021). Nijhoff (2021) demonstrates this process by identifying the following interrelated factors: “demand side: structural embeddedness (market and rules) and supply side: individual resources (human capital) and social/relational embeddedness (social capital)" (p. 1059). Thus, the refugee entrepreneur is situated between the host country's market and policies and their own economic and social capital (Nijhoff, 2021). In response to the dichotomising push and pull framework of mixed embeddedness, Harima et al. (2021) conceptualise embeddedness based on multiple factors, starting with an orientation that refugees are "active entrepreneurial agents who construct opportunities," and thus, formulate the following typology: "value creation with homeland resources; transnational middleman minorities; integration facilitation; qualification transfers; homeland problem-solving; and creative innovation" (p. 631, p. 644). These types of entrepreneurial activities are comprehensive and dynamically show the level of embeddedness between the country of origin and host country. The efficacy of embeddedness and entrepreneurship may be negatively impacted by having to compete for scarce resources with both native citizens and other refugees (see Bjørkhaug, 2020). Zighan (2021) highlights that the promising idea of entrepreneurship is limited by "investors [who] want to see innovative ideas, entrepreneurs and skilled workers and wish to ensure their investment is not subject to failure" (p. 542). Refugee entrepreneurs may also be limited to certain fields, such as the service sector (see Billore, 2011; Mueller, 2014). Yet, Almohammad et al. (2021) reveal that refugee entrepreneurship can improve outcomes of "earning money, chances of obtaining citizenship, improving language skills, and integration with the host society" (p. 70). The limited viable economic options for refugees reveal that entrepreneurship may be a precarious, yet sole pathway for economic security.

Employing the mixed embeddedness framework and characterisations of entrepreneurship as both a necessity and an opportunity, we can focus on the pathway of refugee women pursuing entrepreneurship. Research has shown that immigrants experience difficulties accessing host countries' formal labour markets due to the inability to have foreign degrees recognised in host countries (Almohammad et al., 2021; Harima et al., 2021; Hillmann & Toğral Koca, 2021; Naicker & Nsengimana, 2020; Senthanar et al., 2021; Stumpf et al., 2020; Sweetman et al., 2015; Wauters & Lambrecht, 2008; Zighan, 2021). In research on highly qualified, female refugees in Germany conducted by Hillmann and Toğral Koca (2021), they found that "most men had participated in the labour market before coming to Germany (80%), while only 40% of women had done so" (p. 6). Hillman and Toğral Koca (2021) also factor in that women have responsibilities of child-rearing. As such, women have relatively limited access to the formal workplace when compared to men, and this is further exacerbated by their refugee status in a new host country.

Refugees generally experience challenges with access to the formal economy, yet pursuing entrepreneurship has its own economic barriers. Brieger and Gielnik (2021) conclude from their study of 11,471 immigrants that women have less ability to pursue entrepreneurship compared to men. As with policy barriers in the formal economy, starting a business means having adequate capital (Nijhoff, 2021; van Kooy, 2016). Mehtap et al. (2019) find that none of women in their study had a business plan for their entrepreneurship activities. Their activities were also situated in gendered family roles, meaning that many women had to seek approval from their husbands and, in cases where the husband did not approve, women continued their entrepreneurship discreetly (Mehtap et al., 2019).

Refugee women experience unique cultural, family, and gender responsibilities that do not always afford them opportunities for paid work. Almohammad et al. (2021) find that "the informal sector helps Syrian refugees start and sustain a small business [in Türkiye] without bureaucratic problems" (p. 71). Further, entrepreneurship when aimed at women has emphasised feminine activities and familiar, private locations, such as the home (Datta, 2019; Senthanar et al., 2021; Sidhva et al., 2021). In the study by Sidhva et al. (2021) on Syrian women in Jordan, they found that middle-aged refugee women identified a niche in entrepreneurship due to cultural norms of women having "control of resources" and the challenges faced by men in "accessing work permits, and low wages in the informal economy" (pp. 10–11). Similarly, a study of Syrian refugees in Canada shows that while entrepreneurship may be sought out of necessity, it did enable some women to have "flexibility of working hours and cash-in-hand payments" (Senthanar et al., 2021, p. 839). Syrian refugees in Lebanon exploited an opportunity in the market to offer craftsmanship connected with their previous work experience (Alexandre et al., 2019). And among refugees in Germany, France, and Ireland, risk-taking was evident in response to the "loss of resources, assets, and loved ones in their home countries" (Harima et al., 2021, p. 642). These findings reveal the agency of women refugees to respond to restrictive policies and limited economic security by finding ways to initiate income-generating activities. To further minimise barriers non-citizens face in beginning entrepreneurship, research has tended to support policies that would increase access to "fast-tracked work visas, entrepreneur visas, and special startup visa programs" (Sak et al., 2018, p. 10).

Context

The 2016 alleged coup attempt in Türkiye intensified the emigration of professionals, as the government cracked down on alleged dissidents (see Aydiner & Rider, 2022). These often include educators, journalists, scholars, business professionals, and members of the judiciary. As a result, many individuals from various professions sought refuge or employment opportunities abroad to avoid persecution or job loss. Exiles are individuals who have been forced to leave their country either formally (no choice) or informally, choosing to leave before facing potential imprisonment or other consequences (Baser & Ozturk, 2022).

The US has seen an increase in refugees and asylees from Türkiye, especially after the 2016 alleged coup attempt, with approximately a total of 5,000 arrivals between 2017 and 2021 (DHS, 2020). These numbers do not include illegal entries and asylum seekers. The population of Turkish individuals in the US is approximately 350,000 (Turkish Coalition of America, 2023). The US has a variety of programmes designed to support refugees, including entrepreneurial support. This can take the form of business training, microloans, and other financial services tailored to the needs of refugees looking to start businesses. In addition to federal programmes, there are also local organisations and non-government organisations (NGOs) that offer mentorship, business training, and financial support to refugees to promote self-sufficiency and economic integration.

Methodology

The researchers worked with a small group of Turkish male and female individuals who were forced to leave or were exiled from their country following alleged coup attempt events on July 15, 2016, due to their opposition to the ruling party in Türkiye (Aydiner & Rider, 2021, 2022). Six participants have been drawn from a previous project of 45 people collected at two different times. The Institutional Review Board approved the study, and semi-structured interviews were completed in two tracks in late 2019 and 2022 (see Aydiner & Rider, 2022 for detailed recruitment procedure and methodology).

The researchers used a purposive sampling method to identify six women refugees in the US for in-depth interviews. An interview guide was developed to ensure that all participants were asked the same set of questions for each region and to maintain consistency across the interviews. The interviews were conducted in person and were recorded for later transcription and analysis. Participants were asked to describe their experiences with entrepreneurship. Follow-up prompts were used to facilitate the conversation for additional information. The researchers preferred to conduct the interviews in Turkish and then translate them into English using a professional transcription and translation service provider to fully reflect the feelings of the Turkish participants. To derive meaningful themes from the qualitative data, a systematic approach grounded in Charmaz's (2014) theoretical design was employed. Initially, the data were meticulously transcribed and then subjected to a coding process using the Atlas Ti software. During this phase, emphasis was placed on phrases, terms, and topics that recurred in the unstructured conversations. By identifying these recurrent elements and organising them, overarching themes emerged. These themes not only encapsulated the shared experiences of the participants but also provided a structured framework to understand and interpret their narratives more deeply.

The six women entrepreneurs were all highly educated (a minimum of a four-year university/college degree, and three had graduate degrees) and had English language abilities to different levels. Three participants had full professional proficiency, two had professional working proficiency, and one participant had limited working proficiency. They were residing among the historically highly Turkish-populated states (more than 10,000) of New York

(2), Virginia (2), Pennsylvania (1), and Texas (1). All were of legal status (asylum seeker, asylee, or employment or education-related visa) in the US. Table 7.1 provides detailed demographic information about the participants.

Due to their sudden migration or exile, the participants had little to no financial capital to start a business. Only two participants had limited experience or prior education related to their new business ideas in the US. The other four participants had worked in different fields to collect enough capital to start their first businesses. Throughout their entrepreneurial activity, they experienced working in different market models: in-person, hybrid, and online service/sales. The COVID-19 period brought about both challenges of store closures and changing business fields, and opportunities of access to state benefits for small businesses/individuals/families to start a new business and transferring their business to a hybrid or online environments. We identified several themes that correspond to tensions and triumphs impacting women refugee entrepreneurship in the US. The themes are empowerment and opportunistic environment, networking and mentorship, never giving up and taking risks, gendered norms, language skills, and legal and financial challenges.

Results

Participants in our sample were forced to leave Türkiye urgently and entered the US using different legal statuses, including a tourist visa for one. We also found that the use of the "refugee" term was offensive to the participants because it was connected to anti-immigrant actors' rhetoric. Our participants did not feel like they were someone who must take refuge somewhere else. In response to Türkiye's developing anti-democratic stance, it was considered "normal" to move somewhere else that best fitted their background and education. The participants describe themselves as free women entrepreneurs who contribute to places wherever they live.

Empowerment and opportunistic environment

The US historically provides an opportunistic environment for hardworking individuals. There are many different types of job opportunities for women refugee entrepreneurs. Most of these opportunities varied from state to state and are created by governmental (federal, state, city), non-governmental, not-for-profit, or private sector organisations. Refugees and asylees are eligible to acquire working authorisation in the US and the legal status affords them different types of support for a limited time. There are mainstream federal support such as cash or food assistance for refugees and asylees, in addition to support services (i.e., employment preparation, English-language training, and cash assistance) provided by the Office of Refugee Resettlement (ORR) under the US Department of Health and Human Services (HHS). The ORR programme has state partners that provide these services. The majority

Table 7.1 List of participants

Abbr.	*Age (year)*	*Arrival*	*Business Date*	*Education*	*Vocation Background*	*Business Idea*
US-1	45–54	2016	2019	Elementary School Teaching	Teacher	Women's sportswear
US-2	35–44	2016	2018	Mathematics	Teacher	Fashion store and gift products
US-3	25–34	2019	2022	Mechanical Engineering Business Administration	HR	Software for wholesalers
US-4	35–44	2020	2023	Psychological Counselling	Researcher	IT company
US-5	35–44	2017	2018	Psychology, PhD	Instructor	Academic support for graduate students
US-6	25–34	2015	2018	Primary Teacher education	HR	Photography, handmade products

of programme supporter partners are non-profit organisations such as the International Rescue Committee, World Relief, and religious organisations (i.e., Catholic Charities, Lutheran Community Services, Jewish Family Service, and Interfaith Ministries). In addition to federal and state financial and service assistance, there are also private and not-for-profit organisations, such as Upwardly (2023) and Femigrants (2023).

One of the participants had support from a non-profit in her region:

> *When my case [asylum granted] was approved, I applied for benefits at Catholic Charity [Coordinating organisation designated by ORR]. It was good to see two women administrators who have similar experiences to me [Refugees from Mexico and Bosnia a long time ago]. We had a good relationship and communication. One helped with healthcare, and one helped with cash aid and employment for a few months.*
>
> (US-6)

Since US-6 is competent in English, she did not take English courses provided by a partner organisation. However, she was happy with the contacting officials' manner and the other benefits provided by the organisation prior to her attaining a work permit, which took more than six months. She, therefore, had time to think about business ideas and engage in some small work trials, such as selling varied products on social media marketplaces.

The Small Business Administration (SBA) is an independent agency of the federal government that supports individuals to start or grow a small business through loans, grants, mentorship, and other services (SBA, 2023). The programme also provided COVID-19 small business loans. All participants received temporary COVID-19 benefits for financial assistance and two received unemployment benefits and SBA loans. US-3 describes her business idea and how she received a SBA grant as follows:

> *While I was doing my internship, we received a request. A large meat wholesaler supplies meat all over Europe but takes orders by phone, text message, and e-mail. And the man, every night, goes back to work at 12 o'clock and till 8 in the morning struggles with computerising the orders. He asked us for a system that would automate this. ... so, the idea that came to my mind then is that the sales representative who goes to this market should not enter the order, the market itself should enter the order. Then the salesperson will be out of the way. The vehicle, the cost of the vehicle, which is used to get there, will be removed. They have e-terminals they use; these will disappear, and a more efficient system will emerge. I came to America with this idea, there is the same problem here, there is such a thing here. I got an SBA grant to realise my idea. I started to research it. I probably talked to 60 companies, as wholesalers and markets. Same problem here. 70% of wholesalers or brands need such a solution. It will be an app and a website, and I am currently trying to release software for them.*
>
> (US-3)

The US-3 example describes the process of using her previous work experience to develop a business idea and then seek funding support. Another participant used COVID-19 financial assistance as well.

> *We received unemployment benefits at that time [COVID-19]. I entered the jewellery business. On Etsy, I started selling gold. Personalised gold, jewellery, necklace, bracelet. In that job actually, I succeeded, it was going well. In 2–3 months, we made 600–700 sales. It was a profitable business.*
>
> (US-2)

The COVID-19 period was a challenging time span for all people, but the main concern of the women entrepreneurs was financial issues and creating a stable business. They used the COVID-19 pandemic time and related funding resources to start a business or realise their innovative ideas. Also, SBA grants/loans supported some of them to implement their business plans.

Networking and mentorship

Networking and mentorship are two important support systems that facilitate entrepreneurship. Women entrepreneurs need help with legal procedures to open a business in different states, learn the market needs, identify a product or service, and other topics such as selling online using various platforms (i.e., Amazon, Etsy, Facebook). In our study, participants were supported by immigrants and refugees of the same origin who helped to acquire the required information (Aydiner & Rider, 2021). US-3 stated:

> *[name of a Turkish immigrant], God bless him, taught me how to make an Amazon. I did it [transferring business to an online platform] on Amazon. In that, I really think I was successful [Laughter]. I've made quite a bit of money. So, thank God, we earned enough to support our family.*

US-1 also received mentorship from another refugee woman entrepreneur who started a business before her:

> *[US-2] shared with me everything she knows. She helped me a lot. Provided information about which products sell well, where to buy them, how to make logistics cheaper, and other things she knows. Also, she sent some of her products to me to see the demand in my living area.*
>
> (US-1)

Participants agreed that networking and mentorship was important in making the migration process easier by facilitating business entrepreneurship and/or supporting integration (Aydiner & Rider, 2021; Dekker & Engbersen, 2013). These networking experiences were also based on connecting to individuals from their home country.

Never giving up and taking risks

Women entrepreneurs were open to taking risks and not giving up even after failed trials. Several participants experienced sacrifices in initiating their businesses, including for one participant who experienced an impact on their health. US-1 shared her experience of sacrifice.

> *While we were preparing for retirement the events [alleged coup attempt on July 15, 2016] happened. We lost everything [...] But, I've never been cut off from life. I've always been in it. I tried everything.[...] I got my American's driver license. I delivered packages on Amazon. I opened my own store. Now, I have two stores and 5 employees.*
>
> (US-1)

US-6 used the early COVID-19 period to realise her business idea and made sacrifices. She was knitting handmade facemasks on soft fabric using superhero and comic designs for kids.

> *[...] started to take hundreds of orders daily after taking great reviews from first customers. [...] knitting for hours without sleep but making thousands of dollars.*
>
> (US-1)

US-3 did not give up after trying several different business ideas. She expresses her thoughts as:

> *I had already come here with the idea of an enterprise. I was trying to implement that work. As I had a type B visa, I was interviewing other companies. But of course, there was no direct financial return at that time. I started a company and rented a house. Renting a house was also difficult. Then we started to run that. We made good money for 2 months. Then the corona started, and the tourists did not come. We went bankrupt. [Laughing] When the tourist didn't come, there was no one to stay. The whole city was already empty. We were left without money there. We went down, we went down a lot. [Laughing] We were in debt, we were breaking. Then [Long pause] how were we going to pay off debts? Tried another thing [...].*
>
> (US-3)

Participants took many risks, made sacrifices, and failed multiple times, but they did not give up. Some of them described the reason for taking these risks and making sacrifices with the following phrase, "*...because you have to.*" In a typical business model, the entrepreneur may create a detailed business plan and undertake the market research required for a business start-up. However, refugees do not have enough time to do all of these steps. US-1 experience was:

> *I sold Turkish handmade items like lamps, bags, etc. However, it didn't go well. Then [after studying the market needs], I opened two stores of women's sportswear.*

Although challenges and failures were common, the participants seemed motivated to continue the entrepreneur pathway by capitalising on innovation and by learning and adapting to the needs of the market.

Gender norms

The participants come from a non-Western Muslim majority country with some degree of traditional gender role norms. Although they have college degrees, some of them could not find a job related to their degrees, yet had to support their family:

> *The main breadwinner [in home country] was my husband although I had a university education. I didn't do a job related to my degree and supported my husband in his career, and take care of the kids. However, things have changed when we come here [laughing].*
>
> (US-1)

US-1 experienced a shift in gender role expectations. For other participants, work was interrupted by pregnancy. US-3 found an appropriate environment to accomplish her diverse ideas from Airbnb to custom jewellery and Amazon sales to software development for wholesalers. However, she also had to take a break from her work, despite its success, during her pregnancy.

> *In a short time, I made a great profit in the personalised jewellery business. Then the pregnancy started. The most difficult period for me here was pregnancy.*
>
> (US-1)

Similarly, US-4 had her pregnancy in the US during COVID-19, which added additional stress. However, she could also find time to think more about business ideas:

> *I just couldn't decide where to start. I'm also not scared to start a new career here. I could learn something from scratch. It was easy here. I was not in a pessimistic mood thinking that I could not do it, but I could not decide in a short time which would be more beneficial for both me and people.*
>
> (US-4)

Women entrepreneurs found a better environment in the US in which to start a business. Half of the participants' gender roles have changed and they are now the main breadwinner at home (see Alexandre et al., 2019; Senthanar et al., 2021; Sidhva et al., 2021; Mehtap et al., 2019). However, due to pregnancy, two participants had to take a break from their own businesses, bringing a temporary end to its income generation and their health care coverage, consequences that would have been avoided if they had been in full-time employment.

Language skills

Contrary to the literature regarding language barriers, our highly educated participants did not have issues with language in starting their business. They had full or working proficiency in English:

> *Since I have been studying English all my life and I have been teaching English, I did not have difficulty here. And I was ready to do any kind of work. For a certain amount of money, I started mentorship and academic writing support to graduate students who are working on their dissertations.*
>
> (US-5)

Although US-1 had limited working proficiency in English, she also did not have any issues with English. She states,

> *My English was not good, but it was not a barrier for me. I was communicating somehow. On the other hand, I was working to improve my English.*

Language tends to be a significant barrier to job market participation for immigrants in the literature (Lang, 2022). However, in our sample, participants' human capital and education was adequate to support them.

Challenges for entrepreneurship in the US

Legal issues

Although the participants were not fully aware of their rights, they learned that they could start a business, acquire legal documents, and begin working in a respectively short time. However, they encountered challenges in this process. For example, US-5 states,

> *I thought that I could easily find a job with a very small budget to support my family. But after coming here, that is, things are not like that […]. Because I came here as a tourist. The biggest disappointment was learning that I am not allowed to work on a tourist visa.*

The main problem for our participants was the sudden and unexpected nature of their migration. They did not have enough time to obtain appropriate information about their legal status, rights, other paperwork that varied by state, and their entry classification.

Financial sources

Due to the exile, participants lacked adequate planning and social capital in order to move to the US and pursue a business venture. They have little to no financial sources to support their business ideas and some could not get or did not apply for financial support from the government (i.e., SBA) or private organisations. As a result, they had to temporarily take on odd jobs in order to build financial capital:

> *I delivered packages on Amazon to make money for the business. Did many other jobs [...] Then, I opened my own store.*
>
> (US-1)

Financial support is an essential part of business ideas (Owusu et al., 2021). To start a business, the participants needed financial resources. Some sought governmental programmes; however, it was still a challenging. A few participants sold items to help collect enough capital for their business ideas.

Discussion and conclusion

The dynamics of the entrepreneurial behaviour of women asylum seekers in our study connected to previous refugee literature that has identified entrepreneurship as both a necessity and opportunity (Desai et al., 2021; Zighan, 2021). As we discovered, to pursue entrepreneurship, additional obstacles were surfaced regarding limited start-up knowledge and access to resources, including lack of familiarity with the context of a new host country. However, we found that their entrepreneurial motivation and resilience were unique in seeking out a niche in a business that was personally meaningful. For some participants, their pathway was not initially successful as they had to abandon one failed business to pursue another. Yet, they continued their entrepreneurial endeavour by identifying a new start-up opportunity.

Applying the typology of multiple embeddedness, we argue that Turkish women exiles with an accumulation of higher forms of human capital pursued specific forms of entrepreneurial activity that correspond to the following types: mobilisation of homeland resources, qualification transfers, and creative innovation (Harima et al., 2021, pp. 638, 652). Women entrepreneurs in this study sought to develop goods related to their culture, use specific skills based on their education and previous professions, or pursue creative services to benefit the demand of a target market in the host country. As a result, they engaged in agency to find ways to overcome formal labour market obstacles. Entrepreneurship gave them a sense of purpose and enabled them to receive an income. Women in this study demonstrated their knowledgeability and resourcefulness by finding a niche in the market to establish a needed service.

The focus on exiled people, or force migration, is an important contribution to the broader literature on refugees. The 2016 alleged coup attempt in Türkiye intensified the emigration of professionals, as the government cracked down on alleged dissidents. Particularly targeted were individuals affiliated with, or perceived to be supporters of, the Gülen movement, which the government accused of orchestrating the alleged coup attempt. Those standing for democracy, state officials who exposed the government's dirty deeds and corruption, left-leaning intellectuals, and citizens of Kurdish origin were also targeted. Another targeted group was the signatories of the "peace petition" (also known as the "Academics for Peace" which included more than 2,000 scholars in Turkey). The signatories criticised the Turkish government's operations in the Kurdish-majority south-eastern regions and called for a peaceful resolution. After the alleged coup attempt in 2016, many of those signatories faced legal actions, dismissals from their academic positions, and other forms of backlash. As a result, many individuals from various professions sought refuge or employment opportunities abroad to avoid persecution or joblessness.

The population of Turkish exiled individuals had higher human capital which may not be as common among other forms of refugees. The forced migration pattern is different as many refugees often flee to nearby countries that are characterised as "low to middle-income" (UNHCR, 2022, p. 2). In our study, Turkish migrants crossed an international border to relocate to the US, a high-income country. They were, to some extent, able to transfer their human capital based on skill sets adaptable for establishing businesses, the use of social networks, and proficiency in English. Additionally, many had some familiarity with the US or other European countries due to their educational and work experiences abroad prior to the alleged coup attempt. Thus, Turkish individuals' experiences of forced migration may not be as dire as some of the experiences faced by the majority of refugee communities, but we do identify that the urgency of forced migration, temporary loss of status and income, and adjustment to a host country involved trauma, temporary poverty, and general economic insecurity (see Aydiner & Rider 2022).

Limitations and future directions

While this study contributes to the literature through first-hand accounts of women refugee entrepreneurs, a hard-to-reach and small population, the number of participants is small, and the demographics were based on individuals with higher forms of human capital (education and professional skills). Further qualitative and quantitative research would be beneficial to document a wider range of experiences, patterns, and themes drawing on longitudinal data. This could focus on the long-term sustainability and profitability of women refugee entrepreneurs as they become more integrated over time and hone their business skills. Other research could explore the disconnect between previous specialised careers and refugee entrepreneurship and what this means for job satisfaction. The study of women refugees as entrepreneurs is an underexplored area in the literature, and our study provides insights into women refugees' agency.

Acknowledgements

This research was partially supported through Embry-Riddle Aeronautical University's Faculty Innovative Research in Science and Technology (FIRST) Program.

References

Alexandre, L., Salloum, C., & Alalam, A. (2019). An investigation of migrant entrepreneurs: The case of Syrian refugees in Lebanon. *International Journal of Entrepreneurial Behaviour & Research*, *25*(5), 1147–1164. https://doi.org/10.1108/IJEBR-03-2018-0171

Almohammad, D., Durrah, O., & Ahmed, F. (2021). Deciphering the motives, barriers and integration of Syrian refugee entrepreneurs into Turkish society: A SEM approach. *Digital Policy, Regulation and Governance*, *23*(1), 59–76. https://doi.org/10.1108/DPRG-05-2020-0066

American Immigration Council. (2022). *Asylum in the United States*. www.americanimmigrationcouncil.org/research/asylum-united-states

Atasü-Topcuoğlu, R. (2019). Syrian refugee entrepreneurship in Turkey: Integration and the use of immigrant capital in the informal economy. *Social Inclusion*, *7*(4), 200–210. https://doi.org/10.17645/si.v7i4.2346

Aydiner, C., & Rider, E. (2021). Migration policies and practices at job market participation: Perspectives of highly educated Turks in the U.S., Canada and Europe. *International Journal of Sociology and Social Policy*, *42*(5), 399–415. https://doi.org/10.1108/IJSSP-02-2021-0044

Aydiner C., & Rider, E. (2022). Reskilled and integrated, but how? Navigating trauma and temporary hardships. *International Journal of Environmental Research and Public Health*, *19*(20), 136–175. https://doi.org/10.3390/ijerph192013675

Baser, B., & Ozturk, A. (2022). From exit to voice: Reflections on exile through the accounts of Turkey's intelligentsia. *Middle East Critique*, *31*(4), 401–415. https://doi.org/10.1080/19436149.2022.2132193

Billore, S. (2011). Female immigrant entrepreneurship: Exploring international entrepreneurship through the status of Indian women entrepreneurs in Japan. *International Journal of Gender and Entrepreneurship*, *3*(1), 38–55. https://doi.org/10.1108/17566261111114971.

Bjørkhaug, I. (2020). Revisiting the refugee–host relationship in Nakivale refugee settlement: A dialogue with the Oxford Refugee Studies Centre. *Journal on Migration and Human Security*, *8*(3), 266–281. https://doi.org/10.1177/2331502420948465

Brieger, S., & Gielnik, M. (2021). Understanding the gender gap in immigrant entrepreneurship: A multi-country study of immigrants' embeddedness in economic, social, and institutional contexts. *Small Business Economics*, *56*(3), 1007–1031. https://doi.org/10.1007/s11187-019-00314-x

Charmaz, K. (2014). *Constructing Grounded Theory*. Los Angles: Sage.

Datta, A. (2019). Useful and earning citizens? Gender, state, and the market in post-colonial Delhi. *Modern Asian Studies*, *53*(6), 1924–1955. https://doi.org/10.1017/S0026749X18000562

de Graauw, E., & Bloemraad, I. (2017). Working together: Successful policy and program partnerships for immigrant integration. *Journal of Migration and Human Security*, *5*, 105–123. https://doi.org/10.1177/2331502417005001
Dekker, R., & Engberson, G. (2013). How social media transform migrant networks and facilitate migration. *Global Networks*, *14*(4), 401–418. https://doi.org/10.1111/glob.12040
Desai, S., Naudé, W., & Stel, N. (2021). Refugee entrepreneurship: Context and directions for future research. *Small Business Economics*, *56*(3), 933–945. https://doi.org/10.1007/s11187-019-00310-1
DHS. (2020). *Yearbook of immigration statistics 2020*. Retrieved August 17, 2023, from www.dhs.gov/immigration-statistics/yearbook/2020
Femigrants. (2023). *About us*. Retrieved August 19, 2023, from https://femigrants.com/about-us/
Harima, A., Periac, F., Murphy, T., & Picard, S. (2021). Entrepreneurial opportunities of refugees in Germany, France, and Ireland: Multiple embeddedness framework. *International Entrepreneurship and Management Journal*, *17*(2), 625–663. https://doi.org/10.1007/s11365-020-00707-5
Hedberg, C., & Pettersson, K. (2012). Disadvantage, ethnic niching or pursuit of a vision?: Motives of immigrant women care entrepreneurs in the ageing Swedish society. *Journal of International Migration and Integration*, *13*(4), 423–440. https://doi.org/10.1007/s12134-011-0217-1
Hillmann, F., & Toğral Koca, B. (2021). By women, for women, and with women: On the integration of highly qualified female refugees into the labour markets of Berlin and Brandenburg. *Comparative Migration Studies*, *9*(1), 1–18. https://doi.org/10.1186/s40878-020-00211-3
Lang, J. (2022). Employment effects of language training for unemployed immigrants. *Journal of Population Economics*, 35, 719–754. https://doi.org/10.1007/s00148-021-00832-7
Mehtap, S., Ozmenekse, L., & Caputo, A. (2019). I'm a stay at home businesswoman: An insight into informal entrepreneurship in Jordan. *Journal of Entrepreneurship in Emerging Economies*, *11*(1), 44–65. https://doi.org/10.1108/JEEE-10-2017-0080
Mueller, E. (2014). Entrepreneurs from low-skilled immigrant groups in knowledge-intensive industries: Company characteristics, survival and innovative performance. *Small Business Economics*, *42*(4), 871–889. https://doi.org/10.1007/s11187-013-9498-4
Naicker, V., & Nsengimana, S. (2020). Factors that constrains women entrepreneurs in Kigali Rwanda. *Academy of Entrepreneurship Journal*, *26*(2), 1–18. www.abacademies.org/articles/factors-that-constraints-women-entrepreneurs-in-kigali-rwanda-9265.html
Nijhoff, K. (2021). Refugees starting a business: Experiences of barriers and needs in the Netherlands. *Journal of Small Business and Enterprise Development*, *28*(7), 1057–1074. https://doi.org/10.1108/JSBED-09-2020-0314
Owusu, J., Ansah, W. O., Djan, K. O., & Anin, E. K. | Taghizadeh-Hesary, F. (Reviewing editor) (2021) Impact of financial resource building effort on financial resource availability among small and medium enterprises. *Cogent Business &Management*, 8, 1. DOI: 10.1080/23311975.2021.1920676

Sak, G., Kaymaz, T., Kadkoy, O., & Kenanoglu, M. (2018). Forced migrants: Labour market integration and entrepreneurship. *Economics*, *12*(32), 1–13. https://doi.org/10.5018/economics-ejournal.ja.2018-32

Senthanar, S., MacEachen, E., Premji, S., & Bigelow, P. (2021). Entrepreneurial experiences of Syrian refugee women in Canada: A feminist grounded qualitative study. *Small Business Economics*, *57*(2), 835–847. https://doi.org/10.1007/s11187-020-00385-1

Sidhva, D., Zuntz, A. C., al Akash, R., Nashwan, A, & Al-Majali, A. (2021). In exile, the woman became everything: Middle-aged Syrian women's contributions to family livelihoods during protracted displacement in Jordan. *Journal of Humanitarian Affairs*, *3*(1), 4–15. https://doi.org/10.7227/JHA.054

Small Business Administration. (2023). *About SBA*. Retrieved August 17, 2023, from www.sba.gov/

Street, C., Poh, Y., & Al-Dajani, H. (2022). Refugee women business mentors: New evidence for women's empowerment. *Sustainability*, *14*(15), 1–21. https://doi.org/10.3390/su14159154

Stumpf, F., Damelang, A., Abraham, M., Ebensperger, S. (2020). How national institutions shape skilled immigrants' chances of getting hired: Evidence from harmonised factorial surveys with employers in Germany and England. *KZfSS Kölner Z. Für Soziologie und Sozial Psychologie*, *72*, 351–373.

Sweetman, A., McDonald, T., Hawthorne, L. (2015). Regulated occupations and foreign qualification recognition: An overview. *Canadian Public Policy*, *41*, 1–13. www.jstor.org/stable/43697447

Turkish Coalition of America. (2023). *The Turkish American community*. Retrieved August 17, 2023, from www.tc-america.org

Turner, L. (2020). #Refugees can be entrepreneurs too! Humanitarianism, race, and the marketing of Syrian refugees. *Review of International Studies*, *46*(1), 137–155. https://doi.org/10.1017/S0260210519000342

UNHCR. (2020). *What is a refugee?* Retrieved August 25, 2023, from https://unhcr.org/what-is-a-refugee.html

UNHCR. (2022). *Global trends report 2022*. Retrieved August 25, 2023, from www.unhcr.org/global-trends-report-2022

Upwardly. (2023). *About us*. Retrieved August 25, 2023, from www.upwardlyglobal.org/about-us/

van Kooy, J. (2016). Refugee women as entrepreneurs in Australia. *Forced Migration Review*, *53*, 71–73. www.fmreview.org/community-protection/vankooy#:~:text=URL%3A%20https%3A%2F%2Fwww.fmreview.org%2Fcommunity

Wauters, B., & Lambrecht, J. (2008). Barriers to refugee entrepreneurship in Belgium: Towards an explanatory model. *Journal of Ethnic and Migration Studies*, *34*(6), 895–915. https://doi.org/10.1080/13691830802211190

Zighan, S. (2021). Challenges faced by necessity entrepreneurship, the case of Syrian refugees in Jordan. *Journal of Enterprising Communities*, *15*(4), 531–547. https://doi.org/10.1108/JEC-09-2020-0168

8 Towards digital entrepreneurship

Opportunities and challenges for female refugee entrepreneurs in Sweden

Ghazal Zalkat

Introduction

Digitalisation in the business world in the late twentieth and early twenty-first centuries has created opportunities and challenges for entrepreneurship (Baker & Welter, 2020; Bi et al., 2017; Giones & Brem, 2017; Khajeheian, 2013; Troise et al., 2022). These opportunities and challenges are prominent among female entrepreneurs (Kelly & McAdam, 2022; Lechman & Popowska, 2020; McAdam et al., 2020; McAdam et al., 2019; Ughetto et al., 2020) and immigrant entrepreneurs (Anwar & Daniel, 2016; Duan et al., 2020; Evansluong et al., 2023; Melnikova et al., 2019). Moreover, digital tools (DTs) are important for socially marginalised entrepreneurs and under-represented groups of entrepreneurs such as "refugee entrepreneurs" (Georgiou, 2019). DTs provide a competitive advantage and bring improvements to their lives in terms of access to information, communication, e-services, and employment opportunities (Alam & Imran, 2015). Thus, immigrant/refugee entrepreneurs can mitigate barriers using DTs (Evansluong et al., 2023; Strategic Direction, 2023), enabling them to overcome the negative aspects of social marginality (Dy et al., 2017).

Although digital entrepreneurship provides opportunities in promoting successful labour market integration (Evansluong et al., 2023; Melnikova et al., 2019), both refugees and females are under-represented among digital entrepreneurs in the European Union (EU) (The Organization for Economic Co-operation and Development: OECD/EU, 2019). Overall, refugees are slightly less likely to be entrepreneurs than other immigrants as they often face more challenges to entrepreneurship (e.g., they have lower social and financial capital, their legal status and eligibility to work, etc.) (OECD/EU, 2019; The United Nations High Commissioner for Refugees: UNHCR, 2011). It seems that digital barriers could increase traditional barriers to entrepreneurship among those who experience double discrimination, such as females and forced immigrants/refugees (OECD/EU, 2019). These challenges appear when female refugee entrepreneurs (FREs) lack both essential digital skills and digital entrepreneurship role models (OECD/EU, 2019). Thus, DTs could

DOI: 10.4324/9781003368540-10

exclude vulnerable groups such as refugee women from the market (Bueno Doral et al., 2022).

Extant literature highlights that more research is needed to study how entrepreneurs create and do business in this new digitised context, how they effectively use social media technologies, and how they adapt their business processes and practices (Dy et al., 2018; Horst & Murschetz, 2019; Kraus et al., 2019). More research is also needed that focuses on how women use digitalisation and social media in their entrepreneurships (Olsson & Bernhard, 2021). Hence, we do not have sufficient understanding of both phenomenon of female digital entrepreneurship (Kelly & McAdam, 2022) and immigrant digital entrepreneurship (Duan et al., 2020). More specifically, forced immigrant entrepreneurs (refugee entrepreneurs) have been neglected in current research. Thus, this deficiency in research is doubled for FREs as they experience a double disadvantage effect (gender and spatially concentrated deprivation) within the digital context because of intense competition and professional precarity (Georgiou, 2019). In addition, the intersectional matrix of social positions associated with race, ethnicity, and class issues complicates gender issues (Dy et al., 2017). Therefore, both gender and race are detectable and influential in the digital context which reproduce socio-economic resource disparity (Dy et al., 2017).

DTs form enabling or constraining mechanisms for refugee entrepreneurship, and these mechanisms work differently at various levels (individual, technological, or social) based on context (Brown et al., 2022). Hence, Desai et al. (2021) and Zaheer et al. (2019) advocate for digital entrepreneurship research to take a socio-material and digital technology perspective that applies multiple and cross-levels of analysis and embraces ideas and concepts from various disciplines. Using this interdisciplinary perspective may help in explaining this phenomenon of digital entrepreneurship more comprehensively. Similarly, Brown et al. (2022) highlighted the multilevel and multidimensional nature of refugee entrepreneurship which Desai et al. (2021) advocated for. In addition, refugees' entrepreneurship activities are context-specific (OECD/EU, 2019). Thus, if we want to study refugee entrepreneurship in a digital context (or even in any other context), we need to disentangle the multiple and multilevel factors that can affect refugee entrepreneurship by studying the influence of different levels (individual, market, country, and technology) (Desai et al., 2021). For example, at the micro-individual level, refugees' psychological and psychosocial dimensions play an important role in explaining their entrepreneurial activities. While at the macro-institutional level, policies, regulations, and legal and financial institutions are relevant, they affect refugee entrepreneurship directly and indirectly. This has not been examined in the refugee context, which presents an opportunity for potential research (Desai et al., 2021).

This chapter focuses on the intermingling of human, social, and DTs to study how entrepreneurs seize business opportunities in an increasingly digitised context (Nambisan, 2017). Thus, a mixed embeddedness approach

entrepreneurs, they pose extra challenges for refugees (Brown et al., 2022). For example, due to their refugee status, refugees could have some safety and security concerns about using the DTs (e.g., internet). Moreover, refugees' lack of technological and linguistic skills and limited access to internet can impede their business expansion plans (Brown et al., 2022).

Theoretical framework

Both intersectional perspective and mixed embeddedness could provide a better understanding of how FREs use digital techniques in the host countries from micro (individual), meso (business/market), and macro (environment) perspectives (Anwar & Daniel, 2017; Desai et al., 2021).

Intersectionality demonstrates the interconnectedness of the gender and foreignness of FREs (Crenshaw, 1991; Dy et al., 2017) and provides a way to examine the links among social, cultural, and political contexts (Bastia, 2014; Dy & Agwunobi, 2018; Heizmann & Liu, 2020; Pei et al., 2021). Intersectionality shows the interrelation and overlap of different social categories such as gender, class, and ethnicity alongside digital technology (Christensen & Jensen, 2012; Crenshaw, 1991; Webster & Zhang, 2020). According to Collins (2015), intersectionality can be used as an analytical strategy to provide new perspectives on social phenomena. In this study, FREs have different experiences of using DTs because of their intersectional identity as females and as refugees (Crenshaw, 1991, 2005). For example, in the digital context, refugees use their ethnicity as an asset rather than a liability in entrepreneurship (Evansluong et al., 2023). Conversely, digital barriers increase traditional entrepreneurship barriers of FREs; they experience double discrimination as females and as refugees (OECD/EU, 2019). This is consistent with Dy et al. (2017), which indicates that the intersection of social positions of gender, race, and class status influence the FREs, and the digital context reproduces offline inequalities. Thus, this study adopts an intersectional perspective to explain how DTs are embedded in the entrepreneurial activities of FREs.

The mixed embeddedness approach, which has been used to study refugee entrepreneurship, can also be used to explore the gender gap in refugee entrepreneurship (Anwar & Daniel, 2017; Bagwell, 2018; Barberis & Solano, 2018; Brieger & Gielnik, 2021, Meister & Mauer, 2019; Ram et al., 2017). The mixed embeddedness approach matches refugee entrepreneurs' resources to time and place of entrepreneurial opportunities (Kloosterman, 2006). FREs' economic, political, social, and cultural embeddedness, in interaction with their resources, influences their entrepreneurial outcomes. Thus, the mixed embeddedness approach links the micro-individual level (the refugee entrepreneurs' resource structure), and the meso-business level (the opportunity structure) with the macro-environmental level (institutional structures) (Anwar & Daniel, 2017; Deng et al., 2020; Kloosterman, 2010; Kogut & Mejri, 2021; Ojong et al., 2021).

Research methods and data analysis

This study used qualitative data collection and analysis techniques to answer the research question, "how FREs in Sweden perceived and experienced the use of DTs in their businesses". Since FREs are a hard-to-reach population, the study encountered some difficulties while assembling the participant sample. First, female refugees hesitate to allow outsiders to meddle in their affairs as they have often experienced double discrimination (against their gender and foreignness) in the marketplace (Haandrikman & Webster, 2020; Webster & Haandrikman, 2017). Second, refugees are a mixed group regarding their digital skill levels (OECD, 2019). Third, refugees vary significantly in their education, prior business experience, length of residency in Sweden, and business type; making it challenging to identify patterns or themes. Furthermore, because of the difficulty in obtaining employment, refugee women become self-employed (Webster, 2020). They often operate their businesses on a part-time basis mainly because of their family responsibilities.

Sampling

To reach this hard-to-reach population, the study used virtual network sampling (Facebook, Instagram, and websites) with snowball sampling over a three-month period in Sweden. Virtual network sampling was useful in reaching potential participants, while snowball sampling, where research participants identified other potential participants, improved the representativeness of these results (Baltar & Brunet, 2012; Brickman-Bhutta, 2012; Fenner et al., 2014; Gelinas et al., 2017).

The sampling criteria included FREs who have been living in Sweden for less than ten years and use (or have used) digital technology in their businesses. The sample included FREs who used DTs in their business models to produce products/services, manage their customer/partner relationships, and to create value propositions and/or revenue streams (Nambisan et al., 2017; Sahut et al., 2021). Table 8.1 presents the demographic characteristics of the study's participants.

The sample includes 16 FREs coming from different Arabic countries: Syria, Palestine, Iraq, Egypt, Lebanon, and Jorden. They range in age from early twenties to mid-forties and they have a wide range of educational and professional backgrounds. Most of the FREs have one or more children and live in different Swedish cities. According to the typology of digital entrepreneurship (Hull et al., 2007), FREs in this sample belonged to mild and moderate digital entrepreneurship categories. Most of the FREs in the sample used social media for their business where they spot new opportunities in various social media (Van Horne et al., 2016).

Table 8.1 Demographic characteristics of the participants

Interview #	*Age*	*Marital status*[a]	*Country of origin*	*Time in Sweden*	*Level of education*[b]	*Background*	*Entre. Exp*	*Year of establishment*	*Type of business*	*Working part/ full time*
1	29	M	Iraq	9 years	Low	Nurse	No	2021	Cake and candy	Employee
2	26	M	Syria	6 years	Middle	Marketing	No	2020	Art	Entrepreneur, not registered yet
3	34	M	Palestine	6 years	High	Teacher	No	2020	Party planner	Entrepreneurs, SC
4	34	S	Jordan	7 years	High	Teacher	No	2020	Tourism and integration	Employee and entrepreneur, SC
5	21	M	Syria	5 years	Low	Restaurant chef	Yes	2017	Restaurant and catering	Employee/ student/ entrepreneur, SC/LC
6	36	M	Syria	5 years	High	Teacher	No	2019	Education and service center	Student and entrepreneur, SC
7	40	D	Lebanon	9 years	Middle	Beauty services	Yes	2020	Beauty and Spa	Entrepreneur, SC
8	30	M	Syria	6 years	Low	Trade/ marketing	Yes	2017	Boutique	Entrepreneur, SC
9	34	M	Syria	6 years	High	IT engineer	No	2018	Boutique	Entrepreneur, SC
10	30	M	Syria	6 years	High	Architect	No	2020	Beauty cosmetics/ services	Employee and entrepreneur, SC

(*Continued*)

Table 8.1 (Continued)

Interview #	*Age*	*Marital status*[a]	*Country of origin*	*Time in Sweden*	*Level of education*[b]	*Background*	*Entre. Exp*	*Year of establishment*	*Type of business*	*Working part/ full time*
11	22	S	Syria	9 years	High	HR	No	2020	Clothes sales and trading	Student and entrepreneur, SC
12	22	M	Egypt	8 years	High	Dentist	Yes	2020	Cafeteria	Student and entrepreneur, LC
13	33	M	Syria	4 years	High	Trade/ marketing	Yes	2019	Curtains company	Student and entrepreneur, SC
14	33	M	Palestine	6 years	High	Business manager	Yes	2018	Restaurant and catering	Entrepreneur, SC then LC
15	35	M	Palestine	6 Years	High	HR	No	2020	Coffee shop and candy	entrepreneur, SC
16	45	M	Egypt	6 Years	High	Marketing	No	2015	Marketing/ consultancy	Student and entrepreneur, LC

Abbreviations: SC, sole company; LC, limited company.

Notes

a M, married; S, single; D, divorced.

b Education level: Low, fewer than 12 years in school; Middle, 12 years in school; High, university study.

Interviews

Between January and March 2022, 16 in-depth semi-structured interviews were conducted by telephone, online calls, and a workplace visit with the participants who met the eligibility criteria. The interviews began with general questions about the participants' backgrounds, followed by questions focusing on their entrepreneurial experiences, with an emphasis on the opportunities and challenges encountered in using DTs. The interviews were conducted in Arabic, were digitally recorded, and then translated and transcribed into English. The study supplemented interview data with notes taken during the interviews, data from the businesses' websites and social media platforms, and information from Swedish website "allabolag.se".

Data analysis

The study used thematic techniques (Braun & Clarke, 2006) to analyse data. Thematic analysis is suitable for qualitative data (Nowell et al., 2017), involving an iterative process of moving in and out of the data, identifying themes, and coding them (Braun et al., 2019). In this study, the analytical framework combined the micro-individual-level factors of the entrepreneur (resources and various forms of social, financial, and cultural/human capital); the meso-business-level factors associated with the local opportunity structure (market characteristics and product/services demand); and macro-environmental-level factors associated with the host country (the social, economic, political, and institutional environment). The opportunities and challenges were coded according to these three levels by taking into account the intersectional perspective.

Findings

This section reports on FREs' perceived opportunities and challenges according to the micro-individual level, the meso-business level, and the macro-environmental level. This section, where applicable, also points to intersectional identities of female refugees (see Table 8.2).

Opportunities

The micro-individual-level perspective

All the participants in this study are members of under-represented and disadvantaged groups because of their intersectional identity of being female refugees. However, the use of DTs gave FREs more flexibility, self-confidence, and independence in their lives. These opportunities varied depending on their personal, business, and educational backgrounds.

Some FREs in this study used their education and prior business experience advantageously during the entrepreneurial process. A participant who had been an IT engineer in her home country said:

Table 8.2 Opportunities and challenges for FREs in digitising their businesses

Level	*Opportunities*	*Challenges*
Micro-individual level	• Flexibility • Self-confidence • Independence • Semi-anonymity	• Work–life imbalance • Lack of digital knowledge and skills
Meso-market/ business level	• Increase market access • Building network with customers and suppliers • Provide customers services	• Heterogeneous customers base and preferences
Macro-environmental level	• Respond rapidly to sudden market crises • Wide access to policies and regulations	• Bureaucratic regulations and policies • Unethical online behaviours

> *My previous education as an IT engineer helped me to create a website for selling clothes online throughout Sweden. I also started a Facebook page where I display all my products.*
>
> (Interview 9)

The use of DTs in their businesses offered them the opportunity to overcome challenges related to their intersectional identity because of the semi-anonymity that digital platforms provide. Elaborating on this, a female refugee entrepreneur said:

> *When I sell my products online. no one knows where I come from. I don't experience discrimination in the market as a refugee woman.*
>
> (Interview 2)

In addition, DTs allowed mothers who often lack family support for childcare in their host countries to take care of their pre-school children while working from home. A mother with three children said:

> *I am alone here, and I don't have any family to help me with my children, so I decided to work online from home. My online boutique allows me to be at home, have more time to be with my children and manage my business.*
>
> (Interview 8)

The meso-business-level perspective

The participants used digital channels and social media for marketing and building network with customers and suppliers. The participants said that DTs offer a cheap market platform such as websites and social media channels. These technologies were beneficial for the participants with limited financial resources because they were inexpensive, cost-free, or they didn't require a dedicated physical infrastructure. Eight participants operate their online businesses from home, and eight participants conduct their activities at their business sites (e.g., beauty salons and restaurants).

DTs can also be useful tools for FREs who cannot afford to employ people to manage orders, bookings, and other automatable tasks. The participants lacked, at least initially, the funds to hire administrative support. This was emphasised by a participant who owns a beauty salon and spa:

> *I don't have enough resources to hire a secretary to manage the bookings. I have a website where customers can make their own bookings.*
>
> (Interview 7)

DTs, especially social media, also offer networking opportunities for refugees in their host countries. A participant who owns a restaurant and catering service posts cooking videos on YouTube. A participant with a cake and candy business said:

> *When I created my Instagram account – with photos of my homemade cakes – I was surprised by how many people placed orders for my products and services. Because of social media marketing, my customers network has greatly increased.*
>
> (Interview 1)

Similarly, a participant who owns a restaurant said:

> *My YouTube channel has received more than 130.000 views. My Instagram page has 5.000 followers. Online business has given my restaurant a presence among other restaurants. Following this success, I started an online catering business.*
>
> (Interview 14)

The macro-environmental-level perspective

Because DTs provide access to information and other networks, FREs can use them to establish their market presence and to respond rapidly to sudden market crises (e.g., the Covid-19 pandemic). DTs provide access to a wealth of information, online courses, and resources that can enhance business knowledge and skills. A female entrepreneur working with marketing and consultancy services said:

> *I was inspired by the huge amount of information that I could get online which helped me to start my business in marketing and consultancy.*
>
> (Interview 16)

FREs have wide online access to policies and regulations which they could not manage to get easily as they are not familiar with the host country system, and they experienced discrimination situations while asking others about it.

Challenges

The micro-individual-level perspective

Despite the flexible time-and-space opportunities that DTs provide, many FREs suffer from work–life balance stress. This stress stems from long working hours, unreliable childcare arrangements, and, for those working from home, the lack of clear boundaries between work and personal life (Interviews 1, 3, 6, 13). They are also challenged by the constant need to be present on digital channels and platforms and by their lack of digital knowledge and skills required for the optimal use of DTs. FREs with limited experience with DTs sought assistance from friends and family members. While others hired digital technology experts to support them.

The meso-business-level perspective

The diversity in customer preferences and markets creates challenges for FREs. Customers and markets may be local and international, ethnic and nonethnic, and even retail and wholesale. The participants must tailor their online marketing to meet all these customers and market interests. For example, ethnic customers may be less familiar with, and more suspicious of, online marketing compared to nonethnic customers (Interviews 1, 4, 11, 13).

The macro-environmental-level perspective

FREs engaged in international sales face numerous challenges. For example, international sales require the management of complicated logistics and compliance with bureaucratic regulations and policies. In addition, taxes on goods and services vary depending on the international customers and market. FREs lack the information needed to manage international transactions and regulations while using digital marketing. An owner of a beauty cosmetics online boutique mentioned the following:

> *I have many costumers in different countries in EU and I use to make all the marketing, sells and transactions online but sometimes I face many challenges related to different policies and regulations between countries.*
>
> (Interview 10)

Further challenges emerge from the unethical customer behaviour on social media and from the questionable effect of online shopping. An owner for curtains company said that:

> *I have an online boutique and a Facebook group where I sell my curtains. This online business helps me so well, but I face some issues when some people realize who I am and what is my identity as an owner "female refugee", so they start sending bad comments and posting them on my Facebook group. The worst is when they stop trusting my business.*
>
> (Interview 13)

Discussion and implications

This study of FREs in Sweden offers new perspectives on the opportunities and challenges that arise when they use DTs in their businesses. This is an area of entrepreneurship research that requires more attention as many female refugees are seeking greater economic independence and personal growth by operating their own businesses. DTs can level the playing field for FREs, providing them with the tools and resources to overcome challenges and succeed in their businesses. By harnessing the potential of these technologies, female entrepreneurs can enhance their economic independence and contribute to their host communities' growth and development.

By applying the mixed embeddedness approach, combined with intersectionality, this study contributes to refugee entrepreneurship literature from a gender perspective. The study provides FREs' perspectives about challenges and opportunities related to the use of DTs from macro-, meso-, and micro levels. In digital space, these three levels are intimately connected (Desai et al., 2021). This study concludes that the intersection of gender and refugee status impacts DTs challenges and opportunities experienced by FREs.

FREs' utilisation of DTs reveals various noteworthy opportunities for entrepreneurs. All participants highlighted the potential of DTs in fostering the integration of their businesses within the market of their host country. The semi-anonymity provided by digital platforms offers FREs opportunities to integrate into the host country's market increases their market access and supports the ability to provide customers with their services and products without experiencing discrimination related to their intersectional identity. The participants acknowledge that the use of DTs positively impacted their personal growth, by fostering their self-confidence and independence within their entrepreneurial endeavours. Furthermore, DTs simplify and expedite certain automatable tasks, including ordering and booking processes.

The use of DTs helps minimize the disadvantages associated with FREs' intersectional identity such as gender stereotyping and refugeeness. Nevertheless, FREs face challenges in utilising DTs due to their intersectional identity. These challenges include lack of technical knowledge and skills (OECD/EU, 2019), the unethical online behaviour by some customers, and the complexity of managing online marketing and sales to a heterogeneous customer base. Other challenges, less directly related to their intersectional identity, include emotional and physical stress from work–life imbalance, particularly the constant need to maintain a presence on social media platforms.

Effective public policies in entrepreneurship can play a crucial role in overcoming the challenges faced by under represented and disadvantaged entrepreneurs. These entrepreneurs experience challenges and opportunities based on their intersectional identity (i.e., female refugees) when they digitise their businesses. Thus, this study provides policymakers' insights into female refugee entrepreneurship that could help in when recrafting government immigration and integration policies (Honig, 2020). Policymakers, who promote the cultural and economic integration of refugees, can focus on providing more technical support given that FREs face double discrimination while using DTs because of their gender and ethnicity. This study recommends the development of technical skill programmes for new and aspiring FREs with a focus on how to use DTs to create, market, and distribute their products and services. Aligning with OECD/EU initiatives (2019), the study also recommends policymakers to improve digital connectivity, stimulate digital innovation, and strengthen the regulatory environment for digital entrepreneurship.

Conclusions

This chapter contributes to refugee and digital entrepreneurship literature from a gender perspective. It offers an overview of digital entrepreneurship among female refugees in Sweden by highlighting opportunities and challenges at individual, business, and environmental levels. DTs can be used to overcome some of the traditional challenges that FREs experience, such as discrimination. However, they also introduce new challenges such as lack of digital skills, work–life balance, and stress. Some challenges can be managed if education and guidelines on the use of DTs are provided. FREs can benefit from an increased awareness of these opportunities and challenges. The findings can assist policymakers to design appropriate solutions to promote the use of DTs among disadvantaged groups of entrepreneurs who experience challenges and opportunities due to their intersectional identities of being a female and a refugee.

References

AbuJarour, S.A., Wiesche, M., Díaz Andrade, A., Fedorowicz, J., Krasnova, H., Olbrich, S., Tan, C., Urquhart, C., & Venkatesh, V. (2019). ICT-enabled refugee integration: A research agenda. *Communications of the Association for Information Systems*, *44*, 874–891. https://doi.org/10.17705/1CAIS.04440

Alam, K., & Imran, S. (2015). The digital divide and social inclusion among refugee migrants: A case in regional Australia. *Information Technology & People*, *28*(2), 344–365. https://doi.org/10.1108/ITP-04-2014-0083

Alencar, A. (2017). Refugee integration and social media: A local and experiential perspective. *Information, Communication & Society*, *21*(11), 1588–1603. https://doi.org/10.1080/1369118X.2017.1340500

Alencar, A. (2020). Mobile communication and refugees: An analytical review of academic literature. *Sociology Compass*, *14*(8). https://doi.org/10.1111/soc4.12802

Alencar, A., & Tsagkroni, V. (2019). Prospects of refugee integration in the Netherlands: Social capital, information practices and digital media. *Media and Communication*, *7*(2), 184–194. https://doi.org/10.13140/RG.2.2.25033.39524

Anwar, M.N., & Daniel, E. (2016). Entrepreneurial marketing in online businesses: The case of ethnic minority entrepreneurs in the UK. *Qualitative Market Research*, *19*(3), 310–338. https://doi.org/10.1108/QMR-04-2015-0029

Anwar, M.N., & Daniel, E.M. (2017). Ethnic entrepreneurs and online home-based businesses: An exploratory study. *Journal of Global Entrepreneurship Research*, *7*(1), 1–21. https://doi.org/10.1186/s40497-017-0065-3

Bagwell, S. (2018). From mixed embeddedness to transnational mixed embeddedness: An exploration of Vietnamese businesses in London. *International Journal of Entrepreneurial Behavior & Research*, *24*(1), 104–120. https://doi.org/10.1108/IJEBR-01-2017-0035

Baker, T., & Welter, F. (2020). *Contextualizing Entrepreneurship Theory*. New York: Routledge.

Baltar, F., & Brunet, I. (2012). Social research 2.0: Virtual snowball sampling method using Facebook. *Internet Research*, *22*(1), 57–74. https://doi.org/10.1108/10662241211199960

Barberis, E., & Solano, G. (2018). Mixed embeddedness and migrant entrepreneurship: Hints on past and future directions. An Introduction. *Sociologica*, *12*(2), 1–22. https://doi.org/10.6092/issn.1971-8853/8617

Bastia, T. (2014). Intersectionality, migration and development. *Progress in Development Studies*, *14*(3), 237–248. https://doi.org/10.1177/1464993414521330

Bi, R., Davison, R.M., & Smyrnios, K.X. (2017). E-business and fast-growth SMEs. *Small Business Economics*, *48*(3), 559–576. https://doi.org/10.1007/s11187-016-9788-8

Bock, J.G., Haque, Z., & McMahon, K.A. (2020). Displaced and dismayed: How ICTs are helping refugees and migrants, and how we can do better. *Information Technology for Development*, *26*(4), 670–691. https://doi.org/10.1080/02681102.2020.1727827

Braun, V., & Clarke, V. (2006). Using thematic analysis in psychology. *Qualitative Research in Psychology*, *3*(2), 77–101. https://doi.org/10.1191/1478088706qp063oa

Braun, V., Clarke, V., Hayfield, N., & Terry, G. (2019). Thematic analysis. In Liamputtong, P. (Ed.), *Handbook of Research Methods in Health Social Sciences* (pp. 843–860). Singapore: Springer. https://doi.org/10.1007/978-981-10-5251-4_103

Brickman-Bhutta, C. (2012). Not by the book: Facebook as sampling frame. *Sociological Methods & Research*, *41*(1), 57–88. https://doi:10.1177/0049124112440795

Brieger, S.A., & Gielnik, M.M. (2021). Understanding the gender gap in immigrant entrepreneurship: A multi-country study of immigrants' embeddedness in economic, social, and institutional contexts. *Small Business Economics*, 56, 1007–1031. https://doi.org/10.1007/s11187-019-00314-x

Brown, S. & Desire, P. (2020). Entrepreneurs and ICT Technology in the Dzaleka Refugee camp. In Bandi, R.K., Ranjini, C.R., Klein, S., Madon, S., & Monteiro, E. (Eds.), *The Future of Digital Work: The Challenge of Inequality*. IFIPJWC 2020.

IFIP Advances in Information and Communication Technology, vol. 601, pp. 38–49. Cham: Springer.

Brown, S., Hussain, F., & Masoumifar, A.M. (2019). Refugees and ICTs: Identifying the key trends and gaps in peer-reviewed scholarship. In Nielsen, P., Kimaro, H.C. (Eds.), *Information and Communication Technologies for Development: Strengthening Southern-Driven Cooperation as a Catalyst for ICT4D*. ICT4D 2019. IFIP Advances in Information and Communication Technology, vol. 551, pp. 687–697. Cham: Springer. https://doi.org/10.1007/978-3-030-18400-1_56

Brown, S., Saxena, D., & Wall, P.J. (2022). The role of information and communications technology in refugee entrepreneurship: A critical realist case study. *The Electronic Journal of Information Systems in Developing Countries*, *88*(1), e12195. https://doi.org/10.1002/isd2.12195

Bueno Doral, T., Francia Ferrero, R., & García-Castillo, N. (2022). Methodological proposal for an inclusive education: Co-design of a training in digital skills with refugee women. *Human Review/International Humanities Review/Revista Internacional De Humanidades*, *12*(1), 1–12. https://doi.org/10.37467/revhuman.v11.3904

Cesaroni, F.M., & Consoli, D. (2015). Are small businesses able to take advantage of social media?. *Electronic Journal of Knowledge Management*, *13*(4), 257–268. https://academic-publishing.org/index.php/ejkm/article/view/1062

Christensen, A.D., & Jensen, S.Q. (2012). doing intersectional analysis: methodological implications for qualitative research. *NORA - Nordic Journal of Feminist and Gender Research*, *20*(2), 109–125. https://doi.org/10.1080/08038740.2012.673505

Collins, P.H. (2015). Intersectionality's definitional dilemmas. *Annual Review of Sociology*, *41*(1), 1–20. https://doi.org/10.1146/annurev-soc-073014-112142

Crenshaw, K. (1991). Mapping the margins: Intersectionality, identity politics, and violence against women of color. *Stanford Law Review*, *43*(6), 1241–1299. www.jstor.org/stable/1229039

Crenshaw, K. (2005). Mapping the margins: Intersectionality, identity politics, and violence against women of color (1994). In Bergen, R.K., Edleson, J.L., & Renzetti, C.M. (Eds.), *Violence against Women: Classic Papers* (pp. 282–313). Auckland: Pearson Education New Zealand.

Deng, W., Liang, Q., Li, J., & Wang, W. (2020). Science mapping: A bibliometric analysis of female entrepreneurship studies. *Gender in Management*, *36*(1), 61–86. https://doi.org/10.1108/GM-12-2019-0240

Desai, S., Naudé, W., & Stel, N. (2021). Refugee entrepreneurship: Context and directions for future research. *Small Business Economics*, *56*, 933–945. https://doi.org/10.1007/s11187-019-00310-1

Díaz Andrade, A., & Doolin, B. (2016). Information and communication technology and the social inclusion of refugees. *MIS Quarterly*, *40*(2), 405–416. www.jstor.org/stable/26628912

Duan, C., Kotey, B., & Sandhu, K. (2020). Digital entrepreneurship for immigrants: Motivation, strategies, ecosystems, and performance. In K. Sandhu (Ed.), *Leadership, Management, and Adoption Techniques for Digital Service Innovation* (pp. 162–181). Hershey: IGI Global Publisher of Time Knowledge. https://doi.org/10.4018/978-1-7998-2799-3.ch009

Dy, A.M. (2019). Levelling the playing field? Towards a critical-social perspective on digital entrepreneurship. *Futures*, *135*, 102438. https://doi.org/10.1016/j.futures.2019.102438

Dy, A.M., & Agwunobi, A.J. (2018). Intersectionality and mixed methods for social context in entrepreneurship. *International Journal of Entrepreneurial Behavior & Research*, *25*(8), 1727–1747. https://doi.org/10.1108/IJEBR-12-2017-0498

Dy, A.M., Marlow, S., & Martin, L. (2017). A web of opportunity or the same old story? Women digital entrepreneurs and intersectionality theory. *Human Relations*, *70*(3), 286–311. https://doi:10.1177/0018726716650730

Dy, A.M., Martin, L., & Marlow, S. (2018). Emancipation through digital entrepreneurship: A critical realist analysis. *Organization*, *25*(5), 585–608. https://doi.org/10.1177/1350508418777891

Evansluong, Q., Grip, L., & Karayianni, E. (2023). Digital ethnicity affordances: From a liability to an asset in immigrant entrepreneurship. *International Journal of Entrepreneurial Behavior & Research*. https://doi.org/10.1108/IJEBR-02-2022-0207

Fenner, Y., Garland, S.M., Moore, E.E., Jayasinghe, Y., Fletcher, A., Tabrizi, S.N., & Wark, J.D. (2014). Web-based recruiting for health research using a social networking site: An exploratory study. *Journal of Medical Internet Research*, *14*(1), e20. https://doi.org/10.2196/jmir.1978

Gelinas, L., Pierce, R., Winkler, S., Cohen, I.G., Fernandez Lynch, H., & Bierer, B.E. (2017). Using social media as a research recruitment tool: Ethical issues and recommendations. *American Journal of Bioethics*, *17*(3), 3–14. https://doi:10.1080/15265161.2016.1276644

Georgiou, M. (2019). City of refuge or digital order? *Television & New Media*, *20*(6), 600–616. https://doi.org/10.1177/1527476419857683

Giones, F., & Brem, A. (2017). Digital technology entrepreneurship: A definition and research agenda. *Technology Innovation Management Review*, *7*(5), 44–51. https://ssrn.com/abstract=2984542

Greene, A. (2019). Mobiles and 'making do': Exploring the affective, digital practices of refugee women waiting in Greece. *European Journal of Cultural Studies*, *23*(5), 731–748. https://doi.org/10.1177/1367549419869346

Haandrikman, K., & Webster, N.A. (2020). *Migrant, Woman and Business Owner: A Heterogeneous Group with Diverse Needs*. Working Paper 2020:1 Kulturgeografiskt Seminarium. Stockholm University.

Heis, A., & Dannecker, P. (2022). The meaning of being a migrant entrepreneur: An intersectional approach to mixed embeddedness theory. In Faghih, N., & Forouharfar, A. (Eds.), *Contextual Strategic Entrepreneurship Contributions to Management Science* (pp. 95–118). Cham: Springer. https://doi.org/10.1007/978-3-030-86028-8_6

Heizmann, H., & Liu, H. (2020). Bloody Wonder Woman!: Identity performances of elite women entrepreneurs on Instagram. *Human Relations*, *75*(3), 411–440. https://doi.org/10.1177/0018726720979034

Honig, B. (2020). Exploring the intersection of transnational, ethnic, and migration entrepreneurship. *Journal of Ethnic and Migration Studies*, *46*(10), 1974–1990. https://doi.org/10.1080/1369183X.2018.1559993

Horst, S-O., Järventie-Thesleff, R., & Perez-Latre, F.J. (2020). Entrepreneurial identity development through digital media. *Journal of Media Business Studies*, *17*(2), 87–112. https://doi:10.1080/16522354.2019.1689767

Horst, S.-O., & Murschetz, P.C. (2019). Strategic media entrepreneurship: Theory development and problematization. *Journal of Media Management and Entrepreneurship*, *1*(1), 1–26. https://doi.org/10.4018/JMME.2019010101

Hull, C.E., Hung, Y.-T.C., Hair, N., Perotti, V., & DeMartino, R. (2007). Taking advantage of digital opportunities: A typology of digital entrepreneurship. *International Journal of Networking and Virtual Organisations*, *4*(3), 290–303. https://doi.org/10.1504/IJNVO.2007.015166

Kaplan, A., & Haenlein, M.M. (2010). Users of the world, unite! The challenges and opportunities of social media. *Business Horizons*, *53*(1), 59–68. https://doi.org/10.1016/j.bushor.2009.09.003

Kelly, G., & McAdam, M. (2022). Scaffolding liminality: The lived experience of women entrepreneurs in digital spaces. *Technovation*, *118*, 102537. https://doi.org/10.1016/j.technovation.2022.102537

Khajeheian, D. (2013). New venture creation in social media platform: Towards a framework for media entrepreneurship. In Friedrichsen, M., & Mühl-Benninghaus, W. (Eds.), *Handbook of Social Media Management: Media Business and Innovation* (pp 125–142). Berlin Heidelberg: Springer. https://doi.org/10.1007/978-3-642-28897-5_8.

Kloosterman, R. (2006). *Mixed Embeddedness as a Conceptual Framework for Exploring Immigrant Entrepreneurship*. Eurex Lecture No. 8. Amsterdam Institute of Metropolitan and International Development Studies.

Kloosterman, R. (2010). Matching opportunities with resources: A framework for analysing (migrant) entrepreneurship from a mixed embeddedness perspective. *Entrepreneurship & Regional Development*, *22*(1), 25–45. https://doi.org/10.1080/08985620903220488

Kogut, C.S., & Mejri, K. (2021). Female entrepreneurship in emerging markets: Challenges of running a business in turbulent contexts and times. *International Journal of Gender and Entrepreneurship*, *14*(1), 95–116. https://doi.org/10.1108/IJGE-03-2021-0052

Kraus, S., Palmer, C., Kailer, N., Kallinger, F.L. & Spitzer, J. (2019). Digital entrepreneurship: A research agenda on new business models for the twenty-first century. *International Journal of Entrepreneurial Behavior & Research*, *25*(2), 353–375. https://doi.org/10.1108/IJEBR-06-2018-0425

Lechman, E., & Popowska, M. (2020). Enhancing women's engagement in economic activities through information and communication technology deployment: Evidence from Central Eastern European countries. *Gender, Technology and Development*, *24*(3), 314–340. https://doi.org/10.1080/09718524.2020.1824568

McAdam, M., Crowley, C., & Harrison, R.J. (2019). To boldly go where no [man] has gone before—Institutional voids and the development of women's digital entrepreneurship. *Technological Forecasting and Social Change*, *146*, 912–922. https://doi.org/10.1016/j.techfore.2018.07.051

McAdam, M., Crowley, C., & Harrison, R.T. (2020). Digital girl: Cyberfeminism and the emancipatory potential of digital entrepreneurship in emerging economies. *Small Business Economics*, *55*, 349–362. https://doi.org/10.1007/s11187-019-00301-2

Meister, A.D., & Maurer, R. (2019). Understanding refugee entrepreneurship incubation: An embeddedness perspective. *International Journal of Behaviour and Research*, *25*(5), 1065–1092. https://doi.org/10.1108/IJEBR-02-2018-0108

Melnikova, J., Jurgaityte, V., Zaščerinska, J., Aleksejeva, L., Leete, A., Koppel, H., Rohdin, I., & Olsson, A. (2019). Immigrants and asylum seekers' digital entrepreneurship competence: Evaluation of the theoretical framework. In Vasile, K.C., Grünwald, N., & Lobont, L. (Eds.), *9th Balkan Region Conference on Engineering and Business Education (BRCEBE) & 12th International Conference on Engineering and Business Education (ICEBE)* (pp. 408–416). România: Sibiu. ISSN: 1843-6730. https://doi.org/10.2478/cplbu-2020-0047

Michell, D., Szorenyi, A., Falkner, K., & Szabo, C. (2017). Broadening participation not border protection: How universities can support women in computer science. *Journal of Higher Education Policy and Management*, *39*(4), 406–422. https://doi:10.1080/1360080X.2017.1330821

Mohanty, E., & Mishra, A.J. (2020). Understanding the gendered nature of developing country MSMEs' access, adoption and use of information and communication technologies for development (ICT4D). *International Journal of Gender and Entrepreneurship*, *12*(3), 273–295. https://doi.org/10.1108/IJGE-07-2019-0117

Murzacheva, E., Sahasranamam, S., & Levie, J. (2020). Doubly disadvantaged: Gender, spatially concentrated deprivation and nascent entrepreneurial activity. *European Management Review*, *17*(3), 669–685. https://doi.org/10.1111/emre.12370

Nambisan, S. (2017). Digital entrepreneurship: Toward a digital technology perspective of entrepreneurship. *Entrepreneurship: Theory and Practice*, *41*(6), 1029–1055. https://doi.org/10.1111/etap.12254

Nambisan, S., Lyytinen, K., Majchrzak, A., & Song, M. (2017). Digital innovation management: Reinventing innovation management research in a digital world. *MIS Quarterly*, *41*(1), 223–238. www.jstor.org/stable/26629644

Naudé, W., Marchand, K., & Siegel., M. (2017). Migration, entrepreneurship and development: Critical questions. *IZA Journal of Development and Migration*, *6*(5). https://doi.org/10.1186/s40176-016-0077-8

Nobre, H., & Silva, D. (2014). Social network marketing strategy and SME strategy benefits. *Journal of Transnational Management*, *19*(2), 138–151. https://doi.org/10.1080/15475778.2014.904658

Nowell, L.S., Norris, J.M., White, D.E., & Moules, N.J. (2017). Thematic analysis: Striving to meet the trustworthiness criteria. *International Journal of Qualitative Methods*, *16*(1), https://doi.org/10.1177/1609406917733847

OECD. (2019). Policy brief on refugee entrepreneurship. *OECD SME and Entrepreneurship Papers*, No. 14, OECD Publishing, Paris, https://dx.doi.org/10.1787/70571d6f-en

OECD/European Union. (2019). *The Missing Entrepreneurs 2019: Policies for Inclusive Entrepreneurship*. Paris: OECD Publishing. https://doi.org/10.1787/3ed84801-en

Ojong, N., Simba, A., & Dana, L.-P. (2021). Female entrepreneurship in Africa: A review, trends, and future research directions. *Journal of Business Research*, *132*, 233–248. https://doi.org/10.1016/j.jbusres.2021.04.032

Olsson, A.K., & Bernhard, I. (2021). Keeping up the pace of digitalization in small businesses – Women entrepreneurs' knowledge and use of social media. *International Journal of Entrepreneurial Behavior & Research*, *27*(2), 378–396. https://doi.org/10.1108/IJEBR-10-2019-0615

Paoloni, P., Secundo, G., Ndou, V., & Modaffari, G. (2019) Women entrepreneurship and digital Technologies: Towards a research agenda. In Paoloni, P., & Lombardi, R. (Eds.), *Advances in Gender and Cultural Research in Business and Economics*. IPAZIA 2018. Springer Proceedings in Business and Economics. Cham: Springer. https://doi.org/10.1007/978-3-030-00335-7_12

Pappas, M.A., Papagerasimou, Y., Drigas, A., Raftopoulos, D., & Nikolaidis, P. (2017). ICT-based innovation and employability for women. *International Journal of Engineering Pedagogy*, *7*(2), 36–47. https://doi.org/10.3991/ijep.v7i2.6758

Pei, X., Chib, A., & Ling, R. (2021). Covert resistance beyond# Metoo: Mobile practices of marginalized migrant women to negotiate sexual harassment in the workplace. *Information, Communication & Society*, 1–18. https://doi.org/10.1080/1369118X.2021.1874036

Pergelova, A., Manolova, T., Simeonova-Ganeva, & Yordanova. (2019). Democratizing entrepreneurship? Digital technologies and the internationalization of female-led SMEs. *Journal of Small Business Management*, *57*(1), 14–39. https://doi.org/10.1111/jsbm.12494

Rajahonka, M., & Villman, K. (2019). Women managers and entrepreneurs and digitalization: On the verge of a new era or a nervous breakdown? *Technology Innovation Management Review*, *9*(6), 14–24. https://doi.org/10.22215/TIMREVIEW/1246

Ram, M., Jones, T., & Villares-Varela, M. (2017). Migrant entrepreneurship: Reflections on research and practice. *International Small Business Journal*, *35*(1), 3–18. https://doi.org/10.1177/0266242616678051

Ritchie, H.A. (2022). An institutional perspective to bridging the divide: The case of Somali women refugees fostering digital inclusion in the volatile context of urban Kenya. *New Media and Society*, *24*(2), 345–364. https://doi.org/10.1177/1461444821106318

Sahut, J.-M., Iandoli, L., Teulon, F. (2021). The age of digital entrepreneurship. *Small Business Economics*, *56*(3), 1159–1169. https://doi.org/10.1007/s11187-019-00260-8

Strategic Direction. (2023). Diversity quandary: Making ethnicity and diversity a competitive advantage in the entrepreneurial digital age. *Strategic Direction*, *39*(5),1–2. https://doi.org/10.1108/SD-03-2023-0046

Swartz, E.M., Scheepers, C.B., & Toefy, T. (2022). Women entrepreneurs' opportunity identification of digital platform start-ups: Emerging evidence from South Africa. *International Journal of Gender and Entrepreneurship*, *14*(3), 352–374. https://doi.org/10.1108/IJGE-06-2021-0096

Troise, C., Ben-Hafaïedh, C., Tani, M.Y., & Yablonsky, S.A. (2022). Guest editorial: New technologies and entrepreneurship: Exploring entrepreneurial behavior in the digital transformation era. *International Journal of Entrepreneurial Behavior and Research*, *28*(5), 1129–1137. https://doi.org/10.1108/IJEBR-08-2022-999

Udwan, G., Leurs, K., & Alencar, A. (2020). Digital resilience tactics of Syrian refugees in the Netherlands: Social media for social support, health, and identity. *Social Media + Society*, *6*. https://doi.org/10.1177/2056305120915587

Ughetto, E., Rossi, M., Audretsch, D., & Lehmann, E.E. (2020). Female entrepreneurship in the digital era. *Small Business Economics*, *55*(2), 305–312. https://doi.org/10.1007/s11187-019-00298-8

UNHCR. (2011). *UNHCR Resettlement Handbook*. Geneva: United Nations High Commissioner for Refugees.

Van Horne, C., Dutot, V., & Zhang, Y. (2016). Young entrepreneurs and the digital space: Case studies from the UAE. *International Journal of Business and Management Studies*, *5*(2), 293–300. https://ssrn.com/abstract=2892236

Vasileiadou, E. M., & Missler-Behr, M. (2011). Virtual embeddedness and social media as a basis for the relational capital management of new ventures. *The Electronic Journal of Knowledge Management*, *9*(3), 188–203. https://academic-publishing.org/index.php/ejkm/article/view/932

Veronis, L., Tabler, Z., & Ahmed, R. (2018). Syrian refugee youth use social media: Building transcultural spaces and connections for resettlement in Ottawa, Canada. *Canadian Ethnic Studies*, *50*(2), 79–99. https://doi.org/10.1353/ces.2018.0016

Wang, Y., & Warn, J. (2018). Chinese immigrant entrepreneurship: Embeddedness and the interaction of resources with the wider social and economic context. *International Small Business Journal*, *36*(2), 131–148. https://doi.org/10.1177/0266242617726364

Webster, A.N. (2020). Migrant women entrepreneurs and emotional encounters in policy fields. *Emotion, Space and Society*, *37*, 100730. https://doi.org/10.1016/j.emospa.2020.100730

Webster, N.A., & Haandrikman, K. (2017). Thai women entrepreneurs in Sweden: Critical perspectives on migrant small businesses. *Women's Studies International Forum*, 60, 17–27. https://doi: 10.1016/j.wsif.2016.11.001

Webster, N.A., & Zhang, Q. (2020). Careers delivered from the kitchen? Immigrant women small-scale entrepreneurs working in the growing Nordic platform economy. *Nordic Journal of Feminist and Gender Research*. https://doi.org/10.1080/08038740.2020.1714725

Zaheer, H., Breyer, Y., & Dumay, J. (2019). Digital entrepreneurship: An interdisciplinary structured literature review and research agenda. *Technological Forecasting and Social Change*, *148*, 119735. https://doi.org/10.1016/j.techfore.2019.119735

Section 3

The personal, economic, and social value of refugee entrepreneurship

This section concentrates on the value and impact of refugee entrepreneurship (RE) at the micro (personal) and meso/macro (economic and social) levels. The three chapters illustrate the significance of RE in the host countries in which they settled and answer the 'why' question of needing to invest in refugee entrepreneurship.

In Chapter 9, Junaid and Jurado demonstrate the interconnectedness between well-being, entrepreneurship, and social integration. By examining enablers and disenablers of RE in New Zealand, the authors contribute by demonstrating the symbiotic nature of entrepreneurship and well-being.

Ramachandran et al. (Chapter 10) focus on 'refugee economies' and elaborate on the productive role that refugee entrepreneurs play in the informal economy of South Africa. The authors explain that refugee entrepreneurs generate employment and conduct other economic activities linked to local production and distribution systems which generate multiple, positive spinoff effects.

Schemschat's chapter (Chapter 11) outlines the long-term impact of RE and how civic action and (social) entrepreneurship can contribute to urban revitalisation. In examining the case of the US city of Akron (Ohio), which had undergone a large-scale deindustrialisation resulting in urban decline, the author demonstrates the role of refugee entrepreneurs and their businesses, in conjunction with local policies, social networks, and do-it-yourself practices, can drive local development and community revitalisation.

DOI: 10.4324/9781003368540-11

9 Well-being, entrepreneurship, and the social integration of women refugee entrepreneurs

Fatima Junaid and Tanya Jurado

Introduction

The relationship between well-being and entrepreneurship is ambivalent (Ryff, 2019). On the one hand, entrepreneurship can provide refugee women with financial independence, economic empowerment, and the ability to support themselves and their families while contributing to their communities and wider economy (Abebe, 2023; International Monetary Fund, 2018). This can have a positive impact on their well-being, providing a sense of purpose and self-worth as they seek to integrate into a new country. On the other hand, entrepreneurship can also create stress and financial insecurity, which negatively impact on well-being (Wiklund et al., 2019). Furthermore, many refugee women already face challenges when engaging with entrepreneurship and come from highly patriarchal societies where becoming independent challenges traditional, rigid gender roles. They may also have experienced prior trauma which makes it difficult for them to deal with stress (Hajdukowski-Ahmed et al., 2009). However, concepts such as defiance in terms of traditional gender norms and stereotypical refugee expectations in the context of refugee entrepreneurship and well-being are under-researched areas (Al-Dajani et al., 2019).

Our research motivation is to understand the role of entrepreneurship as a vehicle to support women refugees' integration into society and its positive impact on their well-being. The research question framing this study is: What is the role of personal well-being in the entrepreneurship journey of refugee women and how does entrepreneurship influence their well-being? We explore factors that enable and disenable refugee women in their entrepreneurial endeavours in Aotearoa New Zealand (NZ). This study intersects several fields of research: migrant and refugee entrepreneurs, women entrepreneurs, and well-being and entrepreneurship (Al-Dajani, 2022). Moreover, our research aligns with the NZ government's refugee settlement strategy which has self-sufficiency, participation, and well-being as key goals (Immigration New Zealand, 2022a). The study also aligns with the United Nations' Sustainable Development Goals (SDG 8): the decent work for economic growth (United Nations, 2023). Similarly, with the exacerbated consequences of COVID-19,

DOI: 10.4324/9781003368540-12

this study's findings provide insights regarding the well-being of a vulnerable population and the support needed to improve their economic outcomes.

Refugee entrepreneurship

Refugee entrepreneurship has been defined as "entrepreneurial activity undertaken in a new host country by individuals who are forcibly displaced from their homes due to war, conflict, and persecution" (Abebe, 2023, pp. 315–316). Having engaged in considerable risk to flee their countries, refugees are no strangers to risk and identifying opportunities, aspects of entrepreneurial behaviour that have implications for long term involvement in entrepreneurship (Alvarez & Barney, 2014). A major motivation for refugees to engage in entrepreneurship is to escape from the constraints of their situation, where challenges such as poor language skills and racism impede their access to employment (Desai et al., 2021; Jones et al., 2014).

Recent studies confirm the negative role that racism plays in excluding immigrant/refugee entrepreneurs from parts of the economy (de Vries et al., 2021; Ram et al., 2022; Refai & McElwee, 2022).

When engaging in entrepreneurship, refugee entrepreneurs face challenges that are common to other entrepreneurs, namely, accessing capital, building human capital, capabilities, and potentially scaling up (Organisation for Economic Co-operation and Development: OECD, 2019). In addition to these challenges, refugees are encumbered by discrimination, skill mismatch, and limited access to markets (Pécoud, 2002). They also encounter language difficulties, lack of networks, and face greater difficulties than other entrepreneurs in accessing finance and navigating institutions in the new home country (Wauters & Lambrecht, 2008). Providing support to entrepreneurs in general, and to women refugee entrepreneurs in particular, can lead to higher levels of perceived self-confidence and self-efficacy, which in turn can increase their well-being and integration into the new country (Benight & Bandura, 2004; Marchand & Dijkhuizen, 2018). Further, the benefits of entrepreneurship for the integration of refugees have been linked to building social capital (Bizri, 2017), developing skills, and exposure to the host country's culture (Alrawadieh et al., 2021; OECD, 2019). In contrast, self-employment by refugees has been criticised because it remains too focused on their ethnic communities, and not the wider community. Finally, it is important to note that umbrella terms such as 'refugee entrepreneurs' mask the diversity of refugees which has important implications for social and human capital and concomitant consequences for their entrepreneurial journey and their well-being (Collins, 2021).

Women refugee entrepreneurship

Women refugee entrepreneurship is a subset of two domains of the entrepreneurship literature: migrant/refugee entrepreneurship and women entrepreneurship. The themes that emerge from the migrant/refugee entrepreneurship literature, identify that typically, refugee entrepreneurs operate in low-value market sectors (Ram et al., 2022) and that entrepreneurship is a vehicle to autonomy and financial independence (Sandberg et al., 2019). As with women entrepreneurs, in general, refugee women regain their sense of self-worth through entrepreneurship as they become self-sufficient and can support others within their family units. Being independent enhances self-worth, resourcefulness, and the chances of better social integration (Huq & Venugopal, 2021). Thus, entrepreneurial pursuits help to improve well-being if women find meaning in their entrepreneurial endeavours, which can not only serve to provide a livelihood but also provide an intrinsic drive to become socially included and economically independent (Dijkhuizen, 2019).

As entrepreneurs, woman refugees can recreate themselves in this new role and this contributes to integration through enhanced well-being and social economic status, even though gendered constraints add to difficulties accessing entrepreneurial resources (Adeeko & Treanor, 2022). Many refugee women come from highly patriarchal societies where becoming independent women may be challenging their gender roles (Habash & Omata, 2022; Vershinina & Discua Cruz, 2021). These aspects do not operate in isolation, that is, better financial independence and well-being contribute to the promotion of social inclusion and the breaking down of barriers between refugees and the wider community (United Nations Development Program, 2022).

Existing research has focused on refugee women's well-being (Shishehgar et al., 2017), entrepreneurship and well-being (Ryff, 2019), and refugee entrepreneurship (Freiling & Harima, 2019). However, the literature focusing on refugee women entrepreneurs and their well-being is sparce (Dijkhuizen, 2019). Refugee women face a unique set of challenges in resettlement and integration into their host countries (Mangrio et al., 2019). These challenges can include cultural differences, language barriers, limited access to resources and support networks, discrimination, and limited access to financial capital. These barriers can have a negative impact on their well-being, making it difficult for them to achieve social inclusion and settlement. Studies have identified examples of refugee resilience through their involvement with their own entrepreneurial ventures (Yeshi et al., 2022). Yet, most refugee integration studies are gender blind or generalise findings by considering refugee women as a homogenous group (Crawley, 2022). We note that ethnocentric assumptions about non-Western communities can also impede the capture of contextual entrepreneurial behaviour such as that of women refugees (Muñoz & Kimmit, 2018). Furthermore, for refugee women, context plays an important part (Desai et al., 2021; Welter, 2011; Wiklund et al., 2019) and there is a need for a context-related understanding of the dynamics of refugee settlement, one focusing on refugee women and their experiences (Habash & Omata, 2022).

Well-being and entrepreneurship

There is limited literature relating well-being and entrepreneurship in the context of self-employed refugee women (Dijkhuizen, 2019). Self-employed refugee women experience the tension of being financially sustainable when operating on their own in a financially constrained situation while having to contend with the competitive pressures from the external product and factor markets. These challenges can either enhance or deplete their well-being. It is the paradox of refugee entrepreneurship that it leads to financial sustainability that helps well-being, but also places demands on the entrepreneur's emotional, physical, mental resources which can undermine their wellbeing (Atalay & Tanova, 2022). Further, refugee entrepreneurship is often driven by necessity to enable the entrepreneur to advance personal goals, family security, and personal growth. For women, this necessity is also an opportunity to alleviate their circumstances and improve their living conditions and independence (Al-Dajani & Marlow, 2010). Entrepreneurial activity provides a sense of agency and independence that allows them to play a role in the community and increase their well-being (Alrawadieh et al., 2021). Although there is cause to believe that well-being can play a significant role in entrepreneurial outcomes (Ryff, 2019), there has been little research into well-being and refugee entrepreneurs. Although there has been progress in the study of entrepreneurial well-being, there is still room for more and context-specific research (Stephan et al., 2022).

Ryff's Psychological Well-Being (PWB) model (Ryff, 1989) provides a comprehensive framework for understanding the multidimensional aspects of eudaemonic well-being. The model consists of six dimensions: autonomy, environmental mastery, personal growth, positive relationships, purpose in life, and self-acceptance (Ryff, 1989). Each dimension contributes to the overall experience of well-being. In the context of refugee women entrepreneurship, Ryff's PWB model can be used to understand how entrepreneurship and well-being are symbiotic, given that entrepreneurial activity can include well-being dimensions such as a sense of purpose, mastery, and autonomy. At the same time, the experience of entrepreneurship and success can contribute to an individual's sense of self-acceptance and personal growth (Ryff, 2019).

In drawing from these three domains of literature discussed earlier (migrant/refugee entrepreneurship, women entrepreneurship, and well-being), our project explores the factors that enable and disenable refugee women in their entrepreneurial endeavours in Aotearoa NZ, with special consideration to the role of their personal well-being in their entrepreneurship journey. Entrepreneurship and its interplay with well-being can become a means for refugee women's social integration and cohesion within the larger community, and these are areas that need to be researched (Khademi et al., 2022). In the context of this study, the NZ government identifies the following attributes as important aspects of social integration: *belonging* – a sense of being part of the community, trust in others and respect for law and human rights; *inclusion* – equity of opportunities and outcomes in work, income, education, health, and housing; *participation* – involvement in social and community activities and in political and civic life; *recognition* – valuing diversity and respecting differences; and *legitimacy*– confidence in public institutions (Immigration New Zealand, 2022a).

Methodology

The starting point of this research was our own life experience as two women who have experienced migration. One of the authors has a family history of displacement from rural to urban areas, an event that changed the course of her paternal family forever, leaving behind a way of life that could not be replicated in the big city. This is analogous to refugees who come to host countries that are very different to their own lived experiences and must readapt and develop new skills if they are to thrive. The other author of this research is a Pakistani migrant, who is settled in NZ along with her family and has close links to other migrants in her community from all walks of life, including refugees. She comes from the part of Pakistan which shares a long border with Afghanistan that had the largest number of Afghans as refugees.

This study takes a qualitative, interpretative approach to account for the complex make-up of the refugee population of NZ in which this study is embedded (Drakopoulou-dodd et al., 2014). In NZ, between 1987 and 2017, 750 refugees came every year, until in 2018 when the refugee quota was increased to 1,000, and then further increased to 1,500 in 2020 (Immigration New Zealand, 2022a). The main nationalities that have settled in NZ in the last five years come from Myanmar, Pakistan, Syria, Colombia, Afghanistan, Palestine, Eritrea, Bhutan, and Somalia (Immigration New Zealand, 2022b).

Taking reflexivity and the diversity of the refugee population into account, we ask 'how and why' questions to collect rich data (Bryman, 2004). How and why did refugee women undertake the entrepreneurial journey and what are their reflections on what enabled or hindered them at various stages of this journey? How did this impact on their sense of well-being? Data were collected via semi-structured interviews with eight key informants (KIs) who worked in community non-government organisations (NGOs) supporting refugees. The KIs were in Auckland, Wellington, Christchurch, and Dunedin. Two were men, and the rest were women. Four of our KIs were former refugees, and they were in a vulnerable position due to experiencing trauma and hardships. These sensitivities required a period of trust and relationship-building to establish reciprocity between researchers and informants. The other four key informants were not former refugees, and we were aware that they inferred motivation and behaviours in others. For both groups it was imperative that we were clear with them as to our motivations and objectives and only proceeded to interviews when they were comfortable with the interview process. Following Māori traditions in NZ, we also included *koha* (a small offering) as a token of reciprocity and respect.

Data were analysed using a thematic technique by identifying first-order and then second-order codes (Gioia et al., 2013). We used narrative tools (Ahl & Marlow, 2012) to analyse transcripts of interviews to understand how women refugee entrepreneurs experienced their entrepreneurial journey in terms of their well-being. Our analysis focused on how participants perceived their experiences and was conducted by the authors, with one having expertise in entrepreneurship and the other having expertise in well-being. The analysis was iterative with transcriptions to extract as much insight as possible. Each researcher analysed the transcripts for themes, and we cross-checked with each other to synthesise emerging themes. The first-order codes included themes that emerged from the participants. These themes included sense of belonging, financial imperative, view of the host country as home, building on what they already know, community support, language barriers, access to resources, family obligations, home country cultural barriers, and concerns over social welfare dependency. These themes were organised into second-order categories using the framework on well-being and entrepreneurship as a theoretical basis. We report on these findings in the following section.

Findings

Key themes identified through our interviews fell into the broad categories of enablers and disenablers. We further grouped the disenablers into challenges to start a business and cultural challenges.

Enablers

Motivations for becoming entrepreneurs

The women who did start a business had self-belief in their ability to deliver the service or product in common. Their businesses were rooted in traditional domestic settings, such as cooking, sewing, and hairdressing. KIs reported that women who had been active in their home country were more likely to transfer those entrepreneurial activities to NZ. Faced with barriers that inhibit their activities, women resorted to other avenues:

> *You revert to[...] your small business [...] you have the skill set, and if I think of one particular sister, she has the knowledge base around spices and groceries from back home. She started the importation business, so building on the skills that they have got from back home.*
>
> (Jasmine)[1]

KIs observed that women combined self-belief with their social capital. In one case, the entrepreneur had undertaken tertiary studies which gave her some degree of agency, but was also able to see opportunities in what an everyday domestic activity in her home country is:

> *She studied [at university] for a couple of years and [...] she does braids. One of her dreams is to have her hairdress[ing salon] and [serve people] who like their braids in their hair. And she manifested it as a hobby, but she needs to generate income [...] through something that she likes and that she feels has the talent and that she is good at it.*
>
> (Cynthia)

For many refugee women, their previous skills and experiences, such as cooking, stitching, or running businesses in their home countries, often form the foundation for their entrepreneurial ventures in the host country:

> *Many [...] were also doing some form of small business back home. Helping out in family businesses [...] or something that they had initiated themselves, such as restaurants, stores or crafts [...] they had that experience back home, and if they spent time in refugee camps [...], they would set up little shops there as well.*
>
> (Jasmine)

Women's entrepreneurship is driven by the need to support their families financially when they face limited job opportunities due to language barriers, lack of experience, and cultural differences. Often the catalyst is a financial crisis or ongoing family commitments with the home country family members:

> *What motivates them [are] financial benefits because [...] making something on the side financially starting from home [...] helps the family income, and [...] if there's demand there's growth [...] you're able to branch out into renting a smaller shop or smaller space.*
>
> (Jasmine)

Resilience and determination

KIs reported on the resilience they noted in the women refugee entrepreneurs and their ability to persevere despite the challenges they have endured and emphasised their determination to overcome obstacles and succeed in entrepreneurship:

> *I think mentally they keep on [...] they don't want it to stop [...] they're very resilient [...] that resilience keeps them going [...] They had up and down at the beginning and at the end are very successful.*
>
> (Jane)

This resilience is manifested by the innate strength of the women. They can act and defy any challenges that come their way because they are grounded in the community, in particular in the initial stages of the entrepreneurial journey:

> *They don't want it to stop because they're very resilient. By the way, you know, those refugee community [...] they are kind of open minded, and hope that things will get better, and I think that resilience keeps them going.*
>
> (Jane)

Being resilient went beyond past traumas or language difficulties; it also meant overcoming the deficit connotation of the 'refugee' label and deploying their other capabilities. They are determined to realise their aspirations:

> *The title refugee can sometimes be perceived [...]in a deficit context [...] They have their own intelligence and their own right [...] Nothing has got in their way; they are so determined [...] very motivated. They have aspirations. They want something more for themselves and for their children as well.*
>
> (Jasmine)

Our KIs mentioned that entrepreneurship provides a way for women to connect with others and break out of isolation. This has mental health benefits:

> *Obviously if you get to work then you are not as depressed because you can get out of the house. You're communicating with people. And also, you're not so anxious about the bills? Like winter is coming. If they're not working that depressed and they're also anxious that you know The Unknown.*
>
> (Susan)

> *It's also important to mention [...] for wellbeing, so sitting at home, women just thinking, oh, what am I going to do? And what I'm not going to do. So, in a way this is quite healing, too, if they can set up something small.*
>
> (Jasmine)

The role of community and family networks

The KIs mention the importance of community support for refugee women's business endeavours. Community NGOs were crucial in helping to pave the way for capacity building in both the formal and informal aspects of business, enabling refugee women in their entrepreneurship journey. First, NGOs are supporting in establishing a formal enterprise. Second, NGOs provide assistance in working with their social capital networks, especially for funding, which included family and communities based overseas:

> *If you're going to move from your home [...] into hiring or renting a place [...] you've got to formalise it [...] you have to have the structures [...] the Council certification. You need [...] funds [...]. One thing I like about our refugee communities is their networks [are] spread globally so they can draw*

> *on funds [...] the banks are [not] going to give you a loan because you're a beneficiary. So, I might have my mother or somebody living in the States, who will be able to loan me that money, or even give that money.*
>
> (Jasmine)

The support also came from children who grow up within the system, as the second generation help their mothers and families. Peer support within the community is an important factor that plays a role in empowering women, sharing knowledge and experiences, and learning from others who have succeeded in entrepreneurship.

Empowerment and participation

KIs reported that women refugee entrepreneurs felt validated and empowered as they were both receiving support and contributing to ethnic and wider community through their businesses. This gave them a sense of purpose which enabled their self-belief to try new things, as well as bolstering their sense of autonomy and belonging:

> *One of the reasons is the issue of autonomy [...] Somehow, they validate themselves as active members of the community, not as passive members, not as guests, but by feeling like a productive entity within society [...] Here [in NZ] they realised that because of the need to have economic autonomy, to want to feel more part of the community, they discovered certain potentialities that they had.*
>
> (Philip)

Entrepreneurship enabled women to actively participate in the community (as customers) and act as cultural ambassadors through their service provision to the wider community:

> *I have learnt so much about them and buy from them. I love that without travelling you get exposed to so much.*
>
> (Jasmine)

> *It's through the networks that they're able to take orders. So, you know this one's (lady) very good at Middle East, and [...] another Pakistani. So, there's quite a few of those ones, too, operating from home, and then, I think, on a smaller scale. Catering from home, Mehndi (henna), tailoring from home, another does this calligraphy, not to a large scale [...] as the community grows, I'm talking about the Muslim community, the demand for groceries, clothing grows, and so people have their networks back home, so they're able to import and set up, and they could be selling from home as well.*
>
> (Jasmine)

Peer support within the community is an important factor that plays a role in empowering women, sharing knowledge and experiences, and learning from others who have succeeded in entrepreneurship. Community support plays a crucial role in enabling refugee women to pursue entrepreneurship, which provides them with empowerment and agency. Based on KIs' information, we noticed that in places like Auckland, where there are bigger communities of refugees, there was a bigger client base to start a business informally, whereas in Christchurch, the women didn't have a big client base and therefore struggled more in their entrepreneurial endeavours. The KIs mentioned that the support provided by communities of the refugees in navigating the challenges of starting businesses in a new country often enables the refugee women in building relationships and connections and in overcoming obstacles.

> *My young and other young ones, the mothers, the youth, we have trained them. We want them to be the leaders in community and now they're becoming leaders in community. You know, I want to go in advocacy. Mothers have leadership. They can run any initiatives. So, I know now that I can go in advocacy and, you know, I'm contacting political leaders. I am lobbying. And I'm working with the educated youth. To be advocates in political decisions. I have learned that. For us to be able to do things we have to get to the decision makers, I have learned this in the last 22 years.*
>
> (Felicity)

> *And my work is worth it, because the time I spend making this bread that you're eating now, has its price and here people pay for it. So, from there I also said wow. And yes, she is a person who also has a history of refuge, former refugee, but she also felt very empowered, and it was like look, my work is worth, and we are in New Zealand, we are not in Chile.*
>
> (Cynthia)

Disenablers

Challenges overlapping gender, settlement, finance, and capability

KIs identified overlapping challenges that former refugees faced when starting and running a business which could also hinder their ability to establish formal, as opposed to informal, businesses. These included language, childcare, mobility, housing costs, financial constraints, and tech issues:

> *They can only do [business] within the school hours [...] that really limits them. The other thing that limits them is transport. They [...] want to learn English because language is a big barrier [...] but they also want to work a couple of days or three days because they are struggling with the bills [...] Housing prices [...] are so expensive [...] finding the house is very difficult [...] and the rent is very high. So, we basically struggle even for them to have basic needs like a*

> *warm home [...]. They're not very tech savvy because they don't even know how to use an EFTPOS machine [...]. They only have Facebook to stay in touch with family [...] they don't know Trademe or Marketplace.*
>
> (Susan)

Supporting women through basic resettlement processes had a toll on those who support the former refugees, leaving them feeling isolated:

> *But what makes it a bit challenging [...]is knowing the New Zealand system of running the small business like You've got to have an account, and [...] you have to have the health certificate and all that.*
>
> (Jasmine)

Fear and trauma

The KIs recognised that fear and trauma from their experiences in their home countries can impact refugee women's confidence and motivation to start businesses. They mentioned that past authoritarian regimes and oppressive environments contribute to their apprehension and fear of authority figures, but that encouragement can make all the difference in their sense of agency:

> *If I think of the first generation, [they] have come with trauma* (Jasmine).
>
> *These women, they are scared. They came from dictatorship countries [...] over there, if a person makes a mistake, they would kill them or put them in a prison [...] So, if they get [...] encourage[ment]either the Government or the NGOs or a private person [...] they can do very good, very good, very good work. They are hard workers.*
>
> (Andrew)

Inadequate assistance in entrepreneurship

The challenges faced by women in starting and formalising their businesses point towards a lack of support from government agencies or NGOs and the need for resources, such as funding and training. One KI explained the resettlement strategy in NZ focuses on settling from a human rights perspective, and there is no explicit focus on entrepreneurship.

> *The resettlement focuses on good settlement and connect[ing] to the people [...] It's not about the business. So, connecting to people means schools, health, the marae, the iwi. And not job. So, one of the things that we do is to help the refugee to get jobs.*
>
> (Andrew)

Some women took several years to gain the confidence and empowerment necessary to expand their businesses concentrating on their immediate communities:

The community here is much smaller […] Wellington and Auckland [are] bigger and their businesses are […] for their own community. So yes, they're only making commodities for their own communities because it's so much easier. They know the community […]. It is more like people are looking for you rather than her looking for people.

(Susan)

The community […] is young less than 7 years that refugees have been coming here, this might the reason why there are no entrepreneur women that I know of.

(Lilian)

KIs pointed out that some assistance was inadequate or lacking, including technology orientation along aside the language assistance. As explained by Jasmine, language is a barrier and assistance is required to learn the language. For others even well-intentioned policies, such as a government grant available to refugee entrepreneurs, were not on target:

I had experience with refugees when I worked in [NGO] from doing […] projects that give them 10,000 dollars to […] start [their] own company. [It] was very cumbersome […] and it was a little discriminatory for them to do the whole process.

(Margaret)

Polices are sometimes issued in isolation without taking the whole context into account. In this case, the mental health context assistance was needed to enable women to be entrepreneurial and access the government support:

I went to teach them entrepreneurship classes […]. The issue is when there is no mental [health] support [..] They are good leaders in their commune, but because of these mental problems they cannot arise […]. The truth is that they do have a lot of help from the government, but they don't know how to handle that help […]. You can give a lot of money to a person […] and that person won't be able to emerge because they're not going to know how to use it.

(Margaret)

I find that the country is very maternalistic or paternalistic with refugees, but of bad parenting […]. The government should give them a service that helps them understand the system here, because if not all their lives they will be refugees and they will not live what it is to live here

(Margaret)

There are mixed feelings on how agencies, service providers, and both ethnic and non-ethnic communities engage with former refugee communities. While acknowledging the support given to former refugees, there persists a lack of understanding of the challenges faced by refugees. There is work to be done in consultation with refugee communities to address contextual needs of refugee populations:

> *A lot of the providers still don't know, and there is still a lot of big gaps for them to understand this whole refugee journey and the settlement challenges. I know the Government is putting money a lot of money here, but a lot of the providers need the personal development (PD) sessions. So, for some of the providers I go and do a PD Sessions for them around the refugee settlements, the challenges they face, and how can they better understand those challenges? And so that will enable them to [...] provide services to them, which are more effective than just having a general service. So, I'm a former refugee, too, and I know I didn't see much.*
>
> (Jane)

Discrimination and exclusion

Refugee women face challenges due to cultural and religious beliefs and discrimination. The KIs pointed towards religious discrimination being a disabler, with an example of a Muslim refugee woman facing challenges in a business partnership due to her ethnicity and religion, which had an impact on her confidence and well-being. Not being able to get into the formal economy becomes an incentive to engage in entrepreneurship:

> *They're not going to get employment. Let's be open about the fact because they wear a headscarf. They have Muslim names. Who's going to give them employment? There are so much of structural barriers and racism. So, the best thing you do is then you revert to something, you know, which is your small business.*
>
> (Jasmine)

Discussion

This study seeks to understand the role of personal well-being in the entrepreneurship journey of refugee women and how entrepreneurship influences their well-being. Our synthesis of the interview findings demonstrates the ways in which entrepreneurial journey is enabled by factors that contribute to well-being and disenabled by those that diminish well-being, resulting the relationship between well-being and entrepreneurship as a symbiotic one. See Figure 9.1.

In identifying factors that enable and disenable refugee women in their entrepreneurial endeavours in NZ, we found that women's motivation, resilience and determination, and networks and level of empowerment enabled them to use their social capital. The women's social capital enabled their entrepreneurial journey as it involved building relationships and trust through community activity (Bizri, 2017; Putnam, 2000). Women refugee entrepreneurs were often reliant on their community, or other ethnic minority communities,

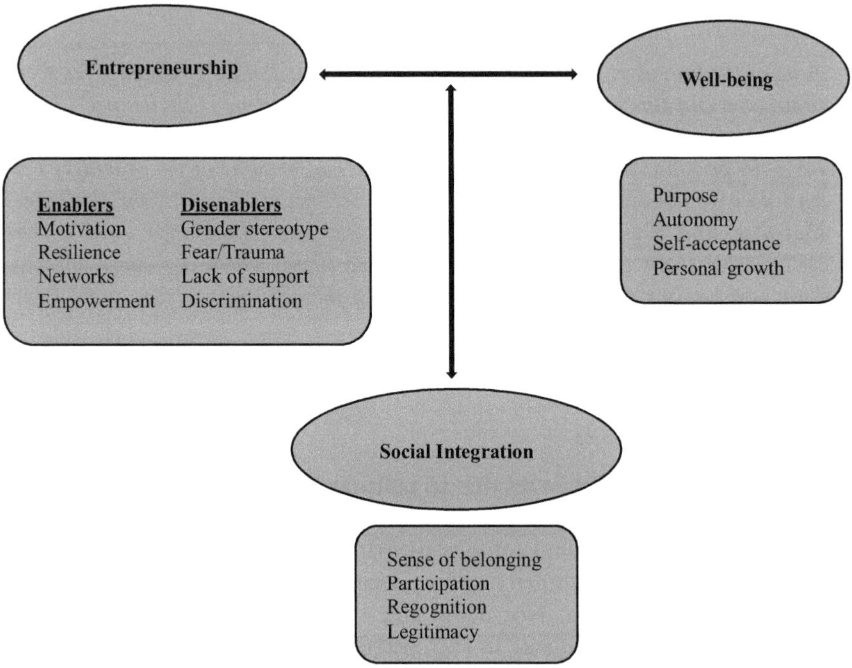

Figure 9.1 Symbiotic relationship between well-being and entrepreneurship.

Source: Developed by authors.

as customers, and were effective at developing and maintaining these links. Social capital included networks that existed before arriving in Aotearoa NZ. We found that support for the venture from the community and family and the centrality of networks (past and present) were important in enabling ventures to eventuate (de Vries et al., 2021; Sandberg et al., 2019).

Another key factor was financial need, as is often the case with necessity entrepreneurship (Al-Dajani & Marlow, 2010). The financial need was often brought to a head by the cultural expectation to send financial aid to family in the home country, and by difficulties in securing paid employment. The experience of social exclusion and discrimination within the formal economy pushed many women refugee entrepreneurs into starting a new venture.

Prior knowledge was important in the decision to embark on the enterprise. Women refugees transferred the skills they gained in their childhood or from conducting domestic tasks to entrepreneurship. Having these capabilities developed their confidence to have a go at running a business. Previous experience or exposure (through family business, for example) with running a small business was also critical in enabling women to start a business (Wauters & Lambrecht, 2008).

Cultural expectations meant that women were constantly navigating stereotypical ideals about entrepreneurs rooted in patriarchal institutions (Marlow & McAdam, 2013). Refugee women entrepreneurs have an added layer of complexity as they navigate expectations that originate in different contexts, for example, expectations from their ethnic community and from the home country's society. Furthermore, many refugees come with their own cultural challenges, and the stigma of refugee status is a barrier to their integration. Finally, newly arrived women refugees experience degrees of exclusion and discrimination which can take a toll on their well-being.

We find that personal well-being and entrepreneurship are interlinked. Despite the numerous factors that disenable the entrepreneurship of refugee women, KIs reported that these women took agency by establishing a business even if it involved defying traditional gender roles (Al-Adjani, 2022). We found that these cultural expectations worked both ways, as the expectation to provide cultural continuity (as evidenced by businesses revolving around food, sewing, spices, hairdressing, and crafts) was combined with their determination to build on what they know, not just rely on what they already know. Having a clear role in the community as a provider of goods and services and being able to overcome numerous challenges to start a new venture enhanced their eudaemonic well-being, which, in turn, fed into their ability to stay on the entrepreneurial journey.

KIs identified qualities such as openness to take up opportunities, such as further training and development, or funding, as contributors to the women's autonomy and mastery of the environment. These dimensions enhanced sense of belonging and self-efficacy (Allport, 1961; Jahoda,1959). Moreover, the entrepreneur took on the dual roles of businesswoman and enabler of the continuation of cultural practices, for instance, through the provision of catering services. In this regard entrepreneurship served as a vehicle to build ethnic communities and to create a bridge with the wider community, thereby contributing to their sense of belonging (Wauter & Lambrecht, 2006) and contributing to social integration. This is an example of eudaemonic well-being, both contributing to the venture creation and feeding from the entrepreneurial experience. Women refugee entrepreneurs display autonomy, confidence, sense of belonging, and personal growth through their involvement in entrepreneurial ventures. In some cases, KIs reported that women who started their entrepreneurial ventures not only experienced a sense of autonomy and purpose but were also able to embark on activities closed to them in their home countries due to rigid gender roles, and this self-acceptance and growth helped to enhance their well-being (Huq & Venugopal, 2021).

From the KI's responses, we learned that women refugee entrepreneurs have a clear sense of purpose, which is linked to increased well-being (Ryff, 2019; Ryff et al., 2021; Ryff & Keyes, 1995). This resonates with our KIs' reports on the resilience of women refugee entrepreneurs. While challenging, entrepreneurship also contributed to their well-being by providing a sense of purpose and increasing their sense of belonging. The increased autonomy, financial contribution, and connection with the community contributed to their eudaemonic well-being. Moreover, the ability to be able to network and meet with other people provided enjoyment and relief from stressors and increased a sense of connection. On the other hand, limited access to resources, discrimination, and other challenges associated with being a refugee can negatively impact the well-being of refugee women entrepreneurs.

For the most part, KIs reported that women were pushed into becoming entrepreneurs because of their life circumstances and lack of financial sustainability which has positive and negative implications for well-being. On the one hand, to have some degree of agency within rigid traditions gives them a space to redefine themselves, while also earning and supporting family can provide a sense of autonomy and pride which impacts positively on well-being. On the other hand, their sense of identity has changed due to displacement and settlement. The breaking with old traditions can be daunting and psychologically depleting: The woman may feel more aligned with the value system of the host country (which generates social integration), but she may not also feel comfortable in her close ethnic community circle. These findings are in line with recent work on the integration of refugees and on how refugee women redefine their roles in the private sphere (Habash & Omata, 2022).

Enabling former refugee women to access training and resources that allow them to upskill and grow their business can aid in their integration and enhance social integration. While NGOs and other community groups provide training, workshops, and resources which can empower women refugees to develop skills, navigate cultural differences, and meet the standards of the host country, women's business success depends on access to information, resources, and networking opportunities. Public policies that have input from the diverse communities are also needed to enhance entrepreneurship. Policies that support women refugees into entrepreneurship will need to include upskilling and start-up support (Collins, 2021) to enhance their empowerment (Al-Dajani, 2022) and readiness for self-employment (Refai & McElwee, 2022). Finally, it is important to acknowledge language barriers faced by refugees and the implications this barrier has on former refugee women to access customers and business support offered by government agencies.

Contribution and future directions

Our chapter contributes by connecting the fields of refugee entrepreneurship, women entrepreneurship, and their well-being. We highlight how entrepreneurship links with belongingness; this is an important aspect of well-being and integration (Khademi et al., 2022). As the global research looks at sustainable steps for building better well-being within marginalised communities, our study contributes by highlighting how entrepreneurship can be a means and end towards well-being of women refugees. Our chapter did not go explicitly into the discussion about intersectionality, being women, refugee, and entrepreneurs, but our study offers some interesting insights. Women refugee entrepreneurs are enabled to become entrepreneurs by their existing strengths and knowledge, their resilience, and the support of their ethnic community. Factors that deplete their well-being (such as exclusion and discrimination) can also push them towards entrepreneurship, because they are left with no other choice when they encounter difficulties in securing employment. The exclusion from mainstream. job market and support from their community along with other factors can lead refugee women going closer to their trusted circle. This has implications for them and the larger community. If we wish to have social integration, the structures and the policies need to be inclusive for them. From a policy perspective, we provide insights to policymakers, about the enabling factors that build the refugee women entrepreneurs' well-being. This feeds into social integration initiatives and the settlement strategy.

An avenue for future research is to pursue the study of social cohesion, well-being, and refugee settlement models. Moreover, it is possible that women refugees from some countries may be more disadvantaged than others in terms of integration in Aotearoa NZ, and further research into the role that entrepreneurship can play in terms of social integration and well-being is needed. This should consider factors such as their cultural background, language proficiency, level of education, and the length of time they have been in the host country. These all have relevance in terms of enabling women to access settlement services, including entrepreneurial support, pointing to the need for discussions that enable systemic solutions that are embedded in the refugee settlement strategy.

Conclusion

In this chapter, we have analysed the interplay between well-being and entrepreneurship among women refugee entrepreneurs and found that it is complex and can have a significant impact on their social inclusion and settlement. The findings of this research would not have been possible without our positionality which allowed for a more nuanced understanding of the experiences of refugee women in Aotearoa NZ. We have provided insights into the challenges women refugee entrepreneurs face, such as language barriers, discrimination, lack of access to resources and networks, and cultural differences, which can inform more effective and inclusive policy design initiatives that better meet the needs of refugee women. We highlight the underutilisation of human capital in the women refugee entrepreneurs as limiting mutual benefits for refugees and host country communities and challenging social integration. Lastly, keeping the sustainable goals under consideration, entrepreneurship and well-being can contribute to the promotion of gender equality and help to challenge gender-based barriers and inequalities. Entrepreneurship has the potential of not only providing women refugee entrepreneurs a means of survival but also bolstering their well-being as they integrate into their host countries (Dijkhuizen, 2019; Marchand & Dijkhuizen, 2018). This can only help to create more inclusive and equitable outcomes for refugee women in Aotearoa NZ.

Note

1 All names used in this study are pseudonyms.

References

Abebe, S.A. (2023). Refugee entrepreneurship: Systematic and thematic analyses and a research agenda. *Small Business Economics*, 60, 315–350. https://doi.org/10.1007/s11187-022-00636-3

Adeeko, N., & Treanor, L. (2022). Negotiating stigmatised identities: Enterprising refugee women in the United Kingdom. *International Small Business Journal*, *40*(1), 23–46. https://doi.org/10.1177/026624262199703

Ahl, H., & Marlow, S. (2012). Exploring the dynamics of gender, feminism and entrepreneurship: Advancing debate to escape a dead end?. *Organization*, *19*(5), 543–562. https://doi.org/10.1177/1350508412448695

Al-Dajani, H. (2022). Refugee women's entrepreneurship: Where from and where to next? *International Journal of Gender and Entrepreneurship*, *14*(4), 489–498. https://doi.org/10.1108/IJGE-06-2022-0090

Al-Dajani, H., Akbar, H., Carter, S., & Shaw, E. (2019). Defying contextual embeddedness: Evidence from displaced women entrepreneurs in Jordan. *Entrepreneurship & Regional Development*, *31*(3–4), 198–212. https://doi.org/10.1080/08985626.2018.1551788

Al-Dajani, H., & Marlow, S. (2010). Impact of women's home-based enterprise on family dynamics: Evidence from Jordan. *International Small Business Journal*, *28*(5), 470–486. https://doi.org/10.1177/026624261037039

Allport, G.W. (1961). *Pattern and Growth in Personality*. New York: Holt, Reinhart & Winston.

Alrawadieh, Z., Altinay, L., Cetin, G., & Şimşek, D. (2021). The interface between hospitality and tourism entrepreneurship, integration, and wellbeing: A study of refugee entrepreneurs. *International Journal of Hospitality Management*, *97*, 103013. https://doi.org/10.1016/j.ijhm.2021.103013

Alvarez, S.A., & Barney, J.B. (2014). Entrepreneurial opportunities and poverty alleviation. *Entrepreneurship Theory and Practice*, *38*(1), 159–184. https://doi.org/10.1111/etap.12078

Atalay, I., & Tanova, C. (2022). Opportunity entrepreneurship and subjective well-being: The role of psychological functioning. Does individualism change this relationship? *Applied Research in Quality of Life*, *17*(3), 1247–1267. https://doi.org/10.1007/s11482-021-09962-2

Benight, C. C., & Bandura, A. (2004). Social cognitive theory of posttraumatic recovery: The role of perceived self-efficacy. *Behaviour Research and Therapy*, *42*, 1129–1148. https://doi.org/10.1016/j.brat.2003.08.008

Bizri, R.M. (2017). Refugee-entrepreneurship: A social capital perspective. *Entrepreneurship & Regional Development*, *29*(9–10), 847–868. https://doi.org/10.1080/08985626.2017.1364787

Bryman, A. (2004). *Social Research Methods*. Oxford: Oxford University Press.

Collins, J. (2021). Immigrant entrepreneurship in Sydney: Australia's leading global city. In C.Y. Liu (Ed.), *Immigrant Entrepreneurship in Cities: Global Perspectives* (pp. 47–65). Cham: Springer. https://doi.org/10.1007/978-3-030-50363-5_3

Crawley, H. (2022). Saving brown women from brown men? "Refugee women", gender and the racialised politics of protection. *Refugee Survey Quarterly*, *41*(3), 355–380. https://doi.org/10.1093/rsq/hdac021

Desai, S., Naudé, W., & Stel, N. (2021). Refugee entrepreneurship: Context and directions for future research. *Small Business Economics*, *56* (3), 933–945. https://doi.org/10.1007/s11187-019-00310-1

de Vries, H.P., Ranabahu, N., & Basharati, Z. (2021). From taking flight to putting down roots: A narrative perspective of the entrepreneurial journey of a refugee. In T. Cooney (Ed.), *Palgrave Handbook on Minority Entrepreneurship* (pp. 365–389). Cham: Palgrave Macmillan. http://dx.doi.org/10.1007/978-3-030-66603-3_17

Dijkhuizen, J. (2019). Exploring degrees of wellbeing of women entrepreneurs in refugee settlements in the Middle East: A personal account. In M.T. Lepely, K. Kuschel, N. Beutell, N. Pouw, & E.L. Eijdenberg (Eds.), *The Wellbeing of Women in Entrepreneurship* (pp. 345–356). Oxon: Routledge.

Drakopoulou-dodd, S., Mcdonald, S., Mcelwee, G., & Smith, R. (2014). A Bourdieuan Analysis of Qualitative Authorship in Entrepreneurship Scholarship. *Journal of Small Business Management*, *52*(4), 633–654. https://doi.org/10.1111/jsbm.12125

Eastmond, M. (2007). Stories as lived experience: Narratives in forced migration research. *Journal of Refugee Studies*, *20*(2), 248–264. https://doi.org/10.1093/jrs/fem007

Freiling, J., & Harima, A. (2019). Refugee entrepreneurship: Learning from case studies. In Heilbrunn, S., Freiling, J., & Harima, A. (Eds.), *Entrepreneurship – A Case-based Topography* (pp. 255–278). Cham: Palgrave McMillan.

Gioia, D.A., Corley, K.G., & Hamilton, A.L. (2013). Seeking qualitative rigor in inductive research: Notes on the Gioia methodology. *Organizational Research Methods*, *16*(1), 15–31.

Habash, D., & Omata, N. (2022). The 'private' sphere of integration? Reconfiguring gender roles within Syrian refugee families in the UK. *Journal of International Migration and Integration*, *24*, 969–988. https://doi.org/10.1007/s12134-022-00982-x

Hajdukowski-Ahmed, M., Khanlou, N., & Moussa, H. (Eds.). (2009). *Not Born a Refugee Woman: Contesting Identities, Rethinking Practices* (NED-New edition, 1). Berghahn Books. www.jstor.org/stable/j.ctt9qcvc2

Huq, A., & Venugopal, V. (2021). DIY entrepreneurship? – Self-reliance for women refugees in Australia. *International Migration*, *59*(1), 126–142. https://doi.org/10.1111/imig.12727

Immigration New Zealand. (2022a). *NZ Migrant Settlement Integration Strategy and NZ Refugee Resettlement Strategy Refresh Project*. www.immigration.govt.nz/about-us/what-we-do/our-strategies-and-projects/refugee-resettlement-strategy/the-nz-migrant-settlement-integration-strategy-and-nz-refugee-resettlement-strategy-refresh-project

Immigration New Zealand. (2022b). *Refugee and Protection: Statistics Pack*. www.immigration.govt.nz/about-us/research-and-statistics/statistics

International Monetary Fund. (2018). *Pursuing Women's Economic Empowerment*. www.imf.org/en/Publications/Policy-Papers/Issues/2018/05/31/pp053118pursuing-womens-economic-empowerment

Jahoda, M. (1959). Current concepts of positive mental health. *Journal of Occupational and Environmental Medicine*, *1*(10), 565. https://journals.lww.com/joem/Citation/1959/10000/CURRENT_CONCEPTS_OF_POSITIVE_MENTAL_HEALTH.12.aspx

Jones, T., Ram, M., Edwards, P., Kiselinchev, A., & Muchenje, L. (2014). Mixed embeddedness and new migrant enterprise in the UK. *Entrepreneurship & Regional Development*, *26*(5–6), 500–520. https://doi.org/10.1080/08985626.2014.950697

Khademi, S., Essers, C., & van Nieuwkerk, K. (2022). Iranian refugee entrepreneurship and inclusion in the Netherlands, *Journal of Refugee Studies*, *36* (1), 105–127. https://doi.org/10.1093/jrs/feac058

Mangrio, E., Zdravkovic, S., & Carlson, E. (2019). Refugee women's experience of the resettlement process: A qualitative study. *BMC Women's Health*, *19*(1), 1–6. https://doi.org/10.1186/s12905-019-0843-x

Marchand, K., & Dijkhuizen, J. (2018). Entrepreneurship as a tool for a new beginning: Entrepreneurship training for refugees in a new homeland. In N. Apostolopoulos, H. Al-Dajani, D. Holt, P. Jones, & R. Newbery (Eds.), *Entrepreneurship and the Sustainable Development Goals (Contemporary Issues in Entrepreneurship Research, 8)* (pp. 135–149). Bingley: Emerald Publishing Limited. https://doi-org.ezproxy.massey.ac.nz/10.1108/S2040-724620180000008013

Marlow, S., & McAdam, M. (2013). Gender and entrepreneurship: Advancing debate and challenging myths; exploring the mystery of the under-performing female entrepreneur. *International Journal of Entrepreneurial Behaviour and Research*, *19*(1), 114–124. https://doi.org/10.1108/13552551311299288

Muñoz, P., & Kimmit, J. (2018). Entrepreneurship and the rest: The missing debate. *Journal of Business Venturing Insights*, *9*, 100–106. https://doi.org/10.1016/j.jbvi.2018.03.003

OECD: Organisation for Economic Co-operation and Development. (2019). *Policy Brief on Refugee Entrepreneurship*. https://doi.org/10.1787/7057/1d6f-en

Pécoud, A. (2002). Cosmopolitanism and business among German-Turks in Berlin. *Journal of the Society for the Anthropology of Europe*, *2*(1), 2–12. https://doi.org/10.1525/jsae.2002.2.1.2

Putnam, R.D. (2000). *Bowling Alone: The Collapse and Revival of American Community*. New York: Simon and Schuster.

Ram, M., Jones, T, Doldor, S., Villares-Varela, M., & Li, H. (2022). What happens to refugee-origin entrepreneurs? Combining mixed embeddedness and strategy perspectives in a longitudinal study. *Ethnic and Racial Studies*, *45*(16), 1–27. https://doi.org/10.1080/01419870.2021.1991970

Refai, D., & McElwee, G. (2022). Refugee subentrepreneurship: The emergence of a liquid cage. *Work, Employment and Society*, *37*(4), 1032–1051. https://doi.org/10.1177/09500170211062814

Ryff, C. (1989). Happiness is everything, or is it? Explorations on the meaning of psychological wellbeing. *Journal of Personality and Social Psychology*, *57*(6), 1069–1081. https://doi.org/10.1037/0022-3514.57.6.1069

Ryff, C. (2019). Entrepreneurship and eudaimonic wellbeing: Five venues for new science. *Journal of Business Venturing*, *34*(4), 646–663. https://doi.org/10.1016/j.jbusvent.2018.09.003

Ryff, C.D., Boylan, J.M., & Kirsch, J.A. (2021). Eudaimonic and hedonic well-being: An integrative perspective with linkages to sociodemographic factors and health. In M.T. Lee, L.D. Kubzansky, & T.J. VanderWeele (Eds.), *Measuring Well-Being: Interdisciplinary Perspectives from the Social Sciences and the Humanities* (pp. 92–135). New York: Oxford University Press. https://doi.org/10.1093/oso/9780197512531.003.0005

Ryff, C.D., & Keyes, C.L.M. (1995). The structure of psychological wellbeing revisited. *Journal of Personality and Social Psychology*, *69*(4), 719–727. https://doi.org/10.1037/0022-3514.69.4.719

Sandberg, S., Immonen, R., & Kok, S. (2019). Refugee entrepreneurship: Taking a social network view on immigrants with refugee backgrounds starting transnational businesses in Sweden. *International Journal of Entrepreneurship and Small Business*, *36*(1–2), 216–241.

Shishehgar, S., Gholizadeh, L., DiGiacomo, M., Green, A., & Davidson, P.M. (2017). Health and socio-cultural experiences of refugee women: An integrative review. *Journal of Immigrant and Minority Health*, *19*, 959–973. https://doi.org/10.1007/s10903-016-0379-1

Stephan U., Rauch, A., & Hatak, I. (2022). Happy entrepreneurs? Everywhere? A meta-analysis of entrepreneurship and wellbeing. *Entrepreneurship Theory and Practice*, *47*(2), 553–593. https://doi.org/10.1177/1042258721107279

United Nations. (2023). *Envision2030 Goal 8: Decent Work and Economic Growth.* United Nations Sustainable Development Goals. https://social.desa.un.org/issues/disability/envision-2030/envision2030-goal-8-decent-work-and-economic-growth

United Nations Development Program. (2022). *Breaking Down Barriers, Empowering People.* www.undp.org/guinea-bissau/news/breaking-down-barriers-empowering-people

Vershinina, N., & Discua Cruz, A. (2021). Researching migrant entrepreneurship communities: A reflection through collaborative (auto)ethnographies. *International Entrepreneurship and Management Journal*, *17*, 507–526. https://doi.org/10.1007/s11365-020-00706-6

Wauters, B., & Lambrecht, J. (2006). Refugee entrepreneurship in Belgium: Potential and practice. *The International Entrepreneurship and Management Journal*, *2*, 509–525. https://doi.org/10.1007/s11365-006-0008-x

Wauters, B., & Lambrecht, J. (2008). Barriers to refugee entrepreneurship in Belgium: Towards an explanatory model. *Journal of Ethnic and Migration Studies*, *34*(2), 895–915. https://doi.org/10.1080/13691830802211190

Welter, F. (2011). Contextualizing entrepreneurship – Conceptual challenges and ways forward. *Entrepreneurship Theory and Practice*, *35*(1), 165–184. https://doi.org/10.1111/j.1540-6520.2010.0042

Wiklund, J., Nikolaev, B., Shir, N., Foo, M.D., & Bradley, S. (2019). Entrepreneurship and wellbeing: Past, present, and future. *Journal of Business Venturing*, *34*(4), 579–588. https://doi.org/10.1016/j.jbusvent.2019.01.002

Yeshi, T., Harima, A., & Freiling, J. (2022). Resilience on an emotional rollercoaster: Refugee entrepreneurship under adversity. *European Management Journal*, S026323732200175X. https://doi.org/10.1016/j.emj.2022.12.009

Young, M., Chan, K. (2015). The psychological experience of refugees: A gender and cultural analysis. In S. Safdar & N. Kosakowska-Berezecka (Eds.), *Psychology of Gender through the Lens of Culture*. Cham: Springer. https://doi.org/10.1007/978-3-319-14005-6_2

10 Refugee entrepreneurship and entrepreneurial economies in South Africa

Sujata Ramachandran, Abel Chikanda, and Jonathan Crush

Introduction

The entrepreneurial activities undertaken by individuals forcibly displaced from their homes due to war, conflict, and persecution represent the latest emerging global phenomenon (Desai et al., 2020; Heilbrunn & Iannone, 2019, 2020). Entrepreneurship allows refugees, asylum seekers, and other forced migrants to address the socioeconomic and institutional obstacles in the destination country and has become an important mechanism for facilitating their social and economic inclusion in the destination country (Abebe, 2023; Lee et al., 2020). The United Nations High Commissioner for Refugees: UNHCR (2022a) has noted that refugees often prefer to adopt the entrepreneurial route rather than waged employment in situations of high unemployment and limited economic opportunities in the labour market of host countries.

A focus on the entrepreneurial activities of forced migrants is important for several reasons. First, forced migrants have more than doubled globally over the last decade, rising from about 43 million to 108.4 million (UNHCR, 2022b). Some refugee cohorts are from origin countries experiencing protracted conflict and crisis circumstances and the possibilities of safe return are absent. Hence, it is important to investigate the livelihood strategies of this growing group in the destination countries. Second, since an estimated 60% of the global refugees reside in urban areas, there is an obvious imperative to understand their economic impacts on their destination countries. Third, as noted by Desai et al. (2020) in their comprehensive review of over 130 peer-reviewed publications on refugee entrepreneurship, there is a sizable knowledge gap on how refugees enter entrepreneurship and their general experiences in running businesses. Thus, research is needed that documents various factors that motivate refugees to start their businesses along with the challenges and successes of their businesses.

Entrepreneurship has been associated with wider economic independence for refugees in destination societies, reducing their reliance on government or other assistance (Rukuni et al., 2022). However, limited access to business capital has been cited as a major barrier to refugee entrepreneurship (Newman et al., 2023; Raijman & Barak-Bianco, 2015). In some contexts,

DOI: 10.4324/9781003368540-13

social networks have constituted an important source of business financing. But, it is not clear whether this is enough to help offset the disadvantages that refugees face in their business operations.

Moreover, refugee entrepreneurial activities cannot be detached from the broader economic participation of forced migrants in the receiving countries. Host country policies and attitudes towards refugees and asylum claimants, the rights and entitlements refugees and asylum-seekers can avail, and the social, economic, and working environments in which they operate their businesses are all vital aspects that shape refugee entrepreneurship, its emergence, and growth in the refugee-hosting countries.

This chapter examines the experiences of refugees who have established informal businesses in the city of Cape Town. It begins by examining the influence of various factors in drawing refugees towards informal entrepreneurship. The chapter then discusses how they established their businesses, paying attention to the various sources of capital used to start the business. Drawing on the concept of refugee entrepreneurial economies (Crush et al., 2017a), it discusses some benefits of refugee entrepreneurship to the South African economy. Finally, it addresses the environment in which the refugees operate their businesses, including their experiences with xenophobia.

Refugees in South Africa

Post-apartheid South Africa has become one of the leading destinations for forced migrants from several African countries. The UNHCR (2023) data show that the refugee population grew from 15,058 in 2000 to 75,512 by 2021, while the number of asylum seekers similarly rose from 15,139 to 167,411. In 2021, the major source countries of refugees and asylum seekers were Ethiopia (61,407), the Democratic Republic of Congo (DRC) (56,735), Somalia (27,070), and Zimbabwe (14,433).

South Africa's Refugee Act of 1998 governs the protection of forced migrants who seek refuge in the country. Refugee status determination is accorded either through *prima facie* procedures, which gives the minister of refugee affairs the power to declare any class of persons to be refugees under any acceptable definition, or through individual status determination of applications submitted by individuals seeking asylum (Crush & Chikanda, 2014). South Africa also follows a 'self-settlement' approach which allows refugees to reside in a geographical location of their choice in the country, which means they have to compete with South Africans for jobs and other basic life necessities. Unemployment levels among black South Africans are high and have risen in recent years, and non-citizens are often blamed for exacerbating this problem (World Bank, 2018).

South Africa's refugee legislation provides the pathway to permanent residency for successful asylum claimants (Department of Home Affairs, 2015). While refugees (and asylum seekers until 2017) are legally permitted to work in South Africa, in practice they struggle to find decent jobs in the formal sector, mainly due to the prevailing anti-immigrant attitudes and institutional barriers (Ferraro & Weideman, 2020; Kavuro, 2022) and South African employers' suspicion of their employment permits (Northcote & Dodson, 2015). This often channels refugees and asylum seekers into informal economic activities such as street trading, sale of art, and curios, as well as operation of small convenience stores, locally known as spazas.

Data sources

The chapter is based primarily on the results of a study that was conducted by the Southern African Migration Programme (SAMP) in 2015. The Growing Informal Cities (GIC) project sought to examine the origins, operations, and problems facing migrant entrepreneurs operating in Cape Town's informal economy. While the research results have been published elsewhere (see Crush et al., 2017a, 2017b, 2017c), these findings not distinguish between entrepreneurs who arrived in South Africa as migrants or as refugees and asylum seekers. The SAMP survey data was re-analysed to select only those who arrived in South Africa as refugees and asylum seekers. Out of the original 518 survey responses, 320 were identified as refugee entrepreneurs. The businesses that were included in the original survey met the basic definition of a micro-enterprise in South Africa: (a) owned by a non-South African; (b) in operation for at least two years to allow for a retrospective analysis of the start-up, problems, and opportunities; and (c) not registered with the South African Revenue Services (SARS).

The participants were purposely selected from urban sites where informal entrepreneurs operate such as Bellville (32.5%), the city centre (27.8%), Imzamo Yethu (20.6%), and Philippi (19.1%). Survey data were supplemented with 30 in-depth interviews with selected survey participants. Two focus group discussions were held in the Cape Town CBD (seven participants) and Philippi (six participants) to acquire detailed knowledge on the experiences operating businesses in the informal economy in the city.

An overwhelming majority of refugee entrepreneurs are male (75%), although this male dominance varies by country of origin. Male entrepreneurs dominate the cohorts from Ethiopia (87%) and Somalia (85%) compared with those from the DRC (69%) and Zimbabwe (68%). Two-thirds of the entrepreneurs originated from only four countries: Zimbabwe (19%), Somalia (19%), DRC (18%), and Ethiopia (9%). Other significant source countries of the refugee entrepreneurs are Nigeria (6%), Malawi (6%), Congo (Brazzaville) (4%), Uganda (3%), Cameroon (2%), Ghana (2%), and Kenya (2%). The sample was relatively well-educated in comparison with South Africans, although the cohort with post-secondary education was not large. Over half (56.5%) had completed at least secondary or high school against just 46.5% of the general South African population. Entrepreneurs from the DRC (63%), Ethiopia (59%), and Zimbabwe (59%) had completed at least secondary school education compared with those from Somalia (42%), a country whose education system has been disrupted by three decades of civil war. Retail, trade, and wholesale (64%) dominate in the economic activities of the entrepreneurs, while services (27%) and manufacturing (9%) were also significant. Entrepreneurs from Somalia (22%), Zimbabwe (18%), the DRC (15%), and Ethiopia (11%) dominate in the retail, trade, and wholesale sector, while entrepreneurs from the DRC (23%), Zimbabwe (19%), Congo (Brazzaville) (11%), Nigeria (8%), and Uganda (8%) made up the bulk of those engaging in the informal service sector, providing services such as car wash and repair, shoe repair, and hairdressing.

Refugees in South Africa's informal economy

Motivation to start a business

Several studies have examined various reasons why people establish businesses with a view to identify the 'entrepreneurial triggers' (Robichaud et al., 2001; Mitchell, 2004; Khosa & Kalitanyi, 2015). Refugee entrepreneurs were asked to rank various factors that influenced them to start their business on a scale ranging from 1 (not important) to 5 (extremely important). Table 10.1

Table 10.1 The motivation to start a business

Factor	*Mean score*
Financial benefits/security	
I needed more money just to survive	4.1
I have always wanted to run my own business	3.9
I wanted to give my family greater financial security	3.8
I wanted to make more money to send to my family in my home country	3.8
Entrepreneurial orientation and personal rewards	
I wanted more control over my own time/to be my own boss	4.0
I have the right personality to run my own business	3.9
I like to challenge myself	3.7
I like to learn new skills	3.7
I enjoy taking risks	3.5
I wanted to do something new and challenging	3.5
I wanted to compete with others and be the best	3.3
Creating employment	
I was unemployed and unable to find a job	2.9
I wanted to provide employment for members of my family	2.6
I wanted to provide employment for South Africans	2.6
I had a job but it did not pay enough	2.5
I wanted to provide employment for other people from my home country	2.3
I had a job but it did not suit my qualifications and experience	2.1

presents respondents' mean scores for entrepreneurial motivation factors derived from previous studies (Robichaud et al., 2001; Shane et al., 2003; Vijaya & Kamalanabhan, 1998). These factors were grouped into three general categories: financial benefits and security, entrepreneurial orientation and personal rewards, and creating employment.

Financial factors exerted the greatest push towards entrepreneurship. The most important reason was the need for extra money to survive and meet their individual and household's living expenses (4.1). Another high-scoring factor was the long-term desire to run their own business (at 3.9), an additional sign of independence, and intrinsic reward. Even though the entrepreneurs cited individualistic reasons for establishing their businesses, they also took a social stance showing the benefits of the business in ensuring greater financial security for the family (3.8) and making money to remit to the home country (3.8). Personal motivations and rewards consistently scored the highest with every factor rating over 3.0. The highest scores were in the entrepreneurial orientation and personal rewards category, including 'being one's own boss' (at 4.0 and second highest mean score), having the right personality to run a business (3.9), and a desire to challenge oneself (3.7). This result suggests that refugee entrepreneurs tended to go into business because they felt that they were personally suited to this kind of activity, as independent-minded people looking for a challenge, wanting to learn new skills, and willing to take risks. Creating employment scored the lowest with all factors. Unemployment and employment generation for others did not rate particularly highly as motives for entrepreneurship. It should be highlighted that creating jobs for family members and for South Africans both scored 2.5, better than creating jobs for other people from the home country at 2.3.

Business ownership and strategies

The survey collected detailed information on the history of the enterprise, including how the business was started, amount and source of start-up capital, and current value of the business. Most refugee entrepreneurs started the business on their own, consistent with individualism in the context of entrepreneurial motivation noted in Table 10.2. Only 15.4% started their business with

Table 10.2 Establishment of business enterprise

	Number	*% of total*
I started it alone	210	60.0
I started it with people from my home country	54	15.4
I started it with my family	53	15.1
I started it with people from other countries	17	4.9
I bought this business from a non-South African	7	2.0
I started it with South African business partners	5	1.4
I bought this business from a South African	4	1.1

people from their home country and 15.1% with family members. Partnerships with people from other countries (4.9%) and South Africans (1.4%) were even less common. More importantly, these findings confirm that refugee entrepreneurs are not taking over businesses started by South Africans.

Obtaining the capital to start a business can be quite challenging for refugees in South Africa as most do not have the necessary collateral to acquire a business loan from a financial institution. Only a small proportion of the entrepreneurs (0.2%) were able to acquire a loan to start a business from a financial institution. Lack of access to credit was highlighted by one focus group participant who noted that 'The banks do not see us as business people. They see us as foreigners first, so you may not even get the chance to say I am a business person, so please can I have money' (Focus group participant). Therefore, most relied on their personal savings (61.4%), loans from relatives (24.1%), or non-relatives (11.5%) to start their business. One respondent in the interviews noted that:

> *I started by saving little by little until I had something big enough to start something consistent. So I started very small. I kept on saving and increasing the quantity of my products until I became like this. As for others, I think they get help from their families. But there is no one who just gets free money.*

Refugee entrepreneurs earned profits of about ZAR4,063 per month on average or nearly ZAR49,000 per year from their business activities. This is equivalent to USD475 per month or USD5,000 per year based on the 2015 exchange rate of 1USD:ZAR10.8472. Notwithstanding the challenges that refugee entrepreneurs face in accessing business capital, the survey results showed significant growth in capitalisation for refugee-owned businesses. While two-thirds used less than ZAR10,000 to start their businesses, only 29% valued their businesses at less than ZAR10,000. On the other hand, while only 7.6% used at least ZAR30,000 to start their businesses, as many as 30.7% valued their businesses at more than ZAR30,000. This shows that many refugee-owned businesses in Cape Town have scaled up their operations and are growing in value, demonstrating that informal entrepreneurship is more than a survivalist activity.

Contributions to local economy

Refugees and migrants have been scapegoated by politicians and others and are perceived to undermine the livelihoods of citizens (Piper & Charman, 2016; Tevera, 2013; Tawodzera et al., 2015). The negative discourse around refugees and migrants in the South African economy have fuelled widespread xenophobic sentiments (Crush et al., 2015; Northcote & Dodson, 2015). Our chapter has attempted to document the contributions of refugee entrepreneurs to the South African economy through three important indicators: purchasing arrangements, rent payments, and employment creation.

Table 10.3 Source of goods sold by entrepreneurs

	Number	*% of total*
Suppliers		
Wholesalers	226	70.6
Small shops/retailers	62	19.4
Direct from factory	51	15.9
Supermarkets	47	14.7
Epping fresh produce market	35	10.9
Direct from farmers	8	2.5
Other		
Make or grow them myself	50	15.6
From other informal sector producer/retailer	42	13.1
From another country	28	8.8
From home country	22	6.9
N	320	

Note: multiple response question

First, the purchasing arrangements of the entrepreneurs can be used to gauge their contribution to the local economy. Manufacturers in South Africa, for instance, depend on both large-scale and small-scale retailers to market their manufactured goods. In this way, refugee entrepreneurs arguably play an important role in supporting local jobs by buying products from the South African manufacturers. The survey results established that most of the entrepreneurs sourced their goods locally from wholesalers (70.6%), small shops and retailers (19.4%), directly from factories (15.9%), and from supermarkets (14.7%) (Table 10.3). A small proportion of the entrepreneurs sourced their products from the Epping fresh produce market in Cape Town (10.9%). Even less common was the importation of goods either from another country (8.8%) or the entrepreneurs' home country (6.9%).

Refugee and immigrant entrepreneurs have also been accused of engaging in group buying, where they pool their resources together in order to get a good deal from manufacturers or wholesalers (Fatoki, 2013; Ikuomola & Zaaiman, 2016). Group buying translates into lower prices for consumers but may pit them against entrepreneurs not engaging in the practice and selling their goods at higher prices. About 36% of refugee entrepreneurs engaged in group buying which shows that this is not a widespread practice.

Second, occupancy and tenure status of the business premises from which they operate also offer insights into the contributions of refugee entrepreneurs to the local economy. Our survey results showed that only 17.2% of the refugee entrepreneurs owned the premises from which they operate. The vast majority paid rent to the city council or municipality (38.1%) or South African private owners (32.8%). Only a small minority did not pay any rent. On average, they paid a mean monthly rental of ZAR2,336.20 (USD 215), varying from a low of ZAR50.00 to a high of ZAR29,000.00. The refugee entrepreneurs

Table 10.4 Jobs created by refugee entrepreneurs

	South Africans		*Family members*		*Home country peers*		*People from other countries*		*Total*	
	No.	*%*	*No.*	*%*	*No.*	*%*	*No.*	*%*	*No.*	*%*
Full time	128	29.8	90	20.9	72	16.7	33	7.7	323	75.1
Part time	45	10.5	31	7.2	16	3.7	15	3.5	107	24.9
Total	**173**	**40.2**	**121**	**28.1**	**88**	**20.5**	**48**	**11.2**	**430**	**100.0**

in our sample collectively paid a mean monthly rent of ZAR591,058 or ZAR6.7 million per year. Of this, ZAR530,317 per month or ZAR6.4 million per year went directly to South African landlords, providing clear evidence of the downstream impacts of their business activities on South Africans and the South African economy.

Third, refugee entrepreneurs clearly contributed to employment generation in Cape Town. However, not much is known about their contribution to employment creation beyond family employment opportunities (Charman et al., 2012; Kalitanyi, 2007). The refugee entrepreneurs surveyed collectively created 430 jobs distributed as follows: 121 jobs (28.1%) went to family members, 88 jobs (20.5%) to people from their home country, 48 jobs (11.2%) to people from other countries, and 173 jobs (40.2%) to South Africans (Table 10.4). In all, 71.9% of the jobs created by these entrepreneurs went to non-family members, confirming that they are an important source of employment creation in South Africa. The majority of the jobs were on a full-time basis (75.1%). For the total sample, one business on average generated 1.34 jobs or 0.97 non-family jobs. It is notable that there were more jobs created for males (59.8%) than females (40.2%), which may be due to the physical nature of this economic activity, including hauling large loads of goods to and from storage rooms and sometimes engaging in running battles with municipal police. A significant number of the female employees (38.2%) are South African, which demonstrates the potential of refugee-owned businesses in alleviating unemployment among marginalised groups in the South African society.

Xenophobia and entrepreneurial activities

Xenophobia continues to be a persistent and significant challenge facing immigrants and refugees and negatively affects their social and economic activities to a considerable extent (Crush et al., 2017b; Crush & Ramachandran, 2015). Migrants, refugees, and asylum seekers, especially the poorer cohorts, have faced xenophobic harassment along with physical and verbal attacks in various public and private places in post-apartheid South Africa. Small businesses operated by refugees and asylum seekers have been especially at risk of xenophobic violence and experienced frequent episodes of attacks, involving loss of store inventory through arson and looting, damage and destruction of shop edifices, forced store closures, temporary or permanent displacement, physical injuries, and loss of life (Crush & Ramachandran, 2015). Yet, these recurring attacks have been treated largely as isolated acts of criminality by South African government agencies (Crush & Ramachandran, 2015). This regular pattern of violence targeting refugee and migrant businesses has resulted in the relocation of some entrepreneurs to smaller urban centres (Crush et al., 2017a, 2017c). Gastrow's (2022) new study of Somali refugee traders shows how their difficult social status as 'pariahs' or unwanted outsiders in marginal neighbourhoods marked by high levels of poverty, crime, and weak rule of law makes them easy targets of common criminal activities and frequent xenophobic anger.

Our survey respondents indicated that prejudice against their nationality (52.8% often/sometimes) and verbal assaults against their businesses (35.4%) were the main social challenges. Security challenges related mostly to theft of goods with 27.3% participants saying that they often experience the problem while 49.5% sometimes experience this problem. One respondent felt that their group was targeted because of their vulnerability:

> *They do not steal from us just because we are foreigners. They are just thieves and they steal everywhere. But maybe they know that foreigners will not be helped by police and they steal.*
>
> (Interview with Cameroonian entrepreneur)

Physical attacks by South Africans were also reported as occurring 'often' by 8.3% and 'sometimes' by 31.9% of the entrepreneurs. Thus, nearly 40% of entrepreneurs were exposed to some form of violence in their business operations. Another Somali entrepreneur noted that business competition sometimes resulted in violence from their South African counterparts:

> *The main problem that we are facing is competition, which is creating hatred between local business owners and Somali business owners, whereby locals are trying to mobilise the community around them to take advantage of that process.*
>
> (Interview with Somali entrepreneur)

Non-citizen entrepreneurs, especially those operating small formal and informal businesses, also encounter routine harassment from police and government officials in addition to regular citizens. Recent Human Rights Watch (HRW) reports have noted that the South African Police Service (SAPS) and Metro Police seized the stock of refugee and migrant-owned businesses in

Johannesburg using the claim of locating counterfeit goods (HRW, 2020, 2021). The confiscated goods were later sold back to the entrepreneurs. Because of their disproportionate vulnerability to xenophobic discrimination and its violent forms, refugee entrepreneurs have also been victims of extortion and forced to make regular payments to ensure the safety and security of their businesses. Local authorities, including police and municipal officials, have been known to collude with South African shopkeepers to restrict or prevent the entrepreneurial activities of refugees and migrants by demanding unnecessary special permits and other similar actions (Gastrow, 2022). Some studies have suggested that all small businesses are vulnerable to looting and other forms of criminal activity (Piper & Sharman, 2016). However, refugee entrepreneurs are far more likely to experience security risks and adopt mitigation measures such as payment to police and others for protection (Ramachandran et al., 2017). In the SAMP survey, as many as 21.3% of participants indicated that xenophobia had affected their business 'a great deal' while 26.2% were affected 'to some extent'. Thus, nearly half of the respondents (47.9%) had their business operations affected to some degree by xenophobic actions.

Recent developments in business operating environment

South Africa's draft *National Labour Migration Policy* acknowledges the country's obligations to refugees and other forcibly displaced persons under various international frameworks (GRSA, 2022). This includes key frameworks such as the ILO (2016) *Guiding Principles on the Access of Refugees and Other Forcibly Displaced Persons to the Labour Market*. This framework upholds decent work opportunities to all persons, including refugees and other forcibly displaced persons, in refugee-hosting countries like South Africa. Accordingly, South Africa is expected to develop national policies and action plans to ensure the protection of refugees and other categories of forced migrants in the labour market, including access to decent forms of work and livelihoods along with other measures that foster refugee economic self-reliance (p. 8). Another related recommendation is that receiving countries like South Africa should develop concrete measures to improve access of refugees and other forced migrants to skill development and upgrading opportunities along with programmes to promote entrepreneurship and business start-up training for them (p. 10). Refugee entrepreneurship has thus been identified as an important dimension of the socioeconomic participation and integration of forced migrants.

However, recent policy shifts clearly undermine these principles of equal treatment and inclusion of refugees and asylum seekers. Recommended by its latest immigration policy, the White Paper on International Migration, and later introduced through the Refugee Amendment Act No. 11 of 2017, the right of asylum seekers to seek employment in South Africa has been severely curtailed (GRSA, 2017). This right may be rejected especially if asylum claimants have the financial resources to support themselves and their dependents through friends, relatives, or charitable organisations. Asylum seekers are now required to obtain special permission from the Standing Committee for Refugee Affairs to seek employment while their claims are being adjudicated. Notably, as asylum seekers, they are not allowed to operate any businesses in the country (Gastrow, 2018). These latest changes further contradict key judgments by South African courts, which have treated the ability of registered asylums seekers to seek self-employment as being vital to their fundamental and Constitutional rights of dignity and equality (Kavuro, 2022).

The growth and relative success of refugee and migrant-owned small businesses has long been a source of anxiety in South Africa for various state and non-state actors. The CEO of the North-West province's Chamber of Commerce claimed in 2019 that 82% of that area's small- and medium-sized enterprises (SMEs) were owned by non-citizens (PMG, 2022b). South Africa's Parliamentary Portfolio Committee for the Department of Small Business Development similarly expressed their concern in April 2022 about 'foreign nationals taking over the small business sector' and ongoing tensions between South African and non-citizen small-scale entrepreneurs (PMG, 2022a). There have been several attempts to severely limit the entrepreneurial activities of refugees, asylum seekers, and other migrants by way of new restrictive by-laws and stringent requirements selectively imposed on non-citizen-owned small businesses. The Department of Trade and Industry introduced a Licensing of Business Bill in March 2013, which would require all businesses selling goods or services, including hawkers or street vendors, to hold special licences in an obvious attempt to strongly limit entrepreneurial activities of non-citizens in the informal economy (Gastrow, 2018). This bill was later withdrawn after strong protests. In 2015, then Small Business Development Minister Lindiwe Zulu argued that non-citizens should not be permitted to run small or large businesses without complying with a special set of requirements. More recently, the Minister of Small Business Development informed South Africa's National Assembly that only non-citizens who qualify for a business visa by being able to make a minimum financial or capital investment of R5 million (approx. USD 262,000) should be allowed to work as entrepreneurs, and that this requirement also extended to those operating small informal businesses (PMG, 2022b). The department is reviewing the Businesses Act no. 71 of 1991 to introduce new restrictions on non-citizen-operated small businesses and offer enhanced protectionist measures for South African informal traders.

A latest vexed development is the emergence of a new vigilante group named Operation Dudula, whose members have been organising frequent violent actions against refugee and migrant traders and businesses, accusing them of unlawful practices and insisting that their entrepreneurial activities harm the economic prospects of South Africans. Launched in 2021 as an online campaign and now expanded as a political organisation, Dudula is a isiZulu term which means expel or push out. In June 2022, Operation Dudula members demanded that only South Africans be allowed to operate businesses at the Johannesburg Park Station in this city, which is a popular destination for migrants and refugees (Majola, 2022). Two days earlier, the Yeoville market in Johannesburg was destroyed by an apparent arson attack soon after its refugee and migrant business operators received threats from this group's members to vacate the area and surrender their businesses to South Africans (Mutandiro, 2022; Seleka, 2022).

Discussion and conclusion

We have analysed some key elements of refugee entrepreneurship in South Africa in this chapter. This research contributes to a very small body of literature on refugee entrepreneurship in the major hosting countries in the global South. Our findings underscore the individual and collective agency and initiative of refugee entrepreneurs to rebuild their lives in South Africa, gain financial independence, and their dedicated efforts to achieve their entrepreneurial aspirations. We further document the multiple, yet often overlooked, positive contributions of refugee entrepreneurial activities to local economies.

Unlike some other host country settings, the entrepreneurial activities of refugees and asylum seekers have attracted significant attention in South Africa for a decade or so. However, much of this scrutiny has not been in a constructive vein, with refugee entrepreneurs regularly accused of unfair advantage and using illegal activities to both establish and build their businesses. The emergence of refugee entrepreneurship and economic integration of refugees is perceived as being detrimental to the development of South African SMEs. As a result, refugee entrepreneurs operate their businesses in a difficult, often hostile, social, economic, and political environment. This situation has not improved since 2015, with new attempts by non-state and state actors to severely control and curtail these entrepreneurial activities. Addressing xenophobic discrimination and public violence are vital to creating a positive and supportive environment for refugee entrepreneurship in this prominent hosting country.

Finally, we identify two aspects that need further research attention. A key feature of refugee entrepreneurship in South Africa is the regular exposure of refugee-owned or operated businesses to various forms of discrimination and xenophobic violence. Violence-affected entrepreneurs are forced to rebuild their businesses after such episodes. It is unclear just how many refugee business operators can successfully recover from such regular losses. This is an aspect that requires further examination. Most of the sample of respondents in the SAMP survey were operating their businesses for only about a decade. A second dimension that requires greater attention is the extent to and ways in which refugee entrepreneurs can transition out of survivalist mode. This is an important neglected aspect, especially since refugee entrepreneurs face an additional set of challenges in operating their businesses in South Africa.

References

Abebe, S.A. (2023). Refugee entrepreneurship: Systematic and thematic analyses and a research agenda. *Small Business Economics*, *60*, 315–350. https://doi.org/10.1007/s11187-022-00636-3

Charman, A., Petersen, L., & Piper, L. (2012). From local survivalism to foreign entrepreneurship: The transformation of the spaza sector in Delft, Cape Town. *Transformation: Critical Perspectives on Southern Africa*, *78*(1), 47–73. https://doi.org/10.1353/trn.2012.0035

Crush, J., & Chikanda, A. (2014). Forced migration in Southern Africa. In E. Fiddian-Qasmiyeh, G. Loescher, K. Long, & N. Sigona (Eds.), *The Oxford Handbook of Refugee and Forced Migration Studies* (pp. 554–570). Oxford: Oxford University Press.

Crush, J., Chikanda, A., & Skinner, C. (2015). *Mean Streets: Migration, Xenophobia and Informality in South Africa*. Ottawa: IDRC.

Crush, J., & Ramachandran, S. (2015). Doing business with xenophobia. In J. Crush, A. Chikanda, & C. Skinner (Eds.), *Mean Streets: Migration, Xenophobia and Informality in South Africa* (pp. 25–59). Waterloo and Cape Town: Southern African Migration Programme, African Centre for Cities and International Development Research Centre.

Crush, J., Tawodzera, G., McCordic, C., & Ramachandran, S. (2017a). Refugee Entrepreneurial Economies in Urban South Africa. *SAMP Migration Policy Series No. 76*. Waterloo: Southern African Migration Programme and Balsillie School of International Affairs.

Crush, J., Tawodzera, G., Chikanda, A., & Tevera, D. (2017b). The owners of xenophobia: Zimbabwean informal enterprise and xenophobic violence in South Africa. *African Human Mobility Review*, *3*(2), 879–909. https://epubs.ac.za/index.php/ahmr/article/download/831/618

Crush, J., Tawodzera, G., McCordic, C., & Ramachandran, S. (2017c). *Comparing Refugees and South Africans in the Urban Informal Sector. SAMP Migration Policy Series No. 78*. Waterloo: Southern African Migration Programme and Balsillie School of International Affairs.

Department of Home Affairs. (2015). *2015 Asylum Statistics: Analysis and Trends for the Period January to December: Presentation to the Portfolio Committee of Home Affairs*. Pretoria: Department of Home Affairs, Republic of South Africa.

Desai, S., Naudé, W., & Stel, N. (2020). Refugee entrepreneurship: Context and directions for future research. *Small Business Economics*, *56*, 933–945. https://doi.org/10.1007/s11187-019-00310-1

Fatoki, O. (2013). An investigation into the financial bootstrapping methods used by immigrant entrepreneurs in South Africa. *Journal of Economics*, *4*(2), 89–96. https://doi.org/10.1080/09765239.2013.11884968

Ferraro, F., & Weideman, M. (2020). Labour-related experiences of migrants and refugees in South Africa. In R. Vitillo, & I. Alasino (Eds.), *The Future of Work: Labour Migrants in the 21st Century*. https://icmc.net/future-of-work/report/04-south-africa/

Gastrow, V. (2018). *Problematizing the Foreign Shop: Justifications for Restricting the Migrant Spaza Sector in South Africa. SAMP Migration Policy Series No. 80.* Waterloo and Cape Town: Southern African Migration Programme and African Centre for Cities.

Gastrow, V. (2022). *Citizen and Pariah: Somali Traders and the Regulation of Difference in South Africa.* New York: New York University Press.

GRSA. Government of the Republic of South Africa. (2017). *White Paper on International Migration for South Africa.* www.dha.gov.za/WhitePaper-Gazette_z.pdf

GRSA. Government of the Republic of South Africa. (2022). *Draft National Labour Migration Policy for South Africa.* www.labour.gov.za/DocumentCenter/Publications/Public%20Employment%20Services/National%20Labour%20Migration%20Policy%202021%202.pdf

Heilbrunn, S., & Iannone, R. (2019). Introduction. In S. Heilbrunn, J. Freiling, & A. Harima (Eds.), *Refugee Entrepreneurship: A Case-Based Topography* (pp. 1–26). Cham: Springer.

Heilbrunn, S., & Iannone, R. (2020). From centre to periphery and back again: A systematic literature review of refugee entrepreneurship. *Sustainability*, *12*(18), 7658. https://doi.org/10.3390/su12187658

HRW. Human Rights Watch. (2020). *"They Have Robbed Me of My Life": Xenophobic Violence against Non-Nationals in South Africa.* New York: Human Rights Watch.

HRW. Human Rights Watch. (2021). *World Report 2021.* www.hrw.org/world-report/2021/country-chapters/south-africa#90de97

Ikuomola, A.D., & Zaaiman, J. (2016). We have come to stay and we shall find all means to live and work in this country: Nigerian migrants and life challenges in South Africa. *Issues in Ethnology and Anthropology*, *9*, 371–389. https://eap-iea.org/index.php/eap/article/view/498

ILO. International Labour Organisation. (2016). *Guiding Principles on the Access of Refugees and Other Forcibly Displaced Persons to the Labour Market.* www.ilo.org/publications/guiding-principles-access-refugees-and-other-forcibly-displaced-persons

Kalitanyi, V. (2007). *Evaluation of Employment Creation by African Immigrant Entrepreneurs for Unemployed South Africans in Cape Town.* Cape Town: University of the Western Cape.

Kavuro, C. (2022). The disappearance of refugee rights in South Africa. *Obiter*, *43*(1), 49–79. www.scielo.org.za/pdf/obiter/v43n1/03.pdf

Khosa, R., & Kalitanyi, V. (2015). Migration reasons, traits and entrepreneurial motivation of African immigrant entrepreneurs. *Journal of Enterprising Communities: People and Places in the Global Economy*, *9*(2), 132–155. https://doi.org/10.1108/JEC-07-2014-0011

Lee, E.S., Szkudlarek, B., Nguyen, D.C., & Nardon, L. (2020). Unveiling the canvas ceiling: A multidisciplinary literature review of refugee employment and workforce integration. *International Journal of Management Reviews*, *22*(2), 193–216. https://doi.org/10.1111/ijmr.12222.

Majola, D. (2022). "One Voice of All Hawkers' Association criticizes attacks on foreign nationals". *Eyewitness News*, 24 June. https://ewn.co.za/2022/06/24/one-voice-of-all-hawkers-association-criticises-attacks-on-foreign-nationals

Mitchell, B. (2004). Motives of entrepreneurs: A case study of South Africa. *Journal of Entrepreneurship*, *13*(2), 167–183. https://doi.org/10.1177/097135570401300202

Mutandiro, K. (2022). "Yeoville market fire was a xenophobic attack, say activists and stall owners". *Ground Up*, 22 June. www.groundup.org.za/article/yeoville-market-fire-was-a-xenophobic-attack-say-activists-and-stall-owners/

Newman, A., Macaulay, L., & Dunwoodie, K. (2023). Refugee entrepreneurship: A systematic review of prior research and agenda for future research. *International Migration Review*. https://doi.org/10.1177/01979183231182669

Northcote, M., & Dodson, B. (2015). Refugees and asylum seekers in Cape Town's informal economy. In J. Crush, A. Chikanda, & C. Skinner, (Eds.), *Mean Streets Migration, Xenophobia and Informality in South Africa* (pp. 145–161). Waterloo: Southern African Migration Programme.

Piper, L., & Charman, A. (2016). Xenophobia, price competition and violence in the spaza sector in South Africa. *African Human Mobility Review*, *2*(1), 332–361. https://sihma.org.za/journals/Piper-Charman.pdf

PMG. Parliamentary Monitoring Group. (2022a). Department of Small Business Development 2022/23 Performance Plan, Portfolio Committee Meeting with Deputy Minister. 29 April.

PMG. Parliamentary Monitoring Group. (2022b). Question NW2884 to the Minister of Small Business Development. 26 October.

Raijman, R., & Barak-Bianco, A. (2015). Asylum seeker entrepreneurs in Israel. *Economic Sociology Newsletter*, *16*(2), 4–13. http://hdl.handle.net/10419/156049

Ramachandran, S., Crush, J., & Tawodzera, G. (2017). Security risk and xenophobia in the urban informal sector. *African Human Mobility Review*, *3*(2), 854–878. https://sihma.org.za/journals/4_Security-Risk-and-Xenophobia-in-the-Urban-Informal-Sector-min.pdf

Robichaud, Y., McGraw E. & Roger, A. (2001). Toward the development of a measuring instrument for entrepreneurial motivation. *Journal of Development Entrepreneurship*, *6*(2), 189–201. www.proquest.com/scholarly-journals/toward-development-measuring-instrument/docview/208438787/se-2

Rukuni, T., Maziriri, E., Dhlamlenze, M., & Benedict, E. (2022). Entrepreneurship as a strategy for refugees in South Africa. *International Entrepreneurship Review*, *8*(2), 37–50. https://doi.org/10.15678/IER.2022.0802.03

Seleka, N. (2022). 'We have lost everything': Vendors count the costs after Joburg's Yeoville Market gutted in fire. News24, 22 June. www.news24.com/news24/southafrica/news/we-have-lost-everything-vendors-count-the-costs-after-joburgs-yeoville-market-gutted-in-fire-20220622

Shane, S., Locke, E.A., & Collins, C. (2003). Entrepreneurial motivation. *Human Resource Management Review*, *13*(2), 257–279. https://doi.org/10.1016/S1053-4822(03)00017-2

Tawodzera, G., Chikanda, A., Crush, J., & Tengeh, R. (2015). *International Migrants and Refugees in Cape Town's Informal Economy. SAMP Migration Policy Series No. 70*. Waterloo: Southern African Migration Programme.

Tevera, D. (2013). African migrants, xenophobia and urban violence in postapartheid South Africa. *Alternation*, *7*, 9–26. https://repository.uwc.ac.za/xmlui/handle/10566/1632

UNHCR. (2022a). *Global Roadmap for Refugee Entrepreneurship*. Geneva: UNHCR.

UNHCR. (2022b). *Global Trends: Forced Displacement in 2022*. Geneva: UNHCR.

UNHCR: United Nations High Commissioner for Refugees (2023). *Refugee Data Finder*. Geneva: UNHCR. Available on www.unhcr.org/refugee-statistics/ (Accessed September 21, 2023).

Vijaya, V., & Kamalanabhan, T.J. (1998). A scale to assess entrepreneurial motivation. *The Journal of Entrepreneurship*, *7*(2), 183–198. https://doi.org/10.1177/097135579800700204

World Bank. (2018). *Mixed Migration, Forced Displacement and Job Outcomes in South Africa*. Washington, DC: World Bank.

11 Refugee (social) entrepreneurship and civic action in the context of urban shrinkage

Insights from the US city of Akron (OH)

Norma Schemschat

Introduction

Research on refugee entrepreneurship has proliferated in recent years, and depending on the context, it is discussed as a path towards integration, a driver of urban change, or a challenge for local migration governance in cities (Abebe, 2023; Atasü-Topcuoğlu, 2019; Bizri, 2017; Desai et al., 2021; Harb et al., 2019; Heilbrunn & Iannone, 2020; Price & Chacko, 2009; Senthanar et al., 2021; Wauters & Lambrecht, 2008). In the context of shrinking cities,[1] refugee entrepreneurship is largely put forward as opportunity through stories of refugees as 'saviours', redressing population decline and boosting local economies. As a result, refugee-centred revitalisation as a strategy to halt demographic and economic decline has entered planning and policy debates in recent years (Housel et al., 2018; Judelsohn et al., 2017; Kühn, 2018; Pottie-Sherman, 2018; Pottie-Sherman, 2020; Pottie-Sherman & Graham, 2021; Sampedro & Camarero, 2018).[2]

Shrinking cities are ambivalent places for arriving refugees. On the one hand, they can be spaces of opportunities, thanks to residential or commercial vacancies. On the other, they can pose challenges to refugee emplacement, including tight municipal budgets, socio-political challenges, and economic constraints. Under such conditions, (social) entrepreneurship can be a means for refugees to regain autonomy, omit structural barriers, and – as we shall see – enact agency. Sometimes, such activities can be co-opted by local decision-makers who put individuals and their success stories on pedestals, increasing the pressures on local community members to follow such examples, thus feeding into what Hackl (2022) coined "conditionality of belonging". And yet, numerous examples of refugee-centred revitalisation exist, turning shrinking cities into interesting laboratories for analysing the complexities tied to refugee entrepreneurship, how it relates to civic action, and how it shapes urban development.

In the US, the Rust Belt region provides examples of shrinking cities that pursued revitalisation by including refugee arrivals into local revitalisation strategies. In this context, refugee-centred revitalisation is discussed predominantly as a top-down strategy, through which the leadership of a shrinking

DOI: 10.4324/9781003368540-14

city opts for inclusive communication strategies. They portray their city as welcoming and immigrant-friendly to attract newcomers who they hope will launch businesses and revitalise the local economy, even if they cannot provide the same offers as growing gateway cities. For example, refugees in Buffalo (NY) are viewed as essential for tackling population loss and invigorating the economy (Judelsohn et al., 2017), as they are in Cleveland's *Dream Neighborhood* project (Day, 2017; Blanco, 2017; Nightengale, 2015). Pottie-Sherman (2018, 2020) has worked extensively on refugees and their integration in revitalisation efforts of cities in the former manufacturing belts of the US and Canada. Further investigated here is Akron's North Hill district, a neighbourhood now known as Akron's *International District*. Through engaged local actors, widespread vacancies and comparatively low real estate prices, numerous refugees found a home and succeeded in opening businesses there. As a result, the neighbourhood is now known for its international atmosphere and for being home to a diverse refugee community.

This study aims to understand how a close-knit network of socially responsive entrepreneurial actors, who are linked to or part of the local refugee population, are driving neighbourhood revitalisation in North Hill. The positive neighbourhood change has led the municipal government to embrace refugee populations in 're-scaling' efforts. The analysis is based on interviews with local refugee entrepreneurs, community leaders, and actors at the junction of economic and urban development, as well as planning documents and media articles. It critics neoliberal resettlement policies in the US and examines how shrinking city governments' diversity-centred rhetoric are entangled and increasingly incorporate bottom-up practices by refugee populations. Through such efforts, refugees enact agency and drive emplacement while becoming part of increasingly neoliberal urban governance, in which diversity is used by urban planners as asset. The analysis will look closely at the complex interrelations between bottom-up place-making by activists and refugee entrepreneurs, and neoliberal restructuring, with the goal to contribute to research on refugee entrepreneurship and civic action in spaces of institutional withdrawal. Place-making, here, will be understood in the Lefebvrian sense: as spatial practice of making place through daily practices of living in space (Lefebvre, 1991).

The chapter will show that (social) entrepreneurship within Akron's refugee community is embedded culturally, economically, geographically, and socially, and that the local context facilitates the activities of some groups, while structural inequalities hinder those of others. In focusing on the North Hill neighbourhood, where a resettlement agency was present for a long time and which has been characterised by widespread residential and commercial vacancy, this chapter investigates the revitalisation that took place over the past 20 years. This revitalisation was driven by the resettlement of refugees who not only found homes in vacant housing but also opened business in commercial vacancies. The chapter argues that while refugee entrepreneurship contributes significantly to local urban revitalisation, a place-based, historically sensitive, political, and social approach is needed to understand the challenges and opportunities of refugee entrepreneurship in places affected by urban decline, and to move from welcoming rhetoric towards welcoming action.

Investigating refugee entrepreneurship at the nexus of resettlement and local development

Within the research on migrant entrepreneurship, refugee entrepreneurial activities have received less attention, even though the forced nature of their mobility may well be influencing their entrepreneurial activities and how it impacts cities. Hence, recent years have seen a steep rise in research activity on refugee entrepreneurship (Abebe, 2023; Atasü-Topcuoğlu, 2019; Bizri, 2017; Desai et al., 2021; Harb et al., 2019; Heilbrunn & Iannone, 2020; Price & Chacko, 2009; Senthanar et al., 2021; Wauters & Lambrecht, 2008). For example, in their research on Syrian entrepreneurs, Harb et al. (2019) find that entrepreneurship was chosen by some refugees for its capacity to provide flexibility, or for the simple fact that they had been self-employed before (Harb et al., 2019). Like for other migrant groups, the literature shows that entrepreneurship can be a source of agency and self-sufficiency for refugees. However, Desai et al. (2021) emphasise that research has yet to further investigate "how refugees engage in entrepreneurship – and in economic activity more broadly", calling it "a sizable knowledge gap" (2021, p. 935).

What is still to be understood, however, is just how refugee entrepreneurship shapes local development (see Siviş, 2021; Cremaschi et al., 2020). In the US, debates on the impact of refugees on local economies considers costs and benefits of refugee resettlement, while discussions are marked largely by questions of 'burden sharing' in Europe. Besides such narratives, refugee arrival is at times discussed for its potential positive impact on local economies. The rationales behind various national refugee dispersal schemes, ranging from early examples in Canada to more recent ones in France, underline that national policies of refugee integration increasingly consider how resettlement can benefit local development. In the US context, Evans and Fitzgerald (2017) find that while resettled refugees face low employment levels at first, the high dependence on welfare changes as time passes. In their study of American Community Survey (ACS) data, they find that refugees show higher employment rates than other migrant groups after six years of being resettled, with welfare costs being covered by tax returns within 20 years.

The work of the pro-immigration think tank *New American Economy* (NAE), a non-profit and bi-partisan advocacy and research organisation that works on the connection between immigration and economic development, equally builds on ACS data. They analysed the economic impact of roughly 2.3 million refugees that resettled to the US between the years 1975 and 2017 and found that household income rose significantly after 25 years: from $22,000 for refugee households who were in the US for five years to $67,000 for households that were in the country for 25 years

(NAE, 2017). The NAE is also active in promoting the positive impact refugee resettlement has on Akron's local economy, advocating for the significant role refugee entrepreneurship has played in local revitalisation. NAE research puts forward the role refugees play in Akron's demographic and economic stabilisation, stating that a 30.8% rise in the foreign-born population between 2007 and 2013 slowed Akron's demographic decline (NAE, 2017, p. 4), and that 5.6% of manufacturing and 6.7% of service industry workers are refugees. These industries, according to the NAE, are still key industries in Akron (NAE, 2017, p. 11).

This chapter connects to this growing debate on the role of refugee entrepreneurship in revitalisation processes and considers both entrepreneurship and social entrepreneurship in Akron's North Hill neighbourhood. The latter will be investigated from the perspective of non-profit and social activist forms of entrepreneurial activity and its impact on urban development. The analysis will follow Murphy and Chatzipanagiotidou (2020, p. 4) in referring to social entrepreneurship as a "continuum" within which social entrepreneurship is generally defined as activities which base the measurement of value in terms of social impact.

Despite its limited scope, this examination of (social) entrepreneurship and civic action in Akron (OH) follows Desai et al.'s (2021) call for more evidence on refugee entrepreneurship that could inform local policies. It seeks to close a knowledge gap on what we know about how newly arrived refugees' entrepreneurial activities shape shrinking places and drive revitalisation – including the opportunities and challenges tied to it. We will show that refugee entrepreneurship and bottom-up civic action are tightly linked in a setting marked by urban shrinkage and the devolution of social services, including those targeted at refugee populations.

Methodology

To learn more about the interrelations of refugee entrepreneurship, civic action, and urban revitalisation in Akron (OH), various qualitative data were triangulated (Flick, 2011) to achieve and in-depth understanding of local action in the context of urban growth and decline. As method of data analysis, a critical discourse analysis (CDA) (Fairclough, 2012) was applied. The choice of CDA lay in its focus on the rich contextualisation of verbal and written text, and hence going beyond textual analysis through the inclusion of historical, spatial, and socio-economic data. As a result, six policy and planning documents were analysed, including the Welcoming Plan put forward by the City of Akron and Summit County. To situate local action in a historical and geographical context, online archival materials, images derived from *Google Street View* (GVS), 63 local and national media articles, and Census and Community Survey Data were analysed.

Further, a total of 14 semi-structured interviews of durations between 45 minutes and two hours were conducted and build the main data set for this analysis. Due to the pandemic and subsequent travel restrictions, these interviews were held via Zoom. Thanks to the openness of local actors and the successful snowball sampling, the online interviews were continued even when travel restrictions were lifted, allowing for exchanges covering three years (from February 2020 to April 2023). The actors interviewed include policymakers in urban planning and economic development, members of local non-governmental organisations (NGOs), members of regional foundations, members of the local refugee community, refugee community leaders, and members of two local community development corporations (CDCs). Written consent was obtained from all interview participants. To ensure participants' anonymity, broad job descriptions were used for local policymakers and members of local institutions, as well as pseudonyms for members of the refugee community. Interviews were transcribed and subsequently analysed with the qualitative data analysis software *MaxQDA* to identify common themes, patterns, and sub-discourses.

To understand and localise refugee place-making in Akron and the role entrepreneurship and civic action play in it, the next section offers the rich contextualisation demanded by CDA. In a first step, a description of the cities trajectory of urban growth and decline is presented, upon which a brief overview of immigration and refugee arrival in Akron (OH) will be given to understand how it gained importance in planning and revitalisation strategies. The section hence traces Akron's urban trajectory and development into a place for refugees' arrivals.

Urban growth and decline in the former 'rubber capital of the world'

Akron (OH) is a mid-sized city located in the US Great Lakes Region. At approximately 165.2 km^2, it is the fifth largest city in the state of Ohio. Located about 65 km south of Cleveland and 80 km west of Youngstown, Akron is firmly embedded in a region strongly affected by urban shrinkage. Emblematic of so-called 'legacy' cities, Akron grew rapidly in the early 20th century, thanks to the booming local rubber industry. Once one of the fastest-growing cities in the US its population grew from 69,067 to 208,435 inhabitants between 1910 and 1920 alone. At a time when the automotive industry in the Great Lakes region took off, Akron's tire manufacturers became the main suppliers in the US: "By 1930, 40 percent of the nation's tires were built in Akron" (Love & Giffels, 1999, p. xiv). This rapid development boosted Akron in terms of scale and resulted in its nickname, 'Rubber Capital of the world'.[3]

At that time, immigration was needed and encouraged, and workers of various nationalities found work in local factories. However, due to globalisation and the outsourcing of rubber production to the US Sunbelt, all rubber manufacturers apart from General Tires had shut down by1982. With the out-migration of young people and increasing financial pressures, the city was "burdened by the hardest times since the Depression" (Love & Giffels, 1999,

p. xiv). With rapidly advancing deindustrialisation, Akron experienced a continuous demographic decline after reaching its population peak of 290,000 inhabitants in 1960. With an estimated population of 188,701 in 2023 (US Bureau of the Census, 2024), the city has lost almost 35% of its population. The shrinkage effects have been considerable with a low population density, high residential and commercial vacancy rates, and socio-economic difficulties.[4]

While Akron was once an expanding city, thanks to large-scale manufacturing, today, the manufacturing sector provided only 37,900 jobs in August 2023, according to the US Bureau of Labour Statistics (2023). Most jobs today can be found in the sectors of trade, transportation, and utilities (68,600 jobs), the service sector, including professional and business services (49,400 jobs), education and health services (56,900 jobs), and leisure and hospitality (33,500 jobs) (US Bureau of Labor Statistics, 2023). While residential vacancy rates have dropped over time, the foreclosure crisis in combination with an old housing stock in the city has led to the re-emergence of elevated residential vacancy rates in the recent years. According to the American Community Survey, 14.6% of Akron's housing was vacant, excluding abandoned structures (Planning to Grow Akron, 2017, p. 10).

The city is employing several policies and strategies to tackle urban decline. In Akron, the foreign-born population is small but growing, making immigration an important factor in tackling demographic decline, with international immigration being strongly shaped by refugee resettlement through the arrival of both primary and secondary refugees. While the former are refugees resettled directly to Akron, the latter move there upon having been previously resettled to other US cities. Secondary refugee arrival is high because the North Hill neighbourhood has become increasingly attractive for refugees due to the tightly knit network of refugees and local actors working with them.

This international immigration has increasingly shaped Akron's demographics since the early 2000s. Table 11.1 shows how the White population is steadily declining, how the Black population saw an increase until 2010 upon

Table 11.1 Population development by race in Akron (OH)

Population group	*Year*					
	1970	*1980*	*1990*	*2000*	*2010*	*2021*
White	226.362	182.114	164.493	145.925	123.879	112.605
Black	48.205	52.719	54.656	61.827	62.648	56.969
Asian	-	-	2.701	3.257	4.218	8.955
Hispanic	-	1.534	1.601	2.513	4.255	5.906
Other	858	1.118	566	1.832	1.543	-
Total	275.425	237.177	223.019	217.074	199.110	190.534

Source: US Bureau of the Census, years 1970–2021, own representation.

when it fell, while Hispanic and other populations are increasing, with the Asian population in Akron more than doubling between 2010 and 2021. The Asian American and Pacific Islanders (AAPI)[5] community in Akron experienced the greatest growth, driven largely by a growing South Asian refugee population.

For many shrinking Rust Belt cities, immigration is discussed as a promising response to depopulation: "Across the Midwest, 37% of all metro population growth during the 2012–2017 period is attributed to immigrants" (Pottie-Sherman, 2020, p. 4). In Akron, the share of newcomers grew by 77.4% while the native-born population shrunk by 0.7% between 2000 and 2015 (Paral, 2017).

The city has, together with Summit County, launched a *Welcoming Akron and Summit County* plan through which the city has joined the Welcoming America network. The plan stems from combined efforts by local organisations such as *Global Ties Akron* and *Asian Services in Action Inc.* (ASIA Inc.), as well as the *IIA*, Summit County, and the mayor's office in Akron. In participating in the *Gateways for Growth Challenge*, the involved actors obtained funding and technical assistance from the Washington-based pro-immigration non-profit *American Immigration Council* and *Welcome America* networks, the two institutions initiating the Gateways competition. The goal of the welcoming plan is for Summit County and Akron to integrate refugees and other migrants – mainly in terms of economic integration. While the report speaks about increasing refugees' and other newcomers' sense of belonging, it is also strongly connected to local economic development. The introductory letter to the plan reads:

> Immigrants and refugees are a vital part of our community. They bring fresh perspective and new ideas, start-up businesses, and they contribute to the vibrant diversity we all value. Communities across the country are constantly competing to attract the human capital that will allow them to thrive in a global economy. More importantly, communities around the world are grappling with how they will live their values in an age of growing migration.
>
> (Welcoming Summit County & Akron, 2017)

A report by the previously mentioned think thank NAE estimates that up to 27% of the foreign-born population in Akron are refugees (NAE, 2017, p. 4). Vulnerable to policies at the federal level, the restrictive immigration policies of former President Trump and the lowering of refugee admission caps led to a dramatic decline in refugee arrivals in Akron, leading to the shutdown of one out of two local resettlement agencies. As put by Shrider, the lowering of refugee admission caps led to "[t]he one trusty source of immigrants – refugees – is being cut off" (Shrider, 2017, p. 131) putting refugee-centred revitalisation policies at risk.

The remaining resettlement agency is the *International Institute Akron* (IIA), which is involved during the first 90 days of refugees' arrival, providing first financial assistance, support in financial literacy, housing, and other support needed upon immediate arrival. Given the complex challenges refugees face upon being resettled, this period is too short, resulting in the emergence of a local support structure primarily driven by local organisations and refugees themselves.

As the review of literature and the contextualisation showed, refugees play an important role in Akron's economy, with revitalisation spatially concentrated in the North Hill neighbourhood. Focussing on this local level, the following section will investigate these processes more closely by focusing on refugee (social) entrepreneurship and civic action taking place in and shaping North Hill.

Place-making in Akron's North Hill neighbourhood through refugee (social) entrepreneurship and civic Action

Various forms of refugee-led commercial and civic action have contributed to local revitalisation in Akron's North Hill, in which three business strips centre around East Tallmadge Avenue, North Main Street, and East Cuyahoga Falls Avenue. This forms the so-called Temple Square and with it the centre of economic revitalisation in the neighbourhood. Within Temple Square numerous shops, restaurants, and service providers have opened which cater to the local refugee population and other diverse populations surrounding it. Towards its west, residents comprise mainly African Americans and Latinx populations, separated from largely White populations to its North, where housing costs rise in direction of more middle-class suburbs such as Cuyahoga Falls. Refugees are centred in the Southern central part of the neighbourhood.

A virtual walk via GSV in close consultation of local business directories and information provided by governmental initiatives such as Great Streets Akron (2018) reveal at least 11 shops catering to refugee populations by providing specific groceries or access to traditional clothing. At least three associations address the needs of refugee groups (e.g., culturally sensitive healthcare services), which show how refugee (social) entrepreneurship and civic action manifest locally in North Hill.

Refugee entrepreneurship in Akron

While it is crucial to go beyond the conception of refugee-led revitalisation as a strategy based solely on refugees' economic contributions, it must be acknowledged that refugee entrepreneurship plays a role in revitalising shrinking cities. In North Hill, we find that high commercial vacancy rates allowed our interview participants to meet unmet needs in their shrinking places of arrival. The stories of our participants show how self-employment was a way to enact agency by filling gaps in services and finding recognition in economic activities that support the local refugee population. An example of this is opening supermarkets that cater to the consumption habits of New Americans.

In the following, we illuminate on the example of Pema, a local refugee community leader from Bhutan, and his story of entrepreneurship and contribution to North Hill's revitalisation. Upon increasing arrival of Bhutanese refugees, Pema realised that a variety of products he and his ethnic community generally consumed were not readily available locally:

> *Initially, it was just my family who came here, later on, followed by my friends from the refugee camps in Bhutan, my neighbours, etc. And so they would look for food they were used to eating in the camps, but they wouldn't find it here, and I needed to drive to places as far as Cleveland where there were a few places where we could find products similar to what we were used to eating.*
>
> (Pema, Interview Akron, February 2021)

After offering a driving service between Akron and Cleveland for community members interested in buying products and other items for Bhutanese cuisine, he relatively quickly decided that this approach was not sustainable. He recalls that he and his wife would drive other community members to Cleveland, but "when the population grew, that became a full-time job […] more than a full-time job […]". At this point, they "knew that there was a need for ethnic foods" (Pema, Interview Akron, February 2021) in Akron, so that he and his family started to wonder:

> *[…] about how we could solve this problem. And since the refugee population [was] growing and the needs [were] growing, the demands [were] growing, and so we thought, 'Well, this is too much. How about we collect all the food and get it all in one place? How about we open a store?' So, I spoke with my brother and my nephew, and we ended up opening this grocery store. In the meantime, we also got self-employed. So that's how it began. There was a demand. There was a need.*

The collective need among newcomers for known foods and products, as described in Pema's story, and the important role they play in home- and place-making are subject to increasing scholarly interest. While research on food security in the context of refugee arrival is still limited, Judelsohn et al. (2021) establish in their study on food security of resettled refugees in the US that:

> New Americans may have had limited access to processed foods, health care, and a balanced diet in their previous homes. Transition into the US may lead to shifts in food experiences, with a paradoxical outcome: while new Americans may find refuge from political and legal persecution, they

may find themselves at risk of diet-related chronic disease in the long term, especially for those with children at home.

(Judelsohn et al., 2021, p. 3)

That Pema and his family, like other refugees in North Hill, took matters into their own hands is also because municipalities still need to engage with the food-related needs of newcomers. Pema has by now opened a second branch of his shop and actively contributes to what Judelsohn et al. (2021) refer to as 'food systems of belonging'. His was only the first of many shops to open in North Hill, thanks to the coming together of new needs, demands, and commercial vacancies. As such, Pema's story is of enacting agency not only for himself but for other members of the North Hill community. The granting of access to food and other produce has been only the beginning of a larger process of transforming the retail landscape in North Hill from a location strongly marked by vacancies towards a retail hub specialised on groceries and other products catering to the needs of the growing refugee population. The following excerpt from our conversation with Pema underlines this:

Interviewer: *How much self-employment is there? It was mentioned that vacant shopfronts would gradually disappear. Was this due to the new shop owners?*

Pema: *Exactly, yeah! There are many groceries like mine now, many of them, there are several restaurants, there are gift shops… There are places where they offer dancing and singing classes and language classes. And there are several home care agencies set up which were launched by refugees.*

Interviewer: *That sounds like an entire industry of services emerged thanks to refugee arrival.*

Pema: *Yes!*

(Pema, Interview Akron, February 2021)

Pema's businesses depend on the local socio-economic and institutional contexts. A well-established network of refugees, local organisations, and the steady arrival of newcomers allowed his business to stabilise and expand by now. The past years of reduced refugee arrival and the pandemic have posed challenges to Pema, but he and his partners used these challenges to offer their shop as a space for information and exchange. Overall, Pema considers the refugee-driven retail landscape in North Hill stable:

Businesses increased in number, and potentially in revenue. It is not only the Bhutanese community that founds businesses, but Burmese and Congolese refugee communities, too. I have stopped counting the businesses: there are groceries, restaurants and bars, gift shops. […]

(Pema, Interview Akron, April 2023)

For Pema, establishing his business and filling gaps in local service provision is considered part of his 'job' as a New American: "As US citizen I have the obligation to make my place better".

Entrepreneurs like Pema do not work entirely independent from other local actors. A major coordinating actor in local activities between economic and civic action is the *North Hill Community Development Corporation (NHCDC)*. Its self-ascribed role is to "empower" the North Hill communities and "amplify their diverse voices, share their lived experience", and "create a community they dream of" (NHCDC, 2022). This is a mammoth task in a city that underwent such rapid changes. One of the CDC's major projects is the *Exchange House*. A formerly vacant house, today it serves as a meeting place for refugees and other local groups, and simultaneously serves as Hostel for travellers who are interested in the *International District*.

Part of the NHCDC's work aims to improve social cohesion, including for non-refugee residents who sometimes feel 'left behind'. This problem was mentioned by Pema:

> *Refugee entrepreneurship has only positive effects for a place. That said, in 2008 no local business was ready to hire refugees due to language barriers or a lack in mobility. However, once businesses saw how hard-working, honest, and loyal refugees were, they over time increasingly hired refugees and New Americans. Over time, this even led to local American-born workers being 'left behind'.*
>
> (Pema, Interview Akron, April 2023)

At the NHCDC, technical support for refugee entrepreneurs, civic action, and neighbourhood development go hand in hand. In the next section, we will look more closely at these socially centred forms of entrepreneurship and civic action.

Service provision by and for refugees: Refugee social entrepreneurship in Akron

Besides the above-described entrepreneurial activities exemplified by Pema, we find that refugee emplacement in Akron is also driven by refugee-led associations and social enterprises which cater to the social needs of refugees (Murphy & Chazipanagiotidou, 2020). Notable actors here are the aforementioned NHCDC and other community development agencies such as *Legacies of Success*, organisations such as *Asian Services in Action (ASIA) Inc.*, and smaller actors such Pema's grocery store which evolved into an important meeting place for Bhutanese and Nepalese refugees in the North Hill neighbourhood and beyond. Other smaller refugee-led social organisations such as the *Ka'ren Community of Akron* or the HALCA – the *Himalayan Arts Language & Cultural Academy* – a cultural centre in North Hill, provide programmes targeted at the preservation of cultural identity through arts, music, and dance classes.

Interviews conducted have shown that these spatial manifestations of refugee arrival reflect a desire by the community to make a place. When the *IIA* stops assisting refugees, these actors support refugees through social care provision, translation services, or providing a space for cultural manifestations and practices. Interviews further suggested that these organisations are often run by members of the South Asian refugee community and practice largely independent of the city administration.

The actor who works most closely with the city and the *IIA* is *ASIA Inc.*, a local organisation providing culturally sensitive social services to refugees of Southeast Asian descent and the AAPI community at large. *ASIA Inc.* has been mentioned by numerous interview participants, underlining its importance for the refugee community. The organisation also provides volunteering opportunities for local youth. Many interview participants reported how helpful the practice of volunteering was in their quest to be recognised as more than a "refugee". The interviews and observations showed that volunteer work can take on different forms: from organised activities in the framework of local or national NGOs to more low-threshold forms of participation in cafés or schools. At the heart of all the activities reported lies a desire to shape one's environment actively. To help others based on one's own, often traumatic, experiences helps to break out of the everyday reality of new immigrants often described as isolating. Wood et al. (2019) state that next to employment, volunteering can be a source for refugees to "forg[ing] meaningful relationships and expand[ing] their social circles" (Wood et al., 2019, p. 10). Findings from our case study confirm this. Volunteering activities can facilitate entering the job market if volunteering is linked to previous professional experiences. Since finding employment is challenging and stressful for many refugees, such volunteer work can ease psychological and emotional burdens. As such, refugee (social) entrepreneurship in North Hill and volunteering are linked by their ability to provide refugees with the opportunity to enact agency.

Much research has been conducted on arts- and culture-based projects aiming to facilitate social cohesion, inclusion, and emplacement and serve urban revitalisation. Cities often use culture and arts in their social cohesion policies as they render places more attractive and support local identity-making (García et al., 2015). In the context of urban development, culture can serve several purposes, ranging from a simple means of external communication and marketing to more internal processes, such as identity and social cohesion building. Finally, arts can also be a means of social innovation (André et al., 2013). The literature on the intersections of art, place, and migration focuses on different forms of creative expression. For example, in her work on artistic interventions in the urban environment to target the exclusion of migrants, Mekdjian employs the term "artivism", which she defines as "a critical process that destabilises everyday urban interactions and practices" (2018, p. 39). Lewis et al. explore "the art-making process as a community-building strategy that is both inclusive and accessible" (2018, p. 7) in their research on refugee youth in Canada. Both approaches described can be found in Akron, where theatre performances are combined with outreach and educational activities and where different social enterprise actors are engaged in artivism and culture-based approaches to neighbourhood revitalisation. An example in Akron is the Gum-Dip, an important hub for theatre projects dedicated to bringing across the story of the local refugee communities via two recent projects, *Brokers without Borders* and *Three Countries, One Mother*. While *Brokers without Borders* deals with the inclusion and exclusion of refugees upon arrival, the play *Three Countries, One Mother* presents the protagonist's story of forced displacement and his journey from a refugee camp in Nepal to Akron. *Three Countries, One Mother* engages with the experiences and stories of Bhutanese-Nepali refugees who were displaced and arrived in Akron. The play is inspired by the protagonist's family, who are:

> Members of the Tamang tribe, an ethnic group in the Bhutanese-Nepali community. [...] Spanning generations and countries, this deeply personal narrative weaves together family stories and shamanic ritual to explore the impact of cultural legacy on an individual.
>
> (Gum-Dip Theatre, 2024, n.p.)[6]

Equally directed by the Gum-Dip Theatre project, the play *Brokers without Borders* also engages with New Americans' stories. It is described on the theatre's website as:

> A multiethnic, theatrical ensemble of former refugees who identify as cultural brokers, meaning that they act as a bridge between their own culture and another by translating and interpreting regularly for their family and community members. This project addresses the divide by creating a cross-cultural original play that demonstrates the experience of navigating an entirely new world and the celebrations of finding success in a globalized community.
>
> (Gum-Dip Theatre, 2024, n.p.)[7]

Besides the theatre plays, Gum-Dip organises conferences and offers workshops and speaking circles where attendees can share their North Hill-related stories. As such, the project and its plays are important elements in the local negotiation of diasporic identity and sites for creating mutual cultural understanding in a context of increasing diversity. In the context of Akron's revitalisation, the Gum-Dip Theatre is a fascinating example of refugee-led arts-based projects in shrinking cities. At once a theatre project which is deeply embedded at the local level – gum-dipping describes a process in tire manufacturing, relating the theatre's name to Akron's industrial heritage – while decisively promoting a positive stance on the increasing diversity in Akron and its North Hill neighbourhood. The theatre aims to "celebrate, challenge, and reinvent community identity through choose-what-you-pay performances, story circles, workshops, and multicultural events". A form of social and artistic entrepreneurship, the project envisions a change of dominant narratives by "elevating voices and identities that are not included in the mainstream" (Gum-Dip Theatre, 2024).[8] With strong connections to the *Exchange House* at the managerial level of the two projects, theatre groups rehearse and meet there frequently.

Other actors provide culture-based offers, too, hence supporting local forms of cultural expression and place-making. One example is *The Himalayan Arts Language & Cultural Academy* (HALCA), a place dedicated to maintaining Nepalese culture for residents in Akron. Its goal is to produce content which creates a better understanding of the realities refugees are facing upon arrival and can thus be understood as a form of migrant activism.

Our findings confirm that culture-based projects play an important role in refugee emplacement and urban regeneration processes and have a positive impact at neighbourhood level. Some of the presented organisations are deeply connected with Akron's local history, and all embrace and promote the increasing diversity refugee arrival has brought about.

Reconnecting to the story of Pema, laid out in the previous section, and to Judelsohn et al.'s (2021) findings that refugee populations resettled to the US face particular health risks due to ultra-processed foods, other actors have emerged who engage with complex issues around food equity as "expansive idea that people have the ability, resources, and agency, broadly defined, to control their food environment [...]" (Judelsohn et al., 2021, p. 4). Through the readily available vacant lots, shrinking cities increasingly become sites of social enterprise projects and coalitions aiming at food security through urban agriculture practices on these lots. In Akron such a project exists through *Akron Cooperative Farms* (ACF) in North Hill, where underused land of a former baseball field has been repurposed into an urban farm. The *ACF* project was launched when locals who were in touch with refugee households observed how newcomers would sometimes use small parts of their property for cultivation – be it for growing food or for keeping poultry. In combination with local programmes fighting food injustice, e.g., *Let's Grow Akron*,[9] ACF emerged via a bottom-up process: locals in touch with Bhutanese, Burmese, and Nepalese refugee communities understood the value of reusing vacant land for urban farming to facilitate place- and home-making practices of refugees. Agricultural and urban farming has provided spaces for collective place-making while ensuring access to fresh produce for vulnerable groups.

In the next section, we will discuss the findings from looking into Akron's North Hill neighbourhood and reflect on what it teaches us about refugee (social) entrepreneurship in shrinking cities.

Discussion: Challenges and opportunities of refugee-centred revitalisation and (social) entrepreneurship in shrinking cities

What refugee arrival and urban shrinkage have in common is the emergence of associative and informal actors and practices as permanent features of local governance (see Cremaschi et al., 2020; Kinder, 2017). Our investigation into Akron showed that refugee (social) entrepreneurship and civic action form an important part of this. Local decision-makers are getting increasingly involved in these processes with a local government presenting itself as immigrant-friendly and tolerant while remaining largely uninvolved in activities at the neighbourhood level, where local and regional foundations increasingly shape and finance civic action. As an old industrial region, there have been times of great capital accumulation, from which influential regional foundations emerged. In Akron, too, this strong philanthropic tissue supports the identified web of civil society actors and refugee-led organisations which address the needs emerging during and after refugee arrivals in places affected by long-term decline. The analysis shows that local actor constellations and their support structure are hence place specific and that local, regional, and national foundations play an important role in refugee emplacement in North Hill.

Refugee entrepreneurship, whether in form of opening shops or in its more social actions, contributes to local revitalisation, and in doing so shows that social entrepreneurship can be a means to fill gaps the States leave behind (Murphy & Chatzipanagiotidou, 2020). In our case study, social refugee entrepreneurship emerged to fill gaps left from the resettlement system. For example, the culturally sensitive social services provision through organisations like *ASIA Inc.*, more strongly arts-based forms of social entrepreneurship such as the Gum-Dip Theatre, or activities offered by the *NHCDC*, which serve as spaces for expression and the creation of mutual understanding. However, these activities remain firmly embedded in re-scaling efforts of the city and risk turning into bits and pieces of neoliberal urban governance. This brings about further local action, for example, in the form of CDCs like Legacies of Success, who fight against predatory investors that put newcomers at risk of expulsion. Refugee (social) entrepreneurship is both included into local revitalisation strategies of the city and becomes a frame through which emplacement efforts are individualised. This resonates with Murphy and Chatzipanagiotidou who conclude from their research on refugee entrepreneurs in Istanbul that an "overemphasis on the economic resilience of refugees can also be read as an attempt to defer responsibility for addressing the protracted crisis situations of asylum seekers and refugees" (Murphy & Chatzipanagiotidou, 2020, p. 6). The two authors criticise that policies pushing for refugee entrepreneurship oftentimes serve as nothing more than "rhetorical flourish" (ibid.) without tackling the underlying problem of barriers to adequate long-term integration to labour markets. Our examination of the Akron's *International District* brought about similar results in that while the city's inclusive rhetoric was welcomed by some refugees, it served as not much more than just that – a 'rhetorical flourish' for others.

Concluding remarks

Academic literature suggests that while refugees tend to need support in the first years upon arrival in a new community, this dependence decreases significantly over time with refugees ultimately contributing to local economies (see Evans & Fitzgerald, 2017). This invites an in-depth engagement with the economic activity of refugees and how it impacts local development.

What is understood is that refugee entrepreneurship contributes to Akron's revitalisation with notable positive effects in North Hill, where commercial vacancies slowly disappear and social entrepreneurship fills the gaps left from years of shrinkage and the devolution of public services. In this region, refugee (social) entrepreneurship, (social) services provision, place-making, and civic engagement are entangled. It is difficult – if not impossible – to disconnect local entrepreneurial activities by and for refugee populations from broader efforts for recognition and inclusion for refugees on the one hand and urban governmental efforts for rescaling on the other.

More than simply boosters of local economies, the actors interviewed in this study were newcomers who reconstructed their lives under challenging conditions. To support this reconstruction, much of the services for the refugee community are provided by civil society actors and local organisations working at times in cooperation with, but largely independent from, the municipality. These organisations', corporations', and foundations' work often intersect with the established environment and local development. While some agencies and local development corporations focus on supporting refugee entrepreneurship, others focus on rehabilitating old homes, and yet others promote culture-led revitalisation.

Common for Rust Belt cities, Akron's government has jumped on the bandwagon of refugee-led revitalisation. However, interviews with participants have shown that local refugee populations often feel that municipal action takes place almost disconnected from needs and aspirations formulated by refugees at neighbourhood level. This, in combination with public government discourses that centre on single success stories and put the individuals behind them on pedestals, aggravates risks of refugee entrepreneurship being increasingly incorporated into a neoliberal urban governance in shrinking cities in which diversity is merely 'rhetorical flourish'.

While refugee entrepreneurship can serve as exit strategy from state-support systems that keep individuals close to the poverty line and as means to drive local urban revitalisation, narratives centring around the *boosterism* of refugee-led revitalisation overlook the challenges inherent in place-making after displacement and the historical local inequalities that persist in downscaled cities. Refugee (social) entrepreneurship in shrinking cities, then, is complex and merits further investigation regarding the specific socio-spatial and socio-economic conditions that shrinking cities pose to newcomers, and also regarding the potentials inherent in the various forms of place-making as practices by refugees.

Notes

1 A shrinking city is "[...] an urban area – a city, part of a city, an entire metropolitan area or a town – that has experienced population loss, economic downturn, employment decline and social problems as symptoms of a structural crisis" (Martinez-Fernandez et al., 2012, p. 214). As emphasised by Martinez-Fernandez and colleagues, the term shrinking city underlines the fact that we deal with a phenomenon that is a "multi-dimensional process with multi-dimensional effects" (ibid.), with "economic, demographic, geographic, social and physical dimensions" (ibid.). They understand these processes as ongoing due to continuous global restructuring.

2 In Europe, immigration in depopulating areas is predominantly discussed in the contexts of ageing populations and shortages in skilled labour, and also within the wider discussion of how to enable resettlement given increasingly anti-immigrant tendencies in public attitudes (see Strang & Ager, 2010; Steele & Abdelaaty, 2019). Cases such as the Italian Riace or the German Altena made headlines: two small towns which integrated refugees into their local development processes with notable success.

3 Local tire manufacturers would drive the city's economic growth and actively shape its urban development (Love & Giffels, 1999, p. 18): the neighbourhoods Firestone Park and Goodyear Heights are a testament of the impact tire manufacturers had on the city.

4 According to recent Census data, Akron has a population density of 3,075 persons per square mile, like other shrinking cities in the region. The poverty rate is 23%, compared to 11.4% nationally based on the most recent Census data. The unemployment rate is slightly higher than the national average, with 4.3% in July 2022 vs. 3.5% nationally.

5 AAPI stands for Asian American and Pacific Islanders. In this chapter, we borrow the term as it was a means for self-identification for interview participants from South Asian countries with forced migration biographies. While this chapter focuses on the entrepreneurial activities of this community, consisting mainly of Bhutanese, Burmese, Nepali, and Ka'ren refugees, Akron has become home to refugees from a variety of national backgrounds, including those from the DRC, Afghanistan, Syria, Iraq, Iran, Ukraine, and other countries.

6 Gum-Dip Theatre (2024). Online. www.gumdiptheatre.com/mission, last accessed 29/07/2024.

7 Gum-Dip Theatre (2024). Online. www.gumdiptheatre.com/mission, last accessed 29/07/2024.

8 Gum-Dip Theatre (2024). Online. www.gumdiptheatre.com/mission, last accessed 29/07/2024.

9 Let's Grow Akron is a non-profit organisation established as early as 1988 to repurpose vacant lots in Akron's inner-city neighbourhoods. For more information on the programme, see http://letsgrowakron.org/about/, last accessed 26/12/2022.

References

Abebe, S. A. (2023). Refugee entrepreneurship: Systematic and thematic analyses and a research agenda. *Small Business Economics*, *60*(1), 315–350. https://doi.org/10.1007/s11187-022-00636-3

André, I., Abreu, A., & Carmo, A. (2013). Social innovation through the arts in rural areas: The case of Montemor-o-Novo: Collective action, social learning and transdisciplinary research. In F. Moulaert, D. MacCallum, A. Mehmood, & A. Hamdouch (Eds.), *The International Handbook on Social Innovation Collective Action, Social Learning and Transdisciplinary Research.* Cheltenham, UK: Edward Elgar Publishing. Retrieved Jul 29, 2024, from https://doi.org/10.4337/9781849809993.00032

Atasü-Topcuoğlu, R. (2019). Syrian refugee entrepreneurship in Turkey: Integration and the use of immigrant capital in the informal economy. *Social Inclusion*, *7*(4), 200–210. https://doi.org/10.17645/si.v7i4.2346

Bizri, R. M. (2017). Refugee-entrepreneurship: A social capital perspective. *Entrepreneurship & Regional Development*, *29*(9–10), 847–868. https://doi.org/10.1080/08985626.2017.1364787

Blanco, O. (2017, February 9). How immigrants helped save the economy of Akron, Ohio. CNNMoney. Online: https://money.cnn.com/2017/02/09/news/economy/immigrants-refugeesakron/index.html (Accessed 29/07/2024).

Cremaschi, M., Albanese, F., & Artero, M. (2020). Migrants and refugees: Bottom-up and DIY spaces in Italy. *Urban Planning*, *5*(3), 189–199. https://doi.org/10.17645/up.v5i3.2921

Day, D. (2017). Dream in progress: The Cleveland Dream Neighborhood. *MUP Capstone.* Department of Urban and Regional Planning, University of Illinois at Urbana-Champaign.

Desai, S., Naudé, W., & Stel, N. (2021). Refugee entrepreneurship: Context and directions for future research. *Small Business Economics*, *56*(3), 933–945. https://doi.org/10.1007/s11187-019-00310-1

Evans, W., & Fitzgerald, D. (2017). *The Economic and Social Outcomes of Refugees in the United States: Evidence from the ACS* (w23498; p. w23498). National Bureau of Economic Research. https://doi.org/10.3386/w23498.

Fairclough, N. (2012). Critical discourse analysis. In M. Handford, & J.P. Gee (Eds.), *The Routledge Handbook of Discourse Analysis* (2nd ed.) (pp. 9–20). New York: Routledge.

Flick, U. (2011). *Triangulation.* Wiesbaden: VS Verlag.

García, M., Eizaguirre, S., & Pradel, M. (2015). Social innovation and creativity in cities: A socially inclusive governance approach in two peripheral spaces of Barcelona. *City, Culture and Society*, *6*(4), 93–100. https://doi.org/10.1016/j.ccs.2015.07.001

Great Streets Akron (2018). Temple Square – North Hill. District Info, online: www.greatstreetsakron.com/district/temple-square-north-hill (Accessed 11/08/2023).

Gum-Dip Theatre (2024). About. Online. www.gumdiptheatre.com/mission (Accessed 29/07

Hackl, A. (2022). Good immigrants, permitted outsiders: Conditional inclusion and citizenship in comparison. *Ethnic and Racial Studies*, *45*(6), 989–1010. https://doi.org/10.1080/01419870.2021.2011938

Harb, M., Kassem, A., & Najdi, W. (2019). Entrepreneurial refugees and the city: Brief encounters in Beirut. *Journal of Refugee Studies*, *32*(1), 23–41. https://doi.org/10.1093/jrs/fey003

Heilbrunn, S., & Iannone, R. L. (2020). From center to periphery and back again: A systematic literature review of refugee entrepreneurship. *Sustainability*, *12*(18), 7658. https://doi.org/10.3390/su12187658

Housel, J., Saxen, C., & Wahlrab, T. (2018). Experiencing intentional recognition: Welcoming immigrants in Dayton, Ohio. *Urban Studies*, *55*(2), 384–405. https://doi.org/10.1177/0042098016653724

Judelsohn, A., Orom, H., Kim, I., Na Sa, A. B., Khan, H., Devito, R., Diaz Del Carpio, R. O., & Raja, S. (2017). Planning the city of good (and new) neighbours: Refugees' experiences of the food environment in Buffalo, New York. *Built Environment*, *43*(3), 402–416. https://doi.org/10.2148/benv.43.3.402

Judelsohn, A., Orom, H., Leon, D., & Raja, S. (2021). Refuge in new food environments? The role of urban planning in facilitating food equity for new Americans. *Journal of Urban Affairs*, *43*(6), 872–889. https://doi.org/10.1080/07352166.2019.1705845

Kinder, K. (2017). DIY urbanism in shrinking cities: Or, what neighbors are left with when markets withdraw and governments contract. *Metropolitics*. https://metropolitics.org/DIY-Urbanism-in-Shrinking-Cities.html

Kühn, M. (2018). Immigration strategies of cities: Local growth policies and urban planning in Germany. *European Planning Studies*, *26*(9), 1747–1762. https://doi.org/10.1080/09654313.2018.1484428

Lefebvre, H. (1991). *Critique of Everyday Life*. Vol. 1. Translated by John Moore. London: Verso.

Lewis, L. B., McLeod, H., & Li, X. (2018). The open studio: Exploring immigrant and refugee youth experiences of belonging through community-based arts practice. *Cultural and Pedagogical Inquiry*, *10*(1). doi: 10.18733/cpi29363

Love, S. & Giffels, D. (1999). *Wheels of Fortune: The Story of Rubber in Akron*. University of Akron Press, 44. https://ideaexchange.uakron.edu/uapress_publications/44

Martinez-Fernandez, C., Audirac, I., Fol, S., & Cunningham-Sabot, E. (2012). Shrinking cities: Urban challenges of globalization. *International Journal of Urban and Regional Research*, *36*(2), 213–225. https://doi.org/10.1111/j.1468-2427.2011.01092.x

Mekdjian, S. (2018). Urban artivism and migrations. Disrupting spatial and political segregation of migrants in European cities. *Cities*, *77*, 39–48. https://doi.org/10.1016/j.cities.2017.05.008

Murphy, F., & Chatzipanagiotidou, E. (2020). Crafting the entrepreneurial self: Refugees, displaced livelihoods, and the politics of labor in Turkey. *Society for the Anthropology of Work*. https://doi.org/10.21428/1d6be30e.bebc21a2

NAE. (2017). *From Struggle to Resilience: The Economic Impact of Refugees in America*, online: www.newamericaneconomy.org/wp-content/uploads/2017/06/NAE_Refugees_V5.pdf, last accessed 31/07/2023.

NHCDC. (2022). About North Hill CDC – North Hill CDC. https://northhillcdc.org/about/, last accessed 02/02/2023.

Nightengale, K. (2015, May 28). Akron Better Block: Transforming North Hill Into A Vibrant International District. The Better Block. https://www.betterblock.org/post/akron-betterblock-transforming-north-hill-into-a-vibrant-international-district, last accessed 02/02/2023.

Paral, R. (2017). *Immigration a Demographic Lifeline in Midwestern Metros* [Research]. The Chicago Council on Global Affairs. www.thechicagocouncil.org/research/report/immigration-demographic-lifeline-midwestern-metros

Planning to Grow Akron (2017). Akron Housing Strategy. Akron Mayor Office. Online: https://cms2.revize.com/revize/akronoh/Departments/Planning%20And%20Urban%20Development/Plans%20Reports%20And%20Maps/planning_to_grow_akron_report_final.pdf.

Pottie-Sherman, Y. (2018). Austerity urbanism and the promise of immigrant- and refugee-centered urban revitalization in the US Rust Belt. *Urban Geography*, *39*(3), 438–457. https://doi.org/10.1080/02723638.2017.1342398

Pottie-Sherman, Y. (2020). Rust and reinvention: Im/migration and urban change in the American Rust Belt. *Geography Compass*, *14*(3). https://doi.org/10.1111/gec3.12482

Pottie-Sherman, Y., & Graham, N. (2021). Live, work, and stay? Geographies of immigrant receptivity in Atlantic Canada's aspiring gateways. *Geographical Review*, *111*(2), 287–307. https://doi.org/10.1080/00167428.2020.1804301

Powers, K., Korfhage, M., Sullivan Borelli, K., & Schuhmacher, T. (2022). *Resettling Main Street: Refugees Bring Revitalization to Some of America's Small Cities. USA Today Network*, online: https://eu.democratandchronicle.com/in-depth/news/2022/01/10/refugees-pa-lancaster-pennsylvania-dutch-image/8765556002/, last accessed 19/04/2023.

Price, M., & Chacko, E. (2009). The mixed embeddedness of ethnic entrepreneurs in a new immigrant gateway. *Journal of Immigrant & Refugee Studies*, *7*(3), 328–346. https://doi.org/10.1080/15562940903150105

Sampedro, R., & Camarero, L. (2018). Foreign immigrants in depopulated rural areas: Local social services and the construction of welcoming communities. *Social Inclusion*, *6*(3), 337–346. https://doi.org/10.17645/si.v6i3.1530

Senthanar, S., MacEachen, E., Premji, S., & Bigelow, P. (2021). Entrepreneurial experiences of Syrian refugee women in Canada: A feminist grounded qualitative study. *Small Business Economics*, *57*(2), 835–847. https://doi.org/10.1007/s11187-020-00385-1

Shrider, E. A. (2017). *Can Immigrants Save the Rust Belt? Struggling Cities, Immigration, and Revitalization*. Ohio State University.

Siviş, S. (2021). Integrating bottom-up into top-down: The role of local actors in labour market integration of Syrian refugees in Turkey. *International Migration*, *59*(4), 190–206. https://doi.org/10.1111/imig.12775

Steele, L. G., & Abdelaaty, L. (2019). Ethnic diversity and attitudes towards refugees. *Journal of Ethnic and Migration Studies*, *45*(11), 1833–1856. https://doi.org/10.1080/1369183X.2018.1513785

Strang, A., & Ager, A. (2010). Refugee integration: Emerging trends and remaining agendas. *Journal of Refugee Studies*, *23*(4), Article 4. https://doi.org/10.1093/jrs/feq046

U.S. Bureau of the Census (2024). Quick facts. Akron city, Ohio, and Dayton city, Ohio. Online: www.census.gov/quickfacts/fact/table/akroncityohio,daytoncityohio/POP645222.

U.S. Bureau of Labor Statistics (2023). Economy at a glance. Akron, OH, online: www.bls.gov/eag/eag.oh_akron_msa.htm#eag_oh_akron_msa.f.3, last accessed 31/10/2023.

Wauters, B., & Lambrecht, J. (2008). Barriers to refugee entrepreneurship in Belgium: Towards an explanatory model. *Journal of Ethnic and Migration Studies, 34*(6), 895–915. https://doi.org/10.1080/13691830802211190

Welcoming Summit County & Akron (2017). Strategic Welcome Plan for the City of Akron and the County of Summit. https://static1.squarespace.com/static/59244a7fe3df285163464984/t/5ae72de788251bd2b3098019/1525100014556/WelcomingSummitCountyAkron.pdf

Wood, N., Charlwood, G., Zecchin, C., Hansen, V., Douglas, M., & Pit, S. W. (2019). Qualitative exploration of the impact of employment and volunteering upon the health and wellbeing of African refugees settled in regional Australia: A refugee perspective. *BMC Public Health, 19*(1), 143. https://doi.org/10.1186/s12889-018-6328-2

Section 4

Supporting and developing refugee entrepreneurship

Refugee or asylum-seeking journeys lead to trauma and stress and shape refugees' well-being, resilience, and adaptability. The five chapters in this section are about means of supporting and developing entrepreneurship among refugees while taking their experience of trauma into account.

In Chapter 12, Newman and Jones Christensen discuss the role of trauma-informed care when encouraging refugees to engage in entrepreneurship. They, further, point out that business start-ups and ongoing development of the venture can affect an individual's mental and physical health. The authors conclude that enhancing refugee entrepreneurs' well-being requires trauma-informed entrepreneurial support systems.

Subramanian and Finsterwalder (Chapter 13), then, outline the need for adequate resettlement services (e.g., healthcare, education, housing, and other support services) as precursors to operating successful businesses, as they contribute to resettled refugees' well-being. This chapter outlines barriers and enablers to finding work or establishing businesses in the service sector.

Kansikas and Seikkula-Leino, in Chapter 14, discuss refugees' resilience and how resilience needs to be considered in the design and delivery of entrepreneurship education programmes targeted at refugees. They point out that psychological resilience facilitates how these entrepreneurs cope with changing circumstances, anxiety, and stress. The authors suggest refugee entrepreneurship education initiatives should take into account the refugees' experiences, asylum-seeking journey-induced resilience, and social capital.

Next, Aktas et al (Chapter 15) elaborate on entrepreneurial resilience and how refugees' social capital shape their business practices. The authors point out that non-governmental organisations (NGOs) play a crucial role in enabling refugees to access support and social capital. Yet, difficulties in attaining bridging and linking capitals hinder refugee women's access to support networks and target markets within a host society.

The final chapter in this section (Chapter 16) discusses child-friendly workshops for refugee women entrepreneurs. In their discussion, Street

DOI: 10.4324/9781003368540-15

and Ng describe the benefits of refugee women entrepreneurs mentoring other refugee women. The authors also suggest that creating women-only spaces, providing on-site childcare, and eliminating educational and cultural barriers through mindfulness and intercultural dialogue are essential steps in supporting and empowering refugee women entrepreneurs.

12 The role of trauma-informed care in sustaining the well-being of refugee entrepreneurs

Arielle Badger Newman and
Lisa Jones Christensen

Introduction

A global refugee crisis is creating the highest number of forcibly displaced persons in history, presenting a global "grand challenge" and one of the most pressing issues of our time (Salehyan, 2019). As of October 2022, there are over 103 million individuals forcibly displaced worldwide, including 5 million asylum seekers, 32.5 million refugees, 53 million internally displaced people, and 5 million people in need of international protection (United Nation High Commissioner for Refugees: UNHCR, 2023). Consequently, international humanitarian efforts are strained in terms of providing longer-term support for this vulnerable and often traumatised population (Alrawedieh et al., 2018). With such large and growing numbers, there is a concomitant strategic focus on enhancing refugee livelihoods and fostering economic self-reliance (Easton-Calabria & Omata, 2018). As part of this endeavour, many governments, non-profit organisations, and other stakeholders promote entrepreneurship among refugees to enable self-reliance and ease integration into the host country (Brown & Scribner, 2014; Fong et al., 2007; Gold, 1992; Jones Christensen & Newman, 2024; Jones Christensen et al., 2019; Kloosterman & van der Leun, 1999; Newman & Jones Christensen, 2021).

For many stakeholders, including the UNHCR, entrepreneurship is seen as a panacea for achieving economic self-reliance and alleviating the pressures from this massive refugee influx on existing humanitarian institutions (Jones Christensen & Newman, 2024; Newman & Jones Christensen, 2021). In some cases, entrepreneurship allows refugees to maximise income using extant skills, qualifications, experience, knowledge, and abilities that can be expressed more easily through entrepreneurship than in the formal labour force in the new location (Alrawedieh et al., 2018; Krahn et al., 2000; Levie, 2007; Mesthenos & Ionnidi, 2002). Notably, entrepreneurship as self-employment can enable refugees to be economically engaged in a manner that avoids some of the discrimination, harassment, xenophobia, and racism that often pervade the relocation and hiring process (Alrawedieh et al., 2018; Guo et al., 2020). Management scholars note that the freedom and self-direction associated with entrepreneurship can often correlate with individual growth, personal

DOI: 10.4324/9781003368540-16

development, and the opportunity to increase satisfaction with life (Shir, 2015; Wiklund et al., 2019). These benefits collectively constitute entrepreneurial well-being (Wiklund et al., 2019). Due to these advantages and their implications for economic well-being, the United Nations and other non-profit organisations endorse entrepreneurship for refugees, affirming that entrepreneurship can help overcome the various challenges of economic and social inclusion for refugees worldwide (United Nations Conference on Trade and Development: UNTAD, 2018).

However, many extant claims about the financial and non-financial benefits of entrepreneurship stem from data from populations very different from refugees. Refugees are involuntary migrants, meaning they were *forced* to flee their home, and thus refugees are likely to face trauma due to the involuntary nature of their migration and potentially dangerous journey to a new (potentially hostile) host community (Jones Christensen & Newman, 2024; Keyes, 2000; Newman & Jones Christensen, 2021). This trauma experienced pre- and post-migration, in combination with data that suggest entrepreneurship, leads to high levels of stress, depression, and overall poorer mental health, and creates issues for pro-entrepreneurship stakeholders (Cubbon et al., 2020; Freeman et al., 2019; Kollman et al., 2019; Newman & Jones Christensen, 2021; Saarni et al., 2018; Schonfeld & Mazzola, 2015). Such experiences compound already fragile psychological states of well-being and feelings of loss and depression from the deprivation of social networks, community, and families (Bemak & Chung, 2014; Bemak et al., 2003). When considering entrepreneurial well-being for refugees, we note that compared to the general population, refugees over-utilise mental health services and have higher rates of psychopathology (Keyes, 2000). We posit that this could have a significant impact on the entrepreneurial journey for refugees. Accordingly, the relationship between trauma, entrepreneurship, and well-being for refugee entrepreneurs requires further investigation.

This chapter explores the topic of trauma in the context of entrepreneurship and covers both the promises and "dark side" of refugee entrepreneurship. To guide this exploration, we ask: What are the consequences of trauma for refugee entrepreneurship? How can support organisations encourage well-being (or mitigate ill-being) for entrepreneurial refugees? To answer these questions, we begin by emphasising the increased risk of trauma exposure inherent to the refugee condition. With this backdrop, we explore the advantages and disadvantages of entrepreneurship and how it may affect refugee entrepreneurs with significant trauma exposure. Finally, we question the effect of entrepreneurship on refugees' well-being. In doing so, we propose how organisations supporting refugee entrepreneurship incorporate trauma-informed practices.

Trauma and the refugee experience

Refugees are individuals forcibly displaced "due to war and conflict, but also due to political, religious, and other persecution; national or man-made disasters;

development-induced displacement; smuggling and human trafficking; and/or environmental displacement" (Reed, 2018, p. 2). Refugees who are officially resettled receive the guarantee to become permanent residents within the host country (UNHCR, 2018; International Rescue Committee, 2019). The international humanitarian community is struggling to support this vulnerable population, as the influx of refugees continues to overwhelm resource-constrained humanitarian institutions (Alrawedieh et al., 2018). Therefore, in attempts to manage the influx of refugees, many governments, non-profit organisations, and other stakeholders encourage entrepreneurship on the part of refugees in order to facilitate self-reliance and integration into the host country (Brown & Scribner, 2014; Fong et al., 2007; Gold, 1992; Jones Christensen et al., 2019; Kloosterman & van der Leun, 1999). To meet this growing need for self-employment, many governments and donors created policies and programmes to encourage entrepreneurship for refugees (Brown & Scribner, 2014). This occurs as organisations, public and private, facilitate entrepreneurship among refugees in order to integrate them culturally and economically into society (Heilbrunn & Ionnone, 2020 Jones Christensen & Newman, 2024; Jones Christensen et al., 2019; Wauters & Lambrecht, 2008). Such programmes exist to enhance and build the economic and non-economic well-being of refugee entrepreneurs.

However, the conditions that tend to exist prior to a forced departure from the home country mean that refugees, more than any other migrant group, tend to experience and witness trauma as part of the migration journey (Bemak et al., 2003; Bemak & Chung, 2014; Leong et al., 2014). Refugees typically experience trauma related to physical deprivation (i.e., food and shelter); physical injury and/or torture (including assault); or due to incarceration, re-education, and other types of violence (Hollifield et al., 2002; Mollica et al., 1987).

Furthermore, refugees can experience *post-migration* trauma when they are legally or extra-legally resettled into a new host country. Specifically, refugees can face racial hostility in the host society, cultural difficulties in attempting to navigate a new culture (sometimes without language proficiency), and trauma from the loss of social networks, community, and family (Bemak & Chung, 2014; Bemak et al., 2003). Refugees generally lack the ability to choose their resettled location, leaving resettled refugees with limited social support in their healing process (IRC, 2019; Newman & Jones Christensen, 2021). Overall, this leads to a higher incidence of mental illness for refugees as compared to other populations – largely due to trauma exposure (Bemak & Chung, 2014; Leong et al., 2014).

This trauma-related heightened vulnerability of refugees can have a profound impact on the entrepreneurial journey. Trauma is defined as "*exposure to actual or threatened death, serious injury, or sexual violence*" (DSM-V of American Psychiatric Association, 2013, p. 271), or as "*an event overwhelms the ordinary systems of care that give people a sense of control, connection and meaning*" (Herman, 1992, p. 34). Such experiences result in reactions such as fear, helplessness, loss of control, and concerns about annihilation (Kaplan & Sadock, 1989). Traumatic events stand out because they can so completely overwhelm "ordinary adaptations to life" and create profound and lasting changes in physiological arousal, emotion, cognition, and memory (Herman, 1992, p. 34). Trauma exposure can affect the ability of refugees to utilise education, connect with others, and assemble funds, all of which are crucial to entrepreneurship (Bemak & Chung, 2014; Leong et al., 2014). Furthermore, scholars have established that trauma can have deleterious effects on both physical and mental health (Herman, 1992; Mate, 2022; Smith et al., 2018; van der Kolk, 2015).

While each individual experiences and manifests trauma differently, individuals who have experienced trauma are susceptible to three primary reactions: hyperarousal, intrusion, and constriction (Herman, 1992). When experiencing hyperarousal, the individual is in a hypervigilant state, always looking for danger for fear of the recurrence of trauma (Frewen & Lanius, 2006); they may appear anxious, irritable, easily angered, startled, or scared (Zaleski et al., 2016). Intrusion is episodic, vivid flashbacks are triggered that interrupt daily functioning (Iyadurai et al., 2019). Individuals tend to avoid situations where a sudden reminder could trigger intrusive episodes. Finally, some individuals completely disconnect from emotions to avoid the traumatic memory and associated feelings of pain, avoiding triggers while maintaining an overall sense of indifference (Cozolino, 2014). This may lead to the abuse of alcohol, drugs, or other substances that "numb" the pain of the trauma (Herman, 1992).

These manifestations of trauma can interfere with entrepreneurial activities. The inability to focus may make it difficult for hyperaroused individuals to make quick informed decisions. An individual suffering from intrusive episodes may avoid important social events for fear of encountering triggers (see Jones Christensen et al., 2023). These impacts of trauma for the refugee population need further exploration to understand the consequences of trauma on entrepreneurship.

Entrepreneurship: A complex "solution" for refugee populations

Interestingly, there can also be trauma associated with the pursuit of entrepreneurship, despite how often the topic is discussed as solely positive. Scholars have established that entrepreneurship can have deleterious effects for an individual's mental and physical health (Lerner et al., 2018; Shepherd & Patzelt, 2015; Zhang & Cueto, 2017). Data suggest that entrepreneurs experience high uncertainty, time pressure, high emotional involvement, and stress from making decisions that decide the fate of their venture (Lerner et al., 2018; Shepherd & Patzelt, 2015; Zhang & Cueto, 2017). This nuance and potential for negative externalities means that if not approached with care, endorsing entrepreneurship for refugees could trigger more trauma. We propose that while entrepreneurship has the potential to contribute to the well-being of refugees when it provides a comparatively rapid way for refugees to begin to survive financially, this connection to refugee entrepreneurial well-being is complex, nuanced, and sometimes problematic. In the next section, we delve deeper into this complexity, exploring both the potential benefits and challenges of entrepreneurship for refugees with trauma exposure followed by a discussion of ways to better help refugee entrepreneurs through trauma-informed practices.

Entrepreneurship: The panacea?

Entrepreneurship is a value creating process that allows an individual to take control and utilise agency. In this way, entrepreneurship can be emancipatory from past experiences as individuals' author their new lives (Rindova et al., 2009). Moreover, the very act of entrepreneurial success could counteract the trauma-related sense of powerlessness, rebuilding their self-confidence and self-efficacy (cf. Haynie & Shepherd, 2011). Achieving entrepreneurial success would give refugees a tangible demonstration of their abilities and potential, thereby challenging trauma-induced negative self-perceptions and fostering a renewed sense of agency and self-efficacy (Shepherd & Patzelt, 2015).

Furthermore, entrepreneurs enjoy autonomy as they craft their jobs and daily work (Baron, 2010; Wiklund et al., 2018), allowing individuals to self-actualise as they craft their jobs to their individual needs (Wiklund et al., 2018). This high level of autonomy can also lead to higher job satisfaction (Benz & Frey, 2008). Overall, entrepreneurship allows individuals opportunities for personal fulfilment, flexibility, and freedom (Shir, 2015), all of which could translate to higher levels of happiness and life satisfaction (Wiklund et al., 2019).

In addition to the above-mentioned individual (sometimes emancipatory) benefits from entrepreneurship and its associated autonomy, by creating their own venture, refugees can avoid the discrimination, harassment, underemployment, xenophobia, and racism often blatantly found in the search for formal employment (Alrawedieh et al., 2018; Guo et al., 2020). Exclusion from traditional employment leads some refugees to feel trapped in the host countries, unable to find stable employment, and escape the associated poverty (Kroon & Paauwe, 2014), and entrepreneurship enables these individuals to avoid this potential pain and frustration.

Furthermore, entrepreneurship can offer refugees a powerful means of regaining a sense of control and purpose in their lives, which may contribute to healing from trauma. Successful entrepreneurship may also provide a sense of accomplishment and personal worth, potentially countering feelings of helplessness or insignificance that often accompany traumatic experiences. Additionally, the process of building a business can offer meaningful engagement and distract from negative and intrusive thoughts related to trauma. These positive benefits are associated with the concept of "well-being", in this case, "entrepreneurial well-being".

Entrepreneurial (ill)well-being

While many studies point to the positive benefits of entrepreneurship listed above, new literature is also exploring the "dark side" of entrepreneurship, to understand the "ill-being" of entrepreneurs (Williamson et al., 2021). Aside from the potential benefits outlined above, entrepreneurship is inherently uncertain and rife with challenges (Cardon & Patel, 2015). Poor firm performance and failure is emotionally taxing (Shepherd & Cardon, 2009), and this can impede an entrepreneur's autonomy (van Gelderen, 2016). Furthermore, as entrepreneurs create and pursue opportunities, the intense process can create heightened emotions (Gregoire et al., 2015), potentially resulting in high levels of stress and other negative emotions for entrepreneurs (Brundin & Gustafsson, 2013). Being an entrepreneur has been associated with poorer mental health (Cubbon et al., 2020; Freeman et al., 2019; Saarni et al., 2008), and depression is common due to the stressors and strains many entrepreneurs experience (Freeman et al., 2021; Schonfeld & Mazzola, 2015). In addition, entrepreneurs tend to experience long working hours, unpredictable business environments, and responsibility for ensuring that all tasks are handled (Kollman et al., 2019). Such stressors can have negative impacts on both physical and psychological health (Kollman et al., 2019).

Specific to refugees, the inherent uncertainties and pressures of entrepreneurship could also potentially trigger trauma symptoms. The fear of failure, for instance, might intensify feelings of insecurity and anxiety that are already present due to past traumatic experiences. Similarly, the stress associated with managing a business could exacerbate trauma-related mental health issues, such as depression or post-traumatic stress disorder for refugees.

Overall, the research on entrepreneurial well-being paints a paradoxical picture – entrepreneurs report life and work satisfaction and overall happiness (Benz & Frey, 2004; Stephen & Roesler, 2010), while simultaneously, entrepreneurship is one of the most stressful jobs leading to poor mental and physical health (Cardon & Patel, 2015; Patzelt & Shepherd, 2011; Stephan, 2018). These considerations regarding the potential costs and benefits for entrepreneurial well-being have yet to be understood in the refugee context. As stated before, refugees are a unique population that, due to the involuntary nature of their migration coupled with a fraught journey fleeing their home to a new (potentially hostile) host community, have a much higher likelihood of trauma exposure, fragile mental health, and overall ill-being. When this population engages in entrepreneurship, key questions emerge: Is it emancipatory from the trauma of refugee circumstances, or is it triggering? How is it both? How can entrepreneurship lead to higher levels of positive well-being, or to ill-being?

These questions, and the data herein about how entrepreneurship is not always beneficial to the entrepreneur, imply that while entrepreneurship may offer opportunities for healing and empowerment for refugees; the practice is not without significant challenges. Applied to the context of refugee entrepreneurship, it appears crucial to approach the subject with a nuanced understanding of these complexities that can ensure that support is in place to help refugees maximise the potential benefits of entrepreneurial efforts. We propose that organisations interested in facilitating refugee entrepreneurship focus on known tactics with established benefits in terms of mitigating the effects of trauma on individuals, as outlined below.

Entrepreneurship: Ways to address the trauma without creating more

We suggest that organisations interested in helping refugees with the process of entrepreneurship must first focus on incorporating trauma-informed practices. Many programmes focused on facilitating refugee entrepreneurship overlook the potential exposure to trauma inherent in the refugee experience (Newman & Jones Christensen, 2021). Scholars and practitioners face a dialectic tension associated with trauma – there is pressure to address the existence of trauma and simultaneous pressure to deny trauma (Herman, 1992). Notwithstanding, we challenge stakeholders surrounding refugee entrepreneurs to push against the temptation to ignore the uncomfortable reality, that is, trauma, and to instead embrace trauma-informed practices.

Trauma researchers, practitioners, and survivors have established that context contributes to the long-term outcomes for trauma survivors either in supporting them or hindering their ability to thrive. In 2014, representatives of each of these stakeholder groups convened to co-create and formalise a definition of what it means to be a "trauma-informed" entity or service provider. Their definition states:

> a program, organization, or system that is trauma-informed realizes the widespread impact of trauma and understands potential paths for recovery; recognizes the signs and symptoms of trauma in clients, families, staff, and others involved with the system; and responds by fully integrating knowledge about trauma into policies, procedures, and practices; and seeks to actively resist re-traumatization.
>
> (Huang et al., 2014, p. 9)

It is important to note that the principles and associated practices associated with trauma-informed care can be helpful even if participants, in this case refugees, do not admit or discuss any specifics about trauma exposure (Herman, 1992; van der Kolk, 2015).

Said differently, there are four "Rs" to being trauma-informed, and they correspond to realisation, recognition, response, and resistance to re-traumatisation (Huang et al., 2014). Organisations focusing on fostering refugee entrepreneurship need to engage the four Rs of being trauma-informed and create an environment that enhances entrepreneurial well-being. We first outline these four concepts of trauma-informed practices, and then lay out six guiding principles that organisations can follow to deliver on the promises of the four Rs.

Background work: Engage the four Rs of being trauma-informed

Realisation

The first requirement for an organisation to be trauma-informed is "realisation". This means that every individual supporting refugee entrepreneur needs to understand trauma and its effects on families, communities, groups, and individuals. This understanding includes realising that trauma is not confined to certain societal subgroups, and that addressing it is not solely a responsibility of mental health specialists. An environment imbued with this level of awareness interprets experiences and behaviours of refugees in the context of coping mechanisms developed in response to adversity. This awareness covers past, present, and vicarious trauma experiences.

Recognition

After "realising" the pervasiveness of trauma and its effects, the next step is to "recognise" its signs and symptoms. These trauma manifestations vary based on gender, age, or specific contexts. Utilising trauma screenings and assessments can be helpful, albeit with careful timing to avoid causing harm or retriggering trauma. When manifesting trauma, the individual can be highly anxious, irritable, easily angered, quickly startled or scared, and have difficulty concentrating, relaxing, or sleeping (Herman, 1992; Zaleski et al., 2016). At other times, an individual may experience an "intrusive episode", or a "flashback" where an entrepreneur is actively experiencing the traumatic memory and is mentally and physically unable to do anything else during that time (Cahill, 1997). At other times, the individual may be withdrawn and emotionally detached (Cozolino, 2014).

Respond

The third "R" associated with being trauma-informed refers to situations where

> staff in every part of the organization, from the person who greets clients to the executives and the governance board, have changed their language, behaviours, and policies to take into consideration the experiences of trauma among children and adult users of the products or services and among the staff providing the services.
>
> (Huang et al., 2014, p. 10)

Resist re-traumatisation

The final "R" refers to ensuring that responses also "resist re-traumatisation". It requires specific and dedicated actions, some not in the scope of this chapter, to avoid triggering or potentially re-traumatising a previously traumatised refugee. Organisations such as entrepreneurial incubators, mentorship programmes, or other entrepreneurial programmes can inadvertently create stressful or toxic environments that halt or delay the recovery of refugee entrepreneurs (e.g., when they pressure refugees to decide quickly, ask then numerous questions, or to imagine a different future). Gendered power dynamics also create stress and staff need to be educated on how practices as simple as inadvertent touching or raising voices can trigger painful memories or potentially re-traumatise entrepreneurs (Herman, 1992).

Putting even the most basic awareness of these principles at the centre of any planning or training in refugee support organisations will help to ensure that such organisations promote well-being for the individual entrepreneur and enhance the healing and emancipatory benefits of entrepreneurship for refugees. However, these above features could easily be mistaken for describing both the necessary and sufficient requirements for an organisation to execute "trauma-informed" care for refugee entrepreneurs. The four Rs enable an organisation to realise the role of trauma, recognise how it manifests, and respond without re-triggering the trauma. Yet, the four Rs only describe the nature of being "trauma-informed". In other words, the four Rs encompass the spirit of what it means to be trauma-informed. For an individual or organisation to be considered as *delivering* trauma-informed care, they must embody and adhere to the following six related principles as well.

Programme design: Incorporate the six principles of trauma-informed care

The National Center for Trauma-Informed Care and the Substance Abuse and Mental Health Services Administration in the United States (Huang et al., 2014) jointly published six guiding principles that establish best practices for working with trauma survivors that enable an organisation to fulfil the promises of the four Rs. These principles include: (1) safety, (2) trustworthiness and transparency, (3) peer support, (4) collaboration and mutuality, (5) empowerment, voice, and choice, and (6) cultural, historical, and gender issues (Huang et al., 2014, p. 10) These principles, when implemented in entrepreneurial ecosystems, can foster an environment conducive for refugee entrepreneurs.

Safety stresses creating an environment of both physical and psychological safety for refugee entrepreneurs. Understanding how different entrepreneurs define "safety" is essential, as it is the traumatised entrepreneur who must feel that the organisation and the entrepreneurial ecosystem is safe for them. When an entrepreneur feels safe, it is less likely to *re-trigger* the trauma, and it is the first and essential step to an organisation's *response* to ensure trauma-informed care.

Trustworthiness and transparency emphasises building a culture of trustworthiness through predictability and transparency in decision-making processes. In many ways, this extends the first principle of safety, as this principle focuses on restoring any lost sense of predictability and trust that the traumatised entrepreneur feels as part of the organisation's *response* strategy to not *re-trigger* trauma.

Peer support, the third principle, utilises the power of community to establish safety and hope, thereby continuing to build trust and enhance collaboration. Peer support is about connecting traumatised individuals with others in the entrepreneurial ecosystem. As traumatised individuals learn to trust their surroundings, including the people within the organisation and entrepreneurial ecosystem at large, they can begin to regulate their own nervous systems. When a person with a trauma history can downregulate and move to a less hyperaroused state of being, there is greater opportunity to connect, collaborate, innovate, and generally perform. This peer support is amplified when members of the community *realise* the role of trauma and *recognise* how trauma may manifest in those around them to provide this needed peer support.

Collaboration and mutuality highlights the importance of partnering and levelling power differences. This principle is also based on the belief that healing happens in relationships and in meaningful exchanges; these exchanges are made easier when the power differentials that people face are mitigated. Given that a trauma history refers to a time when one was powerless to stop an experience from occurring, the power differentials in an organisation become very salient in the context of trauma-informed care. Again, this relates back to the initial R of *realisation*, understanding the role of trauma, and how to not *re-trigger* it through the perpetuation of power differentials in organisational practices.

Empowerment, voice, and choice encourages identifying and building upon individuals' strengths and experiences while engaging with the organisation and entrepreneurial ecosystem. It involves supporting refugee entrepreneurs in shared decision-making, choice, and goal setting, fostering a sense of control over their entrepreneurial journey. The organisation fosters a belief in the ability of the refugee to heal and recover from trauma as the entrepreneurial process facilitates recovery but does not mandate or control it. This organisational *response* to the trauma not only avoids *re-triggering* of the trauma but also can help in the healing process and build resilience for refugee entrepreneurs.

Cultural, historical, and gender issues focus on respecting cultural, historical, and gender diversity. It's about providing access to services responsive to specific, contextual needs and leveraging the healing value of traditional cultural practices and connections. It also requires the organisation to *recognise* and address historical trauma as the organisation works to move past cultural stereotypes and biases based on race, age, sexual orientation, age, religion, gender identity, and geography.

The above principles highlight the best practices for implementing the four Rs of trauma-informed care in organisations that work with refugee entrepreneurs. These guiding principles, when implemented and lived by these organisations, can create an entrepreneurial ecosystem that is understanding and responsive to the needs of traumatised individuals, leading to their successful integration and growth as refugee entrepreneurs. In Figure 12.1, we provide examples of how leaders can utilise these principles and how they can be applied in an entrepreneurial setting.

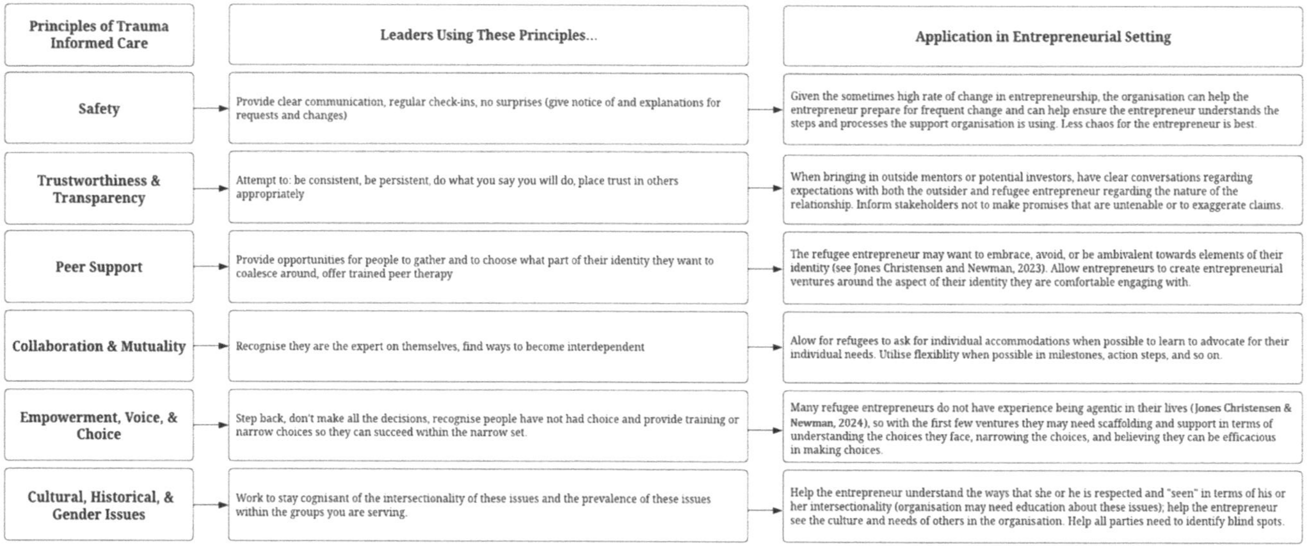

Figure 12.1 Applying trauma-informed care to refugee entrepreneurship.

Source: Compiled by authors.

These fundamental values of trauma-informed care are currently being implemented in many settings, most notably in education (Bailey et al., 2023; Davidson, 2017; Jacobson, 2021), and in social work through counselling and support for resettling in a host community (Im & Swan, 2020, 2021; Im et al., 2021; Ostrander et al., 2017). However, the application of trauma-informed care, as outlined above, for refugee entrepreneurs has yet to be studied in the management literature to understand how trauma-informed care impacts the well-being of the refugee entrepreneur and the entrepreneurial endeavour (Jones Christensen & Newman, 2024; Harima et al., 2019; Jürgens et al., 2022; Newman & Jones Christensen, 2021). We echo these calls for the incorporation of trauma-informed care into entrepreneurial settings for refugees, as well as for other vulnerable populations that have increased chances of trauma exposure.

Future research should examine how organisations facilitating refugee entrepreneurship, such as incubators, training workshops, and mentoring, could benefit from implementing these principles and engaging in the proposed behaviours. In so doing, we can move away from a focus solely on the health and well-being of the venture to a wholistic approach that values the well-being of the individual refugee entrepreneur as well.

Conclusion

The six trauma-informed principles can apply to *any* organisation that seeks to support individuals with trauma exposure. They are becoming increasingly discussed in management conversations, suggesting that in the future, they may simply become descriptors of expected management practice. Yet, the refugee crisis is so extreme that refugee support organisations cannot wait for others to promote these ideas. Instead, we encourage refugee support organisations, particularly those focused on entrepreneurship, to lead in incorporating trauma-informed practices. The traumas inherent in the pursuit of entrepreneurship and in the process of forced relocation can all be addressed with the principles introduced herein. It is our goal for readers to recognise that there are attainable practices that simultaneously encourage the "bright side" outcomes associated with entrepreneurship and mitigate its dark side potential. We assert that when stakeholders incorporate the ideas and ideals associated with being trauma-informed, the organisations they lead can better deliver on the positive promises associated with encouraging refugee entrepreneurship.

References

Alrawadieh, Z., Karayilan, E., & Cetin, G. (2018). Understanding the challenges of refugee entrepreneurship in tourism and hospitality. *The Service Industries Journal*, *39*, 9–10. https://doi.org/10.1080/02642069.2018.1440550

American Psychiatric Association, DSM-5 Task Force. (2013). *Diagnostic and Statistical Manual of Mental Disorders: DSM-5™* (5th ed.). American Psychiatric Publishing, Inc. https://doi.org/10.1176/appi.books.9780890425596

Bailey, M., Kim, W., Koury, S.P., Green, S.A., & Kim, I. (2023). Cultivating trauma-informed educational practices for students with refugee backgrounds. *Children & Schools*, *45*(4), 223–232. https://doi.org/10.1093/cs/cdad017

Baron, R.A. (2010). Job design and entrepreneurship: Why closer connections= mutual gains. *Journal of Organizational Behavior*, *31*(2/3), 370–378. www.jstor.org/stable/41683914

Bemak, F., & Chung, R.C.-Y. (2014). Immigrants and refugees. In F.T.L. Leong, L. Comas-Díaz, G.C. Nagayama Hall, V.C. McLoyd, & J.E. Trimble (Eds.), *APA Handbook of Multicultural Psychology, Vol. 1. Theory and Research* (pp. 503–517). American Psychological Association. https://doi.org/10.1037/14189-027

Bemak, F., Chung, R.C.Y., & Pedersen, P. (2003). *Counseling Refugees: A Psychosocial Approach to Innovative Multicultural Interventions* (No. 40). Westport, CT: Greenwood Publishing.

Benz, M., & Frey, B.S. (2004). Being independent raises happiness at work. *Swedish Economic Policy Review*, *11*(2), 95–134.

Benz, M., & Frey, B.S. (2008). The value of doing what you like: Evidence from the self-employed in 23 countries. *Journal of Economic Behavior & Organization*, *68*(3–4), 445–455. https://doi.org/10.1016/j.jebo.2006.10.014

Bort, J., Stephan, U., & Wiklund, J. (2020). The well-being of entrepreneurs and their stakeholders. In M.M. Gielnik, M.S. Cardon, & M. Frese (Eds.), *The Psychology of Entrepreneurship* (pp. 340–356). New York: Routledge. https://kclpure.kcl.ac.uk/portal/en/publications/the-well-being-of-entrepreneurs-and-their-stakeholders

Brown, R., & Mawson, S. (2016). Targeted support for high growth firms: Theoretical constraints, unintended consequences and future policy challenges. *Environment and Planning C: Government and Policy*, *34*(5), 816–836. https://doi.org/10.1177/0263774X15614680

Brown, A., & Scribner, T. (2014). Unfulfilled promises, future possibilities: The refugee resettlement system in the United States. *Journal on Migration and Human Security*, *2*(2), 101–120. https://doi.org/10.1177/233150241400200203

Brundin, E., & Gustafsson, V. (2013). Entrepreneurs' decision making under different levels of uncertainty: The role of emotions. *International Journal of Entrepreneurial Behavior & Research*, *19*(6), 568–591. https://doi.org/10.1108/IJEBR-07-2012-0074

Cahill, L. (1997). The neurobiology of emotionally influenced memory: Implications for understanding traumatic memory. *Annals of the New York Academy of Sciences*, *821*, 238–246.

Campion, E.D. (2018). The career adaptive refugee: Exploring the structural and personal barriers to refugee resettlement. *Journal of Vocational Behavior*, *105*, 6–16. https://doi.org/10.1016/j.jvb.2017.10.008

Cardon, M.S., & Patel, P.C. (2015). Is stress worth it? Stress-related health and wealth trade-offs for entrepreneurs. *Applied Psychology*, *64*(2), 379–420. https://doi.org/10.1111/apps.12021

Cozolino, L. (2014). *The Neuroscience of Human Relationships: Attachment and the Developing Social Brain (Norton Series on Interpersonal Neurobiology)*. New York: WW Norton & Company.

Cubbon, L., Darga, K., Wisnesky, U.D., Dennett, L., & Guptill, C. (2020). Depression among entrepreneurs: A scoping review. *Small Business Economics*, 1–25. https://doi.org/10.1007/s11187-020-00382-4

Davidson, S. (2017). Trauma-informed practices for postsecondary education: A guide. *Education Northwest*, *5*, 3–24. https://ecampusontario.pressbooks.pub/app/uploads/sites/1721/2021/10/trauma-informed-practices-postsecondary-508.pdf

Easton-Calabria, E., & Omata, N. (2018). Panacea for the refugee crisis? Rethinking the promotion of 'self-reliance for refugees. *Third World Quarterly*, *39*(8), 1458–1474. https://doi.org/10.1080/01436597.2018.1458301

Fong, R., Busch, N.B., Armour, M., Heffron, L.C., & Chanmugam, A. (2007). Pathways to self-sufficiency: Successful entrepreneurship for refugees. *Journal of Ethnic & Cultural Diversity in Social Work*, *16*(1–2), 127–159. https://doi.org/10.1300/J051v16n01_05

Fredrickson, B.L. (2001). The role of positive emotions in positive psychology: The broaden-and-build theory of positive emotions. *The American Psychologist*, *56*(3), 218–226. https://doi.org/10.1037//0003-066x.56.3.218

Freeman, R.E., Dmytriyev, S.D., & Phillips, R.A. (2021). Stakeholder theory and the resource-based view of the firm. *Journal of Management*, *47*(7), 1757–1770. https://doi.org/10.1177/0149206321993576

Freeman, M.A., Staudenmaier, P.J., Zisser, M.R., & Andresen, L.A. (2019). The prevalence and co-occurrence of psychiatric conditions among entrepreneurs and their families. *Small Business Economics*, *53*(2), 323–342. https://doi.org/10.1007/s11187-018-0059-8

Frewen, P.A., & Lanius, R.A. (2006). Toward a psychobiology of posttraumatic self-dysregulation: Reexperiencing, hyperarousal, dissociation, and emotional numbing. *Annals of the New York Academy of Sciences*, *1071*(1), 110–124. https://doi.org/10.1196/annals.1364.010

Gold, S.J. (1992). The employment potential of refugee entrepreneurship: Soviet Jews and Vietnamese in California. *Review of Policy Research*, *11*(2), 176–186. https://doi.org/10.1111/j.1541-1338.1992.tb00400.x

Goodwin-Gill, G.S. (2014). The international law of refugee protection. *The Oxford Handbook of Refugee and Forced Migration Studies*, 36–47. https://doi.org/10.1093/oxfordhb/9780199652433.013.0021

Grégoire, D.A., Cornelissen, J., Dimov, D., & Van Burg, E. (2015). The mind in the middle: Taking stock of affect and cognition research in entrepreneurship. *International Journal of Management Reviews*, *17*(2), 125–142. https://doi.org/10.1111/ijmr.12060

Guo, G.C., Al Ariss, A., & Brewster, C. (2020). Understanding the global refugee crisis: Managerial consequences and policy implications. *Academy of Management Perspectives*, *34*(4), 531–545. https://doi.org/10.5465/amp.2019.0013

Harima, A., Freudenberg, J., & Halberstadt, J. (2019). Functional domains of business incubators for refugee entrepreneurs. *Journal of Enterprising Communities: People and Places in the Global Economy*, *14*(5), 687–711. https://doi.org/10.1108/JEC-11-2018-0081

Hartman, C. & Schilling, K. (2019). *Cham Saar: The first Syrian-German cheese manufacturer*. In S. Heilbrunn, J. Freiling, & A. Harima (Eds.), *Refugee Entrepreneurship: A Case-Based Topography* (pp. 39–53). Boston: Springer.

Haynie, J.M., & Shepherd, D. (2011). Toward a theory of discontinuous career transition: Investigating career transitions necessitated by traumatic life events. *Journal of Applied Psychology*, *96*(3), 501–524. https://doi.org/10.1037/a0021450

Heilbrunn, S., & Iannone, R.L. (2020). From center to periphery and back again: A systematic literature review of refugee entrepreneurship. *Sustainability*, *12*(18), 7658. https://doi.org/10.3390/su12187658

Herman, J.L. (1992). *Trauma and Recovery: The Aftermath of Violence—from Domestic Abuse to Political Terror*. New York: Basic Books.

Hollifield, M., Warner, T., Lian, N., Krakow, B., Jenkins, J., Kesler, J., & Westermeyer, J. (2002). Measuring trauma and health status in refugees: A critical review. *JAMA*, *288*(5), 611–621. https://doi.org/10.1001/jama.288.5.611

Huang, L.N., Flatow, R., Biggs, T., Afayee, S., Smith, K., Clark, T., & Blake, M. (2014). *SAMHSA's Concept of Trauma and Guidance for a Trauma-Informed Approach*. https://ncsacw.acf.hhs.gov/userfiles/files/SAMHSA_Trauma.pdf

Im, H., Rodriguez, C., & Grumbine, J.M. (2021). A multitier model of refugee mental health and psychosocial support in resettlement: Toward trauma-informed and culture-informed systems of care. *Psychological Services*, *18*(3), 345–364. https://doi.org/10.1037/ser0000412

Im, H., & Swan, L. (2020) Capacity building for refugee mental health in resettlement: Implementation and evaluation of cross-cultural trauma-informed care training. *Journal of Immigrant and Minority Health*, *22*(5), 923–934. 10.1007/s10903-020-00992-w

Im, H., & Swan, L. (2021). Working towards culturally responsive trauma-informed care in the refugee resettlement process: Qualitative inquiry with refugee-serving professionals in the United States. *Behavioral Sciences*, *11*(11), 155. https://doi.org/10.3390/bs11110155

International Rescue Committee (IRC). (2019). Migrants, exiles, refugees and immigrants: What's the difference?. Retrieved January 15, 2019 from www.rescue.org/article/migrants-asylum-seekers-refugees-and-immigrants-whats-difference

Iyadurai, L., Visser, R.M., Lau-Zhu, A., Porcheret, K., Horsch, A., Holmes, E.A., & James, E.L. (2019). Intrusive memories of trauma: A target for research bridging cognitive science and its clinical application. *Clinical Psychology Review*, *69*, 67–82. https://doi.org/10.1016/j.cpr.2018.08.005

Jacobson, M.R. (2021). An exploratory analysis of the necessity and utility of trauma-informed practices in education. *Preventing School Failure: Alternative Education for Children and Youth*, *65*(2), 124–134. https://doi.org/10.1080/1045988X.2020.1848776

Jones Christensen, L., Embrey, E., Newman, A., Godfrey, P. (2023). *If the Body Keeps the Score, What Happens When You Bring the Body to Work? Exploring the Effects of Trauma on Employee Human Capital*. [Unpublished Manuscript].

Jones Christensen, L., & Newman, A. (2024). Who do I want to be now that I'm here? Refugee entrepreneurs, identity, and acculturation. *Business & Society*, *63*(1), 242–275. https://doi.org/10.1177/00076503231158611

Jones Christensen, L., Newman, A.B., Herrick, H., & Godfrey, P. (2019). Separate but not equal: Toward a nomological net for migrants and migrant entrepreneurship. *Journal of International Business Policy*, *3*(1), 1–22. https://doi.org/10.1057/s42214-019-00041-w

Jürgens, C., Ramalingam, A., Zarembski, R., Harima, A., & Yeshi, T. (2022). Relational dynamics within refugee business incubators: Bridging refugee entrepreneurs to the host-country entrepreneurial ecosystem. In D.G. Pickernell, M. Battisti, Z. Dann, & C. Ekinsmyth (Eds.), *Disadvantaged Entrepreneurship and the Entrepreneurial*

Ecosystem (Contemporary Issues in Entrepreneurship Research, Vol. 14) (pp. 147–169). Leeds: Emerald Publishing Limited.

Kaplan, H. I., & Sadock, B.J. (1989). *Comprehensive Textbook of Psychiatry, Vols. 1–2.* Baltimore, MA: Williams & Wilkins Co.

Keyes, C.L. (2013). *Mental Well-Being: International Contributions to the Study of Positive Mental Health* (Vol. 8). Dordrecht: Springer.

Keyes, E.F. (2000). Mental health status in refugees: An integrative review of current research. *Issues in Mental Health Nursing, 21*(4), 397–410. https://doi.org/10.1080/016128400248013

Kloosterman, R., Van Der Leun, J., & Rath, J. (1999). Mixed embeddedness: (In) formal economic activities and immigrant businesses in the Netherlands. *International Journal of Urban and Regional Research, 23*(2), 252–266. https://doi.org/10.1111/1468-2427.00194

Kollmann, T., Stockmann, C, & Kensbock, J. (2019). I can't get no sleep – The differential impact of entrepreneurial stressors on work-home interference and insomnia among experienced versus novice entrepreneurs. *Journal of Business Venturing, 34*(4), 692–708. https://doi.org/10.1016/j.jbusvent.2018.08.001

Krahn, H., Derwing, T., Mulder, M., & Wilkinson, L. (2000). Educated and underemployed: Refugee integration into the Canadian labour market. *Journal of International Migration and Integration/Revue de l'integration et de la migration internationale, 1*(1), 59–84. https://doi.org/10.1007/s12134-000-1008-2

Kroon, B., & Paauwe, J. (2014). Structuration of precarious employment in economically constrained firms: The case of Dutch agriculture. *Human Resource Management Journal, 24*(1), 19–37. https://doi.org/10.1111/1748-8583.12024

Leong, F.T., Eggerth, D.E., & Flynn, M.A. (2014). A life course perspective on immigrant occupational health and well-being. *Contemporary Occupational Health Psychology: Global Perspectives on Research and Practice, 3*, 97–113. https://doi.org/10.1002/9781118713860.ch7

Lerner, D.A., Hunt, R.A., & Dimov, D. (2018). Action! Moving beyond the intendedly-rational logics of entrepreneurship. *Journal of Business Venturing, 33*(1), 52–69. https://doi.org/10.1016/j.jbusvent.2017.10.002

Levie, J. (2007). Immigration, in-migration, ethnicity and entrepreneurship in the United Kingdom. *Small Business Economics, 28*, 143–169. https://doi.org/10.1007/s11187-006-9013-2

Maté, G. (2022). *The Myth of the Normal: Trauma, Illness and Healing in a Toxic Culture.* New York: Penguin Random House.

Mestheneos, E., & Ioannidi, E. (2002). Obstacles to refugee integration in the European Union member states. *Journal of Refugee Studies, 15*(3), 304–320. https://doi.org/10.1093/jrs/15.3.304

Mollica, R.F., Wyshak, G., & Lavelle, J. (1987). The psychosocial impact of war trauma and torture on Southeast Asian refugees. *The American Journal of Psychiatry, 144*(12), 1567–1572. https://doi.org/10.1176/ajp.144.12.1567

Newman, A.B., & Christensen, L.J. (2021). Doing it right, but getting it wrong: Best practices for refugee focused incubators. *Journal of Developmental Entrepreneurship, 26*(03), 2150019. https://doi.org/10.1142/S1084946721500199

Ostrander, J., Melville, A., & Berthold, S.M. (2017). Working with refugees in the US: Trauma-informed and structurally competent social work approaches. *Advances in Social Work, 18*(1), 66–79. https://doi.org/10.18060/21282

Patel, P.C., Wolfe, M.T., & Williams, T.A. (2019). Self-employment and allostatic load. *Journal of Business Venturing*, *34*(4), 731–751. https://doi.org/10.1016/j.jbusvent.2018.05.004

Patzelt, H., & Shepherd, D.A. (2011). Recognizing opportunities for sustainable development. *Entrepreneurship Theory and Practice*, *35*(4), 631–652. https://doi.org/10.1111/j.1540-6520.2010.00386.x

Reed, H. (2018). Forced migration and undocumented migration and development. *United Nations Department of Economic and Social Affairs, Nueva York, 2.*

Rindova, V., Barry, D., & Ketchen Jr, D.J. (2009). Entrepreneuring as emancipation. *Academy of Management Review*, *34*(3), 477–491. https://doi.org/10.5465/amr.2009.40632647

Saarni, S.I., Saarni, E.S., & Saarni, H. (2008). Quality of life, work ability, and self employment: A population survey of entrepreneurs, farmers, and salary earners. *Occupational and Environmental Medicine*, *65*(2), 98–103. https://doi.org/10.1136/oem.2007.033423

Salehyan, I. (2019). Conclusion: What academia can contribute to refugee policy. *Journal of Peace Research*, *56*(1), 146–151. https://doi.org/10.1177/002234331881297

Sandberg, S, Immonen, R., & Kok, S. (2018). Refugee entrepreneurship: Taking a social network view on immigrants with refugee backgrounds starting transnational businesses in Sweden. *International Journal of Small Business*, *36*(1–2), 216–241. https://doi.org/10.1504/IJESB.2019.096967

Schonfeld, I.S., & Mazzola, J.J. (2015). A qualitative study of stress in individuals self-employed in solo businesses. *Journal of Occupational Health Psychology*, *20*(4), 501–513. https://doi.org/10.1037/a0038804

Shepherd, D.A., & Cardon, M.S. (2009). Negative emotional reactions to project failure and the self-compassion to learn from the experience. *Journal of Management Studies*, *46*(6), 923–949. https://doi.org/10.1111/j.1467-6486.2009.00821.x

Shepherd, D.A., & Patzelt, H. (2015). The "heart" of entrepreneurship: The impact of entrepreneurial action on health and health on entrepreneurial action. *Journal of Business Venturing Insights*, *4*, 22–29. https://doi.org/10.1016/j.jbvi.2015.08.001

Shepherd, D.A., Saade, F.P., & Wincent, J. (2020). How to circumvent adversity? Refugee-entrepreneurs' resilience in the face of substantial and persistent adversity. *Journal of Business Venturing*, *35*(4), 105940. https://doi.org/10.1016/j.jbusvent.2019.06.001

Shir, N. (2015). *Entrepreneurial Well-being: The Payoff Structure of Business Creation.* Stockholm School of Economics.

Smith, S.G., Zhang, X., Basile, K.C., Merrick, M.T., Wang, J., Kresnow, M., & Chen, J. (2018). *The National Intimate Partner and Sexual Violence Survey: 2015 Data Brief– Updated Release.* Atlanta: National Center for Injury Prevention and Control, Centers for Disease Control and Prevention. Retrieved from www.cdc.gov/violenceprevention/pdf/2015data-brief508.pdf

Stephan, U. (2018). Entrepreneurs' mental health and well-being: A review and research agenda. *Academy of Management Perspectives*, *32*(3), 290–322. https://doi.org/10.5465/amp.2017.0001

Stephan, U., & Roesler, U. (2010). Health of entrepreneurs versus employees in a national representative sample. *Journal of Occupational and Organizational Psychology*, *83*(3), 717–738. https://doi.org/10.1348/096317909X472067

UNCTAD. (2018). Policy Guide on Entrepreneurship for Migrants and Refugees. [unctad.org/en/PublicationsLibrary/diae2018d2_en.pdf].
UNHCR. (2018). Resettlement. Retrieved January 15, 2019 from www.unhcr.org/en-us/resettlement.html
UNHCR. (2023). Refugee Data Finder. Retrieved May 28, 2023 from www.unhcr.org/refugee-statistics/
Van der Kolk, B.A. (2015). *The Body Keeps the Score: Brain, Mind, and Body in the Healing of Trauma*. New York: Penguin Books.
Van Gelderen, M. (2016). Entrepreneurial autonomy and its dynamics. *Applied Psychology*, *65*(3), 541–567. https://doi.org/10.1111/apps.12066
Wach, D., Stephan, U., Weinberger, E., & Wegge, J. (2021). Entrepreneurs' stressors and well-being: A recovery perspective and diary study. *Journal of Business Venturing*, *36*(5), 106016. https://doi.org/10.1016/j.jbusvent.2020.106016
Warr, P. (2013). How to think about and measure psychological well-being. In M. Wang, R.R. Sinclair, & L.E. Tetrick (Eds.), *Research Methods in Occupational Health Psychology: Measurement, Design and Data Analysis* (pp. 76–90). New York: Routledge.
Wauters, B., & Lambrecht, J. (2006). Refugee entrepreneurship in Belgium: Potential and practice. *The International Entrepreneurship and Management Journal*, *2*(4), 509–525. https://doi.org/10.1007/s11365-006-0008-x
Wauters, B., & Lambrecht, J. (2008). Barriers to refugee entrepreneurship in Belgium: Towards an explanatory model. *Journal of Ethnic and Migration Studies*, *34*(6), 895–915. https://doi.org/10.1080/13691830802211190
Wiklund, J., Hatak, I., Patzelt, H., & Shepherd, D.A. (2018). Mental disorders in the entrepreneurship context: When being different can be an advantage. *Academy of Management Perspectives*, *32*(2), 182–206. https://doi.org/10.5465/amp.2017.0063
Wiklund, J., Nikolaev, B., Shir, N., Foo, M.D., & Bradley, S. (2019). Entrepreneurship and well-being: Past, present, and future. *Journal of Business Venturing*, *34*(4), 579–588. https://doi.org/10.1016/j.jbusvent.2019.01.002
Williamson, A.J., Gish, J.J., & Stephan, U. (2021). Let's focus on solutions to entrepreneurial ill-being! Recovery interventions to enhance entrepreneurial well-being. *Entrepreneurship Theory and Practice*, *45*(6), 1307–1338. https://doi.org/10.1177/1042258721100064
Zaleski, K.L., Johnson, D.K., & Klein, J.T. (2016). Grounding Judith Herman's trauma theory within interpersonal neuroscience and evidence-based practice modalities for trauma treatment. *Smith College Studies in Social Work*, *86*(4), 377–393. https://doi.org/10.1080/00377317.2016.1222110
Zhang, S.X., & Cueto, J. (2017). The study of bias in entrepreneurship. *Entrepreneurship Theory and Practice*, *41*(3), 419–454. https://doi.org/10.1111/etap.12212

13 Well-being barriers and enablers of refugees and refugee service industry entrepreneurs

Ilayaraja Subramanian and Jörg Finsterwalder

Introduction

Globally, there is an unprecedented refugee crisis, caused by factors such as conflicts, violation of human rights, environmental shifts, economic inequality, and desperation (United Nations High Commissioner for Refugees [UNHCR], 2023). As of June 2022, approximately 103 million individuals had been displaced from their homes against their will. Of this population, 32.5 million were forced to leave their home countries as refugees. Furthermore, over 40% of these were minors below 18 years of age, and nearly 69% of refugees are hosted by neighbouring countries (UNHCR, n.d.-a). The refugee crisis is a complex humanitarian problem (Boenigk et al., 2021) and one of the most pressing global issues for both developed and developing countries alike (Finsterwalder, 2017). Since the early 2000s, various development agencies, donor governments, and humanitarian non-governmental organisations (NGOs), such as the UNHCR, the International Labour Organization, and the World Bank, have been advocating for the development of refugees' self-reliance as an important objective for both individual refugees and their communities (Skran & Easton-Calabria, 2020). "Self-reliance is the social and economic ability of an individual, a household or a community to meet essential needs (including protection, food, water, shelter, personal safety, health and education) in a sustainable manner and with dignity" (UNHCR, 2005, p. 1). Some form of employment plays an important role in developing self-reliance, yet it has been well documented that there are numerous constraints and obstacles (host country language fluency, lack of formal education, etc.) to refugees finding employment in their host countries; therefore, entrepreneurship has emerged as an alternate means to attain self-reliance (Skran & Easton-Calabria, 2020).

Although refugees are often viewed as a liability for countries that host them, they should be regarded as a resource (Finsterwalder et al., 2021) as their entrepreneurial ventures can make noteworthy contributions to local economies (Alrawadieh et al., 2019). Such contributions refer to the social and economic co-creation of value (Shneikat & Alrawadieh, 2019) and cultural

DOI: 10.4324/9781003368540-17

value (Ranabahu et al., 2023), as they bring human capital and skills to the host country (Skran & Easton-Calabria, 2020). In this chapter, we focus on a subset of refugee entrepreneurs, that is, those who operate businesses in the service industry. We call them refugee service industry entrepreneurs. The aim of this chapter is to elaborate on the status quo of refugee well-being in establishing oneself a host country and the barriers and enablers to finding work or establishing flourishing enterprises. We consider both the system level of refugee employment services and refugee entry into the service industry of a region or country as well as the individual level of refugee well-being. At the individual level, we specifically look at the resources they can bring to a society as service industry entrepreneurs (Finsterwalder & Kuppelwieser, 2020). The approach taken can best be described as a service ecosystems approach (Finsterwalder et al., 2022). The chapter aligns with the Sustainable Development Goals (SDGs) 3 – Good Health and Well-being, 8 – Decent Work and Economic Growth, 10 – Reduced Inequalities, and 11 – Sustainable Cities and Communities (UN, 2023).

The chapter is structured as follows. Firstly, it provides some background information on refugees and their need for transformative services. Then, it outlines the barriers to refugee wellbeing and refugee service industry entrepreneurship. This is followed by explaining the enablers of refugee well-being and refugee service industry entrepreneurship. Implications are then outlined before the chapter concludes.

Refugees and their need for transformative services

A refugee is "someone who has been forced to flee his or her home country because of persecution, war, or violence" (UNHCR, n.d.-b). The majority of these refugees embark on an arduous and/or dangerous journey that is often lengthy (BenEzer & Zetter, 2015). In this chapter, the notion of the refugee service journey, proposed by Boenigk et al. (2021), is utilised. It consists of three phases: entry, transition, and exit. The initial service phase, *entry* phase, refers to the time when an individual chooses to relocate or prepares to seek asylum in a different country (Boenigk et al., 2021). In this phase, refugees require services to meet basic needs such as food, water, shelter, medical care, and travel information (Finsterwalder et al., 2021). The *transition* phase refers to the act of relocating physically from one location to another (Boenigk et al., 2021). UNHCR often assists refugees to stay in temporary shelters or camps and offers services to meet their basic and temporary needs (Nasr & Fisk, 2018). The *exit* phase refers to concluding the service journey by permanently resettling in a new country (Boenigk et al., 2021). This chapter focuses on the *exit* phase of the refugee service journey and discusses the specific issues and challenges faced by refugees, as they resettle in host countries, regaining or maintaining their well-being, and finding employment or entrepreneurial opportunities.

According to Ager and Strang (2008), countries that host refugees tend to offer support services that are tailored to the needs of their citizens rather than catering to the specific requirements of newly arrived refugees. The service needs of refugees in a host country are distinct from those of their citizens, as refugees experience more obstacles due to limited personal resources and their painful refugee (service) journey experiences. Because of the mass scale of the refugee movement globally, host countries may face challenges in providing the level of resettlement services needed (Finsterwalder, 2017). Compared to refugees established in their host country, newly arrived refugees are more vulnerable due to the recent completion of the refugee service journey entry and transition phases (Dodds et al., 2022). In addition, due to lack of social, cultural, and economic resources, newly arrived refugees are vulnerable to and experience significant challenges in their resettlement journeys. Fair and equitable access to service provision can help decrease their vulnerability (Boenigk et al., 2021; Hepi et al., 2017) and enhance their well-being (Finsterwalder et al., 2021).

Farmaki and Christou (2019) propose that future studies concerning the global refugee crisis should be based on principles of Transformative Service Research (Kuppelwieser & Finsterwalder, 2016), which focuses on bringing "uplifting changes and improvements in the well-being of individuals, collectives, and ecosystems" (Anderson et al., 2011, p. 9). This objective indicates that the Transformative Service Research approach, possibly in comparison to other approaches (Kuppelwieser & Finsterwalder, 2016), is especially appropriate for analysing vulnerable groups, such as refugees, due to the significant role services play in their survival and well-being throughout their service journey (Boenigk et al., 2021). According to Nasr and Fisk (2018), the fundamental principle of Transformative Service Research is that services like healthcare, social services, and disaster relief systems are ubiquitous and have the ability to enhance the overall welfare of refugees, whether at individual, collective, or wider societal level. To enhance refugees' well-being and ensure successful integration into the host society, some Transformative Service Research scholars advocate for the inclusion of refugees in a nation's service ecosystem, which entails a dedicated approach for refugees (Boenigk et al., 2021; Finsterwalder et al., 2021; Fisk et al., 2018).

Refugee entrepreneurship refers to the pursuit of entrepreneurial ventures by people who have been compelled to leave their homes because of war, conflict, or persecution, and have settled in a transition or host country (Abebe, 2023; Fuller-Love et al., 2006). Despite refugee entrepreneurs' positive impact on host countries, they often experience various obstacles and challenges in their effort to establish new ventures. Such challenges can be legislative and administrative, financial, sociocultural, and market-related (Alrawadieh et al., 2019). Furthermore, refugees struggle to regain or maintain their well-being. However, it can be argued that only healthy and content refugees can successfully start and operate "healthy" businesses.

Barriers of refugee well-being

To ensure successful integration and enhanced well-being of refugees, government agencies, Non Government organisations (NGOs), for-profit organisations, quasi-government agencies, religious bodies, and formal and informal volunteer groups offer resettlement services (Fozdar & Hartley, 2014). The effectiveness, relevance, and timeliness of these service providers' efforts to meet the service needs of refugees, in accordance with SDG 10 – Reduced Inequalities (UN, 2023), determine how quickly refugees can integrate into the host society. However, there are many gaps in these resettlement services (Subramanian et al., 2022) that negatively affect the refugees' integration process and well-being, which can subsequently create barriers to refugees becoming entrepreneurs. These barriers are highlighted in Subramanian et al.'s (2022) systematic literature review. It also identified that transformative resettlement services are required to enhance the well-being of refugees in the areas of healthcare, education, interpretation and communication, employment and entrepreneurship, housing, and regional and rural resettlement services. We discuss these areas by aligning with Boenigk et al.'s (2021) exit phase of the refugee service journey.

Healthcare service provision

Subramanian et al. (2022) suggest that good health is important for refugees to actively participate in their new host society, including engaging in a service industry entrepreneurship venture, in line with SDG 3 (Good Health and Well-being) and SDG 8 (Decent Work and Economic Growth) (UN, 2023). Access to effective healthcare services is crucial to refugees' well-being, and these services must be available, approachable, acceptable, accommodative, affordable, and appropriate (Levesque et al., 2013). However, the literature (Au et al., 2019; Levesque et al., 2013; Paisi et al., 2020) shows that refugees face significant barriers to accessing and engaging with general healthcare services. These include language and interpretation difficulties (the most common barrier for refugees), cultural differences in service delivery, transportation, lack of trust, limited understanding, healthcare coverage and cost, time pressures, lack of social support, employment obligations, and not having continuity of care. These are contrary to meeting SDG 10 – Reduced Inequalities. Additionally, some refugees face unique barriers in accessing specialised services and care. For example, dental anxiety and beliefs conflicting with oral health can act as barriers for accessing dental care services and/or medical treatment (Paisi et al., 2020). To deal with these barriers, resettlement agencies and healthcare service providers need to work collaboratively (Fehsenfeld & Levinsen, 2019).

Educational services

Ager and Strang's (2008) study shows that education and training can provide skills and knowledge that can help refugees finding employment and/or self-employment. Marcu (2018) examines both the role of higher educational institutions in refugee integration and the problems refugees face in accessing higher education. Problems include the loss of proof of previous qualifications, non-recognition of qualifications, language difficulties, insufficient advice and individual guidance, inadequate information on courses, and lack of adequate financing (Naidoo, 2012; Pugh et al., 2012; Rah et al., 2009).

Andrade and Doolin (2016) state that information and communications technology (ICT) education can contribute to adult refugees' social inclusion in line with SDG 10 – Reduced Inequalities. It is beneficial to participate in an information society, to communicate effectively, to understand a new society, to be socially connected, and to express cultural identity. In relation to economic activities, ICT education promotes participation in productive activities, such as entrepreneurship. However, refugees' problems in accessing higher education also exist in pursuing ICT education. Moreover, in particular, female refugees face specific barriers in accessing educational services, such as transportation issues, long waiting times, the inadequacy of the hours allocated to studies and learning support, and limited or lack of childcare arrangements (Shrestha-Ranjit et al., 2020).

Interpretation and communication services

The literature indicates that resettlement service providers often experience difficulties in providing sociocultural and linguistically effective interpretation services (Subramanian et al., 2022). Language barriers affect refugees accessing crucial services, such as healthcare. One of the common problems is the lack of availability of professional interpreters who could cater to refugee communication needs. Such lack of services affects achievement of SDG 10 – Reduced Inequalities. For example, due to the lack of face-to-face translators, refugees often miss their healthcare services appointments and then have to wait a long time to re-enter healthcare services. Moreover, there is a lack of cultural sensitivity when interpreting services are offered to refugees. For example, same-gender interpreters may not be available for female refugees who prefer to only speak to these translators (Shrestha-Ranjit et al., 2020). The use of ICT tools can improve the efficiency of interpretation services for refugees. Therefore, it is important that interpreters are well-informed and proficient in using the latest electronic tools (Atabekova et al., 2018). When there are no interpreters available, some refugees arrange for informal interpreters such as friends or family members. However, when accessing healthcare services, it is recommended to use professional interpreters as informal ones are not considered effective (Shrestha-Ranjit et al., 2020).

Housing services

Subramanian et al. (2022) show that providing safe, affordable, and appropriate housing is crucial for the successful integration and well-being of refugees. However, refugees often struggle to find suitable housing due to high costs, limited availability of rental properties, poor-quality housing, negative attitudes from real estate agents, and complex tenancy procedures (Fozdar & Hartley, 2014). It is important for housing service providers and resettlement agencies to know about the necessary requirements for successful housing integration and well-being of refugees, such as a housing orientation process, ongoing support, relocation assistance, and addressing potential harassment (Phillips, 2006), thereby aligning service provision with SDG 11 – Sustainable Cities and Communities. Furthermore, Subramanian et al. (2022) found that most of the research conducted on the housing needs of refugees focus on families and general issues relating to housing service provision. However, there is insufficient research on the housing needs of unaccompanied youth refugees and single male or female refugees, who may face their own unique challenges in finding suitable housing.

Employment and entrepreneurship services

For refugees to become economically independent via (self-)employment and successfully integrate into their new country, resettlement agencies and employment service providers conduct programmes to develop refugees' language skills, job skills, work readiness, and job application prowess (Subramanian et al., 2022). These services are vital to cater to SDG 8 – Decent Work and Economic Growth, and seek to address inadequate host country language proficiency, limitations in local work experience, lack of professional networks, and difficulties in navigating a new employment system as common barriers to entering the self-employment. For example, Alrawadieh et al.'s (2019) study shows that some refugee service industry entrepreneurs in the tourism and hospitality domains face challenges, such as legislative and administrative obstacles, lack of resources, and difficulty in accessing the labour market. Greater coordination between different agencies is essential to meet the individual needs of refugees who are looking for employment or self-employment opportunities (Diedrich & Styhre, 2008). However, finding opportunities is just the first step and refugees will need further mentoring programmes to sustain and progress their careers. Månsson and Delander (2017) reveal that mentorship has a positive impact on male refugees' income levels. Further, Daunfeldt et al.'s (2019) study shows that service industries are more likely to have more opportunities for refugees than high-tech and manufacturing industries. Also, as identified previously, foreign credentials and work experience are mostly ignored by employers, and female refugees face greater challenges in gaining employment than male refugees, often due to a lack of transportation, caregiving, and domestic responsibilities (Senthanar et al., 2020). Such issues need to be mitigated to adhere to SDG 10 –Reduced Inequalities.

Regional and rural resettlement services

Refugees who resettle in regional and rural areas face greater challenges when compared to those in metropolitan areas. For example, Jewson et al. (2015)

show that refugees resettling in rural Australian areas have limited access to resettlement services if they do not have a driving license. Furthermore, the authors reveal that certain services are not available, such as translators, due to the fact that resettlement service providers have difficulty attracting interpreters in rural areas. Therefore, a greater level of complex and integrated support is needed to increase the effectiveness of existing services. In general, rural agencies offer a limited number of services owing to resource constraints, such as limited funding and accessibility to professional skills, which result in further widening the gap of inequality (SDG 10). Another Australian study by Kandasamy and Soldatic (2018) confirms that metropolitan resettlement service agencies offer a wider range of services than the rural areas, such as driving courses, ICT training, English language lessons, sport and recreation related services, and healthcare counselling. A full array of services is important in closing any SDG 11– Sustainable Cities and Communities gaps.

In summary, to enable refugees to embark on a successful service industry entrepreneurship journey, it is important to identify and eliminate the various barriers to their well-being. Government refugee resettlement agencies, NGOs, and various organisations play a crucial role in providing resettlement services to refugees, which help them to integrate into host societies and their readiness for entrepreneurship. However, substantial gaps exist within these resettlement services which can delay refugees' progress towards becoming entrepreneurs. These barriers are intricately connected to the refugees' well-being and can be found in several key areas: healthcare, education, interpretation and communication services, housing, and employment and entrepreneurship services. To effectively circumvent these barriers, fostering collaboration among resettlement agencies, healthcare service providers, educational institutions, employment service providers as well as fellow refugees or refugee entrepreneurs becomes crucial. This collaborative effort is vital in establishing an enabling environment for refugees to engage in service industry entrepreneurship and ensure their well-being.

Enablers of refugee entrepreneurship

Various factors enable refugee entrepreneurship, such as access to resources, access to markets, and community support. These act as pull factors that motivate refugees to start their own businesses (Kirkwood, 2009). Other pull factors include the presence of entrepreneurial role models which include fellow refugees, mentoring (de Vries et al., 2015), and social networks, both within and outside refugees' ethnic community (Alexandre et al., 2019). Among these factors, social networks are highly important as they provide refugees with access to vital information, knowledge, capital, and access to other social networks (Elfring & Hulsink, 2003) as well as stability (Bizri, 2017). Referring to entrepreneurship instead of seeking employment, refugees may be drawn to entrepreneurship due to the desire for greater control over their lives (Embiricos, 2020), higher earning potential, increased independence, social status, and flexibility in their working schedule to accommodate family needs. At a personal level, refugees' human capital, such as their skills, education, knowledge, and experience, can also drive them to pursue entrepreneurship (Ilhan-Nas et al., 2011). Additionally, financial support from the host country's government and/or their family may motivate refugees to start a venture (Barth & Zalkat, 2021). The type of refugee entrepreneurship that is driven by pull factors is known as *opportunity entrepreneurship*, which involves taking advantage of favourable opportunities (Skran & Easton-Calabria, 2020).

Personal or external factors (e.g., dissatisfaction with the current situation, lack of opportunity and employment, and marginalisation) that lead to starting a business are called *push factors* (Kirkwood, 2009). These can be difficulties in securing employment due to the lack of local language proficiency, work experience, or formal or incompatible qualifications (Zehra & Usmani, 2023). Refugee entrepreneurship driven by push factors is also known as *necessity entrepreneurship*, as refugees are forced to start ventures (Skran & Easton-Calabria, 2020). The differentiation between pull factors (opportunity entrepreneurship) and push factors (necessity entrepreneurship) hinges on the opportunity cost principle which is critical for entrepreneurial decision-making (Mickiewicz et al., 2017). Opportunity cost refers to the trade-off between investments in different options (Schapper et al., 2014). Amit et al.'s (1995) study finds a link between lower opportunity costs and heightened push factors (necessity), indicating a stronger inclination towards engaging in entrepreneurial activities, whereas higher opportunity cost, reflecting ample high-quality opportunities and increased identification, strengthens pull (opportunity) factors (Fredström et al., 2021).

Both push and pull factors may differ for refugee entrepreneurs based on situational, social, and individual variables (Cetin et al., 2022). *Necessity entrepreneurship* situations may produce fewer benefits for refugees when they are forced to start a venture without adequate resources. However, *opportunity entrepreneurship* may deliver better outcomes for refugees and help develop a more lasting, large-scale enterprise that ultimately employs other refugees (Skran & Easton-Calabria, 2020). Whether *opportunity or necessity entrepreneurs*, refugees need support, guidance, training, and instructions from resettlement agencies, NGOs, and refugee entrepreneurship support agencies to ensure their well-being needs are met. For instance, social enterprises such as "Willkommenskultur" (i.e., welcome culture) in Germany provide assistance to refugees who want to start a business venture. This includes mentoring schemes, professional networking opportunities, and, most importantly, financial assistance from the German Chamber of Commerce and the European Union. These enterprises are leveraging technology to provide accurate information, networking opportunities, and training to enhance refugees' skills and knowledge. The networking opportunities created by these social enterprises help refugees to access information from a range of actors and mentors to deal with their lack of knowledge as well as their lack of social networks (Embiricos, 2020).

Service industry entrepreneurship

Compared to immigrant entrepreneurs, refugee entrepreneurs have traditionally had fewer opportunities to start businesses (Wauters & Lambrecht, 2008). However, in recent years, this has changed with the positive impact of refugees on host countries, particularly within service industries. Such entrepreneurship creates economic and social opportunities for both refugees and the host society (Shneikat & Alrawadieh, 2019), and provides a fast track to economic security and social integration (Barth & Zalkat, 2021). The service industry (hospitality, transport, healthcare, etc.) supports more refugees than the manufacturing industry (Daunfeldt et al., 2019).

While there are various sectors in the service industries, the tourism and hospitality service sector appears to be a promising area for refugee entrepreneurship (Alrawadieh et al., 2021). Shneikat and Alrawadieh (2019) examined the role of entrepreneurship in refugee integration in the tourism and hospitality services industry, specifically in the Turkish context, and identified key factors that enable refugee entrepreneurship, including survivability, the desire for independence, access to resources, access to the labour market, adequate starting capital, opportunity recognition, prior experience, and recommendations from others.

Survivability is a critical enabler for refugee entrepreneurship, as refugees face significant challenges to their existence in a foreign country. Becoming economically self-sufficient is difficult for refugees, which motivates them to become entrepreneurs. The push–pull entrepreneurship theory suggests that the desire for independence is a key driver of new venture creation. To this end, access to resources such as knowledge, experience, expertise, and financial capital are important enablers for refugee entrepreneurship. Having reasonable assess to money (from personal savings, financial support from friends and family, partnerships, etc.) is also crucial for refugee entrepreneurs (Shneikat & Alrawadieh, 2019).

Implications

Prioritising refugees' well-being through collaborative efforts in healthcare, education, and support services is crucial before they can embark on their entrepreneurial pathway. To lower or remove healthcare service barriers that refugees and refugee entrepreneurs face, resettlement agencies, healthcare service providers, and other stakeholders involved in the integration of refugees must work collaboratively and exchange knowledge and information to ensure that refugees receive the necessary healthcare services to support their entrepreneurship venture and its well-being (Fehsenfeld & Levinsen, 2019). There is a need for resettlement agencies, policymakers, and educational institutions to address challenges related to accessing educational services by creating more inclusive and accessible training programmes for refugees, especially for females (Pugh et al., 2012). This requires developing and implementing innovative approaches to recognising and validating refugees' prior learning and qualifications, providing language support, individual guidance, and ensuring access to childcare facilities and flexible schedules. To improve interpretation services, policymakers and service providers should invest in the recruitment, training, and retention of professional interpreters, and provide them with access to the latest technologies (Atabekova et al., 2018). To help refugees progress in their careers and setting up entrepreneurship ventures, mentoring programmes can be implemented, which have been found to have a positive impact on income levels and success in starting new ventures (Månsson & Delander, 2017).

Both *refugee opportunity and necessity entrepreneurs* require support, guidance, training, and instructions from resettlement agencies, NGOs, refugee entrepreneurship support agencies, as well as fellow refugee entrepreneurs to ensure their well-being (Skran & Easton-Calabria, 2020; Subramanian et al., 2022). Social enterprises can provide mentoring and networking to help refugees start and sustain their own businesses. Compared to immigrant entrepreneurs, refugees have limited opportunities to start businesses, but their impact on the service industry has been positive and can create economic and social opportunities for both refugees and the host society (Embiricos, 2020). The service industries are more likely to employ refugees than other industries, such as the high-tech and manufacturing domains (Daunfeldt et al., 2019).

Conclusion

Access to services such as healthcare, housing, interpretation, employment, entrepreneurship agencies, and education is essential for the well-being of refugees, enabling them to rebuild their lives. However, refugees face significant challenges and barriers in accessing and utilising these services, hindering their ability to become service entrepreneurs. Transformative Service Researchers have suggested that incorporating refugees into service systems can promote their well-being and lay the groundwork for refugee entrepreneurship (Fisk et al., 2018; Finsterwalder et al., 2021). Necessity and opportunity entrepreneurship both offer pathways for refugees to start new businesses, but they require support, guidance, training, mentoring, and networking opportunities from resettlement agencies, NGOs, refugee entrepreneurship support agencies, social enterprises, as well as fellow refugee entrepreneurs to succeed (Skran & Easton-Calabria, 2020; Subramanian et al., 2022). Among the various industries, the service sector appears to be very appealing to refugee entrepreneurs (Daunfeldt et al., 2019).

Despite the barriers faced, it is important that refugees feel encouraged to take ownership of their well-being (Chen et al., 2021) as well as their pathway as entrepreneurs, and view themselves as a valuable (and not a vulnerable) resource by drawing on their strengths (Finsterwalder et al., 2017; 2021) and contributing to the local economy and community of a host country.

References

Abebe, S.A. (2023). Refugee entrepreneurship: Systematic and thematic analyses and a research agenda. *Small Business Economics*, *60*(1), 315–350. https://doi.org/10.1007/s11187-022-00636-3

Ager, A., & Strang, A. (2008). Understanding integration: A conceptual framework. *Journal of Refugee Studies*, *21*(2), 166–191. https://doi.org/10.1093/jrs/fen016

Alexandre, L., Salloum, C., & Alalam, A. (2019). An investigation of migrant entrepreneurs: The case of Syrian refugees in Lebanon. *International Journal of Entrepreneurial Behaviour & Research*, *25*(5), 1147–1164. https://doi.org/10.1108/IJEBR-03-2018-0171

Alrawadieh, Z., Altinay, L., Cetin, G., & Şimşek, D. (2021). The interface between hospitality and tourism entrepreneurship, integration and well-being: A study of refugee entrepreneurs. *International Journal of Hospitality Management*, *97*, 1–12. https://doi.org/10.1016/j.ijhm.2021.103013

Alrawadieh, Z., Karayilan, E., & Cetin, G. (2019). Understanding the challenges of refugee entrepreneurship in tourism and hospitality. *The Service Industries Journal*, *39*(9–10), 717–740. https://doi.org/10.1080/02642069.2018.1440550

Amit, R., Muller, E., & Cockburn, I. (1995). Opportunity costs and entrepreneurial activity. *Journal of Business Venturing*, *10*(2), 95–106. https://doi.org/10.1016/0883-9026(94)00017-O

Anderson, L., Ostrom, A.L., & Bitner, M.J. (2011). *Surrounded by services: A new lens for examining the influence of services as social structures on well-being*. Working paper. W. P. Carey School of Business, Arizona State University.

Andrade, A.D., & Doolin, B. (2016). Information and communication technology and the social inclusion of refugees. *MIS Quarterly: Management Information Systems*, *40*(2), 405–416. https://doi.org/10.25300/MISQ/2016/40.2.06

Atabekova, A.A., Gorbatenko, R.G., Shoustikova, T.V., & Valero-Garcés, C. (2018). Cross-cultural mediation with refugees in emergency settings: ICT use by language service providers. *Journal of Social Studies Education Research*, *9*(3), 351–369. https://doi.org/10.17499/jsser.71392

Au, M., Anandakumar, A.D., Preston, R., Ray, R.A., & Davis, M. (2019). A model explaining refugee experiences of the Australian healthcare system. *BMC International Health and Human Rights*, *19*(1), 22–23. https://doi.org/10.1186/s12914-019-0206-6

Barth, H., & Zalkat, G. (2021). Refugee entrepreneurship in the agri-food industry: The Swedish experience. *Journal of Rural Studies*, *86*, 189–197. https://doi.org/10.1016/j.jrurstud.2021.06.011

BenEzer, G., & Zetter, R. (2015). Searching for directions: Conceptual and methodological challenges in researching refugee journeys. *Journal of Refugee Studies*, *28*(3), 297–318. https://doi.org/10.1093/jrs/feu022

Boenigk, S., Fisk, R.P., Kabadayi, S., Alkire, L., Cheung, L., Corus, C., Finsterwalder, J., Kreimer, A.A., Luca, N., Omeira, M., Paul, P., Santos, M.F., & Smidt, N. (2021). Rethinking service systems and public policy: A transformative refugee service experience framework. *Journal of Public Policy & Marketing*, *40*(2), 165–183. https://doi.org/10.1177/0743915620962815

Bizri, R.M. (2017). Refugee-entrepreneurship: A social capital perspective. *Entrepreneurship and Regional Development*, *29*(9–10), 847–868. https://doi.org/10.1080/08985626.2017.1364787

Cetin, G., Altinay, L., Alrawadieh, Z., & Ali, F. (2022). Entrepreneurial motives, entrepreneurial success and life satisfaction of refugees venturing in tourism and hospitality. *International Journal of Contemporary Hospitality Management*, *34*(6), 2227–2249. https://doi.org/10.1108/IJCHM-11-2021-1363

Chen, T., Dodds, S., Finsterwalder, J., Witell, L., Cheung, L., Falter, M., Garry, T., Snyder, H., & McColl-Kennedy, J. R. (2021). Dynamics of wellbeing co-creation: A psychological ownership perspective. *Journal of Service Management*, *32*(3), 383–406. https://doi.org/10.1108/JOSM-09-2019-0297

Daunfeldt, S., Johansson, D., & Seerar Westerberg, H. (2019). Which firms provide jobs for unemployed non-western immigrants? *The Service Industries Journal*, *39*(9–10), 762–778. https://doi.org/10.1080/02642069.2018.1534961

de Vries, H.P., Hamilton, R.T., & Voges, K. (2015). Antecedents of ethnic minority entrepreneurship in New Zealand: An intergroup comparison. *Journal of Small Business Management*, *53*(S1), 95–114. https://doi.org/10.1111/jsbm.12195

Diedrich, A., & Styhre, A. (2008). Making the refugee multiple: The effects of classification work. *Scandinavian Journal of Management*, *24*(4), 330–342. https://doi.org/10.1016/j.scaman.2008.05.003

Dodds, S., Finsterwalder, J., Prayag, G., & Subramanian, I. (2023). Transformative service research methodologies for vulnerable participants. *International Journal of Market Research*, *65*(2–3), 279–296. https://doi.org/10.1177/14707853221139204

Elfring, T., & Hulsink, W. (2003). Networks in entrepreneurship: The case of high-technology firms. *Small Business Economics*, *21*(4), 409–422. https://doi.org/10.1023/A:1026180418357

Embiricos, A. (2020). From refugee to entrepreneur? Challenges to refugee self-reliance in Berlin, Germany. *Journal of Refugee Studies*, *33*(1), 245–267. https://doi.org/10.1093/jrs/fez073

Farmaki, A., & Christou, P. (2019). Refugee migration and service industries: Advancing the research agenda. *The Service Industries Journal*, *39*(9–10), 668–683. https://doi.org/10.1080/02642069.2018.1435643.

Fehsenfeld, M., & Levinsen, K. (2019). Taking care of the refugees: Exploring advocacy and cross-sector collaboration in service provision for refugees. *Voluntas*, *30*(2), 422–435. https://doi.org/10.1007/s11266-019-00097-5

Finsterwalder, J. (2017). Refugee influx: Repercussions and research agenda for service scholars. *Journal of Retailing and Consumer Services*, *37*(July), 177–181. https://doi.org/10.1016/j.jretconser.2016.11.001

Finsterwalder, J., Foote, J., Nicholas, G., Taylor, A., Hepi, M., Baker, V., & Dayal, N. (2017). Conceptual underpinnings for transformative research in a service ecosystems context to resolve social issues–framework foundations and extensions. *The Service Industries Journal*, *37*(11–12), 766–782. https://doi.org/10.1080/02642069.2017.1351550

Finsterwalder, J., Kabadayi, S., Fisk, R.P., & Boenigk, S. (2021). Creating hospitable service systems for refugees during a pandemic: Leveraging resources for service inclusion. *Journal of Service Theory and Practice*, *31*(2), 247–263. https://doi.org/10.1108/JSTP-07-2020-0175

Finsterwalder, J., & Kuppelwieser, V.G. (2020). Equilibrating resources and challenges during crises: A framework for service ecosystem well-being. *Journal of Service Management*, *31*(6), 1107–1129. https://doi.org/10.1108/JOSM-06-2020-0201

Finsterwalder, J., Kuppelwieser, V.G., & Fisk, R.P. (2022). Dynamics of individual actors' self, social, and task pre-dispositions in multi-actor service ecosystems. *Journal of Business Research, 147*(August), 518–531. https://doi.org/10.1016/j.jbusres.2022.04.023

Fisk, R.P., Dean, A.M., Alkire (née Nasr), L., Joubert, A., Previte, J., Robertson, N., & Rosenbaum, M. S. (2018). Design for service inclusion: Creating inclusive service systems by 2050. *Journal of Service Management*, *29*(5), 834–858. https://doi.org/10.1108/JOSM-05-2018-0121

Fozdar, F., & Hartley, L. (2014). Housing and the creation of home for refugees in Western Australia. *Housing, Theory and Society*, *31*(2), 148–173. https://doi.org/10.1080/14036096.2013.830985

Fredström, A., Peltonen, J., & Wincent, J. (2021). A country-level institutional perspective on entrepreneurship productivity: The effects of informal economy and regulation. *Journal of Business Venturing*, *36*(5), 1–15. https://doi.org/10.1016/j.jbusvent.2020.106002

Fuller-Love, N., Lim, L., & Akehurst, G. (2006). Guest editorial: Female and ethnic minority entrepreneurship. *International Entrepreneurship and Management Journal*, *2*(4), 429–439. https://doi.org/10.1007/s11365-006-0007-y

Hepi, M., Foote, J., Finsterwalder, J., Carswell, S., & Baker, V. (2017). An integrative transformative service framework to improve engagement in a social service ecosystem: The case of He Waka Tapu. *Journal of Services Marketing*, *31*(4/5), 423–437. https://doi.org/10.1108/JSM-06-2016-0222

Ilhan-Nas, T., Sahin, K., & Cilingir, Z. (2011). International ethnic entrepreneurship: Antecedents, outcomes and environmental context. *International Business Review*, *20*(6), 614–626. https://doi.org/10.1016/j.ibusrev.2011.02.011

Jewson, A., Lamaro, G., Crisp, B.R., Hanna, L., & Taket, A. (2015). Service providers' experiences and needs in working with refugees in the Geelong region: A qualitative study. *Australian Journal of Primary Health*, *21*(2), 233–238. https://doi.org/10.1071/PY12132

Kandasamy, N., & Soldatic, K. (2018). Implications for practice: Exploring the impacts of government contracts on refugee settlement services in rural and urban Australia. *Australian Social Work*, *71*(1), 111–119. https://doi.org/10.1080/0312407X.2017.1357079

Kirkwood, J. (2009). Motivational factors in a push-pull theory of entrepreneurship. *Gender in Management – An International Journal*, *24*(5), 346–364.

Kuppelwieser, V.G., & Finsterwalder, J. (2016). Transformative service research and service dominant logic: Quo Vaditis? *Journal of Retailing and Consumer Services*, *28*, 91–98. https://doi.org/10.1016/j.jretconser.2015.08.011

Levesque, J., Harris, M.F., & Russell, G. (2013). Patient centered access to health care. *International Journal for Equity in Health*, *12*(18). https://doi.10.1186/14759276-12-18

Månsson, J., & Delander, L. (2017). Mentoring as a way of integrating refugees into the labour market—Evidence from a Swedish pilot scheme. *Economic Analysis and Policy*, *56*, 51–59. https://doi.org/10.1016/j.eap.2017.08.002

Marcu, S. (2018). Refugee students in Spain: The role of universities as sustainable actors in institutional integration. *Sustainability*, *10*(6), 1–21. https://doi.org/10.3390/su10062082

Mickiewicz, T., Nyakudya, F.W., Theodorakopoulos, N., & Hart, M. (2017). Resource endowment and opportunity cost effects along the stages of entrepreneurship. *Small Business Economics*, *48*(4), 953–976. https://doi.org/10.1007/s11187-016-9806-x

Naidoo, L. (2012). Refugee action support: Crossing borders in preparing pre-service teachers for literacy teaching in secondary schools in Greater Western Sydney. *International Journal of Pedagogies and Learning*, *7*(3), 266–274. https://doi.org/10.5172/ijpl.2012.7.3.266

Nasr, L., & Fisk, R.P. (2018). The global refugee crisis: how can transformative service researchers help?, *The Service Industries Journal*, *39*(9–10), 684–700. https://doi.org/10.1080/02642069.2018.1445224

Paisi, M., Baines, R., Burns, L., Plessas, A., Radford, P., Shawe, J., & Witton, R. (2020). Barriers and facilitators to dental care access among asylum seekers and refugees in highly developed countries: A systematic review. *BMC Oral Health*, *20*(337), 1–10. https://doi.org/10.1186/s12903-020-01321-1

Phillips, D. (2006). Moving towards integration: The housing of asylum seekers and refugees in Britain. *Housing Studies*, *21*(4), 539–553. https://doi.org/10.1080/02673030600709074

Pugh, K., Every, D., & Hattam, R. (2012). Inclusive education for students with refugee experience: Whole school reform in a south Australian primary school. *Australian Educational Researcher*, *39*(2), 125–141. https://doi.org/10.1007/s13384-011-0048-2

Rah, Y., Choi, S. & Nguyễn, T.S.T. (2009). Building bridges between refugee parents and schools. *International Journal of Leadership in Education*, *12*(4), 347–365. https://doi.org/10.1080/13603120802609867

Ranabahu, N., de Vries, H.P., & Basharati, Z. (2023). Refugee-owned small businesses: A typology for blended value creation. *International Migration*, *61*(4), 37–56. https://doi.org/10.1111/imig.13072

Schapper, M., Volery, T., Weber, P., & Gibson, B. (2014). *Entrepreneurship and small business* (4th ed.). Wiley.

Senthanar, S., MacEachen, E., Premji, S., & Bigelow, P. (2020). Can someone help me? Refugee women's experiences of using settlement agencies to find work in Canada. *Journal of International Migration and Integration*, *21*(1), 273–294. https://doi.org/10.1007/s12134-019-00729-1

Shneikat, B. & Alrawadieh, Z. (2019). Unravelling refugee entrepreneurship and its role in integration: Empirical evidence from the hospitality industry. *Service Industries Journal*, *39*(9–10), 741–761. https://doi.org/10.1080/02642069.2019.1571046

Shneikat, B., & Ryan, C. (2019). Syrian refugees and their re-entry to 'normality': The role of service industries. *Service Industries Journal*, *38*(3–4), 201–227. https://doi.org/10.1080/02642069.2017.1387539

Shrestha-Ranjit, J., Payne, D., Koziol-McLain, J., Crezee, I., & Manias, E. (2020). Availability, accessibility, acceptability, and quality of interpreting services to refugeewomen in New Zealand. *Qualitative Health Research*, *30*(11), 1697–1709. https://doi.org/10.1177/1049732320924360

Skran, C., & Easton-Calabria, E. (2020). Old concepts making new history: Refugee self-reliance, livelihoods and the 'Refugee entrepreneur'. *Journal of Refugee Studies*, *33*(1), 1–21. https://doi.org/10.1093/jrs/fez061

Subramanian, I., Finsterwalder, J., & Hall, C. M. (2022). A systematic literature review of service-related research on refugees. *The Journal of Services Marketing*, *36*(7), 908–939. https://doi.org/10.1108/JSM-09-2021-0312

UN. (2023). *The 17 goals.* https://sdgs.un.org/goals

UNHCR. (2005). *Handbook for self-reliance.* https://reliefweb.int/report/world/handbook-self-reliance

UNHCR. (2023). *Projected Global Resettlement Needs 2023.* www.unhcr.org/en-au/protection/resettlement/62b18e714/projected-global-resettlement-needs-2023.html

UNHCR. (n.d.-a). *Refugee data finder.* www.unhcr.org/refugee-statistics/

UNHCR. (n.d.-b). *What is a refugee?* www.unhcr.org/what-is-a-refugee.html

Wauters, B., & Lambrecht, J. (2008). Barriers to refugee entrepreneurship in Belgium: Towards an explanatory model. *Journal of Ethnic and Migration Studies, 34*(6), 895–915. https://doi.org/10.1080/13691830802211190

Zehra, K., & Usmani, S. (2023). Not without family: Refugee family entrepreneurship and economic integration process. *Journal of Enterprising Communities, 17*(1), 158–181. https://doi.org/10.1108/JEC-03-2020-0044

14 Entrepreneurship education for refugees

Suggestions on individual resilience development

Juha Kansikas and Jaana Seikkula-Leino

Introduction

The aim of this study is to understand how to build on and support refugee entrepreneurs' individual resilience through entrepreneurship education. Refugee entrepreneurs are persons who have left their home country seeking refuge in another country in which they have become self-employed by starting a business (Abebe, 2023). Potential refugee entrepreneurs are those persons who consider starting a business, but who have not yet started it, in the host country that they settled in. In this chapter we focus on potential refugee entrepreneurs and their individual resilience. We seek to study what type of entrepreneurship education could foster their individual resilience and what kinds of benefits or disadvantages individual resilience might create for potential refugee entrepreneurs.

Individuals who have been forced to migrate face a variety of challenges when starting a business, including limited access to financial resources, language barriers, discrimination, and a lack of social networks (see Nayak et al., 2019). These difficulties can be magnified for refugees who are also dealing with trauma and other psychological stressors (Atari-Khan et al., 2021; Yeshi et al., 2022). Individual resilience, on one hand, can assist refugee entrepreneurs in overcoming these challenges by providing them with the emotional and cognitive skills required to manage personal failures and survive crises (De Cock et al., 2020; Jones & Underwood, 2017; Lackéus, 2014; Othman et al. 2020; Zampetakis et al., 2017). On the other hand, emotional capabilities seem to have a role in individual resilience and how to survive both during and after an enterprise failure (Shepherd, 2004). Furthermore, previous jobs, projects, ventures, and start-ups can foster resilience and provide a foundation for future success (Klyver et al., 2022).

Individual resilience is a personal-driven psychological asset, which varies between entrepreneurs (Salvato et al., 2020). It enables entrepreneurs to cope with crises emotionally and to continue their vision-building. Resilient behaviour supports the birth of entrepreneurial intentions and serves as a starting point for entrepreneuring (Gonzalez-Lopez et al., 2019). Individual resilience reflects an entrepreneur's ability to cope with uncertainty and the stressful

DOI: 10.4324/9781003368540-18

circumstances associated with individual entrepreneurship (Ayala & Manzano, 2014). Resilience is meaningful in goal achievement and high performance as it has a positive influence on small firm performance (Santoro et al., 2021). Yet, Corner et al. (2017) argue that resilience does not necessarily increase success of owner-managers, but it is a mental asset for entrepreneurs to restart – and to retry – in business, without giving up when struggling with difficult times. In business, potential refugee entrepreneurs need resilience because it enables the flexibility and mental stamina needed for the long-term commitment. Resilience is reflected in mental abilities to survive setbacks and negative emotions. As a high level of personal resilience enables entrepreneurs to re-start after failures in a new business, entrepreneurs who are more resilient have an advantage in coping with uncertain circumstances.

Refugee entrepreneurs may be better equipped to navigate the challenges of starting a business in a new context if they develop individual resilience through targeted education and support programmes (Zehra & Usmani, 2023). Thus, this chapter answers the following research question: *How can entrepreneurial education build on and foster individual resilience for refugee entrepreneurship?* The chapter uses an integrative literature review and contributes by developing propositions to understand individual resilience and the role of entrepreneurship education in supporting potential refugee entrepreneurs (Prihadi et al., 2018).

Methodological choice and process: Integrative literature review

An integrative literature review is employed to study entrepreneurship education and its opportunities and challenges for refugee entrepreneurship. We use the integrative review technique to review, criticise, and synthesise literature related to our research focus (Snyder, 2019). This leads to a research agenda and future actions based on relevant literature on individual resilience, entrepreneurship education, and refugee entrepreneurship (Torraco, 2005; Torraco, 2016a).

We have elaborated research agenda and future actions by following three steps. First, we have derived propositions from the current literature, which is typical for integrative literature review technique (Reineholm et al., 2023). We conducted this by selecting literature carefully related to the research question (Snyder, 2019; Torraco, 2005). Second, we have recognised that there is a need for review studies to develop propositions. Hence, the purpose of this integrative literature review is to synthesise current literature and its findings, rather than to summarise them (Torraco, 2005). Third, after deriving propositions, we have elaborated future research actions by describing how to proceed with testing propositions using empirical research. Thus, we follow Klarin and Suseno's (2023) suggestion to formulate future research directions as an outcome of the integrative literature review.

Callahan (2010), Torraco and Lundgren (2020), and Torraco (2016b) list prerequisites and principles for integrative literature review methodology.

By following these principles, the authors conducted a literature search and evaluation during two time periods: February 15–26, 2021 and March 15–21, 2021. The author(s) also conducted a new search from June 14 to 16, 2023 to add latest articles for the analysis. We used several keywords to guide our search: resilience, resilient, entrepreneur, refugee, entrepreneurship, entrepreneurship education, entrepreneurial behaviour, and entrepreneurial. The search was conducted using Boolean searches on Google Scholar and the University of Jyvaskyla library journal databases (including Web of Science, Ebsco, Scopus, Wiley, SAGE, ProQuest, Ebook Central, and Emerald).

We used inclusion and exclusion criteria typical for an integrative literature review (Hamilton & Torraco, 2013). First, we selected articles related to the field, published in FT50 journal list such as *Entrepreneurship: Theory and Practice*. Second, because the number of articles related to resilience was limited in FT50 journals, other high-quality journals were chosen for the analysis (Ardichvili & Jondle, 2009). We prioritised business and economics journals (with ABS journal ranking 1–4) to understand the status of the entrepreneurship education literature (Kastanakis et al., 2022). We excluded working papers, theses, conference papers, and other publications without a refereeing process. We did not define any time span (related to the publishing year) for the data collection, since the material was relatively limited. We then removed duplicates from the data (5 articles) and then excluded 27 articles after examining full text availability, title, and the abstract, due to lack of contribution on the refugee entrepreneurship, individual resilience, or entrepreneurship education. Then we examined full text articles and excluded ten articles because of lack of contribution to the topic. Finally, 45 articles were included for the integrative literature review.

Refugee entrepreneurs' resilience

As mentioned above, resilience is one of the psychological assets that individuals need when facing difficulties and drawbacks (Zampetakis et al., 2017). Entrepreneurship research has studied resilience through individual (Duchek, 2018; Korber & McNaughton, 2018), organisational (Manfield & Newey, 2018), and regional perspectives (Williams & Vorley, 2014) by exploring concepts such as behaviour, failure, evolution, and strategies (Reinmoeller & van Baardwijk, 2005). Individual resilience focuses on entrepreneurs' personal capabilities to cope with challenging circumstances (Korber & McNaughton, 2018). However, so far definitions of entrepreneurial resilience are broad, reflecting multiple factors such as learning, experience, behaviour, and work attitudes (Duchek, 2018). Organisational and strategic studies analyse firm characteristics of resilience, and resilience in networks, such as in entrepreneurial ecosystems (Roundy et al., 2017). Studies on regional resilience focus on understanding the survival of economies or geographical areas in severe crises (Manfield & Newey, 2018). While refugees' experiences of trauma and displacement may present challenges to their entrepreneurial endeavours, they can also develop and maintain resilience through their entrepreneurial activities (Yeshi et al., 2022). Therefore, refugee entrepreneur resilience is not just related to individual characteristics, but it is a reflection of institutional characteristics such as country- and business-specific factors, and relational issues such as social connectedness and refugee role in a society (Yeshi et al., 2022).

Even though there are many barriers for refugee entrepreneurship, there can be some potential for developing entrepreneurship among refugees (e.g., Abebe, 2023; Embiricos, 2020; Mawson, & Kasem, 2019; UNESCO, 2018). We found that the following dimensions associated with resilience facilitate entrepreneurship:

- *Overcoming adversity:* Refugees have already shown immense resilience by surviving and overcoming the hardships of displacement. This ability to persevere and adapt to challenging circumstances can be an asset in entrepreneurship.
- *Adaptability*: Resilience often goes hand in hand with adaptability. Refugees are frequently forced to adapt to new environments, cultures, and economic systems. This adaptability can be a crucial characteristic for entrepreneurs.
- *Creativity and resourcefulness*: Refugees often need more resources and support systems when they arrive in a new country. To overcome these challenges, they develop resourcefulness and creative problem-solving skills. Refugees' ability to think creatively and use available resources best can contribute to their entrepreneurial resilience.
- *Determination and motivation*: Many refugees have a strong sense of determination and motivation to rebuild their lives and provide a better future for themselves and their families. This drive can translate into entrepreneurial endeavours.
- *Unique perspectives and market opportunities*: Refugees bring diverse backgrounds, experiences, and cultural insights to the entrepreneurial landscape. Their unique perspectives can give them a competitive advantage by identifying untapped market opportunities or niche markets that others may overlook.

Thus, there is currently a huge potential for entrepreneurship among refugees (e.g., Abebe, 2023; Embiricos, 2020; Mawson, & Kasem, 2019; UNESCO, 2018). Those refugees who want to start a business, however, might benefit from existing entrepreneurship support and education services as stated in Organisation for Economic Co-operation and Development:

> The individuals identified have reasonably good host country language skills and prior work and entrepreneurial experience. These services and other tailored programs can help build these individuals' local skill sets and networks. An emphasis on networking and mentoring can help them. Furthermore, it is suggested that psychosocial support and training for

> building self-confidence and self-efficacy are critical (especially for women refugees) who want to become entrepreneurs.
>
> (Chliova et al., 2018, p. 19)

With this conceptual foundation, we focus on how entrepreneurial education programmes should build on and foster individual resilience among potential refugee entrepreneurs.

Entrepreneurship education programmes and refugee resilience

Building on potential refugee entrepreneurs' resilience and self-efficacy

Resilience relates directly to "psychological robustness and energy". It has impact on entrepreneurial attitudes such as risk-taking propensity and self-efficacy (Obschonka et al., 2018). The study by Obcschonka et al. (2018) hypothesises that risk-taking and self-efficacy positively predict entrepreneurial alertness among newly arrived refugees. Therefore, it can be inferred that a refugee's resilience plays an important role in influencing their entrepreneurial resilience. Correspondingly, Bergenholtz et al. (2023), Bullough et al. (2014), Klyver et al. (2022), and Obschonka et al. (2018) emphasise the role of self-efficacy in refugees' adaption in new environments. It is needed in high-risk circumstances, as in the case of pandemics (Bergenholtz et al., 2023) and societal crisis like war (Bullough et al., 2014). The entrepreneurial self-efficacy also contributes to new venture start-ups and a person's intention to become an entrepreneur. Thus, refugee entrepreneurs who have a high self-efficacy are more likely to have high ability to adapt to novelty. Thus, self-efficacy is stressed in this study as one of the goals entrepreneurship education should aim for (Bullough et al., 2014).

Understanding one's own identity can create tools for potential refugee entrepreneurs to survive in crises, and to do business simultaneously. This also shapes a person's self-efficacy. Because self-efficacy supports individual resilience (Renko et al., 2021), entrepreneurship education can be designed for enhancing self-efficacy. All teaching supporting self-efficacy, however, does not necessarily lead to an increase in individual resilience. The resilience of refugees results from their transitional experiences of fleeing, displacement, and resettlement. These experiences and actions have an impact on refugee identities (Atari-Khan et al., 2021). Hence, entrepreneurial education programmes need to support self-identity building by tailoring teaching modules to enhance resilience together with self-efficacy.

Together with self-efficacy, entrepreneurs typically need well-being and social capital for high levels of individual resilience (Branicki et al., 2018). In addition, age and professional and industry experiences increase resilience among refugees for entrepreneurial behaviour. Furthermore, social connections and networks, as safety nets, explain why some entrepreneurs survive in crises while the others do not (Bullough et al., 2014). The social connections, experiential learning, and well-being of refugees, therefore, create safety nets in maintaining individual resilience (Zamfir et al., 2018). Therefore, resilience requires change management skills, flexibility, social capital, and learning skills to cope with the changing circumstances.

In summary, self-efficacy and resilience need to be considered in entrepreneurial education and hence our first proposition:

Proposition 1. Entrepreneurship education should promote self-efficacy, physical and psychological well-being, and self-management skills to foster individual resilience among potential refugee entrepreneurs.

Fostering potential refugee entrepreneurs' resilience through teaching and learning

The culture and society in which young entrepreneurs start their businesses influence learning and teaching, including resilience (Sadewo et al., 2020). Yet, we continue to lack sufficient empirical evidence about how entrepreneurship education could promote social capital skills, such as business networking, and also how it could develop capabilities to maintain strong relations, such as family ties (Chrisman et al., 2011). Especially in individualistic cultures, supporting family cohesiveness and social capital management could strengthen networks increasing the likelihood of individual resilience among potential refugee entrepreneurs.

Social capital creates safety nets for potential refugee entrepreneurs. For this reason, entrepreneurship education needs to include activities promoting social networking and the growth of social capital to promote individual resilience (Bullough & Renko, 2013). Social interaction is meaningful and a motivating factor for refugees to participate in business (Street et al., 2022). Therefore, peer support and peer mentoring seem to be powerful tools in increasing refugee resilience (Paloma et al., 2020).

Potential entrepreneurs' cultural shock and misunderstandings influence business start-ups in a new market. Therefore, entrepreneurship education can be tailored using cultural characteristics and society or market-based needs. These education programmes need not only value-based characteristics, but also religious and communicational features (Ratten, 2020). Every culture has legends, myths, and stories about resilient individuals who have battled against the odds. Moreover, the media presents celebrities who can serve as cultural role models of individual resilience. Refugee entrepreneurs can learn individual resilience through the heroic behaviour of cultural legends, both past and present. Pedagogic solutions can reflect these inspiring attitude and persistence of heroic celebrities (Fisher et al., 2016).

Additionally, supporting refugees through entrepreneurship education is a key policy priority. For example, UNHCR, The UN Refugee Agency (2018) suggests to:

> a) Develop, adapt and focus entrepreneurship training for specific refugee target groups and contexts; b) Develop effective entrepreneurship curricula and content to develop an entrepreneurial mindset; c) Engage skilled and experienced trainers; and d) Strengthen synergies between programmes of entrepreneurship training for refugees and migrants, vocational education programmes, and support for basic needs.
>
> (p. 9)

However, the current entrepreneurship education programmes do not specifically focus on refugee entrepreneurship. Nayak et al. (2019, p. 84), who studied Tibetan refugees in India, suggest that "self-regulated or self-directed learning theories" could be used to develop education tailored for the refugees. In environments with scarce resources, self-management or self-directed learning may be more appropriate.

Nayak et al. (2019) also highlight the importance of taking a holistic approach to refugee education and entrepreneurship programmes considering the unique needs and challenges refugees face in pursuing economic stability and social integration. Additionally, the study underscores the need for ongoing evaluation and reflection on such programmes to ensure that they stay responsive to the evolving needs of refugee communities. In many countries, entrepreneurship education is governed by local ministries and political institutions. The formal curriculum network displays the aims of the degrees and their disciplines, leaving little space for skills and tools which could promote individual resilience in the context of entrepreneurship education. Thus, resilience education is extra-curriculum, and it is not formally included in the teaching programme or course outlines. Pedagogical content which could support skills related to individual resilience struggles with a very limited number of curriculum hours. Special topics such as entrepreneurship education therefore receive an insufficient amount of teaching resources.

For these reasons, propositions 2a and 2b are formulated as follows:

Proposition 2a. Entrepreneurship education should recognise social and cultural characteristics such as inspiring role models and communicational, religious, and value-driven characteristics in course development to enhance potential refugee entrepreneurs' resilience.

Proposition 2b. Entrepreneurship education programmes should capacitate potential refugee entrepreneurs for opportunity recognition, evaluation, and low risk ways to test opportunities enhance their resilience.

Emotional regulation for potential refugee entrepreneurs' resilience

Entrepreneurial actions take place in uncertain and risky circumstances. In such circumstances, entrepreneurs feel negative emotions, such as fear and anger (Zampetakis et al., 2017), and they require skills as well as resources for survival and for changing strategic thinking in the new markets. Emotions influence decision-making, including the process of recognising and evaluating opportunities (Othman et al., 2020). Emotional capabilities are also needed to survive during and after the entrepreneurial failure (Shepherd, 2004) and manage personal and business difficulties. Therefore, entrepreneurial resilience is not just about having the abilities to cope with ongoing crises and finding an advantage in it (Hedner et al., 2011), but also coping with emotions. It also means that entrepreneurs require a set of skills and a mindset which help small businesses to recover, and to even perform better, during and after a severe crisis (Ratten & Jones, 2021). Thus, entrepreneurship education programmes for refugees have a role in developing entrepreneurial competencies (Lackéus, 2014) to manage their emotions to survive in a crisis and to develop new ventures (De Cock et al., 2020; Jones & Underwood, 2017), and thereby foster individual resilience by developing skills to manage failures emotionally (Zehrer & Leiss, 2019).

We propose that individual resilience is needed in coping with the new circumstances, anxiety, and negative emotions that potential refugee entrepreneurs face. Especially resilient entrepreneurs have an advantage when developing business turnaround strategies during problems or potential business failures. Thus, individual resilience is an asset that reflects subjective entrepreneurial behaviour (Nevalainen et al., 2021), which leads to Proposition 3.

Proposition 3. Entrepreneurship education programmes should support and train potential refugee entrepreneurs on self-management skills that can help in managing negative emotions and stress contributing to enhanced individual resilience.

Discussion

Based on the above propositions (see Table 14.1), we formulated future research agenda and actions related to refugee entrepreneurship education. The aim of the research agenda is to outline what type of entrepreneurship education is needed for a refugee business start-up and its survival during and after crisis situations.

Individual resilience is a multidisciplinary concept, and it also reflects not only emotions, psychology, and physical condition, but also opportunity evaluation and calculations, along with social skills and social competence. Teaching individual resilience in the future will consist of the mixture of the crisis survival skills and social skills, such as family and family business management. The role of strong family ties during a crisis formulates the basis for individual resilience, both mentally and financially.

When developing refugee resilience through entrepreneurship education, we should consider an individual's psychological factors, such as self-regulation skills and self-efficacy. In addition, when planning educational programmes, one should consider the comprehensiveness of the curricula and the possibilities

Table 14.1 Propositions, needs for research, and future actions

Proposition	*References*	*Needs for research*	*Future action*
1. Entrepreneurship education should promote self-efficacy, physical and psychological well-being, and self-management skills to foster individual resilience among potential refugee entrepreneurs.	Othman et al. (2020), Lackéus (2014), Jones and Underwood (2017), Shepherd (2004), De Cock et al. (2020), Ratten and Jones (2021), Hedner et al. (2011)	Adopting self-efficacy and self-management skills during and after the crisis	Refugee entrepreneurship education and its role in promoting physical and psychological well-being among refugee entrepreneurs
2a. Entrepreneurship education should recognise cultural characteristics such as inspiring role models and communicational, religious, and value-driven characteristics in course development to enhance potential refugee entrepreneurs' resilience.	Sadewo et al. (2020), Ratten (2020), Lee and Wang (2017)	How do the domestic and international cultures influence the teaching of individual resilience?	Culture, norms, and society in teaching individual resilience in refugee entrepreneurship education
2b. Entrepreneurship education programmes should capacitate potential refugee entrepreneurs for opportunity recognition, evaluation, and low-risk ways to test opportunities enhance their resilience.	Street et al. (2022), Paloma et al. (2020)	How do refugee entrepreneurs recognise, evaluate, and test opportunities?	Analysis combining literature and empirical data on refugee entrepreneur opportunities
3. Entrepreneurship education programmes should support and train potential refugee entrepreneurs on self-management skills that can help in managing negative emotions and stress contributing to enhanced individual resilience.	Bagiatis et al. (2020), Nevalainen et al. (2021), Bullough and Renko (2013)	How to design, and implement entrepreneurship education programmes tailored for refugees?	Data collection, design processes with refugees and pedagogists, evaluation mechanisms of refugee entrepreneurship education programmes

of differentiating the programmes based on individual needs since refugees are not a unified group. In terms of education, refugees need comprehensive support, for example, financial advice, business training and mentoring, language and cultural training, legal assistance, training, and opportunities to develop networks, and social space to enhance integration. Moreover, professional coaching and mentoring play a crucial role in the success of entrepreneurship education programmes targeted for refugees. When it comes to refugee entrepreneurs, there may be more demands on them in terms of their individual resilience due to their traumatic journeys.

The theoretical implications of this study relate to the heterogeneity of individual resilience as a concept. Emotional resilience among individual refugees is related to coping with emotions during and after a crisis. Emotions are powerful, and a part of the emotional individual resilience is to accept fear, anger, and sorrow in times of failure and losses (De Cock et al., 2020; Jones & Underwood, 2017; Lackéus, 2014; Othman et al., 2020; Shepherd, 2004; Zampetakis et al., 2017). Culture-related resilience among individual refugee entrepreneurs reflects the power of culture and communication styles as engines to foster individual resilience. It can be in the form of legends and myths which inspire individuals to find role models for personal resilience, or even business models which can be further developed locally (Sadewo et al., 2020; Ratten, 2020).

In future education studies, individual resilience in refugee entrepreneurship should be studied empirically in multiple ways. Individual resilience is unique to each person, and for this reason qualitative tools and research settings increase our understanding of how teaching should be designed. Learning from the negative as well as the positive small and medium-sized business case studies on how to survive can contribute to course material on refugee entrepreneurship education. Additionally, understanding what parts of individual resilience cannot be taught through entrepreneurship education could be valuable for the research community. Future studies should also answer the following research questions: Is individual resilience only good for refugees participating in entrepreneurship education? What are the occasions when individual resilience created poor results? What are the dark sides of individual resilience in relation to entrepreneurial behaviour of refugees.

Pragmatically, pedagogy of teaching needs to consider refugee participants' characteristics and their expectations. As resilience is influenced socially, contextually, and individually, these aspects need to be understood to develop pedagogical solutions. Teaching content of entrepreneurship education programmes for refugees will have a specificity to their needs that is not evident in generic entrepreneurship classes. There is a need for a new type of entrepreneurship teaching based on empowering experiences, mentoring, social support, and integration mechanisms into the surrounding society as family, friends, and other social contexts foster individual resilience. As many of the refugees have suffered due to war, poverty, violence, and various types of traumas, it is important to provide health services for these people when needed. Being an entrepreneur in a new culture is stressful and a demanding task, and it is not meant for everyone.

Conclusion

This study answered the following research question: "How can entrepreneurial education build on and foster individual resilience for refugee entrepreneurship?" Individual resilience in entrepreneurship education is unique for each student. The emotional and cognitive skills in managing personal failures create a basis for resilience and to survive a crisis. Experiences and the experiential learning typical for entrepreneurs foster resilience; hence, previous jobs, projects, ventures, and start-ups have a role in individual resilience. Understanding the role of social ties can also foster individual resilience. Individual resilience in refugee entrepreneurship education is a unique, experience and social capital-based emotional and cognitive asset needed for survival. We conclude by reemphasising the fact that among refugees individual resilience is a complex entrepreneurial asset that can be fostered through educational initiatives.

References

Abebe, S.A. (2023). Refugee entrepreneurship: Systematic and thematic analyses and a research agenda. *Small Business Economics, 60*, 315–350. https://doi.org/10.1007/s11187-022-00636-3

Ardichvili, A. & Jondle, D. (2009). Ethical business cultures: A literature review and implications for HRD. *Human Resource Development Review, 8*(2), 223–244. https://doi.org/10.1177/1534484309334098

Atari-Khan, R., Covington, A.H., Gerstein, L.H., al Herz, H., Varner, B.R., Brasfield, C., Shurigar, B., Hinnenkamp, S.F., Devia, M., Barrera, S., & Deogracias-Schleich, A. (2021). Concepts of resilience among trauma-exposed Syrian refugees. *The Counseling Psychologist, 49*(2), 233–268. https://doi.org/10.1177/0011000020970522

Ayala, J.-C., & Manzano, G. (2014). The resilience of the entrepreneur. Influence on the success of the business. A longitudinal analysis. *Journal of Economic Psychology, 42*(2), 126–135. https://doi.org/10.1016/j.joep.2014.02.004

Bagiatis, C., Saiti, A., & Chletsos, M. (2020). Entrepreneurship, economic crisis, and the role of higher education: Evidence from Greece. *Industry and Higher Education, 34*(3), 177–189. https://doi.org/10.1177/0950422219883832

Bergenholtz, C., Klyver, K., & Vuculescu, O. (2023). Self-efficacy in disrupted environments: Covid-19 as a natural experiment. *Entrepreneurship Theory and Practice, 47*(3), 724–750. https://doi.org/10.1177/10422587211046548

Branicki, L.J., Sullivan-Taylor, B., & Livschitz, S.R. (2018). How entrepreneurial resilience generates resilient SMEs. *International Journal of Entrepreneurial Behaviour & Research, 24*(7), 1244–1263. https://doi.org/10.1108/IJEBR-11-2016-0396

Bullough, A., & Renko, M. (2013). Entrepreneurial resilience during challenging times. *Business Horizon, 56*(3), 343–350. https://doi.org/10.1016/j.bushor.2013.01.001

Bullough, A., Renko, M., & Myatt, T. (2014). Danger zone entrepreneurs: The importance of resilience and self-efficacy for entrepreneurial intentions. *Entrepreneurship: Theory & Practice, 38*(3), 473–493. https://doi.org/10.1111/etap.12006

Callahan, J.L. (2010). Constructing a manuscript: Distinguishing integrative literature reviews and conceptual and theory articles (Instructor's corner). *Human Resource Development Review, 9*(3), 300–304. https://doi.org/10.1177/1534484310371492

Chliova, M., Farny, S., & Salmivaara, V. (2018). *Supporting refugees in entrepreneurship: Prepared for the OECD Centre for Entrepreneurship, SMEs, Regions and Cities*. OECD.

Chrisman, J.J., Chua, J.H., & Steier, L.P. (2011). Resilience of family firms: An introduction. *Entrepreneurship: Theory & Practice, 35*(6), 1107–1119. https://doi.org/10.1111/j.1540-6520.2011.00493.x

Corner, P.D., Singh, S., & Pavlovich, K. (2017). Entrepreneurial resilience and venture failure. *International Small Business Journal, 35*(5), 687–708. https://doi.org/10.1177/0266242616685604

De Cock, R., Denoo, L., & Clarysse, B. (2020). Surviving the emotional rollercoaster called entrepreneurship: The role of emotion regulation. *Journal of Business Venturing, 35*(2), 1–18. https://doi.org/10.1016/j.jbusvent.2019.04.004

Duchek, S. (2018). Entrepreneurial resilience: A biographical analysis of successful entrepreneurs. *International Entrepreneurship and Management Journal, 14*(2), 429–455. https://doi.org/10.1007/s11365-017-0467-2

Embiricos, A. (2020). From refugee to entrepreneur? Challenges to refugee self-reliance in berlin, Germany. *Journal of Refugee Studies, 33*(1), 245–267. https://doi.org/10.1093/jrs/fez073

Fisher, R., Maritz, A., & Lobo, A. (2016). Does individual resilience influence entrepreneurial success? *Academy of Entrepreneurship Journal, 22*(2), 39–53.

Gonzalez-Lopez, M.J., Perez-Lopez, M.C., & Rodriguez-Ariza, L. (2019). Clearing the hurdles in the entrepreneurial race: The role of resilience in entrepreneurship education. *Academy of Management Learning and Education, 18*(3), 457–483. https://doi.org/10.5465/amle.2016.0377

Hamilton, D.W., & Torraco, R.J. (2013). Integrative review of the literature on adults with limited education and skills and the implications for human resource development. *Human Resource Development Review, 12*(3), 308–328. https://doi.org/10.1177/1534484312471135

Hedner, T., Abouzeedan, A., & Klofsten, M. (2011). Entrepreneurial resilience. *Annals of Innovation & Entrepreneurship, 2*(1), 1–4. https://doi.org/10.3402/aie.v2i1.6002

Jones, S., & Underwood, S. (2017). Understanding students' emotional reactions to entrepreneurship education. A conceptual framework. *Education and Training, 59*(7–8), 657–671. https://doi.org/10.1108/ET-07-2016-0128

Kastanakis, M.N., Magrizos, S., & Kampouri, K. (2022). Pain (and pleasure) in marketing and consumption: An integrative literature review and directions for future research. *Journal of Business Research, 140*, 189–201. https://doi.org/10.1016/j.jbusres.2021.11.071

Klarin, A., & Suseno, Y. (2023). An integrative literature review of social entrepreneurship research: Mapping the literature and future research directions. *Business & Society, 62*(3), 565–611. https://doi.org/10.1177/00076503221101611

Klyver, K., Steffens, P., & Honig, B. (2022). Psychological factors explaining Ukrainian refugee entrepreneurs' venture idea novelty. *Journal of Business Venturing Insights, 18*, e00348. https://doi.org/10.1016/j.jbvi.2022.e00348

Korber, S., & McNaughton, R.B. (2018). Resilience and entrepreneurship: A systematic literature review. *International Journal of Entrepreneurial Behaviour & Research, 24*(7), 1129–1154. https://doi.org/10.1108/IJEBR-10-2016-0356

Lackéus, M. (2014). An emotion based approach to assessing entrepreneurial education. *International Journal of Management Education, 12*(3), 374–396. https://doi.org/10.1016/j.ijme.2014.06.005

Lee, J., & Wang, J. (2017). Developing entrepreneurial resilience: Implications for human resource development. *European Journal of Training and Development, 41*(6), 519–539. https://doi.org/10.1108/EJTD-12-2016-0090

Manfield, R.C., & Newey, L.R. (2018). Resilience as an entrepreneurial capability: Integrating insights from a cross-disciplinary comparison. *International Journal of Entrepreneurial Behaviour & Research, 24*(7), 1155–1180. https://doi.org/10.1108/IJEBR-11-2016-0368

Mawson, S., & Kasem, L. (2019). Exploring the entrepreneurial intentions of Syrian refugees in the UK. *International Journal of Entrepreneurial Behavior & Research*, 25(5), 1128–1146. https://doi.org/10.1108/IJEBR-02-2018-0103

Nayak, G., Salovaara, I.M., & Wade, J. (2019). Self-regulated learning in refugee entrepreneurship education: A university-based program for Tibetan entrepreneurs in India. *Diaspora, Indigenous, and Minority Education, 13*(2), 81–96. https://doi.org/10.1080/15595692.2018.1557632

Nevalainen, T., Seikkula-Leino, J., & Salomaa, M. (2021). Team learning as a model for facilitating entrepreneurial competences in higher education: The case of Proakatemia. *Sustainability, 13*(13), 7373. https://doi.org/10.3390/su13137373

Obschonka, M., Hahn, E., & Bajwa, N.U.H. (2018). Personal agency in newly arrived refugees: The role of personality, entrepreneurial cognitions and intentions, and career adaptability. *Journal of Vocational Behavior, 105*, 173–184. https://doi.org/10.1016/j.jvb.2018.01.003

Othman, N.H., Othman, N., & Juhdi, N.H. (2020). The mediating effect of emotion on entrepreneurship education and business opportunity recognition. *International Journal of Business and Society, 21*(3), 1479–1493. https://doi.org/10.33736/ijbs.3365.2020

Paloma, V., de la Morena, I., Sladkova, J., & López-Torres, C. (2020). A peer support and peer mentoring approach to enhancing resilience and empowerment among refugees settled in southern Spain. *Journal of Community Psychology, 48*(5), 1438–1451. https://doi.org/10.1002/jcop.22338

Prihadi, K., Cheow, D.Z.Y., Yong, J.H.E., & Sundrasagran, M. (2018). Improving resilience and self-esteem among university students with entrepreneurship simulation board game. *International Journal of Evaluation and Research in Education, 7*(1), 48–56. http://doi.org/10.11591/ijere.v7i1.11406

Ratten, V. (2020). Coronavirus (Covid-19) and the entrepreneurship education community. *Journal of Enterprising Communities: People and Places in the Global Economy, 14*(5), 753–764. https://doi.org/10.1108/JEC-06-2020-0121

Ratten, V., & Jones, P. (2021). Covid-19 and entrepreneurship education: Implications for advancing research and practice. *The International Journal of Management Education, 19*(1), 1–10. https://doi.org/10.1016/j.ijme.2020.100432

Reineholm, C., Lundqvist, D., & Wallo, A. (2023). Managers' development environments: An integrative literature review. *Journal of Workplace Learning, 35*(9), 117–133. https://doi.org/10.1108/JWL-09-2022-0124

Reinmoeller, P., & van Baardwijk, N. (2005). The link between diversity and resilience. *MIT Sloan Management Review, 46*(4), 60–66.

Renko, M., Bullough, A., & Saeed, S. (2021). How do resilience and self-efficacy relate to entrepreneurial intentions in countries with varying degrees of fragility? A six-country study. *International Small Business Journal, 39*(2), 130–156. https://doi.org/10.1177/0266242620960456

Roundy, P.T., Brockman, B.K., & Bradshaw, M. (2017). The resilience of entrepreneurial ecosystems. *Journal of Business Venturing Insights, 8*(11), 99–104. https://doi.org/10.1016/j.jbvi.2017.08.002

Sadewo, Y.D., Purnasari, P.D., & Dimmera, B.G. (2020). Development of entrepreneurship education teaching material based on the national resilience and Amare culture. *Journal of Education Teaching and Learning, 5*(1), 41–45. http://dx.doi.org/10.26737/jetl.v5i1.1258

Salvato, C., Sargiacomo, M., Amore, M.D., & Minichilli, A. (2020). Natural disasters as a source of entrepreneurial opportunity: Family business resilience after an earthquake. *Strategic Entrepreneurship Journal, 14*(4), 594–615. https://doi.org/10.1002/sej.1368

Santoro, G., Messeni-Petruzzelli, A., & Del Giudice, M. (2021). Searching for resilience: The impact of employee-level and entrepreneur-level resilience on firm performance in small family firms. *Small Business Economics, 57*(1), 455–471. https://doi.org/10.1007/s11187-020-00319-x

Shepherd, D. (2004). Educating entrepreneurship students about emotion and learning from failure. *Academy of Management Learning and Education, 3*(3), 274–287. www.jstor.org/stable/40214116

Snyder, H. (2019). Literature review as a research methodology: An overview and guidelines. *Journal of Business Research, 104*, 333–339. https://doi.org/10.1016/j.jbusres.2019.07.039

Street, C.P., Ng, P.Y., & Al-Dajani, H. (2022). Refugee women business mentors: New evidence for women's empowerment. *Sustainability, 14*, 9154. https://doi.org/10.3390/su14159154

Torraco, R.J. (2005). Writing integrative literature reviews: Guidelines and examples. *Human Resource Development Review, 4*(3), 356–367. https://doi.org/10.1177/1534484305278283

Torraco, R.J. (2016a). The persistence of working poor families in a changing U.S. job market. An integrative review of the literature. *Human Resource Development Review, 15*(1), 55–76. https://doi.org/10.1177/1534484316630459

Torraco, R.J. (2016b). Writing integrative literature review: Using the past and present to explore the future. *Human Resource Development Review, 15*(4), 404–428. https://doi.org/10.1177/1534484316671606

Torraco, R.J. & Lundgren, H. (2020). What HRD is doing – What HRD should be doing: The case for transforming HRD. *Human Resource Development Review, 19*(1), 39–65. https://doi.org/10.1177/1534484319877058

Williams, N., & Vorley, T. (2014). Economic resilience and entrepreneurship: Lessons from the Sheffield City region. *Entrepreneurship & Regional Development, 26*(3–4), 257–281. https://doi.org/10.1080/08985626.2014.894129

Zamfir, A.-M., Mocanu, C., & Grigorescu, A. (2018). Resilient entrepreneurship among European higher education graduates. *Sustainability, 10*(8), 1–24. https://doi.org/10.3390/su10082594

Zampetakis, L.A., Kafetsios, K., Lerakis, M., & Moustakis, V.S. (2017). An emotional experience of entrepreneurship: Self-construal, emotion regulation, and expressions to anticipatory emotions. *Journal of Career Development, 44*(2), 144–158. https://doi.org/10.1177/0894845316640898

Zehra, K., & Usmani, S. (2023). Not without family: Refugee family entrepreneurship and economic integration process. *Journal of Enterprising Communities: People and Places in the Global Economy, 17*(1), 158–181. https://doi.org/10.1108/JEC-03-2020-0044

Zehrer, A., & Leiss, G. (2019). Family entrepreneurial resilience – An intergenerational learning approach. *Journal of Family Business Management* [ahead-of-print]. https://doi.org/10.1108/JFBM-09-2018-0037

UNESCO. (2018). *A lifeline to learning: Leveraging mobile technology to support education for refugees.* ISBN 978-92-3-100262-5. Paris: UNESCO.

UNHCR. The UN Refugee Agency. (2018). Policy guide on entrepreneurship for migrants and refugees, United Nations, [New York], viewed 23 May 2023. http://publications.iom.int/books/policy-guide-entrepreneurship-migrants-and-refugees

Yeshi, T., Harima, A., & Freiling, J. (2022). Resilience on an emotional rollercoaster: Refugee entrepreneurship under adversity. *European Management Journal, 42*(2), 173–185. S026323732200175X. https://doi.org/10.1016/j.emj.2022.12.009

15 Social capital, NGOs, and the resilience of refugee women entrepreneurs

Fatih Aktas, Erin Rider, and Fatih Yilmaz

Introduction

Refugee entrepreneurs need specific skills when starting a business, as they commonly have little to no background experience in a new and unfamiliar place. They do not have the knowledge of local laws and regulations, the ability to research potential markets for products or services, access to finance options available through government/local grants or micro-loans, or networks with other professionals within the social environment (The United Nations High Commissioner for Refugees [UNHCR], 2022a). Therefore, local non-government organisations (NGOs) serve as important intermediaries between refugees and the labour market by filling the knowledge gap, and contributing to an entrepreneurship ecosystem (World Bank, 2023).

This research follows refugee women's entrepreneurial journey, focusing particularly on the role of social capital used by refugee entrepreneurs who have relocated to the Netherlands and Belgium. The research is guided by two questions: *What is the role of social capital in refugee women's entrepreneurship, and how does NGO engagement influence this?* Derived from eight semi-structured interviews with refugee women entrepreneurs, this research illuminates three types of capital: *bonding* to help adapt, *bridging* to increase integration, and *linking* to seek out instrumental resources for economic needs (Putnam, 2000; Szreter & Woolcock, 2004). We argue that refugee women's agency is salient in seeking entrepreneurial pathways. Those pathways are strengthened by purposeful connections to NGOs that support and build social capital. Such social capital is instrumental to their ability to start and sustain a business. This study provides insights into the suitable support needed by refugee women in their entrepreneurial journey in the host society.

Literature review

Among refugees and asylum seekers, the forced migration process and entry into an unfamiliar host country undermine social capital accumulation (see Yeasmin & Hasanat, 2022). Wahlbeck (2013, p. 491) asserts that "social

DOI: 10.4324/9781003368540-19

capital is usually and primarily a local asset" and forced migration leads to a likelihood of social capital loss. Regenerating social capital can be difficult due to their lack of human capital and networks, "newness and foreignness to the host country, and institutional differences between the home and host country" (Harima et al., 2021, p. 626).

Refugees, however, use unique ways to develop social capital in translating their entrepreneurial intentions into business activities (Mawson & Kasem, 2019). They garner their own home country connections, use support networks, and motivate themselves to gain economic security in host countries (Wauters & Lambrecht, 2008). Backman et al. (2021, p. 963) used a longitudinal study over two decades to examine workforce entry among refugees in Sweden and found that while "one-third of refugees experience a successful labour market integration pathway, an equally large share face less fruitful employment outcomes". Hence, entrepreneurial intention and activity are driven by either necessity (Desai et al, 2021; Senthanar et al., 2021; Street et al., 2022; Zighan, 2021) or opportunity (Turner, 2020; Sidhva et al., 2021; Mehtap et al., 2019; Hillmann & Toğral Koca, 2021). However, Atasü-Topcuoğlu (2019, p. 208) critiques "informal entrepreneurship [because] it provides informal jobs and some money for the daily survival of immigrant workers. Such businesses tend to remain small, hence having a limited effect on economic and social integration".

Entrepreneurship can empower refugee women and enhance their economic and social integration. While refugee women are more likely to be excluded from participation in the formal economy, the type of activities they do are better suited for entrepreneurship. For example, they engage in the informal economy and conduct activities that give them more control (Datta, 2019; Senthanar et al., 2021; Sidhva et al., 2021). Such tasks mitigate the need for work permits, overcome barriers to the formal economy, and provide ways to manage economic tasks along with family responsibilities (Alexandre et al., 2019; Mehtap et al., 2019; Senthanar et al., 2021; Sidhva et al., 2021). Although refugee women can encounter barriers in entrepreneur activities (e.g., adequate start-up capital, lack of entrepreneurial skills, and limited social networks), they are highly motivated and use social capital to start businesses (Harima et al., 2021; Sidhva et al., 2021; van Kooy, 2016). For example, strategies can include the use of ethnic ties, discovery of niche markets to provide direct services to an ethnic community or native citizens, and linkages made to organisations for more formal support (Bizri, 2017; Hack-Polay & Igwe, 2019; Surgani, 2022). International and state programmes also rely on similar social capital development strategies when increasing women's participation in labour markets through entrepreneurship and microfinance (Turner, 2020).

Social capital helps in transferring entrepreneurial intent to activity (Mawson & Kasem, 2019). Putnam (1995, p. 67) defines social capital as "networks, norms, and social trust that facilitate coordination and cooperation for mutual benefit". As introduced previously, social capital comprises bonding, bridging, and linking capital (Putnam, 2000; Szreter & Woolcock, 2004). Bonding capital is the traditional social support networks that exist between individuals from the same home country and/or ethnic community (Putnam, 2000). These tend to be strong and refugees further develop these networks in a host country. For example, Wahlbeck (2013) shows that Turkish immigrants in Finland discovered a niche in the kebab food industry and strengthened their bonding capital through hiring other Turkish immigrants. Similarly, refugees form co-ethnic ties and engage in activities that provide services to fellow refugees (Bizri, 2017).

Bridging capital refers to the formation of support networks within the host society (Putnam, 2000). This type of capital may be more challenging to initiate as it requires interactions and communications. Hanley et al. (2018) found that among Syrian refugees in Canada, bonding capital was prevalent and more salient, while bridging capital formed as they formed friendships with citizens. Atasü-Topcuoğlu (2019) asserts that entrepreneurial activity in the informal economy undermines the formation of bridging capital because it limits the opportunities for interactions between refugees and citizens. Bridging capital may be less accessible to refugee women due to gender and cultural restrictions (Goodson & Phillimore, 2008). Yet, Wahlbeck (2013) explains that Turkish immigrants gained bridging capital through marriage to Finnish native citizens, which afforded them greater access to information and institutions in Finland. If refugees are targeting only other refugees in their business, their bonding capital may be limited and affect their entrepreneurial capacity. In contrast, refugees' bridging capital can be increased by providing business services to a general market in the host country. Fontefrancesco and Mendonce (2022) demonstrate that Bangladeshi migrant vendors in Italy provided food products to meet the needs of both migrant and Italian communities, therefore increasing bridging capital through interactions and work experience.

Linking capital situates individuals with organisational actors, who have access to institutional power and authority (Szreter & Woolcock, 2004). Claridge (2018, p. 5) asserts that "NGOs become brokers of linking capital". However, refugees may find NGOs difficult to access and navigate (Zihnioğlu & Dalkıran, 2022). Sri Lankan women immigrants in London found entrepreneurship as challenging due to their inability to generate "start-up capital" with traditional "financial institutions" and, as a result, had to rely on "a limited personal network" with "co-ethnic relatives and acquaintances" (Surangi, 2022, p. 206). Zighan (2021) found that refugees experience barriers in navigating NGO assistance programmes. The author refers to difficulties in meeting the request of these organisations and non-availability of advisory and training services to establish businesses (Zighan, 2021). Even after business training, networking, or mentoring programmes, refugee women often do not have financial means to start a business or those who start a business earn sufficient income or were employing staff (van Kooy, 2016). Refugees' lack of trust on third-party institutions, as NGOs, may also affect linking capital (Hanley et al., 2018).

NGOs are identified as humanitarian agencies as they offer greater compassion than traditional bureaucratic institutions (Hack-Polay & Igwe, 2019). Harima et al. (2021, p. 643) found that while refugee organisations provide increased support, "several refugee entrepreneurs were over-embedded in single support organization contexts", thus limiting more robust networks. NGOs have to rely on their own bridging networks for funding refugee support, but they tend to be unstainable funding sources (see Zihnioğlu & Dalkıran, 2022; Hack-Polay & Igwe, 2019). Goodson and Phillimore (2008) suggest that it is common for refugees to reach out to organisations when they have less social bonding capital. Low and Shah (2023) similarly find that due to refugee women experiencing hostile local relationships, volunteering with local organisations provides an alternative (or only) utilises linking capital to access bridging capital. Zihnioğlu and Dalkıran (2022) show that NGO intracommunal activities can foster interaction between refugees and native citizens, yet long-term impact may be limited due to infrequent availability of such services.

Context

The focus here is on refugee women entrepreneurs in the Netherlands and Belgium. The European Commission promotes social and inclusive entrepreneurship, including refugee entrepreneur support, to promote job creation, work integration, and inclusive and sustainable growth. Specifically, the European Union (EU) provides microfinance and social enterprise finance providers with both repayable and non-repayable funds (European Commission, 2023a). Additionally, organisations such as the UNHCR and various institutions (such as VluchtelingenWerk Nederland and universities) actively collaborate with local governments in the Netherlands and Belgium to provide tailored support for refugee women entrepreneurs.

Although European governments have introduced appropriate financial measures to support businesses, such as financial support during the COVID-19 pandemic, including efforts to close the gender gap in entrepreneurship, significant challenges remain in reaching certain populations. This is particularly so for the self-employed, smaller and younger firms, and women and minority entrepreneurs (European Commission, 2023b,c). For example, in Europe, the proportion of female migrant entrepreneurs employing others has hardly increased since 2015 (European Commission, 2023b,c).

The narrative of refugee women's journey towards economic empowerment is an intriguing storyline in the challenging tapestry of global migration. Central to this narrative in this study are NGOs who play critical roles in determining their paths to entrepreneurship in the Netherlands and Belgium. According to the UNHCR (2022b,c), there were 35,535 individuals who sought asylum in the Netherlands and 36,871 in Belgium in 2022. Both countries saw an increase of 10,000 asylum seekers compared to 2021 (UNHCR, 2022b,c). In both countries, refugee women with diverse skill sets have the potential to fill local labour market shortages in specialised sectors, such as medical care, schooling, and technology. In the context of refugee women's entrepreneurial journey in the Netherlands and Belgium, we see a delicate interplay between bonding capital within refugee communities and the transformative potential of bridging capital through cross-cultural encounters with local individuals. Further, NGOs are qualified to deal with these challenges, acting as catalysts for capital creation and empowerment, further substantiating the importance of linking capital.

Methodology

The following research questions guided this study: *What is the role of social capital in refugee women's entrepreneurship, and how does NGO engagement influence this?* We conducted a series of in-depth interviews with eight refugee entrepreneurs in the Netherlands and Belgium to answer these questions (see Table 15.1).

All participants were recognised as refugees in their new countries. We contacted refugee entrepreneurs through NGOs and personal networks. Initial contact was made via phone calls, emails, or face-to-face meetings. The in-depth interviews were conducted conversationally with the interviewees. Prompts were used to gather more details as needed, such as "Have you received any help from the government or friends?" The researchers paraphrased participant responses in the third person for consistency and clarity due to Dutch and English language barriers. This approach ensured accuracy and clarity in presenting responses. Interviewee transcripts were based on their lived experiences and analysed inductively to enhance the study's authenticity and depth.

As Table 15.1 illustrates, our participants were from Palestine, Azerbaijan, Syria, Armenia, Iran, and Türkiye. One key feature that we accept distinguishes our informants from other refugee women is their higher education levels: All had bachelor degrees, and one had a master's degree.

We analysed the interview data inductively and found local language proficiency, supportive networks, entrepreneurial spirit, resilience of individual women, market perceptions, and ethnic community solidarity related to the context shape women's entrepreneurship. The NGO links and municipal support shape development of their social capital. These help in overcoming adversity and facilitate entrepreneurship in the EU context. We report on these findings in the next section.

Table 15.1 Interviewee details

Interviewee #	*Age (year)*	*Country*	*Host Country*	*Arrival Year*	*Business Date*	*Education*	*Vocation Background*	*Business Concept*
F1	25–34	Azerbaijan	Netherlands	2016	2022	Journalism, BA	Journalist	Media
F2	35–44	Palestinian	Netherlands	2016	2022	Sustainability, MA	HR	Sustainable edible products
F3	35–44	Azerbaijan	Netherlands	2018	2020	Medicine, BA	Paediatric	Tourism
F4	25–34	Syria	Netherlands	2016	2018	Pharmacy, BA	Pharmacist	Restaurant
F5	45–54	Armenia	Belgium	2010	2018	Accountancy, BA	Shop worker	Sewing shop
F6	45–54	Iran	Belgium	2011	2016	Dentistry, BA	Dentist	Fast-food restaurant
F7	35–44	Türkiye	Belgium	2016	2018	Elementary School Teaching, BA	Teacher	Laundrette
F8	35–44	Türkiye	Belgium	2016	2020	Political Science, International Human Rights Law, BA	Civil servant	Social entrepreneurship (NGO)

Findings

Factors related to individual women

Local language proficiency

Women immigrant entrepreneurs face language-related challenges that significantly impact their business sustainability. Adequate knowledge of the local language is crucial to operating effectively in the local market, communicating with clients and stakeholders, and learning the vocational language, thus the need to develop stronger forms of bridging and linking capital. Speaking with a non-native accent can also create obstacles, such as discrimination or social exclusion, as seen in Participant F2's experience.

> *When I began my business, I had recently finished my Dutch language courses and was still speaking in broken Dutch. This led to some criticism from my neighboring Dutch company owners as well as a few of my customers.*

Another important issue is that educated newcomers are expected to quickly achieve local language fluency without accent, as experienced by Participants F4 and F1. This expectation arises from highly educated migrants' desire for positions commensurate with their qualifications but is difficult to achieve. This situation not only drives people towards entrepreneurship as an option, but also creates a further dilemma. If they are not entrepreneurial, their job-seeking behaviour leads them to jobs that do not require their educational skills, and thus jeopardises their career goals as a result of underemployment. Even then, such applications for lesser jobs are often rejected due to over-qualification, further complicating their career path.

Supportive networks

Entrepreneurship can be a challenging journey for women due to limited access to supportive networks and mentorship opportunities (see Yeasmin & Hasanat, 2022). However, the experiences of women entrepreneurs vary widely depending on their personal networks and the availability of supportive infrastructure in their local context.

For instance, Participant F4 was able to successfully open her restaurant without significant challenges in accessing supportive networks or resources. Her personal relationships in the Netherlands played a crucial role in facilitating the necessary connections and providing the support she needed to start her business. In contrast, F1 has struggled to access similar levels of support. Although she benefited from the help of fellow immigrants from her home country when starting her venture, she found it difficult to expand her local network and bridging capital. For Participant F8, setting up her own business would have been almost impossible without support via the creation of trusted relationships and networks. In these cases, different trajectories emerge within the entrepreneurial aspirations of the participants studied through the analysis of bonding, bridging, and linking capital. With minimal barriers to accessing supportive networks and resources, F4 skilfully navigated the establishment of her restaurant. Her success can be attributed to the pivotal role of personal relationships cultivated within the Dutch community, which served as a conduit for essential connections and the support that was required. In contrast, while F1 initially relied on the support of fellow migrants to get her business started (bonding capital), expanding to a local network (bridging capital) proved to be a formidable undertaking. Alternatively, for F8, the very viability of her entrepreneurial social enterprise depends on the cultivation of substantial support structures. Clearly, her entrepreneurial aspirations underscore the indispensability of network capital in circumventing the barriers that would otherwise render her entrepreneurial aspirations insurmountable.

Entrepreneurial spirit

Entrepreneurial spirit and motivation are key factors exhibited by women in this study. F1's entrepreneurial journey started by giving brief interviews about her own country to a not-for-profit organisation based in Germany. This inspired her to believe that she could start her own business and earn money in order to survive in a foreign country. Her primary motivation for starting a journalism venture arises from the lack of democracy in her home country. She claimed that the opportunity to report freely and independently in her country is very limited and dangerous due to a rigid political environment. F1 personifies the entrepreneurial ethos, displaying a willingness to undertake risks, a zeal for creativity, and a devotion to accomplishment. Similar to many other women refugee entrepreneurs, her drive stems from a longing for financial independence, a desire for autonomy, and a determination to have a positive impact on the host society.

Entrepreneurial spirit and motivation are often intertwined, with one driving the other. For example, a strong entrepreneurial spirit may motivate female entrepreneurs to start their own businesses (F1, F3, and F4), while the motivation to create a positive impact may drive the development of innovative products or services (F2). The entrepreneurial spirit prepared F2, who has a master's degree in sustainability in her own country, to design edible products in her new country, and establish her own production company. She said that she promises to overcome the plastic problems together with innovative products. This is achieved by manufacturing and selling edible cutlery and crockery that is sustainable and natural as well as innovative and practical. F2 said:

> *The inability to find a job suitable for my education level is a common motivation for female refugee entrepreneurs to start their own businesses. Like F2, her many entrepreneur friends try to start their own businesses out of frustration with the labour market or a desire to create opportunities for themselves.*

F2 learned from experience as she strived to meet the sustainable food needs in her target market. Entrepreneurship provides a platform for individuals to act on their ideas using their social capital. Disappointment with the limitations of the host labour market may motivate individuals (see Almohammad et al., 2021), such as F2 who created their own opportunities based on her qualifications and education, which were not valued in the host country's labour market.

Resilience

Refugees are people who face complex and immediate challenges. A rebuilt life in a host country is viewed as a second chance by numerous refugee entrepreneurs, and as a result a unique form of resilience. Participants spoke about the resilience and self-confidence required for entrepreneurship. In the course of the struggle with market obstacles, the ability to overcome challenges and bounce back from setbacks is a key factor. According to F1, finding a job with a salary is problematic. She believes that she had been discriminated against when applying for jobs – she had made over 20 job applications but failed in each case. But this situation did not negatively affect her, and it was one of her motivations. In addition, women's entrepreneurship provides them with a path to more independence. F1 draws attention to the fact that having a career also increases women's sense of self-confidence, while a spousal life limits women's freedom.

Our research participants were keenly aware of the value of the things that they have lost in their past and the emphasis on regaining them. F8 lamented that:

> *I think one of the biggest challenges of migrants is to always live in their past life and not have enough passion to use their competence to start their own business or to find a job.*

Like many of our participants, F3 demonstrated remarkable determination in her efforts to rebuild her life. She had valuable insights into the needs of her new geography, as well as the ability to navigate institutional, cultural, and linguistic barriers that can be obstacles. The Netherlands, a country with relatively long asylum procedures, is a case in point.

> *I lived in a refugee camp for about two years with my husband and two young daughters. During this long period, I had psychological problems and had to divorce my husband. Actually, these problems were a starting/exit point for me to be an entrepreneur. I had to stand on my own feet.*
>
> (F3)

F3's experience highlights the challenges that refugees face when living in asylum camps for extended periods of time. Long-term asylum procedures can cause significant stress and anxiety for refugees, which can lead to mental health problems. However, F3's experience also shows the potential for developing resilience in overcoming these challenges. By starting her own business, F3 was able to take control of her own life and become self-sufficient with her two children.

> *I wanted to find a job [Having spent two years in a refugee camp] that let me communicate with people and travel frequently. Therefore, I set up a tourism business offering advice to Russian citizens, as I was fluent in the Russian language and culture. Despite lacking experience, I researched Amsterdam's history and culture and visited historical places to prepare for my new role as a guide.*
>
> (F3)

Her enthusiasm, adaptability, and self-confidence enabled her to overcome challenges and gradually build her business. Further, F3 started her tourism company by offering lower prices and attracting customers through Airbnb. Despite getting lost during her first city tour with Russian tourists, she showed resilience and was able to end the tour successfully. During the COVID-19 pandemic, her business was supported by the municipality, and she found unexpected demand from wealthy Russian tourists fleeing the Ukraine war. F3 covered their financial losses and continued to guide them.

While the pandemic and Ukraine war caused numerous businesses to come to a standstill, in F3's experience, the Ukraine war created an unexpected surge in demand as wealthy Russian tourists left their country due to the conflict and gained residence in Amsterdam. Through adaptability and resilience, F3 was able to consider this unforeseen demand and cover her fiscal losses during the pandemic period. She utilised her connections with Russians, allowing her to broaden her bonding capital.

Context-related factors

Market perceptions

Although previous studies have revealed that immigrant entrepreneurship is primarily male-dominated (Brieger & Gielnik, 2021), women's exclusion from the formal market prompts them to consider entrepreneurship. According to F8, women are lagging behind in innovative entrepreneurship and encounter specific challenges. Women's ideas for innovation are as marketable as men's, but innovative ideas are not recognised by predominantly male stakeholders. Stereotypes about women in innovative sectors and difficulties in balancing work and family still persist. Stakeholders are not aware of women's different needs and there are no measures attempting to attract women for entrepreneurship. F4 stated that individuals facing financial constraints, lack of networks, and gender differences can surmount these obstacles through work experience in their country of origin and acquiring proficiency in the local language. However, according to F1, gender is not a problem for entrepreneurship, and it does not require higher education. Even an uneducated woman can start by cleaning first and can establish her own cleaning company in a few years due to the entrepreneurial commercial structure of the Netherlands.

Other market-related challenges also affect female refugees' entrepreneurship. The success of F1 serves as an inspiring example of how determination can help overcome these challenges. However, financial constraints and a lack of entrepreneurial skills can still pose obstacles for women entrepreneurs, as exemplified by F4's struggles to understand business regulations. Furthermore, starting a business as a woman entrepreneur highlights obstacles, such as higher educational background, cultural differences, language barriers, and limited work experience. Nonetheless, F4 was able to leverage her bilingualism in upper-intermediate language proficiency and past experience as a pharmacist in Syria to successfully launch her own restaurant in the Netherlands.

Ethnic community solidarity

Entrepreneur refugees often have stronger solidarity with other immigrants or refugees in their networks (bonding capital) than with the local community (bridging capital) due to shared negative experiences, such as language barriers and discrimination (Hanley et al., 2018). However, this does not mean that they do not value the support of the local community, and as barriers disappear and integration increases, stronger ties may emerge (Hanley et al., 2018). After 2 years in business F3's and F4's networks had developed rapidly. F4 had more clients than at the beginning, and when there was excess demand F3 shared additional demand with other refugee entrepreneurs and received a commission from them. When F3's demand was low, her colleagues shared their high demand and a quazi-professional solidarity took place. They also received commissions from the commercial establishments to which they took tourists.

In the case of F8 she was able to set up an NGO with a group of migrants and contacts within the host society (bonding and bridging capital):

> *At this point, setting up your own business or finding a job is very difficult without support, the creation of trust relationships and networks. With a group of migrants, we set up an NGO to implement our ideas to help newly arrived migrants with their economic, social, and cultural integration. In our journey, we got support both from experienced migrants who already set up their businesses and experts in different fields that we met in the host society. We did not get support from the government, but we benefited from the good practices that the government or international organizations supported.*

Further, F3's, F4's, and F8's experiences indicate the significance of solidarity, networking, and collaboration for new entrepreneurs in developing their start-ups. Sharing excess demand and receiving commissions from other refugee entrepreneurs (bonding capital facilitated through linking capital from NGOs) allowed F3 to develop solidarity in the new market environment and provide better service to clients. F3's commissions from local shops also show the potency of refugee entrepreneurship in contributing to the local economy (bridging capital).

NGO links and municipal support

Our research question focused on the role of social capital in refugee women's entrepreneurship and how NGO engagement influences this. Our research revealed that several non-profit organisations in the Netherlands and Belgium offer direct support to immigrant entrepreneurs, such as the Amsterdam Centre for Entrepreneurship, Start2Startup, and StartupDelta. These organisations offer networking, mentoring, financing opportunities, and guidance on dealing with regulations and marketing strategies specifically tailored to an immigrant audience. The multiple resources provided by NGOs provide strong forms of linking capital, whereas access to professional services may be more difficult to gain via bonding and bridging capital. For example, the streamlined business registration process and simplified work permit processes in the Netherlands have made it easier for refugees to start their own businesses. New entrepreneurs can be registered via the Chamber of Commerce.

> *I arrived in the Netherlands in 2016 via family reunification, established my own media company in 2022. Also, although the municipality does not have financial support, the official company formation procedures in the Netherlands have a short duration, a start-up can be established by making an individual application and then for building a new company in the Netherlands you only need an accountant!*
>
> (F1)

She indicates how this process was seemingly accessible and achievable, Similarly, F2 states:

> *Before starting my business, I was contacted and supported by Kennispoort. Kennispoort is a valuable resource for entrepreneurs in the Zwolle region, providing support and assistance in a range of areas that are crucial for starting and growing a successful business. In addition to providing guidance and advice on developing business ideas, arranging finance, and making connections with other entrepreneurs, Kennispoort also offers access to a range of resources and services that can help entrepreneurs navigate the challenges of starting a new business.*

Importantly, Kennispoort and other NGOs offer a one-stop place for accessing comprehensive resources. Saeed Zwolle is another organisation that empowers refugee entrepreneurs in the Zwolle region, providing them with resources to succeed in Dutch society. Saeed Zwolle has supported skilled immigrant chefs in beginning their own restaurants by assisting with business planning, management, and networking. F4 received support from Saeed, which helped overcome networking and local communication challenges and achieve entrepreneurial success.

Project AZO in Belgium offered entrepreneurial guidance to asylum seekers and refugees in the Flanders region. Through information sessions, they were instructed on how to do business in Belgium. Then, after an evaluation of entrepreneurial competencies and aspirations, refugees could receive individual counselling. Through an intensive process with a range of specialisations, they could start their own business. Once started, the refugee entrepreneur could still contact the counsellor for aftercare. F5 was able to transform her entrepreneurial idea into a business by obtaining intensive support from an NGO which received government funding for this project. Without this support, she said, it would be almost impossible to start her own business. Because of that she received a lot of advice, was able to test her idea, and secure a loan.

F8 participated in another Belgian support programme and was then able to set up an NGO with a group of other migrants.

> *In my case, it took three years to adapt to the new host country's system. I was lucky to have a chance to attend a Fresh Start program which provided me with all I needed ranging from legal/financial support, how to implement my business ideas to networking. Most importantly with Fresh Start, I realized that my experience can be valued by the host society.*

In F3's company, city tours are based in Amsterdam. F3 stated that after obtaining a legal residence permit, she wanted to live in Amsterdam. The refugee camp management responded by securing a house that she rented from the municipality. In the Netherland refugee camp system, residence permits are initially obtained and then a municipality determines residency location. This is usually a municipality within 60 km of the refugee camp. The ruling was broadened for F3, so she could live in the location suited to her business aspirations. The camp administration had trusted her and arranged legal procedures for her new social and business life. The camp management's positive reaction to F3's request for housing in Amsterdam highlights the importance of local support for refugee entrepreneurship. Despite strict bureaucratic challenges in the asylum process, flexibility was evident in the camp administration's support of F3's choice of Amsterdam as her preferred municipality.

Moreover, municipalities in the Netherlands provide assistance for entrepreneurs, including refugees who want to start their own businesses. This support can take various forms, such as direct funding, advice, and networking opportunities. The financial assistance offered by municipalities can be up to

40,000 euros. However, to be eligible, this requires a well-prepared feasibility study and business plan. F2 stated:

> *I received 40,000 euros credit from the municipality to establish my company due to a well-prepared feasibility proposal;" and F3 said, "During the COVID-19 period, my business came to a standstill, but during this period, the municipality supported me financially and I fulfilled an additional job.*

Linking capital became an essential part of the process for refugees in our study. Without direct support from NGOs in terms of providing information, support, and financial resources, women refugees may have been unable to initiate or work through difficulties in their business start-ups. The leverage, expertise, and capacity of NGOs demonstrate why linking capital may be critical compared to bonding and bridging capital.

Discussion

We sought to answer two main research questions in this study: *What is the role of social capital in refugee women's entrepreneurship and how does NGO engagement influence this?* In answering the first research question, our findings reveal the adversities our women entrepreneurs encountered and how these factors contributed to their entrepreneurial success. These women entrepreneurs encountered some traditional barriers commonly extrapolated in the literature, particularly gender inequities, language skills, and inadequate access to support networks (see Brieger & Gielnik, 2021; Mehtap et al., 2019). However, a significant aspect of their success was the internal factors related to entrepreneurial determination, self-confidence, and self-reliance. External facilitating factors were also significant and based on direct support from NGOs (bridging capital) and interaction with other refugees (bonding capital). NGOs gave these refugee women access to information, resources, and contacts (linking capital). However, the presence of labour, gender, and cultural exclusion contributing to widespread lack of trust among female refugees poses a formidable hurdle to effective NGO engagement (Hanley et al., 2018; Zihnioğlu & Dalkıran, 2022). While NGOs can foster support for initiating entrepreneurship, we anticipate that there may be different challenges to how this support can be engaged in for longer periods of time to assist refugee women in their entrepreneurship sustainability. Nonetheless, NGOs (compared to government support organisations) stand as providers of an alternative avenue for economic empowerment among refugee women due to their specific humanitarian mission and values (Hack-Polay & Igwe, 2019).

In our second research question, we explored how NGO engagement influences refugee women's social capital. The process of rebuilding and adapting this social capital to the economic landscape of the host country is arduous. The prominence of bonding capital within the refugee community, forged upon shared experiences and cultural affinities, shows the importance of familiar networks during the resettlement period (Hanley et al., 2018). However, increasing interaction with locals can generate bridging capital that helps break down cultural barriers and increase business services to the local community (Fontefrancesco & Mendonce, 2022; Hanley et al., 2018; Wahlbeck, 2013). Surprisingly, informal economic ventures inside refugee communities might unintentionally harm the formation of bridging and linking capital due to the exclusionary, homogeneous space (Hanley et al., 2018; Putnam, 2000). Nonetheless, this challenge can be mitigated through local NGOs understanding the incongruity. These organisations foster linking capital between refugees and other host organisations and individuals by strengthening their connections (Claridge, 2018). These dynamics not only demonstrate the adaptive capacity of refugees to enhance several forms of social capital, but also underpin the function of several types of actors (refugee groups, local community, and host organisations) in fostering economic integration.

In evaluating the important role that each form of social capital can play in economic integration of refugees, gender itself complicates this process of social capital accumulation. Specifically examining the experiences of refugee women revealed that they may lack opportunities to access and build bonding, bridging, and linking capital due to gender and cultural norms. While refugee communities generally may have access to bonding capital in a more immediate sense (see Hanley et al., 2018), gendered norms and restrictions undermine women refugees and, therefore, linking capital may be a better avenue to access information and resources via NGO's outreach (see Claridge, 2018). Local NGOs emerge as vital intermediaries between refugee women and the prospect of successful ventures. NGOs lessen obstacles, promote cross-cultural connections, and enable refugee women to display resilience in their entrepreneurial trajectories. The prominence of bonding, bridging, and linking capital within this narrative unveils the transformative potential of interactions, whether through friendships with refugees and locals or engagement with NGOs.

Conclusion

In conclusion, this research advances our understanding of the relationship between refugee women, NGOs, and entrepreneurship. It offers learning for decision-makers, practitioners, and stakeholders for creating pathways that maximise the NGOs' potential for assisting refugee women entrepreneurs in achieving local economic independence and self-confidence. As we navigate the challenging terrain of refugee integration, the role of NGOs emerges as a beacon of hope, offering not only resources but also connections, trust, and chances for refugee women to forge their own paths to success.

References

Alexandre, L., Salloum, C., & Alalam, A. (2019). An investigation of migrant entrepreneurs: The case of Syrian refugees in Lebanon. *International Journal of Entrepreneurial Behaviour & Research, 25*(5), 1147–1164. https://doi.org/10.1108/IJEBR-03-2018-0171.

Almohammad, D., Durrah, O., & Ahmed, F. (2021). Deciphering the motives, barriers and integration of Syrian refugee entrepreneurs into Turkish society: A SEM approach. *Digital Policy, Regulation and Governance, 23*(1), 59–76. https://doi.org/10.1108/DPRG-05-2020-0066.

Atasü-Topcuoğlu, R. (2019). Syrian refugee entrepreneurship in Turkey: Integration and the use of immigrant capital in the informal economy. *Social Inclusion, 7*(4), 200–210. https://doi.org/10.17645/si.v7i4.2346.

Backman, M., Lopez, E., & Rowe, F. (2021). The occupational trajectories and outcomes of forced migrants in Sweden. Entrepreneurship, employment or persistent inactivity? *Small Business Economics, 56*(3), 963–983. https://doi.org/10.1007/s11187-019-00312-z.

Bizri, R.M. (2017). Refugee-entrepreneurship: A social capital perspective. *Entrepreneurship & Regional Development, 29*(9–10), 847–868. https://doi.org/10.1080/08985626.2017.1364787

Brieger, S., & Gielnik, M. (2021). Understanding the gender gap in immigrant entrepreneurship: A multi-country study of immigrants' embeddedness in economic, social, and institutional contexts. *Small Business Economics, 56*(3), 1007–1031. https://doi.org/10.1007/s11187-019-00314-x

Claridge, T. (2018). Functions of social capital - bonding, bridging, linking. *Social Capital Research, 20*, 1–7. https://doi.org/10.5281/zenodo.7993853.

Datta, A. (2019). Useful and earning citizens? Gender, state, and the market in post-colonial Delhi. *Modern Asian Studies, 53*(6), 1924–1955. https://doi.org/10.1017/S0026749X18000562.

Desai, S., Naudé, W., & Stel, N. (2021). Refugee entrepreneurship: Context and directions for future research. *Small Business Economics, 56*(3), 933–945. https://doi.org/10.1007/s11187-019-00310-1

European Commission. (2023a). *Social economy and inclusive entrepreneurship.* https://ec.europa.eu/social/main.jsp?catId=952&langId=en

European Commission. (2023b). *2023 report on gender equality in the EU.* https://commission.europa.eu/system/files/2023-04/annual_report_GE_2023_web_EN.pdf

European Commission. (2023c). *Welcome to eurostat.* https://ec.europa.eu/eurostat

Fontefrancesco, M., & Mendonce, S. (2022). Migrant entrepreneurship and social integration: A case-study analysis among Bangladeshi vendors in Rome. *Societies, 12*(5), 1–12. https://doi.org/10.3390/soc12050139

Goodson, L., & Phillimore, J. (2008). Social capital and integration: The importance of social relationships and social space to refugee women. *International Journal of Diversity in Organizations, Communities, and Nations, 7*(6), 181–194. https://doi.org/10.18848/1447-9532/CGP/v07i06/39510

Hack-Polay, D., & Agu Igwe, P. (2019). Beyond words and rhetoric – Small voluntary organisations and effective refugee integration in the communities. *Journal of Enterprising Communities, 13*(1), 5–23. https://doi.org/10.1108/JEC-11-2018-0084

Hanley, J., Al Mhamied, A., Cleveland, J., Hajjar, O., Hassan, G., Ives, N., Khyar, R., & Harima, A., Periac, F., Murphy, T., & Picard, S. (2021). Entrepreneurial opportunities of refugees in Germany, France, and Ireland: Multiple embeddedness framework. *International Entrepreneurship and Management Journal, 17*(2), 625–663. https://doi.org/10.1007/s11365-020-00707-5

Hillmann, F., & Toğral Koca, B. (2021). By women, for women, and with women: On the integration of highly qualified female refugees into the labour markets of Berlin and Brandenburg. *Comparative Migration Studies, 9*(1), 1–18. https://doi.org/10.1186/s40878-020-00211-3

Hynie, M. (2018). The social networks, social support and social capital of Syrian refugees privately sponsored to settle in Montreal: Indications for employment and housing during their early experiences of integration. *Canadian Ethnic Studies, 50*(2), 123–149. https://doi.org/10.1353/ces.2018.0018

Low, C., & Shah, B. (2023). Refugee women's volunteering as resistance practice to micro-aggressions and social exclusion in the UK. *Social Inclusion, 11*(2), 69–79. https://doi.org/10.17645/si.v11i2.6309

Mawson, S., & Kasem, L. (2019). Exploring the entrepreneurial intentions of Syrian refugees in the UK. *International Journal of Entrepreneurial Behaviour & Research, 25*(5), 1128–1146. https://doi.org/10.1108/IJEBR-02-2018-0103

Mehtap, S., Ozmenekse, L., & Caputo, A. (2019). I'm a stay at home businesswoman: An insight into informal entrepreneurship in Jordan. *Journal of Entrepreneurship in Emerging Economies, 11*(1), 44–65. https://doi.org/10.1108/JEEE-10-2017-0080

Putnam, R. (1995). Bowling alone: America's declining social capital. *Journal of Democracy, 6*(1), 65–78. https://doi.org/10.1353/jod.1995.0002

Putnam, R. (2000). *Bowling alone: The collapse and revival of American community.* New York: Simon & Schuster.

Senthanar, S., MacEachen, E., Premji, S., & Bigelow, P. (2021). Entrepreneurial experiences of Syrian refugee women in Canada: A feminist grounded qualitative study. *Small Business Economics, 57*(2), 835–847. https://doi.org/10.1007/s11187-020-00385-1

Sidhva, D., Zuntz, A.C., al Akash, R., Nashwan, A., & Al-Majali, A. (2021). In exile, the woman became everything: Middle-aged Syrian women's contributions to family livelihoods during protracted displacement in Jordan. *Journal of Humanitarian Affairs, 3*(1), 4–15. https://doi.org/10.7227/JHA.054

Street, C., Poh, Y., & Al-Dajani, H. (2022). Refugee women business mentors: New evidence for women's empowerment. *Sustainability, 14*(15), 1–21. https://doi.org/10.3390/su14159154

Surangi, H. (2022). Are gender and immigration a double disadvantage? Exploring the experiences of Sri Lankan female immigrant entrepreneurs in London, United Kingdom. *Journal of Ethnic and Cultural Studies, 9*(2), 199–215. https://doi.org/10.29333/ejecs/1159

Szreter, S., & Woolcock, M. (2004). Health by association? Social capital, social theory, and the political economy of public health. *International Journal of Epidemiology, 33*(4), 650–667. https://doi.org/10.1093/ije/dyh013

Turner, L. (2020). #Refugees can be entrepreneurs too! Humanitarianism, race, and the marketing of Syrian refugees. *Review of International Studies, 46*(1), 137–155. https://doi.org/10.1017/S0260210519000342

UNHCR. (2022a). *A global roadmap for refugee entrepreneurship*. www.unhcr.org/sites/default/files/legacy-pdf/63565bc94.pdf

UNHCR. (2022b). *The Netherlands: Numbers*. www.unhcr.org/nl/wie-we-zijn/cijfers/.

UNHCR. (2022c). *Belgium*. www.unhcr.org/be/nl

van Kooy, J. (2016). Refugee women as entrepreneurs in Australia. *Forced Migration Review*, *53*, 71–73. www.proquest.com/scholarly-journals/refugee-women-as-entrepreneurs-australia/docview/1837169889/se-2

Wahlbeck, Ö. (2013). Mixed embeddedness and the dynamics of self-employment among Turkish immigrants in Finland. *Polish Sociological Review*, *184*, 487–503. www.jstor.org/stable/24371564

Wauters, B., & Lambrecht, J. (2008). Barriers to refugee entrepreneurship in Belgium: Towards an explanatory model. *Journal of Ethnic and Migration Studies*, *34*(6), 895–915. https://doi.org/10.1080/13691830802211190

World Bank. (2023). Advancing refugee entrepreneurship: Guidelines for the private sector, governments, and the development community. *Private Sector for Refugees (PS4R) Platform*. https://thedocs.worldbank.org/en/doc/848f8400f8c614057e83ea130d050ebc-0570012023/original/FINAL-PS4R-Refugee-Entrepreneurship-Paper.pdf

Yeasmin, N., & Hasanat, W. (2022). Understanding inclusive entrepreneurship: With special reference to women immigrants in arctic Finland. *Finnish Yearbook of Population Research*, *56*, 91–114. http://lib-proxy.jsu.edu/login?url=https://www.proquest.com/scholarly-journals/understanding-inclusive-entrepreneurship-with/docview/2682878997/se-2

Zighan, S. (2021). Challenges faced by necessity entrepreneurship, the case of Syrian refugees in Jordan. *Journal of Enterprising Communities*, *15*(4), 531–547. https://doi.org/10.1108/JEC-09-2020-0168

Zihnioğlu, Ö., & Dalkıran, M. (2022). From social capital to social cohesion: Syrian refugees in Turkey and the role of NGOs as intermediaries. *Journal of Ethnic and Migration Studies*, *48*(11), 2455–2472. https://doi.org/10.1080/1369183X.2022.2047908

16 Nurturing entrepreneurs

Designing child-friendly workshops for refugee women

Claire P. Street and Poh Yen Ng

Introduction

The entrepreneurship workshop is a popular method to develop entrepreneurial intention (Pruett, 2012), and research has evidence of its effectiveness in building nascent entrepreneurs (Onjewu et al., 2021). Entrepreneurship workshops have empowered marginalised groups, including female refugees, to establish their businesses in the last few decades (Dlaske, 2022). However, traditional entrepreneurship training provision is often fragmented and fails to address refugee women's unique needs and challenges (Albrecht et al., 2021; Apicella et al., 2021; Liebig & Tronstad, 2021). This chapter proposes a rethinking of how entrepreneurship workshops for marginalised women are designed and actualised, focusing on a two-day entrepreneurship workshop for refugee women in the United Kingdom (UK), which also incorporated a mentoring programme for the participants.

Literature review

Entrepreneurship has long been recognised as a potent tool for economic empowerment and self-sufficiency of refugees (Marchand & Dijkhuizen, 2018; Megersa, 2020). Among various support mechanisms for nascent entrepreneurs, mentoring has emerged as a particularly effective method for fostering entrepreneurial success (Meister & Mauer, 2019; Solano et al., 2019; Street et al., 2022). In many instances, the entrepreneurship workshop has been used to introduce the mentoring mechanism, allowing the participants to get to know one another and make meaningful connections (Gimmon, 2014; Pruett, 2012).

Entrepreneurial mentoring is a dynamic relationship where experienced entrepreneurs guide novices through the complexities of initiating and growing a business (Crompton, 2012; Man et al., 2022; Terjesen & Sullivan,, 2011). Its importance in the entrepreneurial landscape cannot be overstated, as studies have shown that start-ups with mentorship have a higher probability of success than those without mentorship (Isaak, 2020). Mentoring offers nascent entrepreneurs a wealth of benefits, from gaining insights into market

DOI: 10.4324/9781003368540-20

trends to understanding nuances of business strategy (Sullivan, 2000). Various forms of mentoring exist, ranging from formal arrangements in incubators to more casual guidance from industry veterans (Clutterbuck, 2014).

Due to their unique circumstances, refugee women face distinct challenges in the entrepreneurial arena. These challenges range from language barriers and unfamiliarity with market dynamics to limited access to financial resources (Gower et al., 2022). Given these challenges, the value proposition of mentoring becomes even more pronounced for refugees, acting as a beacon of support in an unfamiliar terrain. For refugee women, the entrepreneurial journey is characterised by an intersection of gender and refugee-specific challenges. They grapple with the societal norms restricting women's economic roles and the inherent difficulties their refugee status poses (Adeeko & Treanor, 2022). Tailored mentoring programmes, therefore, are crucial. Such initiatives that address both gender and refugee-related challenges have shown promising results in the few studies that have been conducted (Meister & Mauer, 2019; Street et al., 2022; van Kooy, 2016). These programmes offer opportunities for refugee women to connect with established business owners acting as mentors who could provide guidance, support, and advice. Nevertheless, many mentoring programmes utilise host nation entrepreneurs who may be unable to relate to the intersectionality challenges faced by refugee women, thus limiting their long-term impact on their entrepreneurial journey.

The context

The UK government has long been criticised for implementing policies hostile to asylum seekers and refugees (Allsopp et al., 2014; Mayblin & James, 2019; Mulvey, 2010). One example of the UK's restrictive immigration stance is the hostile environment policy introduced in 2012 (Webber, 2019). The approach makes it difficult for refugees to live and work in the UK by denying them access to essential services such as housing, healthcare, and bank accounts. The policy also made it a requirement for landlords, employers, and banks to check the immigration status of their tenants, employees, and customers. The government also prohibits asylum seekers from working or setting up their businesses, thereby creating a climate of fear and mistrust among immigrants, leading to discrimination against people who looked or sounded "foreign" (Goodfellow, 2020; Yuval-Davis, 2018). These policies have also been widely criticised for being inhumane and putting the lives of refugees and migrants at risk (Goodfellow, 2020).

On the other hand, there has been a progressive development in channelling refugees into entrepreneurship pathways in recent years. For example, the Home Office and National Lottery Community funded the Refugee Entrepreneurship Pilot scheme in 2018 for a year-long, tailored business support programme for refugees. The objective was to support refugee entrepreneurship in the UK by proving the effectiveness of refugee entrepreneurship programmes and trialling different delivery models (Richey et al., 2021). The UK government's Startup Loans programme also provides loans and mentoring to entrepreneurs, including refugees starting a new venture. Non-profit organisations such as Caritas' Aspire Business and The Entrepreneurial Refugee Network, teamed with the UP Collective, have provided training and support to help refugees develop their business ideas. Social Integration of Refugees through Education and Self Employment supports refugees interested in starting their businesses with tailored support, such as practical workshops, mentoring, and networking opportunities. Their implementation would largely depend on government support and available budgets. The organisation and running of these programmes are also institution-driven and seldom engage the targeted refugee groups in developing such workshops and activities. Furthermore, many of these initiatives are not gender specific.

Workshop objectives and settings

Considering the shortcomings of current initiatives, a two-day workshop led by refugee women entrepreneurs who had settled in the UK was conducted. The workshop covered a broad range of entrepreneurship topics. This endeavour was a joint initiative between the University of Essex and the Interreg project named "Accelerating Women's Enterprise". This project ran from April to October 2019. The targeted participants of this project were refugee women based in Kent and London who had entrepreneurial intent or were in the early stages of entrepreneurship. In other words, the participants were those who were about to start, or had started, a business within the last two years in the UK. They were identified through multiple channels, such as refugee charities, networks, and local councils. The workshop's main objective was to inspire refugee women to consider entrepreneurship by providing them with the necessary tools and resources to overcome the barriers they may face. In addition, the workshop was designed to be a safe and accessible space for refugee women and mothers to explore their entrepreneurial potential and receive encouragement and validation for their ideas.

During the workshop, the fundamental elements of a business model were introduced with simplified language to make it more accessible to women with limited education and English language skills. Key topics covered included defining a product or service, identifying potential customers, essential financial planning, and developing soft skills such as communication, problem-solving, and resilience. The workshop aimed to create basic business start-up skills and an entrepreneurial mindset by fostering social, interpersonal, and intercultural collaboration. The workshop also spoke about the financial barriers that refugee women often face in starting their businesses, including limited access to capital and financial services and a lack of financial literacy. Participants were provided financial education through budgeting advice and information about financial resources. Table 16.1 outlines the workshop scheduled on September 21 and 22, 2019.

Table 16.1 Workshop schedule

Period	*Activity*	*Topic/themes*	*Objectives*
Day 1	Pre-workshop breakfast meeting	Briefing for mentors	
	Icebreaker		
	Mindfulness with counsellor/coach		
	Coffee break		
	Entrepreneurial stories by refugee mentors	Have you ever dreamed of starting your own business?	Entrepreneurial ideas and goals
	Entrepreneurial stories by refugee mentors	Preparing your story	Marketing and social media
	Lunch		
	Mindfulness with counsellor/coach		
	Entrepreneurial stories by refugee mentors	Keeping track of what you earn and spend	Budgeting and record-keeping
	Entrepreneurial stories by refugee mentors	Pitching your idea	Business development plan
Day 2	Mindfulness with counsellor/coach		
	Q&A	Legal requirements for business setup	
	Coffee break		
	Entrepreneurial stories by refugee mentors	I thought of that first!	Protecting your business idea
	Entrepreneurial stories by refugee mentors	Finding money for your business	Setting up and financing your business
	Inspiring stories by refugee mentors		
	Lunch		
	Mindfulness with counsellor/coach		
	Entrepreneurial stories by refugee mentors	It's who you know!	Networking
	Counsellor/coach	Juggling your time	Work–life Balance
	Final Address – End of workshop		

The activities were designed to promote collaboration and creative thinking among the participants. They were also encouraged to develop and record business ideas using business model canvases. According to Haase and Lautenschlager (2011), the most effective learning environments for entrepreneurs are those that replicate real-life situations as closely as possible. Four entrepreneurial stories were told by refugee women entrepreneurs who

imposed on women's capacity to be fully human in patriarchal environments. Earlier work by Willis and Daisley (1997) found that women belonging to ethnic minorities expressed a greater degree of positivity and enthusiasm towards the women-only aspect of training workshops. They also posited that many women believe that they benefit from women-only development courses and that the single-sex nature of the methods enhances their learning. However, the effort to incorporate women-only space in refugee support programmes, particularly for aspiring entrepreneurs, is scarce.

Before the workshop, four refugee entrepreneurs who also acted as mentors in the programme were invited to a planning session to design the workshop. During this session, they expressed the need for a women-only workshop. Aisha insisted: "*We want to share as women and hear the stories of other successful women.*" The facilitators recognised that asserting mixed-gender training and workshops could exclude women of faith, especially those from Muslim backgrounds. They understood that creating a safe and inclusive space was crucial for the women to feel comfortable and participate fully in the workshop activities. As such, they worked together to design a workshop that met the specific needs of the refugee women. They created a women-only space with collective agreement and support as they understood the cultural sensitivities and conditions of the refugee women. The space was designed to be accommodating and inclusive, with a range of activities and resources that met the specific needs of the women.

The mentors and mentees highlighted the importance of a women-only space in their reflections on their experiences. One mentee, Fatana, shared, "*I am glad we were sharing as women*", highlighting the sense of community and support that comes from being in a space with other women. Another mentee, Hala, found the workshop helped provide "*new ways of thinking*" and the "*courage to carry on*" by being around "*successful women*". Huda remarked that being in a women-only space allowed her to be in the company of "*other women who are positive and full of energy*". From the workshop, we were surprised that many mentees had rarely encountered working women in their home countries, let alone women who owned businesses. During initial interviews, especially with the women from Afghanistan, the interpreter had to provide detailed explanations for the term "entrepreneur", as the mentees often confused it with simply having a job. One of the mentees, Lina, reflected, "*I've always seen these ideas on YouTube and have never really met anybody who has done it live, and I'm really excited to see face-to-face someone who's done it.*"

Sana, one of the mentors, spoke about how being in a space with other refugee women is "super inspirational" and reinforces her desire to give back to her community. Similarly, Zarina noted that creating a space for women to discuss their hopes and dreams is important, as knowing how to pursue them can be challenging. Layla also expressed feeling empowered to be in an all-women setup:

> *It's unusual we don't experience that on a daily basis; it's a reminder that we are valuable, and the guidance we give is more valuable if we are relatable role models. Men are important, but it is just as important for women to feel in a safe space and feel like you are valuable.*

Overall, the women found the women-only space helpful and motivating in pursuing their entrepreneurial dreams.

Based on the participants' reflections, the significance of women-only space reinforced prior research (Lewis et al., 2015; Willis & Daisley, 1997) and extended to the refugee women context. Mentors and mentees felt more comfortable sharing their experiences and asking questions in a women-only space. This setting is crucial for refugee women due to their vulnerable background and limited social contact that prevents them from speaking openly. In addition, many refugee women are from Muslim backgrounds, prohibiting them from interacting with other non-related men.

Catering for childcare needs

During a pre-workshop interview, one of the mentees asked:

> *What kind of business can I do with my children? Do I leave my children at home? How can I do it? My problems are money and, language, and childcare. I am still confused about what I want to do.*
>
> Maryam)

As a refugee in the UK without access to childcare benefits and extended family support, it is unsurprising to hear about this frustration. Another participant, Farida, shared a similar sentiment: *"Having babies and kids stops me from starting my own business."* These concerns emphasised the need for accessible childcare during the workshop, as some had expressed hesitancy in attending due to the lack of childcare options. This childcare issue was again highlighted when two mentors had to bring their children with them to the workshop planning session. As they spoke and planned the workshop, the five children present ran around, laughing and playing. Despite the noise and chaos, they all adapted and continued their work.

A manager of a local charity shared an interesting model she had witnessed in their English classes during the pre-workshop discussion. *"The women brought their children with them and played in the same room while their mothers learned English"*. As a group, it was decided to base the workshop on this model to eliminate the stress and additional worries of mothers having to leave their children or provide external childcare for the participants.

In the end, 13 children, including a five-month-old baby, attended the workshop with their mothers. A childcare was set up in the same space as the workshop. This arrangement created a fluid flow where mothers could see their children, and children could always access them. Interestingly, there were minimal disruptions as the children were engaged with activities and rarely moved across to their mothers. The childcare provision for the workshop was carefully thought out and executed to ensure the safety and well-being of the children. To this end, a play therapist was recruited to run the childcare, given refugee children's specific needs and circumstances. Having a specialist like her was essential to provide a safe environment for the children and cater to their unique needs. She facilitated age-appropriate play activities for all the children while working with refugee women volunteers to assist her. It ensured that the children were safe, engaged, and happy throughout the workshop.

The on-site childcare service provided during the workshop received positive feedback from mentors and mentees alike. One mentee, Parwana, expressed her satisfaction as follows: "*I am happy; before I could not attend, I did not want to leave my children with my husband.*" Another participant echoed this sentiment: "*It was so helpful to have the childcare. I could learn without worrying about my children*" (Amal). The presence of children at the workshop also positively impacted the overall atmosphere. A mentee observed:

> *Such lovely, active, full of positive energy women, they just give me more positive feelings and energy to encourage me to work for my future. I'm not just going to sit back and relax now that I had my children.*
>
> (Soraya)

This sense of community was further exemplified when the baby was passed around to others so that the mother could focus on the workshop.

One of the mentors, Sana, had experienced first-hand the difficulties of accessing entrepreneurial training without accessible childcare. She commented that the on-site childcare service would have been a great help to her. "*Childcare was a significant barrier to my access of entrepreneurial training. If a childcare service like this were available, it would have been so helpful to me,*" she said. Sana's experience highlights the importance of providing such services to remove barriers that prevent individuals from accessing valuable training and networking opportunities.

The idea that women's childcare responsibilities hold them back is often used as an excuse to avoid addressing gender inequality in the entrepreneurial sector, as Coate and Howson (2016) argue. It is a prevalent problem faced by women entrepreneurs with children. As a result, childcare becomes a burden for women entrepreneurs, which might affect their businesses (APEC Project, 2013). Furthermore, refugee women face additional challenges due to traditional norms and inadequate childcare provision, which can limit their access to support services (Lovell & Nguyen, 1987). Due to the restrictive government policy that does not pay for their childcare cost and limited family support in a new country, refugee women must take care of their children most of the time. By including the childcare facility in a workshop for refugee women, many expressed their gratitude for the service and its impact on their ability to attend and engage with the workshop. Accessible childcare was critical in facilitating a supportive and inclusive environment for women refugees to access entrepreneurship opportunities. However, many refugee support programmes fail to provide adequate support due to ignorance of cultural norms governing women's roles within their families and communities. Addressing the barrier of childcare responsibilities could increase refugee women's access to entrepreneurial training, ultimately promoting gender equality and creating more opportunities for women entrepreneurs.

Eliminating education and culture as barriers

Rudhumbu et al. (2020) claim that the significance of providing entrepreneurship education to female entrepreneurs cannot be overstated. They explain that this is primarily because they have not had access to sufficient opportunities for vocational and technical education and training in entrepreneurship, which has traditionally been viewed as a male-dominated sector. As a result, many women lack the practical knowledge and skills needed to run their businesses effectively. It is even more relevant for refugee women. The workshop was designed to eliminate education and culture as barriers to participation. Refugee women entrepreneurs were invited to act as mentors and facilitate the design and content creation of the workshop. The education disparity among the refugee women was significant, ranging from those who had received less than two years of formal education under the Taliban to those who held doctorates. To address this issue and create an equitable and inclusive environment, the mentors suggested using oral storytelling to diminish any education discrepancies. Layla emphasised, "*We need to make this relevant to these women; otherwise, what is the point?*"

The language used in the workshop was deliberately simplified, and the entrepreneurs' stories were presented casually and relaxed, encouraging open discussion. An Afghan Pashto interpreter was available to ensure inclusivity among the participants, and the mentors spoke fluent Arabic and English. The mentees came from diverse backgrounds, including Afghanistan, Iraq, and Syria, while the facilitators hailed from Eritrea, Palestine, Iraq, and Yemen. To bring everyone together and foster a sense of unity, the first day of the workshop began by teaching everyone in the room a Swahili song and dance.

Mentors and mentees alike found the initiative to be a valuable and motivating experience. Zarina initially had reservations about what she could teach these women: "*Initially, I looked at these women; they were all married with children, and I thought, what can I teach these women? I know nothing.*" However, sharing personal encounters and perspectives proved to be just as significant. Layla noted: "*The exchange of life experience is just as important; you learn something from them that might not be professional.*" Sana related to the mentees' traditional lifestyles and emphasised the importance of complementing each other, saying: "*I learned from my mother to never look down on these people; their life experiences were different, but we could complement each other.*" Aisha appreciated the opportunity to empower and boost confidence in the mentees: "*I loved that they were sharing their hopes and dreams. Teaching people to empower themselves boosting confidence is an opportunity to question and ask why? Women don't question.*"

When asked to reflect on the most valuable part of the workshop, the mentees expressed their gratitude for learning how to start their businesses, gain freedom, and meet refugee women with businesses. One mentee, Noor, said: "*Learn and show how to be a good, successful woman and get freedom.*" Another mentee, Samar, appreciated the opportunity to network: "*The best part of the workshop was talking with women who had already started their businesses. How they did it.*"

Using storytelling and simplified language helped to level the playing field and encourage participation from all attendees, regardless of their education level or cultural background. The workshop illustrates the importance of eliminating barriers to education and culture to empower refugee women entrepreneurs.

Mindfulness approach

Working with vulnerable women in a workshop setting requires a particular approach. To ensure that the mental health and well-being of the women were addressed, the organiser recruited a trained counsellor who provided support throughout the workshop. The counsellor incorporated mindfulness practices and short meditations, which helped the women to relax and feel more comfortable, enabling them to engage more fully in the workshop activities. These sessions focused on breathing exercises to help participants ground themselves in the present moment. Mindfulness was gradually introduced to the participants throughout the two days, especially as they were unfamiliar with the practice. By creating a calm and supportive environment, emphasising confidentiality, and encouraging active listening and respectful communication, mindfulness sessions provided a safe and welcoming space for participants. The workshop used mindfulness to help the women focus on the present moment and become more aware of their thoughts and feelings. The counsellor was available to support and guide all the refugee women, including the facilitators and participants, to promote their mental well-being. The counsellor's role was to help the women manage any stress, anxiety, or trauma they may have experienced and create a safe and supportive environment for them to share their feelings and emotions. By incorporating mindfulness into the workshop and having a trained counsellor available, the organisers were able to provide a holistic approach to supporting vulnerable women.

Based on the researcher's observation, the women had difficulty focusing on the breathing exercises at the start of the mindfulness sessions. There was a lot of giggling and a lack of concentration, which could be attributed to various factors such as cultural barriers, language differences, or the unfamiliarity of the practice. However, as the mindfulness sessions continued, it became apparent that the women started to understand the importance of self-reflection in managing stress. They began showing more interest and enthusiasm in the practice and could stay focused on the exercises longer. The mindfulness sessions' coach played a vital role in facilitating the women's comprehension of the training and its advantages while establishing a secure and encouraging atmosphere for their engagement. By the end of the sessions, the women appeared to understand better mindfulness and how it can improve their well-being and cope with stress, which could positively impact their personal and entrepreneurial lives.

Refugee women as contributors

Refugee women have often been portrayed as passive recipients of aid and support programmes, perpetuating their perception as victims rather than active contributors to society. However, the workshop positioned refugee women as contributors in a support programme, as the women who had established businesses led the workshop and shared their experiences with those at the nascent stage of entrepreneurship. This approach suggests a radical rethinking to raising entrepreneurial opportunities in the refugee community and highlights the potential of refugees to contribute to society. It also aligns with UNCTAD's (2018, p. IX) recommendation to "support programs that link new refugees and migrants with established refugee and migrant entrepreneurs as mentors and coaches to nascent entrepreneurs". By connecting new refugees and migrants with established entrepreneurs, such programmes facilitate mentorship and coaching opportunities that empower refugee women entrepreneurs to leverage their skills and experience to support their communities. It is imperative, given that, as Bloch (2007) notes, refugees with significant skill levels and qualifications often find themselves in positions that do not match their expertise or educational background. Programmes that recognise and support the potential of refugee women as contributors can help address this issue and create pathways for refugees to thrive as entrepreneurs and community members.

As the mentors reflected on their experiences, they emphasised the importance of peer mentoring in allowing individuals to share knowledge, gain insights, and empower one another. One mentor, Sana, stated:

> *Mentoring means guiding and helping them figure out their own path and what they want to do. I think it's important because I come from a culture that spoon-feeds, so I want to empower women from similar cultures and backgrounds to question and make their own life decisions.*

This sentiment was echoed by Layla, who felt a connection with the Syrian and Iraqi refugee women and wanted to help them live everyday lives. She said:

> *I felt so grateful that I was so privileged. I have no issues with the language; I have a degree and a Master's. I had a lot of empathy for them. I totally*

> *understood; through the whole asylum process, I spent a lot of time with other refugees, and this reminded me of those days.*

The mentees also found the mentoring sessions valuable, with one mentee, Samar, saying she was inspired "*[t]o meet refugee ladies with business*" and another stating, "*Talking to Layla about her food business. She helped me a lot*" (Jamila). Ultimately, as mentor Zarina reflected: "*This felt different. I could share what I had learnt and all the knowledge I had gained through my experiences, and they listened and were interested in what I had to say.*"

What happened next?

After the workshop, the mentors navigated unique challenges, with some achieving their initial business goals and others finding alternate paths in their entrepreneurial journey. Layla from Yemen continued her UK pop-up restaurant and YouTube channel, with mentoring programmes enhancing her network. She also works full-time as a social media specialist for a government department and pursues her entrepreneurial interests on the side. Aisha continued her online business, gaining success and steady growth. Sana, a single mother who had shifted from a Science, Technology, Engineering, and Mathematics (STEM) themed clothing line to an eco-friendly e-commerce business, left entrepreneurship to pursue her career and is now the chief operating officer for a charity focused on East African refugees. Zarina, a Palestinian who concentrates on arts, moved from entrepreneurial goals to teaching functional skills.

Due to constraints during the COVID-19 pandemic, tracking all the participants' progress was impossible. Nonetheless, two of the mentees enrolled in a Foundation year at a nearby university, pursuing studies in childcare and nursing. Another mentee, Maryam, who once aspired to launch her food truck, faced health issues which sidelined her entrepreneurial plans. She is now employed by a Syrian businessman and, alongside her husband, operates his food truck. Yet another mentee secured employment as a delivery person for an online food ordering company.

Entrepreneurship often transcends the tangible success of a business venture. Though the workshop and mentoring programme did not translate to immediate venture success, its empowering effect on individuals, especially women, can be transformative. This empowerment and confidence-building journey can vividly be seen through Sana's evolution. In 2019, Sana described a moment of deep vulnerability and uncertainty: "*I had no confidence. I remember volunteering for a race equality charity. I couldn't do the task given to me to make phone calls. I physically couldn't make the phone call; I was so nervous.*" Such hesitation and lack of self-belief starkly contrast with her reflections from 2023, where she confidently states, "*Throughout my professional career and entrepreneurial journey, I've had the opportunity to take part in various conferences, pitch competitions, and events, each fuelled by my passion for refugee issues, women's empowerment, and sustainability and innovation.*" Even if entrepreneurship is not the end goal for every individual, its empowering journey can undeniably serve as a platform for personal growth and building self-confidence.

Advancing entrepreneurship refugee research

There is a consistent call to develop a gender-aware framework for women's entrepreneurship and to examine contextual factors (Brush et al., 2009; Henry et al., 2016; Welter, 2011). This chapter advances the current discourse on gender and entrepreneurship by showing a case example of how an entrepreneurship workshop can be gender-aware and deliberate on the unique situations of refugee women. Through a supportive environment that eliminated barriers to participation and using mindfulness as a strategy to work with vulnerable women in a workshop setting, we addressed women's distinctive needs and challenges, particularly women refugees. By creating a women-only space, providing on-site childcare, addressing the education and cultural barriers, and offering networking and mentoring opportunities, the workshop enabled refugee women to overcome the obstacles to entrepreneurship and progress in their goals. It also opens a new avenue of research to develop more studies on refugee integration to explore the effectiveness of women-only entrepreneurship workshops and programmes and the provision of on-site childcare for women refugees as strategies for promoting their economic and social integration.

This chapter features the role of refugee women as contributors rather than beneficiaries in a support programme, suggesting a different approach to developing entrepreneurial prospects in the refugee community. Women entrepreneurs who were refugees were asked to facilitate the workshop and become a mentor to other refugee women seeking to start a business. Currently, there is a lack of research looking at the contributions of refugees in supporting each other. Findings from this chapter reveal a strong sense of collectiveness and willingness to help among refugee women. Using their lived experiences and entrepreneurial journey, the women mentors developed self-confidence and empowerment when they offered to support nascent entrepreneurs. Hence, this chapter expands the boundaries of refugee entrepreneurship research by showing the societal and community impacts provided by the refugee women who act as mentors and workshop curators.

Moving forward, it would be valuable to investigate the outcomes of such workshops. While funders and policymakers would be keen to evaluate the impact of entrepreneurship programmes using the number of successful startups, it is also crucial to assess the transformative power gained by the women, such as the transfer of knowledge and skills between the participants and the overall social and economic benefits for the refugee community. Our findings show that some have successfully integrated into society by pursuing higher qualifications and securing permanent employment, producing social and economic benefits for the UK society. Additionally, exploring the challenges and barriers faced by refugee women entrepreneurs, such as language barriers, lack of access to resources and networks, and discrimination, could help identify ways to support and empower this group further.

The findings of this chapter offer valuable insights for policymakers and practitioners working to support refugee women entrepreneurs. For example, establishing women-only spaces can create a supportive and inclusive environment that addresses refugee women's unique needs and challenges in accessing entrepreneurship opportunities. It could involve providing language support, training, mentorship, and networking opportunities tailored to refugee women entrepreneurs' needs. On-site childcare provision is crucial to removing barriers preventing refugee women with children from accessing valuable training and networking opportunities. Policymakers and practitioners could consider implementing childcare services at entrepreneurship events and workshops to make it easier for refugee women with children to attend and engage with the content without worrying about childcare. The findings also underscore the effectiveness of eliminating educational and cultural barriers through mindfulness and intercultural dialogue. It is crucial to provide culturally sensitive training and mentorship keeping in mind refugee women's unique challenges. By addressing the specific needs and challenges that women refugees face, effective programmes can be crafted to empower them to achieve their entrepreneurial goals, contribute to their communities, and build more inclusive and equitable societies. Finally, it is essential to recognise refugee women as contributors and empower them to share their skills and knowledge. Policymakers and practitioners should work collaboratively to create opportunities for refugee women to showcase their skills and knowledge, whether through networking events, mentoring programmes, or other initiatives. It can help build confidence and provide a platform for refugee women entrepreneurs to share their experiences and expertise.

The workshop emphasised the significance of inclusive, equitable, and culturally sensitive approaches to entrepreneurship training, which can empower women and promote gender equality. Although the workshop was successful, the organiser identified areas for improvement, such as including a specialist in each group to fill any knowledge gaps the facilitators might have. Additionally, the need for in-depth learning could be met by extending the workshop and incorporating more specialised sessions. One of the authors has developed meaningful relationships with several participants and has been continuously tracking their progress. These relationships will form the basis of a longitudinal study examining the entrepreneurial journey of refugee women and determining the factors that influence their success or failure in becoming entrepreneurs.

References

Adeeko, N., & Treanor, L. (2022). Negotiating stigmatised identities: Enterprising refugee women in the United Kingdom. *International Small Business Journal*, *40*(1), 23–46. https://journals.sagepub.com/doi/pdf/10.1177/0266242621997033

Albrecht, C., Pérez, M.H., & Stitteneder, T. (2021). The integration challenges of female refugees and migrants: Where do we stand? In A. Narlikar, L. Flach, B. Hoekman, R. Wolfe, J. Matthes, & A. García-Herrero (Eds.), *CESifo Forum* (Vol. 22, No. 02, pp. 39–46). München: ifo Institut-Leibniz-Institut für. Wirtschaftsforschung an der Universität München.

Allsopp, J., Sigona, N., & Phillimore, J. (2014). *Poverty among refugees and asylum seekers in the UK: An evidence and policy review*. Birmingham: University of Birmingham, Institute for Research into Superdiversity. www.birmingham.ac.uk/Documents/college-social-sciences/social-policy/iris/2014/working-paper-series/IRiS-WP-1-2014.pdf

Apicella, L., Moreira, J., Zughool, S., Saad, S., Serdinšek, S., Bowman, S., & Kirakossian, S. (2021). Understanding the needs of migrant and refugee women in entrepreneurship and the creative sectors. *Erasmus & Anefore International Report, 101*, January 2021.

Asia Pacific Economic Cooperation (APEC) Project. (2013). *Access to trade and growth of women's SMEs in APEC developing economies: Evaluating business environments in Malaysia-Philippines-Thailand*. Available at: http://publications.apec.org/publicationdetail.php?pub_id1388 (accessed 3 March 2023).

Bloch, A. (2007). Refugees in the UK UK labour market: The conflict between economic integration and policy-led labour market restriction. *Journal of Social Policy*, *37*(1), 21–36. https://doi.org/10.1017/S004727940700147X

Brush, C.G., de Bruin, A., & Welter, F. (2009). A gender-aware framework for women's entrepreneurship. *International Journal of Gender and Entrepreneurship*, *1*(1), 8–24. https://doi.org/10.1108/17566260910942318

Clutterbuck, D. (2014). *Everyone needs a mentor*. London: CIPD Publishing.

Coate, K., & Howson, C.K. (2016). Indicators of esteem: Gender and prestige in academic work. *British Journal of Sociology of Education*, *37*(4), 567–585. https://doi.org/10.1080/01425692.2014.955082

Crompton, B. (2012). *The effect of business coaching and mentoring on small-to-medium enterprise performance and growth* (Doctoral dissertation, RMIT University). https://researchrepository.rmit.edu.au/esploro/outputs/9921858957601341

Dlaske, K. (2022). Language, (em)power(ment) and affective capitalism: The case of an entrepreneurship workshop for refugees in Germany. *International Journal of the Sociology of Language*, *2022*(276), 69–91. https://doi.org/10.1515/ijsl-2021-0092

Gimmon, E. (2014). Mentoring as a practical training in higher education of entrepreneurship. Education +Training, 56(8–9), 814–825.

Goodfellow, M. (2020). *Hostile environment: How immigrants became scapegoats*. London: Verso Books.

Gower, S., Jeemi, Z., Wickramasinghe, N., Kebble, P., Forbes, D., & Dantas, J.A. (2022). Impact of a pilot peer-mentoring empowerment program on personal well-being for migrant and refugee women in Western Australia. *International Journal of Environmental Research and Public Health*, *19*(6), 3338. https://doi.org/10.3390/ijerph19063338

Haase, H., & Lautenschläger, A. (2011). The 'teachability dilemma'of entrepreneurship. *International Entrepreneurship and Management Journal*, *7*, 145–162. https://link.springer.com/article/10.1007/s11365-010-0150-3

Henry, C., Foss, L., & Ahl, H. (2016). Gender and entrepreneurship research: A review of methodological approaches. *International Small Business Journal*, *34*(3), 217–241. https://journals.sagepub.com/doi/epub/10.1177/0266242614549779

Isaak, A. (2020). An explorative study of refugee entrepreneurship and start-up consulting in German-speaking Europe: A resource-based perspective. In M. M. Pellegrini, L. Gnan, H. Lundberg, M. Raith, L. Songini, & M. Starnawska (Eds.), *European Entrepreneurship Research and Practice: A Multifaceted Effort towards Integration of Different Perspectives* (pp. 23–54). Information Age Publishing, Inc.

Lewis, R., Sharp, E., Remnant, J., & Redpath, R. (2015). "Safe spaces": Experiences of feminist women-only space. *Sociological Research Online*, *20*(4), 105–118. https://doi.org/10.5153/sro.3781

Liebig, T., & Tronstad, K. (2018). Triple disadvantage?: A first overview of the integration of refugee women. *OECD Social, Employment and Migration Working Papers* (No. 216). Paris: OECD Publishing. https://doi.org/10.1787/3f3a9612-en.

Lovell, M.L., Tran, T., & Nguyen, C.D. (1987). Refugee women: Lives in transition. *International Social Work*, *30*(4), 317–325. https://doi.org/10.1177/002087288703000405

Man, T.W.Y., Berger, R., & Rachamim, M. (2022). A social constructivist perspective on novice entrepreneurial learning in business incubators. *International Journal of Emerging Markets*, *19*(5), 1281–1305. www.emerald.com/insight/content/doi/10.1108/IJOEM-11-2021-1784/full/html

Marchand, K., & Dijkhuizen, J. (2018). Entrepreneurship as a tool for a new beginning–Entrepreneurship training for refugees in a New Homeland. In N. Apostolopoulos, H. Al-Dajani, D. Holt, P. Jones, & R. Newbery (Eds.), *Entrepreneurship and the Sustainable Development Goals* (pp. 135–149). Emerald Publishing Limited. www.emerald.com/insight/content/doi/10.1108/S2040-724620180000008013/full/html

Mayblin, L., & James, P. (2019). Asylum and refugee support in the UK: Civil society filling the gaps?. *Journal of Ethnic and Migration Studies*, *45*(3), 375–394. www.tandfonline.com/doi/epdf/10.1080/1369183X.2018.1466695?needAccess=true

Megersa, K. (2020). Evidence from interventions to improve the economic self-sufficiency of refugee women. https://opendocs.ids.ac.uk/opendocs/handle/20.500.12413/15383

Meister, A.D., & Mauer, R. (2019). Understanding refugee entrepreneurship incubation–An embeddedness perspective. *International Journal of Entrepreneurial Behavior & Research*, *25*(5), 1065–1092. www.emerald.com/insight/content/doi/10.1108/IJEBR-02-2018-0108/full/pdf?title=understanding-refugee-entrepreneurship-incubation-an-embeddedness-perspective

Mulvey, G. (2010). When policy creates politics: The problematizing of immigration and the consequences for refugee integration in the UK. *Journal of Refugee Studies*, *23*(4), 437–462. https://academic.oup.com/jrs/article/23/4/437/1530930

Onjewu, A.K.E., Haddoud, M.Y., & Nowiński, W. (2021). The effect of entrepreneurship education on nascent entrepreneurship. *Industry and Higher Education*, *35*(4), 419–431. https://doi.org/10.1177/0950422221101403

Pruett, M. (2012). Entrepreneurship education: Workshops and entrepreneurial intentions. *Journal of Education for Business*, *87*(2), 94–101. https://doi.org/10.1080/08832323.2011.573594

Richey, M., Randall, R., Brooks, J., & Ravishankar, M.N. (2021). UK Refugee Entrepreneurship Pilot Scheme. Center for Entrepreneurs, UK. https://ach.org.uk/sites/default/files/202103/UK%20refugee%20entrepreneurship%20pilot%20scheme.pdf

Rudhumbu, N., Du Plessis, E.C., & Maphosa, C. (2020). Challenges and opportunities for women entrepreneurs in Botswana: Revisiting the role of entrepreneurship education. *Journal of International Education in Business*, *13*(2), 183–201. https://doi.org/10.1108/JIEB-12-2019-0058

Solano, G., Wolffhardt, A., & Xhani, A. (2019). Measures to support early-stage migrant entrepreneurs. *MEGA handbook*. European Union's COSME Programme 2014–2020) www.researchgate.net/profile/Giacomo-Solano/publication/333642044_Measures_to_support_migrant_entrepreneurs/links/5cf8dc5ca6fdcc847508b81f/Measures-to-support-migrant-entrepreneurs.pdf

Street, C.P., Ng, P.Y., & Al-Dajani, H. (2022). Refugee women business mentors: New evidence for women's empowerment. *Sustainability*, *14*(15), 9154. https://doi.org/10.3390/su14159154

Sullivan, R. (2000). Entrepreneurial learning and mentoring. *International Journal of Entrepreneurial Behavior & Research*, *6*(3), 160–175. www.emerald.com/insight/content/doi/10.1108/13552550010346587/full/pdf?title=entrepreneurial-learning-and-mentoring

Terjesen, S., & Sullivan, S. E. (2011). The role of developmental relationships in the transition to entrepreneurship: A qualitative study and agenda for future research. *Career Development International*, *16*(5), 482–506. www.emerald.com/insight/content/doi/10.1108/13620431111168895/full/pdf?title=the-role-of-developmental-relationships-in-the-transition-to-entrepreneurship-a-qualitative-study-and-agenda-for-future-research

United Nations Conference on Trade and Development (UNCTAD). (2018). Policy guide on entrepreneurship for migrants and refugees. Available at: https://unctad.org/en/PublicationsLibrary/diae2018d2_en.pdf

Van Kooy, J. (2016). Refugee women as entrepreneurs in Australia. *Forced Migration Review*, *53*, 71–73. www.fmreview.org/community-protection/vankooy

Webber, F. (2019). On the creation of the UK's 'hostile environment'. *Race & Class*, *60*(4), 76–87. https://journals.sagepub.com/doi/abs/10.1177/0306396819825788

Welter, F. (2011). Contextualizing entrepreneurship—Conceptual challenges and ways forward. *Entrepreneurship Theory and Practice*, *35*(1), 165–184. https://journals.sagepub.com/doi/epub/10.1111/j.1540-6520.2010.00427.x

Willis, L., & Daisley, J. (1997). Women's reactions to women-only training. *Women in Management Review*, *12*(2), 56–60. https://doi.org/10.1108/09649429710162811

Yuval-Davis, N., Wemyss, G., & Cassidy, K. (2018). Everyday bordering, belonging and the reorientation of British immigration legislation. *Sociology*, *52*(2), 228–244. https://journals.sagepub.com/doi/epub/10.1177/0038038517702599

Section 5

Ecosystem and institutional role in refugee entrepreneurship

The final section includes chapters that elaborate on the entrepreneurial ecosystem. The chapters discuss the role of different types of institutions, such as the civil society, the private sector, and the government. The five chapters in this section highlight that these institutions play different roles in developing a supportive environment for refugee entrepreneurship (RE).

Terstriep et al. in Chapter 17 provide a macro view of Europe-wide support infrastructure, as in the entrepreneurial ecosystems and how these can enable RE. The authors emphasise the reciprocal interactions between the regional context and RE. They further emphasise the importance of bridging services, that is, programmes and initiatives that bridge the gap and misalignments between REs and their environment and connect them to actors and opportunities in the ecosystem.

Hatipoglu in Chapter 18 studies Syrian refugees' economic integration in Türkiye and explores how civil society organisations fill service needs. The author finds that civil society organisations facilitate the economic integration of refugees by addressing information asymmetries, expanding enterprises' demand and supply capability, and the survival of enterprises. This chapter illustrates what type of entrepreneurial service these organisations provide and how they initiate and facilitate RE.

In Chapter 19, Chowdhooree and Ferdaus outline a case study of a private-sector entrepreneurial initiative that targets displaced women at Rohingya refugee camp in Bhasan Char, Bangladesh. This initiative, a garment and fashion item production centre operated by a fashion house, is at the incubation stage. The case study elaborates on the opportunities and challenges – economic, social, cultural, and ethical – associated with this business model.

Next, in Chapter 20, Bizri points out the importance of "entrepreneurial alertness". The chapter emphasises that governments need to coordinate and synchronise the fragmented efforts so that the social enterprises could better support RE. This can be done through ecosystem scanning, associating, and evaluating opportunities for synergy. The author advocates for creating policies, bodies, and systems that facilitate synergistic effects.

DOI: 10.4324/9781003368540-21

In the final chapter of this section (Chapter 21), Iannone et al. use entrepreneurial ecosystem-related concepts and theories to propose a forward strategy for multileveled and multidirectional research. The core argument of this chapter is that refugee entrepreneurs are shaped by, and simultaneously shape, their new environments through dynamic processes of co-construction and co-development. The authors propose a conceptual model as a basis for developing future RE research.

17 Does context matter?

Towards a supportive entrepreneurial ecosystem for refugee entrepreneurship

Judith Terstriep, Alexandra David, and Michelle Richey

Introduction

New approaches to managing and resettling large groups of refugees are desperately needed in an "era of displacement" (Betts, 2021), where more than 1% of the world's population are forced to leave their homes. There is a growing recognition that the prevailing global refugee system, primarily reliant on humanitarian aid, has become insufficient. The World Bank (2018) forecasts that 143 million refugees will be displaced by 2050 through conflicts, civil unrest, and climate emergency. To that extent, Europe has recently refocused attention on the role of refugee entrepreneurs, partly fuelled by the ongoing Ukraine conflict. Notably, in February 2022, the arrival of Ukrainian refugees in Germany alone surpassed that of refugees from all other nationalities by nearly fourfold, marking a striking 6.5-fold increase compared to the influx of Syrian refugees in December 2015.

Adding to this, in certain countries, refugees face an average waiting period of 17–20 years for a mandate (World Bank, 2018). The substantial influx of refugees poses multifaceted challenges for European policymakers tasked with providing housing, education, and healthcare and facilitating social integration. A key facet of integration is refugees' access to labour markets, as it not only cultivates dignity and security but also unleashes their innate human potential and creativity (David & Coenen, 2017; Riemsdijk & Alexsson, 2021). To enhance sustainability amid the mounting number of refugees, it is essential to complement humanitarian aid with opportunities that enable refugees to harness their innate talents and skills for dignified livelihoods (Richey et al., 2022; Richey & Brooks, 2023). Scholars underscore that refugees' rapid labour market integration is a catalyst for unlocking human potential, nurturing creativity, facilitating knowledge acquisition, and driving innovation (Cheung & Phillimore, 2013; Riemsdijk & Axelsson, 2021). It promotes meaningful and productive lives, enabling refugees to engage in society actively and give them a profound sense of security and dignity.

Refugee entrepreneurship is a recognised pathway towards self-reliance, economic independence, and social and labour market integration (David & Coenen, 2017; Hartmann & Philipp, 2022; Ranabahu et al., 2021). It

DOI: 10.4324/9781003368540-22

empowers refugees to utilise their skills, knowledge, and creativity while addressing their (often) high unemployment rates (Degler & Liebig, 2017; Fóti & Fromm, 2016; Liebig & Rose Tronstad, 2018). Given the challenges refugees face in accessing decent employment (Lee et al., 2020; Nardon et al., 2021; Szkudlarek et al., 2021), many turn to self-employment as a means of integration and self-sufficiency (Desai et al., 2021; Harima et al., 2021; Hartmann & Phillip, 2022).

A burgeoning literature studies the unique attributes of refugee entrepreneurship (Bernard, 1976; Desai et al., 2021; Hauff & Vaglum, 1993; Newman et al., 2023; Ranabahu et al., 2022; Yeshi et al., 2024). Refugees' embeddedness, manifested in their networks and relations, distinguishes them from other migrant groups. Thus far, the prevailing framework for understanding refugee entrepreneurs' circumstances and opportunity structures has been mixed embeddedness theory (Kloosterman et al., 1999). However, this approach has faced criticism for its static and structurally deterministic nature (Harima, 2022; Sepulveda et al., 2011), failing to capture the dynamic interactions between refugee entrepreneurs and their contexts. Addressing these limitations is crucial to advancing understanding of refugees' opportunities, especially in a field that increasingly seeks to establish mutually beneficial systems for refugees and broader society (Betts, 2021). Therefore, exploring the concept of entrepreneurial ecosystems (EEs) as the context and breeding ground for refugee businesses offers a complementary perspective that may enhance our understanding and capacity to support refugee entrepreneurship.

While refugee entrepreneurship is a global phenomenon (Sinkovics & Reuber, 2021) and policymakers and researchers acknowledge its potential in host countries, the specific regulations, policies, and institutional voids of individual countries significantly shape the opportunities available to refugee entrepreneurs (Elo et al., 2022). In many countries, international and national organisations such as the European Commission, the Organisation for Economic Co-operation and Development (OECD), and regional governments have implemented policy initiatives to support refugee entrepreneurs (Solano, 2021). These initiatives include business start-up grants, mentorship and training programmes, and access to business networks and markets (David & Terstriep, 2023; Richey et al., 2022). However, there has been limited exploration of the spatial and contextual aspects of refugee entrepreneurship (David & Schäfer, 2022) and a lack of attention given to the impact of EEs and specialised support structures such as hubs and accelerators on refugee entrepreneurship (David & Terstriep, 2023; Desai et al., 2021; Harima, 2022). Against this backdrop, calls for a Europe-wide support infrastructure in the form of ecosystems are rising (Ashoka – Hello Europe, 2022; Richey et al., 2022). In response to these calls, this chapter discusses exemplary context specifics of different regions in Germany, the Netherlands, Ireland, and France and their impact on shaping a supportive infrastructure for refugee entrepreneurship.[1]

In the following, we start with a literature review to position our study in the scientific discourse of context specifics, regional innovation systems, and EEs. We then introduce the research design and present our main results. Finally, we conclude by discussing our findings and its consequences.

Context matters: Entrepreneurial ecosystems

Dating back to Marshall (1920), the notion of EE emphasises that context is pivotal for all entrepreneurs and their business endeavours (Audretsch & Belitski, 2021; Desai et al., 2021; Krüger & David, 2020). Entrepreneurial opportunities are rooted in specific spatial entities. The knowledge spill-over theory of entrepreneurship (KSTE) presents a promising approach to understanding the context-specific nature of refugees' entrepreneurial activities (Acs et al., 2013; Audretsch & Keilbach, 2007). Hence, Acs et al. (2013: 757) posit that the environment in which decisions are made can influence "one's determination to become an entrepreneur". KSTE rests on the assumption that new knowledge generated by firms and research institutions can create entrepreneurial opportunities when not fully exploited. Some of this knowledge – intentionally or not – spills over to entrepreneurial individuals sensing and utilising it to develop new business ideas. These knowledge spillovers find optimal utility in contexts where motivated individuals identify and exploit them. Anchored in economic geography, sociology, management, and organisational studies, an EE embodies such a conducive context.

The EE concept highlights regional factors that bolster firms' competitiveness and growth. A recent literature review by Wurth et al. (2022) noted that while the term EE is often used metaphorically in research and policies, emphasising symbiotic interdependence between entities like ecological systems, it also centres on productive outcomes emerging from these interdependent relationships (Harms & Groen 2017; Wurth et al., 2022). These outcomes encompass firm growth and broader societal benefits like social and ecological value. This focus on productive outcomes can reshape the discourse around refugee entrepreneurship, shifting the perception of refugees from being seen solely as a humanitarian burden to potential contributors within social systems (Ashoka, 2022).

Within the EE framework, entrepreneurs and other ecosystem actors share a reciprocal relationship with their contexts, continuously influencing and being influenced by them (Roundy et al., 2018). Although initial steps have been taken to comprehend the recursive nature of entrepreneurship following forced displacement (Shepherd et al., 2020), productive outcomes have been primarily recognised at the individual level, with limited extension to a broader set of actors or resettlement regions. EE research identifies several entities crucial for understanding how productive outcomes materialise in different regions, particularly emphasising organisations bridging micro- and meso-level actors and macro-level institutions. These boundary-spanning actors encompass accelerators (Goswami et al., 2018), universities (Schaeffer & Matt,

2016; Pugh et al., 2018), government departments (Motoyama & Knowlton, 2016), networks, and anchor organisations (Colombelli et al., 2019). Beyond facilitating exchanges across different ecosystem levels (micro-meso-macro), these actors also reap their own benefits from enhanced relational exchanges. Despite EE effectively identifying actors of interest and outlining their spatial contexts and outcomes, a consensus has yet to emerge regarding a comprehensive measure of ecosystem performance. Wurth et al. (2022) advocate for studies integrating output measures with process and interactional insights to provide real-time indications of ecosystem development and enable timely intervention if required.

The EE perspective opens new avenues for refugee entrepreneurship studies and policy. Focusing on recursive, interdependent relationships encourages an opportunity-centric outlook on how regions can gain from hosting resettled refugees and supporting their businesses. Notably, many EE actors relevant to refugee entrepreneurship have already been explored in refugee entrepreneurship studies, albeit in isolation rather than as part of a cohesive ecosystem.

In the following, we share the findings of a research project during the European refugee integration project "Enter to Transform (E2T)", funded by Interreg NWE and ask: How can regional EEs, as spatial contextual entities, better integrate refugee entrepreneurs?

Methodology

This study employs three existing indexes and a global survey to explore how favourable aspects of EEs can be made more accessible to refugee entrepreneurs. Initially, we focused on identifying European regions that meet two criteria: (1) receiving a significant number of forcibly displaced individuals and (2) having a substantial non-EU migrant population, as detailed in Table 17.1. The cross-country research combines desk research with secondary data analysis to illuminate the factors influencing regional competitiveness, innovation system performance, and regional social progress, which in turn shape the economic, social, cultural, and institutional contexts of EEs.

In line with the principles of purposive sampling, we also wanted to focus on regions where we were most likely to be able to gather data on refugees and other minority business owners' activities. As European indexes do not capture refugee business activity, we focused on regional levels of foreign-born self-employment (as a proxy for entrepreneurial activity) compared to host country nationals (see Table 17.2). Based on initial indications that several regions were particularly vibrant for self-employment among non-native populations, we focused more closely on seven NUTS-2 regions[2] in France (Île de France, Lorraine, and Pays de la Loire), Germany (Muenster and Arnsberg), the Netherlands (Noord Holland), and Ireland (Northern Western). We collected data on these regions during 2020 as part of the E2T project.

Table 17.1 Migration flows

Region	*TCNs*[a]	*Share of TP*[b]	*Immigration/asylum applications*[c]		*Share of EU-immigration*	
			2021	*2019*	*2021*	*2019*
France	3,735,239	5.5%	336,398	385,591	14.6%	12.8%
			103,790	*138,290*	*19.3%*	*21.9%*
Germany	6,122,299	7.4%	874,367	886,341	38.1 %	29.4%
			271,735	*142,450*	*50.6%*	*22.6%*
Ireland	299,242	6.0%	80,732	85,630	3.5%	2.8%
			2,615	*4,740*	*0.5%*	*0.8%*
Netherlands	565,821	3.2%	214,185	215,756	9.3%	7.1%
			24,725	*22,485*	*4.6%*	*3.6%*
EU-27	23,902,827	5.3%	2,297,117	3,018,198	n/a	n/a
			537,355	*631,285*		

Source: Eurostat, 2023a, 2023b (MIGR_IMM1CTZ, MIGR_ASYAPPCTZA).

[a]TCNs = Third country nationals on January 1, 2021; [b]TP = total population; [c]First time asylum applicants (shown in italics).

Next, we identified indices that could act as proxies for the contextual factors elaborated in the literature that generally support a thriving EE. We sought indices and survey measures that could expand on the bidirectional nature of contextual and individual EE factors (Guerrero et al., 2016) for refugee entrepreneurs. No single indices fit this requirement, but together, several indices unpacked characteristics of the regions of interest and shed light on how refugees might access supportive EEs.

The first index, the *European Regional Competitiveness Index* (RCI), offers a proxy for the attractive and sustainable formal and informal ecosystem characteristics that make a region appealing to any entrepreneur hoping to set up a new business. Competitiveness scores range from 0 to 100 (Annoni & Dijstra, 2019), with higher scores indicating a more attractive, competitive business environment. RCI data was complemented with data from the *European Regional Innovation Scoreboard* (RIS), which assesses the performance of innovation systems, indicating the innovation outputs of businesses in each region. Regions are scored against an EU average baseline score to indicate the relative innovativeness of an area, acting as a pull factor for potential entrepreneurs. Migrant and refugee entrepreneurship studies have suggested that entrepreneurs' access to EE opportunity structures is also subject to society's openness towards newcomers (Ram et al., 2013; 2017). In this regard, the *EU Social Progress Index (EU-SPI)* represents a direct measure of social progress. It tracks micro-level and cultural factors that impact refugee entrepreneurship, including societal tolerance and inclusiveness indicators (Annoni & Bolsi, 2020). It includes dimensions related to "basic human needs", "foundations of well-being", and "opportunity", scoring regions between 0 and 100, with higher scores indicating more tolerant, inclusive, and socially progressive regional attitudes.

Finally, we compared the index scores with a survey of global refugee entrepreneurship (Andres & Swain, 2019). While the survey differs in form from the other data sources, it offers a granular analysis of targeted business programming for refugee entrepreneurs in the focus regions. We take the existence of refugee entrepreneurship programming to indicate proactive efforts to integrate refugees into an EE. In the following section, we combine these four sources of regional contextual data to form a regional picture of EEs and refugee entrepreneurship support.

Regions' snapshot

Migration flows

Western Europe's migration history reveals distinct migrant cohorts within countries, often linked to colonial legacies (e.g., France and the Netherlands) or mid-20th-century guest worker recruitment strategies, as seen in Germany. Geopolitical and geo-economic shifts, along with events like the Syrian refugee crisis (2015–2017), the EU's eastward expansion, and the recent Ukraine war, have significantly influenced migration patterns.

In 2021, international immigration to the EU recorded 3.7 million arrivals, comprising 2.3 million individuals from non-EU countries and 1.4 million relocating within EU member states (Eurostat & EMN, 2022). As of January 1, 2021, approximately 23.9 million non-EU citizens resided in four EU member states, constituting 5.3% of the EU's population. Notably, once hesitant to consider itself a migration country, Germany had a non-EU citizen population share of 7.4% as of January 1, 2021, followed by Ireland at 6.0% and France at 5.5%. All three countries are above the EU average, the only exception in this study being the Netherlands, with a share of only 3.2%. Migration trends continue, evident in Germany's reception of 38.1% of EU-27 migrants and 50.6% of first-time asylum applicants in 2021, indicating their disproportionate share of non-EU citizens and their economic significance.

Despite migrants, including refugees, often being associated with a higher inclination towards entrepreneurship due to lower risk aversion, self-employment rates between 2019 and 2022 (Table 17.2) as a proxy for entrepreneurial activities demonstrate that this assumption does not always hold true.

In France and the Netherlands, self-employment rates of foreign-born populations are considerably higher than those of natives, while in Germany, they are about the same. In Ireland, self-employment rates of foreign-born populations exceed that of natives by 0.7 in 2019 to 1.5 percentage points in 2022. Despite Germany's overall low self-employment rate, GEM data for 2021 shows that at 14%, the "Total early-stage Entrepreneurial" (TEA)[3] rate of migrants was twice that of the native population (7%) (Sternberg et al., 2022). That is, persons not born in Germany will be significantly more prone

Table 17.2 Self-employment rates of non-EU citizens

Region	*2019a*		*2020*		*2021*		*2022*	
	FOR	*NAT*	*FOR*	*NAT*	*FOR*	*NAT*	*FOR*	*NAT*
France	6.0	4.2	5.7	4.3	6.0	4.5	6.6	4.7
Germany	3.9	3.9	3.3	3.5	3.5	3.5	3.5	3.4
Ireland	6.0	5.3	6.1	5.0	6.0	4.6	6.5	5.0
Netherland	11.4	7.1	10.9	7.3	9.2	6.9	11.6	7.2

Source: Eurostat (2023c, 2023d; LFSA_ESGACOB; MIGR_POP2CTZ); Authors' own calculation.

[a]Self-employment rates = Number of self-employed foreign-born (FOR) and natives (NAT) normalised by population of both groups.

to start a business or are in the process of doing so. It was interesting to see that although the self-employment rates of the foreign-born in Ireland exceed those of the natives, recruiting refugees for the mentoring activities planned in the E2T project was difficult due to a lack of trust and the spatial distribution of potential participants.

Regional competitiveness and innovativeness

The first two indices, the RCI and RIS, track and score what EE literature might label as formal and informal institutional dimensions. The *RCI* is split into three sub-categories. The first, BASICS, captures institutional, macroeconomic, infrastructural, and health-related factors that affect a region's overall quality of life. The second, EFFICIENCY, captures the quality of higher education, training, and lifelong learning. The final category, INNOVATION, is sensitive to a region's technological readiness, business sophistication, and overall innovative output. Collectively, these measures take the pulse of macro-level institutions and factors shaping entrepreneurs' and citizens' opportunities (see Figure 17.1).

The regions' aggregated RCI scores range from 97 (Nord Holland) to 55 (Lorraine) but with some dynamic variations and differences between regions. Notably, education levels in the regions correlate with benefits to regional productivity, growth, and entrepreneurial attainment. Noord-Holland stands out with a score of 97 in the education dimension, while the other regions score between 60 and 64. The existence of sizeable markets for trading also indicates vital opportunity structures for would-be entrepreneurs. In this dimension, Île de France (94) ranks first, while Northern Western records the lowest (37). Muenster, Arnsberg, and Noord-Holland closely follow Île de France, scoring between 86 and 81. In contrast, Lorraine and Pays de la Loire are lagging behind, with scores below the EU average of 65.

Technological readiness and business sophistication scores also denote the capabilities of existing businesses in these regions and their ability to respond to

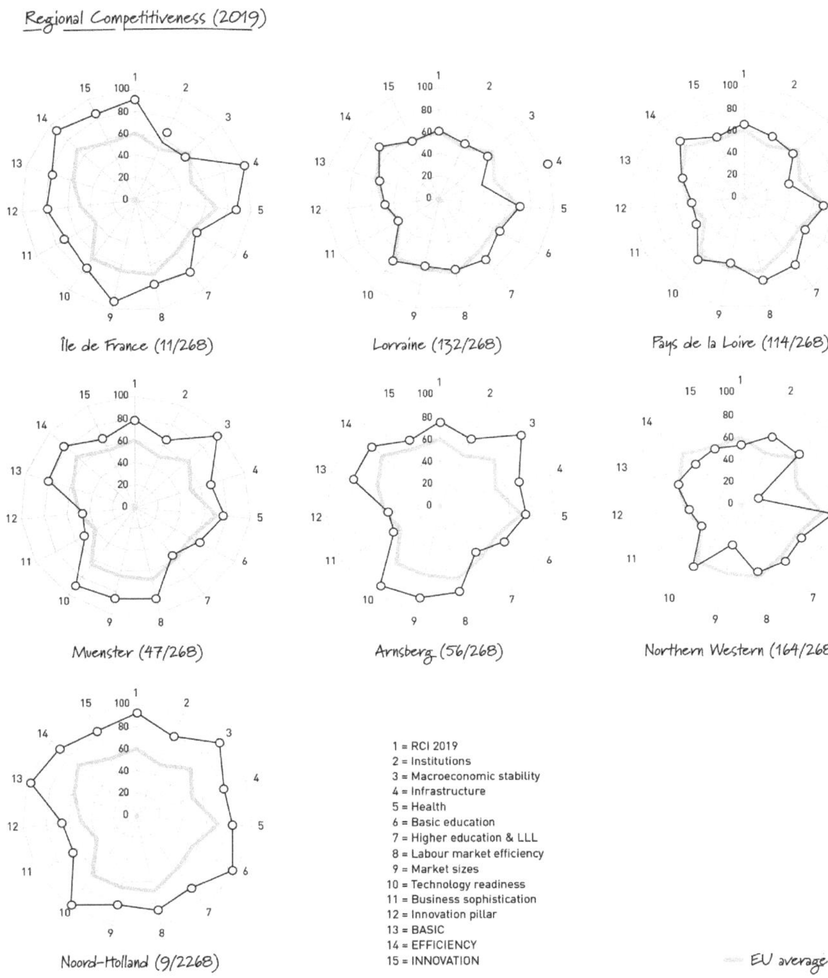

Figure 17.1 E2T regions' competitiveness indices.

Source: Authors' own compilation based on data from RCI 2019.

competitive pressures, such as new entrants and increased market competition. Noord-Holland stands out for its high technology readiness in households and enterprises, scoring 98. Muenster and Arnsberg closely follow with scores of 89. While all other regions also surpass the EU average of 65, Pays de la Loire lags with a value of 69. In the dimension of business sophistication, Île de France takes the lead. This dimension encompasses factors such as gross value added in sectors such as information and communications technology

(ICT) and financial/insurance activities, foreign direct investment, and economic activity clusters that facilitate knowledge spillovers. Understanding business sophistication is crucial for establishing support infrastructures for refugee entrepreneurial activities and comprehending a region's opportunity structures.

The *RIS* index examines innovative dynamics across regions in greater depth (see Figure 17.2). It scores regions against an EU average score and provides additional granularity across several innovation dimensions.

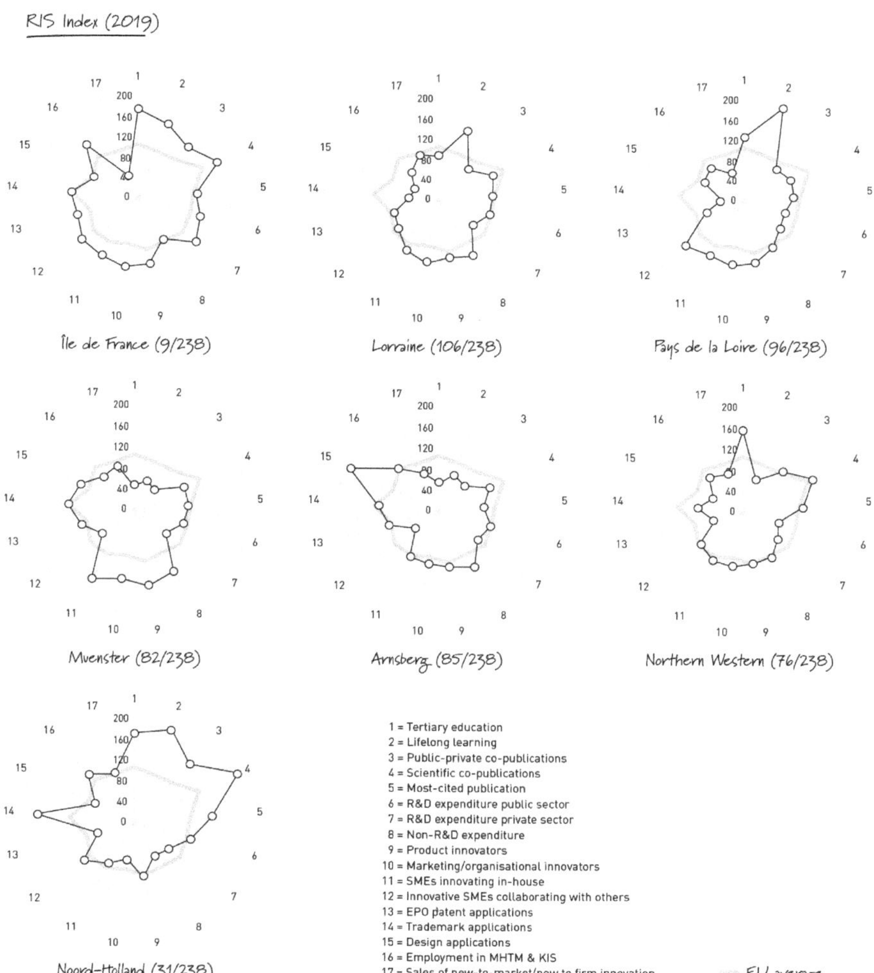

Figure 17.2 Innovation performance of E2T regions.

Source: Authors' own compilation based on data from RIS 2019.

Regarding overall regional innovation performance, Île de France stands out as one of the top ten regions among innovation leaders (rank 9), while Noord-Holland falls within the bottom one-third of this group, holding rank 31. Muenster (82), Arnsberg (85), and Northern Western (76) are in the middle one-third, while Pays de la Loire (96) and Lorraine (106) are located in the bottom one-third of strong innovators. Despite varying performance levels, all regions fall into one of the three innovator groups, demonstrating their diverse capabilities within the regional innovation system. The analysis shows that while regions perform well overall, their innovation profiles are somewhat distinctive, as depicted in Figure 17.2.

For example, business sector research and development expenditure (on equipment, patents, licenses, etc.) indicate differing levels of diffusion and commercialisation of innovations – Muenster takes the lead in this particular dimension, scoring 139.2% above the EU average. Interestingly, despite being in the "Innovation Leaders" group, Noord-Holland's performance is only moderate in some areas, such as "product innovators" with 72.9% of the EU average. Next to private investments, public sector research and development expenditure is pivotal in boosting a region's overall innovation performance by creating new opportunities. It is notably high in Île de France and Noord-Holland, with Northern Western performing moderately. Arnsberg, Lorraine, and Muenster also exhibit strong performances in this dimension, ranging from 102.6% to 90.1% of the EU average.

Considering the bidirectional relationship between entrepreneurship and regional competitiveness, regions with high competitiveness rankings, such as Noord-Holland and Île de France, provide favourable conditions for refugee entrepreneurial activities. Muenster and Arnsberg also offer a supportive framework, albeit with some limitations in the innovation pillar and business sophistication. In contrast, the Northern Western region faces multiple challenges, including market size, infrastructure, innovation, and sophistication. Interestingly, peripheral regions have been observed to offer unique opportunity structures for refugee entrepreneurs to establish businesses more quickly, with less competition among newly arrived individuals. Likewise, all regions have good innovation system performance, albeit with varying strengths and weaknesses.

Paying attention to these differences in contextual factors gives an idea of the latent opportunities that exist in areas that refugees resettle in and also the competitive nature of the EEs they will encounter. Highly technical and complex legal requirements for operating businesses have been identified as barriers to including refugees in formal entrepreneurship (Newman et al., 2023). This is not to say that refugees do not enter competitive industries and sectors, but that micro-level factors like levels of language, educational attainment, and cultural understanding can make or break attempts to access competitive, innovative regions on a level playing field with other entrepreneurs (see Chapter 2 in this book).

Regional social progress

Like the RCI, the EU-SPI is split into three sub-indices that characterise the informal, cultural conditions supporting quality of life and opportunity. These are BASIC factors, such as access to nutrition, shelter, and security; FOUNDATION factors, such as the acquisition of basic knowledge, health provision, and ICT access; and OPPORTUNITY factors, such as tolerance and inclusion, personal freedom and choice, higher education, and personal rights. The regional differences are depicted in Figure 17.3.

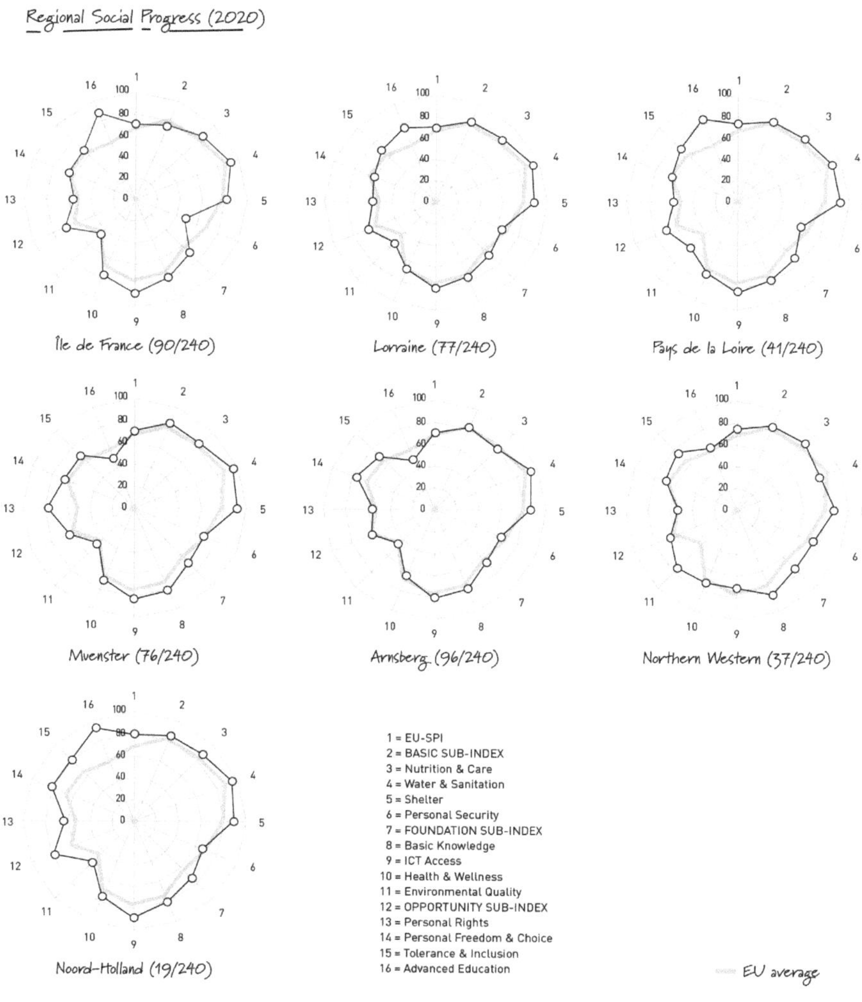

Figure 17.3 E2T regions' social progress.

Source: Authors' own compilation based on data from EU-SPI 2020.

Again, Noord-Holland ranks first with an SPI index of 80, followed by Pays de la Loire and Northern Western, with values of 75. Lorraine and Muenster rank third, each with an index of 72. Île de France and Arnsberg bring up the rear with values of 71. However, the SPI varies across the five regions, though all rank above the EU average SPI of 66.

Particular dimensions within the OPPORTUNITY sub-index, such as tolerance and inclusion, personal freedom and choice, are salient in refugee resettlement and hold significance in research on refugee resettlement and entrepreneurship. In these studies, the concept of self-determination, where individuals perceive themselves as the architects of their choices and opportunities, emerges as a salient motivating factor for refugees embarking on starting businesses (Richey et al., 2022).

Being a key indicator for refugees' business opportunities, Noord-Holland scores highest (79), followed by Pays de la Loire with a 10-point distance. Arnsberg is assigned the lowest value in the OPPORTUNITY sub-index (62), while dynamic variations are evident in the single dimensions. To exemplify, Muenster and Arnsberg share the highest score concerning personal rights (78). However, they rank lowest in advanced education (49), an area where Noord-Holland (93) and Île de France (88) excel. Significant regional variations regarding personal freedom and choice are also evident, encompassing factors such as freedom over life decisions and job opportunities closely tied to refugee entrepreneurial prospects. Tolerance and inclusion, comprising tolerance towards immigrants, are particularly pronounced in Noord-Holland (81) and Northern Western (77), whereas it is significantly lower in Île de France (66). Pays de la Loire and Lorraine scored 72 and 70, while Muenster and Arnsberg scored 68. This dimension encompasses intricate facets of social progress, rendering it difficult to improve through supportive measures.

Interestingly, a positive and high correlation exists between the OPPORTUNITY sub-index and gross domestic product (GDP) per capita (0.62) in the regions. In contrast, the dimension "tolerance and inclusion" declines with a growing population (–0.52). Table 17.3 summarises the findings from the data analysis.

Table 17.3 Summary of regional EEs

Region	*RCI 2019*	*RIS 2019*	*EU-SPI 2020*
Île de France (FR)	91	122.0	71
Lorraine (FR)	61	95.9	72
Pays de la Loire (FR)	66	98.4	75
Muenster (DE)	78	107.4	72
Arnsberg (DE)	77	106.0	71
Northern Western (IE)	53	109.0	75
Noord-Holland (NL)	93	128.9	80
EU average	*60*	*100.0*	*67*

Bringing the EU-SPI together with the RCI and RIS indicess suggests that the regional formal and informal institutions a refugee is likely to encounter are not necessarily well aligned. For example, although Île de France and Noord-Holland are strikingly similar in terms of regional competitiveness and the innovation system, EU-SPI data suggests that refugees are more likely to access relevant resources and networks in Noord-Holland due to its high scores in "tolerance and inclusion" and "personal freedom of choice". From the perspective of potential refugee entrepreneurs, this would make Noord-Holland well-aligned as an EE supportive and inclusive of refugees and Île de France less so. In addition, the EU-SPI opportunity dimension "tolerance and inclusion" implies varying levels of "social legitimacy" for refugees' entrepreneurial activities.

Refugee entrepreneurship research

Assessing whether supportive infrastructures effectively create opportunities for refugee entrepreneurs is essential to complement insights into the (mis) alignment of support features within EEs for refugees. Although no indices for refugee entrepreneurship currently exist, business support initiatives have emerged as a crucial component in establishing a supportive infrastructure for refugee entrepreneurs (David & Terstriep, 2023; Richey & Brooks, 2023). These targeted business support initiatives are often funded by macro-level institutions like governments and philanthropic organisations and executed by meso-level entities such as social enterprises and business networks, making them collaborative and proactive elements within an inclusive EE context for refugees.

Numerous reports, including the Global Refugee Entrepreneurship Study (GRES; Andres & Swain, 2019), assessed refugee business support globally and provided insights into such initiatives' characteristics, accomplishments, and potential worldwide, focusing on the four countries featured in this chapter. The GRES highlights the misalignment of formal and informal institutions within an ecosystem, underscoring the necessity of targeted refugee business support. Notably, 78% of the support programmes surveyed were in Europe (Andres & Swain, 2019), primarily in countries, though not necessarily the specific regions covered by the indices. The surveyed refugee entrepreneurs generally aligned with the formal characteristics previously described, boosting high levels of educational attainment (75%), prior experience (50%) across various business sectors, and strong motivation to establish businesses in their resettled areas. However, they also encountered obstacles to their entrepreneurial aspirations, with limited access to finance and a limited understanding of European markets being the most significant challenges (Andres & Swain, 2019). Targeted refugee business programmes played a critical role in mitigating these challenges through workshops, mentoring, and funding support, with consistently high demand for these programmes compared to available slots. Over a 10-year period, the surveyed programmes collectively supported the launch of 12,960 new refugee businesses, generating 18,127 new jobs. Nevertheless, these programmes reported challenges related to their reliance on government funding and the sustainability of their support initiatives. Overall, the report vividly illustrates the collaborative and proactive EE efforts required to make regional entrepreneurial opportunities accessible and inclusive for refugee newcomers seeking to rebuild their livelihoods through entrepreneurship.

Discussion and conclusions

In this chapter, we asked how regional EEs can better integrate refugee entrepreneurs. Using EE as a theoretical, sensitising lens, we mapped the ecosystems of seven exemplary European EEs in Germany, France, the Netherlands, and Ireland. In doing so, we identified that significant misalignments between formal and informal ecosystem actors could limit the impact of refugee entrepreneurship. In line with earlier findings (David & Schäfer, 2022; Yamamura & Lassalle, 2022), illustrating the seven regions' different economic, social, and cultural baselines, our outcomes underline that context matters in refugee entrepreneurship as it shapes opportunity structures.

Furthermore, our findings suggest not only the "hard" factors of regional competitiveness and the innovation system that shape refugee entrepreneurship but also the "soft" factors that allow refugee entrepreneurs to tap into these potentials by gaining access to the EE. These factors are important in building inclusive EEs, allowing refugees to establish business networks and benefit from economic growth by gaining equal opportunities with proper support through actors' motivation (Lassalle et al., 2020; Zhao et al., 2021). Resources, including knowledge spillovers accessed through refugees' embeddedness, will help the entrepreneurs sense and seize their market potential and successfully launch their business ideas. However, rather than being static, entrepreneurship is a fluid process with changes over time in terms of business development and entrepreneurs' status quo. In the case of refugees becoming entrepreneurs, their recognition of citizenship changes their opportunities and perceptions. Institutional actors as part of the inclusive EE are needed to accelerate this process to drive recognition.

In line with the study by Zhao et al. (2021), we also underscore the importance of programmes and targeted initiatives that bridge misalignments and connect refugee entrepreneurs to other ecosystem actors and opportunities. The EE framework contributes to understanding and designing mutually beneficial resettlement outcomes in regions hosting refugees. When refugees' skills and talents match market demands, sustain social enterprises, and alleviate pressure on social welfare budgets, mutual benefits and functioning interdependence can be achieved. Consequently, we plead for a more fine-grained understanding of the socio-spatial circumstances experienced by refugees envisaging to start a business.

Notes

1 Regarding refugee entrepreneurship, we encompass all businesses established or operated by refugee migrants. For this discussion, refugees include individuals defined in Article 1 of the 1951 Geneva Convention on refugees as those who have fled war, violence, conflict, or persecution and have crossed international borders to find safety in another country (UNHCR, 2023).

2 NUTS-2 (Nomenclature of Territorial Units for Statistics) is a hierarchical system used by the European Union to divide regions for statistical purposes. NUTS-2 regions are the second level of hierarchy (Eurostat, 2022).

3 TEA captures the percentage of the working-age population (typically between 18 and 64 years old) who are either in the process of starting a new business or have recently started and are managing a business that is relatively new, typically less than 3.5 years old.

References

Acs, Z. J., Audretsch, D. B., & Lehmann, E. E. (2013). The knowledge spillover theory of entrepreneurship. *Small Business Economics*, *41*(4), 757–774. https://doi.org/10.1007/s11187-013-9505-9

Andres, F., & Swain, P. (2019). *Global refugee entrepreneurship survey 2019*. London: Centre for Entrepreneurs. https://centreforentrepreneurs.org/wp-content/uploads/2020/04/Global-Refugee-Entrepreneurship-Survey-2019-report.pdf (accessed 01 Sept. 2023).

Annoni, P., & Bolsi, P. (2020). The regional dimension of social progress in Europe: Presenting the new EU Social Progress Index. *Working Paper*, WP 06/2020. Luxembourg: Publications Office of the European Union.

Annoni, P., & Dijstra, L. (2019). The EU Regional Competitiveness Index 2019. *Regional and Urban Policy*. Luxembourg: Publications Office of the European Union.

Ashoka – Hello Europe. (2022). Transforming the field of migration through collaborative framework. *SSRN Electronic Journal*. https://doi.org/10.2139/ssrn.4250438

Audretsch, D. B., & Belitski, M. (2021). Towards an entrepreneurial ecosystem typology for regional economic development: The role of creative class and entrepreneurship. *Regional Studies*, *55*(4), 735–756. https://doi.org/10.1080/00343404.2020.1854711

Audretsch, D. B., & Keilbach, M. (2007). The theory of knowledge spillover entrepreneurship. *Journal of Management Studies*, *44*(7), 1242–1254. https://doi.org/10.1111/j.1467-6486.2007.00722.x

Bernard, W. S. (1976). Immigrants and refugees: Their similarities, differences, and needs. *International Migration*, *14*(4), 267–281. https://doi.org/10.1111/j.1468-2435.1976.tb00947.x

Betts, A. (2021). *The wealth of refugees: How displaced people can build economies*. Oxford: Oxford University Press.

Cheung, S. Y., & Phillimore, J. (2013). Refugees, social capital, and labour market integration in the UK. *Sociology*, *48*(3), 518–536. https://doi.org/10.1177/0038038513491467

Colombelli, A., Paolucci, E., & Ughetto, E. (2019). Hierarchical and relational governance and the life cycle of entrepreneurial ecosystems. *Small Business Economics*, *52*(2), 505–521.

David, A., & Coenen, F. (2017). Immigrant entrepreneurship - A chance for labour market integration of refugees? In A. David & I. Hamburg (Eds.), *Entrepreneurship and entrepreneurial skills in Europe: Examples to improve potential entrepreneurial spirit* (pp. 77–101). Opladen: Budrich.

David, A., & Schäfer, S. (2022). Spatial perspectives on migrant entrepreneurship. *ZFW – Advances in Economic Geography*, *66*(3), 131–136. https://doi.org/10.1515/zfw-2022-0033

David., A. & Terstriep, J. (2023) *Transformational hubs for recognised refugees – Policy recommendations by the Enter to Transform Project.* Gelsenkirchen: Institute for Work and Technology. 6. https://doi.org/10.53190/inno/202301

Degler, E., & Liebig, T. (2017). *Finding their way – Labour market integration of refugees in Germany.* Paris: OECD. www.oecd.org/els/mig/Finding-their-Way-Germany.pdf

Desai, S., Naudé, W., & Stel, N. (2021). Refugee entrepreneurship: Context and directions for future research. *Small Business Economics*, *56*(3), 933–945. https://doi.org/10.1007/s11187-019-00310-1

Elo, M., Täube, F. A., & Servais, P. (2022). Who is doing "transnational diaspora entrepreneurship"? Understanding formal identity and status. *Journal of World Business*, *57*(1). https://doi.org/10.1016/j.jwb.2021.101240

Eurostat. (2022). *Statistical regions in the European Union and partner countries. NUTS and statistical regions 2021.* Luxembourg: Publications Office of the European Union. https://ec.europa.eu/eurostat/documents/3859598/15193590/KS-GQ-22-010-EN-N.pdf/82e738dc-fe63-6594-8b2c-1b131ab3f877?t=1666687530717 (accessed: 29 April 2023).

Eurostat. (2023a). *Immigration by age group, sex and citizenship (migr_imm1ctz).* https://doi.org/ 10.2908/migr_imm1ctz (accessed April 2023)

Eurostat. (2023b). *Asylum applicants by type, citizenship, age and sex – annual aggregated data (migr_asyappctza*). https://doi.org/10.2908/MIGR_ASYAPPCTZA (accessed April 2023).

Eurostat. (2023c). Self-employment by sex, age and country of birth (1 000) (lfsa_esgacob). https://doi.org/10.2908/LFSA_ESGACOB (accessed April 2023).

Eurostat. (2023d). Population on 1 January by age, sex and broad group of citizenship (migr_pop2ctz). https://doi.org/10.2908/MIGR_POP2CTZ (accessed April 2023).

Eurostat & EMN (European Migration Network) (2022). *Annual report on migration and asylum 2021. Statistical Annex.* Luxembourg: Publications Office of the European Union. https://doi.org/10.2785/790447

Fóti, K., & Fromm, A. (2016). *Approaches to the labour market integration of refugees and asylum seekers.* Luxembourg: Publications Office of the European Commission. https://doi.org/10.2806/42171

Goswami, K., Mitchell, J. R., & Bhagavatula, S. (2018). Accelerator expertise: Understanding the intermediary role of accelerators in the development of the Bangalore entrepreneurial ecosystem. *Strategic Entrepreneurship Journal*, *12*(1), 117–150. https://doi.org/10.1002/sej.1281

Guerrero, M., Urbano, D., & Fayolle, A. (2016). Entrepreneurial activity and regional competitiveness: Evidence from European entrepreneurial universities. *The Journal of Technology Transfer*, *41*(1), 105–131. https://doi.org/10.1007/s10961-014-9377-4

Harima, A. (2022). Theorizing disembedding and re-embedding: Resource mobilization in refugee entrepreneurship. *Entrepreneurship & Regional Development*, *34*(3–4), 269–293. https://doi.org/10.1080/08985626.2022.2047799

Harima, A., Periac, F., Murphy, T., & Picard, S. (2021). Entrepreneurial Opportunities of Refugees in Germany, France, and Ireland: Multiple Embeddedness Framework. *International Entrepreneurship and Management Journal*, *17*(2), 625–663. https://doi.org/10.1007/s11365-020-00707-5

Harms, R., & Groen A. (2017). Loosen up? Cultural tightness and national entrepreneurial activity. *Technological Forecasting and Social Change*, *121*, 196–204. https://doi.org/10.1016/j.techfore.2016.04.13

Hartmann, C., & Philipp, R. (2022). Lost in space? Refugee entrepreneurship and cultural diversity in spatial contexts. *ZFW – Advances in Economic Geography*, *66*(3), 151–171. https://doi.org/10.1515/zfw-2021-0017

Hauff, E., & Vaglum, P. (1993). Vietnamese boat refugees: The influence of war and flight traumatization on mental health on arrival in the country of resettlement. A community cohort study of Vietnamese refugees in Norway. *Acta Psychiatrica Scandinavica*, *88*(3), 162–168. https://doi.org/10.1111/j.1600-0447.1993.tb03432.x

Kloosterman, R., van der Leun, J.P. & Rath, J. (1999). Mixed embeddedness: (In)formal economic activities and immigrant businesses in the Netherlands. *International Journal of Urban and Regional Research*, *23*(2), 252–266. https://doi.org/10.1111/1468-2427.00194

Krüger, D., & David, A. (2020). Entrepreneurial education for persons with disabilities—A social innovation approach for inclusive ecosystems. *Frontiers in Education*, *5*, Article 3. https://doi.org/10.3389/feduc.2020.00003

Lassalle, P., Johanson, M., Nicholson, J. D., & Ratajczak-Mrozek, M. (2020). Migrant entrepreneurship and markets: The dynamic role of embeddedness in networks in the creation of opportunities. *Industrial Marketing Management*, *91*, 523–536. https://doi.org/10.1016/j.indmarman.2020.04.009

Lee, E. S., Szkudlarek, B., Nguyen, D. C., & Nardon, L. (2020). Unveiling the canvas ceiling: A multidisciplinary literature review of refugee employment and workforce integration. *International Journal of Management Reviews*, *22*(2), 193–216. https://doi.org/10.1111/ijmr.12222

Liebig, T., & Rose Tronstad, K. (2018). Triple disadvantage? A first overview of the integration of refugee women. *OECD Social, Employment and Migration Working Papers*, No. 216. Paris: OECD. https://doi.org/10.1787/3f3a9612-en

Marshall, A. (1920). *Principles of Economics*. London: Macmillan.

Motoyama, Y., & Knowlton, K. (2016). From resource munificence to ecosystem integration: The case of government sponsorship in St. Louis. *Entrepreneurship & Regional Development*, *28*(5–6), 448–470. https://doi.org/10.1080/08985626.2016.1186749

Nardon, L., Zhang, H., Szkudlarek, B., & Gulanowski, D. (2021). Identity work in refugee workforce integration: The role of newcomer support organizations. *Human Relations*, *74*(12). https://doi.org/10.1177/0018726720949630

Newman, A., Macaulay, L., & Dunwoodie, K. (2023). Refugee entrepreneurship: A systematic review of prior research and agenda for future research. *International Migration Review*, *0*(0). https://doi.org/10.1177/01979183231182669

Pugh, R., Lamine, W., Jack, S., & Hamilton, E. (2018). The entrepreneurial university and the region: What role for entrepreneurship departments? *European Planning Studies*, *26*(9), 1835–1855. https://doi.org/10.1080/09654313.2018.144755

Ram, M., Jones, T., Edwards, P., Kiselinchev, A., Muchenje, L., & Woldesenbet, K. (2013). Engaging with super-diversity: New migrant businesses and the research-policy nexus. *International Small Business Journal*, *31*(4), 337–356. https://doi.org/10.1177/0266242611429979

Ram, M., Jones, T., & Villares-Varela, M. (2017). Migrant entrepreneurship: Reflections on research and practice. *International Small Business Journal: Researching Entrepreneurship, 35*(1), 3–18. https://doi.org/10.1177/0266242616678051

Ranabahu, N., De Vries, H. P., & Basharati, Z. (2021). The economic integration of women refugee entrepreneurs in New Zealand. In M. McAdam & J. Cunningham (Eds.), *Women and Global Entrepreneurship* (pp. 64–80). New York: Routledge.

Ranabahu, N., De Vries, H. P., & Basharati, Z. (2022). Refugee-owned small businesses: A typology for blended value creation. *International Migration*. https://doi.org/10.1111/imig.13072

Richey, M., & Brooks J. (2023). New development: From aid to empowerment—making refugee policy more sustainable. *Public Money & Management, 44*(1), 85–89. https://doi.org/10.1080/09540962.2023.2238912

Richey, M., Brooks, J., & Ravishankar, M. N. (2022). Building self-determination of disadvantaged groups: Insights from an entrepreneurship focused program for refugees. *International Journal of Entrepreneurial Behavior & Research*, *28*(7), 1828–1850. https://doi.org/10.1108/ijebr-10-2021-0806

Riemsdijk, M., & Axelsson, L. (2021). Introduction “Labour market integration of highly skilled refugees in Sweden, Germany and the Netherlands”. *International Migration*, *59*(4), 3–12. https://doi.org/10.1111/imig.12883

Roundy, P. T., Bradshaw, M., & Brockman, B. K. (2018). The emergence of entrepreneurial ecosystems: A complex adaptive systems approach. *Journal of Business Research*, *86*(1), 1–10. https://doi.org/10.1016/j.jbusres.2018.01.032

Schaeffer, V., & Matt, M. (2016). Development of academic entrepreneurship in a non-mature context: The role of the university as a hub-organisation. *Entrepreneurship & Regional Development*, *28*(9–10), 724–745. https://doi.org/10.1080/08985626.2016.1247915

Sepulveda, L., Syrett, S., & Lyon, F. (2011). Population superdiversity and new migrant enterprise: The case of London. *Entrepreneurship and Regional Development, 23* (7–8), 469–497. https://doi.org/10.1080/08985620903420211

Shepherd, D. A., Saade, F. P., & Wincent, J. (2020). How to circumvent adversity? Refugeeentrepreneurs’resilience in the face of substantial and persistent adversity. *Journal of Business Venturing*, *35*(4), 1–26. https://doi.org/10.1016/j.jbusvent.2019.06.001

Sinkovics, N., & Reuber, A. R. (2021). Beyond disciplinary silos: A systematic analysis of the migrant entrepreneurship literature. *Journal of World Business*, *56*(4), 101223. https://doi.org/10.1016/j.jwb.2021.101223

Solano, G. (2021). A level playing field for migrant entrepreneurs? The legal and policy landscape across EU and OECD countries. *International Migration*, *61*(2), 27–47. https://doi.org/10.1111/imig.12939

Sternberg, R. et al. (2022). *Global entrepreneurship monitor. Unternehmensgründungen im weltweiten Vergleich*. Länderbericht Deutschland 2021/22. Eschborn: RKW.

Szkudlarek, B., Nardon, L., Osland, J. S., Adler, N. J., & Lee, E. S. (2021). When context matters: What happens to international theory when researchers study refugees. *Academy of Management Perspectives, 35*(3), 461–484.

The World Bank. (2018). Annual report. World Bank Group.

UNHCR. (2023). *Persons who are forcibly displaced, stateless and others of concern to UNHCR*. www.unhcr.org/refugee-statistics/methodology/definition/ (accessed: 3 April 2023).

Wurth, B., Stam, E., & Spigel, B. (2022). Toward an entrepreneurial ecosystem research program. *Entrepreneurship Theory and Practice, 46*(3), 729–778. https://doi.org/10.1177/1042258721998948

Yamamura, S., & Lassalle, P. (2022). Extending mixed embeddedness to a multi-dimensional concept of transnational entrepreneurship. *Comparative Migration Studies, 10*(14). https://doi.org/10.1186/s40878-022-00288-y

Yeshi, T., Harima, A., & Freiling, J. (2024). Resilience on an emotional rollercoaster: Refugee entrepreneurship under adversity. *European Management Journal, 42*(2), 173–185. https://doi.org/10.1016/j.emj.2022.12.009

Zhao, W., Wang, A., Chen, Y., & Liu, W. (2021). Investigating inclusive entrepreneurial ecosystem through the lens of bottom of the pyramid (BOP) theory: Case study of Taobao village in China. *Chinese Management Studies, 15*(3), 613–640. https://doi.org/10.1108/CMS-05-2020-0210

18 The contribution of civil society organisations to refugee entrepreneurship in Türkiye

Burcin Hatipoglu

Introduction

This chapter identifies the gaps in the institutional environment for Syrian refugees' economic integration in Türkiye and explores how civil society organisations (CSOs) address some of these gaps. CSOs refer to all the non-state actors in the institutional environment. Refugee entrepreneurship is a relatively new phenomenon in the nation, and in their attempts to integrate refugees into the local markets, CSOs seek strategies to address a social problem in this specific context by filling an institutional void (Hesse et al., 2019).

Ideally, as the primary responsible agency, the state should enable an effective refugee integration process supported by its policies and institutions. In Türkiye's case, the mismatch between the legal frameworks, the refugees' needs, and the institutional framework's inadequacies limits the refugees' participation in the formal workforce (Kirisci & Kolasin, 2019; Knappert et al., 2018; Knappert et al., 2023; Sunata & Tosun, 2019). Many refugees start up new businesses because of their necessity to survive in a foreign land (Lehmann et al., 2022). The success of their businesses is embedded in the institutional environment and has implications for refugees, their communities, and the host society (Heilbrunn, 2019). Along with owners' attributes and motivations, external forces and various types of support offered to them are significant in shaping their entrepreneurship journey (Dana, 1997). Consequently, the active contribution of CSOs in the institutional environment for refugees' economic integration becomes vital, particularly for directing them towards legal and practical ways of finding work or starting up, managing, and maintaining businesses.

This chapter argues that there are gaps in supporting refugee employment/self-employment that are not adequately filled by state agencies, of which some are addressed by CSOs. In adopting a qualitative research design, the chapter exemplifies four cases that pursue initiatives and programmes for refugees in Türkiye. For multiple reasons, the nation is a unique context for examining the institutional environment and CSOs' response systems in refugee economic integration. The research objective of the chapter is to explore the gaps in the institutional system facing refugee entrepreneurs and demonstrate how CSOs

DOI: 10.4324/9781003368540-23

address some of these gaps for the benefit of refugees. The findings of this analysis may be partially generalisable to other nations that host refugees with practical value to their CSOs, governments, and experts.

Literature review

Institutional voids in the context of refugee economic integration

Institutional settings are not homogeneous, and complex relations exist between the organisations and their contexts. Institutional theory studies have established a growing interest in examining organisations and their context, emphasising the nature of contextual features, patterns of compliance, and how legitimacy is constructed (Greenwood et al., 2017). Likewise, contextualising the study of refugee integration and attending to the unique differences posed by internal and external factors and institutional systems have been widely recommended in the literature (Hesse et al., 2019; Karakulak & Faul, 2023; Maalaoui et al., 2020; Mackreath & Sağnıç, 2017; Olarewaju & Fashola, 2020).

The significance of the context in refugees' economic integration is confirmed in different settings that host refugees (Heilbrunn, 2019). A comparative study from ten European Union (EU) countries highlights the pitfalls of mainstreaming refugee integration and recommends policy innovation by learning from what works in other settings and assessing the appropriateness of these examples for each context (Scholten et al., 2017). For these reasons, adopting the institutional theory perspective is useful in the study in explaining the peculiarities of the context and the role of different institutions (e.g., government vs. civil society) (Hack-Polay & Igwe, 2019).

Institutions "are composed of established patterns of communications" (Lammers & Garcia, 2014, p. 195) and include formal and informal institutions and governance systems that shape how organisations behave (Williamson, 2000; Yang et al., 2020). A strong and enabling institutional system will lower the uncertainties for refugee entrepreneurs, ensuring their trust in its effectiveness and encouraging them to take risks to grow their businesses within the market (Mickiewicz & Olarewaju, 2020; Olarewaju & Fashola, 2020). In contrast, the absence or the inadequacy of institutional support can cause refugees to encounter obstacles when they navigate the market.

According to institutional theory, an organisation's actions are shaped by its institutional environment. What is a legitimate behaviour is determined by the social and cultural expectations in the context, and for those reasons, organisations will display limited rational behaviours rather than applying functional rationality (Lammers & Garcia, 2014). As they seek legitimacy while acting within accepted norms and values, they may be more involved in some areas than in others, leaving unattended gaps in the system. Mair and Marti (2009, p. 422) describe institutional voids as "situations where institutional arrangements that support markets are absent, weak, or fail to accomplish the role expected of them". In the context of refugees, the mismatching regulations and the absence of support systems can lead to these institutional voids. For example, the complexity of the regulatory system and governance structure can perplex refugees during new business establishment as they will need to interact with multiple governmental agencies, often using their limited local language skills (OECD/European Commission, 2021). When their support needs are unattended, it can result in refugees directing their job search efforts from formal to informal labour markets or not formalising their businesses, causing them to be excluded from many of their employment, legal, and welfare rights.

Specialised intermediaries will positively affect refugees by assisting them to access opportunities through training activities (e.g., skills training and languages), employment services (e.g., resume writing and assistance with work permits), or mentoring services (e.g., attending tenders and access to finance) (Garkisch et al., 2017; Verwiebe et al., 2019). They can also help them with setting up their businesses. For example, Harima et al. (2019) studied the business incubators for refugees in Germany and noted their crucial role in fostering entrepreneurship. Despite much room for improvement, the authors noted that the incubators offer structured entrepreneurial knowledge, guidance in understanding the institutional system, and encourage refugee entrepreneurs to tap into their social networks.

Following the institutional theory, various agents, such as regulators, intermediaries, and media, can communicate, monitor, and enforce social expectations on organisations (Greenwood et al., 2017). As such, CSOs are a cornerstone of the institutional context. They can inform government policy, support the government in policy implementation, and monitor compliance. CSOs are all those non-state actors that include local and international non-governmental organisations (NGOs), non-profit organisations (NPOs), solidarity and activist groups, and voluntary organisations (Garkisch et al., 2017).

Using the institutional perspective, CSOs will work alongside the government and support the government's and other institutions' efforts for effective migration systems (Bisignano & El-Anis, 2019; Knappert et al., 2023; Lehmann et al., 2022). To fulfil these aims, CSOs may partner with various agents in the context of the institutional environment, such as other CSOs, employer organisations, intermediaries, and local regulatory agencies (Karakulak & Faul, 2023; Özçürümez & Hoxha, 2022; Scholten et al., 2017).

The literature has elaborated on the services CSOs offer refugees within and outside the displacement camps, such as humanitarian aid, healthcare, education, psychological support, and legal services (Hack-Polay & Igwe, 2019). Although there is a growing emphasis on the role of CSOs in supporting the government for refugees' economic integration (Harima et al., 2019; Verwiebe et al., 2019), the effectiveness of their strategies and efforts is poorly addressed in the literature (Garkisch et al., 2017; Nardon et al., 2020; Scholten et al., 2017). We know little about which gaps CSOs target, with whom they build alliances, and how they offer their services. Yet it is understood that a strong institutional environment that enforces the rule of law and in which all relevant agents actively contribute to addressing complex challenges brought by forced migration is elemental for moving forward. Researchers and experts should have a realistic picture of the field and know what works and what does not work through systematic analysis (Hesse et al., 2019).

Context

Refugees in Türkiye

Since the start of the civil unrest in Syria, coupled with an open-door policy, Türkiye has become the largest refugee-hosting country globally, with 3.6 million refugees (United Nations High Commissioner for Refugees (UNHCR, 2022). The government had no prior experience of refuge influx on such a scale and hence it was unprepared for refugee integration and faced many challenges during refugees' mobilisation and settlement. As their stay in the country was considered temporary, the emphasis of the government, as well as the supporting organisations, focused more on providing humanitarian aid (needs-based) than their socio-economic integration (rights-based) (Mackreath & Sağnıç, 2017).

The refugees interviewed in this study reported struggling with inconsistent application at municipal and other local state agencies. Although the Directorate General of Migration Management was formed in 2013, and the government later introduced laws and regulations (Ministry of Interior, 2018), the disconnect across state agencies continued, generating new hurdles for the refugees and employers (Sunata & Tosun, 2019). The regulation for the employment of people under temporary protection status, introduced in 2016, was a good step towards refugee employment. However, it was cumbersome, requiring employers to register each employee; pay fees and renew permits annually; limit the number of Syrians to be employed; and prove that they could not find a qualified local employee for the same position (Kirisci & Kolasin, 2019).

Adding to the challenges, the refugees that stayed in the country were the less educated. While some skilled and educated refugees found home in Western countries via resettlement programmes (e.g., Canada and Sweden), many did not meet these countries' eligibility criteria and thus remained in Türkiye and other neighbouring countries. Integrating a low-skilled workforce is more of a challenge than a skilled one, putting added pressure on the institutional system.

CSOs in the context of refugee economic integration in Türkiye

State and civil society relations have been traditionally complicated in Türkiye, and the arrival of refugees added to the complications (Aras & Duman, 2019). From the start of the refugee arrival, intergovernmental organisations and a wide range of CSOs, including international humanitarian organisations, local NGOs, faith-based organisations, and grassroots initiatives, worked to support the needs of refugees in Türkiye (Mackreath & Sağnıç, 2017). Most international CSOs come from Western countries and are funded by their governments (Aras & Duman, 2019). Some local ones were newly set up to offer services to the refugees, whereas others adapted their ongoing work to meet refugee needs (Sunata & Tosun, 2019). They generally operate around the Syrian border and in cities with most refugees (e.g., Istanbul and Gaziantep), while under the government's close watch (Aras & Duman, 2019).

Following the unrest in Syria and the arrival of refugees to the nation, the Turkish government offered humanitarian services mainly in the camps near the border, and therefore it needed support for those refugees who lived outside of these camps. The CSOs successfully received funding from external sources and distributed it among refugee populations in and outside of camps (Mackreath & Sağnıç, 2017).

Initially, the government welcomed international and local CSOs of many types. However, a series of events occurred that challenged the government's authority, namely, the Gezi Park protests in Istanbul in 2013; the unrest during the Peace Process in Southeast Türkiye in 2015; the coup attempt in 2016; and the trials of Academicians for Peace. After these events the government became more sensitive to organised civil society activities and closed many of the locally founded CSOs that provided migration services (Boztaş, 2019; Sunata & Tosun, 2019). Those that remained were either ideologically aligned to the government or did not challenge the government's migration policies (Mackreath & Sağnıç, 2017). In their study of the Sultanbeyli district in Istanbul (a district with a high refugee population), Danış and Nazlı (2019) observed that over time, "pro-governmental organisations" have risen with close ties to the government.

International NGO operations were also restricted, requiring their permits to be renewed regularly and limiting which activities they would perform and in which cities. For example, language services can be only provided by CSOs that have approval from the Ministry of Education, and courses are to be taught by state-employed trainers (Bache, 2019). Similarly, for providing employment services, the CSOs must be approved by the Turkish Employment Agency (ISKUR), which takes time to pass through (Field Interviews).

Besides managing their relations with the government, CSOs face multiple challenges when providing services for migrants, such as securing funding from support institutions, their access to meaningful jobs, and difficulties in engaging businesses in the employment processes (Nardon et al., 2020). In Türkiye, scholars have criticised the effectiveness of the CSOs' migration services (Knappert et al., 2018). In particular, the lack of coordination among them, lack of transparency, and informality have been observed by the researchers (Aras & Duman, 2019; Danış & Nazlı, 2019; Mackreath & Sağnıç, 2017).

Sunata and Tosun (2019) grouped refugee NGOs in Türkiye into four: migrant NGOs, local NGOs, international NGOs, and professional

NGOs with local activities. Framing the value created for refugees by NGOs, Karakulak and Faul (2023) suggested that NGOs and their partnerships offer value creation activities to answer refugees' needs in three domains: necessities, capabilities, and social and political spheres. According to the authors, whether NGOs and their partners create value and which type of value is created depends on the framing of the refugees in each context. For example, the services offered will be limited when the government and the public do not support capability development for refugees.

There are gaps in refugee employment that are not adequately addressed by state agencies, which leaves space for other agents to perform. Therefore, the central question of this research is as follows: How do CSOs address the gaps in the institutional environment for the economic integration of refugees in Türkiye? Continuing this line of questioning, what actions do they take, and what approaches do they use? In answering these questions, the chapter aims to identify the role of CSOs in refugee economic integration in the context of their entrepreneurial activity.

Methods of the study

This chapter relies on a comparative study of four CSOs known for their proactive engagement in facilitating the integration of Syrian refugees and providing employment and entrepreneurship services in Türkiye.

Selection of participant organisations

The four CSOs were chosen as case studies based on desk research and field studies conducted during 2018–2019. The author connected with KEDV for her research on women's cooperatives, and the other three CSOs were contacted for her more comprehensive research on refugee economic integration. In data collection and analysis, the researcher took great care to establish trustworthiness regarding credibility, transferability, dependability, and confirmability (Lincoln & Guba, 1985). The extended involvement of the researcher during 2018–2023 with the CSOs enhances the study's credibility.

The sample CSOs offer services for refugees' labour market integration and entrepreneurship, which fit the replication logic of theoretical sampling in multiple case study designs (Eisenhardt & Graebner, 2007). The variety of the cases aims to explore which of the governance gaps are filled by the CSO and whether there are contrasting patterns. The four CSOs displayed differences in these criteria: (1) local versus international, (2) target groups, and (3) business forms. The brief descriptions of the sample CSOs are presented next.

Data collection

The multiple case study relies on data derived from face-to-face interviews and online meetings via Zoom (during COVID-19) with the managers and field officers of four CSOs; semi-structured interviews with the partner organisations of the CSOs, their local and refugee beneficiaries, documentary analysis that are collected over the years (2018–2023), and online panel meetings attended during COVID-19 (Table 18.1).

During the meetings, the interview guide functioned as a reference and a final check to ensure the completion of the interview. Using open questions, the interviews centred on the participants' first-hand experiences, perspectives, and suggestions regarding refugee employment/self-employment (Charmaz, 2006). Notes were taken during face-to-face meetings, and telephonic and virtual meetings were recorded with permission of the participants and transcribed to enhance the confirmability of the results. Informant triangulation was

Table 18.1 Case descriptions

Name of the CSO & headquarters and subsidiaries	*Type & founding year*	*Activities*	*Interviewee position & number of interviews*
Foundation for the Support of Women's Work (KEDV)-OXFAM Istanbul	Locally founded social enterprise (1986)	Working with grassroots women's groups in disadvantaged areas National scale	Field Officers & Cooperative Members (8)
Stitching United Work (SUW) Istanbul, Bursa and Izmir offices	Non-profit organisation (NPO), initially funded by the Dutch Minister of Foreign Trade and Development (2017)	It aims to get access to employment for refugees in cooperation with the respective parties.	General Manager & Human Resource (HR) Manager (4)
Building Markets (BM) Istanbul and Gaziantep	USA/Canada-origin NPO (2016)	Offers refugee entrepreneurs support services	General Manager & Field Officers (8)
SADA Women's Cooperative Gaziantep	Cross-sector partnership between the UN Women, ILO, and ASAM* (2019)	Employs refugee and local women as owners/members/employees	Field Officers, Board Members, Consultants & SADA Members (10)

Source: Author's own work.

*United Nations Entity for Gender Equality and Empowerment of Women (UN Women), the International Labor Organisation (ILO) and Gaziantep Metropolitan Municipality, and the Association for Solidarity with Asylum-Seekers and Migrants (ASAM).

ensured by sending transcripts to the interviewees to ensure confirmability of the findings (through member check) based on the interview answers.

The researcher achieved a comprehensive understanding of the phenomenon by employing complementary triangulation. This involved integrating findings from various data sources, such as programme leaders, project owners, social media, and secondary data. Additionally, the researcher utilised multiple data collection techniques, including observations, interviews, and documentary analysis. These collective efforts significantly enhanced the credibility of the study.

Data analysis

The gathered data has been initially synthesised into an activity report encompassing the initiatives and approaches of the CSOs in the field of refugees' economic integration from 2016 to 2023. The empirical data were analysed using grounded theory analytical procedures (Glaser, 2001). An inductive approach was utilised to code the textual data, forming subthemes that emerged during the coding process.

Coding and classifying data in qualitative content analysis require much interpretation by the researcher and can result in inconsistencies in the first coding round. Throughout this analytical process, the researcher read the activity report and asked whether the first-order themes (e.g., registry of businesses) describe the phenomena being examined (addressing the gaps) (Gioia et al., 2013). The sections that fit the second-order themes (e.g., disseminate information) were reviewed in the last reading round. Next, the second-order themes were abstracted to a higher level and gathered into aggregate dimensions (e.g., closing the gaps) (Table 18.2). After finalising the themes and aggregate dimensions, the analysis continued by revisiting the case study's relevant literature and writing. These were necessary steps as they contributed to the transferability criterion of qualitative rigour (Gioia et al., 2013), wherein the researcher could write thick descriptions of the four cases.

Findings

The review of the context-specific literature points to the gaps in the economic integration of refugees unaddressed by the central government in Türkiye. For example, a comprehensive report by TEPAV has shown that as low as 2% of refugees benefited from the job-finding services of ISKUR (national employment agency) (Güven et al., 2018). Only lately, through funding from external sources such as GIZ (German Cooperation Agency) and the World Bank, ISKUR ran several employment programmes for refugees and locals (GIZ, 2023; ISKUR, 2019). Furthermore, refugee entrepreneurs noted difficulties integrating into local supply chains, opening bank accounts, receiving credit from banks, and benefiting from entrepreneurial support programmes from governmental agencies (Building Markets, 2020a). Similar to the case

Table 18.2 Coding scheme

Examples and first-order themes	*Seond order themes*	*Aggregate themes*
Fieldwork Publish reports and newsletters on social media and websites Oral reports, presentations, and webinars	Collect information Disseminate information	Closing the gaps in information asymmetry
Networking events UN Women connecting SADA with international buyers BM preparing entrepreneurs to apply for grants	Awareness-raising activities Invite and engage them in local and international supply chains Invite and engage them in public procurement activities	Demand expansion for refugee-owned enterprises
Work permit costs Business registry costs Work from home and co-operatives. Digital marketing Registry of businesses	Financial support to businesses Develop new business models Training Mentoring	Supply expansion of refugee-owned enterprises
Orientation, coaching, on-the-job training programmes	Adaptation to local business and work environment	Survival of enterprises

Source: Author's own work.

of ISKUR, only very recently, KOSGEB (Small and Medium Enterprises Development Organisation of Türkiye) started entrepreneur support programmes for the refugees.

The following section presents the actions and approaches of CSOs, pointing to the gaps they address in the system.

Actions of CSOs for the economic integration of refugees

The gaps targeted by CSOs are aggregated into four action areas: closing the gaps in information asymmetry, demand and supply expansion for refugee enterprises, and survival of enterprise (Figure 18.1).

Closing the gaps in information asymmetry

To improve information asymmetry, CSOs collect real-time information through fieldwork. For example, BM collects business information through

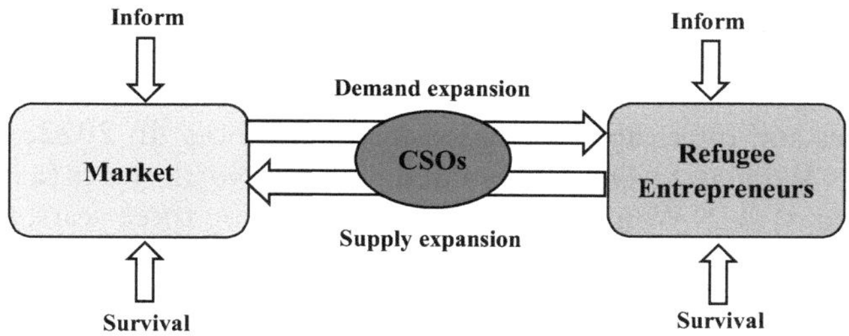

Figure 18.1 CSO actions in the refugees' economic integration.

Source: Developed by the author.

face-to-face surveys with entrepreneurs and verifies this data annually through follow-up visits and calls. The NPO uses all channels to reach refugee entrepreneurs, such as field visits, telephone calls, social media, and online events, to reach out to entrepreneurs. Communications become even more critical during disasters. For example, KEDV has been highly active during COVID-19 (2020–2022) and the Türkiye-Syria earthquakes (2023) by collecting information via phone calls and conducting a needs assessment.

CSOs also disseminate information to the public and entrepreneurs to lessen information asymmetry. They conduct market research and publish reports and newsletters on their websites and social media. For example, SUW publishes a newsletter summarising its engagement with local businesses and refugees. BM provides an open database of refugee-owned businesses on its website and publishes market research and specialised reports. BM's data-driven and evidence-based approach is highly significant as refugee entrepreneurship is a "black box" in the country. There are nearly 10,000 refugee-founded enterprises (Building Markets, 2020b), and BM's database has over 2,330 enterprises, with at least one Syrian owner, that can be searched using city, industry, or size filters. The database is relatively current and highly beneficial for buyers who want to expand their supply chain to refugee-owned enterprises. These efforts help CSOs to build trust with the host community and donors and gain legitimacy.

Expand the demand for refugee enterprises

To expand the demand for refugee enterprises, CSOs engage in awareness-raising activities and invite and engage entrepreneurs in local and international supply chains and public procurement opportunities (Figure 18.1). For example, during 2020–2023, KEDV implemented a programme titled "Empowerment of Low-Income Refugee and Local Women in Türkiye", which was financially supported by the Dutch government. They applied the programme in six cities where refugees mainly resided and provided support activities such as awareness-raising meetings, mentoring programmes, and women's cooperatives and producers entering supply chains.

Project partners guided the SADA Women's Cooperative to visit local governmental agencies and offer catering services to their offices. In 2022, with the support of UN Women, SADA collaborated with 66°North stores (a large retail chain in Iceland) (UN Women, 2022). In the following three years, their unique textile products will be sold at 66°North stores, and SADA's story will be promoted through media (Milliyet, 2022). After the earthquakes in 2023, SADA received funding from the Australian government to make clothing for the earthquake victims in the region (SADA Women's Cooperative, 2023, May 4).

Expand the supply of refugee enterprises

To increase the number of refugee-owned businesses, CSOs work with entrepreneurs and other partners to provide them with various capability development services.

Financial support: Institutions like the Japanese government, the EU, and GIZ funded refugees and local women to establish the SADA Women's Cooperative.

Develop new business models: ILO, UN Women, and ASAM established the SADA Women's Development Centre in Gaziantep in 2017. The women-only centre was unique because it targeted strengthening the socio-economic resilience of women and girls under female leadership (Interview with ILO Manager, 2020). The partners encouraged women in leadership and entrepreneurship. However, the lack of capital and prior business experience prevented women from starting their businesses. Finding a women's cooperative where refugee and local women work collectively was a solution that the programme partners agreed upon. The partners provided specific training modules on collective working and finding and managing cooperatives to prepare them for the task (Interview with Genç İşi Kooperatif, 2020). SADA Women's Cooperative was founded in 2019 as a collaboration between local and refugee women (33 Syrians, 2 Afghans, and 13 locals).

Training services: From 2017 to 2019, KEDV implemented a programme called "Vocational Proficiency of Syrian and Turkish Women" (TAMEB), which received financial backing from Global Project Partners (GPP), a non-profit organisation based in Germany. The TAMEB programme was implemented at two women's cooperatives in Istanbul (Hatipoglu, 2021). During the initial year of the TAMEB programme, the objectives were twofold: enhancing the capacity of women's cooperatives in terms of physical and technical aspects and promoting the engagement of refugee women in diverse training modules offered by these cooperatives. In the subsequent year, TAMEB focused on bolstering the production capabilities of women's cooperatives. These activities were carried out concurrently, involving both refugee and native women. In the follow-up of the study in 2022, the author observed that some of the refugee women continued to work with one of the cooperatives and were involved in their new projects on food production and services.

Mentoring Services: BM supports refugee entrepreneurs in starting the formalisation processes of their businesses. In the following stages, the NPO offers mentoring and training services, such as digital marketing, brand, and financial management, to improve refugee entrepreneurs' chances for survival (Interview with the BM General Manager Türkiye, 2022).

Survival of enterprises

To improve the success and maintain the continuity of refugee businesses, CSOs help them adjust to the local work culture and guide them in doing business locally. They provide specialised orientation and on-the-job training, career coaching, and mentoring services for refugees. Moreover, after helping them set up businesses, CSOs continue to help owners promote their businesses and provide them with business education. These services become even more needed during disasters such as the pandemic, floods, and recent earthquakes, which bring additional challenges for refugee-owned enterprises.

The BM reports, backed by significant field research, display these challenges and entrepreneurs' specific needs. For example, during the COVID-19 pandemic, 38% of the refugee enterprises halted their operations entirely in May 2020, compared to 22% of all the local businesses (Anderson, 2022). Their unique challenges included a lack of available capital, information gaps, language barriers that limit access to support programmes, and a lack of digitalisation during the pandemic.

After the earthquakes of February 2023, BM conducted another survey (via phone) with over 860 enterprises in five cities impacted by the earthquakes – identifying refugee entrepreneurs' immediate situation (e.g., whether their businesses survived or had to leave town) and their needs guided BM' work (Building Markets, 2023). For example, in the following months, they provided online training activities (e.g., making sales calls and finding capital during disasters) for businesses struggling in the region (Interview with BM Account Manager, 2023). Furthermore, they used the funds they received from donors (e.g., Manar Foundation for Community Engagement and Give Directly) to provide financial support to the survivors and empower and enhance the capabilities of community initiatives.

CSO approaches to the economic integration of refugees

The approaches by CSOs are gathered into three domains: Blending logic, intermediary, and development roles (Figure 18.2).

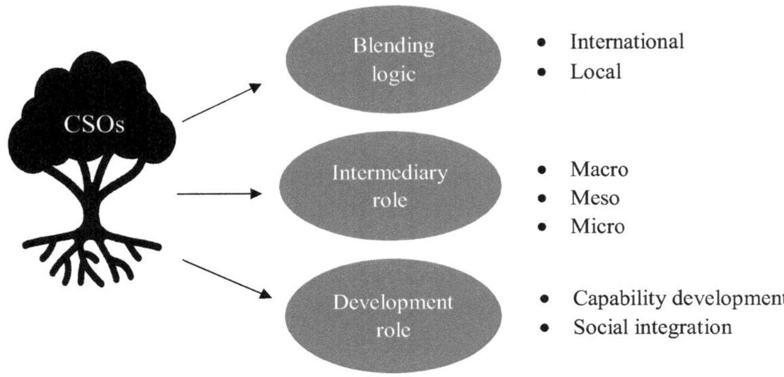

Figure 18.2 CSO approaches to the economic integration of refugees.

Source: Developed by the author.

Blending logic

In their study of refugee integration in Türkiye, Sunata and Tosun (2019) concluded that NGOs with local activation were more successful in delivering their services as they knew the specific refugee needs and how to solve the issues at the local level. The study in this chapter confirms their conclusion about the significance of local expertise. For example, KEDV has nearly four decades of experience and knowledge in assisting women from disadvantaged regions. Their experience conducting realistic needs analysis, localised training materials, and field experts with practical solutions to women's challenges are valuable and highly regarded within the institutional system.

Building on Sunata and Tosun's (2019) study, the findings suggest a blending logic in which CSOs benefit from their local experience and bring knowledge and experiences gained in other contexts to tackle migration management issues. For example, the training modules developed in SUW's Netherlands offices were adapted to the Syrian refugees and the locals in Türkiye. Similarly, KEDV blends its local knowledge with OXFAM's international expertise in humanitarian aid to support the earthquake victims. Building Markets works together with its US headquarters in planning research activities. SADA benefits from the broad experience of UN Women and ILO in decent work, cooperatives, and gender equality. As migration management is a new phenomenon in the country, the blending logic is instrumental in providing the beneficiaries with the most efficient and effective services.

Intermediary role

CSOs act as intermediaries among institutional agents and multiple institutional layers in migration management. For refugees who cannot access correct information or relevant support from government agencies, CSOs help them make sense of their new environment and access services. At the macro level, CSOs are in a position to seek and receive funds from external institutions and governments to aid refugees. All four CSOs have a good reputation and expertise in writing proposals and managing programmes; therefore, they are supported by donors.

They collaborate with urban municipalities, businesses, and other CSOs at the regional and local levels to find refugee employment and self-employment solutions. For example, SUW worked together with Sultanbeyli, Küçükçekmece, and Fatih municipalities in Istanbul. Similarly, Gaziantep municipality has been supportive during the establishment and management of SADA. KEDV worked with Izmir metropolitan municipality and started a bread kiosk, Turkish bath, and tea garden to be operated by the women (KEDV, 2022).

Development role

According to Karakulak and Faul (2023), when it comes to providing value for refugees, CSOs and their partnerships engage in activities that address refugees' needs in capability development. CSOs in this study also follow many awareness-raising and capability development activities to achieve that goal. For example, BM and SUW mentor refugee entrepreneurs in setting up businesses.

The CSOs work on improving refugees' economic integration and developing their capabilities to improve their social integration in their new country. In many cases, CSOs offer support programmes to locals and refugees concurrently, enabling them to bring the two communities together and improve their social cohesion. For example, during the pandemic, KEDV, in partnership with UN Women, implemented the Resilient Communities programme in the Akyol neighbourhood of Gaziantep. The programme encouraged local and refugee women's collective leadership, organising, and solidarity and addressed socio-economic issues in the district (Interview with Field Officer, 2022). Likewise, SADA management and members include women from both communities.

Discussion and conclusion

A systematic approach to refugee employment and entrepreneurship is absent in many nations, resulting in ad hoc and informal services being used (OECD/European Commission, 2021; Scholten et al., 2017). Barriers set by institutional agencies, such as impractical regulations, accessibility, and flexibility of support schemes, can impede refugees' access to formal markets (de la Chaux & Haugh, 2020). In an institutional system where agents ignore the specific needs of the refugees, their market participation will be obstructed (Mair & Marti, 2009), and their business success will be at risk (Hagos et al., 2019).

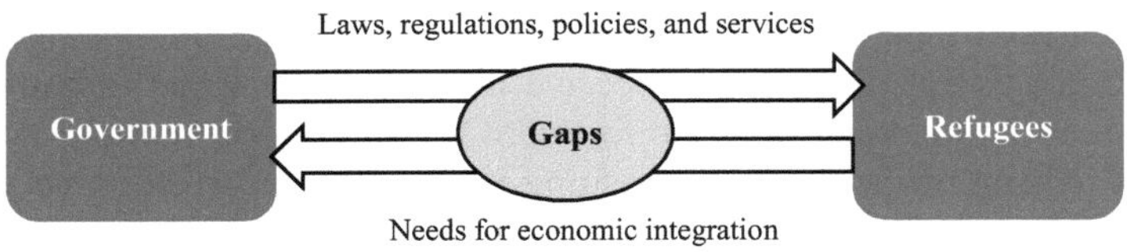

Figure 18.3 Gaps in the refugees' economic integration.

Source: Developed by the author.

This chapter identifies gaps in the institutional environment for Syrian refugees' economic integration in Türkiye. The findings support the existing literature (Kirisci & Kolasin, 2019; Knappert et al., 2018; Knappert et al., 2023; Sunata & Tosun, 2019) in suggesting that the discrepancy among the legal frameworks, the needs of refugees, and the shortcomings of the institutional framework in the country hamper the ability of refugees to fully engage in the formal labour markets or start and maintain a new business (Figure 18.3).

It is not surprising to find institutional gaps in developing nations, particularly when examining a new phenomenon such as refugee entrepreneurship. Yet, what is worrying is the continuance of the issue for an extended period of time. Utilising the institutional theory focus on context (Greenwood et al., 2017), we confirm the peculiarity of the setting in Türkiye. Despite large numbers of refugees residing in the nation for nearly a decade, their economic integration through formal mechanisms remains low. The state, the primary agency responsible, falls short of facilitating a successful integration process for refugees by failing to establish policies or institutions to support such a process. The findings show that transaction costs in emerging and developing countries are higher, the gaps for refugee employment are more significant than expected, and filling institutional voids is more challenging than in developed nations (Mickiewicz & Olarewaju, 2020).

Refugee integration is a complex and multi-faceted issue. In Türkiye, the CSOs needed to examine the gaps in services and the needs of the refugees to maximise the impact of their actions. To address this recently identified social challenge, some even had to take on new roles to extend their services, and others had to innovate new business models to fit the context. Overall, *a blending logic*, in which actors bring in knowledge and experiences gained in other contexts (e.g., developed nations) to harvest and apply with local expertise, is observed in this study.

In developed nations, a mechanism of complementarity operates in which actors not only perform their distinct roles but also contribute by addressing gaps and enhancing the efforts of others to promote refugee economic integration (Knappert et al., 2023). The sample CSOs in Türkiye, working alongside the government, address the gaps by ***lowering the information asymmetry, expanding demand and supply for refugee enterprises,*** and ***supporting the survival of enterprises.*** However, compared to the actors in developed nations, the CSOs in Türkiye perform these actions while maintaining a safe distance from the central government, in not overstepping the state's discourse on refugee management. The patterns of CSOs' compliance (Greenwood et al., 2017) develop under the government's close watch.

Utilising the categorisation of Karakulak and Faul (2023), CSOs in Türkiye focus on the necessities (e.g., humanitarian aid) and partially on the capability development domains (e.g., refugees' language skills and access to social services). Only a few eligible CSOs provide refugee employment services or support for entrepreneurs. CSOs build trust and goodwill by staying within the borders defined by the government and demonstrating that they are there to support local and refugee communities (rather than only refugees). They perform their ***capability development*** role while bringing two communities together and supporting social cohesion. These are messages underlined and communicated by the actions of the CSOs to local society, helping CSOs to construct their legitimacy (Greenwood et al., 2017).

The third domain in the categorisation of Karakulak and Faul (2023), which represents social and political domains, is addressed narrowly by the CSOs. At the macro level, CSOs engage little in advocacy efforts to influence policies and create an enabling environment for their work. Previous studies have recorded that many CSOs felt uneasy (Sunata & Tosun, 2019). Thus, the limitations brought by the central government for CSOs' operations could cause this conclusion. In comparison, within the institutional system, CSOs are more involved in working together or influencing governmental agencies (e.g., municipalities) at the local level. Their ***intermediary role*** between the refugees and the local governmental agencies and their collaborations confirm that multiple agents work together to face the challenges of refugee integration (Knappert et al., 2023; Özçürümez & Hoxha, 2022).

The findings of this chapter highlight CSOs' importance in delivering an enabling economic and social environment for refugees (Hack-Polay & Igwe, 2019). The study makes several contributions. First, it contributes to the literature on refugee integration by providing insights into their economic integration and work adjustment in the host country. Second, it identifies the critical role of the CSOs and their partnerships in fostering economic integration through individual entrepreneurship and collective entrepreneurship. It reminds us of the private sector's responsibility to participate in these cross-sector partnerships. Third, it outlines how CSO's efforts could be developed to support broader and more effective strategies to support refugee integration. Finally, informed by the institutional theory, the study points to governance gaps in refugee entrepreneurship and delivers policy implications.

References

Anderson, A. J. (2022). *The impact of COVID-19 on Syrian businesses in Turkey: Navigating recovery.* Building Markets. www.buildingmarkets.org

Aras, B., & Duman, Y. (2019). I/NGOs' assistance to Syrian refugees in Turkey: Opportunities and challenges. *Journal of Balkan and Near Eastern Studies, 21*(4), 478–491. https://doi.org/10.1080/19448953.2018.1530382

Bache, C. (2019). Challenges to economic integration and social inclusion of Syrian refugees in Turkey. *Career Development International, 25*(1), 14–18. https://doi.org/10.1108/CDI-11-2018-0277

Bisignano, A.P., & El-Anis, I. (2019). Making sense of mixed-embeddedness in migrant informal enterprising. *International Journal of Entrepreneurial Behavior & Research, 25*(5), 974–995. https://doi.org/10.1108/IJEBR-03-2018-0114

Boztaş, Ö. (2019). Shrinking humanitarian space in Turkey: The government of Turkey's agency in shaping the operations of humanitarian NGOs in Turkey. *METU Studies in Development, 46*, 153–174. http://dx.doi.org/10.60165/metusd.v46i2.1053

Building Markets. (2020a). An assessment on the financial inclusion of Syrian-owned enterprises in Turkey. www.buildingmarkets.org

Building Markets. (2020b). Turkish-Syrian business partnerships, Part II. www.buildingmarkets.org

Building Markets. (2023). Rapid needs assessment: The February 2023 earthquake's immediate impact on Syrian SMEs in Türkiye. www.buildingmarkets.org

Charmaz, K. (2006). *Constructing grounded theory: A practical guide through qualitative analysis.* Sage.

Dana, L.P. (1997). The origins of self-employment in ethno-cultural communities: Distinguishing between orthodox entrepreneurship and reactionary enterprise. *Canadian Journal of Administrative Sciences/Revue Canadienne des Sciences de l'Administration, 14*(1), 52–68. https://doi.org/10.1111/j.1936-4490.1997.tb00118.x

Danış, D., & Nazlı, D. (2019). A faithful alliance between the civil society and the state: Actors and mechanisms of accommodating Syrian refugees in Istanbul. *International Migration, 57*(2), 143–157. https://doi.org/10.1111/imig.12495

de la Chaux, M., & Haugh, H. (2020). When formal institutions impede entrepreneurship: how and why refugees establish new ventures in the Dadaab refugee camps. *Entrepreneurship & Regional Development, 32*(9/10), 827–851. https://doi.org/10.1080/08985626.2020.1789752

Eisenhardt, K.M., & Graebner, M.E. (2007). Theory building from cases: Opportunities and challenges. *Academy of Management Journal, 50*(1), 25–32. https://doi.org/10.5465/amj.2007.24160888

Garkisch, M., Heidingsfelder, J., & Beckmann, M. (2017). Third sector organizations and migration: A systematic literature review on the contribution of third sector organizations in view of flight, migration and refugee crises. *Voluntas: International Journal of Voluntary and Nonprofit Organizations, 28*(5), 1839–1880. www.jstor.org/stable/44668922

Gioia, D.A., Corley, K.G., & Hamilton, A.L. (2013). Seeking qualitative rigor in inductive research: Notes on the Gioia methodology. *Organizational Research Methods, 16*(1), 15–31. https://doi.org/10.1177/1094428112452151

GIZ. (2023). *Supporting employment and vocational training for Syrian refugees and host communities.* Retrieved May 8, 2023, from www.giz.de/en/worldwide/40559.html

Glaser, B.G. (2001). *The grounded theory perspective: Conceptualization contrasted with description.* Sociology Press.

Greenwood, R., Oliver, C., Lawrence, T.B., & Meyer, R. (2017). Introduction: Into the fourth decade. In R. Greenwood, C. Oliver, K. Sahlin, & R. Suddaby (Eds.), *The SAGE handbook of organizational institutionalism.* Los Angeles: Sage.

Güven, S., Kenanoğlu, M., Kadkoy, O., & Kurt, T. (2018). *Syrian entrepreneurship and refugee start-ups in Turkey: Leveraging the Turkish experience.* Ankara: TEPAV.

Hack-Polay, D., & Igwe, P.A. (2019). Beyond words and rhetoric–Small voluntary organisations and effective refugee integration in the communities. *Journal of Enterprising Communities: People and Places in the Global Economy, 13*(1/2), 5–23. https://doi.org/10.1108/JEC-11-2018-0084

Hagos, S., Izak, M., & Scott, J.M. (2019). Objective institutionalized barriers and subjective performance factors of new migrant entrepreneurs. *International Journal of Entrepreneurial Behavior & Research, 25*(5), 842–858. https://doi.org/10.1108/IJEBR-06-2018-0405

Harima, A., Freudenberg, J., & Halberstadt, J. (2019). Functional domains of business incubators for refugee entrepreneurs. *Journal of Enterprising Communities: People and Places in the Global Economy, 14*(5), 687–711. https://doi.org/10.1108/JEC-11-2018-0081

Hatipoglu, B.K. (2021). Community-based social enterprises and social innovation: The case of women's cooperatives in Turkey. In D.M. Wasieleski, & J. Weber (Eds.), *Social entrepreneurship* (*Business and Society 360*, vol. 5, pp. 97–118). Bingley: Emerald Publishing Limited.

Heilbrunn, S. (2019). Against all odds: Refugees bricoleuring in the void. *International Journal of Entrepreneurial Behavior & Research, 25*(5), 1045–1064. https://doi.org/10.1108/IJEBR-10-2017-0393

Hesse, A., Kreutzer, K., & Diehl, M.-R. (2019). Dynamics of institutional logics in a cross-sector social partnership: The case of refugee integration in Germany. *Journal of Business Ethics, 159*(3), 679–704. https://doi.org/10.1007/s10551-017-3775-0

ISKUR. (2019). Opening meeting of Employment Support Project for Syrians and Turkish Citizens under Temporary Protection held in Ankara. www.iskur.gov.tr/haberler/gecici-koruma-altindaki-suriyeliler-ve-turk-vatandaslari-icin-istihdam-destegi-projesi-acilis-toplantisi-ankara-da-yapildi/

Karakulak, Ö., & Faul, M.V. (2023). Value creation for refugees by social partnerships: A frames perspective. *Business & Society,* 00076503231157715. https://doi.org/10.1177/00076503231157715

KEDV. (2022). *Empowerment of low-income refugee and local women in Türkiye.* Retrieved May 22, 2023, from www.kedv.org.tr/icerik/eb-turkiyede-yasayan-multeci-ve-yerel-dar-gelirli-kadinlari-guclendirme-projesi

Kirisci, K., & Kolasin, G.U. (2019). *Syrian refugees in Turkey need better access to formal jobs [Web log post].* www.brookings.edu/blog/order-fromchaos/2019/07/18/syrian-refugees-in-turkey-need-better-access-to-formal-jobs/

Knappert, L., Kornau, A., & Figengül, M. (2018). Refugees' exclusion at work and the intersection with gender: Insights from the Turkish-Syrian border. *Journal of Vocational Behavior, 105*, 62–82. https://doi.org/10.1016/j.jvb.2017.11.002

Knappert, L., Ortlieb, R., Kornau, A., Maletzky, M., & van Dijk, H. (2023). The ecosystem of managing refugee employment: Complementarity and its microfoundations. *Academy of Management Discoveries*, *9*(3), 339–362. https://doi.org/10.5465/amd.2020.0157

Lammers, J. C., & Garcia, M. A. (2014). Institutional theory. In J.C. Lammers, M.A. Garcia, L. Putnam, & D. Mumby (Eds.), *The SAGE handbook of organizational communication: Advances in theory, research, and methods* (pp. 195–216). Thousand Oaks, CA: Sage.

Lehmann, T., Albaba, H., & Kreiter-Sammet, S. (2022). Refugee entrepreneurship in Germany: An institutional voids perspective. In L.-P. Dana, N. Khachlouf, A. Maâlaoui, & V. Ratten (Eds.), *Disadvantaged minorities in business. Contributions to management science.* (pp. 129–151). Cham: Springer. doi: https://doi.org/10.1007/978-3-030-97079-6_6.

Lincoln, Y.S., & Guba, E.G. (1985). *Naturalistic inquiry.* Newbury Park, CA: Sage.

Maalaoui, A., Ratten, V., Heilbrunn, S., Brannback, M., & Kraus, S. (2020). Disadvantage entrepreneurship: Decoding a new area of research. *European Management Review, 17*(3), 663–668. https://doi.org/10.1111/emre.12424

Mackreath, H., & Sağnıç, Ş.G. (2017). *Civil society and Syrian refugees in Turkey.* Yurttaşlık Derneği. www.hyd.org.tr/

Mair, J., & Marti, I. (2009). Entrepreneurship in and around institutional voids: A case study from Bangladesh. *Journal of Business Venturing, 24*(5), 419–435. https://doi.org/10.1016/j.jbusvent.2008.04.006

Mickiewicz, T., & Olarewaju, T. (2020). New venture evolution of migrants under institutional voids: Lessons from Shonga Farms in Nigeria. *International Small Business Journal, 38*(5), 404–423. https://doi.org/10.1177/026624261989626

Milliyet. (2022). Onlar üretecek dünya giyecek (They will produce the world will wear). Retrieved May 08, 2023, from www.milliyet.com.tr/gundem/onlar-uretecek-dunya-giyecek-6877511

Ministry of Interior. (2018). Presidency. https://en.goc.gov.tr/about-us

Nardon, L., Zhang, H., Szkudlarek, B., & Gulanowski, D. (2020). Identity work in refugee workforce integration: The role of newcomer support organizations. *Human Relations*, 0018726720949630. https://doi.org/10.1177/0018726720949630

OECD/European Commission. (2021). *The Missing entrepreneurs 2021: Policies for inclusive entrepreneurship and self-employment.* Paris: OECD Publishing. https://doi.org/10.1787/71b7a9bb-en

Olarewaju, T., & Fashola, O. (2020). Migrant entrepreneurship under institutional voids. In W. Leal Filho, A. Azul, L. Brandli, A. Lange Salvia, & T. Wall, (Eds.), *Decent work and economic growth. Encyclopedia of the UN Sustainable Development Goals.* Cham: Springer. https://doi.org/10.1007/978-3-319-71058-7_93-1

Özçürümez, S., & Hoxha, J. (2022). Expanding the boundaries of the local: Entrepreneurial municipalism and migration governance in Turkey. *New Perspectives on Turkey, 68,* 1–19. https://doi.org/10.1017/npt.2022.19

SADA Women's Cooperative [@sadacooperative]. (2023, May 4). *We signed a project with the Australian Ambassador to Turkey Miles Armitage and his delegation. Within the scope of the project, we aim to produce for the clothing needs of earthquake survivors and deliver them to 300 earthquake victims.* Twitter.

Scholten, P., Baggerman, F., Dellouche, L., Kampen, V., Wolf, J., & Ypma, R. (2017). *Policy innovation in refugee integration. A comparative analysis of innovative policy strategies to refugee integration in Europe*. Erasmus Migration and Diversity Institude. Retrieved from http://hdl.handle.net/1765/122531

Sunata, U., & Tosun, S. (2019). Assessing the civil society's role in refugee integration in Turkey: NGO-R as a new typology. *Journal of Refugee Studies, 32*(4), 683–703. https://doi.org/10.1093/jrs/fey047

UN Women. (2022). *SADAxN66: First connection and beyond*. Retrieved from www.youtube.com/watch?v=q2Nr1mYJ0h8

United Nations High Commissioner for Refugees (UNHCR). (2022). Global trends. Retrieved October 09, 2023, from www.unhcr.org/global-trends-report-2022

Verwiebe, R., Kittel, B., Dellinger, F., Liebhart, C., Schiestl, D., Haindorfer, R., & Liedl, B. (2019). Finding your way into employment against all odds? Successful job search of refugees in Austria. *Journal of Ethnic and Migration Studies, 45*(9), 1401–1418. https://doi.org/10.1080/1369183X.2018.1552826

Williamson, O.E. (2000). The new institutional economics: taking stock, looking ahead. *Journal of Economic Literature, 38*(3), 595–613. www.jstor.org/stable/2565421

Yang, A., Liu, W., & Wang, R. (2020). Cross-sector alliances in the global refugee crisis: An institutional theory approach. *Business Ethics: A European Review, 29*(3), 646–660. https://doi.org/10.1111/beer.12288

19 A private sector entrepreneurial initiative for displaced women at Rohingya camp in Bhasan Char, Bangladesh

Imon Chowdhooree and Muhammad Ferdaus

Introduction

Refugees are a group of people that are forcefully displaced because of persecution or a fear of persecution on account of their identity (Ridge et al., 2004). The women in such a group, more so than men, face a number of challenges due to the possibilities of sexual violence, and unequal access to humanitarian assistance (United Nations International Children's Emergency Fund [UNICEF], 2022; United Nations High Commissioner for Refugees [UNHCR], 2002). This is especially so while they are temporarily accommodated in camps with bare minimum facilities expecting to be repatriate to their native locations (Ali et al., 2022 Chaux & Haugh, 2018; Turner, 2014). Over the years, it has become very necessary to create new livelihood opportunities for the displaced population to reduce their dependency on host governments and the humanitarian welfare that is provided in camps (Jacobsen & Fratzke, 2016; Jacobsen, 2002). New livelihood opportunities may also lead to viable and durable solutions for economic development that will influence the repatriation process (Jacobsen & Fratzke, 2016).

It is especially important to empower displaced or refugee women to become economically independent by providing different types of livelihood opportunities through entrepreneurship (Al-Dajani & Marlow, 2013; Jabbar & Zaza, 2016; Mawson & Kasem, 2019; Ritchie, 2018, 2017, 2014; Sepulveda et al., 2011; Street et al., 2022; Senthanar et al., 2022). Such opportunities empower women through increased income, financial independence, new-found confidence, participation in decision-making, reduced vulnerability, and enhanced human security (Christoplos & Hilhorst, 2009; Street et al., 2022; Ritchie, 2018). Empowered women not only enjoy personal success, financial gain, and status, but they also practise social power and agency, which can enact systemic changes in society (Batliwala, 2007).

Working with a well-established corporate is frequently a desirable and fruitful option, as it has the resources and innovative methods for supporting

DOI: 10.4324/9781003368540-24

people (Malik et al., 2018). In certain instances, businesses and marketplaces for consumer products, real estate, education, telecommunications, and many other commodities and services thrive in refugee camp regions despite considerable practical and legal restrictions (Pluess & Victor, 2018; Ray, 2023). Such activity is now being considered as a new business opportunity for refugees, host countries, and the business sector (Pluess & Victor, 2018). Even for-profit businesses are using their corporate social responsibility resources to work with charitable or non-profit organisations to develop job opportunities for displaced people (Malik et al., 2018). An increasing number of businesses have pledged to use their core business assets in addition to charitable donations to advance refugee resilience (Pluess & Victor, 2018).

This chapter studies an entrepreneurial initiative offered by a private sector fashion design house, in collaboration with the Government of Bangladesh. It targets employing the Rohingya women from the camps at Bhasan Char Island, Bangladesh. Although the Rohingya community in Bangladesh is usually referred to as refugees, the Government of Bangladesh defines them as the forcefully displaced population from Myanmar, a neighbouring country of Bangladesh. As their identity is not formally recognised by the Government of Myanmar, their status is that of a stateless people. More than 830,000 Rohingya community members from Myanmar are victims of "crimes against humanity" in their homeland, and therefore crossed the international border and resided in various camps in Bangladesh (UNICEF, 2019). The Government of Bangladesh has prepared planned accommodation on Bhasan Char Island for more than a hundred thousand of these victims.

This study specifically aimed to understand the impact of the initiative on the empowerment of the displaced women on Bhasan Char Island in providing them with livelihood opportunities. The qualitative research, conducted in 2023, systematically reviewed documents and collected primary data through transect walks (i.e., gathering spatial data while walking around an area), observations, and key informant interviews. Ten interviews were undertaken with informants who oversaw the operation of the centre set up by the fashion design house, and various other facilities and services within the camps. They provided information about official procedures, plans, and proposals for the business model behind this entrepreneurial initiative. Because of formal restrictions, it was not possible to conduct organised focus group discussions or interviews with the beneficiaries (displaced women) of the entrepreneurial initiative. Key informants were the main source of information about the reactions of these women. In this case, the tools of systematic observation and a transect walk with the beneficiaries were conducted to understand the impact of new livelihood opportunities on the lives of the beneficiaries. The significance of this study is identification of opportunities for the better performance of similar types of initiatives which target the empowerment of displaced women in any part of the world.

Rohingya population in Bangladesh

Rohingya infringement and settling in Cox's Bazar

The Rohingya is an ethnic minority community of Myanmar, residing predominantly for generations in the state of Rakhine, bordering Bangladesh (see Figure 19.1). This community has faced and is still facing systematic discrimination, repression, statelessness, and organised violence in their native land. Most of this community have become displaced from their homeland because they were victims of crimes against humanity, including mass atrocities, sexual violence, mass killing, and widespread arson conducted by government security forces (Human Right Watch, 2021; United Nations Office for the Coordination of Humanitarian Affairs (OCHA), 2021; Baidya et al., 2020). Huge numbers of Rohingya have crossed the international border and taken shelter in camps established within the territory of Bangladesh (OCHA, 2021).

In 1991, as a consequence of the first known systematic persecution campaign, a huge number of Rohingya people were displaced, and approximately 250,000 entered Cox's Bazar in Bangladesh through its porous border. A further mass-scale intrusion occurred when almost 700,000 Rohingya people entered Bangladesh following the violent operations by the armed forces of Myanmar in late August 2017 (UNICEF, 2019). This newly arrived displaced population joined hundreds of thousands who were already living in unofficially built camps or with local communities. Of this new influx, more than 50% were women and girls, and 60% were children under 18 (Oxford Committee for Famine Relief – OXFAM International, 2023). Gradually, all found shelter in already formed unofficial camps and in some newly built official camps, by clearing the natural forest reservations of the hilly regions of Cox's Bazar region. Despite Bangladesh not having any national law or adhering to any international instruments, this demonstrates a commitment to the principle of non-refoulement – not forcing the displaced population to return to a place where they are likely to face persecution (Macdonald et al., 2023).

Rohingya settlement in Bhasan Char

The Bangladesh government developed planned accommodation for Rohingya people in a secluded area, Bhasan Char Island, as part of the Ashrayan Project. The project, known as the "Sheikh Hasina[1] Model", aims to provide houses and land to the homeless or landless population of Bangladesh (Kayas, 2022; see Figure 19.2). The housing is currently accommodating Rohingya people until the repatriation process begins, and when they return, it will be used for rehabilitating distressed local people (Armed Forces Division, 2023).

The island of Bhasan Char is a newly formed habitable island in the Meghna River Basin on the Bay of Bengal, some 60 km from the mainland. It belongs to the Char Ishwar Union of the Hatiya sub-district of Noakhali district.

Figure 19.1 The map showing the location of Bhasan Char Island in the Bay of Bengal.

Source: Human Right Watch (2021).

Figure 19.2 The layout of shelters (left) and image of shelters (right) in Bhasan Char Island.

Source: The Bangladesh Navy (2023).

The island was uninhabited before the development of the Rohingya camps and there were initial doubts about its safety and liveability because of the fear of inadequate storm and flood protection, risk of food shortages, unreliable water sources, lack of schools and health care, and severe restrictions on freedom of movement. But the Government of Bangladesh has ensured safety by providing all modern amenities, including health care (Human Right Watch, 2021). Further, the occasional ship service is provided to reach the island from Chattogram port, and small rentable boats are available to reach the island from nearby important locations. The total land area of this island is 38.4 km^2, and within this area, 1,702 acres (6.9 km^2) of land is protected by an embankment. It has 1,440 single-storied housing blocks or sheds for accommodating 103,200 people with all necessary facilities (Armed Forces Division, 2023; Human Right Watch, 2021).

The relocation process started in December 2020, and according to UNHCR information, in March 2023, 29,810 people from 7,455 families were living on the island. Among these residents, 52% are females and 48% are males. Approximately 56% of residents are children (UNHCR, 2023).

During the field study at Bhasan Char island camps, it was communicated that the Government of Bangladesh has given special attention to introducing formal livelihood opportunities to the Rohingya people. It has already realised that the repatriation process will take time and, meanwhile, it will be difficult to meet all the residents' needs with national and international aid. This was because of the population's natural growth and the decreasing availability of aid. In recent times, because of the shortfall in donations, the UN World Food Project cut the budget for food allowance. As of March 1, 2023, the Rohingya refugees have been receiving $10 per person per month instead of $12 (Al Jazeera, 2023). This may be a precursor for aid from other sources also being reduced in the future. However, currently it has been observed that every refugee on Bhasan Char Island receives aid which meets their daily basic needs. Despite meeting basic needs, the government is undertaking multiple initiatives to introduce several livelihood options so that Rohingya refugees can become accustomed to earning income to meet other types of needs. This is aimed at preparing them for a future in which they will have to earn money to support themselves.

Various types of agricultural production-based earning options have been introduced on Bhasan Char Island. Further, boats are provided for some Rohingya refugee males to undertake open sea fishing, whilst others are running small shops inside the camp area. Some males operate rickshaw vans, which are used as local modes of transportation within the island. Multiple options of vocational training programmes in industrial sewing machine operation, solar panel repair and maintenance, baking and food processing, and primary health care have been introduced to develop Rohingya refugees' skills as they can gain production-based jobs or run a business in the future. As a part of these vocational training options, a private fashion design house has launched an entrepreneurial initiative in the camp. This initiative is mainly targeting the Rohingya refugee women.

The fashion design house on Bhasan Char Island

This fashion design house was approached by the government to create livelihood opportunities for the Rohingya community that had received government-sponsored skill development courses (see Figure 19.3).

As one of the leading fashion design houses in Bangladesh, it has an established lifestyle brand for designing, manufacturing, and selling fashion wear, fashion accessories, home textiles, handicrafts, and handloom-based products. With strong social commitments, it has been running its business in the country since the early 1990s. The fashion house started its manufacturing operation on Bhasan Char Island just after the arrival of the first group of Rohingya refugees in December 2020. The purpose of this centre is to train Rohingya women and engage them in manufacturing of the fashion design house's products. The participants may also be encouraged to start their own businesses for manufacturing items. Currently, it runs three sections of production:

Figure 19.3 Rohingya women are working at the centre.

Source: Field Survey (2023).

- Tailoring: In which Rohingya women are involved in making dress items.
- *Karchupi* embroidery: A special type of embroidery work on fabric that uses various types of beads and stones with silver and golden threads. Small pieces of embroidery work are prepared to attach to dress items or any other types of fabric items.
- Regular hand-embroidery: Pieces of hand-embroidered fabrics are produced for attaching to dress items or any other types of fabric items.

Within the centre, there is a small unit for block and screen printing on fabric, and about 20 Rohingya males work there. The centre's activities are regularly monitored by the government, and it needs to submit regular reports to the government on the progress of its operations.

Recruitment and training

Recruiting women for training is an important task of this operation. The representatives of the centre go door-to-door to encourage and motivate Rohingya women to participate in the training sessions. They explain what kind of benefits they might get in the future if they receive some training, and how they can earn some money. As most of the representatives are men, they cannot speak directly to the Rohingya women. They need to speak firstly to the male leaders of each group (known as *majhi*), the leaders then speak to the male members of the families; and finally, the male members speak to the female members of their families. If there is interest from the Rohingya women and they receive permission from the male family members (i.e., husband or father), then they may participate in the activities at the centre.

Participants need to attend the training sessions before engaging in manufacturing in the centre. Training is necessary to ensure that the Rohingya women are work ready, as they do not have the necessary skills to produce the types of products desired. Depending on individual performance, participants usually receive 3–6 months of training. Each participant receives a small allowance of BDT[2] 25 every day for attending training sessions. It is in the form of a small food voucher for some refreshments, and it was introduced to spark interest in training. The centre is continuously training the women and, so far, almost 600 Rohingya women have received training.

Manufacturing operations and working hours

Participants normally engage in manufacturing after acquiring the appropriate skills. The women can go to the centre to produce the fashion design house's products or, alternatively, they can take orders to their homes and deliver the products after finishing. In total, 300 women go to the centre regularly for work in the three different sections. Others do not go to the centre regularly as they have been given the option of working from home at their convenience. Some are under 18 years of age and go to school. This group usually goes to the centre after school hours. The centre runs two production shifts: morning to noon and noon to evening. Every participant works 3–4 hours in a single shift. If someone cannot finish their products, they take them home and deliver the finished products whenever they can. As it does not require much space, the women can easily produce or complete the products at home. Payments are on a piece basis. To encourage them to come to the centre to produce the products, participants are given a small allowance as a food voucher for buying refreshments. This allowance is on top of the wage they receive for producing the products.

Impacts of this operation on participants

As previously stated, during training, along with acquiring the skill, the participants receive a small allowance. They also receive this allowance if they come to work in the centre. The official records show that there are women who have earned more than BDT 10,000 per month. The amount of earnings depends on how fast they can produce the products and, on average, most of the women earn BDT 3,000 per month. They receive the standard wage similar to employees in other centres around Bangladesh, although the overall production quality of Rohingya women is poorer than the quality of products from the other centres. They even receive the same wage if they produce defective products or products of unacceptable quality, whereas the employees of its other centres do not receive this benefit.

The key informants mentioned that many participants usually spend their earnings on buying various items, like cosmetics, dresses, and jewellery. As they cannot open bank accounts or buy property, they have typically not developed a habit of saving money for the future. To date, none have shown any interest in running their own business, or starting anything new, or investing their money for any purpose. It is also true that there is no formal opportunity for them to invest their money.

Women also give the money to their parents or husbands, and they spend the money on buying household items. It was highlighted by the key informants that earning money and contributing to family expenses have changed their status within their families. There are cases where the women became very determined to make decision regarding their personal lives. But we need to collect evidence to establish whether those women who earn also play a stronger role in any decision-making.

Challenges

The key informants stated that the overall operation and production has numerous challenges which have caused the overall production cost to increase.

Sociocultural challenges

Culturally, it is not usually acceptable within the Rohingya community that women will go out to earn money. Family members always discourage them from working, and the women also prefer not to get involved in any activities outside their homes. Recruiting women for training and motivating them to work for the centre is, therefore, a difficult task. Overall, these women are not self-motivated to work for an income. Most women preferred to stay at home and only engage in necessary domestic work. Male members of the community are often idle and show little interest in working, which deters women's involvement in any additional activities. The centre needs to work very hard to keep the women motivated and engaged in their work. A further challenge for the centre is that these women face domestic problems at home and suffer from poor mental health, which hampers their work environment and quality of production.

It is also difficult to communicate with these women, as it needs to be via community leaders and male members. Often, it becomes very difficult to know the reason for their discontinuation of training or work and the centre needs to put in extra effort to find out the issues and resolve them.

The centre allows the participants to work at home to resolve some of the issues related to family-based priorities. In other centres in which Bangladeshi women work, they run 8 hours or more daily shifts, and the women work full time with full dedication. But the centre on Bhasan Char Island maintains flexible and shorter shifts. It runs two short shifts of 3–4 hours to accommodate the various needs and priorities of the Rohingya women. Often, school-going females join after school, and others join after finishing other duties. This type of short and flexible working period hampers the total production quality and quantity in the work environment. As a result, the production costs increase.

Geographical challenges

Bhasan Char Island is a remote location and is not connected by regular transport systems. The consequence of this remoteness is that the centre has higher costs for transhipping raw materials and finished products. Raw materials as well as finished products need to be shifted to and from Dhaka, the capital of Bangladesh. Therefore, the overall production costs increase because of high transportation charges.

Economic challenges

The Rohingya community's basic needs are met with aid and they usually do not have any scope to progress in life, buy any property, open a bank account, or invest their money. They, therefore, lack the motivation to engage in any type of work. Often, the Rohingya women do not continue the training or work after training. If any participant does not work after receiving the training, it is considered a loss for the centre.

The centre also suffers due to high operating costs. Although solar power is available for generating electricity, it is not enough to run the centre. To generate adequate electricity, it needs to run a fuel-based generator. This is an additional cost above costs associated with paying salaries to trainers and recruiters, which are not usually needed in other centres. Also there are daily allowances for attending the training sessions and coming to the centre to produce the products. These additional costs add up to the total production cost.

Production quality challenges

Overall, the production quality and efficiency of Rohingya women working for the centre are not at a satisfactory level. On average, 20% of the products produced are not of an acceptable standard. This percentage is considered very high compared with the products produced in other centres around Bangladesh. To meet quality expectations many products are rejected or altered by other skilled workers. As participants are paid for defective products, their performance is low as viewed by our key informants. They are often not told that the quality of their products is unacceptable and that they need to improve, as it is thought that repetitive negative feedback might leave them disheartened or discouraged. The organisation instead encourages them to work more, hoping that this engagement will lead to a gradual improvement in quality.

Legal status challenges

The centre faces challenges in recruiting females under 18 years of age, who are classified as children although there will be no official document to prove their age unless they were born in camps. According to the UNHCR guidelines, it is not possible to employ anyone under 18, yet it is females under 18 who are interested in joining the centre. Studies have also identified that the rate of child marriage is high in the camp areas (Melnikas et al., 2020), and these young women can be mothers of several children before they are 18. However and gradually, humanitarian experts and organisations are beginning to allow the recruitment of females under 18.

Future plans

The centre plans to introduce initiatives to reduce the level of financial loss it currently experiences and, if possible, make profits. There is an initiative to find out the natural or inherent skills or capacities of Rohingya women to produce specialised products that are different from regular products produced in the centre. If skilled women are employed to produce unique products, it may help to reduce the amount of waste.

A further initiative is to brand products that Rohingya women make as refugee-made products. They can then be promoted in a different way so that those products can gain attention from customers concerned of humanitarian causes. This might help to get orders from foreign buyers. In this case, donors and international humanitarian organisations may help to get orders and promote their products in the international market. The centre is also planning to open a retail outlet so that anyone can buy products as souvenirs. There is a further option of developing products or clothing items targeting local Rohingya consumers. In this way, the products will be consumed locally and will not need to be transhipped elsewhere. These are all future plans, and nothing has been implemented yet, and there are no alternative initiatives for improving the skills of the workers and the quality of the products.

Discussion

The Bhasan Char Island case is a study of a private-sector entrepreneurial venture that has collaborated with the Bangladesh government to create livelihood opportunities for the displaced women which empower them. Women's empowerment is considered to be an important factor for social development over the last 30 years (O'Hara & Clement, 2018). Empowerment initiatives are required within systematically disempowered and marginalised communities, where women's participation in decision-making makes it possible to achieve sustainable development goals such as poverty eradication and social integration (United Nations Social Development Network, 2012). Displaced populations that are contained in a confined environment as marginalised groups need assistance to improve their power dynamics capacities (Chowdhooree et al., 2020; Richey et al., 2021). Often women appear as entrepreneurs in the new host country despite different types of challenges, but often influence other fellow refugees (Fuller-Love et al., 2006; Street et.al., 2022), and change their roles in the power dynamics of society.

Globally, there are cases that investigate the successful interplay between the experiences of forced displacement and entrepreneurial ventures in new socio-economic and institutional contexts (Adeeko & Treanor, 2021; Mawson & Kasem, 2019). In the Bhasan Char Island case of Rohingya women, the corporate entrepreneurial initiative did not provide strong evidence that the trained and employed women were able to take part in decision-making, or that their roles in the overall power dynamics have changed, or that they gained roles to make any significant change in the Rohingya refugee community. Their involvement, however, allowed them or their family members to buy some additional items, and there was conjecture that, in some cases, women gained enough confidence to make decisions about their relationships.

This research has some limitations. Due to formal restrictions, this study did not include interviews from Rohingya refugee women. This is at odds with the empowerment research as scholars (e.g., Chowdhooree et al., 2020; Wood et al., 2021) recommend understanding marginalised groups' personal goals before making claims of societal impact. This is specifically applicable to developmental initiatives targeted at marginalised groups. Despite this limitation of the study, it is understood that as every aspect of Rohingya refugee women's lives is taken care of and their activities are monitored in a confined environment, they usually remain less motivated to do anything without any hope for a better future. They also do not have any hope of leaving the camps, acquiring better accommodation, buying properties, having a bank balance, or running a new business. Moreover, women working and earning is usually not appreciated in Rohingya male-dominated culture and society. It is considered as disgraceful for the men of the family if the women need to engage in earning money (Akhter & Kusakabe, 2014). Therefore, some women do not show much interest in earning an income.

Based on these findings, it is concluded that the private sector entrepreneurial initiative is still in its incubation stage. It is not showing many success stories and the business model itself is facing multiple challenges. The centre's production costs are high, and as a business organisation it is running at a loss. There are some planned initiatives for reducing future losses, but none have been introduced to date to address the losses. This begs the question of how long it will be possible for the organisation to provide this service, bearing all losses.

Although it is a common practice for host countries to either refuse to issue work permits to refugees or place restrictions on their employment opportunities, it is encouraging that the Government of Bangladesh has taken the initiative to offer refugee women employment opportunities given the delay in the repatriation process. The private sector entrepreneurial initiative was introduced to integrate the displaced population into the national markets and supply chain and fill the institutional voids of economic opportunities for the displaced population. For displaced people to gain "power", it is important to have access to resources and to use those resources effectively (Uphoff, 2005). The Rohingya women in this case gained access to resources and opportunities, but it is unclear whether they are effectively using those to empower themselves.

Conclusion

The humanitarian crisis of forcefully migrated or displaced populations has become the central part of many global political, social, and academic debates. The Bhasan Char Island case, in addressing the problems of Rohingya refugees and developing suitable livelihood opportunities for them, is considered a very important aspect of sustainable solutions to their problems. It has become necessary to create livelihood opportunities to reduce their dependency on government and humanitarian welfare. As a durable solution, it may also influence the repatriation process, as self-reliant individuals will be more confident in their ability to live a better life after returning to their home country. The current study offers insights into the process and challenges of the business model used in the private sector entrepreneurial initiative for empowering Rohingya women. The private initiative of employing and empowering women is highly challenging due to sociocultural practices, higher cost of production, and poor work performance of the women. Based on the findings, it can be concluded that the entrepreneurial initiative in the private sector is still in the embryonic stage and has a few success stories to date. This study highlights the need to alter the current business model although it is clear that the problems are not easy to resolve.

Notes

1 Shaikh Hasina is the former prime minister of the Government of Bangladesh.
2 1 BDT = 0.0091 USD (August 2023).

References

Adeeko, N., & Treanor, L. (2021). Negotiating stigmatized identities: Enterprising refugee women in the United Kingdom. *International Small Business Journal, 40*(1), 23–46. https://doi.org/10.1177/0266242621997033

Akhter, S., & Kusakabe, K. (2014). Gender-based violence among documented Rohingya refugees in Bangladesh. *Indian Journal of Gender Studies, 21*, 225–246. https://doi.org/10.1177/0971521514525088

Al-Dajani, H., & Marlow, S. (2013). Empowerment and entrepreneurship: A theoretical framework. *International Journal of Entrepreneurial Behavior & Research, 19*(5), 503–524. https://doi.org/10.1108/IJEBR-10-2011-0138

Al Jazeera. (2023). Concerns mount over UN food aid cut for Rohingya in Bangladesh: The UN and the Bangladesh government call for more international aid to help the refugees as they face a ‘difficult year’. www.aljazeera.com/news/2023/3/7/concerns-mount-over-un-food-aid-cut-for-rohingya-in-bangladesh (Accessed April 26, 2023).

Ali, Z.F., Chowdhooree, I., Newaz, S., Ferdaus, M., & Ghani, S.M. (2022). Refugee camps at landslide risk: Studying mitigation measures. In: R. Sarkar, R. Shaw, & B. Pradhan (Eds.), *Impact of climate change, land use, and land cover, and socioeconomic dynamics on landslides*. Singapore: Springer. https://doi.org/10.1007/978-981-16-7314-6_16

Armed Forces Division. (2023). *Ashrayan Project. Prime Minister's Office Armed Forces Division*. The Government of Bangladesh. https://afd.gov.bd/activities/ashrayan-project (Accessed April 21, 2023).

Baidya, E.U., Mahboob, F., Polin, F., & Chowdhooree, I. (2020). Designing spaces with victims of humanitarian crisis: Action research on spaces for children at Rohingya camps in Bangladesh. In: I. Chowdhooree & S.M. Ghani (Eds.), *External interventions for disaster risk reduction: Impacts on local communities. Advances in 21st century human settlements* (pp. 103–112). Singapore: Springer. https://doi.org/10.1007/978-981-15-4948-9_6

Batliwala, S. (2007). Taking the power out of empowerment—An experiential account. *Development in Practice, 17*(4–5), 557–565. www.jstor.org/stable/25548253

Chaux, M.D.L., & Haugh, H. (2018). Organizing refugee camps: “Respected space” and “listening posts”. *Academy of Management Discoveries, 4*(2), 155–179. https://doi.org/10.5465/amd.2017.0040

Chowdhooree, I., Dawes, L., & Sloan, M. (2020). Dependency on external supports: An addition to community vulnerability. In: I. Chowdhooree & S.M. Ghani (Eds.), *External interventions for disaster risk reduction. Advances in 21st century human settlements.* Singapore: Springer. https://doi.org/10.1007/978-981-15-4948-9_3

Christoplos, I., & Hilhorst, D. (2009). *Human security and capacity in fragile states.* Wageningen: Wageningen University.

Fuller-Love, N., Lim, L., & Akehurst, G. (2006). Guest editorial: Female and ethnic minority entrepreneurship. *The International Entrepreneurship & Management Journal, 2*(4), 429–439. https://doi.org/10.1007/s11365-006-0007-y

Human Right Watch. (2021). An Island jail in the middle of the sea. www.hrw.org/report/2021/06/07/island-jail-middle-sea/bangladeshs-relocation-rohingya-refugees-bhasan-char

Jabbar, S.A., & Zaza, H.I. (2016). Evaluating a vocational training programme for women refugees at the Zaatari camp in Jordan: Women empowerment: A journey and not an output. *International Journal of Adolescence and Youth. 21*(3), 304–319. https://doi.org/10.1080/02673843.2015.1077716

Jacobsen, K. (2002). Livelihoods in conflict: The pursuit of livelihoods by refugees and the impact on the human security of host communities. *International Migration, 40*(2), 95–123. https://doi.org/10.1111/1468-2435.00213

Jacobsen, K., & Fratzke, S. (2016). *Building livelihood opportunities for refugee population: Lessons from past practice.* Washington DC: Migration Policy Institute.

Kabeer, N. (1999). Resources, agency, achievements: Reflections on the measurement of women’s empowerment. *Development and Change, 30*(3), 435–464. https://doi.org/10.1111/1467-7660.00125

Kayas, M.M.E. (2022). Ashrayan Project: ‘Sheikh Hasina Model’ in inclusive development. *The Business Standard.* www.tbsnews.net/thoughts/ashrayan-project-sheikh-hasina-model-inclusive-development-489250

Khamphakdy-Brown, S., Jones, L.N., Nilsson, J.E., Russell, E.B., & Klevens, C.L. (2006). The empowerment program: An application of an outreach program for refugee and immigrant Women. *Journal of Mental Health Counselling, 28*(1), 38–47. https://doi.org/10.17744/mehc.28.1.fmc2j3jw5xx1cvbf

Kleist, N. (2010). Negotiating respectable masculinity: Gender and recognition in the Somali diaspora. *African Diaspora, 3*(2), 185–206. https://doi.org/10.1163/187254610X526913

Macdonald, G., Mekker, I. & Mooney, L. (2023). Conflict dynamics between Bangladeshi host communities and Rohingya refugees. Special Report. United States Institute of Peace. www.usip.org/publications/2023/04/conflict-dynamics-between-bangladeshi-host-communities-and-rohingya-refugees.

Malik, A.A., Bernstein, H., Mohr, E., & Irvin-Erickson, Y. (2018). *For-profit Humanitarians IKEA’s partnership with the Jordan River Foundation.* Research Report. Urban Institute, Washington DC.

Marra, T. (2014). *Our diary book.* IKEA Foundation. https://ikeafoundation.org/blog/our-diary-book/

Mawson, S., & Kasem, L. (2019). Exploring the entrepreneurial intentions of Syrian refugees in the UK. *International Journal of Entrepreneurial Behavior & Research, 25*(5), 1128–1146. https://doi.org/10.1108/IJEBR-02-2018-0103

Melnikas, A.J., Ainul, S., Ehsan, I., Haque, E., & Amin, S. (2020). Child marriage practices among the Rohingya in Bangladesh. *Conflict and Health, 14*(28). https://doi.org/10.1186/s13031-020-00274-0

Milner, J., & Loescher, G. (2011). Responding to protracted refugee situations: Lessons from a decade of discussion. *Forced Migration Policy Briefing* 6. Oxford: Refugee Studies Centre, Oxford.

OCHA. (2021). Rohingya refugee crisis. United Nations Office for the Coordination of Humanitarian Affairs. www.unocha.org/rohingya-refugee-crisis

O'Hara, C., & Clement, F. (2018). Power as agency: A critical reflection on the measurement of women's empowerment in the development sector. *World Development, 106*, 111–123. https://doi.org/10.1016/j.worlddev.2018.02.002

OXFAM International. (2023). Bangladesh Rohingya refugee crisis. www.oxfam.org/en/what-we-do/emergencies/bangladesh-rohingya-refugee-crisis (Accessed April 28, 2023).

Pluess, J.D., & Victor, S. (2018). Business models for building refugee resilience. *Stanford Social Innovation Review: Informing and Inspiring Leaders of Social Change.* https://ssir.org/articles/entry/business_models_for_building_refugee_resilience#

Ray, T. (2023). Women entrepreneurs in Kosovo empowered by access to funding: Financial assistance the key ingredient for successful growth. International Finance Corporation: World Bank Group. www.ifc.org/en/types/stories/2023/funding-key-ingredient-successful-growth# (Accessed July 8, 2023).

Richey, M., Randall, R., Brooks, J., & Ravishankar, M.N. (2021). *UK refugee entrepreneurship pilot scheme.* UK: Center for Entrepreneurs. https://ach.org.uk/sites/default/files/2021-03/UK%20refugee%20entrepreneurship%20pilot%20scheme.pdf

Ridge, T., Hale J., & Hoefer, M.D. (2004). *2003 yearbook of immigration statistics.* U.S. Department of Homeland Security.

Ritchie, H.A. (2014). *Rethinking 'entrepreneurship' in fragile environments: Lessons learnt in Somali women's enterprise, human security and inclusion.* Occasional Paper No. 9. IS Academy on Human Security in Fragile States, Wageningen University, Wageningen.

Ritchie, H.A. (2017). *Uncertain livelihoods in refugee environments: Between risk and tradition for Syrian refugee women in Jordan.* Report 15. Secure Livelihoods Research Consortium, Overseas Development Institute, London.

Ritchie, H.A. (2018). Gender and enterprise in fragile refugee settings: Female empowerment amidst male emasculation—a challenge to local integration?. *Disasters, 42*(1), 40–60. https://doi.org/10.1111/disa.12271

Sen, A. (2005). *Development as freedom.* New Delhi: Oxford University Press.

Senthanar, S., MacEachen, E., Premji, S., & Bigelow, P. (2020). Employment integration experiences of Syrian refugee women arriving through Canada's varied refugee protection programmes. *Journal of Ethnic and Migration Studies, 47*(3), 575–595. https://doi.org/10.1080/1369183X.2020.1733945

Sepulveda, L., Syrett, S., & Lyon, F. (2011). Population superdiversity and new migrant enterprise: The case of London. *Entrepreneurship & Regional Development, 23*(7–8), 469–497. https://doi.org/10.1080/08985620903420211

Street, C.P., Ng, P.Y., & Al-Dajani, H. (2022), Refugee women business mentors: New evidence for women's empowerment. *Sustainability, 14*, 9154. https://doi.org/10.3390/su14159154

Turner, S. (2005). *Suspended spaces: Contesting sovereignties in a refugee camp*. In: T.B. Hansen & F. Stepputat (Eds.), *Sovereign bodies: Citizens, migrants, and states in the postcolonial world* (pp. 312–332). Princeton, NJ: University Press.

Turner, S. (2010). *Politics of innocence: Hutu identity. Conflict and camp life*. New York: Berghahn Books.

Turner, S. (2014). Making good citizens from bad life in post-genocide Rwanda. *Development Change, 45*(3), 415–433. https://doi.org/10.1111/dech.12093

UNHCR. (1967, 1951). Convention and protocol relating to the status of refugees. Retrieved from www.unhcr.org/about-unhcr/who-we-are/1951-refugee-convention

UNHCR. (2002). "Refugee Women (EC/GC/02/8)," Global consultations on international protection, UNHCR, 25 April 2002. *Refugee Survey Quarterly. Special Issue on Refugee Women, 21*, 78–86. www.jstor.org/stable/45053861

UNHCR. (2023). Global Report 2023. Asia and Pacific. https://reporting.unhcr.org/global-report-2023/regional-overviews/asia-and-pacific

UNICEF. (2019). *The Rohingya refugee crisis: The humanitarian crisis continues with no immediate solution in sight*. UNICEF Bangladesh. www.unicef.org/bangladesh/en/rohingya-refugee-crisis-0

UNICEF. (2022). Gender-based violence in emergencies: Gender-based violence reaches every corner of the globe. In emergency settings, GBV soars. www.unicef.org/protection/gender-based-violence-in-emergencies

United Nations Social Development Network. (2012). *Empowerment: What does it mean to you?* Department of Economic and Social Affairs, Division for Social Policy and Development. www.un.org/esa/socdev/ngo/outreachmaterials/empowerment-booklet.pdf

Uphoff, N. (2005). Analytical issues in measuring empowerment at the community and local levels. In D. Narayan (Ed.), *Measuring empowerment: Cross-disciplinary perspectives* (pp. 219–246). Washington, DC: World Bank.

Wood, B., Ng, P., & Bastian, B. (2021). Hegemonic conceptualizations of empowerment in entrepreneurship and their suitability for collective contexts. *Administrative Sciences, 11*(1), 28. https://doi.org/10.3390/admsci11010028

20 Social entrepreneurship

A key element of the refugee entrepreneurship ecosystem

Rima M. Bizri

Introduction

The value of a research depends on how capable it is of solving problems. With wars raging in multiple locations worldwide, giving rise to a constantly increasing number of refugees, the world is in dire need of effective solutions that would not only address the displacement-related challenges, but also create and capitalise on potential benefits for the host communities. "Refugee entrepreneurship" has thus become an increasingly relevant topic in academic research as well as in policymaking due to its role in proposing ways for alleviating financial hardship among refugees and creating opportunities for economic and social integration within host communities. However, refugee entrepreneurship does not happen overnight, and being a popular topic does not automatically make it an easily implementable solution. Though research on refugee entrepreneurship exploded with the Syrian refugee crisis (Alexandre et al., 2019; Bizri, 2017; Harima et al., 2021; Mawson & Kasem, 2019; Obschonka et al., 2018; Shepherd et al., 2020; Turner, 2020; Abebe, 2023), very few studies focused on the entrepreneurial ecosystem in which refugee entrepreneurship thrives (Birdthistle et al., 2019; Collins et al., 2017; Harima et al., 2019; Marchand & Dijkhuizen, 2018).

An effective and sustainable ecosystem is necessary to identify, develop, protect, and support refugee entrepreneurs – an ecosystem that understands and appreciates the added value of entrepreneurship within the refugee communities, and is able to diminish the barriers they face along the way. Typically, an entrepreneurial ecosystem comprises interdependent actors and relationships that support the creation of new ventures (Liguori et al., 2019). One of the important actors of the refugee-entrepreneurial ecosystem is the social enterprise which plays a vital role in enhancing the business and social environments in which it operates (Barton et al., 2022; Kilpatrick et al., 2021; Kong, 2019; McKinnon et al, 2020; Meqdadi et al., 2020). In many cases, the social enterprise meets a variety of social and business needs, often playing a role that is traditionally performed by government bodies, thus filling a gap in the ecosystem within the host economy. The possibility of identifying multiple,

DOI: 10.4324/9781003368540-25

and even synergistic, entrepreneurial solutions is dependent on how alert the ecosystem actors are to needs, gaps, and capabilities present in the ecosystem. The higher the alertness of the social entrepreneurs, the more precise the identification of systemic gaps, potential solutions, and latent synergies. In other words, the greater the alertness, the more effective and efficient the ecosystem.

The aim of this chapter is to explore the ways in which social entrepreneurs, being important actors in the entrepreneurial ecosystem, could capitalise on the synergies surrounding the entrepreneurial space to promote sustainable refugee entrepreneurship and facilitate business start-up and growth. This chapter also posits that the creation of policies, bodies, and public sector systems to promote refugee entrepreneurship would deliver better results if combined with "entrepreneurial alertness" which helps to connect the elements of the ecosystem through scanning, associating, and evaluating opportunities for synergy (Tang et al., 2012). Policymakers would need to create "alert" bodies and systems to become better at spotting connections and identifying patterns that would link social enterprises together and to other relevant enterprises within and outside the refugee community. A higher-level view is needed to move from the refugee entrepreneurship landscape out into its ecosystem space where entrepreneurial activity occurs at a collective and much grander level, securing access to human, financial, technological, and professional resources, and leading towards an integrative framework for social enterprise in the refugee entrepreneurship ecosystem.

In a refugee situation and on the ground, the ecosystem is far from entrepreneurial, and refugees are, at best, provided with basic life support and little else. At times like these, the priority always goes to providing sustenance, shelter, and basic infrastructure for the refugee community. It is only afterward that host government authorities begin to consider, evaluate, and possibly engage in promoting refugee entrepreneurship, taking up the role of "after-the-fact" regulator of an existing activity with the purpose of limiting the damage rather than creating potential. Along these lines, the prominent economist Mariana Mazzucato refers to the juxtaposition between government's "market-fixing" and "market-shaping" roles (Mazzucato & Ryan-Collins, 2022). She posits that the public sector (which represents government policy) should not be focused on fixing market inefficiencies but rather on shaping market direction through active and intelligent entrepreneurial participation. She even suggests that, in many cases, this is exactly what the public sector has done, pointing to the huge public sector investments in innovations that have revolutionised industry at large (Mazzucato, 2016).

Today, with raging wars flaming numerous areas around the world, refugee situations are recurring and displaced people have become a common sight. Strategies are being developed and adopted at national, federal, and local government levels to address these situations with the needed readiness, but more proactiveness is needed to turn serious challenges into serious opportunities. Structural systems are necessary to facilitate entrepreneurial activities, and to channel entrepreneurs, their ideas, and skills into the marketplace inside and outside the refugee community. Such a system was pioneered by the United Nations High Commission for Refugees (UNHCR) in Ecuador where a flood of refugees from the Pacific coast of Colombia were directed and trained to become economic players in the refugee community, and later the host community. Eventually, refugee entrepreneurs became facilitators of their own integration in Ecuador, the host economy, contributing to its development through the creation of small businesses which offered products and services needed by both refugee and host communities (Sánchez Piñeiro, 2017).

This model has also been replicated with other forced displacements, such as with Syrian (Senthanar et al., 2021) and Ukrainian refugees (Klyver et al., 2022), where a variety of supportive institutional levers were put in place to facilitate entrepreneurial activity that would ultimately lead to the economic development and integration of refugees into their host communities. However, there have always been limits to what government authorities are able to do to support the entrepreneurial ecosystem due to the constraints of government policy (Mason & Brown, 2014; Soliman et al., 2023) and budgets. Existing policies, procedures, and budgets are often difficult to amend, and may require excessively complex and politically straining processes. This is where social entrepreneurship usually presents an alternate and more feasible pathway.

Social entrepreneurship

Social entrepreneurship involves recognising complex social problems and the inability of existing (government) systems to solve them, while identifying new entrepreneurial models that could better address them (Bornstein & Davis, 2010; Gray et al., 2003). In other words, social entrepreneurs have the ability to detect gaps in the entrepreneurial ecosystem where they could add value and facilitate entrepreneurial activity by using new business models which blend the "for-profit" concept with "community service" motivation. At the personal level, social entrepreneurship has been defined as an individual skill or character trait (Christmann, 2014) which displays a passion for ethics and justice (Mair & Marti, 2006), leading the social entrepreneur to undertake a venture that would contribute to ethical and just social outcomes.

Though much confusion persists on the difference between the impact of the social enterprise and that of governmental efforts in support of entrepreneurship, a comparison by Bornstein and Davis (2010) in their seminal work adds considerable clarity. The authors differentiate between governments and social entrepreneurs by pointing out that the former operate from the top down, while the latter address problems from the bottom up, starting with an interaction with a problem on the ground level leading to an organisation through trial and error, gaining advantage from the nuanced understanding of ground-level detail. Governments on the other hand lack the flexibility of social enterprises as they are constrained by unnecessary rules and protocols.

Thus, the social enterprise that aims to support refugee entrepreneurship appears to have several advantages over similar government initiatives. In fact, due to its sustainability-driven approach, the social enterprise can achieve social objectives without overburdening the government/public sector with unnecessary costs, as other programmes do. Nevertheless, perhaps the most important benefit of social entrepreneurship is community collaboration among the multiple actors of the ecosystem which may, in turn, promote not only refugee entrepreneurship, but also interdependence and social cohesion (Kovanen, 2021), leading to increased social capital in the refugee community.

The aforementioned point is of extreme importance in a refugee entrepreneurship context and warrants further elaboration. Refugee entrepreneurs face enormous challenges that are often insurmountable. Most of the refugee entrepreneurial initiatives do not reach the profit-making stage despite the feasibility and potential of their businesses. Failure is often attributed to issues related to logistics, legalities, or the value chain (Ataei et al., 2020), not to the low usefulness or quality of the product or service offering. In other words, the success or failure of refugee entrepreneurial ventures largely depends on factors related to the entrepreneurial ecosystem in the host community. In the absence of adequate support from the public sector, gaps in the ecosystem are often addressed by social entrepreneurs who capitalise on existing resources and networks to lubricate the entrepreneurial value chain and facilitate entrepreneurial activities in ways that foster interdependence and collaboration. This ultimately leads to the expansion of the social capital base (Bizri, 2017) and to a deeply connected entrepreneurial ecosystem marked by social cohesion and integration. The interdependence among the actors in the ecosystem eventually strengthens the collaborative ties and renders networks of market players more resilient, both economically and socially.

Social entrepreneurship in context

An illustrative example is the *MedUP!* (Maroush et al., 2020). *Promoting Social Entrepreneurship in the Mediterranean Region* project was initiated in 2018 with the objective of enhancing the entrepreneurial ecosystem by focusing on one of its important components, social entrepreneurship, and improving the social entrepreneurship landscape in Lebanon and five other regional nations by drawing enabling policies, capacity-building for support organisations, and by directly enabling a number of social enterprises in the country. The *MedUP!* project focused on two main areas – (1) impact and (2) sustainability – through the creation of a *Social Enterprise Network* (a grant fund to support and mentor social enterprises), the initiation of a public–private dialogue for policy advocacy, and the launch of a landscape study that sets a baseline against which to measure future achievements. With *MedUP!*, the existing entrepreneurial ecosystem in Lebanon was recharged to make a positive impact, though it came rather late, considering the Syrian refugees flowed into Lebanon seven years earlier. It is not hard to imagine the impact and sustainability of social enterprises in Lebanon had this project existed prior to the forced displacement of the Syrian refugees (Maroush et al., 2020). This only accentuates the crucial role of proactiveness in taking measures well in advance of forced displacements, having plans set for implementation and blueprints ready for execution.

In a more recent study of the Lebanese entrepreneurial ecosystem where a large Palestinian refugee population thrives, the authors found that the absence of adequate government regulation and support negatively impacted the development of social entrepreneurial intentions among those refugees (Abou Chakra & Al Jardali, 2022). Though the results of the study were rather intuitive, they were indicative of the need for government regulation that protects and supports refugees' entrepreneurial and social ventures.

Now that the world recognises that refugee crises will continue to exist and recur, it has become clear that some of the most essential structural preparations needed for an effective entrepreneurial ecosystem are government-backed contingency plans for supporting and developing social enterprises in potential refugee communities. In fact, recent studies have indicated that refugee entrepreneurial activity may not be expected to function effectively without social entrepreneurial initiatives (Maroush et al., 2020) designed to address gaps created by existing policy frameworks.

The role of alertness

The value of social entrepreneurs is that they are in touch with what happens on the ground. More often than not, gaps in the ecosystem are "detected" by alert social entrepreneurs who are able to link them with multiple human, financial, and technological capacities in the ecosystem, thereby overcoming existing barriers and facilitating entrepreneurial survival and growth. Entrepreneurial alertness has been described as the situation where entrepreneurs are able to notice factors within their domain of expertise that result in the recognition of opportunities which go unrecognised by others (Ardichvili et al., 2003; Baron & Ensley, 2006).

However, it is important to note the following nuance: Previous research offers the useful analogy where lower-rank employees can induce bottom-up socially inspired innovations in for-profit organisations (Alt & Craig, 2016) because employees on the ground can experience the problems/needs, and possibly the solutions, more closely. The same thing happens with social entrepreneurs except that the latter usually have a ***moral motivation*** to take the risk and move forward with the solution. Social entrepreneurs are indeed "entrepreneurs" who are motivated by the desire to solve a social/communal problem. They possess a sensitivity – an alertness – not only to the needs of their fellow humans but also to the potential connections that may exist, or that *they* might forge, around those needs. Thus, there is a significant link between alertness of social entrepreneurs and their innovative thinking (Zhao et al., 2021).

An example[1] of the alertness of a typical social entrepreneur is Aicha. Aicha is a refugee who works as a registered nurse at a busy medical centre in a distant African refugee camp. Aicha noticed that most of the medical centre staff's children had to wait, unattended, for their parents for an average of 4 hours after school daily before their parents (non-refugees) could punch out and take them home. Weekends were worse as the schools were closed and the children were left unattended for hours on end. Aicha could sense the need/problem/gap, but she could also see the solution. She had a long conversation with the medical centre director who had a conversation with the town's mayor (*it was a small town…*), who pulled a few strings at the local bank which financed the rehabilitation of the medical centre's backside warehouse into a minimalist childcare centre for the staff's children. Naturally, the bank's financing had to be paid back and the operational cost of running the childcare centre required a constant flow of income. This is where her entrepreneurial alertness helped Aicha to connect the dots and create a model whereby the childcare centre employees (mostly refugee-camp mothers) worked 4 hours in the morning in the kitchen corner of the warehouse to produce meals (a profit-making item), and 4 hours in the afternoon caring for the medical staff's children. The modest profits made from meal sales covered the running cost of the childcare centre, children were adequately tended to until their parents picked them up, and the bank loan was paid out in small instalments. By the end of the first year of operation, the quality of the meals had attracted consumers from all around the town and the sales grew to an extent that the warehouse had to be remodelled to accommodate an industrial kitchen. The childcare centre developed an outstanding reputation of quality care and preschool preparation to an extent that employees of other institutions wanted to enrol their children in it and an expansion was underway.

For both projects, human, financial, and technological resources were needed and in an entrepreneurial ecosystem where policies were in place, entrepreneurial activity would be triggered to support these projects. Construction contractors and subcontractors, with their own sets of white- and blue-collar labour, would sprout around these projects offering their services and competing with differentiation in quality and cost. Service providers would emerge to offer transportation for children enrolled from outside the medical centre community, and meal delivery to customers around various parts of the town.

However, in an entrepreneurial ecosystem where alertness is high, many more opportunities for entrepreneurship would be detected. Policymakers would be alerted about the need for recruitment and training of staff, inspection services for food production, and evaluation services of the childcare practices and facilities, in addition to a myriad of other needs – and resources – which could only be identified through a bird's-eye view of the ecosystem. The alertness of various ecosystem participants (regulators, policymakers, social entrepreneurs, and refugee entrepreneurs) is crucial for the dynamic advancement of that ecosystem without duplication, overlap, wastage, or nepotism. Aicha's entrepreneurial alertness was bottom-up, while the policymakers' alertness was top-down, and both types of alertness were needed and acted in a complementary and synergistic fashion. Here again, the critical role of the public sector emerges as a fully-fledged market participant, mostly through Public-Private-Partnerships (PPPs) which ideally promote a coordinated effort that generates innovative market solutions. Traditionally, PPPs have been assigned the task of "de-risking" entrepreneurial projects which, in reality, limits the potential role they ***could*** be playing. Instead, the public sector needs to divert its goal from de-risking towards full-on risk-taking, since "winning policies provide enough rewards to cover the losses, and ... losses are used as lessons to improve and renew future policies" (Mazzucato et al., 2020).

Indeed, there is added value in adjusting the mindsets of regulatory and policymaking bodies and systems in a way that facilitates the synchronisation of the disjointed efforts of social enterprises which often emerge in a disorderly fashion, possibly duplicating efforts and wasting community resources. Even with the best intentions, if not well coordinated, social enterprises may strain their ecosystems and forgo valuable efficiencies, hence the need for synchronisation by *'alert'* regulators with a high view of the ecosystem, its resources, deficiencies, and opportunities for synergy.

This leads to the premise that alertness is not only an attribute of individuals but also of institutions. In a refugee entrepreneurial ecosystem, regulatory institutions have the ability, ***and responsibility***, to scan the entrepreneurial landscape for social enterprises which might have (1) synergistic relationships with refugee start-ups and could move them forward and (2) a positive role in connecting refugee entrepreneurial ventures with host country ventures and *their* ecosystem, ultimately expanding the scope of economic activity.

Adopting this vision of the public sector's role is critical for changing the role's *impact* as well as the role players' *identity*. According to Mazzucato et al. (2020), the traditional discourse has adopted the stand that government activity in the market is that of a mere regulator/policeman, whose purpose is to de-risk market activity more than anything else, limiting potential for outlandish groundbreaking ventures. This aim, described by this "language", will likely attract only employees who fit this profile and seek to follow the stated agenda, employees who prefer stability to risk, and mediocrity to outstanding feats. It becomes a self-fulfilling prophecy where the false premise paves the way for a below-standard status quo which aims to sustain the false premise. In other words, if government bodies accept the role of market guardian and fixer, then that is what they will end up doing, and this is the culture they would be building. However, if government bodies take on the role of "market shaper", then their people would be likewise oriented, and their identities and outcomes would be far more entrepreneurial. "The public sector bears responsibility for the long-term resilience and stability of societies, and for shaping public outcomes through policy-making and public institutions" (Mazzucato & Kattel, 2020, p. 2), suggesting that government role should ideally transcend "market-fixing" to assume the more impactful role of "market-shaping", and this should be reflected in the discourse used around public sector investment.

Social entrepreneurship – Alertness framework

The takeaway of this chapter is how social entrepreneurship could positively impact refugee entrepreneurial activity from within and outside the refugee community, as influenced by the entrepreneurial alertness of multiple actors in the entrepreneurial ecosystem. Entrepreneurial alertness could facilitate social entrepreneurship at three levels: within the refugee community space helping refugee entrepreneurs; in the regulatory space, helping government institutions detect gaps and fill them through joining start-ups together to benefit from synergies; and in the market space, where social entrepreneurs, external to both the refugee community and the regulatory bodies, could detect synergies that aim at filling gaps and meeting social needs (see Figure 20.1). An elaboration is presented below.

Alertness within the entrepreneurial community

There are numerous opportunities for improvement in any refugee community, and those who thrive in those communities are the ones who know best what social and economic gaps exist and what needs are most pressing. When members of those communities can identify those needs and conceptualise and act upon sustainable methods by which to meet them, those members are by definition social entrepreneurs (Bornstein & Davis, 2010) stemming from within the refugee communities.

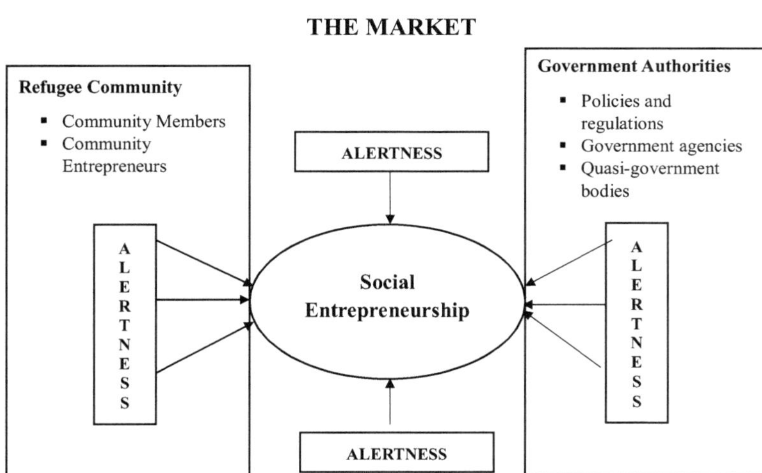

Figure 20.1 Social entrepreneurship – Alertness framework.

Source: Developed by the author.

A social entrepreneurship example[2] was when a refugee farmer living in a vast refugee camp in Turkey noticed an abundance of idle young men within the camp, a large patch of land suitable for agriculture at the edge of the camp, and an availability of other "ingredients" (water, seeds, and sunlight) for a horticulture mini project. Using his eight years' experience growing tropical crops in arid spaces, this entrepreneur invited fellow refugees to join in cultivating the patch to produce tropical crops (organic and pesticide-free) and start selling them to the camp's managing staff at symbolic prices. Over two years, the project grew and became a profit-making venture that met a growing consumer need, employed and provided training to previously idle labours, and generated a small profit to reinvest in the project. Through his alertness, this social entrepreneur was able to recognise an opportunity, conceptualize a solution, and meet a social need that was otherwise unmet. In this example, the alert social entrepreneur, the social need, the solution, and the beneficiaries all came from within the refugee community.

Alertness in the market

The same opportunity could be noticed by a social entrepreneur from *outside* the refugee community, who may be more familiar with the resources (physical, financial, human, and technological) available in the market outside the refugee community. She might be alerted to a connection between a pressing social need within the refugee camp and an outside capability or resource that could meet that need. She might even conceptualise a variety of solutions, given the wider range of inputs and methods available to her in the outside market. In this case, the alert social entrepreneur identifies the solution (capability or resource) from outside the refugee community and makes it available to solve the community's problem. Without the alertness of the social entrepreneur, the refugee community would still be lacking a capability, existing and available but inaccessible for use by that community.

Alertness of regulatory bodies

The third case is where individuals working at regulatory bodies and policymaking institutions are alerted to symbiotic opportunities among potential participants within and outside the refugee community. The roles of regulatory bodies and policymakers currently revolve around fixing market failures, formulating guidelines which govern the interaction between society, the refugee community, and pertinent government agencies, in addition to developing programmes for increasing awareness of the needs, limitations, and requirements of all three entities.

However, government bodies and the public sector are well-positioned to view the entrepreneurial landscape within and external to the refugee community. By taking the *alert* stand of "market-shaper", they can identify refugees' pressing social needs, connect the dots, and link recipients with suitable providers from inside and outside that community, for the purpose of ensuring quality outputs and compliant practices and processes. This capability ultimately widens the scope of interaction among the ecosystem participants and allows the public sector to play a more critical role in identifying, funding, and overseeing risky endeavours which, as suggested by Laplane & Mazzucato (2020), could also be a source of lucrative returns that might be reinvested in new innovative research. Laplane and Mazzucato argue that the public sector should be able to share both risks and returns of its public investments, to allow for the recycling of rewards into ever-revolving investments. A public "innovation fund" might be the logical outcome of all public sector investments, and this is what would likely stimulate the entrepreneurial appetite, and alertness, of that sector.

It may be argued that the entrepreneurial alertness of policymakers could have considerable leverage on social enterprises as the former use their capacities to create appropriate linkages with and among the latter. For example, the entrepreneurial alertness of a regulatory body may flag the potential benefits of connecting two or three social enterprises in a way that offers economies of scope through the utilization of the same value chain, eventually reaping shared benefits at a lower cost per enterprise. The selection of the most suited business partner is made easier, faster, and more efficiently when *"alert"* regulatory systems are already in place. Clearly, alertness on all three levels may be essential for facilitating social entrepreneurship within the entrepreneurial ecosystem.

Systemising alertness: It goes beyond training...

In a study by Ho et al. (2018), entrepreneurial competencies of alertness and efficacy among youth were found to be enhanced through specialised entrepreneurial training. However, it can be argued that honing entrepreneurial alertness may require going beyond mere training to a level of systemisation which aims to enhance the symbiosis and coordination among regulatory, policymaking bodies and social enterprises. Training alone, though helpful, may not provide the intended results. Building systems of scanning, screening, connecting, testing, execution, and assessment might be a useful blueprint for systemising alertness and proactivity in regulatory and policymaking bodies, ultimately leading to an interconnected ecosystem of participants from within and outside the refugee community. So perhaps through the systemisation of alertness, developing processes for scanning and searching for synergies, associating and connecting, evaluating and judging symbiotic proposals, meaningful and effective collaborations could be forged more quickly to promote refugee entrepreneurship in the host community. A useful area to explore is the integration of artificial intelligence (AI) models which might represent a progressive and effective means (Ratten, 2020) of systemising alertness in the ecosystem. Both public and private sectors already have enormous data sets that could be used to train AI systems to perform the abovementioned tasks (de Sousa-Filho et al., 2020), thus revolutionising the involvement of the public sector, making it more *"alert"*, and transforming its role from regulator to partner in the ecosystem.

It may be necessary to draw out the roles of central vs. local/regional government separately as each may have a different focus, approach, and impact. However, this issue may be the subject of another study as a variety of factors may be at play at each level of administration, such as the size and reach of government, allocated budgets, technological acceptance, degree of involvement in the refugee ecosystem, trained human resources, and support systems, to mention a few.

Conclusion

Countries on the border of neighbouring nations known to suffer from internal or external political strife should develop ready-to-implement contingent structural plans for the creation of entrepreneurial ecosystems, which would facilitate the emergence of not only entrepreneurial start-ups but, more importantly, social enterprises designed to support them. Structural plans could range in scope from screening and assessment mechanisms to training and incubation programmes, networking initiatives, and financing schemes. Eventually, we could enhance the suitability of these mechanisms and initiatives to the surrounding environment so that they provide growth opportunities to other elements of the ecosystem without unduly draining its resources.

At the inspirational level, social entrepreneurship is a socio-economic correction tool. It often creates a support system for the underprivileged, unemployed, and under-financed individuals. It combines "*will*" with "*capacity*" to serve the community using a win-win approach. Drayton (2006) described it as having the goal of using socially innovative ideas to rectify social wrongs in this world. This chapter suggests that, armed with entrepreneurial alertness, social entrepreneurship may well be what communities need to promote and advance refugee entrepreneurship.

Given the nature and limitations of this conceptual paper, it might be useful to put the above-proposed relationships to the test in empirical studies to gain some objective insight which would develop this line of thought and move it forward.

Notes

1 Hypothetical example for illustration only.
2 Hypothetical example for illustration only.

References

Abebe, S.A. (2023). Refugee entrepreneurship: Systematic and thematic analyses and a research agenda. *Small Business Economics*, *60*(1), 315–350. https://doi.org/10.1007/s11187-022-00636-3

Abou Chakra, S.M., & Al Jardali, H. (2022). Drivers of social entrepreneurial intentions of Palestinian refugees in Lebanon. *Journal of Research in Marketing and Entrepreneurship*, *24*(2), 242–269. https://doi.org/10.1108/JRME-02-2021-0014

Alexandre, L., Salloum, C., & Alalam, A. (2019). An investigation of migrant entrepreneurs: The case of Syrian refugees in Lebanon. *International Journal of Entrepreneurial Behaviour & Research, 25*(5), 1147–1164. https://doi.org/10.1108/IJEBR-03-2018-0171

Alt, E., & Craig, J. B. (2016). Selling issues with solutions: Igniting social intrapreneurship in for-profit organizations. *Journal of Management Studies*, *53*(5), 794–820. https://doi.org/10.1111/joms.12200

Ardichvili, A., Cardozo, R., & Ray, S. (2003). A theory of entrepreneurial opportunity identification and development. *Journal of Business Venturing*, *18*(1), 105–123. https://doi.org/10.1287/mnsc.1060.0538

Ataei, P., Karimi, H., Ghadermarzi, H., & Norouzi, A. (2020). A conceptual model of entrepreneurial competencies and their impacts on rural youth's intention to launch SMEs. *Journal of Rural Studies*, *75*, 185–195. https://doi.org/10.1016/j.jrurstud.2020.01.023

Baron, R.A., & Ensley, M.D. (2006). Opportunity recognition as the detection of meaningful patterns: Evidence from comparisons of novice and experienced entrepreneurs. *Management Science*, *52*(9), 1331–1344. https://doi.org/10.1287/mnsc.1060.0538

Barton, S., Porter, H., Murphy, S., & Lysaght, R. (2022). Potential outcomes of work integration social enterprises for people who are homeless, at risk of homelessness, or transitioning out of homelessness. *Social Enterprise Journal*, *18*(3), 409–433. https://doi.org/10.1108/SEJ-07-2021-0054

Birdthistle, N., Flynn, A., & Rushworth, S. (2019). From Syria to the land down under–The land of opportunity? *International Journal on Minority and Group Rights, 26*(1), 116–137. www.jstor.org/stable/27001395

Bizri, R.M. (2017). Refugee entrepreneurship: A social capital perspective. *Entrepreneurship & Regional Development*, *29*(9–10), 847–868. https://doi.org/10.1080/08985626.2017.1364787

Bornstein, D., & Davis, S. (2010). *Social entrepreneurship: What everyone needs to know*. Oxford University Press.

Christmann, G. B. (2014). Social entrepreneurs on the periphery: Uncovering emerging pioneers of regional development. *The Planning Review*, *50*(1), 43–55. https://doi.org/10.1080/02513625.2014.926725

Collins, J., Morrison, M., Basu, P.K., & Krivokapic-Skoko, B. (2017). Indigenous culture and entrepreneurship in small businesses in Australia. *Small Enterprise Research*, *24*(1), 36–48. https://doi.org/10.1080/13215906.2017.1289855

de Sousa-Filho, J.M., Matos, S., da Silva Trajano, S., & de Souza Lessa, B. (2020). Determinants of social entrepreneurial intentions in a developing country context. *Journal of Business Venturing Insights*, *14*, e00207. https://doi.org/10.1016/j.jbvi.2020.e00207

Desai, S., Naudé, W., & Stel, N. (2021). Refugee entrepreneurship: Context and directions for future research. *Small Business Economics*, *56*(3), 933–945. https://doi.org/10.1007/s11187-019-00310-1

Drayton, W. (2006). Everyone a changemaker: Social entrepreneurship's ultimate goal. *Innovations: Technology, Governance, Globalization*, *1*(1), 80–96. https://doi.org/10.1162/itgg.2006.1.1.80

Gray, M., Healy, K., & Crofts, P. (2003). Social enterprise: Is it the business of social work?. *Australian Social Work*, *56*(2), 141–154. https://doi.org/10.1046/j.0312-407X.2003.00060.x

Harima, A., Freudenberg, J., & Halberstadt, J. (2019). Functional domains of business incubators for refugee entrepreneurs. *Journal of Enterprising Communities: People and Places in the Global Economy*, *14*(5), 687–711. https://doi.org/10.1108/JEC-11-2018-0081

Harima, A., Periac, F., Murphy, T., & Picard, S. (2021). Entrepreneurial opportunities of refugees in Germany, France, and Ireland: Multiple embeddedness framework. *International Entrepreneurship and Management Journal*, *17*, 625–663. https://doi.org/10.1007/s11365-020-00707-5

Ho, M., Uy, M., Kang, B., & Chan, K. (2018). Impact of entrepreneurship training on entrepreneurial efficacy and alertness among adolescent youth. *Frontiers in Education*, *3*(13). https://doi.org/10.3389/feduc.2018.00013

Isenberg, D.J. (2010). How to start an entrepreneurial revolution. *Harvard Business Review*, *88*(6), 41–50.

Kilpatrick, S., Farmer, J., Emery, S., & DeCotta, T. (2021). Social enterprises and regional cities: Working together for mutual benefit. *Entrepreneurship & Regional Development*, *33*(9–10), 741–757. https://doi.org/10.1080/08985626.2021.1899293

Klyver, K., Steffens, P., & Honig, B. (2022). Psychological factors explaining Ukrainian refugee entrepreneurs' venture idea novelty. *Journal of Business Venturing Insights*, *18*, e00348. https://doi.org/10.1016/j.jbvi.2022.e00348

Kong, E. (2019). Harnessing and advancing knowledge in social enterprises: Theoretical and operational challenges in the refugee settlement experience. *Journal of Social Entrepreneurship*, *10*(2), 193–210. https://doi.org/10.1080/19420676.2018.1541009

Kovanen, S. (2021). Social entrepreneurship as a collaborative practice: Literature review and research agenda. *Journal of Entrepreneurship, Management and Innovation*, *17*(1), 97–128. https://doi.org/10.7341/20211713

Laplane, A., & Mazzucato, M. (2020). Socializing the risks and rewards of public investments: Economic, policy, and legal issues. *Research Policy*, *49*, 1–11. http://doi.org/10.1016/j.repolx.2020.100008

Liguori, E., Bendickson, J., Solomon, S., & McDowell, W.C. (2019). Development of a multi-dimensional measure for assessing entrepreneurial ecosystems. *Entrepreneurship & Regional Development*, *31*(1–2), 7–21. https://doi.org/10.1080/08985626.2018.1537144

Mair, J., & Marti, I. (2006). Social entrepreneurship research: A source of explanation, prediction, and delight. *Journal of World Business*, *41*(1), 36–44. https://doi.org/10.1016/j.jwb.2005.09.002

Marchand, K., & Dijkhuizen, J. (2018). Entrepreneurship as a tool for a new beginning - Entrepreneurship training for refugees in a new homeland. In N. Apostolopoulos, H. Al-Dajani, D. Holt, P. Jones, & R. Newbery (Eds.), *Entrepreneurship and the Sustainable Development Goals* (pp. 135–149). (Contemporary Issues in Entrepreneurship Research, Vol. 8). Emerald Publishing.

Maroush, Z., Wannis, H., Haidar, G., & Ayoub, T. (2020). *Lessons from the Lebanese social entrepreneurship ecosystem*. Oxfam GB. DOI: 10.21201/2020.5839

Mason, C., & Brown, R. (2014). *Entrepreneurship ecosystems and growth-oriented entrepreneurship*. Report for the OECD LEED Programme, Paris.

Mawson, S., & Kasem, L. (2019). Exploring the entrepreneurial intentions of Syrian refugees in the UK. *International Journal of Entrepreneurial Behaviour & Research, 25*(5), 1128–1146. https://doi.org/10.1108/IJEBR-02-2018-0103

Mazzucato, M. (2016). From market fixing to market-creating: A new framework for innovation policy. *Industry and Innovation, 23*(2), 140–156. https://doi.org/10.1080/13662716.2016.1146124

Mazzucato, M., & Kattel, R. (2020). COVID-19 and public-sector capacity. *Oxford Review of Economic Policy, 36* (Supplement_1), S256–S269. https://doi.org/10.1093/oxrep/graa031

Mazzucato, M., Kattel, R., & Collins, J. (2020). Challenge-driven innovation policy: Towards a new policy toolkit. *Journal of Industry, Competition and Trade, 20*, 421–437. https://doi.org/10.1007/s10842-019-00329-w

Mazzucato, M., & Ryan-Collins, J. (2022). Putting value creation back into "public value": From market-fixing to market-shaping. *Journal of Economic Policy Reform, 25*(4), 345–360. https://doi.org/10.1080/17487870.2022.2053537

McKinnon, K., Kennedy, M., Barraket, J., & DeCotta, T. (2020). Is being in work good for wellbeing? Work integration social enterprises in regional Australia. *Australian Geographer, 51*(3), 361–375. https://doi.org/10.1080/00049182.2020.1781322

McKinnon, K., Kennedy, M., & De Cotta, T. (2022). Social enterprises and community wellbeing in regional Australia. *Journal of Sociology, 58*(2), 161–177. https://doi.org/10.1177/14407833211035839

Meqdadi, O., Johnsen, T.E., & Pagell, M. (2020). Relationship configurations for procuring from social enterprises. *International Journal of Operations & Production Management, 40*(6), 819–845. https://doi.org/10.1108/IJOPM-07-2019-0523

Meyer, H.H. (2018). Analysis of entrepreneurial eco-system for refugee entrepreneurial activities in Germany. In O. Dvouletý, M. Lukeš, & J. Mísař (Eds.), *Innovation management, entrepreneurship and sustainability (IMES 2018)* (pp. 669–682). Oeconomica Publishing House.

Obschonka, M., Hahn, E., & Bajwa N.U.H. (2018). Personal agency in newly arrived refugees: The role of personality, entrepreneurial cognitions and intentions, and career adaptability. *Journal of Vocational Behavior, 105*, 173–184. https://doi.org/10.1016/j.jvb.2018.01.003

Ratten, V. (2020). Entrepreneurial ecosystems. *Thunderbird International Business Review, 62*(5), 447–455. https://doi.org/10.1002/tie.22164

Sánchez Piñeiro (2017). How business incubators can facilitate refugee entrepreneurship and integration. *UNHCR Innovation Service*. Retrieved on 31/03/2023, from www.unhcr.org/innovation/how-we-can-use-business-incubators-for-refugee-integration

Senthanar, S., MacEachen, E., Premji, S., & Bigelow, P. (2021). Entrepreneurial experiences of Syrian refugee women in Canada: A feminist grounded qualitative study. *Small Business Economics, 57*, 835–847. https://doi.org/10.1007/s11187-020-00385-1

Shepherd, D.A., Saade, F.P., & Wincent, J. (2020). How to circumvent adversity? Refugee-entrepreneurs' resilience in the face of substantial and persistent adversity. *Journal of Business Venturing, 35*(4), 105940. https://doi.org/10. 1016/j.jbusvent.2019.06.001

Soliman, S., Keles, J.Y., & Fottouh, N. (2023). Refugee entrepreneurship and institutional voids: The case of Syrian refugee entrepreneurs in Egypt. *Academy of Management Discoveries, 9*(3), 363–382. https://doi.org/10.5465/amd.2020.0200

Tang, J., Kacmar, K.M.M., & Busenitz, L. (2012). Entrepreneurial alertness in the pursuit of new opportunities. *Journal of Business Venturing, 27*(1), 77–94. https://doi.org/10.1016/j.jbusvent.2010.07.001

Turner, L. (2020). '#Refugees can be entrepreneurs too!' Humanitarianism, race, and the marketing of Syrian refugees. *Review of International Studies, 46*(1), 137–155. https://doi.org/10.1017/S0260210519000342

UNHCR. (2018). Global trends: Forced displacement in 2018. United Nations High Commissioner for Refugees. www.unhcr.org/globaltrends2018/. Accessed 22 Feb., 2023.

Zayadin, R., Zucchella, A., & Anand, A. (2022). Exploring the emancipatory role of entrepreneurship in a developing context. *International Journal of Entrepreneurial Behaviour & Research, 28*(2), 527–547. https://doi.org/10.1108/IJEBR-08-2021-0642

Zhao, W., Yang, T., Hughes, K.D., & Li, Y. (2021). Entrepreneurial alertness and business model innovation: The role of entrepreneurial learning and risk perception. *International Entrepreneurship and Management Journal, 17*, 839–864. https://doi.org/10.1007/s11365-020-00637-2

21 Refugee entrepreneurship dynamics

Conceptual considerations for research

Rosa Lisa Iannone, Sibylle Heilbrunn, and Elke Murdock

I wish to believe that, if Luxembourg (or any [...] government) would create enabling mechanisms for refugees to start their own businesses, this would de facto facilitate their social and economic integration in the host country.

– Abo Zarifa, Serial entrepreneur and refugee (2016, p. 47)

Prelude: A call for a new conceptualisation

Our history – whatever the conditions – has been characterised by an extraordinary continuum of innovation and entrepreneurial pursuits. How these have manifested across time and contexts continues to provide rich harvests that shape progress while challenging "glocal" interchanges. Nowadays, contemporary societies are increasingly drawing upon entrepreneurship as a worthwhile socio-economic pursuit; one distinct, and sometimes mythical, from other conventional forms of labour market engagement, such as employment. Intricate institutions and systems of norms, actors, services, programmes, and regulatory structures have emerged, characterising the entrepreneurial space as one that arises, grows, and remains dynamic, driven by interconnections.

Amidst unprecedented tides of forcibly displaced populations – estimated at 36.4 million, an increase of 3% from the end of 2022 (United Nations High Commissioner for Refugees: UNHCR, 2023) – entrepreneurial ecosystems (EEs) in both neighbouring and distant host communities must anticipate inflows of new refugee participants (Heilbrunn & Iannone, 2019a; categorisation based on Kunz, 1973). Under these conditions, betwixt the complexities of unauthored global dilemmas and compounded crises, refugees are carving out new entrepreneurial pathways, often in unfamiliar territories, contributing to global entrepreneurial tapestries. Representing extreme cases of entrepreneurial endeavour (Heilbrunn et al., 2019), they have demonstrated an ability to outpace nationals and other migrants in business establishment and performance (Damm & Rosholm, 2010; New American Economy, 2017; Zalkat et al., 2024).

DOI: 10.4324/9781003368540-26

Paralleling these recent, intense refugee waves, related academic studies have increased exponentially since the mid-2010s, including considerations of refugees navigating EEs in new countries of residence (Harima & Freudenberg, 2020; Harima et al., 2019; Jürgens et al., 2022; Meister & Mauer, 2019). Significant attention has also been paid to the barriers as well as enabling factors to refugee entrepreneurship (RE) (de la Chaux & Haugh, 2020; de Lange et al., 2021; Luseno & Kolade, 2023; Salmon & Singleton, 2023; Wauters & Lambrecht, 2008). Nevertheless, our theoretical understandings of the dynamics that characterise and shape these processes remain disparate and disciplinarily marked. For these reasons we are urging for a new conceptualisation.

The score: Organisation of the chapter

This chapter directly addresses a consequential research gap in RE studies by acknowledging that refugee entrepreneurs are shaped by, and simultaneously shape, their host countries, EEs, and social environments. Recent literature reviews have critiqued RE research for being largely descriptive, lacking in longitudinal studies, and for being theoretically underdeveloped (Abebe, 2023; Heilbrunn & Iannone, 2020; Newman et al., 2023). It is thus our position that purposefully shifting from unidirectional research strategies to multidirectional approaches will cast an increased critical outlook onto empirical work, allowing for a more precise understanding of RE processes.

In the next section, we outline the development of RE research and EEs, illustrating that at their foundation, there is a consensus surrounding the fact that refugee enterprises evolve through relational dynamics. Then, we elaborate further on two enveloping features that are intrinsic to these dynamics: (1) a wider neoliberal ideological context and (2) experiences of legitimacy, examined through the lens of epistemic injustice. These precede our conceptual model as they emphasise the main premise for multidirectional research, which we argue is to uncover the simultaneous tensions and transformations that take place through the dynamic processes of refugee entrepreneurs. After that, our conceptual model is presented and discussed including (1) the research loci, followed by (2) considerations of the multileveled, interconnected domains – individual (micro), social (meso), and cultural (macro). That section ends with (3) a summary of analytical tools that can be applied in future empirical work. This leads to a practical research agenda for future studies.

Mise en scène: Panoramas for refugee entrepreneurship

Recent literature from the field of business creation informs us that enterprises evolve in EEs. Initially advanced by Cohen (2005), combined with Isenberg's

(2010) pragmatic insights, our understanding of EEs supplanted the conventional discourse centred on clusters (Porter, 1990, 2000). In turn, the transition from a cluster paradigm to an EE metaphor reflects a broader intellectual trend towards adopting a more ecological lens in the analysis of entrepreneurial phenomena, thereby also broadening the scope of inquiry within the field. The conceptualisation of regional concentrations of entrepreneurial endeavours as EEs likewise signals a notable shift within scholarly discourse (Kuckertz, 2019), since EEs involve the community and cultures in which entrepreneurs interact.

However, EEs are not neutral spaces. Following the myth of meritocracy, entrance to and entrepreneurial success should ideally be based on personal achievement. Yet, critical studies have acknowledged that features such as race, class, and gender also matter and limit the possibilities and opportunities of those who are not part of a dominant EE culture (Jürgen et al., 2022). Refugees are, per definition, not part of the dominant majority in their new countries of residence – they are *the others*. Yet, despite acute institutional voids and severe disparities, some of them "made it" and have become entrepreneurs (Heilbrunn et al., 2019).

In their new contexts and with entrepreneurial trajectories, refugees do not operate in a vacuum. Ethnic enclaves, informal communities, institutions, and civil society (Kloosterman et al., 1999) all interact with them in and around formal structures, within EEs and in the wider contexts of their lived experiences. For example, Jürgen et al. (2022) identify that incubators, along with other actors and forces within EEs, encounter relational dynamics that are distinct from those typically experienced within respective mainstream contexts – creating dilemmas. Their research revealed that selection criteria for participation in EEs may blur EE-related business objectives to satisfy social objectives in attempts for greater inclusion. In turn, they postulated that this could arise from some of the trauma and compounded vulnerabilities characterising refugees that also marginalise them or create dissonance that in turn demands more time and dedication than expected. Importantly, these facets highlight what is rarely discussed, and what is the main focus of our chapter: the inherent two-way or multidirectional transformations that take place in refugee entrepreneurial processes.

Interludes: Encounters onto the scene

In this section, we consider refugee entrepreneurs' encounters in and around their new contexts from two enveloping perspectives: the wider ideological neoliberal context and the varying layers of epistemic injustice refugee entrepreneurs face, impacting their legitimacy. Critically examining the wider and indirectly evidenced implications of refugee entrepreneurs represents an important enhancement of the lines of inquiry that have dominated RE research, bringing features of power and legitimacy into primary focus.

Global neoliberal ideologies

In adopting the progress paradigm of economic growth and sustainable development, entrepreneurship and innovation ostensibly provide solutions to society's problems and challenges (Hallonsten, 2023). Accordingly, the common discourse on entrepreneurship reflects a neoliberal *Weltanschauung* of profit-oriented competition that favours the free-market arrangements of capital, deregulation, and a distancing of government interventions in both business and private activities (Heilbrunn & Iannone, 2019b). Undeniably, neoliberal policies deeply affect all aspects of people's lives and become what is termed by Brown (2015) as "governing rationality" that economises everything. The ideology infiltrates every material and non-material entity, globally. It also penetrates non-wealth-generating spheres such as learning and relationship building and effectively "submits them to market metrics and governs them with market techniques and practices. Above all, it casts people as human capital who must constantly tend to their own present and future value" (Brown in Shenk, 2015, para. 5). Meanwhile, evidence illustrates that a purely neoliberal organisation of society will inevitably create winners and losers (Bal & Dóci, 2018; McGuigan, 2014). This happens primarily because deregulation, privatisation, and governmental withdrawal from social provisions lead to a shift in power from governments to mostly multinational corporations, which are driven by profit interests (George, 2014).

Consequently, work is exchanged as a commodity on the market, often individually, rather than within frameworks of unions, which are perceived as trouble-making interventionists that disturb the "natural" flow of the free market (Heilbrunn, 2022). Players in the neoliberal reality are deemed *homo economicus* (Brown, 2015), rationally and strategically promoting their own interests and goals. This neoliberal rationality transfers the liability of success and failure towards enterprising individuals themselves, and the idea of meritocracy gives this logic a name since it legitimises emerging inequalities and provides an explanation as to why the losers can only blame themselves (Heilbrunn, 2022; Heilbrunn & Iannone, 2019b). Thus, the entrepreneurial culture emerging out of neoliberalism encompasses risk-taking, adaptability, initiative, self-confidence, results-focus, competitiveness, and organisational skills (Pauceanu et al., 2021) that foster a competitive narrative. In combination with the myth of meritocracy, this generates groups of victors and vanquished (Davies, 2014). What is more, because neoliberal rhetoric praises individuals for achievements in entrepreneurship, attributing economic independence as the ideal form of emancipation following the hardships of refuge, it equally blames the individual unfairly for shortcomings that are systemic in nature and completely out of one's control. In effect, the ideology offers an enchanting narrative that alleges equality among all, as rational actors (Gill, 2013), yet it can concurrently strengthen and reproduce unfair systems and codes that are detrimental to those who are most sensitive to shifts in support availability, means and mechanisms.

Moreover, while entrepreneurship is lauded for its potential to spur job creation and economic growth, the empirical evidence regarding its ability to generate significant empowerment for marginalised groups remains extremely limited (Honig, 2017; Naudé, 2011; Nightingale & Coad, 2014; Shane, 2009; Smit & Pretorius, 2023). Furthermore, research suggests that policies aimed at fostering entrepreneurial development through increased job opportunities and reduced poverty have not yielded expected outcomes (Fotopoulos & Storey, 2019; Pretorius et al., 2021).

Given the above, questions arise around how to foster entrepreneurship among refugees, without exacerbating the utterly new and frequently precarious circumstances they find themselves in. The situational facets of refugees are vastly different from other non-forced migrant groups (Desai et al., 2021). Refuge is characterised by restricted and limited choice (Balcilar & Nugent, 2019; Smith, 2015) and refugees' decision-making in transit is complex, compounded by the very fact that they have all been forced to leave their home countries, "owing to well-founded fear of being persecuted" (UNHCR, 1951, p.14), and an inability to access safety within their homeland's borders. In addition, they recurrently lack legal status in their new settings, restricted decision-making, and "...have limited financial resources, and do not enjoy basic rights, such as the right to work and earn a living" – factors that not only narrow their range of choices but may also lead to choices appearing less "rational" (Missbach, 2019, p. 441) to outsiders.

This leads us to consider a second significant, omnipresent feature that refugee entrepreneurs persistently encounter in their new countries of residence: epistemic injustice. Much like the neoliberal ideology that shapes material and non-material aspects of entrepreneurial processes, refugee entrepreneurs contend with an additional layer of power tensions in their new settings, where not only their rationality is doubted, but their fundamental ability *to know* is also put into question. As a starting point and as a relational feature of existence for refugee entrepreneurs seeking legitimacy in non-native countries, this additional layer of unequal power reveals insights from both the refugee perspective and of those providing refuge. Taking into account this multiplicity of perspectives will invariably enhance our critical analyses and ultimate ability to discern deeper principles that are in process in RE.

Layers of identity power and epistemic injustice

We draw upon Fricker's (2007) theoretical work on identity power and epistemic injustice to delve more deeply into the acuteness of REs' starting position upon arrival in their new, "safe", "home" territories. She refers to the harm faced by individuals, consequential to their marginalised status within a given society's systems and institutions. This is in line with the growing body of research on RE that emphasises the precarity refugee entrepreneurs face at every stage of their process of refuge, including their integration and inclusion in their host countries. However, consideration of the power asymmetry between refugee entrepreneurs and the mainstream has rarely been examined beyond aspects of integration through business creation, and the mainstream's enablings towards that end.

Epistemic injustice manifests when individuals are denied very basic opportunities to participate in society, express themselves, or even be considered as *knowers* or as people who can formulate an understanding (Boochani et al., 2020). It represents a very discernible – though overlooked – form of epistemic exclusion, silencing, and subordination that in the case of refugees create rigid, invisible barriers. As entrepreneurial hopefuls, their outset position is one of disadvantage, sometimes stemming from their inescapable legal illegitimacy and barring from formalised work recourses, or other systemic obstructions including linguistic and cultural barriers, limited access to social networks and resources, and prejudiced perceptions of their capabilities and knowledge (Desai et al., 2021). As a result, refugee entrepreneurs face a very confronting struggle to establish themselves as legitimate participants in society, and then as legitimate entrepreneurs in EEs. This has a tangible effect on all aspects of their lives and livelihoods, including access to funding, networks, and other opportunities that are crucial for integration and business success.

One key aspect of epistemic injustice is testimonial injustice which occurs when individuals' testimony is discredited or dismissed based on prejudice or stereotypes about their social identity (Fricker, 2007), entangled with the very status (and associated labels) of being a refugee. In turn, this often translates into a dismissal of entrepreneurial ideas, skills, and experiences that are ultimately undervalued or ignored by potential EE stakeholders, including investors, mentors, and collaborators. In a revelatory example of the interrelations that reinforce inequality, Omran and Yousafzai (2023) expand on the consequences of epistemic injustice, highlighting its effects through considerations of gaslighting in the context of women entrepreneurs from a postcolonial perspective. Their study calls attention to the fact that epistemic injustice can have a compounding effect on individuals who can be identified as members of multiple dejected subgroups.

At the root of testimonial injustice is hermeneutical injustice, which occurs when individuals' experiences are not adequately understood or recognised due to the absence of shared interpretative resources (Fricker, 2007), reflecting the discriminatory power of institutional practices that informally and formally exclude voices and participation of undesirable population segments. It impacts communication, meaning making, and meaning sharing which in extreme circumstances completely quash individual agency (Medina, 2017). In the context of entrepreneurship, this can manifest as a lack of identification and recognition of the unique skills that refugee entrepreneurs offer, as well as the challenges they face. For example, refugee entrepreneurs' experiences of resilience, adaptability, and creativity in overcoming adversity may not be acknowledged or valued within mainstream entrepreneurial and EE narratives, further marginalising them within these spaces (Bailey, 2020).

Altogether, the compounding features of epistemic injustice lead to intense testimonial silencing, wherein individuals are persistently and systematically prevented from participating in knowledge-sharing and decision-making processes – even those that directly affect them. Language and cultural barriers, limited social capital, and inherent host-country discriminatory practices and norms are examples of what contribute to the exacerbation of refugee entrepreneurs' struggle to take authority over and assert their own voices or even peripherally contribute meaningfully to entrepreneurial discussions and activities. As a result, their perspectives and insights will go entirely unheard, further casting them into the shadows of exclusion and inhibiting their ability to fully engage in normal life activities, or any substantive entrepreneurial opportunities (Bloch, 2014; Lyon et al., 2007; Phillimore & Goodson, 2006).

Altogether, addressing epistemic injustice in refugees' entrepreneurial processes elucidates beyond unidirectional research questions that examine the "what" of refugee entrepreneurs. Minding the nuances of epistemic injustice requires concerted, coordinated efforts to recognise and challenge underlying biases and barriers that prevent refugee entrepreneurs from legitimate participation and pathways to prosperity. Decisively considering the "why" and "how" from multilayered, interrelationships between refugee entrepreneurs, mainstream EEs and their wider contexts offers richer insights that are more meaningful and more useful in generating research-based outcomes.

Repertoires: Conceptual considerations for refugee entrepreneurship research

Considering our intention to shift towards more meaningful, multidirectional examinations of RE processes, we have discussed two important contextual features that impact refugee entrepreneurs' unequal positions of power and legitimacy within their new settings of refuge, which recognises them as the *other* within a dominant mainstream. By acknowledging such conditions, we can more appropriately conceptualise the dynamic processes of RE. As we will see, the various aspects of a useful analytical framework for research in this regard must remain sensitive to both the distinct and subtle forces that emerge through interrelationships and interactions, as there exists a gap in our current knowledge of RE regarding tensions in intermediations. This refers to the transitional and transformational actions, spaces, and processes in RE, which we argue must equally consider actors and institutions refugee entrepreneurs engage with. RE studies insufficiently theorise the power relations in multidirectional processes, which invariably strengthens a unidirectional perspective from that of refugee entrepreneurs' endeavours – and obligation – to thrive. The analytical tools discussed in this section have thus been chosen as potential means to overcoming such limits, so that we may enhance the explanatory quality of RE research.

Loci: Examining dynamic processes in RE

The conceptual model we propose for examining RE dynamics is illustrated in Figure 21.1. Taking on an enmeshed multileveled, multidirectional perspective, this model allows us to go beyond the "what" and the perfunctory "how" and "why" of entrepreneurship. It encompasses research loci that focus on the dynamics of interrelationships and intermediations, highlighting the forces of constraint as much as those of assistance. Without an interactive lens, there could be no meaningful understanding of processes. In other words, the conceptual model concerns itself with integration-related forces that make inclusion or exclusion, legitimacy, growth, and other developmental and power-related aspects possible (Ager & Strang, 2008), as well as mixed embeddedness (Kloosterman et al., 1999; Polanyi, 1957). In every instance, considerations centre on the configurations of interactions that occur in, as well as in between (people, domains, institutions, etc.).

This framing strengthens the growing body of knowledge we have that draws upon migrant entrepreneurship research in elucidating the various personal, social, and business-making processes that refugee entrepreneurs experience in their new countries of residence (Abebe, 2023; Heilbrunn & Iannone, 2020; Newman et al., 2023). The mixed embeddedness approach posits that entrepreneurs must become embedded within the social networks and institutional frameworks of their new environments in order to thrive – "encompassing the crucial interplay between the social, economic

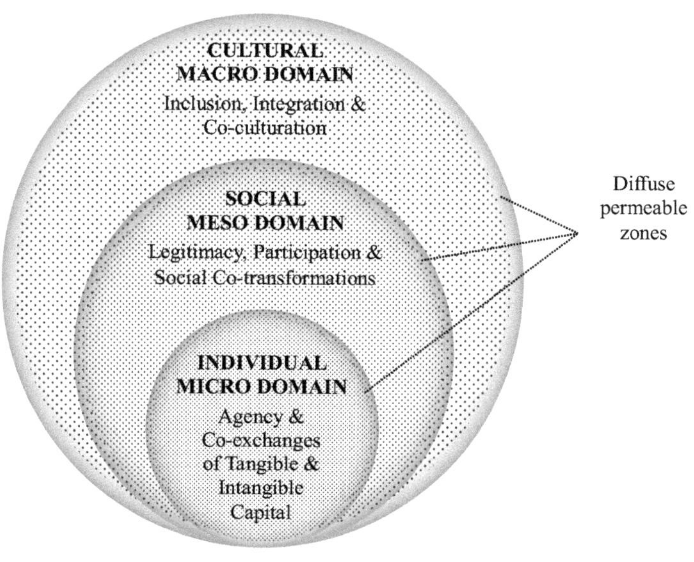

Figure 21.1 Dynamics of refugee entrepreneurship.

Source: Developed by the authors.

Table 21.1 Theoretical lenses to examining the dynamics of RE

Domains	*Suggested Concepts*
Cultural (macro) domain	*Co-culturation* acculturation and enculturation
Social (meso) domain	*Communities of Practice (CoP)* situated learning and legitimate peripheral participation
Individual (micro) domain	*Forms of Capital* all forms of in/tangible capital, including cultural, symbolic, social, economic, political, and human, with particular attention to value homophily, brokers and uncalculating cooperators

and institution contexts" (Kloosterman et al., 1999, p. 257). Within our framework, the central unit of analysis would be on the processes of mixed embeddedness, rather than a given "state" of refugee entrepreneurs. Ager and Strang (2008) equally emphasise that integration entails two-way processes of change, related to the conditions of and participation in all aspects of daily life. This includes healthcare, housing, social safety, education, cultural knowledge and language, and other decision-making and scopes of self-determination. Key to the model is the understanding that not only are refugee entrepreneurs themselves adapting, developing, or transforming, but that the institutions and agents they interact with also become affected by the processes, suggesting multidirectionality. In the following subsections we will elaborate on the domains and components of Figure 21.1, leading to suggestions for more specific analytical tools for future research, summarised in Table 21.1.

Three domains

The dynamics of RE as conceptualised in Figure 21.1 have been grouped into three demarcated domains of conditions and interactive processes. Although the domains are distinctly recognisable, they are interrelated, and thus the boundaries between them are diffused and considered permeable. This is conceptually important, as when examining RE processes we argue that research must also consider multilevel implications, for example, macro effects of individual exchanges. The possibility of supplemental and altered co-constructions of meaning and practices can occur in adaptation processes *between* refugee entrepreneurs and EEs, for example, which is very different from an outlook on adaptation processes as unidirectional, or domain-specific, as in *of* refugee entrepreneurs in EEs. Highlighted in Shneikat and Alrawadieh's (2019) study, entrepreneurial pursuits are highlighted as viable refugee integration strategies. Consequently, significant attention is given to the enablers and barriers of RE integration *into* their host country's "socio-economic environments" (p. 746). Instead, we propose examining entrepreneurship as a constellation of processes *between* legitimate participants in the mainstream society and legitimacy-seeking refugees, for example. Schmich and Mitra (2023) make the concluding remark from their comparative United Kingdom–Germany study that we may already have sufficient "evidence to consider refugee entrepreneurship as an option for economic integration and whether it could contribute to social integration" (p. 25). Thus, adopting the conceptual model from Figure 21.1 would help guide future empirical research in reaching beyond the unidirectional understandings we currently have.

Individual micro domain

Within the individual micro domain, refugee entrepreneurs' agency, capital (such as symbolic, cultural, social, human, and financial), and legitimacy are considered. In their simplest expressions, they manifest as transactional exchanges that can be observed. For example, a social capital lens can shed light upon refugee entrepreneurs' quest for strengthened performance and enriched positioning (Bizri, 2017; Luseno & Kolade, 2022; Mboko, 2020). Individual to individual interactions are especially interesting in this domain, including those with family and close connections, acquaintances with network brokers and other more personally distant intermediaries, as well as exchanges with benevolent, uncalculating cooperators who engage in prosocial activities (Jackson et al., 2012; Jordan et al., 2016; Power & Ready, 2018; Raihani & Power, 2021). Taking into account the heterogeneity and superdiversity of refugee groups (Heilbrunn & Iannone, 2020), activating value homophily (McPherson et al., 2001) engenders relevant cooperation, especially since relative status homophily between refugees and resource-facilitators or -holders in new settings can be characterised as acutely disparate. Thus, a focus on power in multidirectional relations in and around this domain holds the promise of revealing more meaningful insights about processes towards legitimacy and other individual changes that may range between quite small to transformational.

Social meso domain

In this domain, interrelations between refugee entrepreneurs and the mainstream are highlighted. From a relational perspective, our interest resides in the social dynamics which may explain and lead to changes in legitimacy and fluidity of participation in terms of degree, as well as quality. For example, taking part in EEs and engaging with various co-ethnics as well as socially positive host country service organisations privileges refugees to deeper insights into a system's functioning beyond the transactional aspects. Within prosocial activities, this could lead to legitimising pathways in communities of practice (CoPs), whereby newcomers engage in socialising practices through quasi-apprenticeships (Lave & Wenger, 1991) or informal learning in entrepreneurial hubs (Wenger, 1998), where identity formation is also activated along with meaning making.

To avoid unidirectional outlooks upon legitimacy-seeking actions and behaviours, we encourage analysis within this domain to also examine mutual influences of participation. From such a perspective, social constructions overshadow knowledge transfer or theoretical abstraction. Observation, practice, and skills enhancement occur through legitimate peripheral participation in mutually supportive, community processes of expert masters interacting with newcomers. Their relationships involve mutual engagement in shared activities. Then, as newcomers contribute and interact with masters, a sense of identity and belonging develop – shaped by both the expertise of masters and the evolving contributions of newcomers (Wenger, 1998). Along the trajectories, individuals transition smoothly from their positions of peripherality towards central positions of participation – which do not necessarily entail more powerful or dominant positions – as they graduate from novice members of a CoP to experts (Lave & Wenger, 1991). Thus, considerations of power structures within this domain can equally be revelatory, particularly since the transformations that occur directly relate to positionality.

Cultural macro domain

In relation to the widest, macro-level of RE experiences depicted in Figure 21.1, co-culturation (Reinders, 2006) – a concept originating from co-cultural communication theory, or co-cultural theory (Orbe, 1998) – offers a lens through which we can examine the fluid and substantially dynamic nature of inclusion and integration from a phenomenological, co-constructivist perspective. The fundamental principles provide a critical insight into the privilege that is afforded to known segments of society, to which positions of power (including unconscious ones) create circular feedback systems that reinforce *their* dominant perspective. Furthermore, although a society's composition might be characterised by diversity, adopting a co-cultural perspective in analysing interactions confronts persistent marginalisation and underrepresentation. In a given context, these manifest as compelling, exerting or coercing co-cultural group members to strategically adjust their behaviours and patterns of communication in public spheres, so as to strengthen existing schemes and structures. Linking back to the section on interludes above, these frames of reference allow for discerning neoliberal tenets, injected into policies, practices, and norms, helping to reveal the underpinnings of epistemic injustice. Co-culturation also considers fundamental research on acculturation and enculturation – the former encompassing processes of adopting cultural norms, values, and practices of a dominant, mainstream society, and the latter considering the processes and practices of orienting oneself, learning and retaining one's own cultural heritage (Kim & Abreu, 2001; Yoon et al., 2011). Although these two pathways are multidimensional and interactive, they remain independent from one another (Yoon et al., 2020), which is why an application of co-cultural theory within the cultural domains of RE can be enhancing.

Experiences of refugees, other migrants, and ethnic minorities are often depicted in research as experiences of acculturation (Murdock, 2016). To varying degrees, these experiences entail adaptability and a taming, or even subjugation of practices from countries of origin in public spheres, limiting them to socio-ecological niches. This, in turn, may lead to the formation of cultural intermediate worlds (Reinders, 2006). Thus, a co-cultural perspective could facilitate a comprehensive examination of the processes involved in voluntary engagement in a/symmetrical, peer interactions. For instance, newcomers may interact with mentors (through a CoP) and supportive local intermediaries, potentially fostering positive co-culturation (Orbe, 1998; Orbe & Lambert, 2021; Reinders, 2006). Moreover, these interactions may lead to positive outcomes in both the entrepreneurial and personal spheres as well as within the newcomer and mainstream populations alike.

Summary of suggested analytical tools for multidirectional examinations of RE dynamics

The conceptual model we propose (Figure 21.1) for RE research entails a concerted shift towards multidirectional and multileveled analyses regarding the processes of change that occur in and around three permeable, bound domains: micro (individual), meso (social), and macro (cultural). We argue for this shift to avoid unintended, unidirectional perspectives on refugee entrepreneurs that come in the form of rich descriptions that may also intrinsically reinforce the harmful mainstream narratives and practices they seek to confront. Omitting the inherently interactive quality of change, including motivations for change and critical evaluations as to the polymorphic and heterogeneous impacts of change, is too easily accomplished when adopting a line of inquiry that analyses individual refugee entrepreneurs, their entrepreneurships, and their transformational or processes of adaptability in new contexts, from their singular position as the *other* doing the action or overcoming adverse conditions. Instead, we argue that research concerned with revelatory and explanatory insights upon RE dynamics will position refugee entrepreneurs as participatory agents in continuous, albeit unequal, co-actions, and co-exchanges, involved in back-and-forth, continuous processes of co-creation, within a context of change.

This shift in research focus overcomes bounded assumptions while challenging researchers to critically and multidirectionally reexamine features of RE. In a unidirectional light, entrepreneurship endeavours could be accepted as categorically positive, yet still lead to damaging effects in less obvious associations among loosely connected agents or between agents and institutions. For example, examining competing perspectives leads to potential discoveries regarding the unequal applications of power, co-constructions of anti-narratives, obfuscations in pro-social activities, hidden deceptions in processes of increased participation in entrepreneurship or processes of acquiring financial resources and business loans, and uncovering incongruity between legitimacy affordances, despite frequent participation in integration procedures. The shift can liberate research insights from bias legacies and other inadvertent fallacies (Nightingale & Coad, 2014).

We thus contend that Figure 21.1's components can serve as a useful frame of reference to enrich RE research through examinations of the power relations that account for a/synchronous processes of change that evolve through interactions. Complementing the conceptual model is Table 21.1, which summarises related theoretical lenses mentioned earlier in this section. These would acknowledge the mutuality of interrelations that shape RE dynamics and offer a research orientation upon relational co-exchanges of resources (micro), co-construction of practices and meaning (meso), and eventual, co-culturation of individuals and of their wider contexts (macro).

Postlude: A practical research agenda for the future of RE

This chapter was introduced by an insider's quote. As a refugee (serial) entrepreneur, Abo Zarifa surmised the need and opportunity to create "enabling mechanisms for refugees to start their own businesses" (2016, p. 47). Adopting a framework that incorporates different domains and recognises the mutual interactions within a given context may be a compelling step towards understanding the enabling mechanisms she calls for, at the heart of RE dynamics.

This chapter's main objective was thus to harness current approaches in RE research, bringing them back to their essence of actualising studies that make explicit what is so often stated but also so under-theorised: that refugee entrepreneurs are shaped by, and simultaneously shape, their new environments through dynamic processes of co-construction and co-development. As the literature informs us, RE is often idealised amidst adversity, yet is entangled within neoliberal principles that prioritise economic growth and individual agency – of non-refugees who need to adapt to their new environments. Such a perspective falls short of addressing the heterogeneity of experience that is not unidirectional. As we have argued, an inability to methodologically and analytically appraise the inextricably interrelated value of the two (or more) interacting components in an exchange will also lead to problematic, unidirectional insights. For example, encouraging refugees through soft strategies of obligation, for instance, or systematic, formal requirements, to integrate through adaptation, with entrepreneurial pursuits being an identifiable means, may be accepted by mainstream neoliberalism, but may not necessarily lead to greater legitimacy, and certainly neglects the impact that refugees have on the hosting society's populations, systems, and institutions. We thus argue that analysing processes of change as unidirectional provides incomplete knowledge, which may lead to both the conscious and unconscious perpetuation of fallacies. Therefore, our conceptual model precludes unidirectional inquiries, however valuable and rich they may be, and directly addresses persisting RE knowledge gaps. Moreover, the implications of multilevel analyses lend us to possible reformulations of central concepts in RE – such as "power", "legitimacy", and "agency". This leads to research that looks upon and also independently questions long-standing unidirectional axioms, such as the ones that uphold the prescripts of refugee entrepreneurs' ultimate responsibility to thrive.

Future research directions could draw upon techniques that have the ability to examine the social aspects of processes, relationally and multidirectionally, across the three domains discussed: individual (micro), social (meso), and cultural (macro). Moreover, there is a need for longitudinal studies (see Ram et al., 2022 for a pioneering example), and for research that decouples RE from exclusively positive outlooks. Processes of change necessarily entail interrelational negotiations, and in turn, interrelational power, which also entails friction and resistance. Choosing analytical perspectives that put into focus the static components of process holds the potential for a re-examination of discourses on RE and more relational outlooks upon entrepreneurial processes in general, and refugees' experiences within their new contexts. These could include analytical instruments from co-culturation (Orbe, 1998; Orbe & Lambert, 2021; Reinders, 2006), social psychology, such as from CoPs (Lave & Wenger, 1991; Wenger, 1998), and social capital theory (Jackson et al., 2012; McKeever et al., 2014; McPherson et al., 2001; Power & Ready, 2018; Raihani & Power, 2021), as well as from other branches of psychology studying individual development. This could ultimately lead to a reconsideration of normative perspectives in RE research. Framed by a careful consideration of the wider and more micro-contextual forces, such as neoliberal ideologies and their impact on legitimacy and other positions of powerlessness, the future of RE studies holds the promise of more meaningful insights that can lift the veil of unidirectional shortcomings and cultivate the richness of refugee entrepreneurs.

References

Abebe, S. A. (2023). Refugee entrepreneurship: Systematic and thematic analyses and a research agenda. *Small Business Economics, 60,* 315–350. https://doi.org/10.1007/s11187-022-00636-3

Abo Zarifa, W. (2016, May). The new entrepreneurs: Migrants talk about integration strategies and the meaning of home. *Forum, 362*(Mobile people), 46–48. www.forum.lu/issue/mobile-menschen/

Ager, A., & Strang, A. (2008). Understanding integration: A conceptual framework. *Journal* of *Refugee Studies, 21*(2), 166–191. https://doi.org/10.1093/jrs/fen016

Bailey, A. (2020). On gaslighting and epistemic injustice: Editor's introduction. *Hypatia, 35*(4), 667–673. https://ssrn.com/abstract=3811840

Bal, P. M., & Dóci, E. (2018). Neoliberal ideology in work and organizational psychology. *European Journal of Work and Organizational Psychology, 27*(5), 536–548. https://doi.org/10.1080/1359432X.2018.1449108

Balcilar, M., & Nugent, J. B. (2019). The migration of fear: An analysis of migration choices of Syrian refugees. *The Quarterly Review of Economics and Finance, 73,* 95–110. https://doi.org/10.1016/j.qref.2018.09.007

Bizri, R. M. (2017). Refugee-entrepreneurship: A social capital perspective, *Entrepreneurship & Regional Development, 29*(9–10), 847–868. https://doi.org/10.1080/08985626.2017.1364787

Bloch, A. (2014). Living in fear: Rejected asylum seekers living as irregular migrants in England. *Journal of Ethnic and Migration Studies, 40*(10), 1507–1525. https://doi.org/10.1080/1369183X.2013.859070

Boochani, B, Flores, D., Sibanda, A., et al. (2020). Transnational communities for dismantling detention: From Manus Island to the UK. *Community Psychology in Global Perspective, 6*(1), 108–128. http://siba-ese.unisalento.it/index.php/cpgp/article/view/21826

Brown, W. (2015). *Undoing the demos: Neoliberalism's stealth revolution*. Zone Books. https://doi.org/10.2307/j.ctt17kk9p8

Cohen, B. (2005). Sustainable valley entrepreneurial ecosystems. *Business Strategy and the Environment, 15*(1), 1–14. https://doi.org/10.1002/bse.428

Damm, A. P., & Rosholm, M. (2010). Employment effects of spatial dispersal of refugees. *Review of Economics of the Household, 8*, 105–146. https://doi.org/10.1007/s11150-009-9067-4

Davies, W. (2014). *The limits of neoliberalism: Authority, sovereignty and the logic of competition*. SAGE Publications Ltd. https://doi.org/10.4135/9781473906075

de la Chaux, M., & Haugh, H. (2020). When formal institutions impede entrepreneurship: How and why refugees establish new ventures in the Dadaab refugee camps. *Entrepreneurship & Regional Development, 32*(9–10), 827–851. https://doi.org/10.1080/08985626.2020.1789752

de Lange, T., Berntsen, L., Hanoeman, R., & Haidar, O. (2021). Highly skilled entrepreneurial refugees: Legal and practical barriers and enablers to start up in the Netherlands. *International Migration, 59*(4), 74–87. https://doi.org/10.1111/imig.12745

Desai, S., Naudé, W., & Stel, N. (2021). Refugee entrepreneurship: Context and directions for future research. *Small Business Economics, 56*, 933–945. https://doi.org/10.1007/s11187-019-00310-1

Fotopoulos, G., & Storey, D. J. (2019). Public policies to enhance regional entrepreneurship: Another programme failing to deliver? *Small Business Economics, 53*(1), 189–209. www.jstor.org/stable/48702001

Fricker, M. (2007). *Epistemic injustice: Power and the ethics of knowing*. Oxford University Press. https://doi.org/10.1093/acprof:oso/9780198237907.001.0001

George, J. M. (2014). Compassion and capitalism: Implications for organization studies. *Journal of Management, 40*(1), 5–15. https://doi.org/10.1177/0149206313490028

Gill, R. (2013). The evolution of organizational archetypes: From the American to the entrepreneurial dream. *Communication Monographs, 80*(3), 331–353. https://doi.org/10.1080/03637751.2013.788252

Hallonsten, O. (2023). *Empty innovation: Causes and consequences of society's obsession with entrepreneurship and growth*. Palgrave Macmillan. https://doi.org/10.1007/978-3-031-31479-7

Harima, A., & Freudenberg, J. (2020). Co-creation of social entrepreneurial opportunities with refugees. *Journal of Social Entrepreneurship, 11*(1), 40–64. https://doi.org/10.1080/19420676.2018.1561498

Harima, A., Freudenberg, J., & Halberstadt, J. (2019). Functional domains of business incubators for refugee entrepreneurs. *Journal of Enterprising Communities: People and Places in the Global Economy, 4*(5), 687–711. https://doi.org/10.1108/JEC-11-2018-0081

Heilbrunn, S. (2022). *Dark sides of the startup nation: Winners and losers of technological innovation and entrepreneurship in Israel.* Routledge. https://doi.org/10.4324/9781003091042

Heilbrunn, S., Freiling, J., & Harima, A. (Eds.). (2019). *Refugee entrepreneurship: A case-based topography.* Palgrave MacMillan. https://doi.org/10.1007/978-3-319-92534-9

Heilbrunn, S., & Iannone, R. L. (2019a). Introduction. In S. Heilbrunn, J. Freiling, & A. Harima (Eds.), *Refugee entrepreneurship: A case-based topography* (pp. 1–26). Palgrave MacMillan. https://doi.org/10.1007/978-3-319-92534-9_1

Heilbrunn, S., & Iannone, R. L. (2019b). Neoliberalist undercurrents in entrepreneurship policy. *Journal of Entrepreneurship and Innovation in Emerging Economies, 5*(2), 149–162. https://doi.org/10.1177/2393957519861489

Heilbrunn, S., & Iannone, R. L. (2020). From center to periphery and back again: A systematic literature review of refugee entrepreneurship. *Sustainability, 12*(18), 7658. https://doi.org/10.3390/su12187658

Honig, B. (2017). Compensatory entrepreneurship: Avoiding the pitfalls of global isomorphic entrepreneurship research and activities. *REGEPE – Revista de Empreendedorismo e Gestão de Pequenas Empresas [Entrepreneurship and Small Business Journal], 6*(3), 452–465. https://doi.org/10.14211/regepe.v6i3.723

Isenberg, D. J. (2010). The big idea: How to start an entrepreneurial revolution. *Harvard Business Review, 88*(6), 40–50. https://hbr.org/2010/06/the-big-idea-how-to-start-an-entrepreneurial-revolution

Jackson, M. O., Rodriguez-Barraquer, T., & Tan, X. (2012). Social capital and social quilts: Network patterns of favor exchange. *American Economic Review, 102*(5), 1857–1897. https://doi.org/10.1257/aer.102.5.1857

Jürgens, C., Ramalingam, A., Zarembski, R., Harima, A., & Yeshi, T. (2022). Relational dynamics within refugee business incubators: Bridging refugee entrepreneurs to the host-country entrepreneurial ecosystem. In D. G. Pickernell, M. Battisti, Z. Dann, & C. Ekinsmyth (Eds.), *Disadvantaged entrepreneurship and the entrepreneurial ecosystem (Contemporary issues in entrepreneurship research* (Vol. 14, pp. 147–169). Emerald Publishing Limited. https://doi.org/10.1108/S2040-724620220000014007

Jordan, J. J., Hoffman, M., Nowak, M. A., & Rand, D. G. (2016). Uncalculating cooperation is used to signal trustworthiness. *PNAS Proceedings of the National Academy of Sciences of the United States of America, 113*(31), 8658–8663. https://doi.org/10.1073/pnas.1601280113

Kim, B. S. K., & Abreu, J. M. (2001). Acculturation measurement: Theory, current instruments, and future directions. In L. A. Suzuki, J. M. Casas, C. M. Alexander, & J. C. Ponterotto (Eds.), *Handbook of multicultural counseling* (2nd ed., pp. 394–424). Sage Publications, Ind.

Kloosterman, R.C., van der Leun, J., & Rath, J. (1999). Mixed embeddedness: (In)formal economic activities and immigrant businesses in the Netherlands. *International Journal of Urban and Regional Research, 23*(2), 252–266. https://doi.org/10.1111/1468-2427.00194

Kuckertz, A. (2019). Let's take the entrepreneurial ecosystem metaphor seriously! *Journal of Business Venturing Insights, 11*, e00124. https://doi.org/10.1016/j.jbvi.2019.e00124

Kunz, E. F. (1973). The refugee in flight: Kinetic models and forms of displacement. *The International Migration Review, 7*(2), 125–146. https://doi.org/10.1177/019791837300700201

Lave, J., & Wenger, E. (1991). *Situated learning: Legitimate peripheral participation.* Cambridge University Press.

Luseno, T., & Kolade, O. (2022). Barriers and opportunities for refugee entrepreneurship in Africa: A social capital perspective. In O. Kolade, D. Rae, D., Obembe, & K. Woldesenbet Beta (Eds.), *The Palgrave handbook of african entrepreneurship* (pp. 407–435). Palgrave Macmillan. https://doi.org/10.1007/978-3-030-75894-3_17

Luseno, T., & Kolade, O. (2023). Displaced, excluded, and making do: A study of refugee entrepreneurship in Kenya. *Journal of Entrepreneurship in Emerging Economies, 15*(4), 808–834. https://doi.org/10.1108/JEEE-04-2021-0163

Lyon, F., Sepulveda, L., & Syrett, S. (2007). Enterprising refugees: Contributions and challenges in deprived urban areas. *Local Economy, 22*(4), 363–375. https://doi.org/10.1080/02690940701736769

Mboko, S. (2020). Understanding the social capital in refugee entrepreneurs. *Advances in Management, 13*(2), 24–34. www.proquest.com/scholarly-journals/understanding-social-capital-refugee/docview/2406646572/se-2

McGuigan, J. (2014). The neoliberal self. *Culture Unbound, 6*(1), 223–240. https://doi.org/10.3384/cu.2000.1525.146223

McKeever, E., Anderson, A., & Jack, S. (2014). Entrepreneurship and mutuality: Social capital in processes and practices. *Entrepreneurship & Regional Development, 26*(5–6): 453–477. https://doi.org/10.1080/08985626.2014.939536

McPherson, M., Smith-Lovin, L., & Cook, J. M. (2001). Birds of a feather: Homophily in social networks. *Annual Review of Sociology, 27*(1), 415–444. https://doi.org/10.1146/annurev.soc.27.1.415

Medina, J. (2017). Varieties of hermeneutical injustice. In I. J. Kidd, J. Medina, & G. Jr. Pohlhaus (Eds.), *The Routledge handbook of epistemic injustice* (pp. 41–52). Routledge.

Meister, A. D., & Mauer, R. (2019). Understanding refugee entrepreneurship incubation – An embeddedness perspective. *International Journal of Entrepreneurial Behaviour and Research, 25*(5), 1065–1092. https://doi.org/10.1108/IJEBR-02-2018-0108

Missbach, A. (2019). Asylum seekers' and refugees' decision-making in transit in Indonesia: The need for in-depth and longitudinal research. *Bijdragen tot de taal-, l and- en volkenkunde [Journal of the Humanities and Social Sciences of Southeast Asia], 175*(4), 419–445. https://doi.org/10.1163/22134379-17504006

Murdock, E. (2016). *Multiculturalism, identity and difference.* Palgrave Macmillan. https://doi.org/10.1057/978-1-137-59679-6_1

Naudé, W. (2011). Entrepreneurship is not a binding constraint on growth and development in the poorest countries. *World Development, 39*(1), 33–44. https://doi.org/10.1016/j.worlddev.2010.05.005

New American Economy. (2017). *From struggle to resilience: The economic Impact of refugees in America* [Report]. www.newamericaneconomy.org/wp-content/uploads/2017/06/NAE_Refugees_V5.pdf

Newman, A. B., & Christensen, L. J. (2021). Doing it right, but getting it wrong: Best practices for refugee focused incubators. *Journal of Developmental Entrepreneurship, 26*(03), 1–34. https://doi.org/10.1142/s1084946721500199

Newman, A., Macaulay, L., & Dunwoodie, K. (2023). Refugee entrepreneurship: A systematic review of prior research and agenda for future research. *International Migration Review, OnlineFirst.* https://doi.org/10.1177/01979183231182669

Nightingale, P., & Coad, A. (2014). Muppets and gazelles: Political and methodological biases in entrepreneurship research. *Industrial and Corporate Change, 23*(1), 113–143. https://doi.org/10.1093/icc/dtt057

Omran, W., & Yousafzai, S. (2023). Navigating the twisted path of gaslighting: A manifestation of epistemic injustice for Palestinian women entrepreneurs. *Human Relations, OnlineFirst.* https://doi.org/10.1177/00187267231203531

Orbe, M. P. (1998). *Constructing co-cultural theory: An explication of culture, power, and communication.* Sage Publications, Inc. https://doi.org/10.4135/9781483345321

Orbe, M. P., & Lambert, A. A. (2021). Co-cultural theory and communication. *Oxford Bibliographies Online in Communication.* https://10.1093/obo/9780199756841-0259

Pauceanu, A. M., Rabie, N., Moustafa, A., & Jiroveanu, D. C. (2021). Entrepreneurial leadership and sustainable development—a systematic literature review. *Sustainability, 13*(21), 11695. https://doi.org/10.3390/su132111695

Phillimore, J., & Goodson, L. (2006). Problem or opportunity? Asylum seekers, refugees, employment and social exclusion in deprived urban areas. *Urban Studies, 43*(10), 1715–1736. https://doi.org./10.1080/00420980600838606

Polanyi, K. (1957). *The great transformation.* Beacon Press.

Porter, M. E. (1990). The competitive advantage of nations. *Harvard Business Review (March–April)*, 73–91.

Porter, M. E. (2000). Location, competition, and economic development: Local clusters in a global economy. *Economic Development Quarterly, 14*(1), 15–34. https://doi.org/10.1177/089124240001400105

Power, E. A., & Ready, E. (2018). Building bigness: Reputation, prominence, and social capital in rural South India. *American Anthropologist, 120*(3), 444–459. https://doi.org/10.1111/aman.13100

Pretorius, M., Le Roux, I., Rosslyn-Smith, W., & Letsholo, R. (2021). Artificial entrepreneurship and fallacy assumptions that inform enterprise development failure. In G. A. Goldman (Ed.), *Critical management studies in South Africa: Directions and contexts* (pp. 123–142). AOSIS. https://doi.org/10.4102/aosis.2021.BK322.07

Raihani, N. J., & Power, E. A. (2021). No good deed goes unpunished: The social costs of prosocial behaviour. *Evolutionary Human Sciences, 3*, e40. https://doi.org/10.1017/ehs.2021.35

Ram, M., Jones, T., Doldor, S., Villares-Varela, M., & Li, H. (2022). What happens to refugee-origin entrepreneurs? Combining mixed embeddedness and strategy perspectives in a longitudinal study. *Ethnic and Racial Studies, 45*(16), 1–27. https://doi.org/10.1080/01419870.2021.1991970

Reinders, H. (2006). Interethnische Beziehungen im Lebenslauf [Interethnic relationships in the life course]. *Diskurs Kindheit und Jugendforschung [Discourse Childhood and Youth Research], 1*, 7–20. https://doi.org/10.25656/01:999

Salmon, U., & Singleton, A. (2023), Barriers to entrepreneurship: An intersectional analysis of an early-stage refugee entrepreneurship programme in the United Kingdom. *International Journal of Entrepreneurial Behavior & Research,* [ahead-of-print]. https://doi.org/10.1108/IJEBR-11-2022-1048

Schmich, M., & Mitra, J. (2023). Can entrepreneurship enable economic and social integration of refugees? A comparison of the economic, social and policy context for refugee entrepreneurship in the UK and Germany. *Journal of Entrepreneurship and Innovation in Emerging Economies, 9*(1), 9–32. https://doi.org/10.1177/23939575221146848

Shane, S. (2009). Why encouraging more people to become entrepreneurs is bad public policy. *Small Business Economics, 33*, 141–149. https://doi.org/10.1007/s11187-009-9215-5

Shenk, T. (2015, April 2). Booked #3: What exactly is neoliberalism? *Dissent*. www.dissentmagazine.org/blog/booked-3-what-exactly-is-neoliberalism-wendy-brown-undoing-the-demos/

Shneikat, B., & Alrawadieh, Z. (2019). Unraveling refugee entrepreneurship and its role in integration: Empirical evidence from the hospitality industry. *The Service Industries Journal, 9–10*, 741–761. https://doi.org/10.1080/02642069.2019.1571046

Smit, M. M., & Pretorius, M. (2023). When entrepreneurship becomes a tool for political hegemony. *Acta Commercii, 23*(1), a1086. https://doi.org/10.4102/ac.v23i1.1086

Smith, K. (2015). Stories told by, for, and about women refugees: Engendering resistance. *ACME: An International Journal for Critical Geographies, 14*(2), 461–469. https://acme-journal.org/index.php/acme/article/view/1174

UNHCR. (1951). *Convention and protocol relating to the status of refugees; United Nations High Commissioner for Refugees*. Geneva. www.unhcr.org/media/convention-and-protocol-relating-status-refugees

UNHCR. (2023). *Mid-year trends*. www.unhcr.org/mid-year-trends#:~:text=The%20global%20refugee%20population%20reached,from%20the%20end%20of%202022

Wauters, B., & Lambrecht, J. (2008). Barriers to refugee entrepreneurship in Belgium: Towards an explanatory model. *Journal of Ethnic and Migration Studies, 34*(6), 895–915. https://doi.org/10.1080/13691830802211190

Wenger, E. (1998). *Communities of practice: Learning, meaning, and identity*. Cambridge University Press. https://doi.org/10.1017/CBO9780511803932

Yoon, E., Cabirou, L., Galvin, S., Hill, L., Daskalova, P., Bhang, C., Ahmad Mustaffa, E., Dao, A., Thomas, K., & Baltazar, B. (2020). A meta-analysis of acculturation and enculturation: Bilinear, multidimensional, and context-dependent processes. *The Counseling Psychologist, 48*(3), 342–376. https://doi.org/10.1177/0011000019898583

Yoon, E., Langrehr, K., & Ong, L. (2011). Content analysis of acculturation research in counseling and counseling psychology: A 22-year review. *Journal of Counseling Psychology, 58*, 83–96. https://doi.org/10.1037/a0021128

Zalkat, G., Barth, H., & Rashid, L. (2024). Refugee entrepreneurship motivations in Sweden and Germany: A comparative case study. *Small Business Economics, 63*, 477–499. https://doi.org/10.1007/s11187-023-00830-x

22 Conclusion

Looking ahead

Nadeera Ranabahu, Huibert P. de Vries, and Robert T. Hamilton

The chapters in this collection sought to address some of the scholarly, methodological, and empirical issues outlined in Chapter 1 and provide a nuanced understanding of the refugee entrepreneurship (RE) phenomenon. Aligning with refugee migration trends, the chapters present studies of refugees with diverse backgrounds and circumstances. The chapters also bring issues of diverse groups (women, refugees in camps, and resettled refugees) to the forefront. The chapters discuss the characteristics of refugee entrepreneurs and their businesses, the challenges and barriers they face, the impact or value of RE, and the support mechanisms and agencies that help, or in some cases hinder, refugee business opportunities. Each of the chapters provides its own distinctive story which underpins theoretical and/or policy implications for RE research and practice.

Future directions for RE research and practice

The scope of refugee entrepreneurship

Diversity among refugees (such as climate change refugees and internally displaced people)

All chapters in this volume focused on refugees who fled their home countries to new countries for reasons of war, political or religious persecution, or conflicts. Predominantly they are framed using the United Nations High Commissioner for Refugees' (UNHCR's) definition of refugee. There were a few exceptions, such as Aydiner and Rider (Chapter 7) who studied Turkish political asylees with relatively higher education who arrived in the USA via alternative routes to the atypical refugee journey. This said, what is becoming clear is that although we have an emerging understanding of how refugees who move across borders use their ethnic networks in acquiring resources, we do not have enough studies that focus on displaced people within transition and host countries, and their entrepreneurship activities.

DOI: 10.4324/9781003368540-27

In addition, although the UNHCR definition captures the forced migrants, the 1951 Refugee Convention does not cover climate refugees or displaced populations due to climate change or environmental events (Apap & Harju, 2023). This is because climate refugees, in theory, can still rely on the protection offered by their own countries (Apap & Harju, 2023). In contrast, conventional refugees could not rely on their home countries as home country regimes may be the source of persecution (Apap & Harju, 2023) or turn a blind eye to the plight of specific ethnic communities in society. The universal human rights treaties also do not refer to a specific right to a safe and healthy environment (Apap & Harju, 2023). Yet, "the UN human rights treaty bodies all recognise the intrinsic link between the environment and the realisation of a range of human rights, such as the right to life, health, food, water and housing" (Apap & Harju, 2023, p. 7).

We recommend that future studies should place greater emphasis on exploring the impact of entrepreneurial activity on internal displacement, livelihood disruptions, and livelihood restoration. Similar to the work of David and Zaghow (Chapter 2), who provide conceptual and phenomenological clarity for demarcating conventional refugees and immigrants, we recommend studying similarities and differences between conventional refugees, climate refugees, and/or other displaced people. Factors of refugee movement, contextual heterogeneity, and temporality of refugee experience that Abebe et al. (Chapter 3) synthesised will help in this regard.

We also invite future studies to explore business start-up motivation, processes, and practices of these displaced people. As Ranabahu et al. point out in Chapter 4, there are differences between intentions and actions. Hence, future studies can explore how climate refugees' resource positioning shapes the intention–action gap and any subsequent business start-up and development. In addition, we recommend greater engagement in research on displaced communities and the role of entrepreneurship in restarting their livelihoods. If displaced people are existing business owners, how they pivot and modify businesses due to climate events will also be of interest.

Such research can inform the policies and practices of national and international agencies (such as the UNHCR and resettlement agencies in host countries) that seek to address the global refugee crisis. Questions that need answering, but are not limited to, include the following: How can support agency policies and practices address the varying entrepreneurial experience, capability, and needs of diverse refugee communities? Can one-fits-all policies support these communities? Further, how should agencies support people who are displaced by climate change or other natural events to make their regions habitable or restore their livelihoods?

Refugees and their businesses

Pathways for business start-up and development

An overwhelming number of studies in this volume and the broader extant literature point out the necessity-driven nature of RE (e.g., Adiputera et al.,

Chapter 6). Refugees start businesses in sectors with low entry barriers as they often lack resources. These businesses are often subsistence in nature, where women, for example, predominantly enter into entrepreneurship as a temporary fix to address their immediate needs (Huq & Biru, Chapter 5). This is partly due to refugees' lack of financial resources and lack of options for obtaining external funding. This creates a need for innovative ways to fund refugee businesses that emerge as a result of multiplicity of refugee journeys.

Academically, studies that explore novel modes of financing are still emerging (e.g., Emanuel-Correia et al., 2022; Gama et al., 2023). We see the need for further studies on such financing options including microfinance schemes, FinTech initiatives, community-based cooperative financing, and peer-to-peer (P2P) lending for refugees and how to tailor these to refugee's differing needs and circumstances. We also recommend the use and study of blockchain and other technologies which enhance transparency and accountability when financing refugee businesses.

Beyond necessity, we see the need for further studies on alternative entrepreneurship pathways. Resettled refugees, once they become accustomed to context, could also identify emerging or lucrative business opportunities or employ emerging technology in their business ventures. In fact, Aydiner and Rider (Chapter 7) and Zalkat (Chapter 8) illustrate refugees' use of online sales, social media, and other digital tools in businesses. We recommend further exploration on refugee engagement in digital entrepreneurship, social media marketing and sales. Further, RE studies can explore the use of emerging generative or explainable artificial intelligence tools for translation and other functions and how these tools shape refugees' businesses. Refugees also engage in volunteering and the "gig economy" and how these practices contribute to business start-ups can also provide insights into different ways through which refugees venture into entrepreneurship.

The need for multimode data and multimethod data collection

We also affirm the findings of Abebe (2023) and Heilbrunn and Iannone (2020) and call for methodological plurality in future studies. In this volume, inductive and, albeit limited deductive, type studies added to the plurality of methods and methodologies used in exploring the RE phenomenon. The interviews (or in some cases focus group discussions) with a small sample of respondents were the most common data collection tool used in the chapters of this volume. One of the key reasons for the limited variability in data collection tools is that refugees are a hard-to-reach population, and trust-building takes time. Zalkat (Chapter 8) details how digital techniques can be used in identifying and inviting research participants. We recommend that future studies should embrace such strategies and enhance methodological plurality by using multimodel data (e.g., videos, photos, and social media) and using multiple techniques such as auto-ethnographic accounts, discourse or diary analysis, or photo/video journals.

Terstriep et al. (Chapter 17) used quantitative data and provided a comparative and cross-country analysis of the entrepreneurial ecosystem and how this information can be used in RE. Ramachandran et al. (Chapter 10) used a self-administrative survey in their chapter. Taking onboard such strategies, we recommend that future studies should collect quantitative data or make use of existing host country refugee data, such as the host country census or immigration statistics. RE research can also benefit from longitudinal research designs, the use of panel data sets, or cross-national and cross-continental studies.

We also believe that there is a lack of studies that critique RE. For example, Huq and Biru (Chapter 5) and Iannone et al. (Chapter 21) question the neoliberal ideologies of RE. We encourage future researchers to approach RE from a critical realist view and question whether RE is the "last resort" or whether it is a well-planned endeavour within neoliberal societies. Similar to the works of Adiputera et al. (Chapter 6) and Newman et al. (2023), we encourage critics on illegal and informal RE businesses and the constraining nature of refugees' existing social networks.

Personal, economic, and social value of refugee entrepreneurship

The meaning of integration

RE literature explains that business start-up and development facilitate refugees' integration into host communities (e.g., Junaid & Jurado, Chapter 9). Nevertheless, the term "integrated refugees" is ambiguous. For example, do we consider refugees to be integrated when they are accepted by host communities and have the same privileges and rights as all other people?; when they become citizens in the new host country?; or is it when they self-identify that they are fully integrated into the community? We do not have answers to these questions yet and current studies do not provide greater clarity on the meaning of "integrated refugees". We invite future researchers to examine this.

Policy and practice would also benefit from studies on how refugee resettlements shape communities at the meso or macro levels. Ramachandran et al. (Chapter 10) and Schemschat (Chapter 11) explained the economic effects of RE, outlined vital contributions refugees make, how refugees shape local production and distribution, and elaborated on how refugees can revitalise cities affected by the urban decline. We invite future research to continue this tradition and study meso and macro effects, in addition to micro-level (individual refugee level) benefits and impact of RE.

Supporting and developing refugee entrepreneurship

Overall refugee well-being and RE

Newman and Jones Christensen (Chapter 12) and Subramanian and Finsterwalder (Chapter 13) point out the well-being needs of refugees and specifically the need to address trauma and psychological and physical well-being for RE. The framework of Newman and Jones Christensen (Chapter 12) can help practitioners in designing trauma-informed care when promoting entrepreneurship. Transformative health care, education, interpretation and communication, housing, and settlement services are required alongside entrepreneurship support to promote well-being of refugees (Subramanian & Finsterwalder, Chapter 13).

Yet, our understanding of diverse well-being needs and the role of RE is so far limited. For example, on one hand, RE may not be the best option for refugees with post-traumatic disorder, neurodiverse needs, or with physical disabilities. On the other hand, RE may be the only option available for these diverse groups of refugees to engage in economic activities, which enhances social and economic well-being. We recommend that future studies should explore the role of RE among diverse refugee groups with a range of well-being needs and go beyond physical and psychological well-being by considering cultural, social, and environmental well-being. We also invite future studies to look at RE support mechanisms from ethical and human rights perspectives.

Education and training

Kansikas and Seikkula-Leino (Chapter 14) explain the resilience and adaptability of refugees and how educational pedagogies, curricula, and programmes can foster and build on these attributes. In a similar effort, Aktas et al. (Chapter 15) outline the role of NGOs in promoting social capital and resilience, while Street and Ng (Chapter 16) describe how child-friendly workshops and mentoring support refugee women empowerment. These studies focus on strength-based approaches rather than deficit-based explanations. Aligning with the strength-based approaches, we recommend that future studies should focus on institutional level programmes, course design, training services, and how effective they are in addressing the education and capacity needs of the refugees.

In addition, we see the need for skills development in new areas to ensure that resettled refugees are not left behind. We see "green skills" as one such priority (Auktor, 2020). These include engineering and technical skills for eco-buildings and energy-efficient designs, science skills for managing environmental problems, operational management skills for a circular and green economy, and monitoring skills for ensuring legal and technical compliances (Auktor, 2020). Upgrading of refugee skills in these areas is required when transitioning to a low-carbon economy (Auktor, 2020). Thus, we recommend RE scholars to focus on how we can develop these skills among resettled refugees.

Ecosystem and institutional role in refugee entrepreneurship

Gender dynamics and refugee women's access to ecosystem support

Al-Dajani (2022) points out that greater consideration should be given to the exploration of refugee gender dynamics and recommends studying refugee women entrepreneurs' practices by embedding in family, community and host, and home and transition countries. The works of Aydiner and Rider (Chapter 7), Zalkat (Chapter 8), Aktas et al. (Chapter 15), and Street and Ng (Chapter 16) address these concerns. Women refugees procure support from their informal networks rather than from the external entrepreneurial ecosystem. Hence, these studies also reinforce that women's entrepreneurship is not a meritocratic, non-contextual, or neutral activity (Ahl & Marlow, 2012).

We suggest extending this thinking into the ecosystem level. As there are socio-spatial differences in the entrepreneurial ecosystem, the structures, actors, and interdependencies at local, regional, or national levels could exclude refugee women (or even refugees). Hence, future research should explore how local, regional, or national entrepreneurial ecosystem structures, actors, and interdependencies include or exclude refugees. The conceptual framework of Iannone et al. (Chapter 21) can help in this regard.

Intrapreneurship in RE

Finally, we call for future studies associated with intrapreneurship and RE. In this volume, Hatipoglu (Chapter 18), Chowdhooree and Ferdaus (Chapter 19), and Bizri (Chapter 20) explained the roles of different institutions/organisations (e.g., private sector, NGO, and public) in the entrepreneurial ecosystem in promoting RE. Beyond these institution types, there are hardly any RE publications on intrapreneurship initiatives facilitating RE. In practice, however, organisations engage in intrapreneurship or corporate social responsibility activities and support refugees. This is evident in the work of TENT which outlines how more than 400 major multinational companies support refugee initiatives (TENT, 2024). However, as Chowdhooree and Ferdaus point out, not all private-sector initiatives are viable. Hence, we see the need to scrutinise private-sector initiatives, from an intrapreneurship perspective, to identify their effectiveness and efficiency.

Conclusion

In conclusion, this book illustrates that the RE phenomenon has been (and can be) examined from different theoretical perspectives and lenses. The chapters in this volume apply different perspectives to explain the nuances of RE and emphasise that there are still unresolved theoretical and empirical issues to address. In fact, there are new issues emerging with changing global landscapes (environmental, economic, sociocultural, and technological) and the increasing number of refugees. These all fuel a constant need to review policy and practice. We invite future researchers to explore RE to extend the theoretical, conceptual, methodological, and empirical boundaries and contribute to the ongoing advancement of robust, effective, and equitable RE theory and practice.

References

Abebe, S. A. (2023). Refugee entrepreneurship: Systematic and thematic analyses and a research agenda. *Small Business Economics*, *60*(1), 315–350. https://doi.org/10.1007/s11187-022-00636-3

Ahl, H., & Marlow, S. (2012). Exploring the dynamics of gender, feminism and entrepreneurship: Advancing debate to escape a dead end? *Organization*, *19*(5), 543–562. https://doi.org/10.1177/1350508412448695

Al-Dajani, H. (2022). Refugee women's entrepreneurship: Where from and where to next? *International Journal of Gender and Entrepreneurship*, *14*(4), 489–498. https://doi.org/10.1108/IJGE-06-2022-0090

Apap, J. & Harju, S. J. (2023). The concept of 'climate refugee': Towards a possible definition. European parliament briefing. www.europarl.europa.eu/RegData/etudes/BRIE/2021/698753/EPRS_BRI(2021)698753_EN.pdf

Auktor, G. V. (2020). Green industrial skills for substantiable future. *Background Paper for the LKDF Forum 2020.* https://lkdfacility.org/resources/background-paper-for-the-lkdf-forum-2020

Emanuel-Correia, R., Duarte, F., Gama, A. P. M., & Augusto, M. (2022). Does peer-to-peer crowdfunding boost refugee entrepreneurs? *Finance Research Letters*, *46*, 102264. https://doi.org/10.1016/j.frl.2021.102264

Gama, A. P. M., Correia, R. E., Augusto, M., & Duarte, F. (2023). Third-party signals in crowdfunded microfinance: Which microfinance institutions boost crowdfunding among refugee entrepreneurs?. *Small Business Economics*, *61*(2), 559–586. https://doi.org/10.1007/s11187-022-00708-4

Heilbrunn, S., & Iannone, R. L. (2020). From center to periphery and back again: A systematic literature review of refugee entrepreneurship. *Sustainability*, *12*(18). https://doi.org/10.3390/su12187658

Newman, A., Macaulay, L., & Dunwoodie, K. (2023). Refugee entrepreneurship: A systematic review of prior research and agenda for future research. *International Migration Review*, 01979183231182669. https://doi.org/10.1177/01979183231182669

TENT. (2024). TENT partnership for refugees: A global business coalition. www.tent.org/members/

Index

Note: Endnotes are indicated by the page number followed by "n" and the note number e.g., 111n5 refers to note 5 on page 111.